Essential Papers on Hasidism

ESSENTIAL PAPERS ON JEWISH STUDIES
General Editor: Robert M. Seltzer

ESSENTIAL PAPERS ON HASIDISM

Origins to Present

Edited by
Gershon David Hundert

New York University Press
New York and London

Library of Congress Cataloging-in-Publication Data
Essential papers on Hasidism : origins to present / edited by Gershon
    David Hundert.
        p.   cm. — (Essential papers on Jewish studies)
      ISBN 0–8147–3469–3 (alk. paper) — ISBN 0–8147–3470–7
    (pbk. : alk. paper)
          1. Hasidism—History.   I. Hundert, Gershon David, 1946–
    II. Series.
    BM198.E85   1990
    296.8'332'09—dc20   90–5971
                                CIP

New York University Press books are printed on acid-free paper,
and their binding materials are chosen for strength and durability.

Contents

IV. Hasidism in the Twentieth Century

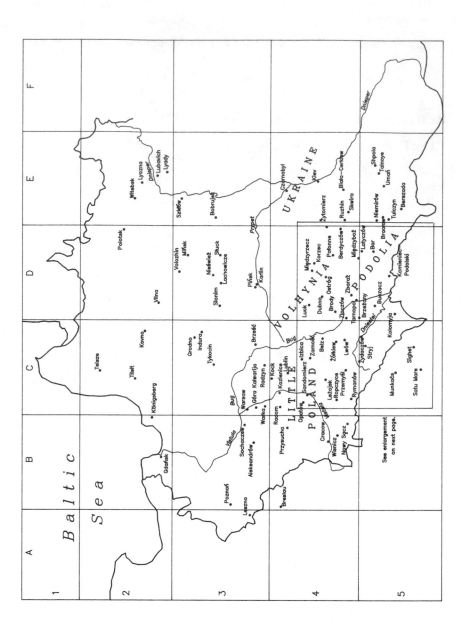

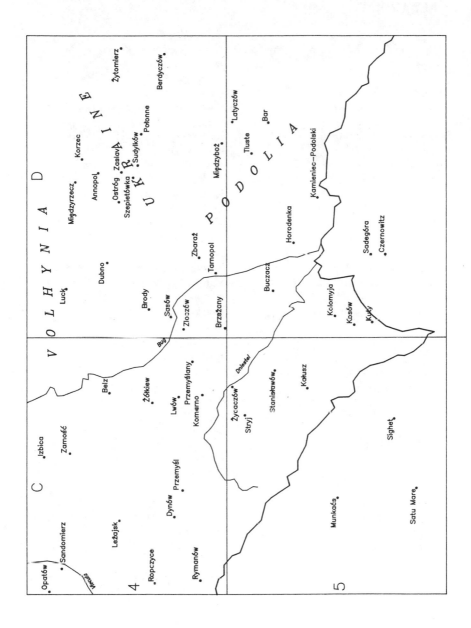

KEY TO MAP

Introduction

Hasidism continues to evoke mixed emotions. The sight of black-frocked, fur-hatted, bearded men with curled sidelocks hanging beside their ears is at once peculiar and familiar to many. After the murder by the Nazis of most European Jews, and, with them, of the majority of the world's Hasidim, the movement has lately regained considerable vitality. Bewilderingly to some, it is actually growing not only in numbers, but also in prominence and influence. Most dramatically, Hasidim play an important role in Israeli politics and society. When the leader (*rebbe* or *zaddik*) of the Belz Hasidim proclaims that peace is more important than territory, or when the leader of the Lubavitch (or Habad) Hasidim says the opposite, their words are reported on the front pages of Israeli newspapers. Some of those who find all this displeasing—among them secularists, religious moderates, and certain non-Hasidic Orthodox Jews—have attacked the Hasidim in language reminiscent of the first bans of excommunication against them in 1772. These opponents speak of false messianism, of misleading the youth, of exploiting the simple, and of endangering the unity of the Jewish people. For all of that, the Hasidim remain, even in Israel, more than a little mysterious to the rest of the population.

There exists no sociological-anthropological treatment of one or another Hasidic group in Israel. Although such communities in the United States, Canada, and Belgium have been studied by sociologists, the lack of such work in Israel may reflect the very seriousness with which they are taken. It is also an indication of the vitality and confidence, even triumphalism, which characterizes these groups in the present day. In Israel at least, they are not a tiny and curious anachronism. And, to be sure, there are not insignificant Hasidic communities in North America and Europe as well.

This book is intended to provide a comprehensive "port òf entry" to the Hasidic world, its history, its values, and its practices. Although many will be interested chiefly in contemporary phenomena, these, surely, cannot be understood without a sense of Hasidism's beginnings, its central ideas, institutions, and customs and some notion of how Hasidism has changed over the past 250 years. In the late eighteenth century, and during most of the following century, Hasidism dominated the religious life of large sections of the Jewish communities of Eastern Europe, which comprised, at the time, the largest concentration of Jews in the world. As a result, most of the present volume is devoted to that period.

The other goal of this book, and of the series of which it forms a part, is to provide a review of the development of scholarship on its subject. In this case, there will emerge as well a sense of the differing ideological uses of Hasidism. These will be clear, for example, in .the memoir of Solomon Maimon (1754–1800), one of the earliest East European Jews to have his thinking shaped by the European Enlightenment. The chapters by Simon Dubnow, a founder of modern Jewish historiography, reflect in some measure his romantic (Diaspora) nationalism mixed with a vestigial Enlightenment-informed revulsion for Hasidism. He first published his history of Hasidism in Russian at the end of the nineteenth century.[1] Benzion Dinur, on the other hand, was an architect of Zionist historiography, and, at one time, Minister of Education in the State of Israel. His landmark study of the origins of Hasidism was first published in Hebrew between 1943 and 1945. Dinur's hypothesis that Hasidism was a messianic movement has been rejected, or at least, modified considerably by subsequent scholarship. Still, many of the issues he was first to raise continue to frame the historiography of the movement, and his methodological innovation—mining the rich literature of homiletics and exegesis *(mussar* and *drush)*—was a pathbreaking and vitally important contribution. Shmuel Ettinger, who, until his death in 1988, was, like Dinur before him, Professor of Jewish History at the Hebrew University in Jerusalem, rejected the two central hypotheses of Dinur's study: that Hasidism was a messianic movement, and that it was a movement of social protest. By the time Ettinger composed the essay included in this volume, he had moved away from the blatantly ideological manifestations of Zionist historiography.

The opening selection in the volume is from the autobiography of Solomon Maimon which he published in German during his lifetime. For all of the disdain this vagabond philosopher had for Hasidism by the time of writing, he nevertheless communicated some feeling of the attractiveness Hasidism held for him as a young man, and, doubtless, for many others. Reflected also are the popular mysticism which characterized the movement, the emphasis on self-annihilation,[2] and the centrality of the rebbe or zaddik.

The chapters by Dubnow, Dinur, and Ettinger all address aspects of the early generations of Hasidism. Murray Jay Rosman's essay, first published only a few years ago, revolutionized the picture of the "founder" of the movement, Israel ben [son of] Eliezer, Baal Shem Tov (the Besht). It would appear from Rosman's study, and that of Emanuel Etkes,[3] that there was no mass movement at all around the Besht. Hasidism, as a movement, began only somewhat later, and its development was inextricably bound up with the institution, or better, with the institutionalization, of the zaddik. Perhaps it would be more accurate not to use the term "movement" at all in describing Hasidism. In view of the substantial differences among Hasidic groups and their leaders in doctrine and orientation, it might be preferable to speak of various Hasidic circles which shared certain characteristics but not others. Mordecai Wilensky's article briefly summarizes the objections of the early opponents (mitnaggedim) to Hasidism. Some of these, as noted, continue to be repeated.

In the second section of the volume, there is a debate of sorts between Gershom Scholem and Ada Rapoport-Albert on the proper understanding of the central idea of devekut (attachment to God) in Hasidic teaching, and of its relation to the role of the zaddik. Indeed, although there were roughly similar theoretical antecedents, it was/is the notion of the zaddik as an actual social institution, which distinguished the movement from all others and gave it its unique characteristics. One was/is not a Hasid, one was/is the Hasid of some particular master. This is what distinguished "Beshtian" Hasidim from the earlier pietist mystics who were also called Hasidim. Scholars will debate precisely when the change came about, but there can be no doubt that by the last decades of the eighteenth century the institution of the zaddik and his followers, who were his followers alone, had begun to distinguish Hasidim from others.

The second part of the second section includes treatments of special aspects of Hasidic life. Louis Jacobs' chapter on prayer provides one such dimension. And, for all of its tendentiousness and eclecticism, Aaron Wertheim's chapter is, to my knowledge, the only presentation of the behavior of a Hasid during the week and on the Sabbath. Here, the reader will learn, among other things, what a *kvitl* is, and why Hasidim try to eat what their rebbe has left on his plate.

The scholarly literature on Hasidism in the nineteenth century is very thin. Although this can be ascribed partly to Dubnow's notion that the creative period of Hasidism ended at the beginning of that century, which idea has been rejected by more recent scholarship, work on the subsequent period has barely begun. Mahler's treatment remains the only sustained history of Hasidism in the nineteenth century. In this section, some of the different "schools" among the Hasidim are described. The reader will note that Mahler's orientation to history was much influenced both by Marxism and by Zionism.

The first of the selections representing the twentieth century is by Martin Buber. It is interesting to contrast Buber's description, "My Way to Hasidism," with Maimon's recollection of his encounter with the Hasidim. For Buber, the main attraction seems to have been the possibility of a truly spiritual life which hallowed the everyday, and which he found in the Hasidic path, reflected particularly in Hasidic tales. For Buber, Hasidism was the quintessence of Judaism itself, and it was he who first presented Hasidism, in his own terms, to Western readers. Some scholars, and particularly Scholem and his followers, rejected Buber's emphasis on one kind of source, to the virtual exclusion of others, as a distortion of the historical reality of Hasidism. Yet, there was and is a valuable corrective to the positivist emphasis on theology and the history of ideas by Scholem and his students in the more phenomenological approach of Martin Buber.[4] In the last chapter, still another orientation is to be found in Stephen Sharot's synthesis of the sociological literature on contemporary Hasidism. He attempts to describe, if not to explain, how the Hasidim manage to maintain their distinctiveness in the face of the surrounding culture.

Expressed as succinctly as possible, Hasidism, at its beginning, was a movement of religious revival with charismatic leadership. One characteristic of Hasidic teaching in general was its emphasis on the rabbinic dictum *leit atar panuy minei*, that is, that the divine presence fills the world in all its aspects and no place is devoid of that presence. The continuous quest for the spiritual, and its personification in the zaddik, was/is perhaps the source of the attractiveness and of the success of Hasidism. Many historians, and particularly those with ideological motives such as Dubnow, Mahler, and Dinur, have, for their own reasons, been drawn to attempts to analyze how a group of religious masters created such a broad "social movement" in such a short time. Many of their conclusions have been rejected; the tools of social history, even when freed from cruder ideological tendencies, can do little more than sketch in the background to Hasidism. They are inadequate for the task of explaining its success.

Though it could not be represented here, there is also a Hasidic historiography of Hasidism. The majority of those works, which are often equipped with all of the standard scholarly apparatus, have emanated from Habad (Lubavitch) circles. Although valuable, they must be treated with the same caution one brings to any other work informed by a specific ideological tendency. Scholarly attention to this problem, and to the interrelationship between "scholarly" and Hasidic versions of the history of Hasidism, has only just begun.[5]

Many of the assumptions, hypotheses, and the conclusions advanced in the work of the authors presented in this volume have been or will be questioned. Nevertheless, if my choices have been correct, the reader will emerge with the beginning of an understanding of Hasidism as a social phenomenon and as a set of spiritual paths. Those who genuinely wish to meet Hasidism must acquire the necessary languages and read the sources themselves.

A word of tribute is due to Dr. Eli Lederhendler of Jerusalem who translated the Hebrew selections so felicitously. Dr. Lederhendler and I have striven to unify the system of transliteration and the spelling of personal and place-names. All of the remaining inconsistencies and infelicities are the responsibility of the editor.

JERUSALEM, MAY 1989

NOTES

1. See Robert Seltzer, "The Secular Appropriation of Hasidism by an East European Jewish Intellectual: Dubnow, Renan and the Besht," *Polin* 1 (1986), 151–162.

2. See Moshe Idel's comments in his *Kabbalah: New Perspectives* (New Haven, Yale U. Press, 1988), 241–242.

3. "Hasidism as a Movement: The First Stage," in *Hasidism: Continuity or Innovation?* ed. B. Safran (Cambridge, Mass., Harvard U. Press, 1988), 1–26.

4. See Maurice Friedman's most recent defence of Buber: "Interpreting Hasidism: The Buber-Scholem Controversy," *Leo Baeck Institute Yearbook* 33(1988), 449–467, and the citations there.

5. Ada Rapoport-Albert, "Hagiography with Footnotes: Edifying Tales and the Writing of History in Hasidism," *History and Theory* 27(1988), 119–159 and the references there.

Instead of a Bibliography

The present book is about one-third the length of the one originally imagined by the editor. Since present circumstances have not permitted the publication of a three-volume work, the only recourse is to list, for the industrious reader, some of the pieces which were not included. In this way, the book as originally imagined will approach real existence. These, then, are most of the items which fell by the wayside in the final and painful "cuts."

PART ONE

Jacob Katz, *Tradition and Crisis: Jewish Society at the End of the Middle Ages.* New York, Schocken Books, 1961, 225–244.

Torsten Ysander, *Studien zum bestischen Hasidismus in seiner religions-geschichtlichen Sonderart.* Uppsala, A-B Ludequistka, 1933, 327–413.

Eliezer Sevi Zweifel, *Shalom al Yisra'el,* ed. Abraham Rubinstein. Jerusalem, Mossad Bialik, 1972, pt. 3, 9–77.

PART TWO

Arthur Green, "The Zaddiq as *Axis Mundi* in Later Judaism," *Journal of the American Academy of Religion* 45 (1977), 328–347.

Mendel Piekarz, "The Messianic Idea in the Period of Early Hasidism" (Hebrew), *The Messianic Idea in Jewish Thought.* Jerusalem, The Israel Academy of Sciences and Humanities, 1982, 237–253.

Gershom Scholem, "The Neutralization of the Messianic Element in

Early Hasidism," in his *The Messianic Idea in Judaism*. New York, Schocken Books, 1971, 176–202.

PART THREE

Yosef Dan, "The Peak Period of the Hasidic Story" (Hebrew), in his *Hasippur ha-hassidi*. Jerusalem, Keter, 1975, 189–263.

Ada Rapoport-Albert, "On Women in Hasidism: S. A. Horodecky and the Maid of Ludmir Tradition," in *Jewish History: Essays in Honour of Chimen Abramsky*, ed. A. Rapoport-Albert. S. J. Zipperstein, London, 1988, 508–525.

Joseph Weiss, "A Late Jewish Utopia of Religious Freedom," in *Studies in Eastern European Jewish Mysticism*, ed. D. Goldstein. Oxford, Oxford U. Press, 1985, 209–248.

PART FOUR

Jacques Gutwirth, "The Structure of a Hasidic Community in Montreal," *Jewish Journal of Sociology* 14 (1972), 43–62.

Jiri Langer, "A Youth from Prague among the Chassidim," in his *Nine Gates to the Chassidic Mysteries*. New York, David McKay, 1961, 3–28.

I

THE SOCIAL AND RELIGIOUS CONTEXT
OF EARLY HASIDISM

1

On a Secret Society, and Therefore a Long Chapter

Solomon Maimon

About this time I became acquainted with a sect of my nation called the *New Hasidim*, which was then coming into prominence. *Hasidim* is the name generally given by the Jews to the *pious*, that is, to those who distinguish themselves by practising the strictest piety. These were, from time immemorial, men who had freed themselves from worldly occupations and pleasures, and devoted their lives to strict observance of the laws of religion and doing penance for their sins. They sought to accomplish this by prayers and other exercises of devotion, by chastisement of the body and similar means.

About this time some of them set up a new sect. They maintained that true piety does not consist in chastisement of the body, which disturbs the spiritual quiet and cheerfulness necessary for the knowledge and love of God. On the contrary, they maintained that man must satisfy all his bodily needs, and seek to enjoy the pleasures of the senses, so far as may be necessary for the development of his feelings, since God has created all for his glory. The true service of God, according to them, consists in exercises of devotion with exertion of all our powers, and annihilation of self before God; for they maintain that man, in accordance with his destiny, can reach the highest perfection only when he regards himself, not as a being that exists and works for himself, but as an organ of the Godhead. Instead, therefore, of spending their lives in separation from the world, in suppression of their natural feelings, and in deadening their powers, they believe that they act much more to the purpose when they develop their natural feelings as much as possible, to exercise their powers and to widen their sphere of work.

It must be acknowledged that both of these opposite methods are based on something true. The basis of the former is obviously Stoicism, that is, an endeavour to determine actions by free will in accordance with a higher principle than passion; the latter is founded on the system of perfection. Both, like everything else in the world, may be abused, and are abused in actual life. Those of the first sect drive their penitential disposition to excess; instead of merely regulating their desires and passions by rules of moderation, they seek to annihilate them; and, instead of endeavouring, like the Stoics, to find the principle of their actions in pure reason, they seek it rather in religion. This is a pure source, it is true; but as these people have false ideas of religion itself, and their virtue has for its foundation merely the future rewards and punishments of an arbitrary tyrannical being who governs by mere caprice, their actions flow from an impure source, namely the principle of interest. Moreover, in their case this interest rests merely on whims, so that, in this respect, they are far below the grossest Epicureans, who have, it is true, a low, but still a real interest as the end of their actions. Religion can only yield a principle of virtue when it is itself founded on the idea of virtue.

The adherents of the second sect have indeed more correct ideas of religion and morals; but since they regulate themselves for the most part in accordance with obscure feelings, and not in accordance with distinct knowledge, they likewise fall into all sorts of extravagances. Self-annihilation cramps their activity, or gives it a false direction. They have no natural science, no acquaintance with psychology; and they are vain enough to consider themselves organs of the Godhead—which of course they are, to an extent limited by the degree of perfection they attain. The result is, that on the credit of the Godhead, they perpetrate the greatest excesses; every extraordinary suggestion is to them a divine inspiration, and every lively impulse a divine call.

These sects were not in fact sects of different religions; their difference consisted merely in their religious practices. But their animosity went so far that they decried each other as heretics, and indulged in mutual persecution. At first the new sect held the upper hand, and extended itself over nearly the whole of Poland, and even beyond. The heads of the sect sent emissaries everywhere, whose duty it was to preach the new doctrine and procure adherents. Now the majority of the Polish Jews are scholars, that is, men devoted to an inactive and contemplative life; for every Polish Jew is destined from birth to be a rabbi, and only the greatest incapacity can exclude him from the office. Moreover this new doctrine was to make the way to blessedness easier, since it declared that fasts and vigils and the constant study of the Talmud are not only useless but even prejudicial to that cheerfulness of spirit which is essential to genuine piety. It was therefore natural that adherence to the doctrine became widespread in a short time.

Pilgrimages were made to holy places where the enlightened leaders of this sect lived. Young people forsook parents, wives and children, and went *en masse* to visit these leaders and hear from their lips the new doctrine. The occasion which led to the rise of this sect was as follows.[1]

I have already remarked that, since the time when the Jews lost their national position and were dispersed among other nations where they are more or less tolerated, they have had no internal form of government except their religious constitution, by which they are held together, and they still form, in spite of their political dispersion, an organic whole. Their leaders, therefore, have been occupied principally with imparting additional strength to this, the only bond of union by which the Jews still constitute a nation. But the doctrines of their faith and the laws of their religion originate in the Holy Scriptures, which leave much that is indefinite in regard to their explosion and application to particular cases. Consequently the aid of tradition is called in, and by this means the method of expounding the Holy Scriptures, as well as the deduction of cases left undetermined by them, is made to appear as if specified in determinate laws. This tradition could not of course be entrusted to the whole nation, but merely to a particular body—a sort of legislative commission.

But this did not avoid the evil. Tradition itself left much that was still indeterminate. The deduction of particular cases from the general, and the new laws demanded by the circumstances of different times, gave occasion for many controversies; but through these very controversies and the mode of their settlement, the laws became more numerous, and their influence on the nation more powerful. The Jewish constitution is therefore in its form aristocratic, and is accordingly exposed to all the abuses of an aristocracy. The unlearned classes of the people, being burdened with the support not only of themselves but also of the indispensable learned class, were unable to give their attention to these abuses. But from time to time men have arisen out of the legislative body itself, who have not only denounced its abuses, but have even called in question its authority.

Of this sort was the founder of the Christian religion, who at the very outset placed himself in opposition to the tyranny of this aristocracy, and brought back the whole ceremonial law to its origin, namely, a pure moral system, to which the ceremonial law stands related as means to end. In this way the reformation at least of a part of the nation was accomplished. Of the same sort also was the notorious Shabbethai Sevi, who at the close of the seventeenth century set himself up as Messiah, and was going to abolish the whole ceremonial law, especially the rabbinical institutions. A moral system founded upon reason would, owing to the deeply rooted prejudices of the nation at that time, have been powerless to work out a wholesome reformation. To prejudice and fanaticism, therefore, it was necessary to oppose prejudice and fanaticism. This was done in the following way.

A secret society, whose founders belonged to the disaffected sections of the nation, had long taken root. A certain French rabbi, named Moses de Leon, is said, according to Rabbi Joseph Candia, to have composed the *Zohar,* and to have foisted it upon the nation as an old book having for its author the celebrated Talmudist, Rabbi Simeon ben Yochai. This book contains an exposition of the Holy Scriptures in accordance with the principles of the Kabbalah; or rather, it contains these principles themselves delivered in the form of an exposition of the Holy Scriptures, and drawn, as it were, from these. It has, like Janus, a double face, and admits, therefore, of a double interpretation.

One is that which is given with great diffuseness in Kabbalistic writings, and has been systematised. Here is a wide field for the imagination, where it can revel at will without being in the end better instructed on the matter than before. Here are delivered, in figurative language, many moral and physical truths, which lose themselves at last in the labyrinth of the hyperphysical. This method of treating the Kabbalah is peculiar to Kabbalistic scholars, and constitutes the lesser mysteries of this secret society.

The second method, on the other hand, concerns the secret political meaning of the Kabbalah, and is known only to the superiors of the secret society. These superiors, as well as their works, remain ever unknown; the rest of the society you may become acquainted with, if you choose. But the latter *cannot* betray political secrets which are unknown to themselves, while the former *will not* do it, because it is against their interest. Only the lesser (purely literary) mysteries are entrusted to the people, and urged upon them as matters of the highest importance. The greater (political) mysteries are not taught, but, as a matter of course, are brought into practice.

A certain Kabbalist, Rabbi Joel Baalshem[2] by name, became very celebrated at this time on account of some lucky cures which he effected by means of his medical knowledge and his conjuring tricks, as he gave out that this was done, not by natural means, but solely through *Kabbalah Ma' asith* (practical Kabbalah), and the use of sacred names. In this way he played a very successful game in Poland. He also took care to have disciples in his art. Among them were some who followed his profession and made themselves a name by successful cures and the detection of robberies. With their cures the process was quite natural. They employed the common means of medicine, but after the usual method of the conjurer they sought to turn the attention of the spectator from these, and direct it to their Kabbalistic hocus-pocus. The robberies they either brought about themselves, or they discovered them by means of their detectives, who were spread all over the country.

Others of greater genius and a nobler mode of thinking formed far grander plans. They saw that their private interest, as well as the general interest, could be best promoted by gaining the people's confidence, and this they sought to do by enlightenment. Their plan was therefore moral and political at the same time.[3] At first it appeared as if they would merely do away with the abuses which had crept into the Jewish system of religion and morals; but this involved a complete abrogation of the whole system. The principal points which they attacked were these:

1. The abuse of rabbinical learning. Instead of simplifying the laws and rendering them capable of being understood by all, the learning of the rabbis leaves them still more confused and indefinite. Moreover, being occupied only with the study of the laws, it gives as much attention to those which are no longer of any application, such as the laws of sacrifice, of purification, etc., as to those which are still in use. Besides, it is not the study, but the observance of the laws, that forms the chief

concern, since the study of them is not an end in itself but merely a means to their observance. And, finally, in the observance of the laws the rabbis have regard merely to the external ceremony, not to the moral end.

2. The abuse of piety on the part of the so-called penitents. These become very zealous, it is true, about the practice of virtue. Their motive for virtue, however, is not that knowledge of God and His perfection, which is based on reason; it consists rather in false representations of God and His attributes. They fail therefore to find true virtue, and hit upon a spurious imitation. Instead of aspiring after likeness to God, and striving to escape from the bondage of sensual passions into the dominion of a free will that finds its motive in reason, they seek to annihilate their passions by annihilating their powers of activity, as I have already shown by some deplorable examples.

On the other hand, those who sought to enlighten the people required, as an indispensable condition of true virtue, a cheerful state of mind disposed to every form of active exertion; and they not only allowed, but even recommended, a moderate enjoyment of all kinds of pleasure as necessary for the attainment of this cheerful disposition. Their worship consisted in a voluntary elevation above the body, that is, in abstracting their thoughts from all things except God, even from the individual self, and in union with God. By this means a kind of self-denial arose among them, which led them to ascribe, not to themselves, but to God alone, all the actions undertaken in this state. Their worship therefore consisted in speculative adoration, for which they held no special time or formula to be necessary, but they left each one to determine it according to the degree of his knowledge. Still they chose for it most commonly the hours set apart for the public worship of God. In their public worship they endeavoured to attain that elevation above the body which has been described; they became so absorbed in the idea of the divine perfection, that they lost the idea of everything else, even of their own body, which became in this state wholly devoid of feeling.

Such abstraction, however, was a very difficult matter; and accordingly, whenever they emerged from this state through new suggestions taking possession of their minds, they laboured, by all sorts of *mechanical operations,* such as movements and cries, to bring themselves back into the state once more, and to keep themselves in it without interruption during the whole time of their worship. It was amusing to observe how they often interrupted their prayers by all sorts of extraordinary tones and comical gestures, which were meant as threats and reproaches against their adversary, the Evil Spirit, who tried to disturb their devotion; and how by this means they wore themselves out to such an extent that, on finishing their prayers, they usually fell down in complete exhaustion.

It is not to be denied that, however sound may be the basis of such a worship, it is subject to abuse just as much as the other. The internal activity following upon cheerfulness of mind, must depend on the degree of knowledge acquired. Self-annihilation before God is only well-founded when a man's thought, owing to the grandeur of its object, is so entirely occupied with that object, that he exists, as it were, outside himself, in the object alone. If, on the contrary, the thought is limited in respect of its object, so that it is incapable of any progress, then the activity mentioned, by being concentrated on this single object, is repressed rather than stimulated. Some simple men of this sect, who sauntered about idly the whole day, pipe in mouth, when asked what they were thinking about all the time, replied, "We are thinking about God." This answer would have been satisfactory if they had constantly sought, by an adequate knowledge of nature, to extend their knowledge of divine perfection. But this was impossible in their case, as their knowledge of nature was extremely limited; and consequently, they concentrated their activity upon an object which, because their capacity was unfruitful, became unnatural. Moreover their actions could be ascribed to God only when they were the result of an accurate knowledge of God; but when they resulted from a very limited knowledge, it was inevitable that all sorts of excesses should be committed, using God as excuse.

The fact that this sect spread so rapidly, and that the new doctrine met with so much approbation, may be very easily explained. The natural inclination to idleness and a life of speculation on the part of the majority, who from birth are destined to study, the dryness and unfruitfulness of rabbinical studies, the great burden of the ceremonial law which the new doctrine promised to lighten, the tendency to fanaticism and the love of the marvellous, which are nourished by this doctrine— these are sufficient to make this phenomenon intelligible.

At first the rabbis and the pietists opposed the spread of this sect; but in spite of this it maintained the upper hand. Hostilities were practised on both sides. Each party sought to gain adherents. A ferment arose in the nation, and opinions were divided.

I could not form any accurate idea of the new sect, and did not know what to think of it, till I met with a young man who had already been initiated into the society and had enjoyed the good fortune of conversing with its superiors. This man happened to be travelling through the place of my abode, and I seized the opportunity of asking for some information about the internal constitution of the society, the mode of admission, and so forth. The stranger was still in the lowest grade of membership, and consequently knew nothing about the internal constitution of the society. He was therefore unable to give me any information on the subject; but, as far as the mode of admission was concerned, he assured me that that was the simplest thing in the world. Any man who felt a desire for perfection, but did not know how to satisfy it, or wished to remove the hindrances to its satisfaction, had nothing to do but apply to the superiors of the society, and automatically he became a member. He did not even require, as you must do on applying to a medical doctor, to say anything to these superiors about his moral weakness, his previous life, and matters of that sort, inasmuch as nothing was unknown to the superiors—they could see into the human heart and discern everything that is concealed in its secret recesses, they could foretell the future, and bring near things that are remote. Their sermons and moral teachings were not, as these things commonly are, thought over and arranged in an orderly manner beforehand. This method is proper only to the man who regards himself as a being existing and working for himself apart from God. The superiors of this sect hold that their teachings are divine and therefore infallible only when they are the result of self-annihilation before God, that is, when they are suggested to them *ex tempore,* by the exigence of circumstances, without their contributing anything themselves.

As I was quite captivated by this description I begged the stranger to communicate to me some of these divine teachings. He clapped his hand on his brow as if he were waiting for inspiration from the Holy Spirit, and turned to me with a solemn mien and his arms half-bared, which he brought into action somewhat like Corporal Trim, when he was reading the sermon. Then he began as follows:

"Sing unto God a new song; and His praise in the congregation of saints" (Psalm cxlix, 1). Our superiors explain this verse in the following way. The attributes of God as the most perfect being must surpass by far the attributes of every finite being; and consequently His praise, as the expression of His attributes, must likewise surpass the praise of any such being. Till the present time the praise of God consisted in ascribing to Him supernatural operations, such as the discovery of what is concealed, the foreseeing of the future, and the production of effects by His will. Now, however, the saints, that is, the superiors, are able to perform such supernatural actions themselves. Accordingly in this respect God has no longer pre-eminence over them; and it is therefore necessary to find some new praise, which is proper to God alone.

Quite charmed with this ingenious method of interpreting the Holy Scriptures, I begged the stranger for some more expositions of the same kind. He proceeded therefore in his inspired manner:

"When the minstrel played, the spirit of God came upon him" (2 Kings iii, 15). This is explained in the following way. As long as a man is self-active, he is incapable of being influenced by the Holy Spirit; for this purpose he must hold himself like an instrument in a purely passive state. The meaning of the passage is therefore this. When the minstrel *(ha-menaggen)* i.e., the servant of God, becomes like his instrument *(ke-naggen)*, then the spirit of God comes upon him.[4]

"Now," said stranger again, "hear the interpretation of a passage from the Mishnah, where it is said: 'The honour of thy neighbour shall be as dear to thee as thine own.' Our teachers explain this in the following way. It is certain that no man will find pleasure in doing honour to himself: this would be altogether ridiculous. But it would be just as ridiculous to make too much of the marks of honour received from another, as these confer on us no more intrinsic worth than we have already. This passage therefore means merely that the honour of thy neighbour (the honour which thy neighbour shows to thee) must be of as little value in thine eyes as thine own (the honour which thou showest to thyself)."

I could not help being astonished at the exquisite refinement of these thoughts; and charmed with the ingenious exegesis by which they were supported. My imagination was strained to the highest pitch by these descriptions, and consequently I wished nothing so much as the pleasure of becoming a member of this honourable society. I resolved therefore to undertake a journey to M———, where the superior B——— resided. I waited with the greatest impatience for the close of my period of service, which lasted still for some weeks. As soon as this came to an end, instead of going home (though I was only two miles away), I started at once on my pilgrimage. The journey extended over some weeks.

At last I arrived at M———, and after having rested from my journey I went to the house of the superior under the impression that I should be introduced to him at once. I was told, however, that he could not speak to me at the time, but that I was invited to his table on Sabbath along with the other strangers who had come to visit him; that I should then have the happiness of seeing the saintly man face to face, and of hearing the sublime teachings from his own mouth; that although this was a public audience, yet, on account of the individual references which I should find made to myself, I might regard it as a special interview.

Accordingly on Sabbath I went to this solemn meal, and found there a large number of respectable men who had gathered from various quarters. At length the awe-inspiring great man appeared, clothed in white satin. Even his shoes and snuffbox were white, this being among the Kabbalists the colour of grace. He gave every newcomer his greeting. We sat down to table and during the meal a solemn silence reigned. After the meal was over, the superior struck up a solemn inspiring melody, held his hand for some time upon his brow, and then began to call out, 'Z——— of H———, M——— or R———,' and so on. Every newcomer was thus called by his own name and the name of his residence, which excited no little astonishment. Each recited, as he was called, some verse of the Holy Scriptures. Thereupon the superior began to deliver a sermon for which the verses recited served as a text, so that although they were disconnected verses taken from different parts of the Holy Scriptures they were combined with as much skill as if they had formed a single whole. What was still more extraordinary, every one of the newcomers believed that he discovered, in that part of the sermon which was founded on his verse, something that had special reference to the facts of his own spiritual life. At this we were of course greatly astonished.

It was not long, however, before I began to qualify the high opinion I had formed of this superior and the whole society. I observed that their ingenious exegesis was at bottom false, and, in addition to that, was limited strictly to their own extravagant principles, such as the doctrine of self-annihilation. When a man had once learned these, there was nothing new for him to hear. The so-called miracles could be very naturally explained. By means of correspondence and spies and a certain knowledge of men, by physiognomy and skilful questions, the superiors were able indirectly to elicit secrets, so that they succeeded with these simple men in obtaining the reputation of being inspired prophets.

The whole society also displeased me not a little by their cynical spirit and the excess of their merriment. A single example of this may suffice. We had met once at the hour of prayer in the house of the superior. One of the company arrived somewhat late, and the others asked him the reason. He replied that he had been detained by his wife having been that evening confined with a daughter. As soon as they heard this, they began to congratulate him in a somewhat uproarious fashion. The superior thereupon came out of his study and asked the cause of the noise. He was told that we were congratulating our friend, because his wife had brought a girl into the world. "A girl!" he answered with the greatest indignation, "he ought to be whipped."[5] The poor fellow protested. He could not comprehend why he should be made to suffer for his wife having brought a girl into the world. But this was of no avail: he was seized, thrown down on the floor, and whipped unmercifully. All except the victim became hilarious over the affair, upon which the superior called them to prayer with the words, "Now, brethren, *serve the Lord with gladness!*"

I would not stay in the place any longer. I sought the superior's blessing, took my leave of the society with the resolution to abandon it forever, and returned home.

Now I shall say something of the internal constitution of the society. The superiors may, according to my experience, be brought under four heads: the prudent, the crafty, the powerful,[6] and the good.

The highest class, which rules all the others, is of course the first. These are men of enlightenment, who have attained a deep knowledge of the weaknesses of men and the motives of their actions, and have early learned the truth that prudence is better than power, inasmuch as power is in part dependent on prudence, while prudence is independent of power. A man may have as many powers and in as high a degree as he will, but his influence is still limited. By prudence, however, and a sort of psychological mechanics, that is, an insight into the best possible use of these powers and their direction, they may be infinitely strengthened. These prudent leaders, therefore, have devoted themselves to the art of ruling free men, that is, of using the will and powers of other men, so that while these believe themselves to be advancing their own ends, they are in reality advancing the ends of their leaders. This can be maintained by a judicious combination and regulation of the powers, so that the slightest touch upon this instrument may produce the greatest effect. There is no deceit in this, for the others reach their own ends also.

The second class, the crafty, also use the will and the powers of others for the attainment of their ends; but in regard to those ends they are more short-sighted or more impetuous than the former class. It often happens, therefore, that they seek to attain their ends at the expense of others; and their skill consists not merely in attaining their own ends, like the first class, but in carefully concealing from others the fact that they have not reached theirs.

The powerful are men who, by their innate or acquired moral force, rule over the weaknesses of others, especially when their force is such as is seldom found in others, as, for example, the control of all the passions but one, which is made the end of their actions.

The good are weak men who are merely passive in respect of their knowledge and will-power, and whose ends are reached, not by controlling, but by allowing themselves to be controlled.

The highest class, that of the prudent, supervising all the others without being under their supervision, rules them all. It makes use of the crafty on their good side, and seeks to make them harmless on their other side by outwitting them, so that when they believe they are deceiving, they themselves are deceived. It makes use, moreover, of the powerful for the attainment of more important ends, but seeks, when necessary, to keep them in check by the opposition of several powers. Finally it makes use of the good for the attainment of its ends, not merely with them but also with others, inasmuch as it commends these weak brethren to the others as an example of submission that is worthy of imitation, and by this means clears out of the way those hindrances that arise from the independent activity of the others.

This highest class usually begins with Stoicism, and ends with Epicureanism. Its members are pious men who have for a considerable time devoted themselves to the strictest exercise of religious and moral laws, and to the control of their desires and passions. But they do not, like the Stoic, look upon Stoicism as an end in itself; they regard it merely as a means to the highest end of man, namely, happiness. They do not therefore remain at the Stoical stage, but, after having obtained from it all that is necessary to the highest end, they hasten to that end itself, the enjoyment of happiness. By their exercise in the strictest Stoicism their sensibility for all sorts of pleasure is heightened and ennobled, instead of becoming duller, as it is with gross Epicureans. By this exercise they are in a position to defer every pleasure that presents itself till they have determined its real worth, which a gross Epicurean will not do.

The first impulse to Stoicism, however, must lie in the temperament, and it is only by a kind of self-deception that it is attributed to voluntary action. But this vanity imparts courage for actual undertakings of a voluntary nature, and this courage is continually fired by their successful outcome. As the superiors of this sect are not men of science, it is not to be supposed that they have hit upon their system by the guidance of reason alone. Rather the motive was, in the first instance, temperament, in the second, religious ideas; and it was only after that, that they could attain to a clear knowledge and practice of their system in its purity.

This sect was, therefore, in regard to its end and its means, a sort of secret society, which had almost acquired dominion over the whole nation; and consequently a great revolution would have been expected, if the excesses of some of its members had not laid bare many weak spots and thus put weapons into the hands of its enemies. Some of them, who wished to pass for genuine Cynics, violated all laws of decency, wandered about naked in the public streets, attended to the wants of nature in the presence of others, and so on. By their practice of extemporising, as a consequence of their principle of self-annihilation, they introduced into their sermons all sorts of foolish unintelligible, confused stuff. Some of them became insane, and believed that they no longer existed. To all this must be added their pride and contempt of others who did not belong to their sect, especially of the rabbis, who, though they had their faults, were still far more active and useful than these ignorant idlers. Men began to find out their weaknesses, to disturb their meetings, and to persecute them everywhere. This was brought about especially by the authority of a celebrated rabbi, Elijah of Vilna, who stood in such great esteem among the Jews that scarcely any traces of the society can now be found.

NOTES

1. In our times, when so much is said both *pro* and *contra* about secret societies, I believe that the history of a particular secret society, in which I was entangled, though but a short time, should not be passed over in this sketch of my life.
2. *Baalshem* is one who occupies himself with the practical Kabbalah, that is, with the conjuration of spirits and the writing of amulets, in which the names of God and of many sorts of spirits are employed.
3. As I never attained the rank of a superior in this society, the exposition of

their plan cannot be regarded as verified by experience, but merely as an inference arrived at by reflection. How far this inference is well founded, can be determined only by analogy according to the rules of probability.

4. The ingenuity of this interpretation consists in the fact that in Hebrew Nagen may stand for the infinitive of *play*, as well as for a *musical instrument*, and that the prefix ke- may be translated either *as*, in the sense of *when*, or *as*, in the sense of *like*. The superiors of this sect, who wrenched passages of the Holy Scriptures from their context, regarding themselves as merely vehicles of their teachings, selected accordingly that interpretation of this passage, which fitted their principle of self-annihilation before God.

5. A trait of these, as of all uncultivated men, is their contempt of the other sex.

6. Of this class I became acquainted with one. He was a young man of twenty-two, of very weak bodily constitution, lean and pale. He travelled in Poland as a missionary. In his look there was something so terrible, so commanding, that he ruled men by means of it quite despotically. Wherever he came he inquired about the constitution of the congregation, rejected whatever displeased him, and made new regulations which were punctiliously followed. The elders of the congregation, for the most part old respectable men, who far excelled him in learning, trembled before his face. A great scholar, who would not believe the infallibility of this superior, was seized with such terror by his threatening look, that he fell into a violent fever of which he died. This man had attained such extraordinary courage and determination merely through early exercises in Stoicism.

2

The Beginnings: The Baal Shem Tov (Besht) and the Center in Podolia

Simon Dubnow

THE MAN AND THE MYTH

The historical image of the progenitor of Hasidism is clouded by a fog of miracle stories with which the folk adorned its beloved hero. The veil woven by the imagination of his contemporaries and of later generations obscures the reality of the Besht's actual character to such an extent that it sometimes seems as if he was not a real person at all, but a myth, an imaginary name attached to the force that created a religious movement that shook the Jewish world. Those conversant with the literature of the time will not, of course, be so foolish as to doubt the existence of the Besht; after all, we have the testimony not only of his disciples and colleagues but also that of several contemporaries who opposed his teachings. (In the last case, however, the life of the founder of Hasidism is but dimly reflected, as we shall see below.) The silhouette of a person of real flesh and blood emerges even from the legendary biography of the Besht, if we know how to read it. We are shown a man who was influenced by his environment and, in turn, left his imprint on it. In passing, we are given a glimpse of life in the eighteenth-century Ukraine.

Fifty-five years after the death of the Besht, a book appeared that purported to relate the events of his life—*Shivhei ha-Besht (In Praise of the Baal Shem Tov)*—comparable to the manner in which the first

Reprinted by permission of Dvir Publishing House from *Toledot ha-hasidut,* by Simon Dubnow, 1944.

gospels of Jesus Christ appeared two generations after his death. The process of gestation for both mythic biographies was the same, despite the seventeen hundred years that separate them. Over the course of some decades, miracle stories began to spread among the folk about the son of Podolia, just as they had about the son of Galilee in his day. Each tale, as it was first told, was not far removed from reality; but as it was transmitted from one teller to the next among the group of true believers, it became embellished and exaggerated. Afterward, the tales were collected and committed to writing in several versions, and began to circulate among the faithful as "sacred scripture" (that, indeed, is how they were referred to, later on, in printers' introductions). Finally, the editors appeared on the scene and collated the different renditions, producing a published work. That is how two editions of *Shivhei ha-Besht* came to be printed in the same year, 1815 (in Kapust, Lithuania, and in Berdyczew, in the Ukraine).[1] Lore became text, legend became scripture: the Genesis of the Hasidim, the book of the "apostles" of the new faith, concealing more than it reveals.

Our task is to attempt to uncover what was concealed, in order to find the kernel of truth that lies buried inside the legend; to discover the actual truth—to the extent that is possible—about the mythic hero. Yet, while doing so, we cannot afford to overlook the legend, either, which was the perceived truth in the eyes of generations of believers. The historian thus has a dual mission to accomplish: to deal with both the *history that became legend* and the *legend that made "history")*.[2]

ISRAEL BEN ELIEZER BEFORE HIS PUBLIC APPEARANCE (APPROXIMATELY 1700–1735)

Toward the end of the seventeenth century, when Podolia was still under Turkish rule (having been ceded to the Turks after the Polish-Turkish war of 1672–1699), a Jewish family that had suffered much from the war lived close to the frontier between Podolia and Moldavia. The father, Eliezer, had been taken prisoner by armed men (apparently a unit of Tatars) who attacked his town, and his wife had fled to another town where she made a living as a midwife. The legendary account tells some rather far-fetched—at times quite absurd—things about Eliezer's adventures while in captivity.[3] His captors took him "to a faraway place where there are no Jews" and there he became a servant in the house of the "viceroy." After a while, he was appointed to be a counselor to the king, who was greatly impressed by his suggestions on military strategy. The daughter of the king was given to him to be his wife, but the pious Jew would not so much as touch a gentile woman, and when he revealed his secret to her, she released him to return home. On the way, Elijah the Prophet appeared to bring him glad tidings: Because of his exemplary conduct, he would father a child "who would bring enlightenment to all Israel." Eliezer returned home to find his wife alive and well, and in their old age (both of them being "close to one hundred years old," as the story, quite sincerely, would have us believe) they were blessed with the birth of the predicted son, whom they named Israel.

If we strip this fairy tale of its fanciful touches, we are left with the bare facts that the birth of the founder of Hasidism was preceded by a period of crisis, and that the child was born after peace had been restored. The Turkish occupation of Podolia ended with the peace agreement signed at Karlowice in 1699, according to which the territory was returned to Polish rule. The child, Israel, was born about that time, as the story informs us, in the town of Okopy, near Kamieniec Podolski— that is, on the Polish side of the Polish-Turkish border (just as it had been before the war). His date of birth may be set at approximately 1700, the threshold of the eighteenth century.[4]

Israel was orphaned in childhood. Eliezer, on his deathbed, told his young son the conventional things: "My beloved son, remember this as long as you live—God is with you. You need not be afraid of anything." The boy took these words to heart and they strengthened his resolve as he embarked on the road of life. He would later come to think of his father's last words as a kind of prophecy and a confirmation of his own teaching that man is in a constant, solitary encounter with his Creator.

The Jewish community took the lad in hand and saw to it that he received a proper education in a private elementary school (heder) or a charity school (talmud torah). The boy showed some aptitude but evidently could not accustom himself to the schoolroom routine. "He would study for a few days, and then would stay away from class." When people went in search of him, they would find him sitting all alone in the woods. They would send him back to his teacher, but after a while he would again flee to the forest to be alone. Perhaps the casuistic art of Talmud study proved unsatisfying to the young dreamer and budding visionary. Perhaps he felt drawn more strongly to lore and legend. Or perhaps he was constitutionally more suited for solitude and was not eager for the company of his classmates. In the end, his would-be benefactors gave up and left him to his own devices.[5]

To support himself, Israel became a teacher's aide, helping to care for young children. His job entailed escorting them to the schoolroom or the study hall *(beit midrash)* and leading them in the recitation of simple prayers. He performed these tasks enthusiastically: On the way to or from school "he would sing to [the children] in a pleasing voice," and he was well loved by his charges. Later on he found another job, as watchman at the *beit midrash*. Here, again, he developed distinctive habits, sleeping while other Jews came to pray or study, and waking at night to engage in solitary prayer and to privately peruse books that caught his interest.[6]

What did the young man study in those long hours of solitude? Evidently it was "practical" kabbala (applied mystical lore) that fired his imagination. Among the works that were popular at the time among Polish Jews were the so-called *Kitvei ha-Ari (Writings of Rabbi Isaac Luria)*. Such esoterica—apocrypha bearing the names of "the holy Ari," Rabbi Hayyim Vital, and other illustrious kabbalists—had been banned from publication by the rabbis, who feared they might lead to heresy and Sabbatian beliefs.[7]

We are told that these secret works found their way into Israel's hands when he was only fourteen. Strange fantasies overlap here with things that might have been true.[8] If we try to discern the factual basis for this story, we come up with the following information: A certain "Rabbi Adam" (a strange name, one that Jews never used) arrived in Okopy one day with a parcel of manuscripts. He had been instructed in his father's will to deliver these to a youth by the name of Israel ben Eliezer, to whom they rightfully belonged. They were "his soul's own spiritual patrimony [lit., 'they belonged to the root of his soul']." The visitor encountered the lad at night at the *beit midrash,* where he handed over the manuscripts. After that, the two would meet in a certain house outside town to study "spiritual and practical kabbala." There they would fast, perform immersions and practice the rites engaged in by the great mystics. It was here, apparently, that Israel learned the formulas that were used by the *baalei shem* ["masters of the holy Name," or spiritual wonder workers]. But before he could become a *baal shem* in his own right, he had to undergo many trials and tribulations.

When the townspeople noticed that the orphan lad had chosen "a proper path" and was showing an interest in study and prayer, they arranged a match for him—as was customary in those days when they would burden fourteen- and fifteen-year-olds with the duty to "increase and multiply." Not long afterward, however, the woman died. Israel then left his native town and set out for Eastern Galicia, toward the nearby district of Brody, where he became a schoolteacher in a community close to that city.[9] He won over everyone he met with his honesty and fairness, and when it was necessary to arrange courts of arbitration for civil suits between Jews of the community, Israel was often chosen to serve as an arbitrator (dayyan).

On one occasion he was involved in arranging a compromise settlement between two litigants, one of whom was the father of the prominent Brody rabbi, Avraham Gershon Kutover. The father had a divorced daughter, and, being favorably impressed by the young dayyan's scholarly mien, proposed to the young man that he marry his daughter. Israel agreed to this, on condition that the matter remain confidential for the time being. In the interim, however, the father of the prospective bride died. His son, the rabbi, was astonished to discover among his father's papers the nuptial agreement that betrothed his sister to an unknown individual, Israel ben Eliezer by name. More shocking still, the prospective bridegroom soon appeared before the rabbi, dressed "as a coarse person" (in "a short fur jacket and a wide belt"), and spoke uncivilly to the rabbi as Jacob had spoken to Laban: "Let me have my wife!" The rabbi asked his sister if she would consent to marry this "boor," to which she replied that she was honor bound to respect her dead father's wishes. During the wedding ceremony, the bridegroom revealed his secret to his bride: that he wished to remain incognito for the time being, so that no one would think of him as a scholar and a kabbalist.

His brother-in-law, Rabbi Avraham Gershon, considered it beneath his dignity to live in close proximity with this "boor," and therefore suggested to his sister that she and her husband leave Brody. He supplied her with a horse and wagon, and the couple went in search of shelter elsewhere.[10]

They settled in one of the villages that lay between Kutów and Kosów, nestled in a valley among the Carpathian mountains. Reb Israel spent most of his time in seclusion, in the hills. Twice a week, his wife brought a horse and wagon up to him. Israel would dig clay out of the hillside and load it onto the wagon for his wife to take to market in the nearby town. The earnings allowed them to barely get by. Fortunately, Reb Israel's needs were scanty: During his days of solitary meditation he would fast most of the time, taking only a bit of bread between fasts.[11] The mystic's thoughts were lost in the upper spheres, while all around him loomed the majestic Carpathians, forested and blanketed with grass on the lower slopes and snow-capped up above. Here, amid the silence of nature, the recluse heard the voice of God. Here he felt His presence permeating the entire universe. This was the setting in which the basic idea underlying his later teachings germinated: "all the world is full of His Glory"—literally.

This solitary existence among the mountains lasted about seven years, according to Hasidic tradition. Possibly this is an allusion to the seven years that the sainted mystic, the Ari, was said to have spent in seclusion in Egypt, according to *Shivhei ha-Ari*. Ultimately, though, the couple grew weary of their life of extreme penury, and they returned to Brody to seek the help of Rabbi Avraham Gershon. The rabbi took his brother-in-law into his household as a servant, but soon found that he was not suited to such work. Therefore (and with a view toward ridding himself once again of this "blemish" on the family name), he rented for the young couple a tavern—a bar and rooms for travelers—in a village near Kutow. Reb Israel's wife ran this small business, to which her husband occasionally lent a hand; but in his spare time he sat in a small shelter on the banks of the Prut and delved into mystic lore,[12] just as the Ari, in his day, had sat in his small house by the side of the Nile. It would seem that the future Baal Shem Tov was consciously modelling himself in the image of the Ari as he knew it from *Shivhei ha-Ari*.

Close to the year 1730, Reb Israel settled in the Galician town of Tluste, where he once again became a schoolteacher. On occasion he would travel to the nearby villages and tutor the sons of the excise men there. Still, he made only a precarious living. The legendary account informs us that his clothes were of coarse, woven stuff and that his toes stuck out of holes in his shoes, he was so poor.[13] For several more years Reb Israel continued to weigh the merits of remaining a "hidden" holy man, as against appearing in public as a *baal shem* who could use the kabbala to perform miraculous acts. Then, after he turned thirty-six, he decided to make himself known to the world.[14] In reality, the timing must not have been calculated until years later, when others took note of the fact that his public appearance took place in his thirty-sixth year, about 1735. That was the event that changed the life of the founder of Hasidism.

THE REVEALED RABBI ISRAEL, THE *BAAL SHEM* (APPROXIMATELY 1735–1745)

In those days numerous *baalei shem* were active in Polish Jewry, especially in the southern areas—Galicia and Podolia. Several of them were very well known, such as Rabbi Yoel, the *baal shem* of Zamość. Most of them, however, enjoyed only a local reputation in the immediate vicinity of their own towns. At a time when trained physicians were rare —indeed, in the small towns and villages they were unheard of—the *baalei shem* took the place of doctors in the treatment of physical and emotional ailments, since the people were steeped in superstition and ignorance. Most of these practitioners used "tried and true" remedies: herbs and potions, charms to recite over injured limbs, amulets and oaths. The more conscientious among them made use of practical kabbala, mystic practices, special prayers and the like. The folk naively believed that these "wonder workers" were capable of exorcising "demons" from the emotionally disturbed, able to prevent death and ward off all sorts of misfortunes. In Galicia there were books containing prescriptions, such as *Toledot adam* and *Mif'alot elohim* (both printed in Żółkiew, 1720 and 1724). These were based on the books of kabbala and on the writings of famous *baalei shem* (Rabbi Yoel, Rabbi Eliyahu, and others). But most often, these books were not printed, and circulated in manuscript as secret writings, known only to the few initiates.

The *baalei shem* exerted a tremendous religious influence among the folk masses who believed implicitly in their remedies and their "miracles." There were many who exploited this blind faith for their own profit, but the best ones considered their work a sacred calling. The healing they performed was not done merely for the sake of their own livelihood, but primarily as a means of redeeming the souls of those who approached them for help, or of disseminating knowledge of the revealed Torah. Such men were instrumental in spreading belief in the Sabbatian movement. And when that movement waned, the early proponents of Hasidism and zaddikim made use of the expertise of the *baalei shem* for their own ends. The zaddikim who established the Hasidic way of life were the heirs of the *baalei shem*.

The first of them, Rabbi Israel Baal Shem, turned to that calling at first out of poverty; but when the Hasidic idea was out of its infancy and he felt the need to bring it to the masses, he realized that the "miracle worker" sobriquet was likely to influence the people to accept his teachings. Is this not similar to other examples we can point to in the history of religions? Would Jesus the Nazarene have become the founder of a new faith had he not worked "miracles" and "wonders," healing the sick, "reviving the dead' and so forth; had he not, that is, made use of the fact that the folk *believed* such miracles had indeed taken place? In like fashion, the creator of Hasidism began from the magic of the *baalei shem* and progressed to the revelation of a new teaching. Rumors of the wonders he had performed laid the groundwork for the acceptance of his ideas. And because he did not deal only with physical ailments— having set himself also to treat those who suffered in spirit and to provide spiritual guidance to those who turned to him—the masses sensed that this was no "ordinary" *baal shem,* but a *baal shem* of particular goodness, a guide and a teacher. That was how he became known as the "Baal Shem Tov" (*tov,* Heb.: "good") or the Besht, for short. It became the special title of the founder of Hasidism.

In the first few years after deciding to make himself known as a *baal shem,* he apparently focused his activities in the town of Tluste, where he continued to live. He would depart on occasional forays, however, into the surrounding communities in Galicia and Podolia: Horodenka, Kutów, Niemirów and Szarogród. Sometimes he turned up even in Volhynian towns: Polonnoe (Polonne), Biala Cerkiew, Zaslaw and others.[15] He traveled mostly to villages, healing the local Jewish excise men and lessees (*arendars*). Even members of the Polish gentry sometimes asked him to call on them for medical purposes. He generally used proven methods, such as bleeding by lancet or leeches. Sometimes he would use a prayer or oath to drive a demon out of the body of a sick person, or out of a house. If the attempt proved unsuccessful, he would tell the family that Satan had intervened, or that he heard a heavenly voice announcing that the person in question had been sentenced to die.

The Besht was wary of doing any healing in a house where a Christian doctor or a Tatar medicine man was also consulted, because such people would sometimes attack him. When a doctor would question him about the source of his knowledge, he would answer simply, "God taught me."[16] The Besht was especially famous for his therapeutic amulets. A formula written on parchment, containing the names of angels and imprecations against hostile forces, was enclosed in a small case made of tin and hung around the neck under the clothing of a sick person, a pregnant woman, or a newborn infant. This was considered by the believers as guaranteed protection against misfortune. Amulets written or signed by the Besht were thought to be the most effective, and there were many who willingly paid quite a bit to "redeem their souls." Letters to the wonder worker were written from all over the Ukraine requesting amulets and advice. There was so much work involved that soon the Besht required the constant assistance of a scribe for writing the amulets and answering letters. Later on, he would have two such scribes.[17]

After having earned a reputation as a "holy man," he turned to simpler methods—those closer to his own inclinations: prayer. In prayer, he would become very animated and would inspire the same passion in onlookers. It is said that when he prayed in a village barn, the barrels of produce surrounding him veritably danced with the force he put into his bodily movements.[18] If asked to give advice or to foretell matters relating to an individual's fate, he would open the book of the Zohar, look in it, and immediately pronounce his answer. Once he succeeded in this manner in pinpointing the location of a man who had departed on a long journey and of whom nothing had been heard since. When people asked him how he was able to answer personal queries by consulting so ancient a book, he replied: "The light God created in the first six days was sufficient (according to the legend in the Talmud) to enable one to see from one end of the universe to the other. When God saw that the earth was too puny to require so much light, He tucked some of it away for the righteous to use in times to come. And where did he hide it? In the Torah, and that is why when I open the book of the Zohar [zohar, Heb.: shining light] I can see anywhere in the world."[19]

In general the Besht confined his journeys to Galicia and the Ukraine, but once he happened to venture into Lithuania. In Sluck, one of the major Jewish communities there, there lived two wealthy brothers who had come there from Galicia to manage the estates belonging to Prince Radziwill. These estate stewards (who were also known to their Lithuanian contemporary, Solomon Maimon, under their Polish name, dzierzawcy) oversaw the affairs of many country Jews who had leased small incomes or taverns from them. The powerful stewards supervised their tenants closely to see that they were diligent and hard-working, and they would raise the rent they charged without any consideration for their poor brethren, who cursed the two as "tyrants." According to the legend told by the Hasidim, the wife of one of the wealthy brothers once invited the Besht to dedicate the impressive house that her husband had built in Sluck. The holy man spent about three weeks there, but sensed that he was not quite trusted and that the Lithuanian Jews did not really believe in his "wonders." Before his departure, the pious wife inquired of him how long they might expect their good fortune to last; to which the Besht replied: twenty-two years. And his prediction proved accurate, for at the end of twenty-two years the prince became angry with his stewards and had them thrown in prison.[20]

Did the Besht himself believe all the wonder-stories that were told about him? Did he actually think he was a prophet and a seer? We would have to penetrate into his innermost soul in order to answer that. But we can say this: A person of that sort, with his thoughts always focused on God, who did not distinguish between God and nature, who saw the visible world as being insolubly linked to the divine sphere, and believed with all his soul that there was constant communication and mutual influence between them—such a person would not be capable of finding anything beyond the range of the "naturally" possible. For him, everything was at one and the same time both natural and divine, physical and metaphysical, simple reality and "miracle of God." The following saying is attributed to him: "When a person is in communion with God's presence, and then directs his thoughts to the upper spheres, he is immediately transported to the upper spheres. For his thoughts determine where he is, and were he not in the upper spheres, he could not truly concentrate his thoughts on them."[21] It was clear to him that the prayer of a holy man, when performed with real passion and directed at achieving true communion with the divine realm, had the potential to influence matters on high.

God did not always change His decision in accordance with such a prayer, however: Sometimes a miracle might occur, and sometimes the prior decision was allowed to stand. Sometimes a seer can predict, but the prediction does not come true. The Hasidic legend tells us quite frankly that the Besht once told a wealthy man that his son would recover from an illness. But when he saw afterward that the boy seemed to be dying, and that the parents wanted to "expose" the holy man as a charlatan, he fled from their house and miraculously traveled an impossible distance, in order that "the matter should not bring him harm elsewhere."[22] What we have here, then, is neither fakery nor madness, but attempts to intervene in the sphere of the divine. When we thoroughly analyze the Besht's teachings, we can understand his thinking in these matters.

At the end of the period we are dealing with, between approximately 1740 and 1745, another change occurred in the life of the Besht. He moved from the Galician town of Tluste to Miedzyboz, in Podolia, where he remained for the rest of his life.[23] For twenty years Miedzyboz became the center of a new religious movement, as Safed had been (in the Land of Israel) in the days of Rabbi Luria (the Ari) and his disciples. With this shift in location came also a substantive change: In Miedzyboz the *baal shem* became a spiritual teacher; the "wonder worker" who had captured the imagination of the folk became the preacher of new ideas to disciples who came from the world of rabbinical learning. Before the move, the Besht roamed the countryside; now, with the reputation he enjoyed, people came to him, not only to benefit from his "wonders" but also to hear his message. Talmud scholars and kabbalists, rabbis and preachers, who could not find satisfaction in scholastic and ascetic religion and sought a new path, found their way to the Besht. Some came with the idea of testing him, and some came to bask in the glow of his religious passion. Among them were the rabbi of a number of Podolia communities, Yaaqov Yosef Ha-Cohen, and a preacher (*maggid*) from Volhynia, Rabbi Dov Ber, who became the pillars of Hasidism after the death of the Besht. It was at that time, too, that the Besht's brother-in-law, Rabbi Avraham Gershon Kutover of Brody, who had once scorned him, made up with him at last. There were those among the Besht's visitors who tried to best him in religious argumentation, but the legends maintain that they were always defeated.[24]

What did the Besht do to disseminate his ideas? Evidently he was not especially gifted in oral preaching or writing, but he was particularly effective in one-on-one discussions and in coining maxims, similar to the practice of the founders of religions in the ancient world. In intimate discussion he was inspired by the "holy spirit," and his thoughts would take form as parables, epigrams, and homilies on biblical passages.

Those who heard him were impressed by his originality, by the depth of his religious feeling, and by the basic idea that made a systematic whole of the various expressions he used. The Besht's words and his maxims remained in the memory of his disciples, who later recorded them in their books, more or less as their master had spoken them. Many of them, however, did become distorted and mixed with later ideas. The historian must therefore approach these materials with caution, attempting to sift (as far as this is possible) the original creation of the founder of Hasidism from accretions added by his disciples.

THE BESHT AS LEADER OF THE HASIDIC SECT IN PODOLIA

In the forties and fifties of the eighteenth century, while the Encyclopedists in Paris were rebelling against clericalism in the name of human reason, a small town in the Ukraine became the hub of a religious movement that flatly denied the efficacy of reason and, instead, sought to subject all of life to the dictates of a mystical faith. A band of Hasidim —kabbala-inspired rabbinical figures who were dissatisfied with their lot (preachers and other second-rung religious functionaries from the small communities)—gathered in Miedzyboz where they imbibed the teachings of their master, the Besht. The Besht and his circle evidently met for prayers in their own synagogue or prayer quorum, where they were joined by some members of the local community. Those of the disciples who returned to their hometowns spread word of the new teaching (either openly or discreetly) and, in their turn, established groups for common prayer—new cells of what became the Hasidic sect.

As the Besht observed his influence spreading, his confidence grew that Heaven itself had singled him out for the task of bringing his brethren back to their Father. His imagination soared and he believed that he "heard heavenly pronouncements," that subtle meanings of Scripture were revealed to him by the ancient prophet, Ahijah the Shilonite, to whom Hasidic legend ascribes the role of teacher to the Besht.[25] He began experiencing trances or "spiritual journeys," visions in which he was "elevated" to the spiritual realm, and later reported what was revealed to him there. He recorded two such episodes, at the New Year of 5507 (September 1746) and at the New Year of 5510 (1749) in a letter, which may be said to represent a proclamation or manifesto of Hasidism. He gave the letter to his faithful disciple Yaaqov Yosef Ha-Cohen, asking him to deliver it to his brother-in-law, Rabbi Avraham

Gershon Kutover, who had since settled in the Holy Land. Because Yaaqov Yosef was detained in Europe and never delivered the letter, it remained in his possession. Several years later he published it in one of his books.[26] Concerning his first experience with "elevating his soul," the Besht reported the following:[27]

On New Year of the year 5507 I effected an elevation of my soul, as you know, and I saw wondrous visions such as I have never seen in all my life. Words cannot properly describe what I beheld and learned, even were we to speak face to face. Upon reaching the lowermost part of Paradise, I saw untold numbers of souls of both the living and the dead, people known and unknown to me . . . and many sinners who had repented of their sins and had been forgiven. . . . And every one of them asked of me the following: "God has graced you with special understanding and a capacity for knowing such matters, so come with us up here and be of help to us." And because of the great joy that I witnessed among them, I made up my mind to join them.

And I saw in my vision that the Satan Samael had come to disturb that incomparable joy with his accusations of sin. He performed his work by seeking to foment persecutions and forcible conversions, so that certain souls would die terrible deaths. I was stricken with horror and almost gave up my soul, and I begged my master and teacher[28] to escort me, for it is a great peril to rise up into the upper spheres.

I arose by stages, until I entered the palace of the Messiah, where the Messiah sits and studies Torah with all the sages and holy ones. There I witnessed great rejoicing. I believed that the rejoicing was over my having left this world behind, but they told me I had not died yet—only that it causes them delight on high when I unite the holy spheres from below through their holy Torah.

And I inquired of the Messiah: How long? And he answered me: "By this shall you know it [the time of my coming], that when your teaching will be widespread and known throughout the world . . . and [others besides you] will be capable of uniting the holy spheres and of elevating souls like you do, then all the impurities [qelipot] will have been removed and the propitious hour for salvation will have come."

I was much taken aback by this and I felt great sorrow over the formidable length of time required for this: When could it possibly take place? But during my sojourn there I did learn three mystical secrets [seggulot] and three secret holy names. . . . And I thought to myself, perhaps this might enable my associates to reach the spiritual level and inner state that I have reached. . . . But I did not receive permission to reveal them as long as I live. . . . I can tell you this, however: When you are at prayer or engaging in study, with every word you speak make the union of the Name [of God] your deep purpose, for each and every letter contains a universe, souls, divinity, and so forth.

To this report of his conversation with the Messiah, the Besht added several statements about the persecutions that terrorized the Jewish communities in the Ukraine at that time:

And I prayed there, also, over what God had done, the effect of which was the consigning of some souls of Israel to Samael to be killed. Of them, some were forcibly baptised and then killed. And I received permission to address Samael personally, and I asked . . . and he answered me that his intentions were pure. And so it happened after this, for our many sins, that a false accusation was lodged against several people in the holy community of Zaslaw. Two of them converted and then they killed them. The rest brought great sanctification to the holy Name and were martyred through awful deaths. And after that there was a false accusation in the holy communities of Sowotowka and Duniawiec; but there the people would not let themselves be converted, having heard of the fate that befell those in the holy community of Zaslaw. All of them were martyred for the sake of the holy Name, and withstood the test.[29]

His second "elevation of the spirit" took place in 1749 and was also connected with troubles. That was when the Haidamaks rose up in the Ukraine: Communities were destroyed in Winnica, Latyczów, Pastów, and several other towns.[30] On this, the Besht wrote:

And on the New Year of 5510 [1749] I performed an elevation of the soul, as you know, and I beheld a great accusation [persecution being prepared against us], with Samael receiving permission to destroy entire communities and districts. So I placed my soul in the balance [lit.: offered my soul] and prayed: Let us fall into the hands of God and not into the hands of men. And my request was granted. Instead [of the marauders] there would be a grave feebleness [disease], a plague in all of Poland and the neighboring countries such as we have never seen. And that was how the feebleness spread so far and wide. . . . I persuaded my group[31] to recite special prayers upon waking in order to deflect the decree. From heaven I was told: But you yourself chose to "fall into the hands of God," so why now are you attempting to annul the decree? Since then I did not say the special prayers or pray especially [to end the plague]. I only went along to the synagogue with everyone on Hoshana Rabba . . . and I prayed that the plague would not spread to our area. And that was how we succeeded, with the help of God.

Here the Besht entangled himself in a claim of "foreknowledge" after the fact: The Haidamaks did indeed destroy a number of communities, and stopped when the plague began to spread. It was then that the Besht was granted the revelation that his prayers had averted the direct danger to Jewish communities, bringing instead a general danger of sickness.

The Besht's letter gives us an insight into the Hasidic answer to the problem of messianism. The national aspect is erased here by the spiritual aspect, particularly by the element of personal salvation: salvation of the soul. Once the teachings of Hasidism would be widely acknowledged and many people would reach the state of holiness attained by the Besht, the "propitious hour for salvation will have come." The Besht was dismayed by the prospect of how long this would take, but found some consolation in the "mystical secrets" he learned, secrets that were associated with achieving the "union" of God's name, with infusing prayer with mystical meaning, and so forth. Thus, the spread of Hasidism is the way to salvation, and the zaddikim, those who learn the "secret," are to be the real saviors, who will prepare the way for the Messiah's arrival.

At the end of his letter to his brother-in-law, the Besht wrote: "I have not given up entirely on going to the Land of Israel, if that is God's will, and being with you there, but the times seem to rule that out." A later Hasidic legend tells us at some length about the Besht's preparations for a journey to the Holy Land. He reached Istanbul with his daughter and his scribe. But on the way a great storm arose and almost sank his boat. Taking this as a sign that Heaven wished to stop him from carrying out his plan—out of fear that his arrival in the Land would force the Messiah to arrive before his appointed time—the Besht decided to return home.[32]

Who were the central members of the Besht's coterie in Miedzyboz? His set companions were Reb Sevi "the scribe," and the famous rabbi, Yaaqov Yosef, from Niemirów. The former answered the Besht's correspondence with advice about mundane matters—cures and amulets for the sick, advice and blessings for those embarking on new ventures, and so on. The latter would set down in writing the Besht's teachings, his parables and his maxims. There was also Reb Aryeh-Leyb of Polonne, known as the "Polonne Preacher," who was among the first to bring the Besht's teachings to other communities.[33]

The group numbered among it several scholars who had originally opposed the Besht—a man who pursued a lowly calling, as they saw it, writing amulets and dealing in all the other remedies of the baalei shem —but his "charms" proved irresistible once they got close enough to know him, and they became his enthusiastic devotees. These were Rabbi Nahman Kosover, Rabbi Yishaq Drohobyczer, Rabbi Wolf Kotzis, and Rabbi David Purkes.[34] The greatest of them all, and the one who inherited the mantle of the Besht's leadership, was a man who joined him only later, at the end of his life: the Maggid (Preacher) Rabbi Dov Ber of Miedzyrzecz (who will be discussed in chapter 3). Some of the Besht's disciples were authorized by him to accept appointments as rabbis and preachers, ritual slaughterers and *hazzanim* (cantors) in the small communities nearby where his influence was strongly felt. All of them made efforts to spread the word of the greatness of their rabbi and sponsor.[35]

Toward the end of his life, the Besht was increasingly preoccupied with Jewish communal affairs. He no longer needed to worry about a livelihood: He received a decent level of support from the flock of the faithful, who would send him money as a "soul redemption" when he provided amulets, cures, prayers, and blessings. For his part, he distributed a great deal of charity to the poor, and in particular took care of ransom payments—that is, paying the debts owed by petty *arendars* to Polish overlords who held the lessee and his family members as ransom against prompt payment of the lease fees.[36]

In those days, when not one Passover passed by without a charge of ritual murder somewhere, the communities had to worry about ransom of a different kind: They needed money to support the families of those imprisoned or martyred in the course of a blood libel. We have seen, in the letter already quoted, how concerned the Besht was over the blood libels in Zaslaw and elsewhere during 1747–48. In 1753 the Ukraine was rocked by a terrible blood libel affair in Zytomierz. (Those arrested in this episode, known as the Pawolocz affair in Hebrew memorials, came mainly from the small town of Pawolocz.)[37] News that the prisoners had been killed (so the Hasidic account tells us) reached Miedzyboz on a Friday and caused the Besht much anguish. The next night he lay on the ground and wailed, until the spirits of the ancient rabbinic martyrs, Rabbi Akiva and all the rest, came to tell him that his cries had caused a commotion in heaven. Nevertheless, the die was cast.[38]

The Besht was sorely troubled by the problems that beset the persecuted and the humiliated Jews. He had no use for the preachers who would berate the people for their sinfulness and threaten them with hellfire and brimstone. He was moved to anger on one occasion when he learned that there was a preacher in the synagogue who was "slandering the people of Israel"—that is, castigating them for their transgressions. Word of the Besht's consternation reached those assembled at the synagogue, who promptly left before the sermon was over. The preacher asked the Besht the next day to explain why he had been so angered. The legend has it that "the Besht sprang from his seat, scattering teardrops from his face, and said: 'You speak ill of the Jews! Don't you realize that the Jew goes out every day to earn a living, and toward evening he begins to hurry because he worries about missing the time for his prayers? So he goes into a house and prays, without even knowing what he is saying, and still the angels of heaven are deeply moved by this prayer.' "[39] Another tale about the Besht relates that he performed an "elevation of the spirit" and saw the angel Michael, the defender of the Jews in the heavenly kingdom, engaged in praising Israel: "Even their demerits are in fact meritorious—their misdeeds [misconduct in business affairs] are done only for the sake of [a holy purpose, such as] enabling their daughters to marry scholars or performing acts of charity, and they do not act out of choice."[40] This defense of "misdemeanors" on the basis of economic necessity or family obligations smacks of "ends justifying the means" when it comes to performing *misvot* (commandments): a failing that is fairly common in Hasidic circles.

The traditionalist rabbis were provoked by the tales that were spread about the "holy man of Miedzyboz" and were perturbed at the way the "ignorant folk" were making so much of his piety and spirituality. It is told that the Besht was summoned to appear at the Council of the Four (Polish) Lands, to account for his behavior. The head of the council, Rabbi Abraham Abba, asked the Besht, "Judging by your conduct, it would seem that you are possessed of a holy spirit, but there are those who say that you are unlettered. Let us now test your expertise in the laws of the Torah." They asked him to explain what is the rule with regard to someone who had omitted to say the "Ya'aleh veyavo" prayer for the new moon. This was a classic test question on which volumes had been written. The one being tested was expected to demonstrate virtuosity in the scholastic literature. The Besht, however, replied with perfect simplicity: "This law has no purpose, for you or for me, for you may well forget to perform something for which the penalty is very great before I forget what prayers I must recite." There is no stronger refutation of rabbinic casuistry than this statement of the simple sincerity of prayer. But the rabbis considered the answer they were given as proof that the Besht was indeed an ignoramus—though the legend adds that, eventually, circumstances led them to understand the Besht's power to understand hidden mysteries.[41] Apart from this story, we have no reliable evidence of personal confrontations between the Besht and the rabbis of his day.[42]

During the last four years of his life the Besht was witness to the activities of the Frankist movement that spread into the same communities in Podolia and Galicia where Hasidism had made inroads. The Frankist sect was a legacy of the Sabbatian heresy against which the rabbis had fought during the Besht's childhood. The young recluse of the Carpathian mountains had evidently engaged in an inner struggle against the temptation to follow the esoteric teachings of the Sabbatians. One Hasidic legend [43] describes, in its own way, this youthful blemish:

Sabbetai Sevi came to the Besht to seek a way to rehabilitate his soul, which could come about only through blending soul with soul, spirit with spirit, being with being. [The Besht] proceeded with great caution, because he feared that he [Sabbetai Sevi] was a great evildoer. Once, when the Besht was asleep, Sabbetai Sevi (may his name be blotted out) came and tempted him so that he managed to hurl him into the lowest part of the netherworld, and the Besht looked around and found himself together with Jesus (of Nazareth) upon a board called a slate. . . . The Besht said that there was a spark of the sacred in Sabbetai Sevi, but that Samael the Satan trapped him in his dungeon.

At a later stage, when the Besht had formulated his ideas in conscious opposition to messianic kabbalism, he was more stringent in his judgment of the Sabbatians. When their book *Hemdat yamim* was published in Poland (a compendium of prayers and sermons attributed to Sabbetai Sevi's prophet, Nathan of Gaza), the Besht warned his disciples that it was "impure" and likely to "pollute the world." He once noticed the book lying on a table in the home of a friend, took it, wrapped it in a dirty rag, and threw it on the floor. [44]

One may therefore understand how overwrought the Besht became when the Frankist sect emerged to spread heresy in the land, starting from its openly anti-Talmudic stand and ending with Christian leanings. The bastion of Hasidism was at the very eye of the storm: The famous disputation between the rabbis and Jacob Frank took place in the summer of 1757 in Kamieniec Podolski, under the eye of the Jew-hating Bishop Dembowski. A consequence of the disputation was the burning of the Talmud (October 1757).

At that time, we are told (in the Hasidic legends a prophecy always precedes the event, though it was really a prophecy after the fact), [45] 'the Besht foresaw a great persecution for Israel that would remove the Oral Law [Talmud] from them." This occurred on the eve of Yom Kippur. The Besht had been particularly distressed all day, and when the elders of the town came to him to receive his blessing, the Besht was unable to utter more than one or two blessings, so great was his grief. In the synagogue afterward, the Besht prostrated himself before the holy ark and cried, "Woe, for they wish to remove the Torah from us! How will we go on living scattered among the nations without the Torah?!" At this point the tradition interpolates a comment that is remarkable, coming from pious believers: "And the Besht was angered at the rabbis, and said that it was their fault for the falsehood in their hearts, and that all the sages of the Talmud, the Tannaim and Amoraim, had been put on trial." What can this mean? Is the Besht, distressed by the troubles caused by a sect of anti-Talmudists, himself accusing the rabbinical scholars and the rabbis of the Talmud? Or rather—and this is more credible—is this a criticism of the rabbis for having placed so much emphasis on the study of Talmud that they, in effect, created a situation in which the burning of *books* could threaten to destroy Judaism itself?

Throughout the day of Yom Kippur the Besht sought to arouse the heavens with mighty feats of prayer. It is said that he "went back and forth from one world to the other," and that with the aid of his "teacher" (Ahijah the Prophet) he reached the palace of the Messiah, who told him that "his prayers were accepted and the accuser of the Jews was silenced (in the heavenly court): All but a faint reminder of the sentence had been lifted"—that is, the punishment would be a light one. "The charge," so we are told by the narrator, "was prompted by the [Jews' response to] the sect of Sabbetai Sevi, may his name be blotted out, and the bishop of Kamieniec had two sets of Talmud burnt" (additional Talmuds were burnt afterward). The bishop, however, who stood close to the flames, was stricken and later died.

That is how the Hasidim perceived or portrayed the events of 1757–58 surrounding the disputation in Kamieniec, the Frankist threat, the burning of the Talmud, and the sudden death of the Podolian bishop. The Hasidim believed that it was the power of their leader that prevented the worst from happening, so that only a few Talmuds were actually consigned to the flames, and the wicked bishop received his just desserts.

What else did the Besht do to counter the threat of the Frankists, apart from rending the heavens with his entreaties? He was, after all, close to the scene of events—first in Podolia, and later in Galicia, in Lwów, where a second disputation took place in the summer of 1759. Of this the legends we have tell only that, "a disputation took place before the bishop of the holy community of Lwów, but the fear of the Torah fell upon him [the bishop] and he undertook no evil. And the entire sect of the wicked was wiped out through conversion to Christianity, after the bishop humiliated them in public by having them shave half their beard and one of their earlocks, so that everyone would know that they were neither Jews nor Christians."[46]

On the basis of one story that originated with anti-Hasidic Jews, the notion that the Besht also participated in the Lwów disputation became widespread. He is said to have been among the rabbis there, led by the rabbi of Lwów, Haim Rapoport. But this tale has been subjected to critical examination and found to be pure fiction.[47] The Besht, it is true, had a role in the tragic dénouement of the Frankist episode, but of another sort entirely: While the rabbis and communal leaders were celebrating the exit of the Frankist sinners from among the ranks of the Jewish people (having been made to accept the Catholic faith), the Besht mourned the loss of Jewish souls. "And because of those who were lost," the narrator tells us (*Shivhei ha-Besht,* p. 8), "the Besht said that the Shekhinah (divine immanence) was grieving and that God said, 'As long as the limb is attached [to the body] there can be hope that it will be cured, but once it is severed there can never be any hope.' For each soul in Israel is like a limb of the Shekhinah."

In that year, when hundreds of weak limbs were cut off due to the baptism of the Frankists, the death of the wise man of Miedzyboz approached. According to Hasidic tradition, "the Besht had to face his end because he exerted himself so much against the sect of Sabbetai Sevi," that is, he was weakened by the magnitude of his distress and by the energy expended in prayer during the disputations at Kamieniec and Lwów, and the baptisms that followed. Close to the Shavuot holiday the Besht took to his bed. His associates and disciples gathered there on the night of Shavuot to keep vigil, a custom dating back to the Ari. The Besht held forth to them on the subject of the revelation of the Torah, and then instructed the men of the burial society on the details of his burial. In the morning he told those around him, "I am not concerned about myself, for I know with certainty that I am going out this door and will immediately enter another one." He then sat up in bed and spoke about the transition from the lower world to the world on high, and prayed to himself. His death throes were brief, and then he expired (on the first day of Shavuot, 1760).[48]

The Besht had a son, Sevi, and a daughter, Hodel. The son was incapable of assuming his father's place at the head of the Hasidim, and the Besht therefore looked in his last days to one of the greatest of his disciples, the preacher (Maggid) Dov Ber of Miedzyrzecz, to lead the movement after him. Later on, when Hodel's sons grew up, they, too, took their place in the leadership of the movement, but they were not the equals of their grandfather's other spiritual heirs.

CONTEMPORARY REPORTS ABOUT THE BESHT

We have endeavored to discern the historical nature of the Besht through the opaque glass of Hasidic legend. We have applied critical analysis to the legend in order, on the basis of internal evidence, to find out something of the true image of the man, but this is not enough. We require some independent observations as well: We must listen to the voices of his contemporaries, those who stood outside the circle of Hasidism—its opponents and those who stood in between—but who either knew the Besht or knew of him. Let us draw the line at the first generation to live under the impact of the Hasidic movement, spanning the forty years following the death of the Besht: 1760–1800.

Much was written at the time by opponents of the movement about Hasidism and about its leaders, but very little about its founder. The Besht himself, during his lifetime, was active only within a circumscribed area and did not elicit a great deal of attention on the part of the rabbis. By the time the Hasidic movement attained significant proportions, its founder was no longer alive and his biography was already being lost in the legendary mists. Whatever the anti-Hasidic writers had to say about the Besht is therefore no more than hearsay. But under the circumstances, even the rumors they heard from first-hand sources may be of value to us, at least in order to establish how the Besht was *perceived* by that first generation.

Information about the Besht from anti-Hasidic sources was not published until the last decade of the eighteenth century, but was written, for the most part, on the basis of what the writers had heard in earlier years. The first instance of this is the reference to the Besht in the autobiography of Solomon Maimon, the philosopher, that was published in Berlin in 1792. In chapter 19 of part one of the book, in which Maimon speaks at length about his experiences as he traveled from his native Lithuania to Volhynia, to see the Besht's successor, R. Dov Ber, the Maggid of Miedzyrzecz, he relates what he heard and saw among the Hasidim there. (See chapter 1 in this volume.) This is what he had to say about the founder of the Hasidic sect:

One of the kabbalists who lived at that time in Poland was Rabbi Joel [sic] Baal Shem,[49] renowned for his cures and other secret remedies which he used in order heal the sick and the handicapped. According to him, he performed these wonders through the use of "practical kabbala" and invoking the holy divine names; but in fact he did all this with medical knowledge that he learned and with the help of magical hocus-pocus. R. Joel [Israel] Baal Shem attracted many disciples who learned his ways and who were also successful at cures, finding stolen objects. . . . But there were those among his disciples for whom this kind of magic was not enough, and who set themselves a more elevated aim. They perceived that with the power they held by virtue of the people's faith in them, it was possible for them to do a greal deal for their own personal good as well as for the general welfare. So they wanted to enlighten the people with their knowledge as well as to hold sway over them with the power of that knowledge.

The Besht, then, was a simple *baal shem* according to Maimon: a healer of the sick and teller of fortunes. But the disciples of the Besht turned these tools into a way to spread the new faith.

A similar opinion of the Besht was rendered by one of the first men in Warsaw who followed the Berlin school of the Enlightenment, Yaaqov (Jacques) Calmanson, in his book, *Essai sur l'état actuel des juifs de Pologne et leur perfectibilité*.[50] He refers to the Hasidim as "a sect of fanatics who became known only twenty years ago."

The sect emerged in Miedzyboz in Podolia, and its founder was a fanatical rabbi who exploited the superstitions of the ignorant common people, always eager for miracles. He was thus able to achieve renown as a prophet. He boasted that he was able to cure any disease through the kabbala. . . . The common people, easily swayed by such empty words, came in large numbers to seek cures from him, but found only deception. Yet, the number of his disciples grew.

The fanatical anti-Hasid from Lithuania, Israel Loebel the Maggid, who began traveling around the communities of Russia, Poland, and Germany in 1798 to preach against the danger of the Hasidic sect[51] and who wrote a number of polemical tracts against Hasidism, had this to say about the Besht in his *Sefer ha-vikuah* (Warsaw, 1798):

There has arisen against us a man known among the Hasidim as R. Israel the Baal Shem Tov, whose influence is greater after his death than it ever was in his

lifetime, who expressed contempt for God's Torah . . . in his heretical writings.
. . . I heard from the old rabbi of the holy community of Miedzyboz . . . who
went to see that terrible inciter [of heresy], R. I. [R. Israel] of Miedzyboz, after
he heard of him, and he found him to be an empty cistern, without a drop of
learning in him, though he purported to know things that he had never seen or
heard. . . .
It is written in their [the Hasidim's] heretical writings that R. I. the great inciter
was taught by Ahijah the Shilonite, the tutor of the prophet Elijah. . . . How
could this be true, if all his life he remained an ignoramus?[52]

In a pamphlet printed in German (in Frankfurt on the Oder in 1799),[53]
Loebel again commented on the Besht, albeit with erroneous chronology.

Between 1760 and 1765[54] a certain rabbi by the name of Israel came to prominence in the Ukrainian town of Miedzyboz. He thirsted for power, but because
he lacked Talmudic learning and other knowledge he had little hope of ever
convincing others of his spiritual qualities, and so he chose another path for
himself: He became one who calls upon spirits, hence the name of *baal shem*.
. . . In order to win the faith of the masses he took on pious ways and assumed a
facade of deep religiosity. The cloud of mystery in which he cloaked himself and
the natural human tendency to seek out hidden wisdom attracted to this new
rabbi, Israel Baal Shem, within the short span of less than ten years over ten
thousand people, whom he called "Hasidim."

The anti-Hasidic preacher continued in this vein, confusing the order
of events. When it became known (he informs us) that this sect of
pseudo-pious people were in reality sinners against law and morality,
the Gaon of Wilno [Vilna], R. Elijah, came out against them, together
with the leaders of the community of Brody, and published the facts of
their treachery in the tract, *Zamir 'arisim ve-harvot surim*. Before his
death, the Gaon made his disciples swear that they would have nothing
to do with this group of sinners. Afterward the "cunning rabbi Israel
Baal Shem" wickedly produced a book called *Savaat ha-ribash [Testa-
ment of R. Israel Baal Shem Tov*—actually published thirty years after
the death of the Besht, and before the death of the Vilna Gaon], which
contained "the laws of the sect." With this, the Hasidim "were torn
completely out of the nation of Israel." After the death of the said *baal
shem* there were a number of leaders of the sect, rather than just one. R.
Israel Loebel names these leaders and wishes to publicize their wickedness.

Thus, he fashioned a distorted history of the forty years following the death of the Besht. This great agitator for the anti-Hasidic camp, who should have known every detail of the religious conflict, in fact knew hardly anything at all about the life of the founder of the sect and erroneously placed him in a direct confrontation with the Vilna Gaon— when in fact the Gaon publicly attacked the sect only some twelve years after the Besht had died.

Greater caution about the Besht's activities was demonstrated by another militant anti-Hasid, the anonymous compiler of the tract, *Zamir 'arisim* (second version, Warsaw, 1798). He called for open warfare

against those new Hasidim who arose after the Ribash, that is Rabbi Israel Baal Shem Tov, for he encouraged many to become his disciples [Hasidim]. . . . He usurped the rightful place of the holy and pure Torah . . . invented a book of remedies . . . and created a stir, calling on people to bring him money to redeem or ransom their souls. (From the declaration at the opening of the book)

In his introduction to the book, the author observed about the Besht that, "there were some people who knew him closely and who said that he was not one of the scholarly sort, but was rather convinced that he was a prophet and a seer, and he knew a bit about remedies and the [manipulation of] holy names, like the other *baalei shem*." In the body of the book itself, the author poked fun at the Besht's supposed trans- ports of the soul to the next world, which the Besht reported in his famous letter, and at the belief of the Besht's disciples that their master had been instructed by Ahijah the Shilonite. The anthologies *Savaat ha- ribash* and *Keter shem tov* are regarded by the anti-Hasidic polemicist as the writings of the Baal Shem Tov himself. He uses these texts to argue that their author "was not versed in the holy tongue and all his words in his books are but debased dialect" (that is, heavily mixed with the vernacular Yiddish).

At about the same time (1798–1800) a collection of letters, polemics, and bans against Hasidism circulated in handwritten copies under var- ious names: *Shever posh'im, Zimrat 'am ha-ares,* and *Zot torat ha- qanaut*.[55] The compiler or editor speaks of the Besht as one would speak of a figure from the distant past:

These impure people (the Hasidim) departed from God's ways and the ways of our ancients and chose themselves a new path, saying that their fathers had told them about a certain man named Israel Baal Shem. . . . And he commanded them to leave the ways of the Jewish people. . . . We know nothing definite about this man Israel and what he was; nor did he leave behind any text or book known to all the Jews. But his disciple Yaaqov Yosef wrote about what he had commanded [them].[56]

A letter from the anti-Hasidic preacher, R. David Maków, to one of the rabbis states as follows:

The beginning of the sect's growth was in the year 1766. The Baal Shem, Israel of Miedzyboz died in 1759 and was famous as a *baal shem*, not as a scholar, and all the great learned men scorned him, except for a very few whose names I know from hearsay, not anyone who was known by reputation. In that year the fame of R. Berush of Miedzyrzecz in Volhynia began to spread, and a number of rabbis and learned scholars *[geonim]* undertook journeys to seek his advice.[57]

Thus, on the threshold of the nineteenth century the anti-Hasidim already seem not to have known anything precise "about this man Israel and what he was." They knew only this: that he was not an educated man, in the rabbinical sense, but, rather, was known as a *baal shem*, a healer of the sick, who made much of his own spiritual talents and of his ability to teach the true faith, and whose doctrine had been explained to the Hasidim in the books of Yaaqov Yosef and Dov Ber of Miedzyrzecz.

From this testimony by the opposing camp it would appear that the fanatical rabbis did not pay any heed to the Besht during his lifetime (with the exception of the story reported earlier, about the confrontation with the head of the Four Lands Council, if this has any historical truth to it); and after his death they knew very little about him indeed. The image they had of the man was unclear, somehow less than real, while among the Hasidim he had already transcended reality.

From the moderates—rabbis who were not part of the Hasidim but who also did not particularly oppose them—we have two sources that suggest a tendency among kabbalist rabbis to believe in the sanctity of the Besht. The rabbi of Ostróg, Meir Margaliot, who was appointed by the king in 1777 as "chief rabbi of the Ukraine and Podolia," had as a youth been close to the Besht and regarded him very highly.[58] Rabbi Margaliot's public position (he was known as a *gaon*—a preeminent scholar—and his great work of responsa and commentaries, *Meir netivot*, was published in 1791–92 in Polonne) inhibited him from actually joining the ranks of the Hasidic sect, but he did not hide his admiration for its founder. In his book on kabbalist matters *Sod yakhin u-bo'az* (Polonne, 1794, p. 5) he wrote:

As my teachers who were great in learning and in piety, including my dear and pious friend, the great one of his generation, our rabbi, R. Israel Besht of blessed memory, admonished me in the matter of the proper frame of mind for studying (Torah) for its own sake, one must concentrate in sanctity and purity on the individual letters (of Torah) in thought and in fact. . . . And when one finds the understanding and is able to focus on the holy letters themselves, he (the student) will be able to understand from the letters even such things as future occurrences. And from my youth, from the day I came to know with such deep affection my dear teacher and friend, our rabbi, that same R. Israel, I realized with certainty that his ways were those of sanctity and purity, full of piety and shorn of worldliness. . . . God's glory is revealed in hidden things.

The final words intimate the author's sympathy for Hasidism and his intention to defend the Besht against the condemnation of the rabbis.

Another kabbalist rabbi, outside of Poland, believed the Besht to have been one of the sainted ones: This was the Jerusalemite traveler, Hayyim Yosef David Azulai, author of the lexicon of rabbinic literature, *Shem ha-gedolim* (1774–98). In two places[59] he mentions "the famous rabbi, one should say of him 'the holy one,' our rabbi R. Israel Baal Shem Tov." He states that the book of the Jerusalem kabbalist R. Hayyim Atar, *Or be-yisrael,* was admired by readers in Poland because "the holy, pious rabbi, our teacher R. I. Baal Shem Tov, used to speak about the greatness of R. H(ayyim)'s soul." Azulai writes with much respect for the books by Yaaqov Yosef Ha-Cohen, "which are greatly revered" due to the fact that their author wrote in the name of his teacher, the Besht. [—translated by Eli Lederhendler.]

NOTES

1. See appendix 2 in Dubnow's *Toledot ha-hasidut* on the sources of *Shivhei ha-Besht.*
2. In his excellent essay on Moses (in *'Al parashat derakhim,* vol. 3, pp. 210ff.), Ahad Ha-Am (pseud.: Asher Ginsburg) distinguishes between the "historical truth" and the "archaeological truth" with respect to the Moses legend. In his view, the "historical truth" is the legend as it became part of history, while "archaeological truth" represents the factual record, to the extent that critical research can discover it. The conceptual distinction is identical to that with which I have approached the history of Hasidism. But I take issue with his terminology, which cannot reasonably be applied even to ancient legends, far less to our own case. We should, rather, draw a distinction between the absolute truth of historical reality and the perceived

or relative truth of myth, as it was accepted among the faithful. Care must be taken to avoid confusing the one with the other, as is so often done regarding the history of Hasidism.

3. *Shivhei ha-Besht,* p. 1 (Kapust and Berdyczew editions, 1815).

4. The exact place and date of the Besht's birth have never been clearly established. *Shivhei ha-Besht* does not mention the name of the town where Rabbi Eliezer lived before his captivity. It is said only that, "He lived in the province of Wallachia, near the border" (p. 1a). Apparently the writer confused Moldavia with its neighbor, Wallachia. The place of the Besht's birth is not noted either, but according to the account he was in Okopy when he was fourteen years old. This would seem to indicate that this was the town of his birth, since he had never left it. Okopy was a fortress town near Kamieniec, and its few Jewish residents were considered to be members of the nearby Jewish community of Zwaniec, the seat of a number of prominent rabbis at that time. (Rabbi Yaaqov Halperin, author of *Beit ya'aqov,* was the rabbi *[av beit din]* there until 1738; fragments of that manuscript are in my possession.) It is most probable that the young Israel ben Eliezer was educated in Zwaniec or another nearby community, because in Okopy itself there seems not to have been an organized Jewish community at any time.

   As to the date of his birth, this fact is missing entirely from *Shivhei ha-Besht,* so we can only make an estimate. It is commonly assumed that he was born between 1690 and 1700. But if we take into account the legend incorporated in the history, the birth must have taken place after the Peace of Karlowice, so we may be justified in dating the event sometime in the year 1700. In Heinrich Graetz's *Geschichte der Juden* (Berlin and Leipzig, 1853–76), vol. 11, app. 2, the date is recorded as 1698. The basis for this statement is a letter written by the Besht in 1750, in which he calls his grandson "bridegroom." This evidence can support our suggested date equally well, however.

5. *Shivhei ha-Besht,* pp. 1, 3.

6. Ibid., pp. 3–4.

7. The majority of these writings were published only after the death of the Besht, under the titles *'Es hayyim* or *Pri 'es hayyim,* by Rabbi Hayyim Vital, in the Hasidic printing house (Korzec, 1784, and other editions).

8. *Shivhei ha-Besht,* pp. 1d, 2a–c.

9. At that time, the Jewish communities of Eastern Galicia and Podolia were federated to the Council of Four Lands (va'ad arba arasot) as one province: the "Land of Rus' " (a section of the Polish Ukraine).

10. *Shivhei ha-Besht,* pp. 2d, 3a.

11. Ibid., p. 3b; table of generations of the Besht's disciples, p. 6.

12. Ibid., pp. 3, 4, records two versions of this story: one as told by Rabbi Shneur Zalman of Liozna and one by the Besht's secretary, Rabbi Alexander Shohet.

13. Ibid., p. 5a.

14. Ibid.

15. These, at least, are places mentioned in *Shivhei ha-Besht*.

16. *Shivhei ha-Besht*, pp. 5, 8, 9, 35, and elsewhere.

17. Ibid., pp. 4, 18, 27, and elsewhere. A contemporary *mitnagged* (opponent of the Hasidim) reported about the Besht that, "I recall that he was known as a non-scholar, he was only a *baal shem* who wrote amulets" (ms, *Zot torat ha-qana'ut*, p. 174; and ms, *Zimrat 'am ha-ares*, at the end—letter of Rabbi David Makow). Another had this to relate: "Some trustworthy people who knew him (the Besht) said that he could not be reckoned among the learned at all, but he was convinced that he was a prophet and seer, and he was acquainted with certain remedies and sacred formulas, like most of the *baalei shem* (*Zamir 'arisim*, p. 2b [Warsaw, 1798]. The author of *Seder ha-dorot he-hadash* tried in vain to prove that the Besht performed his miracles "without oaths and without amulets" (p. 6).

18. *Shivhei ha-Besht*, p. 7.

19. Ibid., p. 6b; see also *Or ha-meir* by Rabbi Ze'ev of Zytomierz, *parashat pekudei* [On Exodus 38:21–40:38]

20. I am summarizing here the tale that begins with the words, "I heard . . . that when the Besht was with the Derzavces in the holy community of Sluck" (*Shivhei ha-Besht*, p. 29), because it contains details that were known to other contemporaries. As already noted, the brothers Dzierzawcy were mentioned by Solomon Maimon in his autobiography (p. 8ff. of the German text, p. 9 in the Hebrew translation by Taviov); and by the author of the ms, *Zot torat ha-qana'ut:* "And whoever wished to know what the future held in store would ask him (the Besht), as an old and great scholar told me . . . that the famous rich men known as Dzierapzes *[sic]*, who became great under the patronage of the great prince . . . and wished to know their future, so they sent for him, and he told them that their greatness would last only fourteen *[sic]* years . . . and that indeed is what happened."

21. *Savaat ha-Ribash*, p. 16 (1793 edition).

22. *Shivhei ha-Besht*, p. 27.

23. The Hasidic legends have no chronological sense, so that it is not possible to determine precisely when the Besht settled in Miedzyboz. Only by an educated guess and by the internal evidence of the stories, which sometimes mention Tluste and other times mention Miedzyboz as the center of his activity, can we assume that after his public debut, about 1735, he lived for several years in Tluste, where he had previously worked as a schoolteacher, and then about 1740 moved to Miedzyboz. At any rate, he was already living in Miedzyboz when he wrote his prophetic letters of 1747 and 1750. [But see below, n. 26-ed.]

24. *Shivhei ha-Besht*, pp. 11, 32, and elsewhere; *Keter shem tov*, pt. 2, pp. 19–20 (1849 edition), pp. 38–39 (Lwów, 1865 edition).

25. *Toledot yaaqov yosef* (Korzec, 1780), "Balaq" [on numbers 22:2–25:9].

26. *Ben porat yosef* (Korzec, 1781), end of the book. The section about the "elevation of the soul" in 1746 was then reprinted in a volume of the

Besht's collected sayings, *Keter shem tov* (Żółkiew, 1784). The authenticity of the letter is supported by the citing of Yaaqov Yosef as the messenger. He himself published the letter during his lifetime in his book *Ben porat yosef*. The letter's contents also argue for its authenticity for, in addition to prophecies and other esoteric matters, the letter refers to well-known events from contemporary Polish Jewish life: the blood libels of 1747 and 1748, and the Haidamak persecutions in the Ukraine of 1749–50. The Besht's letter was written approximately in 1751 in answer to a letter received from his brother-in-law, Rabbi Avraham Gershon Kutover, the previous year. From the letter before us it would appear that the Besht's earlier letters to R. Avraham Gershon, containing various "novellae and mysteries," had similarly failed to reach their destination. The letter was again reprinted, together with a facsimile reproduction from the first edition of *Ben porat yosef,* in the volume *Sefer ha-hasidut* by A. Kahana (Warsaw, 1922), pp. 77–78.

27. I omit some of the less relevant details and have slightly corrected the Hebrew.

28. A reference to Ahijah the Shilonite, as mentioned earlier.

29. On the blood libel in Zaslaw in 1747, see *Evreiskaia starina* 5 (1912), pp. 202ff. There actually was among the Jews arrested and tortured to death one who had accepted baptism in the hopes that this would secure him a lighter punishment, but he was executed after all. The episode in Zaslaw is also mentioned in *Shivhei ha-Besht* pp. 10–11. The trial in Duniawiec or Dunaigrod took place in 1748, but those accused were not imprisoned or executed (*Evreiskaia starina* 4 [1911], pp. 268ff.). Nothing is known about a blood libel in Sowotowka, but such an incident took place in 1748 in Szepietówka, and the spelling was no doubt corrupted in the letter. The case involved the execution of two Jews: see Dubnow, *Divrei yemei 'am 'olam* [Tel Aviv, 1958] vol. 7, sec. 18.

30. *Divrei yemei 'am 'olam,* vol. 7, sec. 17.

31. This demonstrates the presence of a separate conventicle of Hasidim at that time in Miedzyboz.

32. *'Adat zaddikim,* pp. 5ff.

33. *Shivhei ha-Besht,* pp. 11–12.

34. Ibid., pp. 24, 32, 33.

35. Ibid., pp. 4, 5, 23, 26.

36. Ibid., p. 20; and see Dubnow, *Toledot ha-hasidut,* chap. 1, sec. 8.

37. Dubnow, *Divrei yemei 'am 'olam,* vol. 7, sec. 18.

38. *Shivhei ha-Besht,* p. 20.

39. Ibid., p. 25.

40. *Toledot yaaqov yosef,* "Shoftim" [Deut. 16:18–21:9]; *Keter shem tov,* pt. 1, p. 19; pt. 2, p. 5.

41. *Shivhei ha-Besht,* p. 31. This story is partly authenticated by a witness from the opposing side: Rabbi Israel Loebel, in *Sefer ha-vikuah* (Warsaw, 1798), p. 9, states that "the inciter" (his name for the Besht) gave his answer to the

said question of 'Ya'aleh veyavo', saying, 'How would he ever forget (his prayers)? If the obligation is to say it, forgetting it is impermissible.' Asked another question, about food that must be disqualified as nonkosher, he answered, 'Why should I need to know that? The world is not bereft of rabbis, after all.' " Rabbi Loebel relates the affair as one simply involving rabbis, without any mention of the Council of Four Lands. But that does not necessarily mean that this detail is outside the realm of possibility, for in those days, in the 1750s, the council would meet virtually every year in Konstantynów, in Volhynia, and on occasion in Brody (in 1751 and also in 1756). It may be that the Besht had come from Miedzyboz and that he entered into a discussion with the head of the council, Rabbi Avraham ben Hayyim of Lublin, known for his defense of Rabbi Jonathan Eybeschütz in his famous conflict with Rabbi Jacob Emden. At any rate, the story of an examination of the zaddik by the rabbis is well attested in both versions.

42. Among the unpublished writings of the opponents of Hasidism there is a document that contains a hint that another such incident did take place, but there is no other confirmation. In the manuscript collection, *Shever posh'im* that was composed approximately in 1798, and in its later version, *Zimrat 'am ha-ares* (see appendix 3 of Dubnow, *Toledot ha-hasidut*), the document appears under the name: Letter from the holy community of Ostróg about the R. I[srael?] B[aal?] Sh[em?]. Nothing is noted about the letter apart from the year it was written and the names of the signatories. It is addressed to the "leaders and rabbis" and informs them that the community of Ostróg, which could boast of having been home to the great scholar, the Maharsha, two hundred years earlier, had recently been

polluted by the presence of gullible fools [i.e., Hasidim]. Their leader was a wicked one who would destroy Israel, who sometimes said that he had come from Szklów, and another time said he was from Svotch. . . . Here in our town [the letter relates] he preached sermons several times, speaking lies and empty words. We inquired about him and found . . . that he is wicked, a drunken false prophet [*navi shikor*—a play on *shikor* (drunk) and *sheqer* (false)] and deranged. . . . Here his infamy was exposed, for he ate and drank and was drunk during the *yortsayt* [annual day of mourning]. . . . And we, true disciples of God's Torah, imposed the strictest ban upon this wicked man Israel, may his name be blotted out. Therefore, to all into whose presence this letter comes . . . take heed for the glory of God, pursue him, ban him, isolate him from the Jewish people!"

There is no sign in the letter that the person in question was Israel Baal Shem Tov; the founder of Hasidism had never lived in Szklów, and we cannot find any town by the name of Svotch (though the word may be a corruption of something else). What is related here about the conduct of the drunken "prophet," Israel, does not fit what we know about the Besht, a man whose worst enemies did not even resort to such extreme descriptions of him. After examining a number of manuscripts I came to the conclusion that the ban was directed against a Hasid of a later period, who was engaged in spreading Hasidic teachings in Ostróg, and who was on that account persecuted by the anti-Hasidic forces in the town. The compilers of the two collections mentioned were evidently the ones who identified the letter as being related to R. I. B. Sh., and in time it was assumed that the reference was to the Besht himself, who is also known by the same initials. This tripped up the collator of the second collection, *Zimrat 'am ha-ares*, the preacher (maggid) David Maków, who wrote at the end of the collection the following words: "In addition, the ban pronounced in the holy community of Ostróg against Israel Baal Shem during his lifetime may be found in the aforesaid booklet [here the reference is to the well-known anti-Hasidic tract, *Zamir 'arisim ve-harvot surim*, printed in Szklów in 1772, but that book had no reference at all to a supposed ban against the Besht in Ostróg].

43. *Shivhei ha-Besht*, p. 11d.
44. Ibid., p. 11c–d. *Hemdat yamim* was printed in Żółkiew two or three times between 1745 and 1763. See: *Osar ha-sefarim* by I. Ben-Yaaqov (Wilno, 1880), p. 193.
45. Ibid., pp. 7–8.
46. Ibid., p. 8a.
47. In 1769 a selection of writings from the rabbis of the early medieval era was published in Altona. (It included excerpts from R. Saadia Gaon's *Ha-pedut ve-ha-purqan*, Maimonides's *Iggeret teiman*, and other items.) In addition, it contained a small composition called *Ma'aseh nora bepodolia (A Terrible Event in Podolia)*, by R. Avraham of Szarogród, with an introduction by R. Jacob Emden. Emden, who remained a fanatical opponent of Sabbatianism, and of Frankism in particular, even in his old age, had received a visitor from Podolia, Avraham of Szarogród, who related to him what he had heard of the Frank affair. Emden transcribed what he heard, translating it from Yiddish, and published it in the aforesaid collection. The story reveals its author to have been a simple man who was ready to believe just about anything, for the story contains far-fetched rumors and fantasies: supposed "miracles" performed by Jacob Frank, for example, through magic, as well as miraculous acts taken against him by the rabbis, through the Holy Spirit. Inter alia, the story relates that among the Jews who participated in the disputation in Lwów were the chief rabbi of the district, R. Haim Rapoport, R. Ber of Miazlowycz, and "R. Israel of Miedzyboz B[aal] Sh[em]."
    It was this thin reed that supported the contention of the first historians who wrote of the Frankist episode (H. Graetz, in his work on *Frank und die Frankisten* [Breslau, 1868], p. 50; David Kahana in his work *Even ofel*, reprinted in 1914 in his *Toledot ha-mequbbalim* [Odessa], pt. 2, p. 81; and others) and who stated as a matter of fact that the Besht was a participant in the famous disputation. Recently, however, Majer Balaban has examined the question (*Studien zur Geschichte der frankistischen Bewegung* [Warsaw, 1927], a memorial volume in honor of Dr. Poznanski) and found that none of the relevant Polish sources contain a reference to the Besht. The book by Father Pikolski (*Złość Żydowska* [Lwów, 1760]), who had acted as secretary at the Lwów disputation, in particular does not mention the Besht at

all. Similarly, the memoir of Dov Ber of Bolechow (Birkenthal), a contemporary witness who took part in the preparations for the disputation ("Divrei binah," in *Ha-shiloah,* vol. 33, [1917]), does not mention the Besht.

Among the letters by the Besht and his disciples, reprinted in *Ginzei nistarot* (Jerusalem, 1924) there is one from Lwów (no. 59), signed by R. Haim Rapoport, R. Israel Baal Shem of Miedzyboz, and R. Ber of Miazlowycz and dated 27 Tammuz 1759, in which they announce their victory over the Frankists: this collection, however (and others like it) is known to contain many forgeries. This is especially applicable to the Lwów letter. (See Dubnow, "Iggerot ha-Besht ve-talmidav, emet o ziyuf?" in *Qiryat sefer* 2 [1926], pp. 209ff.; cf. Balaban, *Studien,* pp. 71ff.; cf. Dubnow, *Toledot ha-hasidut,* app. 4.)

48. The account of his death in *Shivhei ha-Besht* (pp. 35–36) does not give the year of his death, but in *Zimrat 'am ha-ares o zot torat qana'ut* by the anti-Hasidic maggid David Maków, it is stated that: "The Baal Shem Israel of Miedzyboz died in 1759." Graetz relied on this (vol. 11, p. 597, notes), but it does not seem to square with the facts. The account of the Besht's death that puts it *after* the disputation at Lwów and on the Shavuot holiday cannot be easily dismissed. Since the disputation was in the summer of 1759 (Tammuz—July), the Besht cannot have died during the previous month (Sivan). Logic demands that his death on Shavuot took place the following year, that is, in 1760. In later Hasidic writings I did find one reference to support this. In *Midrash pinhas* (Warsaw, 1876) by Pinhas Koritzer, a disciple of the Besht, we find the following: "The killings in Uman took place in 1765, after the death of the Besht, for he died in 1760."

49. Graetz (*Geschichte,* vol. 11 [1870], p. 597) and others have noted that the name Israel was probably corrupted to produce Joel [a two-letter difference in Hebrew], since the much earlier figure, R. Joel the Baal Shem, does not fit the chronology here. See Maimon, *Lebensgeschichte,* p. 217 in the first edition (Berlin, 1792), and see also the translation by Taviov: *Toledot Shlomo Maimon* (Tel Aviv, 1941), pt. 1, p. 100.

50. Warsaw, 1796.

51. See Dubnow, *Toledot ha-hasidut,* chap. 7, on the conflict between the two sides in 1798; and see the primary sources listed at the end of his book.

52. *Sefer ha-vikuah,* Introduction, p. 1, and also pp. 9–11, in the body of the text. There, too, there is an account of a debate over the Law between the rabbis and the Besht, as mentioned in the notes to section 12.

53. Israel Loebel, *Glaubvirdige Nachricht von der in Polen und Litauen befindlichen Sekte Chasidim genannt;* the tract was reprinted in *Sulamith,* vol. 2 (1807), pp. 308–333.

54. An obvious error, as the Besht died in 1760: It would have been correct to refer to the period from 1750 to 1760.

55. See the appendix of Dubnow, *Toledot ha-hasidut,* item 3.

56. The first selection is from a manuscript of *Shever posh'im* no. 34 (my copy), and is found in another version in *Zot torat ha-qanaut* in the Bodleian

Library at Oxford (from which E. Deinard copied the text for publication in his *Herev hadah,* p. 22). A third version with some late additions may be found in the manuscript of *Zimrat 'am ha-ares,* no. 89 (my copy). In this case, the following words were added by a fanatical anti-Hasid: "We know of a certainty that (the Besht) is an ignoramus and a drunkard," etc.

57. Letter of the Maggid R. D. Maków, found at the end of the ms *Zimrat 'am ha-ares* and ms *Zot torat ha-qanaut:* "Israel Miedzyboz who died in 1759, the year in which I was married. And I recall that he was known not as a scholar but only as a *baal shem,* a writer of amulets, and had not studied at all. . . . And he would go about in the marketplaces and the streets with a stick and a pipe in his mouth and [tobacco] and talk to the womenfolk" (copied from the Oxford ms, appended to volume 11 of Graetz's *Geschichte,* p. 597 of the 1870 edition).

58. See *Qevusat yaaqov* by R. Yaaqov Margaliot (Przemysl, 1897), pp. 51–53: legends about the Besht and his disciple R. Meir Margaliot.

59. *Shem ha-gedolim,* pt. 2: list of books, listings for *Or hayyim* by R. Hayyim Atar and *Sofnat peaneah hadash* by Yaaqov Yosef Ha-Cohen.

3

The Maggid of Miedzyrzecz, His Associates, and the Center in Volhynia (1760–1772)

Simon Dubnow

THE MAGGID DOV BER AND HIS CIRCLE IN MIEDZYRZECZ

Groups of Hasidim had cropped up in most of the towns of Podolia, Volhynia, and Galicia during the last decade of the Besht's life. It is very difficult to estimate how many of these existed. One contemporary observer put the number of the Besht's early followers at ten thousand, reaching forty thousand by the year of his death.[1] But guesses of this sort are highly speculative and unreliable. We may say, however, that from the mid-eighteenth century on, groups of Hasidim multiplied throughout the Ukraine. They prayed in synagogues or prayer quorums of their own in a new, distinctive style: ecstatically shouting and waving themselves about. R. Shlomo of Chelm, one of the older generation of rabbis, complained of this as early as 1751, in introducing his Talmudic study, *Mirkevet ha-mishna* (Frankfurt on the Oder, 1751). Describing various groups or schools of pietists, he singled out one of them for criticism:

And some of them are quite ignorant of any knowledge . . . having studied neither the mysteries (kabbala) nor Gemara and legal codes, stripped bare [intellectually] and wailing aloud, prancing upon the hilltops. And in prayer and supplication [they sing] out loud and change [voice] over and over. Their behavior is strange: They dress in white . . . they make their hands go to and fro and they sway like the trees of the forest. . . . And though they have not studied or

Reprinted by permission of Dvir Publishing House from *Toledot ha-hasidut,* by Simon Dubnow, 1944.

read books, still they call themselves wise and take themselves the title "rabbi." Among them, the more of these swayings and other gestures, the better, and those who perform these are glorified by the women and children, and wax great in the eyes of those who know nothing. . . . They [the ignorant] will praise these people to their face: "O, pious one, o humble one!" And there is no one who realizes that deep down in their hearts lies deceit.

The behavior of the Hasidim at prayer elicited from that great antisectarian crusader, R. Jacob Emden of Altona, these fiery words:

Now upstarts have arisen, a new sect of Hasidim in Volhynia and Podolia, and some of them have even come to this country (Germany). All their interest lies only in the Zohar, and they overextend their prayers, taking up half the day—much more than Hasidim of earlier periods. According to what I have been told, they perform the Eighteen Benedictions with unnatural and improper body movements, groping with their hands and swaying from side to side, their heads bent backward and their faces and eyes looking skyward.[2]

The outstanding rabbis of Poland and Germany draw the same picture: Ecstatic frenzy and wild motions during prayer were the trademarks of the new Hasidism. R. Jacob Emden, who knew Polish Jewry very well after his struggle against Sabbatians and Frankists, spoke of the new sect's growth in Podolia and Volhynia. It is, indeed, true, that during the Besht's lifetime Hasidism was contained within these two provinces, together with Eastern Galicia (then still part of Podolia, in the years prior to the Polish partitions). Podolia was, from the very first, the movement's headquarters: The Besht resided at Miedzyboz and attracted scores of disciples and many who believed in his miracles. His great disciple, Yaaqov Yosef Ha-Cohen, served as a rabbi in the nearby Podolian towns: Szarogród, Raszków, and Niemirów.

After the Besht's death, Miedzyboz experienced a decline. Sevi Hirsh, the only son of the Besht, was not capable of assuming the leadership, and the Besht's followers found themselves a new leader in a new place: in the Volhynian town of Miedzyrzecz, the residence of the Maggid, Dov Ber, who had grown closest of all to the Besht during his last days. This town became the new "capital" of Hasidism, and the 1760s saw Volhynia become the movement's center of gravity, rather than Podolia. Yaaqov Yosef, too, who had been the Besht's first close disciple, moved at that time from Niemirów and took up the post of rabbi in Polonne, in Volhynia. This shift into a province that constituted the border between the Ukraine and the Lithuanian lands had significant consequences:

From that point on the northern provinces—Lithuania and White Russia—were to be drawn into the orbit of Hasidism, which saw itself as
the proper movement to lead all of Jewry.

Prior to his encounter with the Besht, R. Dov Ber had trod the well-
traveled route of the rabbinical scholar. Born in a small Volhynian town
(in 1710, approximately), he studied both the revealed Torah and the
mysteries with rabbinical tutors and kabbalist mentors. He started out
as a schoolteacher in various towns and in the countryside, and later
took up the calling of preacher in a number of Volhynian communities:
Tulczyn, Miedzyrzecz, Korzec, and Rowno.[3]

As a preacher, he followed the basic style of his contemporaries, most
of whom were influenced by the Lurianic kabbala, with its themes of
asceticism, penitence, and purification from sin. And he practiced what
he preached, living the ascetic life, eating hardly any food, sometimes for
days at a time, from one Sabbath to the next while he studied Torah.
His severe regimen of study and fasting weakened him physically. During one spell of illness he took the advice of some friends and went to
see the Besht, who was famous as a healer. The treatment the Besht
proposed for restoring the Maggid's health lay in the spiritual solution
he offered him: He proved to him that true service of God was possible
not through self-affliction and melancholy, but through joy and religious
enthusiasm. This encounter was later retold by the Hasidim in two
wonderful tales about the rebbe and his disciple.

The earlier of the two versions[4] portrays R. Dov Ber as a "great
expert in Talmud and rabbinic literature, with a full measure of knowledge in the kabbala [as well]." The Maggid is said to have regarded the
rumors about the Besht—"that all the people go to him" fully believing
that he "is able to perform wonderful deeds through the power of his
prayer"—with some skepticism, and resolved to go to the Besht "to test
him." After a day or two on the road, he regretted the time wasted on
such a journey, time which he rightfully ought to have devoted to study;
but he took consolation in the thought that perhaps he might hear words
of wisdom from the reputed holy man. He was therefore bewildered,
upon entering the Besht's room, to hear him begin to tell trivial stories
about common folk.

The Besht told about a journey in which he had lost the few provisions he had brought along in his bag, so that there was nothing left to
feed the non-Jewish driver, but he was able to buy more food from

another non-Jew who happened by—and other such stories. The Maggid, being unfamiliar with the Besht's method of explaining deep spiritual truths through simple parables and tales taken from everyday life, decided to stay only the one night and to return home. In the middle of the night, however, the Besht sent his servant to summon him, so that he might ask a question on a point in the kabbala based on R. Hayyim Vital's book, *Es hayyim*. The Maggid examined the text in question, and answered the query in accordance with the simple meaning *[peshat]* of the text. Whereupon the Besht rebuked him, saying that he obviously had not understood it at all! The Maggid then looked again at the passage in question, and responded that "the simple reading was indeed as I stated previously: If you know a different interpretation, let me hear it and I will decide who is right." The Besht then commanded him to stand, because the passage in *Es hayyim* contained the names of several angels. Immediately, "the whole house became suffused with light, a fire burned all around, and they (both) sensed the presence of the angels who had been mentioned." At this point, the Maggid heard the Besht say, "The simple reading is as you say, but your manner of studying the text lacked soul." Afterward, the Maggid remained with the Besht to study "deep and great wisdom."

Another story told by the Hasidim[5] has it that the Besht had already known of the Maggid, and wished to bring him into the circle at Miedzyboz. But the learned Maggid lacked the motivation to become close to the *baal shem* who was so popular with the masses because of his cures and miracles. Finally, the Maggid's friends were able to persuade him to see the Besht and seek his advice about his poor health.

The Besht did not receive this doubting Thomas very nicely at all, and only after some time did he agree to "heal him with words," reading verses of Psalms and other prayers. When these prayers proved ineffective, he decided to apply ordinary cures—herbs and draughts. For this purpose, he assigned lodgings to the Maggid, providing him with twelve zloty a week for expenses. The patient frequently fainted "out of weakness" (perhaps, too, from the "remedies" of the physician); finally, his health improved. Then the two men turned to kabbalistic matters.

"Once, when we were studying the divine chariot *[ma'aseh merkava]*," the Maggid said—according to this story—"I heard loud sounds and I saw lightning and torches, and it was so for about two hours, and I was sorely afraid and I began to faint." The narrator adds here that this was a revelatory experience, like the giving of the Law at Sinai, and it was in this manner that the Besht's other disciple, the rabbi of Polonne, also received their master's Torah.

In the last days of his life, R. Dov Ber himself told his disciple, R. Shlomo of Luck, that the Besht "taught me the language of the birds and the trees and the holy names and formulas for uniting the holy spheres," and had shown him the writing of the angels, and so on.[6]

We may be permitted to doubt that the Besht "revealed" such "secrets" to the Maggid. But there is one secret that he certainly did reveal to him: how to escape the rigors and pessimistic worldview of an ascetic religious regimen, and replace it with a philosophy directed toward joyous communion with God, suffused with spiritual enthusiasm that contained the secret of life itself.[7] The Maggid found in this new teaching a healing power that was spiritual as well as physical. He descended from the lofty heights of kabbalist thought to the "practical world" of everyday people, and his philosophy enabled him to join both worlds into a whole.

The Besht, for his part, also found in his newly won disciple what he had been looking for: someone firmly grounded in all branches of religious literature, with a respectable reputation among the rabbinic scholars, ideally suited for the recruitment of a large following among the elite. At the end of his life the Besht decided that R. Dov Ber was a worthy successor and better able to lead the sect than any of his other disciples and confreres. It is difficult to determine on the basis of the stories whether the Besht, before his death, instructed his followers to accept the primacy of the Maggid of Miedzyrzecz, or whether the initial allegiance of several disciples to the Maggid prompted others to follow their lead. All we are told in the stories is: "Those same fountains of wisdom who had gone to the Besht went to the Maggid."[8] In more realistic terms, the historian may be permitted to state: Those who had gone to seek out the Hasidic way in Miedzyboz continued thereafter to go to Miedzyrzecz.

Miedzyrzecz[9] became the center for the leadership of the Hasidic sect. The shift in location brought in its wake, as well, a shift in the methods used to spread the Hasidic doctrine. If the Besht was endowed with an extraordinary talent for making the new teaching popular among the common folk, the Maggid was in a position to influence the scholars— rabbis and kabbalists—to whom he had a natural affinity by virtue of his education.

There were many, even among this elite group, who were "wayward seekers on the road of life": young men whose zeal had not been cooled by scholastic pursuits, and old men who had not found inner solace in either "revealed" or "hidden" wisdom in the old form. Such "God-seekers" came to the Maggid in Miedzyrzecz, who represented both learning and spirituality. Rabbis and preachers, students of Talmud from *yeshivot* and dabblers in kabbala, all made their way to him from all points of the map—Lithuania and the Ukraine, Galicia and White Russia. Among his disciples were some who would later achieve fame in their own right. From the Ukraine, there were Levi Yishaq of Berdyczew, Nahum of Czarnobyl, and Ze'ev Wolf of Zytomierz; from Galicia, Elimelekh of Lezajsk and R. Mikhl of Zloczów; from Lithuania and White Russia, Aaron of Karlin and Mendel of Witebsk, Avraham of Kalisk and the youngest of the group, Shneur Zalman of Liozno. Most of these were to become the leaders of the next generation, but there were others who came just to learn about the new doctrine without practicing it themselves. The latter included such men as the two brothers Horowitz, Pinhas and Shmelke (Shmuel), who later took up rabbinical posts in major communities outside Poland: in Frankfurt on the Main and in Nikolsburg, Moravia (Mikulov, Czechoslovakia). Of these two Talmudists, the Maggid said: "I found a box full of candles, but they were not lit. I created a spark and at once they all ignited, and there shone forth a great illuminating light." [10] The spiritual fires were banked in the atmosphere prevailing in the German lands. Only one of R. Pinhas Horowitz's friends in Frankfurt—R. Nathan Adler, author of *Ba'al ha-halomot*—tried unsuccessfully to fan the flames again.

The testimony of Hasidim is supplemented by one report by a contemporary opponent of Hasidism, R. David Maków, who wrote the following about the circle in Miedzyrzecz: [11]

The beginning of the sect's growth was in the year 1766. . . . In that year the fame of R. Berush [Ber] of Miedzyrzecz in Volhynia began to spread and a number of rabbis and learned scholars *[geonim]* undertook journeys to seek his advice, and some of them accepted his way, though they did not abandon the righteous path of studying the holy Torah . . . especially the *gaon* R. Raphael Cohen [rabbi of Pinsk until 1771] . . . who was there [in Miedzyrzecz] but did not accept his [R. Dov Ber's] [teachings] and did not stray from the [proper] paths of study and worship. And when he [R. Raphael] was afterward in Vilna, the great Gaon [R. Elijah] inquired of him regarding R. Ber, asking whether he was a great scholar. And he replied: No. And when he asked [whether Dov Ber was steeped in] the mysteries, he replied, "I cannot judge, as I am not a master of that discipline." And after him, the rabbi of Lubavitch went to him several times and asked him to explain a passage in the Zohar, in the famous section on *parashat terumah* [Exodus 25:1–27:19], but from the answer he received he understood that he lacked knowledge.

Despite the differences in the assessments regarding the "great Maggid," even this anti-Hasidic witness bears out that Miedzyrzecz in those days became a center that attracted men of great learning.

The Maggid did not simply wait passively to receive guests and seekers of wisdom; he sent preachers out to the communities to spread knowledge of Hasidism and to attract to Miedzyrzecz the best of those scholars who showed an inclination toward the new system. Legend tells of two friends, Israel and Azriel, who came all the way from Polock, in White Russia, to Miedzyrzecz "to seek truth." When they saw "the holiness of the rabbi, the Maggid," and observed his way of worshipping God, they both decided to become emissaries for a holy purpose: to travel about the country to speak to believers and persuade them to go to Volhynia to learn true Torah and piety. As the two friends went from town to town, Azriel would lead the horses and Israel would sit in the wagon "and delve into his holy thoughts." Everywhere they came, Azriel would participate in group prayer, chanting aloud in a pleasant voice and with great feeling, which aroused the sympathies of those around him. The two would also try to persuade some of the prominent citizens to undertake a trip to see the great Maggid. "And great rabbis and esteemed scholars traveled to Miedzyrzecz on their recommendation" and later became famous zaddikim.[12] The two emissaries, who had come from the far north, apparently did most of their traveling in Lithuania and White Russia. We have an eyewitness's account to substantiate this: Solomon Maimon, who in his youth was "entrapped" in this manner by one of the emissaries from Miedzyrzecz.

Solomon Maimon, from the Lithuanian town of Nieswiez, was about sixteen then, already married, an expert Talmud scholar and a student of kabbala, who made his living as a tutor in a nearby village. In his autobiography[13] he refers to the Beshtians as "the new Hasidim," as distinct from earlier generations of pietists who pursued a life of austerity and penitence, fasting and asceticism. (See the first chapter of this volume.)

Maimon's recollections of his visit to Miedzyrzecz provide us with a portrait of the public side of the Hasidic center: the gatherings of Hasidim around their rabbi, the Maggid's table discourses on Saturday nights, replete with hidden meanings which seemed to the individuals present to be directed to them personally and especially intended to answer their own spiritual needs; and ecstatic prayer that sometimes spilled over into rowdiness by some, who sought thereby to arouse themselves to worship God out of joy. There is nothing in his account about wonder workers and miracles of the kind attributed to the Besht. Even Hasidic legends speak only of the Maggid's prophetic spirit, claiming that he was able to see into the future and to influence the decree of Heaven through prayer: "His prayer and his word were heard—God decreed, but he [the Maggid] brought about a nullification," as his disciple, Shlomo of Luck, said.[14]

The direct influence of the Maggid was focused largely within the intimate circle of his disciples, who would listen to his wisdom not only on the Sabbath, in the company of all and sundry, but also throughout the week, in their rabbi's private chamber. Those days are described in hushed tones of veneration by his disciples: "Several times," Ze'ev Wolf of Zytomierz wrote,

I myself saw that when he opened his mouth to speak words of Torah, he looked as if he was not of this world at all, and the divine Presence spoke out of his throat. And sometimes, even in the midst of saying something, in the middle of a word, he would stop and wait for a while. . . . The Maggid said to us. "I will teach you the way Torah is best taught, not to feel [be conscious of] oneself at all, but to be like a listening ear that hears the world of sound speaking but does not speak itself."[15]

Solomon Maimon gives us a homily of the Maggid's on the biblical passage (2 Kings 3:15), "As the musician played, the hand of the Lord came upon him." This may be read, the Maggid explained, to suggest that the Holy Spirit dwells in man only when he is passive and not active, a vessel for divine influence. The passage may be interpreted: "As the musician *was* played," that is, if the musician can make himself an instrument that can be played upon, only then does the holy spirit come upon him.[16]

This elevated sense of spirituality and self-transcendence enabled the Maggid to leave a deep impression on those who heard him speak, as one disciple recalled:[17]

The holy words of my master, my holy teacher Dov Ber of blessed memory . . . are words that encompass the world itself, words that are measured as the heights are measured, which not all minds can grasp . . . as is known by all those hundreds and thousands of the great ones who heard his wonderful words, and into whose hearts they penetrated like burning fire, spurring them to serve the Creator.

This disciple believed with all his soul that the Besht had revealed the secrets of the world to the Maggid: "He taught him the language of the birds and the trees[18] and the holy names and formulas for uniting the holy spheres; and believed that the prophet Elijah had revealed himself to the Maggid, and so forth.

For twelve years the Maggid led his flock on two levels: He chose the best from among his close disciples, and these became the leaders of Hasidism throughout Poland and Russia; and he inspired the less sophisticated audiences through stirring homilies and sermons. These returned from Miedzyrzecz with the new Torah that they had learned, fortified with mystical excitement and spreading tales of wonders. During the Maggid's lifetime, conventicles of Hasidim emerged in communities that had not previously been touched by the new movement: in Lithuania and White Russia.

This aroused the wrath of the rabbis there, who raised a hue and cry against the "destroyers of Israel" in their midst. In Vilna, the bastion of rabbinism, and in the great community of Brody, which had links to the Hasidic center in Volhynia, a ban was declared against the Hasidic sect and its members were excommunicated.[19] These events date to the spring of 1772.

News of the ban reached the ears of the aged Maggid, and reports began to arrive of persecutions against members of the sect, including some of his own disciples. The old man was pained by the religious strife that had arisen in response to his activities. It did not require a prophetic spirit to realize that danger lay ahead. Afflicted by these depressing thoughts, the Maggid fell ill and died in the town of Annopol, on the 19th of Kislev (December) in the year 5533 (1772). The circle in Miedzyrzecz dispersed, the disciples departed each to his own home district, and each determined to disseminate the teachings of Hasidism to all the communities of Israel, despite the pressures exerted against them by the rabbinical authorities.

RABBI YAAQOV YOSEF OF POLONNE AND THE BEGINNINGS
OF HASIDIC LITERATURE

While the Maggid of Miedzyrzecz was creating a cadre of teachers for the Hasidic movement, men who would soon assume the leadership of the group all over Poland and Russia, his fellow Hasid, Yaaqov Yosef Ha-Cohen, in Podolia (and afterward, in Volhynia), undertook another task of great value: committing the teachings of the Besht to writing.

As a rabbi (for the community of Szarogród) and a scholastic Talmudist since his youth,[20] R. Yaaqov Yosef had at first strongly opposed the Hasidic ideas when they began to percolate out of the Miedzyboz circle around the Besht into surrounding communities in Podolia. But the "wizard" of Miedzyboz cast his eye upon the young rabbi and succeeded in winning him over. According to the legend,[21] the Besht himself made overtures to him and, in addition, approached him indirectly through one of his disciples, Aryeh Loeb, the Preacher of Polonne.

Once, Yaaqov Yosef heard that the Besht had come to Mohylew-on-the-Dniestr and decided he ought to test him. When he arrived in Mohylew on Friday morning, at the time for morning prayers, he found the Besht "smoking a pipe," which stunned him. Afterward, however, having observed him at prayer and heard his words of Torah, he understood that the Besht was inspired by the Holy Spirit. It was then that Yaaqov Yosef began to travel to Miedzyboz to be with the Besht, and the latter "raised" him spiritually to his own level of religious understanding.

When anti-Hasidim in Szarogród took notice of these developments, there occurred a falling-out between the anti-Hasidic townspeople and their "corrupted" rabbi. The split in the community widened daily, until it reached the point that the rabbi was forced to leave town one Friday and take up residence in a nearby village. The Besht happened to be traveling in the district that day and he proposed to his companions that they go to spend the Sabbath in that particular village with the rabbi of Szarogród, to console him in his sorrow. The Preacher of Polonne was there, too, and upon observing Yaaqov Yosef's agitation told him not to grieve: he had heard that Yaaqov Yosef's enemies had been condemned (in Heaven) to die unnatural deaths, and that the whole town of Szarogród would burn. In due course, this prophecy was fulfilled, during the Uman and Ukraine persecutions ("the time of flight") and during the war between Russia and Turkey (1768–72) that followed. We may assume, here again, that this was actually a "prophecy after the fact," for the expulsion of the rabbi of Szarogród took place in 1748, about twenty years before the Uman persecution.[22]

Between 1748 and 1752, approximately, R. Yaaqov Yosef served as rabbi in the small Podolian town of Raszków. Here, too, evidently, there were rumblings of discontent from some opponents of Hasidism, and it became necessary for him once again to find a new situation. At that point he secured a rabbinical post in the oldest Jewish community in Podolia, Niemirów, that dated back before the 1648 persecutions. The Besht and the local Niemirów Hasidim were apparently of some help to him in finding this new position. In Niemirów Yaaqov Yosef finally achieved "a secure seat" for as long as the Besht was alive and for about ten years thereafter. He would often travel to visit his mentor in Miedzyboz and partake of his wisdom, which he would record and later use in his own discourses in Niemirów.

For all his enthusiasm for the new philosophy he had adopted, Yaaqov Yosef found it difficult at first to wean himself from his old ascetic habits. For several years he continued to maintain a partial regimen of self-mortification (fasting during the day and eating only at night, except for Sabbaths), thus weakening himself physically. When the Besht heard of this, he hastened to Niemirów and commanded him to cease his fasting. The legendary account accords with a letter which Yaaqov Yosef kept.[23] On the back of the letter was written: "From the holy community of Miedzyboz to the [holy] community of Niemirów . . . to the rabbi, R. Yaaqov Yosef Ha-Cohen." The text itself read as follows:

To my dear friend, the rabbi . . . , great in piousness [hasidut], . . . Yosef Ha-Cohen. Behold, I have received your letter and I see . . . that you think somehow that you must mortify yourself, which upset me greatly. I insist in the name of God that you do not continue to endanger yourself in this manner, for such deeds are born of a bitter darkness and lead to melancholy, and God's divine Presence dwells not in melancholy but rather in the joy of holy purpose, as you well know from what I have taught time and again. . . . This is my advice to you, and may God be with you: Each morning, while engaged in study, concentrate on each letter (of the Torah) so as to make this an act of worship, and that will alleviate the source of the [misery]. . . . And do not neglect your own flesh, God forbid, by fasting more than is proper or necessary. . . . From one who wishes you well always, Israel Besht.

As rabbi of his community, Yaaqov Yosef's duties involved preaching two public sermons a year, as was customary: on the Sabbath preceding

Passover and on the Sabbath between the New Year and Yom Kippur.[24] But, as was the Hasidic practice, he had a close circle of associates to whom he regularly imparted the teachings of Hasidism, every Saturday evening at the close of the Sabbath. For a long time he continued to disseminate the Besht's ideas orally and did not dare to write them in a book.

Those were the days of frequent persecutions against Jews in the Ukraine, and reflections of these events may be discerned in Yaaqov Yosef's sermons.[25] After the terrible year of 1768, in which several communities in Podolia and other parts of the Ukraine were devastated by the marauding Haidamaks, Yaaqov Yosef left Niemirów and settled in Polonne, a town in Volhynia, where the Hasidic movement was blossoming under the influence of the center in Miedzyrzecz. The previous rabbi there, Aryeh Loeb, died in 1770, and R. Yaaqov Yosef took his place.[26] He remained there until his death (ca. 1782).[27]

The furore caused by the ban declared against Hasidism in 1772 in Vilna and in Brody reached Polonne and greatly upset R. Yaaqov Yosef, who had earlier been the victim of ostracism because of views he held. It was then that he decided to marshal his own ammunition and sally forth to battle. He began to compile a book of his sermons and discourses, based mostly on what he had heard from the Besht.

He had two chief purposes: (1) He wanted to bring his master's teachings to a wider public, and he had at his disposal the notes he had made during his trips to Miedzyboz. (2) He wished to provide a detailed explanation of the Hasidic approach, along with a critique of scholastic rabbinism and its standard-bearers. He set forth most of the Besht's teachings in *Toledot yaaqov yosef,* a collection of sermons arranged according to the annual cycle of Torah readings.[28] Here, Yaaqov Yosef incorporated things he had heard from his master without naming him specifically, sometimes noting only, "as I heard from my teacher" or "as I heard it said in my master's name."[29] The book concluded with a special section with the heading, "These are the words I heard from my teacher, of blessed memory, and I cite them in abbreviated form only, because of my fear, and also because of what I have forgotten." This would indicate that the author took special care not to alter the words of his master, and that he omitted some of them out of "fear"—evidently, he feared he would be accused of heresy or of distorting the Besht's teachings.

R. Yaaqov Yosef's sermons are no different in *form* from those of his
contemporaries: He collects biblical verses and passages from the Talmud, from the Midrash and the Zohar; poses complicated and casuistic
questions and solves them; and sometimes, out of this conglomeration,
there stand out—like islands in a vast ocean—epigrams and other
statements that shed light on the basic underlying idea. The *content* of
his interpretations and homilies, however, does reflect innovation. The
author's critique of the rabbis further sets this book and its intent apart.

Two other books by R. Yaaqov Yosef (*Ben porat yosef* and *Sofnat
peaneah*) include randomly compiled novellae, legal commentary and
aggadic lore, the rabbi's formal sermons delivered on the Sabbaths before Yom Kippur and before Passover, and responsa on points of law.
There is some repetition here of Beshtian material already reported in
Toledot yaaqov yosef, but some of the maxims cited are new. At the end
of *Ben porat yosef* the author included the famous 1750 letter of the
Besht about his "elevation of the soul" and his discussion with the
Messiah (see chapter 2 in this volume).

It may be assumed that some of R. Yaaqov Yosef's writings—especially those reporting the words of the Besht—circulated in manuscript
copies before they were published, just before the author's death.[30] Later
on, people would refer to Yaaqov Yosef as *ba'al* [author of] *ha-toledot,*
or simply, *Ha-toledot*—an indication of the book's fame. This notoriety
owed more, perhaps, to the ire of the anti-Hasidim, who reviled it, than
to the book's inherent appeal among the Hasidim themselves.

This book (copious in size) is basically a polemical work. The author
is a born preacher, someone who took naturally to reminding the leaders
of his day of where they had gone wrong. In commenting on the Torah
portion of "Balaq" (Num. 22:2–25:9) he repeats several times the Talmudic statement (Ta'anit, 20; Sanhedrin, 105–106): "The curse pronounced against Israel by Ahijah the Shilonite was better than the blessing of Balaam the wicked." This, the author explains, reflects his
constructive purpose in exposing the failings of his generation. The
preacher who criticizes in order to prod people to mend their ways is a
true prophet; the hypocrites and flatterers who only sing the praises of
their contemporaries are false prophets. Here, Yaaqov Yosef pauses to
reveal a secret about his master, the Besht: He claims that "Ahijah the
Shilonite was the teacher of Elijah the prophet and the teacher of my
master (the Besht), of blessed memory."[31]

This piece of fantasy, which the anti-Hasidim viewed as blasphemy, reveals more about the character of the disciple than about the teacher. R. Yaaqov Yosef was indeed very close in temperament to the caustic prophet, Ahijah, who foretold the division of the Israelite kingdom: Yaaqov Yosef in turn became the prophet of the *religious* division of the Jewish people. Having suffered all his life at the hands of the rabbis of the old school, he poured all his wrath upon them in his sermons and his books. Along with the remarkable maxims of the Besht, we find in the *Toledot* harsh accusations and defensive apologetics: accusations against the established rabbis and a defense of the Hasidic leaders who are termed "pure masters of Torah" or "zaddikim [righteous]."

There is much truth in the criticism expressed by the rabbi of Polonne. He lashes out at those rabbis who raise themselves above the people and are unconcerned about the spiritual needs of the "ignorant masses." He labels them (in a term borrowed from the Zohar), "Jewish devils *[shedin yehudain]*" and "scourge of the vineyard of Israel." [32] The author speaks of "three forms of exile: the exile of Israel from the nations, the exile of the scholars from the simple people, and the exile of pure masters of Torah from those who are wise for wicked purposes, the Jewish devils."

"With the passage of time," Yaaqov Yosef opines, "the capacity to understand and gain insight has diminished." Most of the rabbinic scholars

use their scholarship to adorn themselves, feeling somewhat proud when [they] master one point of (Talmudic) law, and waxing very proud indeed when [they] master the [difficult] elaborations of the decisors or kabbala. . . . And this allows us to understand the verse (Isaiah 1:5): "Why do you seek further beatings, that you continue to offend?" For the more they hurry to the yeshiva to study, the further they stray from God.

The author speaks with disdain of scholars who "steep themselves in casuistry in order to win recognition among other men of learning" and who enter into conflicts over matters of so-called honor or pride. He reaches such "dangerous" conclusions as:

In earlier times it was thought that God could only be worshipped when a person delves into Torah and engages in prayer, fasting and wailing. And since they saw that there were people who did not behave in this way, their [the scholars'] anger was kindled and they brought anger to the world, until the time came when it was realized that [worship of God] only required that they teach them [the people] to walk a straighter path, the path of compassion, in worship of God and in all facets of social conduct. . . . [Therefore,] Let him not be entirely preoccupied with his studies, let him also involve himself with people, and let him then wear fear of God on his face . . . and let him understand that God is present at all levels and is able to cause an element of worship to characterize all of man's activities. Then he will not debase them in his mind, but on the contrary, he will judge them [the simple people] on their positive merits.[33]

What is the task of a truly spiritual Jewish leader? That is the question that most agitated the rabbi whose unconventional ideas had made him the object of rabbinical wrath. Here he develops an entire system:

Man is created out of matter and form, which are two opposites. For matter instinctively follows the physical demands of the body, but form yearns for things of the spirit. And man's purpose in life is to transform matter into form so that they will be one complementary whole rather than two entities. And just as this is the purpose of each single person, so, too, is this true of the Jewish people as a whole. Those who are called "the masses" and "simple people" ['amei ha-ares—lit., people of the earth], because their lives are mainly devoted to the earthiness of material things, they constitute the matter. This is not so of the zaddikim, who engage in study of the Law and service to God—they are the form, and their purpose is to turn matter into form. And just as this is true of the Jewish people, so, too, may this be said of [their place in] the world as a whole: There are seventy original nations, all of whom take hold of the limbs of the tree of holiness, and Israel grasps the root of the tree. Israel has to bring this plenitude to the rest of the seventy nations. . . . Zaddikim are spirit and form, and the masses of the people are physical matter, and the zaddik must strive to make matter into form. . . . As long as they [the masses] cling to the zaddikim, who provide form for the matter, there can be life for the body because of the soul; that is not true when the body is separate from the soul, for surely that is what we call death. [And that is why it is said, Berakhot 18:] "The wicked are called dead in their lifetime."[34]

In order to breathe life into the body of the people, the zaddik must remain at one with the people, he must stand among the people, not above them as the established rabbis did. How will the rabbi "who comes to preach to people whom he regards as being of little worth and to whom he does not feel a sense of belonging . . . be able to join with them in order to raise them up to their Heavenly Father?" That is why the rabbi should occupy a central position, between the scholars and the masses, so that he will be able to join with the people and elevate it to a higher spiritual level. This was the meaning he attached to the verse (Song of Songs 3:3–4): "I met the watchmen who patrol the town. Have you seen the one I love? Scarcely had I passed them when I found the one I love. I held him fast, I would not let him go till I brought him to my mother's house, to the chamber of her who conceived me." The watchmen are the rabbis, and the zaddik inquires of them whether they have found the way to the Jewish masses and joined together with them, but he receives no answer, for they have not succeeded. Only after he has gone beyond them, beyond the way of the great rabbis of the day, can the zaddik find the way to join together with the people and to bring it to the palace of the king of the universe.[35] "When the zaddik is isolated on the highest rung, he has no point of contact with the commonality of the people; only when he stands on the lowest rung is he able to help them to rise up." This turns out to be reflected, too, in the symbol of "a ladder rising from earth to the heavens" that Jacob saw in his dream (Gen. 28:12).[36]

Zaddikim of this sort suffer the slings and arrows of rabbis and communal leaders, who are jealous of the success of the Hasidic leaders who stand close to the people. Of these rabbis, Yaaqov Yosef wrote that they call to mind the following passage (Ps. 2:1–3): "Why do nations assemble and peoples plot vain things; kings of the earth take their stand and regents intrigue together against the Lord and against His anointed? Let us break the cords of their yoke, shake their ropes from us!"

Why had persecutions against the Jewish people increased? Because the "kings of the earth"—the rabbis who purchase their office from Polish noblemen—and the "regents"—communal leaders—"have assembled together" to persecute the zaddikim "who devote themselves to Torah and divine service, causing them to flee the city, outlawing their prayer meetings, and trying to break the cords of love that bind them to God, all because they [the Hasidim] retire to their own place for study and prayer." Here the author is clearly speaking out of personal experience: "As I myself saw, such a war is always declared against any who wish to pray in their own quorum ... and in our time there were denunciations of [such] people to the [gentile] authorities ... and I, the writer of these lines, may attest to these facts ... in [the case of] Szarogród."[37]

Because the zaddik was the intermediary between God and the masses of the nation, he required time to be alone "to commune with his Master," to pray to Him and to speak in the Jews' favor, to make sure that they would be provided with all their needs. For these purposes, the zaddik needed material support from his devotees, who would provide him with his own needs, so he would not be distracted by concerns about this-worldly vanities. "It is God's will that they [the wealthy and the learned] should have a mutual influence on each other: the one by his wealth, and the other by Torah and spiritual teachings." "The masses, who are called matter, and the keepers of the peace of Israel, who represent form, must influence each other: [this means that] the wealthy ones among the people will act with their wealth to benefit the masters of learning who are poor, and the masters of learning, in turn, benefit the masses through their Torah, by insuring that prosperity will continue to flow from on high." "The giver should realize that he actually receives." "Those who support the scholars give, but in fact they reap the benefit of prosperity for themselves." "Should they (the communities) concur and provide for the spiritual leader of their generation, who chooses to find in solitude the way to join himself to God through Torah and prayer, so that he will be freed of public duties, then this is certainly to the benefit of them all; for they can in turn join themselves to Him through (the zaddik); but if they do not allow him to rest his soul and if they burden him with public duties, then they certainly harm themselves as well as him."[38]

Thus, the function of the zaddik emerges along two lines: on the one hand, solitary communion with God and on the other, union with the people. In the latter case, the zaddik's function is confined to bringing the people's requests up to heaven; he is not expected to participate in other duties of a communal nature. That is to say, the zaddik is bound to seek, through his spiritual activity, the welfare of the individual, more so than that of the public. In making this point, Yaaqov Yosef added a new layer of meaning to the spiritual-philosophical zaddikism as expressed by the Maggid of Miedzyrzecz. In time, the "practical" school of zaddikism would become the basis of absolute rule by the zaddik. This was precisely because of its emphasis on the zaddik's influence over the life of the individual Hasid, who would come to the zaddik not just for the fulfillment of his spiritual needs, but also and much more, perhaps, for the fulfillment of his material needs, so that he might "receive prosperity" through the activity of the zaddik.

R. Yaaqov Yosef, like the Maggid of Miedzyrzecz, was more a theoretician than a practitioner of zaddikism. They both were educators— one relying on the oral word, the other having recourse also to the printed word—and both, through their teachings, elevated the status of the zaddik. But there are no legends about them having performed miracles of a this-worldly nature: healing the sick, visiting barren women, or providing prosperity or "wealth" to their devotees.

In spirit the two men were close to each other, but not so in their personal relations. There is no mention in any of the Maggid's sermons of the rabbi of Polonne, and the latter, for his part, does not explicitly mention by name the Maggid of Miedzyrzecz in any of his books, although he mentioned many others from the Besht's circle (R. Nahman of Horodenka, R. Nahman of Kosów, Menahem Mendel of Przemyślany, R. Loeb Pistiner, R. Yehuda Loeb the Preacher, and others). Evidently, there was ill-feeling or competition between the two most prominent disciples of the Besht after their master's death. The Maggid, who had drawn close to the Besht only in his last years, had taken over as his successor, while R. Yaaqov Yosef remained by himself in his small community and did not even see his own books in print until his final days.

Later legends[39] relate that R. Yaaqov Yosef did not inherit the Besht's mantle because he was too strict. We can discern signs of anger and of bitterness throughout his books. He certainly found a bitterly ironic twist to apply to the blessing given to the people of Israel, "I will make your seed as the sands of the sea": "Just as there is no natural way to make whole strands out of grains of sand, so, too, there is no natural way to create unity between one Jew and another."[40]

OTHER ASSOCIATES AND DISCIPLES OF THE BESHT

Apart from the two outstanding members of the Besht's circle—the Maggid of Miedzyrzecz and R. Yaaqov Yosef—none of the other associates of the Besht or his disciples achieved general renown either in the leadership of the sect or in its literature. Each one, rather, was active in his own particular setting and within the group he gathered around him, to whom he brought the knowledge of Hasidism. The sanctity of the Besht cast a halo upon them as well and in this sense they were remembered by later generations as holy men.

Hasidic lore contains the names of over thirty such confreres and disciples who formed the Besht's personal entourage.[41] Only a few of them were personalities in their own right, however. The oldest in age among them were the Galicians, who had been drawn to the Besht while he still lived in Tluste and who afterward made pilgrimages to him in Miedzyboz. One of these, R. Nahman of Kosów, was known as a kabbalist and had taken sides with R. Jonathan Eybeschütz in his celebrated duel with R. Jacob Emden. The fanatical Emden suspected R. Nahman, too, of heretical Sabbatian beliefs and wrote of him as follows:

Nahman Kosów, whose heresy is known to witnesses and who is an ignoramus, corrupted a holy community when he was sent to Opatów. And when the pure ones detected what he was they spread word that he was a deviant. This caused a furore among the "sons of Korah" [heretics, i.e., the Sabbatians] and for his sake they instigated a bitter controversy.[42]

Nahman of Kosów, like many of his contemporary kabbalists, was at first opposed to the teachings of the Besht. After a while, however, he was attracted to them and became a committed devotee of the Besht. He was among the first ones to publicly use the Lurianic prayerbook. When asked how he dared to alter long-standing custom in such a manner, he replied: "And who can say definitely that they [who followed the Ashkenazi rite] are all in heaven now?"

Nahman was an *arendar* of noblemen's estates and a grain merchant, and he frequently traveled for business throughout Galicia and Podolia.[43] Wherever he went, he recruited others to his new beliefs. R. Yaaqov Yosef quotes him several times in *Toledot yaaqov yosef*. On one occasion, R. Nahman remonstrated with his listeners that they must fulfill the literal meaning of the words, "And I will always have God before me," in the sense that one's thoughts must be constantly focused on God, even while conducting business affairs. When asked how that was possible, he replied: "Isn't it true that when you are in the synagogue for prayer you still find the time to think about all sorts of wares and business transactions? Then you can also do the reverse!" And he also said, "Do not look to [the authority of] the fathers [*avot*, punning on the biblical injunction against witches: *ovot*]—when people say, 'Why have there not been Hasidim among my fathers and grandfathers? Has the Messiah come, then [that we should abandon the old ways]? . . . But had the fathers known that they were misdirected, they would have chosen the path of the sons."[44]

One of the Besht's faithful friends was R. Nahman of Horodenka. This Hasid, whose "faith was as strong as a pillar of iron," was possessed of an indomitable optimism. For every occurrence his response was, "there is some good in this, too"—just like the Nahum in the Talmudic legend. Once, troops were garrisoned in Jewish homes in Miedzyboz. The Besht told Nahum to pray that the decree be annulled, to which R. Nahman answered, "This, too, may be for the best" (thinking, perhaps, that the soldiers would protect the Jews from the marauding Haidamaks). To this, the Besht replied, laughing: "It is good that you did not live at the time of Haman, for you might have reacted to Haman's evil decree by saying that it was for the best!" In criticizing the ascetics, he would say, "There are doctors who cure with a bitter potion, but he who cures with a sweet one is the better physician. Through ascetic self-denial man becomes bitter and cruel, but good thoughts lead him to see other people in a better light."

R. Nahman of Horodenka was in Miedzyboz when the Besht died, and afterward he would often visit the Besht's grave. Later, when he was preparing to leave for the Holy Land, he prayed by the graveside of his master and sought his permission to undertake the journey. Upon returning from the cemetery he announced with joy, "The Besht commanded me to go to the Holy Land."[45] He left in 1764, traveling by boat together with a group of Hasidim from Galicia. When a storm arose at sea, endangering the boat, the passengers gathered in a quorum of ten and R. Nahman, taking a Torah scroll in his arms, said, "If, God forbid, the heavenly court has decreed that we must die, we represent a holy court, too, together with the Godhead and the divine power, and we do not agree to the verdict. Let it be God's will that the sentence be reversed!" Those present answered, "Amen," and on his instructions began to chant Psalms until the storm blew over and the boat made its approach to the port of Haifa.[46] R. Nahman died about ten years later, in Tiberias. In his last years he married a member of the Besht's family: a daughter of the Besht's daughter. Their union produced the famous zaddik, R. Nahman of Bratslav.[47]

The third Galician in the Besht's entourage was R. Mendel of Przemyślany, one of the elders in the first generation of the Hasidic movement.[48] After the death of the Besht he left for the Land of Israel together with R. Nahman of Horodenka, in 1764,[49] where he remained for the rest of his life. Maxims attributed to him were published in *Liqutim yeqarim* (pp. 20–24, 1792 edition), and later in a small tract called *Darkhei yesharim* (Zytomierz, 1805). In both books, R. Mendel repeats things he had heard from the Besht. A deep-seated sense of fatalism is reflected in his words: "A man should not grieve overmuch because of something he had intended to do but was unable to carry out. He should believe that God intended otherwise, and certainly had [the purpose] been a correct one in God's view, He would have assisted him in bringing it to completion." "Another rule is not to overindulge in studying . . . for if we lose sight of the need to cling to God and merely learn a great deal, then we may, God forbid, lose the fear of God, and fear of God is basic." Legend tells of R. Mendel that before his journey to the Holy Land he used to say, "Let it be God's will that I live to pray one proper prayer before God." And after arriving in the Holy Land he wrote: "Let it be God's will that I live to say one proper letter [of prayer] before the Creator of the universe." [50]

One of the Besht's disciples who was particularly close to him was Aryeh Loeb, the Preacher of Polonne. A skilled orator whose sermons of reprimand and exhortations to repentance had been very effective with the people, he turned his talents to the dissemination of Hasidism. On the Besht's instructions he traveled throughout Galicia and the Ukraine, calling for "repentance" in the spirit of the new teaching, for "worship of the heart," for closeness to God and faith in the zaddikim. Legend accords him eloquent successes in sermons he preached in Lwów and other cities.[51] His criticism was directed against the scholastics who sharpened their wits on Talmud and rabbinic legalistic tomes, supposing this to be the essence of Judaism. "For our many sins, they [the rabbis] are all wise and understanding and pious in their own eyes, and they attack the preachers, saying: In this world, the essential [service of God] is to study well, to have a keen and expert knowledge [of Torah], and to make penetrating remarks on the simple meaning of texts. [They believe] that in this way they will merit a place in the world to come, and nothing else is required, and they pridefully look down on anyone who does not agree with them." This is what he wrote in his book Qol aryeh.[52] It would appear that he was very close in his views to that great polemicist, R. Yaaqov Yosef Ha-Cohen, who occupied the rabbinate of Polonne after the death of the Preacher in 1770.

One of the Besht's disciples who occupied a special place in the group was a Jew from Lithuania who had settled in Volhynia: R. Pinhas Shapira of Korzec (Pinhas Koritzer). R. Pinhas and his father frequented the Besht's home, but were suspect in the eyes of the other Hasidim: "Lithuanians," after all, were thought not to have the same spiritual depth and were known to question the holiness of the Besht.[53] As time went on, R. Pinhas became a very devoted Hasid, but in his own characteristic way: He was not full of divine thunder and commotion, nor did he display outward excitement; rather, he expressed his faith in an inward yearning for God, a kind of integrity, and the highest ethical standards.

Once, people asked him why his voice was not audible during prayer and why his body did not move with spiritual frenzy. He replied, "The essence of prayer is longing for contact with the Creator of the universe, and the essence of that longing is to rid oneself of physicality, which is just the same as the departure of the soul from the body."[54] His concern was that his reason would not succeed in being master to his religious emotions. He was wont to say, "I am always afraid that I shall not be more wise than pious." He kept to himself, and was unable to sermonize in public. "Several times great people came to me, but I could not speak words of Torah before them. Now a man has come from Ukraine who is of a lesser stature, and I speak to him . . . for when Torah is united with a zaddik, there is union in the holy spheres, and such union cannot take place before [mere] people." Another Yiddish maxim of his that was recorded was: "I was better able to find perfection [understanding of Torah] when I studied (in the yeshiva) behind the stove. Now that I study up at the front, I hardly understand what is written [on the page]." In his opinion, piety had become more important than learning in the last generation: "In our generation there is not the devotion to Torah that there was in earlier days, for these days the fear of Heaven has become very widespread in the public. In the earlier days, there was not so much fear, and so they spent more time on Torah. There are still places of learning, and there, there is less fear of Heaven" (a reference to the Jews of Lithuania, where Hasidism was less influential). Regarding the split between Hasidim and anti-Hasidim, R. Pinhas advised against speaking about it at all, counseling the wisdom of silence.[55]

This silent one, who did not set himself up as a zaddik, rabbi, or preacher (apparently, he was a schoolteacher), became known as a "holy one" among Volhynian Hasidim. R. Pinhas lived in Korzec, in Ostróg, and in Szepietówka between 1760 and 1790, and died in Szepietówka in 1791, approximately. His disciple was the zaddik Raphael of Bershad, who was later to found a special group of Bershad Hasidim (in Podolia) and quoted the insights he had gleaned from his master. R. Pinhas

Shapira had a son who established a printing house in Slavita, Volhynia, which produced many books, including Hasidic literature. R. Pinhas's grandchildren, known as "the printer-brothers of Slavita," were arrested during the reign of Nicholas I after being denounced for allegedly printing uncensored material and for supposedly being involved in some political transgression. They were sentenced to severe corporal punishment and to hard labor. [—Translated by Eli Lederhendler.]

NOTES

1. The preacher Israel Loebel, in his anti-Hasidic tract *Glaubvirdige Nachricht von der in Polen und Litauen befindlichen Sekte Chasidim genannt* (Frankfurt on the Oder, 1799); printed again in *Sulamith*, 2 (1807), pp. 309, 313; but this is not a reliable source, as he is not even clear on chronology, putting the beginning of the Besht's activity in the period 1760–65, and placing the death of the Besht fifteen years still later (see chapter one, section 13). Loebel's contention was accepted by I. M. Jost in his first book, *Geschichte der Israeliten*, [Leipzig, 1859] vol. 9, p. 45, and even Heinrich Graetz, *Geschichte der Juden* (Berlin and Leipzig, 1853–76), vol. 11, p. 107, used the figure of ten thousand.

2. *Mitpahat sefarim*, p. 31 (Altona, 1768). The book was published after the death of the Besht, but we know that most of it was written beginning in 1758, that is, in the last years of the Besht's life. Hence, it reflects what the author had been told between 1750 and 1760.

3. We know very little about the life of the Maggid before he became close with the Besht, apart from slight hints scattered in various books. See [A. Walden,] *Shem ha-gedolim he-hadash* [Warsaw, 1879], Pt. 1, p. 11; *Shivhei ha-Besht*, p. 11; [M. M. Bodek,] *Seder ha-dorot he-hadash* [Lemberg, 1865], pp. 16, 17, 26. His disciple, Elimelekh of Lezajsk, called him "the Maggid from Rowno" (*No'am elimelekh*, [Lwów, 1788], "Va-yeshev"). One letter by the Maggid is signed, "Dov Ber ben R. Avraham m.m. of the holy community of Miedzyrzecz and the holy community of Korzec" (at the end of *Darkhei yesharim* by R. Mendel of Przemyślany (Lwów, 1862). Israel Loebel in the article printed in *Sulamith* 2 (p. 315), calls him: "Baer Medsirsitz, Rabbiner zu Kortschik"—that is, Korzec, which is situated on the river Korczyk.

4. Cited at the end of volume two of *Keter shem tov* by R. Aaron of Opatów (first printing: Żółkiew, 1795; Lwów edition, 1849, pp. 27–28). The author, who only collects the sayings of the Besht and does not deal with miracle stories, here departs from his norm and relates this story, which he heard from a certain Hasid, who in turn had himself heard it told by

R. Dov Ber. From *Keter shem tov* the story was republished in the second edition of *Maggid devarav le-yaaqov* (Berdyczew, 1808), after the introduction.

5. *Shivhei ha-Besht*, p. 11 (Kapust and Berdyczew, 1815).
6. Dov Ber of Miedzyrzecz, *Maggid devarav le-yaaqov, o liqutei amarim* (Korzec, 1784).
7. The Gaon Elijah of Vilna said that the Besht "used his magic to lead R. Berush astray" (ms, *Zimrat 'am ha-ares,* at the end-letter to R. David Maków).
8. *Shivhei ha-Besht*, p. 26a.
9. In the eighteenth century Miedzyrzecz was considered part of the Korzec district, but in the nineteenth century, part of Rowno. R. Ber served both cities as Maggid.
10. *Seder ha-dorot he-hadash*, p. 31; see also *Shivhei ha-Besht*, p. 14b.
11. In his letter appended to ms, *Zimrat 'am ha-ares* (1800–1805), in both versions.
12. [Bodek,] *Seder ha-dorot he-hadash*, pp. 33–34. The Hasidic author does not mention the source of his information, and I therefore consider his story to be part of the legendary tradition, though it does not contain fantastic elements. One story is worthy of special attention: Once the two friends from Polock came to Vilna and tried the tempt the Gaon, R. Elijah, who was an opponent of Hasidism, to go to Miedzyrzecz to engage the "holy" Maggid in discourse. The Gaon almost agreed, but his students and his mother objected. In this way (the author comments), "Satan" succeeded, and peace was not established between the leaders of Hasidism and its opponents. There is nothing here that departs from the realm of the possible, but since the time of this occurrence is not noted—whether it was prior to 1772 or whether it was connected with the bans declared in Wilno in that year, the last year of the Maggid's life—it may be suspected that the author has collated two events. In 1771 there was an attempt to arrange a debate between the Gaon and R. Mendel of Witebsk, a disciple of the Maggid; and later on, there was an unsuccessful attempt to arrange a truce between the Gaon and the Hasidic leader, R. Shneur Zalman of Liozno, who was prepared to meet the Gaon in Vilna (see Dubnow, *Toledot ha-hasidut,* sections 18, 21, 25).
13. Solomon Maimon's *Lebensgeschichte* (Berlin, 1792), chapter 19, in which he tells of "a hidden fellowship" and his trip to see the leader of the Hasidim. This chapter, and the one following, lack details of chronology and therefore we are left with guesswork. These two chapters, devoted to kabbala and Hasidism, are situated in the book between the account of Maimon's early life in Lithuania and his departure for Königsberg and Berlin. Since that departure took place in 1777, and the Maggid died in 1772, Maimon must have visited Miedzyrzecz in one of the last years of the Maggid's life: between 1770 and 1772, when Maimon was between sixteen and eighteen years old. The contention that he must have become part of

the Hasidim before that does not seem supportable. [See Chapter 1 in this volume.]

14. Introduction to *Maggid devarav le-yaaqov;* see also *Shivhei ha-Besht,* pp. 12–13.

15. *Or ha-meir,* "Sav" [on Leviticus 6:1–8:36].

16. *Toledot shlomo maimon,* chapter 19.

17. R. Shlomo of Luck, recording his sayings in *Maggid devarav le-yaaqov,* introduction.

18. The same thing is said of the Ari in *Shivhei ha-ari,* and there is no doubt that the author here transferred the idea to this case.

19. See Dubnow, *Toledot ha-hasidut,* chapter 3.

20. *Ben porat yosef* includes a section of novellae from his days in the yeshiva (pp. 183–194) and several responsa on questions related to the Talmud and later decisors which are written in casuistic fashion (p. 194ff., in the Piotrków edition, 1884).

21. *Shivhei ha-Besht,* pp. 8–9.

22. Ibid., p. 9b:

Those who were sentenced to die unnatural deaths were killed in the holy community of Uman during the time of flight, and those who were condemned to die by pestilence died in the pestilence that occurred two years after the flight. And they had a stay of execution of about twenty years or more, for I know that he (Yaaqov Yosef) had been rabbi in Niemirów sixteen years prior to the flight, apart from what he had served in Raszków for several years before this event.

This gives us a hint about chronology: the rabbi's expulsion from Szarogród in ca. 1748, his stay in Raszków approximately from 1750 to 1752, and from 1770 to his death, in Polonne.

23. *Shivhei ha-Besht,* p. 8d.

24. Homilies of this type were published in *Ben porat yosef,* some of them including the notation: "Sermons for the Sabbath preceding Yom Kippur for the years 1759, 1760, 1765; for the Sabbaths preceding Passover, 1765–1767 (pp. 211–243, Piotrków edition, 1884).

25. In one sermon from 1753 (*Toledot yaaqov yosef,* "Sav") he says: "Esau was a man of the field, and ruled over the desert, the place of impurities . . . that touched and harmed the martyrs in the land, who were killed, for our many sins, in this year of 1753 in the land of Ukraine"—a reference to the blood libel in Zytomierz in 1753.

26. See reference to the gravestone of the Preacher of Polonne dated 1770, in the book by S. A. Horodetzky, *Ha-hasidut ve-ha-hasidim* [Berlin, 1922], vol. 1, p. 138.

27. After the printing of his three books (1780–82) we hear no further word about his life. On his gravestone, which was preserved in Polonne next to that of the Preacher of Polonne, the date is missing because of worn letters. All that is legible are the words: "A man of life and great in deeds, pious

and humble, a man of God, [a man] who may be called holy, a learned scholar ... the rabbi *[Admor]* Yaaqov Yosef son of Sevi Cohen Zedek, author of the books *Toledot yaaqov yosef, Ben porat yosef* and *Sofnat peaneah*" (ms by M. Biber of Ostróg, in my possession).

28. In the proclamation of the anti-Hasidim issued following the book's publication it is stated that it contains "teachings and novellae that they (the Hasidim) preach according to their way of Torah, at the final Sabbath meal" (ms, *Shever posh'im,* par. 30). It must be assumed that most of the sermons were redone by the author when committed to writing, with additions and corrections, while others were probably originally written down.

29. The name of the Besht is mentioned only on the verso of the title page of the first edition (Korzec, 1780); in later editions, the text there is omitted. See Dubnow, *Toledot ha-hasidut,* appendix on sources, par. 63.

30. About the printing of *Toledot yaaqov yosef* in 1780 and the commotion it aroused among the anti-Hasidim, see Dubnow, *Toledot ha-hasidut,* sec. 22. A later book, *Kutonet passim* (Lwów, 1866), which is attributed to R. Yaaqov Yosef, is suspected of being a forgery. It is merely a mélange of sermons already contained in the *Toledot* and the other books of the rabbi of Polonne.

31. *Toledot yaaqov yosef,* "Balaq" (1780 edition; these lines were omitted in later editions, due to the protests of anti-Hasidim).

32. Ibid., "Va-yishlah," "Sav," "Va-ethanan," "Shoftim," "Ki-tesei", and several other places, from which are drawn the citations herein.

33. *Toledot yaaqov yosef,* "Va-yesei." This elicited the greatest anger among the anti-Hasidim (see *Shever posh'im* and *Zimrat 'am ha-ares,* passages cited in a later section).

34. Ibid., Introduction, and repeated many times throughout the book: "Bereishit," "Yitro," "Ki-tissa," "Ki-tavo," and elsewhere.

35. Ibid., "Yitro"; see also "Bereishit," "Tazri'a."

36. Ibid., "Shoftim," "Va-yesei," and others.

37. Ibid., "Neso," "Be-ha'alotekha," Massa'ei," "Va-ethanan."

38. Ibid., "Bereishit," "Noah," "Yitro," "Va-yaqhel."

39. Published without reference to the source in *Sefer ha-hasidut* by A. Kahana (Warsaw, 1922), pp. 111–112.

40. *Toledot yaaqov yosef,* "Bo."

41. The author of *Seder ha-dorot he-hadash* enumerates thirty-seven "close associates and disciples of the Besht" (pp. 12–26), but they include the names of some men who were not actually part of the Hasidic sect, such as R. Meir Margaliot, or who only joined the group after the time of the Besht and were disciples of the Maggid of Miedzyrzecz. M. L. Rodkinson, in his book, *Or yisrael* ([Koenigsberg, 1876] pp. 30–45) presents a list of sixty-nine disciples and family relations of the Besht. This list includes people mentioned by name in *Shivhei ha-Besht* and in *Shem ha-gedolim he-hadash,* in connection with a legend of the founder of Hasidism, even if they did not always have a direct connection with the Besht personally.

42. *Sefer hitavqut* by J. Emden (Altona, 1762; Lwów edition, 1877, p. 80b).

43. *Shivhei ha-Besht,* pp. 18, 29, 32.

44. *Toledot yaaqov yosef,* "Va-yera," "Bo": "I heard it said in the name of the Hasid, R. Nahman Kosover . . ."

45. *Shivhei ha-Besht,* pp. 21, 23, 36, etc. In *Toledot yaaqov yosef,* "Hayyei sarah," and elsewhere, we find the name R. N. of Horodenka.

46. I found this account in a small, extremely rare book, *Ahavat siyyon* by R. Simha ben R. Yehoshua of Zolozec (near Brody), who wrote the story of his journey to the Holy Land in 1764 in the company of Hasidim from Galicia, the Ukraine, and Lithuania (no place or date of publication is stated). The print is quite old. See pp. 6 and 15.

47. The Besht's grandson, R. Moshe Hayyim Ephraim of Sudylkow, in his book, *Degel mahaneh ephraim* [Jozefów, 1883], quotes a number of maxims attributed to R. N. of Horodenka, whom he calls "my late in-law" ("Lekh-lekha," "Toledot," "Va-yishlah," and elsewhere).

48. In *Shivhei ha-Besht* he is also called by the surname "Premisler" (p. 21), that is, from the city of Przemyśl, Galicia, and the question of his geographic origin is therefore unclear. In *Liqutim yeqarim* [Lemberg, 1865] his name appears on the title page together with the names of the Besht and the Maggid of Miedzyrzecz (appearing again on p. 20c). See *Seder ha-dorot he-hadash,* pp. 15–16.

49. In *Ahavat siyyon* (see n. 46) he is twice referred to as "Mendel of Premysla," in the same context with Nahman of Horodenka and the others who went to the Holy Land.

50. *Darkhei yesharim,* pp. 1–2 (Lwów edition, 1865); *Seder ha-dorot he-hadash,* p. 16.

51. *Shivhei ha-Besht,* pp. 19, 22, 34, etc.

52. Printed in 1798 in Korzec, it did not find a wide readership.

53. *Shivhei ha-Besht,* p. 20c–d: "They knew him (R. Avraham, the father of R. Pinhas) for a Litvak (Lithuanian) and as one who was set in his views, and they feared lest he lead the Besht astray."

54. *Seder ha-dorot he-hadash,* p. 14.

55. The quotations are taken from two sources: *Liqutim mr' pinhas mi-koris,* published as a supplement to *Ner yisrael* by R. Y. of Kozienice (ca. 1835, no place or date of publication stated); and *Midrash pinhas,* printed later with additional comments by his disciple, the zaddik Raphael of Bershad (Warsaw, 1876). Both books are apocryphal: R. Pinhas did not write the things attributed to him—they are written by others either in his name or in his disciple's name (see *Shem ha-gedolim he-hadash,* under "Pinhas"). Horodetzky (*Ha-hasidut ve-ha-hasidim,* Vol. 1, pp. 144ff.) cites passages from a ms attributed to R. Pinhas and his disciple, which evidently was the source for those who published the above-mentioned anthologies. This would suggest that there might be a grain of authenticity in some of the quotations. As some of these were quoted in Yiddish, this may further attest to an oral tradition. *Midrash pinhas* mentions the years 1786–88, giving us

a hint of chronology. On Raphael of Bershad and the Slavita publishers, see *Zikhronot yemei ne'urai* by A. B. Gottlober (*Ha-boqer or,* 1881, no. 1); and see also *Sefer ha-hasidut* by A. Kahana, p. 269ff. The "holy letter" of R. Pinhas Shapira of Ostróg to R. Yeshaya of Duniawyce, published at the end of *Hesed le-avraham* (1855) contains only conventional Hasidic material.

4

The Origins of Hasidism and Its Social and Messianic Foundations

Benzion Dinur

I. THE HISTORICAL CONTEXT OF HASIDISM AND THE SOURCES FOR ITS HISTORY

The Hasidic movement or, as it was known when it first began, the new Hasidism,[1] originated and developed, as we know, in Podolia and Volhynia[2] in the mid-eighteenth century.[3] In fairly short order it grew to embrace tens of thousands and became a massive folk movement. By the second generation the Hasidic sect comprised a significant proportion of the Jewish nation. By the early nineteenth century it dominated the greater part of the East European communities—including almost all the communities in the Ukraine and Eastern Galicia, most of those in Poland, a large number of those in White Russia, Rumania, and Hungary, and a small minority in Lithuania.[4] Its spirit made itself felt even in circles antagonistic toward it.[5] Nor was its victory purely temporary: The movement succeeded in consolidating the masses of its followers in new social frameworks, in molding its own distinct forms, and in providing age-old patterns of life with a new visage. The movement proved able to withstand the fierce opposition of the organized Jewish communal establishment, the rabbinate and the lay leadership, demonstrat-

Reprinted by permission of The Bialik Institute from *Bemifneh ha-dorot*, by Benzion Dinur, 1972.

Benzion Dinur's footnotes have been retained because they are a crucial part of his contribution to the study of Hasidism. They are, however, frequently incomplete and occasionally inaccurate. An effort has been made to supply some of the publication data missing in the original notes, but the references have not been checked. *Caveat lector!*

ing a tremendous strength and a marvelous degree of stability. In facing this struggle it displayed a rare measure of vitality and leadership, not permitting its foes to maneuver it to the fringe of Jewish society or to relegate it to the status of a "sect." Indeed, its influence only increased. Its leaders managed to preserve its individuality, its particular character, and its lifestyle without creating a schism in Judaism or disrupting Jewish religious and institutional unity. Not surprisingly, the movement's successes and consistent strength attracted the attention of scholars and historians: Of all religious movements within Judaism, Hasidism has become the subject of the most broad-ranging and richly developed scholarly literature. Gershom Scholem, in his *Major Trends in Jewish Mysticism,* has asserted that, "Its history, its quarrels with its opponents, the figures of its great saints and leaders and even its decay into a political instrument of reactionary forces—all this is fairly well known today."[6]

But despite the extensive literature of and about Hasidism,[7] I feel that there is still no adequate explanation for its astonishing success. It is true that we have a better understanding now of the movement's historical context. We know that the origins and growth of Hasidism were—from the point of view of time, place, and the social and religious atmosphere —related to two grave crises in Judaism: the fiasco of the Sabbatian movement[8] and the withering of Jewish self-government in Poland.[9] The first reports about the new Hasidism, whether referred to by name or simply described in terms of its distinctive characteristics, date from the forties and fifties of the eighteenth century. Its early growth took place where it began, in the provinces of Podolia and Volhynia and in nearby districts of Eastern Galicia. These were years of ferment and turmoil for the Jewish communities in Poland as a whole, and for those in that region in particular. Many reports exist of the heightened incidence of messianic propaganda and activity on the part of the remnants of the Sabbatians and associated groups in that time of great religious turmoil —the effect of the Sabbatian movement's failure that was felt among broad segments of the nation.[10] Even more numerous are the references to the widening social gap in Jewish society: a gap that was partly a function of the general processes of social disintegration in the country, but which was largely expressed in the decline of Jewish communal self-government and its attendant factors.[11] Both of these elements were especially critical precisely in the districts where Hasidism took root.

Yet, this sketch of the historical context—while it is correct in its general outlines—does not satisfactorily account for the emergence and rise of a new movement. Certainly, the Jews of mid–eighteenth-century Poland were prey to a decaying exilic life that was, in turn, an aspect of the decline of the Polish state and its corrupt regime. The Jews were economically weakened and their circumstances reduced; their community organizations were divided and fragmented; they were caught in a state of religious confusion, stunned and depressed in the national sense. For these reasons they represented a fertile breeding ground for any mass social, religious, or messianic movement. But the social context as such only provided the *potential* for such movements to emerge; it did not necessarily or inevitably *cause* them to do so, nor could it determine the quality of their achievements. Indeed, the background factors could not, by themselves, "produce" such movements. Critical challenges for which the required resources could not be found are not at all rare in the history of nations, including the history of the Jews. The idea that "history" responded to the needs of that generation[12] is just simplistic. What "social decay" actually means is the weakening of social bonds and the tearing of the social fabric; historically significant ideological "confusion" may be defined as the collapse of old assumptions that had once been accepted as veritable pillars of the known world, but were now rocked to their foundations. And any new phenomenon that combines the historical, the social, and the ideological implies a reconstituted social fabric, the formation of new social cells, the forging of alternative societal bonds, and the emergence of a new set of certainties to replace the old, crumbling verities—though these are often constructed from used bricks. Such a social force, if it exists, can grow rapidly in the kind of soil that contains numerous layers of "historical decomposition"— that is, of failed social structures. Historical inquiry into the origins of folk movements cannot simply describe the processes of social and ideological breakdown that "caused" or "necessitated" the emergence of such movements. It must locate and identify those new social elements that, within the overall context of social decomposition, provided the basis for a new societal formation and gave direction to the processes of social reconstruction.

The beginnings of a new movement are marked, from the social point of view, by the emergence of the social bearers of that movement; and from the ideological point of view, by the formulation of the basis for the new teaching, which serves as the platform for a new social and spiritual union. In our case, we must therefore discover: Which groups in Jewish society during the eighteenth century became the bearers of the Hasidic movement, the ones who created its public existence and framed its organizational structure? And, again, what were the organizing principles of the Hasidic philosophy—the principles that provided an ideological platform for the organization of the movement? And yet again: Though the two crises—the social crisis and the religious one—which form the historical context in which the movement arose, ostensibly explain the success of Hasidism and the extent of its influence in the population, simply referring to these crises as contextual elements does not in fact offer an explanation. Hasidism did not solve any of the grave problems that created those crises. Hasidism did not bring the Messiah, nor did it bring reform of the social order of the Jewish community (kehilla). Yet, the measure of the movement's success and its widespread dissemination attest to the fact that it did satisfy the demands of that generation: It drew them out of the bewildered despair into which they had sunk—persecuted and disillusioned about their hopes, yet filled with the exalted ardor of their faith—in the wake of the failure of Sabbatianism; and it also smoothed over and removed some of the bitterness from the sharp social divisions within the community. It does not suffice, then, for historical inquiry to merely describe those crises: Rather, it must also discover what Hasidism contributed toward their resolution. It must examine most carefully and in detail what the early social profile of the movement was in the days in which it came into being; which social elements were its bearers; to what extent were these elements related to the social opposition to the kehilla regime; did they find in the new movement the outlet they needed for their social impulses, and what social benefits did their work in organizing the new movement provide? Research must pay close heed to the beliefs of Hasidism's followers: It must discover the messianic roots of those beliefs, which enabled the people of that generation to free themselves from their depression and despair, from their perplexity, and provided release for their messianic tension. The historian must, in addition, look for the actual mechanisms by which the movement succeeded—through the ideological and organizational forms it took—in combining both the social and messianic elements into a single historical entity: a new Hasidic movement.

This type of approach to the study of early Hasidism clearly requires a different approach, as well, to the historical sources. A reexamination from the ground up is indicated, particularly with regard to the earliest phase of the movement and to the personality of its founder, the Besht. Those who have written in the past on the history of Hasidism have relied almost entirely on literary sources and on the Hasidic tradition. The extensive Hebrew literature of that period—other than that pertaining directly to Hasidism or Haskalah—has been all but ignored. This is true of contemporary *mussar* books (didactic works of religious, moral, and social criticism) and scriptural commentaries (sermons), which were saturated with kabbalist ideas and ascetic values and which, to a great extent, were also "oppositionist" in orientation, full of sharp criticism of the social order in the Jewish community and mindful of the need for reforms. Their historical relevance becomes especially clear in the many cases of authors who lived in the areas where Hasidism originated,[13] and whose books were printed and disseminated in that same geographic region. Similarly, it is to be regretted that historians have paid inadequate attention to books of the "rules of conduct and customs" genre. These represented an essential and popular conduit of kabbalist ideas, introducing mystic customs to a wide population and altering the prevalent religious life-style even before the Hasidic movement arose with a religious style of a specifically Hasidic character; yet these were the very ideas that formed the cornerstone of Hasidism in all its forms.[14]

It would seem that as research into the history of Hasidism developed, the picture that emerged became progressively less clear and remains hidden by an even denser cloud of mystery. The first of the historians to deal with the subject still stressed the connection between the new movement and the offshoots of Sabbatianism, even though their understanding of that connection suffered from a certain "naive realism": Thus, the Besht ostensibly organized into a coherent sect numerous Hasidim of similar bent who felt the need "to find themselves a leader";[15] or even, in another case, "The condemned and persecuted members of the sect of Sabbetai Sevi who at that time became followers of Jacob Leibowicz Frank, but who balked at following him into Catholicism, attached themselves to R. Israel Baal Shem Tov to escape persecution without submitting once more to the burdens of asceticism from which they had freed themselves."[16] Yet Dubnow found that Graetz "incorrectly viewed Hasidism as a kind of continuation of the Sabbatian movement," while he himself believed that messianic elements appeared in Hasidism only as an episodic and eccentric phenomenon during the Napoleonic Wars. Thus, as he puts it, "the answer to the question of messianic salvation in Hasidic teaching" lies "chiefly in the sphere of personal salvation" and "the national component was obliterated by the spiritual component"; and if Hasidism succeeded in "lessening the burdens of exile and oppression in the minds of its believers," that was because Hasidism was directed from the outset at "personal salvation" and wished to fulfill the desire of "the common Jew" to "find release from his troubles as an individual, rather than from the collective problems of the Jewish people."[17] "Hasidism is the final in a series of religious visions that emerged over the past few centuries on the basis of Hebrew mysticism, the last link in the long chain of Hebrew mysticism"; it is "a mystic sect" that "won numerous adherents and achieved a strong and stable position" but which actually rested on the individual, on the Jew as an individual who sought an avenue for "closeness" to God, who "sees God before him at all times," senses God's presence, speaks to Him and pours out his troubles to Him, who "is so much involved with Him as to blot out the realities of his existence." Hasidism is a product of religious imagination, a literary-spiritual creation, like the kabbala, the aggada, the apocalyptic literature, or prophecy.[18] And Buber, too, for whom Hasidism did not only follow Sabbatianism but "its very origin is rooted in the predicament created by the Sabbatian crisis," sees Hasidism, in the final analysis, as a yearning for "a new beginning, the beginning of a life of truth for the sake of the true God in a world of truth."[19]

religious

Even Scholem, who has shed so much light on Sabbatianism—its surprising contradictions, its dilemmas and complexities—and who has so ably mapped this extremely complex world, with all its obscurities, identifying and demonstrating for us where the lines of connection between the offshoots of Sabbatianism and the first sparks of the new movement (Hasidism) lie[20]—even he contends that Hasidism was fundamentally nonmessianic. Scholem insists that he does not wish to imply that "the messianic hope and the belief in the redemption disappeared from the hearts of the Hasidim"; but this qualification hardly alters his essential point. Scholem himself rightly states "there is no single positive element of Jewish religion which is altogether lacking in Hasidism." The main problem is to define the extent to which messianism played a dynamic role in the movement, and to this question Scholem's answer is

G S

unequivocal: that the messianic idea ceased to function as the main driving force in Hasidism, "although some groups and two or three of their leaders transplanted themselves to Palestine."[21] Scholem characterizes the Hasidic approach to messianism as "neutralization"—that is, a relaxation of the messianic tension: Redemption ceased being a matter of such urgency and imminence; "pressing for the end" was no longer on the agenda.

I do not intend to enter here upon a discussion of the accuracy of these views, as they will be taken up in detail further on. I merely cite them here in order to point out an interesting and rather strange phenomenon: The origins of a movement that began in the not-too-distant past, among a population that possessed a varied and substantial literature, has been subjected to a certain mystification by our historiography, which has produced a myth about the nature of Hasidism. The disregard of the real messianic tensions that characterized the movement at its outset is one factor in this mythologization. Legends told of the zaddikim and the Hasidim have been elevated to the status of "sacred tales,"[22] crowned with the title of "folklore" because "they were told in naive wonder until they became legend,"[23] and taken to be the prime documentary sources available for the history of Hasidism. Even Dubnow, the first to place Hasidism into a social-historical context and who warned against the fallacy of mixing legend and fact (as was usual in the case of Hasidism), nevertheless made much of the value of the stories as "legendary accounts which were the perceived reality in the minds of several generations of believers"[24] and used them extensively as historical documents.

Yet, in actual fact, the number of Hasidic wonder-stories that possess authentic folkloristic value is quite small. Even traditions handed down by disciples and believers, reverently preserving a plethora of minute detail—without differentiating the trivial from the significant—must be critically scrutinized, even if they seem to lack a legendary basis. Sometimes the figure of the rebbe or zaddik is painted in these tales not in accordance with reality but rather in line with an ideal type. They elaborate and amplify details more than is required, more than could have been true.[25] Most of the Hasidic stories represent a type of propaganda in a literary-didactic form, directed in general at "reaffirming belief in the zaddikim,"[26] reinforcing faith in the ability of man to reach a higher spiritual plane through his belief in zaddikim; and sometimes they are intended to enhance the influence of certain zaddikim in particular and to heighten the devotion of their followers.[27] Moreover, the religious value of a story about a zaddik and his saintly deeds lies in the telling itself, regardless of any connection to historical reality or to actual events. For by telling such stories one "brings goodness into the world"; one who "speaks about the grace of God awakens it on high, and the opposite—God forbid—is also true."

Telling tales of zaddikim is one method of attempting to influence the divine sphere. They belong to that category of things "about which man ought to speak" and of things as they ought to be. Stories fulfill a certain function under certain circumstances, and that is the reason they are told. A tale about a prisoner set free through the activity of a zaddik is told when a Jew is actually imprisoned, and the zaddik or Hasid who tells the tale—"who speaks the words that bring goodness"—does so with the intention that it help to accomplish an actual release.[28] A lengthy discussion of this is unnecessary; these stories should not be viewed as folktales or legendary reflections of historical events and personalities. Not all of them represent a combination of naïveté and mystical beliefs; they are, as I have said, propaganda of a deliberate sort, the furthest thing from naïveté.

Exaggeration is an intentional artifice. Actions and qualities belonging to other people and other times are assigned to completely different characters. This is done intentionally because it is not only the duty of the Hasid to glorify the zaddik,[29] even endowing him with qualities he lacks, it is also the duty of the zaddik to glorify himself so as to strengthen the faith of those who are spiritually dependent on him.[30] That is why the zaddikim themselves were very often the authors of these stories.[31] And there are stories that are little more than thinly clad lessons, "ideas," "teachings," deliberately cast in literary form. They enabled the teller to disguise certain things that, for reasons related to the particular time and place, were better left unsaid. In addition, stories were an attractive way to popularize an idea.[32]

It should be obvious that the different types of tales vary in their historical significance. Legends may bear witness to the historical perceptions of certain social circles or classes; there may also be a good deal of factual significance in them, if they are straightforward and uncontrived. But the propaganda stories bear witness mainly to themselves. They testify about the religious, intellectual, and ethical character, both of those who were actively involved in the movement, who frequented the "courts" of the zaddikim, who composed the tales and disseminated them, and of the mass public, the target of the stories, for whose sake and in whose spirit they were composed. For that reason, what is significant to us in such stories are those elements that are "typical": the motifs, types of miracles performed, the methods employed by the zaddikim, the literary and folkloric sources that provided material for most of these stories, and the changes that were introduced into the generic legends that were available and upon which the new stories were patterned. The historical "reality"[33] behind these stories lies not in what is told, but in the teller. From a factual point of view, the historical value of the content of such stories is practically nil. They belong to that kind of literature in which the art is calculated and deliberate from the start.

On the other hand, the third kind of Hasidic story does offer evidence of a historical nature: those which are transparent vehicles for a lesson or preaching. These stories have the same value as the sermons spoken by the zaddikim, whose historical value has been underestimated, it seems to me. The sermons, even when published in books (whether by the zaddikim themselves or by their disciples), are essentially an oral document, spoken to a group of disciples or intimates, or before a larger audience at a Sabbath or holiday meal, and only later on revised for publication. They retain the directness of the living rhetorical source— even in their literary form—through maxims, parables, words of advice, and patterns of oral speech.[34] Through the written version we can perceive something of the zaddik, the teacher and guide, but also something of the Hasid, the disciple, the seeker of guidance, to whom the words are addressed; hence, these sermons tell us something about the Hasidic pedagogic style.

The failure to take adequate account of Hasidism's historical context, then, has meant that important source material for the history of the movement has been overlooked and that the sources that were utilized were treated in an undiscriminating and oversimplifying manner. With this in mind, I endeavored to find testimony in the contemporary literature that might illuminate the way in which new social and ideological constructs came into being; to examine, in light of those sources, the Hasidic tradition, to the extent that it has been preserved in reliable form; and to sketch, in general terms, the profile of early Hasidism and its social and messianic foundations, which link it organically with the great crises of that generation—the crises out of which the movement emerged and developed.

II. THE INTERNAL CRISIS OF EIGHTEENTH-CENTURY POLISH JEWRY AND ITS SIGNIFICANCE

The root of the crisis that plagued the autonomous *kehilla* regime in eighteenth-century Polish Jewry was not the oligarchical character of that regime. It was not the takeover by "the *kahal* establishment" of "the entire community," or the "domination of the *kehilla* by a small group, an oligarchy of wealthy elders *[parnasim]* and rabbis,"[35] that caused the crisis. This could not have been the real cause of the problem for a simple reason: the communal regime had always, from its inception, been of an oligarchical nature. Officeholders in the *kehilla*—"chiefs," "elders," "selectmen" or *kahal,* judges, and so forth—were never directly chosen by the citizenry of the communities,[36] but were appointed by special electors chosen for that purpose, either directly or indirectly, by the *kahal* itself: that is, by those same officials whose annual term of office was about to expire.[37] And if it happened that the group that chose the electors co-opted several people who were not already officials of the *kahal,* then they were usually people who had only recently left the ranks of the communal establishment,[38] or else those about to be chosen for office:[39] that is, members of the upper class or of the class just below them (if they happened to be noted scholars).[40] In any event, the inclusion of such "outsiders" was limited, leaving the majority of the voting members safely in the hands of the *kahal* itself, so that it would retain the decisive voice in choosing the electors who, in turn, would nominate the incoming board.[41]

It is true, of course, that in the period we are dealing with new regulations were sometimes passed which reinforced the *kahal* oligarchy. Thus, membership in the communal assembly (the largest public body in the *kehilla*) was restricted; the number of those who could vote for electors was limited;[42] artisans in the larger communities were deprived of the right to vote.[43] But such measures testify, rather, to the desire of the leadership to *preserve* the oligarchical nature of communal government in the face of possible challenge by new social elements, than to an assault against a previous regime or against a class that had in the past participated in communal leadership. Indeed, there are a number of cases we know of in which there were attempts to *broaden* the popular base of the communal assembly,[44] to enlarge it, as well as evidence relating to certain groups that wished, at the very least, to enter and obtain influence in their community government, if not actually take it over.[45] It is in this light that we should see the disenfranchisement of the artisan class or the disbanding of artisan associations [*hevrot*] that took place in some places.[46] These and other *hevrot* constituted (as far as the *kahal* was concerned) the seedbed of friction with and opposition to the regime and, hence, a threat.[47] The regulations mentioned were simply tools utilized by the *kahal* in its struggle against its opponents, which had been going on for some time.[48]

In any case, there is no justification for viewing these measures as the *causes* of social opposition; though, of course, barring artisans from the assembly, disbanding their *hevrot,* and other such devices certainly aggravated the resentment of those social groups and intensified their battle with the *kahal.* The battle as such, and the bitterness it aroused, had been manifested long before this, however. What so enraged the "common crowd" was that such extreme measures of social control had not been applied in the past.

One school of thought has it that, since the *kahal* regime was dependent upon the general social order in the Polish commonwealth, when Polish officials began to pressure the *kahal,* this pressure was in turn applied by the *kahal* against its membership, which elicited cries of protest against the heavy tax burden imposed on the Jews. This does not, in my opinion, sufficiently explain the turmoil that ensued, though the facts underlying this theory are essentially correct. The treasury's demand of greater revenue from the Jews in that period was hardly the only way in which conditions for the Jews' worsened: This was only one instance among many—nor was it the worst among them. In that period, when the Jews were vulnerable from above and from below; when they were the victims of ceaseless blood libels, of the unbridled religious zealotry of churchmen, and of the unrestrained, vulgar arrogance of the gentry; when the Jews were the prey of cruel marauding mobs and vicious violence—and when the Jewish communities carried the awesome burden of "defending a people surrounded by enemies on all sides"[49]—a closer solidarity, if anything, should have developed between the individual Jew and the *kahal* that was his ostensible protector.

What is so remarkable, and thus requires explaining, is that it was precisely at this juncture that we observe mass rebellions against the communal establishment and against "Jewish autonomy and [against] efforts to sustain it": a rebelliousness that was most sharply expressed by the "common people" of Szawle [Siauliai] who asked, "Why do we need a rabbi and kahal-men? To assail us and ruin us?"[50] Yet, it seems to me that the very sharpness of this declaration allows us to understand the nature of the internal crisis of the Jewish community. The essential core of their complaint—"what good is the kahal to us?"—is a simple statement of the utter failure of the kahal to fulfill those functions for which it was created and for the sake of which it had existed until then. The same reasoning applies to the bitterness behind the opposition to the established regime: People are generally inclined to tolerate almost any system of government with a good deal of forbearance as long as it continues to fulfill its basic functions and raison d'être, even if it does so in an exploitative or oppressive manner. Exploitation as such is not usually enough to strain the public's tolerance to the breaking point. Only serious dysfunction in a system will spark rebellious turmoil, for that is when the public's willingness to obey the authorities breaks down, and the regime, in turn, needs to turn to overly repressive means.

Moreover, the breakdown in the functioning of a system inevitably brings with it a process of moral corruption as well, for the regime cannot honestly justify its existence even to itself. Government for the sake of exploitation then replaces exploitation as a byproduct of government. No regime is despised more than that which has failed but continues its cynical exploitation—even augmenting it through its determination to remain in control. That was the condition of the Jewish communities in Poland, especially in Podolia, Volhynia, and White Russia. This was not a constitutional crisis (over the issue of oligarchy) but an emergency in the functioning of the system as such.[51] Historical circumstances had put Jewish self-government to a crucial test, and it had been found wanting. That failure induced the Jews of that period to alter decisively their attitude to the kahal. It was as if it had lost its very justification for existence. It mattered little whether the kahal system in fact shared any responsibility for its own collapse or whether it could have withstood the severe challenges it faced, given the circumstances. The only relevant fact was that it failed and that the people blamed it for its failure. This dealt a body blow—as indicated—to the people's willingness to obey the communal authorities and to bear the burdens imposed by them: the basic conditions for any system of government. The people of that time revolted against and reviled that system and set about casting off its burdens.

We will be in a better position to follow the processes that contributed to this crisis if, taking the historical context into account, we examine the complaints typically lodged by contemporaries against the *kahal* and portrayals of that regime *as manifestations of the trend toward rebellion*. Similarly, as we seek to understand the daunting tasks faced by Jewish self-government in those days, we should assess the accusations against the *kahal*, and the demands made of it, according to each respective aspect of *kahal* responsibility: the residential and the economic basis of the community, the fiscal and the administrative apparatus, and the operation of sociolegal and moral-religious norms.

III. CRITICISM OF THE *KAHAL* AUTHORITIES AND THE MORAL DECLINE OF THE GENERATION: *MUSSAR* LITERATURE AS A SOURCE

Contemporaries' criticism of the social and moral state of Polish Jewry in general and of the communal authorities in particular is recorded mainly in literary sources, especially in collections of *mussar* (preaching) and sermons. The use of such sources as reliable reflections of social conditions requires some explanation. It is natural, perhaps, to assume that these books vastly enhance our ability to comprehend the mentality of an earlier age.

This particular literary genre, more than any other, reveals the essential oneness that binds the generations together. Human nature and human urges have not really changed, after all, and the majority of the passages of rebuke that appear in the books of the Prophets have lost little of their relevance. That is true not only because of the nature of man, who is "wicked from early youth," but also because those human foibles tend to manifest themselves on the social plane in ways that have not really changed, either. Social criticism constantly seems to hark back to the same type of source material, keeps returning to the same themes and in every generation follows similar paths. Ethical indignation; education of the individual toward a higher sensibility; social polemic and partisan advocacy by social classes and ideological groups; social conflict and political friction among parties and factions; attempts to find justification for arbitrary calamities and the search for proper expressions of penitence for the great mass of society—these are all present in the *mussar* literature of every age. The same themes appear over and over again: greed and corruption, bias in legal judgment and unfair trespass, false oaths and lying, breach of promise, favoritism, oppression of widows and orphans and cheating strangers, robbing the blind and exploitation of the poor, usury and profiteering. The familiar litany also includes protest against unethical abuse of positions of trust, misuse of the power of public office, and exploitation of the weak and the helpless— and all this is accompanied by further reproof against frivolousness, moral irresponsibility, uncontrolled appetite for sensual pleasures and possessions, pursuit of luxuries, unrestrained sexuality, and blatant degeneracy. The target for such social criticism is always the same, though appearing under a variety of labels: the "leaders," "chiefs of the House of Jacob," "princes of Israel," "heads of the community," "scholars and chiefs," "priests and prophets," "great sages and rabbis," "the prominent and the great."

The task of the historian is to identify and shed light on what is unique to the social profile of a particular period and to avoid blurring historical distinctions by emphasizing common elements. Therefore, in analyzing literary documents of this genre our first obligation is to ascertain whether—and to what extent—they are to be regarded as a record of actual social realities in the period under examination. It follows that we have to ask whether what is described in the *mussar* literature is usable data, given the fact that this literature, by its very nature, deals with human weaknesses that are common to any period of history. Moreover, it might be argued that this literature focuses upon allegations of sinfulness out of a psychic need to explain, and offer religious justification for, contemporary misfortunes and disasters; hence, such writings may offer a barometer of sociohistorical instability but not a guide to the social history of the period. If *mussar* literature flourished in a period of persecutions and oppression, as, for example, in the period we are discussing, we are entitled to see this as an expression of widespread anxiety and a response to calamity, an outgrowth of a popular need to discover reasons for such suffering and to prescribe penitential behavior, from which people might draw comfort and hope. In other words, we may say that in this literature both form and content are determined more by *ideological* than by *historical* components. The question to be asked, then, is: How may we, nevertheless, uncover the realistic foundations beneath the surface of *mussar* literature which may afford us a reliable glimpse into "the way things were."

Scholars have always followed a simple method in this regard: The factual value of statements in *mussar* literature is measured through a comparison with other contemporary documents. If those other sources confirm the impression given in *mussar* books, the latter may be accepted as further corroboration of the available record. *Mussar* literature is thus treated as a complementary source, one that reveals the way in which contemporaries perceived facts and events, their reactions and their manner of thinking. But, while this method is very satisfactory in seeking to establish the factual record, it does not offer a solution to the overall question we have posed, for it reduces the literary sources to a secondary, auxiliary status. It does not really offer an internal test regarding the distillation of "the facts as they were" from this literature; nor can it guide us in using *mussar* as an independent source in its own right, which may, of course, find corroboration in other sources but which need not necessarily depend on such external testimony.

This problem is not peculiar to *mussar* literature: It applies equally to the historical value of similar types of literary sources.[52] The answer lies, first of all, in addressing each distinct genre according to its own social basis. From the historical point of view it should be remembered that the history of literature is also the history of its readers. It is not just the story of succeeding generations of writers, but also of readers, for the connection between the two is not *a postiori*—it is not an aftereffect of the act of writing—but an organic, *a priori* link, an integral aspect of the act of creation itself and a determinant of the nature of that creation. In each genre, the conduits of influence are not at all unidirectional: the writer's ideas pouring forth to affect his readers. Rather, the transaction is a mutual one: Literature reveals the wishes and desires of the reading public, hints at the probable reactions of the readers (as perceived by the writer) and, thus, tells us something about the influence of the readership on the literary work itself. The form and style of a work is shaped by the audience and the social milieu for which it is intended or which is receptive to such works.[53]

When seeking to analyze works of *mussar*,[54] what we should notice right away is that their literary pattern is that of homiletics. Even in cases where this is not immediately apparent, the model is present as a substratum, and the outward form taken by the literary creation (exegesis, scholarly novellae, discussion arranged by subject matter) is often no more than a later reworking by the author of what had been a primary form.[55] A sermon is directed by a preacher to a particular audience on a particular occasion, whom the preacher endeavors to impress while attempting to strike a note of special relevance to those present. He will weave his general message around this central point or issue. And within his audience's realm of particular concern, he will search for the point of greatest sensitivity, by means of which he intends to draw the interest of his listeners and leave an impact upon them. Having located such a point, the preacher will naturally dwell upon and elaborate it in realistic detail and in the most vivid hues. In other words, the preacher's portrayal of the sins of the age is not necessarily the product of his own observations but rather a reflection of his audience's concerns, his audience's perceptions of what is amiss. Similarly, the descriptive color with which the preacher endows his oration is not only a function of his individual talent: It expresses, as well, the level of the public's feelings about the sins of their contemporaries, preserving for posterity the social temperature regarding the issue at hand.[56]

Complaints, for example, about the lack of internal peace in the Jewish communities—"everyone wishes only to swallow his fellow alive out of jealousy and hatred"[57]—among those most frequently cited in the literature of rebuke and chastisement,[58] actually constitute a special case of the broader category of "senseless hatred," said to have been the cause of the destruction of the Second Temple (itself a recurrent theme in *mussar* literature of every age). The charge is stereotypical, even when a particular preacher berates his generation on this score with a more detailed indictment ("factions gather together, the one against the other, bringing contention and violence to the city, a great commotion, with every one insisting on his victory . . .");[59] one may ascribe the realism of his images to his general perceptiveness. However, when these charges are specified, perhaps by descriptions of those who perpetrate such evil and other characterizations ("they hand over Israel's treasure to strangers"[60] (i.e., bring civil suit against other Jews in gentile courts), "this is, alas, frequently so in our day,"[61] "denunciations and informing" have "become as common as if they were legal"), it is reasonable to assume that that generation was actually plagued by these issues. These more detailed examples flesh out the previously cited formulaic charges about "contention and violence in the city" and "every one insists on his victory." Or, again, one encounters passages on the issue of lending on interest (e.g., that "even prominent people and scholars . . . lend on interest freely"). Although it is clear that this was an actual concern of contemporary public opinion, the charge itself is not enough to indicate the degree of sensitivity which the public had reached on this issue. However, when one takes into account the sharpness and vividness of the language used by the preacher ("the arrogant wealthy dogs have not yet been satiated by the interest they take"),[62] one may also deduce something about the emotional sensitivity of the issue. Use of words like "dogs" and "satiated" are clear indications of that.

If we subject the general complaints and accusations voiced in those days to this sort of examination, we will be able to identify common themes, to distinguish the realistic force of linguistic patterns as they are used to describe moral failings of the day, and to observe the "color" or "temperature" of the preachers' rhetoric. On this basis, we will come to the conclusion that the chief complaints of that generation were that the Jewish community establishment was being overrun by strongmen, habitués of the nobles' courts and those with access to political influence; that the social gap was widening and that public morals were in a decline. And we will conclude that the "temperature" of indignation surrounding these issues indicated that a mass rebellion was brewing against the *kahal* regime, against the authority of the rabbis, and even against some of the cherished assumptions and values that formed the ideological basis of Jewish self-rule.

IV. POLITICAL STRONGMEN WREST CONTROL OF THE COMMUNITIES: THE DECLINING AUTHORITY OF RABBIS AND THE TRADITIONAL LEADERSHIP

The new dominance attained by a parvenu class of men whose power lay in their political connections among the nobility was part and parcel of the general process of disintegration that affected Jewish social cohesion. "[No longer] is Israel one unified body, linking one Jew to the next with bonds of love and brotherhood and mutual support in the accepted Jewish way"; rather, "might makes right."[63]

Given this situation, even informing and denunciations to the authorities were no longer regarded as particularly exceptional. In previous generations leading scholars had assailed such deeds as the wickedness of those who "did violence against the people," claiming that "the [Jews'] law is unable, in the face of such behavior, to assure the proper execution of the law,"[64] and that informing "had greatly increased and wrought havoc in the communities."[65] In the early eighteenth century, such people could hardly be considered exceptions within the society at large; they came, in fact, from the heart of the community itself, either "those of wealth"[66] or the "leaders and dignitaries."[67] "No one is afraid to lord it over everyone in public" and therefore "everyone fears them" and "we are being destroyed and diminished, for our many sins."

The tendency of Jews to take litigation against other Jews into gentile courts was but a subcategory of a more general phenomenon: the far too intimate connections with the authorities cultivated in certain circles which rose to wealth and prominence at a time when most of the people were in dire straits, while civil wars and foreign invasions raged, while personal security and safety were regularly jeopardized, while Jewish communities were wiped out or expelled, and while Jews were subjected to oppressive laws and persecution. Those who managed in those troubled times not only to maintain their status but also to prosper did so by dint of exceptional effort. In the course of their upward scramble they cast aside some of the inhibitions of Jewish tradition and time-honored ethical principles. These were people who were primarily committed to their own enrichment, no matter what, and who pursued worldly pleasures unreservedly. They grew rich, some of them "adopted the life-style of the overlords" and were "satisfied to pursue wickedness and follow the arrogant dictates of their own licentiousness";[68] they "committed every kind of wrongdoing, every sin and every crime, gorging themselves and drinking to excess, fornicating and generally doing as they pleased."[69]

In the nature of things such habits rubbed off on other elements of society, too. the success enjoyed by the wealthier class was a potent lure and set a new standard that was hard to ignore. It should not surprise us, then, that the general view—certainly the prevailing opinion of many, if not of Jewish society as a whole—was that "anyone who does not cheat and work the angles is a fool, anyone who does not lie is a nobody, anyone who does not steal or take profits out of others' pockets is a dullard and will never succeed." In those adverse times it was a byword that "bread is worth risking one's life for," and lying, cheating, violating Jewish laws for the sake of greater income were commonplace.

The word "money" (ma'ah), it was said, stood for "misvot may be annulled" (ma'avirin 'al ha-misvot).[70] People were "mad for money, swore false oaths, made fraudulent claims, lied in court, suborned witnesses, and used dishonest weights"[71] without apparent qualm or scruple. In self-justification it was said, "whoever has this world, will inherit the world to come, too, for whoever is rich can afford to carry out religious obligations, give to charity, and perform altruistic deeds."

The keen desire to become wealthy, to increase one's income, and to achieve a higher status was a consequence of the times the people lived in. It was fed by the many opportunities that existed for those enterprising individuals who had no compunction about the methods they used and who were willing to exploit those opportunities to the full. To make money and grow rich—this became the social ideal; to grow rich, no matter the means or the route, be it well-trod or not: by trade or by moneylending, by profiteering or bribing officials; or by working hand-in-glove with the nobles, who were so numerous and who were a law unto themselves, arrogant and eager to seize profits, who ruled the land but who needed agents and allies and were willing to share their ill-gotten gains with those who did their bidding. It was necessary to make money and grow rich because, as people said, "money is the answer to everything"; "the whole world is not enough," never sufficient, "for the lover of money"; and, as people also said, "This terrestrial world, after all, is a world [worth enjoying], too."[72] One needed to make money and grow rich—no matter how, no matter what.

For the sake of gaining wealth and making their fortune, they disregarded every commandment that safeguarded relations with their fellow-men, with their own relatives, with their friends. The Torah, in consequence, is diminished, its splendor lost. ... We have set our sights upon greed: that is our chief goal and purpose, and many have violated laws in minor and major ways. They are prepared to disregard any of God's laws if they can thereby reap one more miserable coin.[73]

The concomitant denigration of manual crafts that became common among the middle-class householders and in "polite society" was mainly a product of that period.

For our many sins, in our day people resort to all sorts of machinations in order to become a merchant or businessman, to deal in falsehood and vanities, to spend their time on things that are of no value—and all for the sake of being considered "respectable," or what is popularly called "fine people"—and this leads them to commit every sin in the book. . . . People say: Honor is more important than any "Thou shalt not" written in the Torah, and it is unworthy to lower oneself to earn one's living from manual work, which is despicable. . . . Young and old, he is utterly consumed with greed.[74]

Attaining wealth in various ways was the goal of many. "Some buy produce at a low price and save it until prices go up," buying on speculation and thereby insuring that prices would indeed rise and causing suffering to the "poor and the indigent, whose children must bear hunger and thirst." They speculated not only with food, but with salt—a necessity item. Conflicts and disputes of all sorts were also rife, and lending on interest in various forms and guises was widespread. The rabbinic dispensation for "partnership agreements" became virtually a blanket justification that, in effect, erased the biblical prohibition against lending on interest and swept away every limitation in this regard. "People simply add the term 'partnership agreement' to a promissory note, without even knowing what it refers to and what is permitted by it." It was common, as well, to "add the interest to the principal in one lump sum and thus avoid having to use the word 'interest.' " People would mortgage their homes and give the lender use of the house instead of interest. In other cases, "many must pay charges for a few weeks of depreciation-costs"[75]—a form of insurance by which the wealthy protected the value of money they had lent out. Money changing itself, in an age of foreign invading armies and changing governments, was a trade that attracted many people looking for easy enrichment. Promissory notes—of individuals and of the community or a group of communities—became a negotiable item of exchange and a source of handsome profits, as we may infer from the attempts that were made to limit such transactions.[76]

Regulations of the Lithuanian Council (va'ad ha-medina) provide a further inkling of the extent to which lending on interest contributed to the widening social gap among Jews. These communal ordinances all date from the period following the ordeal of 1648.

In the ordinance of the council adopted in 1667, for example, the intention was to assist borrowers "who suffer so greatly from usurious interest" that "they can barely go on living." Maximum interest rates were set at "no more than one Polish zloty per hundred zlotys per week," that is, 50 percent annually. The ordinance goes on to state that in the case of small loans, local leaders "may use their discretion to waive the restriction and permit a higher rate."[77] Ordinances of the following sessions of the council—up to the final one held in 1761—regarding the further limitation of the maximum interest rate[78] and encouraging each local community to set such standards for its own citizens in accordance with prevailing local economic conditions, and the stringent measures taken by the councils against debtors who were not repaying their debts,[79] all demonstrate how sensitive an issue interest rates continued to be.

It is certain, too, that the fact that among those lending money on interest and engaging in sharp business practices rabbis, scholars, and other learned people were significantly represented only heightened Jewish society's sensitivity on this point and contributed to the overall moral turpitude. Preachers excoriated contemporary rabbis whose income derived from lending money on interest; these rabbis "sinned and led many others into sin," both by virtue of the fact that they transgressed the biblical prohibition against usury and because they used their authority to grant themselves dispensations. The communities, nevertheless, felt constrained to accept such men as their rabbis "because of his wealth, since we already owe him thousands"; and because "he will support the community members through loans and through business." The common folk "all say that lying and deceit are characteristics of the religious leadership." And the preacher quoting these views had to admit that "it would seem that they are almost right, for they speak the truth about the way it is in reality, for our many sins, and for that reason even the truly righteous are still considered to be cheats, for they are contaminated [by association]." No wonder, then, that the preachers unanimously made the point that not only did the common people not look up to the rabbis as men of importance deserving the respect of their inferiors, but that "the common folk are contemptuous of the rabbis," and "the coarse, uneducated ones seem to grow steadily in importance while the status of the learned ones declines." And they spoke as well of "ignorant and wicked people who hate the rabbis more than gentiles hate the Jews."[80]

Yet, these wealthy merchants and moneylenders were not the new force that wrested control over the communities. The activity of the former group was rather restricted (excepting those directly linked to the noblemen's and overlords' financial affairs), and thus could not provide a sufficient power base: they did not have backing from outside the community and were not strong enough to win influence within the community. Their importance lay more in the fact that they set the spiritual tone and the social context for the rise of the "strongmen," who enjoyed the patronage of the magnates.

While the Catholic church in general, and monasteries in particular, possessed vast wealth and during that period all but dominated the money-lending business entirely, the magnates tended to look to their Jewish "aides" for expertise in management to a great—and increasing —extent. These Jews participated in the administration of the estates and in the exploitation of the serfs' labor; they saw to the financing of the estates through loans and attended to arrangements for the growing export trade, shipping their lords' produce to other countries. The magnates themselves were hardly in a position to see to such matters personally. They lived like royalty and busied themselves with political affairs; while the Jews—especially those with enterprise, capital, and a network of connections—whose sphere of economic activity was limited by the restrictions placed on them by the gentile burghers, looked increasingly to the countryside, to the villages and in particular to the great estates of the nobles. For their part, the landowners also found their Jewish agents useful in exploiting their Jewish tenants. This was the group that formed the third and most politically aggressive stratum of new leaders and communal officials in Jewish society: men with sufficient clout to impose their will or retain their hold over the communities, and who collaborated with the magnates in an exploitative and oppressive regime that plundered at will whatever Jewish assets could be seized. These men were not always from the respected families that had always in the past combined scholarly attainment and communal leadership. Rather, as I have stated, their power rested upon the external patronage of noble overlords, who at that time exercised absolute rule over their subjects, including the Jews. This sort of Jew, "used his home only for stopovers and actually spent all his time among gentiles, who was habitually with [his patron], night and day, showing him schemes for enrichment and new plans for dominating his subjects, from whom he extracted new taxes and levies."[81] Such people, who rose to power during that period and took the reins of the *kahal* regime, symbolized the moral degradation of that era and turned Jewish self-government into a fiction, a caricature. Worse, the Jewish communal government turned into a system of entrapment, a prison in which the warders took bribes from the

NB

inmates for the privilege of controlling them and profited from outright plunder and pillage.

Indeed, we find much evidence of popular resentment against those who "enjoy the lavish favor of the magnates' purse filled with Jews' money that they turned over to them." Moreover, "If the rabbis and chiefs stood firmly against them with holy wrath instead of kowtowing to them, they would surely pronounce them to be outlaws, wicked men whose lives are forfeit."[82] But the power of the strongmen was on the ascendant, and they proved dominant. At a later stage we hear, "Now that scandals and strife have become so common, the lowest elements are chosen to be communal heads."[83]

Gradually, this class of Polish-style court Jews took control. At first, they entered the leadership because the Jews were so dependent on them. It was said, "The Jews are powerless unless the lords of the land step in [on their behalf]." It was important to know how to "persuade the overlords to cooperate," and few Jews were capable of doing this as well as "those who even get along well and flatter the nuns with gifts." Those were the men who had absorbed the mentality and life-style of the magnates: They placed their own interests above all else.

They devote themselves to their own affairs, and their days are taken up with lords and ladies, with lavish pleasures among the nobles and officials. They never have enough of what they desire, they pursue vanities ceaselessly and their money pursues them in turn.[84]

It was natural that the magnates or overlords who owned the towns and cities were interested in having someone they could trust put in charge of the kahal. They disregarded the traditional etiquette and the accepted practice, enshrined in the charters given to the Jews, allowing them to choose their own leaders; instead they chose one who was to their liking.[85] The kahal either submitted and found a modus vivendi with the new chairman,[86] or else tried to persuade the overlord, who might recall the ancient privileges of the Jews and renew their right to choose their own leaders. During earlier periods, community boards would fight to defend their right to self-government and refused to permit the "court Jews" to ride roughshod over them. But now, when "God's people are full of fear, when it is dangerous to travel and 'the sound of a driven leaf' makes them afraid . . . and there is not a single person who has not had some miraculous escape from the many terrible persecutions, killings, hostage-taking, sieges, and great distress of other sorts . . . [therefore] whoever wishes to rule over them takes control . . . for the Jews are now a poor and downtrodden people."[87] In those times when, apart from more general crises, each locality had gone through its own particular trials, for every lord and every priest had his own method of persecuting the Jews ("innovating" in this realm and thereby winning for himself a place in heaven, as well as more mundane rewards here on earth),[88] there were Jews who, despite their lack of real qualification and power, were able to seize control because of the fear that existed in Jewish society. That rabbi and preacher of the second generation of that era who said, " 'Every troubler of Israel becomes chief' [is literally true], for anyone who comes and troubles them can take control, even if he is weak,"[89] based his observation on his own and the previous generation's experience.

Indeed, as power fell into the hands of those with ties to Polish magnates—who were no more than agents of the "overlords and princes"— a new attitude began to dominate the *kahal* regime in the communities: an attitude of arrogant condescension toward lowly underlings. They adhered strictly to the injunction, "Invest your office with dignity, and let every chairman be like a prince of princes." The leader was "lord over the imposition of all fines and master of all taxes," and "he took his reward for public service, whether openly or under the table through various machinations, for God forbid that he take a single step without assuring his own recompense."

Such attitudes were typical not only of chairmen and officials of the community, but also of rabbis who "expended great sums and bought [themselves] rabbinical posts, which they treated as a fiefdom, full of subordinates; and over a period of several years [they] gain back what they spend in payment to the overlord, by charging fees and taking bribes; once the 'principal' is repaid them, they continue charging as 'interest' due them for the rest of their lives."[90] For "the landowners charge significant sums for approving the appointment of a rabbi for one of their cities or towns; and the rabbis, in turn, charge the community members four times that amount, and thereby oppress the people of the towns, many of which become financially ruined in this manner." "In some areas the rabbinate has become a profit-making job virtually synonymous with farming the customs tolls, and very often control over the rabbinate is out of the Jews' hands entirely."[91]

This was not merely a matter of interference by the Polish authorities in the appointment of rabbis; what we have here is an entire social stratum that captured the rabbinate for itself, just as it captured the lay leadership of the communities and proceeded to exert its control. It was not that rabbis became wealthy, but rather that *the wealthy and power-ful became rabbis,* or else appointed candidates of their own choosing. Or, as one prominent rabbi of the time said, "In our day, for our many sins, the lowly ones are on top, in place of their betters, and are accepted in the large communities through [the influence of] the overlords and money." Another well-known rabbi, chosen for "the sake of heaven and without any expenditure of funds whatsoever," found it necessary to make a point of that, because "everywhere rabbis are appointed because of money which they distribute in large sums to the landowner and to the *kahal.*" The popular anger and rebelliousness directed against the Jewish administration was fanned even more by this new situation in the rabbinate than by the position attained by "lesser" men in the lay leadership. The decline of the rabbinate had a more devastating impact on the public, and preachers devoted much attention to this phenomenon, demanding that it be opposed. They correctly viewed this issue as an expression of the drastic moral decline of their generation.

The rabbi is the foundation stone and the pinnacle, ruling over one and all. His word is law for each Jew in his community, and without his approval no action will be taken. The rabbis are the leaders who must point out the correct path.

Preachers and writers of *mussar* books called upon "the rabbis, the chiefs, the pious and the learned ones, etc., to wage the Lord's battle wherever their influence is felt, to stand firm and strengthen their resolve against rabbis of that ilk . . . who may bear the name of 'rabbi' but are not really entitled to it."[92]

It is obvious that the people at large had no faith in such rabbis. If even in earlier times it was said that the word "rabbi" was an acronym for *rasheha be-shohad yishpotu*—that is, they are judges of bribery— because of the fact that they attained their office through bribing officials, it was now understood in a literal sense, as well.[93] Accusations against Jewish strong-arm tyrants in Poland, who "buy rabbinical posts from the nobles and then rule mercilessly over the people, skinning them alive and crushing their bones" were common. It was generally believed, too, that the rabbis did so, not merely to recoup the expenditures they had been forced to make to buy their office, "but also to increase their power, their wealth and the status of their family. Their house is full of deceit, and so they wax great and grow rich, ruling the poor folk high-handedly and strictly, and squeezing them."[94]

Actually, the phenomenon of rabbis winning their posts through bribing the nobility, giving payoffs to the *kahal,* or trading on the power of influential individuals was not entirely new. Earlier regulations of the intercommunal councils threatened to "punish[,] condemn[,] and ex-communicate" anyone "who tries to lobby the king for rabbinical or other appointments." The earliest examples date from the end of the sixteenth century and these were confirmed and restated a number of times.[95] It would appear that the problem was a common one even then. One of the rabbinical leaders of that time contended that "this sin and transgression has recently come among us," and related that "our teach-ers mentioned this violation in connection with drastic punishments and fines, lest anyone attain his office of rabbi and teacher for silver and gold, whether he pays individuals or groups." Yet, there is an essential difference between the two phenomena. At the end of the sixteenth century and the early seventeenth, "there were very many scholars, each of whom desired to become a rabbi or chief rabbi of a city," and since "the householders are the ones who choose and appoint whom they please, according to their own wishes, and most of all in consideration of money,"[96] there were candidates for the rabbinate who used this situation to further their own careers. But the situation in the rabbinate at the end of the seventeenth and the beginning of the eighteenth century was something else again: Now it was part and parcel of the rise to power of the local political "muscle" in each community, far more than it was simply a question of the decline of standards in the rabbinate. The new breed of rabbis were "flesh of their flesh" and "bone of their bone" —quite literally: the brothers, sons, sons-in-law, and brothers-in-law of the upstart group in charge of communal affairs.[97] [The chief function of the rabbi was to serve as head of the communal judiciary system, hence his title—*av beit din,* "head of the court." In addition to these courts which took decisions in accordance with rabbinic traditions there were lay, communal (kahal) courts which were essentially arbitration courts. The distinctions in jurisdiction were vague.—ED.]

This was a deliberate and calculated campaign on the part of the new lay leadership to capture another important arm of social control: the judicial arm. This would assure them the retention of power and allow them to fully exploit its possibilities. If the rabbis they chose were not worthy, some of them too young and inexperienced,[98] or less than illustrious as scholars,[99] or perhaps not of sterling moral character,[100] this was no real impediment. Quite the contrary: Such rabbis were bound to be more malleable and cooperative. The *kahal* was jealous indeed of the independence of the judiciary. They were not at all pleased with the division of labor that traditionally obtained in the Jewish community—lay leaders seeing to social affairs; judges, to legal matters (especially civil cases); and assessors, to the distribution of the tax burden. The intercommunal councils sought to preserve intact the independence of the courts as well as that of the assessors. The "strongmen" were out to subordinate both of these realms to their own power, however, for only thus could they attain their objective.

And attain it they did. The rabbis of the time had no standing vis-à-vis the *kahal* and its leaders, who began to intervene directly in civil suits. The courts became simply part of the lay administration: not, it is true, in matters of religious decision, but in cases of arbitration undertaken by the *kahal*.[101] Matters of tax assessment (previously handled by specially appointed assessors, who worked with a free hand, sometimes anonymously) were now undertaken directly by the *kahal,* in spite of efforts by the councils to bar such practices.[102] The leaders made full use of the opportunity to turn that institution into a constant producer of revenue, which proved quite lucrative because it was "not something open to public view"; and this enabled them, again, to reinforce their own power by rewarding friends and punishing their opponents.

The literature of the day is, indeed, filled with resentment against scandalous conduct of this sort and against the abuse of power by the *kahal* in the various spheres of Jewish self-government: administration, the courts, and the tax structure.

In our day it has become permissible for chairmen, chiefs of the community and leaders to live at the public expense. They consume the earnings [of the people], taking food from the mouths of babes and oppressing the multitude through taxes and municipal rates, and behave like lords toward the Jewish people.

Moreover, "the communal heads do not share the burden of paying the taxes of the king and the magnates"; "he exempts his entire family, and anyone who needs to speak to him must approach him with servility"; "people are obsequious to the rich because of [their control over] taxes and municipal rates, and they are cruel and haughty to the poor, extracting from them [their last cent] with all manner of coercive measures." Not even the money they collect satisfies them: they treat (the poor) however they please. "They eat and drink from the cream of the money at their disposal. And when it comes to accounting for the *kahal* expenses, the deficit is supposed to be paid from the negligible amounts left over." The communal heads routinely "influence the verdict [in civil suits] and give biased judgment, favoring their friends and taking revenge upon their opponents as far as they are able, making those whom they wish to pressure pay large sums in the capitation and other taxes." "Once a man becomes the head of the community, he determines all assessments and levies to be paid, and he gives money where he wishes, and all that he desires to do, is done." "It is not enough for him that he is exempt from paying the tax of the king and the magnates, he even takes money for himself from the funds that are brought to his house by the townspeople, and no one knows what he does in secret, and he eats and drinks at public expense." "And their wives and children, too, have a say in the outcome of a verdict, and they speak arrogantly to the poor." "They say that they have the power, and thereby weaken the force of law and Torah." If anyone crosses these tyrants, "their sin is remembered for all time, and they will never be treated with any kindness or mercy." "At the time of a council session, some of them [rabbis and leaders of provincial councils] accept gifts from the community [representatives] who come before them with a case for litigation, or else the powerful leader of a province will, for the payment of such a gift, go lightly in apportioning the taxes for the communities in question, and demand much more of the communities whose representatives arrive [at the council] empty-handed." "Such a council is not worthy of the title 'holy' [kodesh], but rather should be termed 'harlot' [kadesh/kedesha]." The author of these remarks found it necessary to add: "Although I know of some rabbis and leaders of provincial councils who are honest and take no gifts or bribes, what I have written applies in most cases."[103]

Naturally, "self-government" of this sort possessed no authority with the people at large, nor was it properly prepared to deal with the extraordinary tasks placed before Polish Jewry during this period. It represented one more factor in the widening social gap and the moral decline in public life.

V. THE WIDENING SOCIAL GAP AND MORAL DECADENCE

The Jewish community's social profile was significantly altered, as well, because of the sharp differences in living standard between the various classes. The "wicked of the earth,"[104] those "with ties to the magnates," aspired to imitate their patrons in everything, including their standard of living, their everyday occupations, and their attitude to their underlings. They, too, like the estate-owners, lived a life of extravagance: their homes "are decorated like the palaces of royalty," and their carriages "are drawn by many brown horses" like those of royal officials. They thus "kindle the jealousy of the gentiles against us, . . . their families eat delicacies to their fill, they dress in finery, they use golden utensils, living a life full of pleasures and delights"; for they, "the heads and leaders of the people, . . . enjoy the best of everything, their faces are always ruddy, fat and healthy because they indulge their appetites." Even those of a lesser status "desire spacious homes and delights that Jews were formerly strictly careful to avoid," but now such Jews "wish to rival the nobility, building homes with large upper stories, surrounded with gardens and orchards."[105]

Along with mounting wealth and power, such hedonistic tendencies became more widespread in this class. As already noted, the popular saying was, "This [terrestrial] world, after all, is a world [worth enjoying], too."[106] The life-style that expressed this appreciation for worldly pleasures reflected what these Jews learned from the example of the nobles.

As one critical preacher put it,

Recently a new fashion has been started and has spread far and wide, that Jews dress in gentile clothes, so that one cannot tell if a woman is a Jew or not. . . . Jewish women go about in finer clothes than even the aristocracy . . . very decolleté, naked from the throat to their bosom. . . . Violators among the people go about in gentiles' fashions, and even worse, shave their beards . . . and they teach their children French and other languages.[107]

But above all, it was the nobles' attitude toward the population at large that the new Jewish leadership absorbed. In the previous generation one already heard complaints of "the fault of the generation": "Whoever attains any standing of authority—immediately his fellows dare not speak up in his presence."[108] In the period we are dealing with, the *mussar* books are simply filled with comments of this sort, decrying

"leaders and heads of the generation who lord it over the community
. . . [each one of them] speaks haughtily with pride and contempt to the
Jews of his city, relying on the fact that no individual will dare to say a
word against him, lest he take his revenge."

This arrogance was expressed not only in speaking to individuals:
"Leaders and chiefs are contemptuous of the Jewish communities" who
come to the councils for judgment and who depend on their help (even
though) "they are holy congregations, the chosen people of God, the
children of Abraham, Isaac and Jacob." "Their own self-pride prevents
them from showing the proper courtesy and dignity."[109] Preachers often
warned that, "those who are prideful at the expense of others because of
the honor of their office, who are haughty because they happen to be
communal leaders and who do not show the proper attitude of respect
toward the people, are destined to pay a penalty"; but it would seem
that these warnings were in vain. There is a simple explanation here: It
was not only the communal leaders who behaved arrogantly—this was
the case for most of "society" and became part of the culture. "Some are
prideful because of their wealth, some because of their wisdom, some
because of their learning." Regardless of the reason, they all believed
themselves to be superior to the common folk and behaved rudely and
contemptuously toward them.

"Everyone places his hope in money," because "they see that the poor
are the lowest of the low, and the rich take the power for themselves,
and consider the poor to be simply an obstacle in their path." For that
reason "the servile multiply among us and set their hopes on the wealthy."
The wealthy and powerful also knew how to use popular maxims to
their advantage: "Do not be a pious fool" and "in this world one flatters
the wicked." And they set up parties of supporters made up of those
who "for the sake of the food and drink they get from them are willing
to let their words and actions pass, and they tell them, 'well done.' 'well
put.' Of such people it is said: You call wickedness good, and goodness
wicked." Even when they know full well that "all his words are wicked
and all his works are vengefulness and robbery, sin and evil, vanity and
abomination and vileness and never for good," not only do they not
protest, "but, on the contrary, they shower him with praise and honor."
Moreover, all those "who eat from what the wealthy ones provide—
puffed up as they [the wealthy] are and however lustful their ways—
[those dependents] cover up their [patrons'] abominations and vanities

... [and] even learn their ways, out of a convergence of character based on the benefits they derive from them."[110]

Part of the "aristocratic style" was a penchant for living beyond one's means, and this became a widespread tendency in various social circles, as many sources in the *mussar* literature testify. Everyone (the preachers wrote) "strives to show off ... in fine clothing" and to dress their children "in princely clothes, so that people would take notice and look up to them in respect," even though such luxury "is pleasant for the moment, but turns into trouble and distress by the morrow."[111]

It was not only the preachers who tirelessly inveighed against luxuries: the community boards and councils also approved regulations, time and again, comprising detailed rules about clothing and jewelry—what was and was not permitted, and what finery was appropriate for celebrations and holidays.[112] Outside observers, too, reported their own or others' impressions that the Jews of Poland, like other folk of "high status," were living well beyond their means and, therefore, were so deeply in debt.[113]

Clearly, this situation was bound to lead to degeneracy in public morals. This applied first and foremost to the leadership of the communities, who (as already noted) had absorbed some of the life-style of the nobility. Along with the highest communal officials, this extended to all the other officeholders and various public figures in Jewish society.

In this connection, the following example is quite typical. In drawing up the sworn agreement between the community of Dubno and its *shtadlan* [political spokesman], it was stipulated that he never "engage in falsehood of any kind, whether in a Jewish tongue or in Polish, nothing that the mind can conceive and the mouth give speech to"; that he never "render assistance to an individual [litigant] in gentile courts"[114] in any matter that "contravenes a verdict rendered by the rabbi in authority or is directed against the leaders of the community." In addition, the *shtadlan* was not to write petitions directed against the leaders, nor was he to delay returning any "documents or charters that belong to the *kahal*." These formulations undoubtedly reflect the bitter experiences of communities (not only Dubno) with regard to the aristocratic comportment of numerous *shtadlanim* and other communal appointees.

We have other testimony, as well (particularly from *mussar* literature) regarding the sort of behavior communal officials, *shtadlanim*, wardens, and the like were apt to engage in. They were accused of "spreading gossip abroad and revealing confidential information about the *kahal* and playing up to the wealthy regarding taxes, but estrange themselves from the poor and deal cruelly with them." Moreover, "the [public] funds mean nothing to them, for they do with them as they please, eating and drinking out of the [community] purse." And while it may be that some expenses of the *kahal* were truly large, this, too—according to the preachers—was partly the fault of the officers, "for they are not sparing with the public funds entrusted to them, and instead they pay Jewish money to gentiles just in order to square accounts."[115]

That is not to say, however, that corruption was to be found only among the ranks of communal appointees. There is enough evidence to suggest that their superiors in the hierarchy ("officers and chiefs," leaders of communities, and provincial council chairmen) were no better. A court verdict from Dubno, involving a litigation between "the honorable leader of the community, Rabbi Meir of Dubno, and the venerable chairman, Rabbi Yirmiah of the same city [on the one hand] and the leaders of the province of Volhynia, on the other, is unfortunately revealing about the state of affairs at the time. Among the allegations we find are: the chairman of the Four Lands Council[116] received a double salary: one from the council and one from the province he represents; the chairmen received exaggerated expense accounts, far more than they actually spent; of the funds they collected in order to provide gifts to the magnates and Polish authorities "for the good of the province," only a small portion was ever used for its destined purpose—and even then, the bribes paid were sometimes given for private aims, for the sake of securing their appointments, etc.

Given such facts, we should not be surprised by what other contemporaries reported: that "during meetings of provincial leaders and rabbis, some of them accept gifts from the community representatives who come to them for a verdict"; that "a powerful provincial chairman would take bribes from the communities, by sending assessors into the communities to lighten the tax burden on those that provide gifts, and raise the burden on those communities that do not provide such gifts to the assessor." This state of affairs, the preacher in question admits, may not have been true of all the leaders and rabbis, but it was true in the main.[117]

These statements, which at the time aroused the wrath of the Four Lands Council board, may have included a measure of exaggeration and distortion. Yet, it cannot be doubted that the practices alluded to were part of "everyday life," and in light of these allegations we ought to take a more serious look at similar, if isolated, charges elsewhere in the contemporary literature. Each such accusation should be collated, one by one, into a general overall portrait of the "ways of the aristocrats." Thus, we should see in this context the report of "a great scholar" who "refused to obey the emissaries of the rabbinical court, and they submitted to him"; and the case of an attempt to bribe (with "twenty red zlotys") one of the most prominent rabbis, who was serving on the council;[118] and the terse verdict of the Treasury tribunal that the Jewish provincial leaders had collected tax revenue from the Jews but had embezzled funds for their own private purposes, and that they had overtaxed the poor.[119] These items indicate a cold and bitter reality. In this light, the seemingly rhetorical flourishes of Rabbi Israel of Zamość (about a certain individual who entertained his household "after dinner, with tales of how he had done out another man, how he had cleverly diverted him and sucked his blood, and about the money that he had recovered from a friend and cheated his family"[120]—and that everyone in attendance "congratulated him heartily for the abomination he had committed, as if, God forbid, all laws and limits had been suspended") take on a newly appreciated semblance of realism. The "aristocratic ways" of the wealthy, the officers of the community, and the politicians put into bold relief (sometimes, indeed, quite deliberately)[121] the level of demoralization to which the bulk of Polish Jewry had sunk. The decadence in the upper strata affected, as well, the moral probity of much broader segments of society.

The many references we find in the literature of the time regarding the multitudes of poor people, who are "on the lowest possible rung," can hardly be considered mere rhetoric, either. Forced idleness, neglect and abandonment, a languishing and debilitating poverty, constant hunger (literally)—these were the facts of life for masses of people. At the end of the eighteenth century we hear of "great numbers of Jews without work" who are a burden on their communities; of "families who must support these people at their own expense"; of "people out of work, who [pass you on the street and] say *sholem aleichem* [greetings to you]"; of the poor and the destitute "in every town and city."[122] Such remarks are relevant for the entire period, ever since the depredations of 1648–49 and continuing under the new conditions in the country as a whole and on its frontiers, in the years that followed.

Polish Jewry constituted a large population, and the largest concentration of all was located in the Ukrainian areas (Volhynia, Podolia, and Kiev). Here one found the oldest-established communities. This pattern was not basically altered by the massacres (of the mid-seventeenth century), although many of those who survived had to move elsewhere. Exiled and homeless refugees and victims wandered far and wide from town to town, which had a negative impact on the social stability of the rest of the Jewish communities. It proved difficult to absorb so many newcomers: often the gates were shut before them, and some communities were actually compelled to deny them entry.[123] Therefore, many refugees ultimately returned to their former homes, once the Poles had reestablished their rule in those areas. Jewish arendars and tavern-keepers returned to the inns and taverns, where the blood of the slaughtered still stained the floorboards.[124] They had no choice but to return—they had nowhere else to go. However, even the renewed string of settlements in the western Ukraine—with all the encouragement they were given by influential circles in the nobility and the clergy—were able to absorb only a small portion of the refugee population.

Here lay the origin of the problem that plagued so many of the poor, "whose main need is to be given employment." This large social stratum served as a tremendous floating source of labor. Within this very large group, there were gradations of poverty. The most unfortunate of all were the "poorest of the poor," beggars of one sort or another. They lived on the very margins of society—virtual outsiders. These were people whose poverty was their occupation, the basis for whatever livelihood they could manage to eke out. Some would beg from door to door in their own town or district. Others wandered further afield, giving rise to those scruffy bands of *Betteljuden* who traveled with their families, sometimes even with wagons of their own, from city to city and even from country to country. They would find all doors and gates closed to them, but would somehow manage to lodge themselves in nooks and crannies. In the second and third generation, some of them actually established themselves on a firmer footing.

Above this group stood the "poor and the unfortunate," for whom poverty was but a "supplemental" source of income. They tended to make their principal living (if at all) from tutoring or teaching young children, as street vendors of fruit and other wares; but they would on occasion—Sabbath eve or before holidays, new moons, and other times of special privation—go alms-seeking from door to door, despite the restrictions that some localities instituted. This stratum of the "employed poor" was by no means small. One typical city (which was neither especially well-established nor known for the kind of prosperity that would have attracted large numbers of refugees) contained a population of "employed poor" that comprised 8 percent of all the local Jews.[125]

At the next level up we find the servant class: again, a fairly numerous group[126] and one whose status was rather deplorable. They included domestics as well as shop assistants, servants to toll-farmers, messengers, and so forth. Many of them were "newcomers" (that is, refugees), orphans, and widows.[127] Some of them were also educated, but having reached a town where no one knew them, they took on such jobs as assistant to tax-farmers. This work was not only degrading, it was also sometimes without emolument. Often "they are not paid, or they are accused of having stolen something, or otherwise tormented, in order to get rid of them without paying them their due."

The following incident gives us some indication of the prevalent attitudes of householders toward their servants. A householder sent his servant to the marketplace demanding payment from some artisans there who owed him money. This took place at night, during a storm, "the snow and the wind were so bad that it was almost impossible to walk." Everyone else was going home, including this particular householder, and his servant begged him not to be cruel and to allow him, too, to go home. The master demanded, however, that the servant go as he had been instructed. The servant did so, and froze to death. He was not the only one: there were two other servants who also froze. The rabbi who recounted the episode wrote that "the master of the house at first expressed no regret, for they did not, he claimed, die by his hand." For that reason, the rabbi counseled that the matter be treated with "utmost severity and published abroad, for this is a veritable plague among us, for our many sins."[128]

Data from the 1765 Polish census regarding the occupational stratification of the Jewish population have never been fully published, nor have they been the object of scholarly investigation. We can therefore make no precise judgment about the size of the personal service class. But from the fragmentary data that have appeared in various publications, and judging by the amount of attention devoted to the topic in a variety of contemporary sources, we may state with some certainty that the servant class (both male and female) was fairly large.[129]

The largest and the most respectable segment of the urban Jewish working population was the artisan class. Numerically, artisans represented a significant portion of the urban Jewish population.[130] In the aftermath of the catastrophe of 1648–49, large numbers of Jews who had been left without livelihoods streamed into the manual crafts. There was hardly any craft that Jews did not ply, and there were some in which Jews specialized, becoming the majority in that particular field.[131] It is in this period, therefore, that we tend to hear more and more about conflicts and competition between Jewish and Christian artisans—an important component in the overall conflict between the Jews and the burghers. Similarly, it is not surprising that most of the Jewish artisan associations *(hevrot)* were founded during the seventeenth and eighteenth centuries.[132] One factor behind the organization of the *hevrot* was the desire to regulate the crafts and protect established artisans from the influx of "new" craftsmen. The latter, who were hard-pressed to earn a living, were willing to do anything, anywhere, regardless of prevailing standards. One writer tells us that everywhere one went in those days one encountered Jews traveling through the country offering their services as tailors for men's and women's clothing, and (ironically, given their own long beards) as barbers. The details he furnishes are objective reflections of his time.[133]

Although the literature of the late eighteenth and early nineteenth century *(Sefer ha-berit* by Pinhas Eliyahu Hurwitz, or the works of Menashe of Iliya) exhorts Jews to learn manual trades, this should not be taken as an indication that there were few Jewish craftsmen or that they were badly off. On the contrary, if we examine these injunctions to acquire a craft, we will arrive at two basic conclusions:

1. When they were addressed to "most of the people" who "do not wish to learn a craft," they were directed at two types of people in particular: to merchants and those educated Jews "who feel that only business is a pursuit worthy of their status," and to those "who rely on the expectation that their sons will be rabbis or rabbinical judges."

2. Crafts are considered to be a decent source of income, and whoever makes his livelihood in this manner "is not dependent on others." The material conditions for craftsmen were more stable and their status more honorable than that of any other segment of the urban working population,[134] including those lower-middle-class elements

that filled posts such as *hevrot*-rabbis, teachers, preachers, and the like—a sort of intellectual proletariat whose actual socioeconomic status was among the lowest of all, even if (from the point of view of Jewish social values) they belonged to the "elite" and felt that they deserved to be treated as such.

Indeed, only a very small portion of these "rabbis, preachers, judges, teachers and the like" (in Solomon Maimon's categorization)[135] could possibly have been content with their lot. During the period we are discussing, this group experienced a decline in status, both financial and social. The official rabbinate became, as we have seen, the preserve of the privileged and an arena of intense friction with a lay leadership that was bent upon using the rabbinate to their own advantage. Community rabbis of the day tried to obtain personal documents of protection and patronage in order to resist *kahal* control.[136] There were only a few rabbis in each large community, but there were so many Jewish communities in Poland; and besides rabbinical appointments there were openings for rabbinical judges, for preachers, and in each community there were several *hevrot*, each of which had a president, who received at least some emolument from this post.[137] No wonder, then, that so many "depended on the expectation that their children would be rabbis or judges."[138]

In addition, there was a third category, apart from educated Jews who made their living from their Torah studies. There were, as Solomon Maimon described, those whose learnedness was enough of an asset in the matrimonial stakes that well-to-do but uneducated parents welcomed them as sons-in-laws, and whose wives worked to support them and their children (usually by tavern-keeping or the retail trade). They, too, "do not want to teach their sons a [manual] trade, just Torah."

All these groups of Jews with a Torah education fed the swelling ranks of elementary school teachers, far beyond the available demand.

There are more teachers than pupils, and therefore they do not succeed in earning even half a decent income. Their homes are bare of food and clothing. Some of them also do some business on the side, some of them give private lessons in the better homes, and some of them must travel far away from their wives to find students in another land. And there are some who go abroad but find no students there either, and their wives and children starve to death. Some travel far and wide, one becoming a preacher, giving sermons, another may beg alms from Jews wherever he goes, another will become a scribe—and all of those who travel for sustenance to cities far away seek nothing but food for their families.[139]

That description, dating from the end of the eighteenth century, is relevant to the entire period. That much is attested by contemporaries who noted as a matter of course that teachers "do not stop working day or night, and they are not paid their fees . . . [and] therefore they are forced to travel abroad." There were some, of course, for whom going abroad to teach was but an intermediate stage toward a higher goal: By the end of the seventeenth century we already note criticism in the *mussar* literature directed against those who "abandon their wives and go to foreign lands to teach children and then they turn to business, working until they succeed in becoming wealthy."[140] These, however, were the exception. Most were poor, and in socioeconomic terms they were directly associated with the masses of the unemployed poor who "do not even make half a decent income." It is no wonder, then, that in all the social turmoil in the Jewish communities of the eighteenth century we find evidence of active participation by teachers and preachers. They were the articulate spokesmen for this large poverty-stricken population which also included the poorer tavern-keepers and innkeepers, middle-men, and other agents[141] who were so numerous in Jewish society. They helped these strata to organize themselves into a social unit and lent character and form to the "opposition" in the Jewish communities.

The poverty of these strata was dire. Preachers warned, for example, against not giving enough bread to children on their way to school, because so many children were going hungry;[142] and the literature of the time is filled with factual comments related to the demoralization that afflicted Jewish society at large, beginning with but not limited to the moral decline among the "strongmen," the leaders, and the community chairmen. Indeed, one rabbi wrote about "most of the poorest people are generally assumed to be thieves," and further testimony adds that "thieves and robbers have multiplied beyond counting." One woman demanded that her husband divorce her after "he joined in a gang of villains, robbers, and forgers." Elsewhere we find a Jew accused of being in league with killers who "murder Jews."[143] Evidence from various places in the Ukraine, Podolia, and White Russia indicates that there were Jews "with links to those bandits," and that there were "apostates and [Jewish] highwaymen" who joined such gangs.

Conversion in general was more widespread than we might think, a phenomenon that was linked to the deepening social divisions in Polish Jewry. An example we know of, of a housemaid "who stole money and valuables" and then married one of the Haidamak leaders, is probably not the only one of its kind. The conversions that occurred in this period suggest a common theme of rebellion: deliberate heresy as protest and provocation. Among Jews who joined up with Polish military forces, not a few probably converted.[144] The degree to which conversion was seen as an acknowledged facet of Jewish life at the time may be inferred from the following typical incident: In 1777, during a fire, the "illustrious and scholarly son of the martyr, Rabbi Menahem Mendel" and "son-in-law of the great and generous rabbi, R. Shmuel-Shmelke Katz of Ostroha [Ostróg],"[145] disappeared. A rumor immediately spread that he had converted and that he had been seen alive in Dubno. Upon investigation, it transpired that the son had been killed; but we learn that there was also a female convert and her son-in-law, who had become the priest Anthony Shofet in the same community.

Instances of conversion were hardly limited to the lower classes, of course, and also took place among the well-to-do, particularly in the countryside. In the sources we encounter converted Jews who controlled "town[s] and the nearby villages," or who ran taverns as agents of the royal treasury.[146]

Naturally, such cases of voluntary conversion (or cases in which the convert may have initially been forcibly baptized but then acquiesced voluntarily and remained a Christian) should be seen in the context of closer links and more intimate relations established between Jews and non-Jews at various levels of society—especially at the margins of society. On this, too, we have numerous references in the sources that seem to reveal only the tip of the iceberg. Thus, we should take note of complaints about those:

who openly exploit our labor and oppress us, and mix with the gentiles and learn their ways—not only by going to their homes to eat and drink, and thus demonstrating that they are no kin to Joseph [who did not eat with the Egyptians], but also by creating true confusion in the world through their sexual promiscuity, for our many sins, for through this there arises a confusion of the distinctions between the profane and the sacred, Israel standing for the sacred.[147]

In light of these phenomena, the more restricted case of actual conversion may be seen as part of a broader social reality and as a manifestation of the processes of decline and decadence that affected Polish Jewry.

But those processes touched off popular revulsion and resistance, as well. Those who expressed this resistance came mostly from the class that suffered the most: Jews from the countryside, from the urban poor, from the ranks of the educated but underemployed. They represented the "opposition" in Jewish society and they supplied the proponents and champions of the various new sects and movements that arose. These strata were also very active in founding *hevrot* and other associations with a reformatory character. By juxtaposing an examination of this social opposition and its activities with a thorough investigation of the social composition of the early Hasidic movement, we should be able to achieve a new and more realistic appreciation for the social component in Hasidic teachings. This, in turn, should allow for a new understanding of the social forces underlying Hasidism generally.

VI. THE COMMUNAL OPPOSITION: BASIC UNITS AND SOCIAL PROFILE

A social opposition in Polish-Lithuanian Jewry was nothing new. It was actually the constant mirror image of the oligarchical regime in the *kahal*. Evidence for the existence of this opposition emerges from, among other sources, the regulations enacted by the provincial councils and bylaws of the communities. We also find it mentioned or implied in the *mussar* literature and sermons of the period. From these hints and facts it is possible to get a sense of the "oppositional style" in Jewish society over long periods.

The Lithuanian Council, for example, mentioned in its resolutions of 1623 an "age-old ban" against "forming cliques and factions with others in order to oppose or counter the community board and its activities, to say nothing of opposition to leaders of the provincial councils and their decisions." "Factions" of this sort were not necessarily aimed at deposing the incumbent leadership: quite often it was simply a matter of some of the more prominent community members gathering together to discuss public affairs and criticize what they felt was amiss. "They tell each other, 'We should strengthen our resolve and go as a group to bring up the matter before the *kahal* leaders' "; or they simply "gather together privately [i.e., behind the back of the *kahal*] before they come before the *kahal* leaders."

Among the common folk, who had no direct means of bringing

matters before the *kahal,* we find "numerous small groups assembling everywhere—on the street and in the market—and they bitterly denounce or mock certain [individuals] and their actions . . . they laugh at the leaders of the *kahal* in scorn."[148] "There are many who fall into this iniquity" because "it is the common people's way to speak ill and arouse opinion against the majority [i.e., the established leaders]." Those who leveled criticism or invective against the leadership and took them to task ("he curses the majority and defies all Israel . . . he makes all the community's affairs appear [in a] negative [light]") were not exceptional at all. Such "trouble makers" are described as "smooth talkers who say appealing things," and preachers warned "anyone who fears the word of the Lord" to shun such folk, to "spurn their company and listen not to their words."[149] The Lithuanian Council demanded that the local communal leaders "repair the breach, . . . break in the gnashing teeth of those wicked ones through severe punishment, no matter where they are, isolate them and ostracize them and do everything possible to keep them at a distance."[150]

Indeed, we find many resolutions of the councils and the local communities imposing stiff penalties on anyone "belittling and shaming any of the communal heads or board members, whether in public or in private";[151] against "rumor-mongers spreading maliciousness between one person and another, or between some person and the rabbi or one of the leaders in order to cause trouble," and similarly against those who spread evil opinions about the communal establishment "by which they cause injury to the community at large."[152] This applied, in equal measure, to "anyone who dares make derogatory remarks against the chiefs and leaders."[153] The purpose of such regulations was to shore up the authority of the *kahal* and buttress its structural integrity. To that end, public criticism had to be squelched and decisions of the community board had to be treated as sacronsanct. The only concession the established leaders were willing to make to any "who find there is a certain matter which they believe to be improperly resolved, God forbid" and who wished to raise the issue "at the pure table of the congregation's heads," was that they could come, "singly or at most two people," to discuss the matter with the leader of the community himself or to a committee of two board members.[154] However, it was strictly forbidden to engage in any collective agreements ("conspiracies," "gangs") regarding communal affairs, outside the statutory frameworks. Any subgroup or intermediary group was regarded as divisive, interposing itself between the *kahal* regime and the individual. Such factional activity was held to be "mutinous," an offense for which—in addition to the punishment prescribed by the leaders "of old"—the community was empowered to mete out new disciplinary measures.

Yet, the frequency with which the regulations aimed at "conspiracies" and "gangs" were renewed and reiterated seems to indicate that these measures were less than successful at quashing a thriving social opposition. Moreover, the additional provisions attached to existing statutes, the stiffer punishments that were mandated, and the adoption of broader definitions of punishable offenses[155] imply that the opposition forces continued to grow in strength and popular base, becoming a permanent and serious threat to the *kahal* regime.[156]

Popular preachers played a significant role in the crystallization of oppositionary sentiment. Their influence had grown during that period. It was not the general practice for the official rabbinate to appoint preachers: "Anyone whose pure-hearted intentions moved him to rove the country to make straight what had become bent" became a peripatetic, self-appointed social critic "without license of the rabbinical court —but with a license from God."[157] Nevertheless, there were some preachers who enjoyed a semi- or quasi-official status in their communities. Statements about "the early days [when] each town and city would appoint a preacher of righteousness, a devout man of God, who would hold forth on Sabbaths and holidays and any suitable occasion, speaking words of wisdom and castigation in order to arouse the people's hearts and prevent them from falling into sin,"[158] were not necessarily meant as reference to the far-distant past. (Jewish communities had in the past adhered to the rule, as expressed by Maimonides, that Jewish law required them "to appoint a wise, pious, and learned elder who is admired by them and who would preach in public to cause people to better their ways.")[159] What our author referred to as "the early days" is likely to have been the generation before his, "before the division and dispersal" which led communities to cease appointing their own official preachers.

The status of the preacher was second to that of the rabbi. References in the literature to "one of the select ones in the congregation of the Lord" specifically mean "the presiding judge of the rabbinical court [i.e., the community rabbi] or the preacher." The task assigned to the preacher was to educate and to interpret the tradition, to instruct the people in

God's law, and to inspire fear of God in them. Sermons were delivered especially on Sabbaths, after the morning meal ("for that is the set time for reading the Prophets and to study works of *aggada* [rabbinic lore]"). It was deemed especially important to take this opportunity to address manual workers and businesspeople who had no chance to engage in Torah study throughout the week.[160] In some cases the preacher also gave a daily religious lesson to the common folk, and on Sabbaths would expand on the biblical theme of the week.

In addition, however, the preachers saw it as their duty

to arouse the great scholars of the generation and the leaders and teachers to action, lest they fail to repair the breach and prevent the people from sinning. They must teach the people the right path to follow and proper conduct. . . . Of what avail is it for them to shut themselves up in their studies and thus fail to correct transgressions—in that way they will lose the whole people. . . .

The people at large are to be considered as one [collective] individual: Someone who has had some of his limbs broken feels the pain of those limbs in the healthy parts of his body, and the pain will continue until some cure is found for the injury; for they are all part of one body.

But most of the rabbis "make light of this and believe the society can cure itself without them," nor do they appoint preachers any more, "they are not concerned about it"; they certainly do not take care "to rebuke the lay heads and leaders of the generation."

The preachers, however (as we have seen), were quite ready to confront the established leaders over their misconduct, and even challenged the rabbis themselves. The latter, for their part, "seem surprised [by this], and not only do they not support [the preacher-social critic], they actually condemn him, [asking] 'Who gave you the right to criticize?' "[161] Moreover, while the status of the preacher was an honorable one, his calling (as noted) was far indeed from being lucrative. This was especially the case in the eighteenth century, when preachers could barely eke out a living. Preachers were generally paid out of the dues funds of the *hevrot* whom they addressed, or else from charity funds or special bequests.[162] No wonder, then, that preachers were often forced to wander far and wide as itinerants, like other educated Jews "who receive no support."[163]

In addition, the position of social critic cannot be said to have enhanced the status of the preacher or brought him peace of mind:

A scholar who preaches to and castigates his generation is of dark visage, he is always in difficult straits and ill health, his physical strength is sapped by constant worry lest wicked ones come to curse, vilify, or beat him. For the wicked ones hate the preacher so much that sometimes they become a threat to his very life or they libel him with false accusations.

Even when the rabbi himself is the preacher he cannot feel secure, "because it happened several times to rabbis who wished to rebuke people that false charges were made against them, so that the prince took everything he owned and had him removed from his post as rabbi." [164]

The situation of preachers who were dependent upon the funds of the *hevrot* was similarly unenviable, for,

if they should attempt to rebuke them over some transgression or wickedness, they are in mortal danger because they stand to be deprived of a source of income. People say: This person is a troubler and presents himself as righteous and pious and pure—shall he take money from us, to boot? Does he think he is better than the rabbi, who is our teacher, chosen to instruct us in the proper way to live? Can someone be a rabbi to Israel if he wages war against them?

Many preachers, therefore, endeavored "to ingratiate themselves with the uncultivated people," agreeing with their opinions and mingling with them. [165]

This was not necessarily due to a desire to "fawn upon the ignorant mob," as one particularly puritanical *mussar* writer charged. The closeness between the preachers and the simple people was quite natural. The lives of the preachers were lives of penury which they shared with their humble public. The "half an income" that they lived on was paid for by those selfsame strata of the poor and the uneducated. From a social point of view, the intimacy between them was inevitable. Someone whose function is that of religious teacher and ethical guide to the common people and who lives their life, suffering along with them, sharing their everyday cares and concerns, celebrating with them in their times of joy, cannot, when finding cause to remonstrate with them, see only their faults and close his eyes to the rampant corruption of the upper strata, from which he, too, suffers. His intimate attachment to them cannot be limited to the way he "chastises them in mild tones and with due respect, forbearing to invoke God's wrath, heaven forbid." [166] Those among them who were blessed with a strong social conscience— and by the nature of things, there were quite a few in this category— viewed the poor masses as the ideal social base for their own mission.

"Scholars who desired to rebuke rabbis and lay leaders but who feared being placed under a ban" could find here the support they needed "so that they might not fear their bans." They could follow the advice of one preacher who counseled his colleagues: in the event that they excommunicate you, respond in kind, and then the ban will be upon them [instead]."[167] That response "in kind" took on social force by virtue of their identification with and reliance on their popular base. This, indeed, became the social reality behind the status of the preachers. Those who "as a matter of course were not allowed to approach the pulpit"—or if they were permitted in principle to do so but could never be sure that they would get a chance to preach because at their approach the congregation would hurriedly intone the next part of the service, "leaving the learned [preacher] shamed and angry"[168]—found among the poor and the artisans a free pulpit, ready listeners, their own synagogue or prayer room where they were free to teach and instruct, and a social environment that lent their words a positive resonance.

In this manner the preachers grew in influence and began to play a greater public role. They became more of a fixture in the life of the folk, an integral part of its social and religious existence. As such they were instrumental in forging those segments or cells of the social landscape which, in due course, began to assume a separate organizational identity —albeit still within the framework of the community and under its regime—that clearly reflected a certain independence: a new community in-the-making.

The initial cells of this community in-the-making were the *hevrot,* the artisan guilds or voluntary societies *(havurot),* and the small prayer quorums. Despite the constant struggle of the *kahal* against "conspirators who form societies of their own," such groups multiplied quite rapidly and succeeded in establishing themselves as bulwarks between the individual and the *kahal* authorities. At times they not only lent support to those subjected to administrative pressure, but actually reduced the power of the community's authority over the citizen.

The various artisan societies sought to remove from the *kahal's* purview all matters pertaining to their members. Similarly, they sought control over matters related to apprenticeships and to out-of-town craftsmen seeking to establish themselves locally—although these issues, in principle, fell under the *kahal's* regulatory function of *hezqat ha-yishuv* (granting and safeguarding the right of domicile). Every written constitution or book of regulations adopted by *havurot* specifically insisted that all conflicts that arose among the artisans themselves, any complaint lodged by one against another, would be arbitrated by the *havurah* (society) itself, without the need to go before either the *kahal* or the rabbi. The notion that the rabbi's function was limited to areas relevant only to the entire community was another typical feature; appeals against an arbitration conducted by the *havurah* went before the court of the local landowner, rather than that of the *kahal* or the rabbi.

The artisans had the right to build a study and prayer hall *[beit midrash]* in the immediate vicinity of the main synagogue and to appoint religious functionaries of their own to help organize prayer services, as was the Jewish custom everywhere.[169] The charters of the artisan societies show a general tendency to assert their autonomy from the religious supervision of the *kahal*. The *kahal*, for its part, endeavored to retain such control through the appointment of one of its functionaries as ex officio president or "patron" of each artisan association.[170]

The preacher engaged by such an association was expected to address the members on Sabbaths and holidays, and attendance was mandatory (just as it was incumbent upon the members to attend daily prayers at the association's prayer hall). This formal provision aided the societies in maintaining separate prayer quorums and the prayer hall itself, for although they became widespread in the Jewish communities,[171] the *kahal* was never very pleased with the idea and in some cases actually tried to disallow such separate gatherings.[172] From the perspective of the *kahal*, the societies' religious services constituted a new means of evading some of the fees and charges imposed on the public for the community benefit,[173] in addition to creating new organizational units outside the direct control of the *kahal*. In view of this, the *kahal* leaders were extremely careful to screen the electors for the annual vote: that is, to exclude those who regularly prayed anywhere but in the main synagogue.[174]

Indeed, the artisan societies were not the only ones to be active in the field of mutual assistance and protection of professional interests. We know of examples of tavern-keepers' societies, whose charters were meant to regulate and safeguard members' rights in matters of leasehold.[175] Similarly, some middle-class householders banded together: "Each one [was required] to donate whatever sum he could afford upon the founding of the society, to be deposited with the warden [treasurer] . . .

for interest-free loans in accordance with the religious law, so that [in times of need] they need not be completely bankrupt and become dependent on charity." Such groups existed in several localities.[176]

In addition, there were many societies whose function was not related to social services, but rather to liturgical or educational activities.[177] The *kahal,* as noted, saw to it that proper supervision was provided for these groups. The Lithuanian Council meeting of 1670 decided that, "Every association or society, no matter who they are, must appoint two wardens from among the members, and two from the *kahal."* The job of these officers was to insure the "political" conformity of the association. The *kahal* was empowered, in appointing its two representatives or wardens, to choose anyone "from within the *hevrah* (guild) or from outside it."

It would appear, though, that the societies strove, for their part, to minimize or neutralize interference by the *kahal.* They increased the number of their wardens so that the two *kahal*-appointed men remained in the minority. This prompted the Lithuanian Council of 1687 to add further stipulations regarding the *kahal's* right to supervise the societies, specifying that "there shall be only two wardens from the society, and two shall be chosen by the leaders of the community." This regulation placed the societies under more stringent control, in effect giving an equal say in their management to a body outside their own membership. Moreover, the same session of the council stipulated that the "secretary shall also be chosen according to the wishes [of the *kahal]."* [178]

As the oppositionist spirit became more evident, the insecurity of the *kahal* grew apace, and its attitude toward the multiplicity of societies in the community became increasingly distrustful. Evidently, the established leadership attempted to obstruct the founding of new associations. To employ the language of the time: They sought to prevent "the group of the select few whose spirit has moved them to work for a sacred purpose" from "performing a righteous act." [179] There were some communities in which the *kahal* introduced measures against already-existing societies. The same motivations probably explain the regulation introduced in Przemyślany, according to which, "No member of the society *[havurah]* who does not have the right to vote shall be appointed as elector, and the electors themselves shall not appoint to any post or job whatsoever anyone who does not have the right to vote." [180]

It would, indeed, appear that the *kahal* successfully defended its power over the community, despite the decline in its moral authority and in the effectiveness of its regime. The newer social structures were unable to free themselves from the stigma and the attendant restrictions against "conspirators and factions," and thus never constituted more than a tentative beginning. The strongest economic segments of Jewish society—Jews in the rural settlements—remained outside the framework of these embryonic cells of a new social order. They were rarely in contact with preachers. The leading religious leaders, who should have traveled the circuit of their own localities and smaller communities that belonged to their jurisdiction, did not fulfill that obligation. As for those who did go out to the countryside "for the sake of earning something to eat and a bit of money," [181] they did little teaching. The idealized image (or perhaps it was a custom practiced in much older periods) of the great rabbis taking the time once a year or once every two years "to teach the isolated individual Jewish *arendar* the laws and customs of our holy Torah, such as the proper observance of the Sabbath, the laws of Passover and the proper mode of prayer," may not in reality have been of much practical importance.

The preachers, despite their ability to attract large crowds of listeners, appear to have made only a minimal impact with their message. "[There were] many who run with enthusiasm [to hear] words of Torah lore [but] their hearts are not touched by the preacher's words." That the preachers' comments fell on deaf ears was apparently not only because people were willing to listen to sermons only to the extent that they provided diversion (and the preachers, wishing to accommodate the people's tastes, fulfilled their expectations in this regard—"It is their way to mix their words of chastisement with humorous talk that makes the people laugh, so that there is almost no difference between them and the jesters who entertain at weddings"). The fact is that the rabbinic lore preached in these sermons seems to have been the subject of doubt and skepticism:

The common folk scorn the words of our righteous sages, and say that they cannot believe the things that they are told, which are nothing but nonsense or exaggeration . . .

The common folk laugh and mock us, and say, "Just as the words of Rabba Bar Bar Hamma are an exaggeration, so, indeed, is the entire Talmud."

The same applied to preachers' descriptions of the punishments and torments of the afterlife, about which all the preachers felt duty-bound to give due warning, "in order to convince those on a lower level to repent and return to a proper way of life."[182] Such talk apparently lost its effectiveness. "The people say, 'It is impossible that things will be as bad as the *mussar* books say, which is meant only to frighten people.'"

The people at large opened the prayer halls to the preachers and brought large audiences to hear them, but did not give serious thought to their rebukes and their scolding. The gap between the simple people and the learned classes remained as palpable as before. Rabbi Yaaqov Yosef, the preacher from Polonne, spoke of "the hatred shown by the common people to the learned scholars" and used a parable about the angels and Jacob to illustrate his point:

[The angels said,] We came to your brother Esau, whom you treat with brotherly affection in order to draw him closer to a life of holiness, but he behaves toward you as Esau the wicked, out of his great hatred for you.[183]

This encapsulates the essential experience of an entire generation of preachers who chastised and condemned and urged the people to embrace an ascetic ideal. They did succeed in helping certain new social structures to emerge in Jewish society, and even appeared to draw some of these closer to one another; but they proved unable to weld and forge them into a single new entity.

VII. THE SOCIAL OUTLOOK OF THE HASIDIC MOVEMENT

The Hasidic movement formed a part of the opposition forces in Jewish communal life. That this was so may be confirmed from three sets of data: (1) the social context that forms the background for early Hasidic legends;[184] (2) the movement's social composition, as reflected in the class origins of the movement's leaders, local figures, and rank and file members; and (3) the public activity of the movement's leaders, to the extent that the few reported details we know of permit us to draw any conclusions.

The image of Jewish life, as portrayed in Hasidic legends about the Besht and about his first disciples, as well as in the preaching done by those early disciples, is identical to the image of social dislocation and disintegration that we have distilled from the materials already examined (and which were quite independent of sources related to the Hasidic movement). Here, in Hasidic lore, we again confront the same picture.

The wealthiest members of the communities are all-powerful; Sabbath eve prayers would not begin until they make their entrance. The important *arendars* (the *derzhavtses*) live on very friendly terms with the "princes" and the magnates, who owe them large sums of money and whose affairs are entirely in their Jewish agents' hands (even the Polish assistants of the nobles are afraid of them, wary of their influence, even when they are no longer at the height of their power, and seek their favor). But the Jews of their own communities hate them and wish them no good, even in times of danger. Successful merchants abandon commerce to take up leaseholding and tax farming, at the invitation of the landowners. Secondary tenants, who rent taverns from the *arendars,* are mostly downtrodden and exploited, and are sometimes called upon to assist their bosses in the landowner's court and in the countryside.[185] The "fabulously wealthy" travel to the fairs at Leipzig and Breslau (Wrocław) for business. There are many "wicked men" who offer to pay the landowners a great deal more than the actual rental for a lease, and thereby squeeze out the poorer *arendars,* including widows, and make their lives miserable. No amount of pleading affects them. The leaseholds of the wealthy merchants—the "aristocrats," the *arendars,* the customs collectors, and tavern-keepers—constitute the central economic support for a host of other Jews: poor meat slaughterers who go from village to village in search of work, schoolteachers in the countryside, and even rabbis who "make the round of villages in pursuit of gifts [fees or contributions]." The status of the educated scholars has dwindled so that "scholars rise early to knock on the doors of generous people. . . . The scholar must go begging for a position, asking to be allowed to study and to teach the community." "Teachers must go to parents to solicit pupils, and cantors must go looking for people to hear them lead prayers." Artisans are mentioned only infrequently: mainly the poorest of their class (smiths, bakers, wives who must sell rolls in the market, stocking makers, and wool cleaners, "who do not leave their homes at all except to go to pray," and they receive the wool at home from the shopkeepers . . .). We find, as well, examples of the moral degeneracy that we have already noted: informers, women involved in intimate relations with the gentry, frivolous and drunken meat-slaughterers whose lack of attention to their task leads the people into unwitting sin (through violations of kashrut),[186] and so forth.

The identification of the Hasidic movement as an organic part of the

Jewish social opposition comes through even more in the social standing of its leading figures and representatives. The earliest stories about the Besht, up to the time of his public advent, deal with all the elements of society with links to the opposition, as we have described them. His parents were captives and refugees; his mother, "out of poverty," took up midwifery; his father, when he enjoyed a period of success, drew close to the authorities as an *arendar* in a village.[187] The Besht himself was an orphan lad, who went through all the lowest positions in the social hierarchy: a teacher's aide, a night watchman at a *beit midrash,* a domestic servant, a schoolteacher, a meat-slaughterer in the countryside, and a destitute leaseholder running a village inn.[188]

One must assume that some of these descriptions are taken directly from the family traditions of the Besht and his relatives. But it seems to me fair to say that the inclusion of this variety of occupations in the Besht's life story is also a "collective portrait" of the Hasidic movement, which depicted its leader in accordance with the social profile of the movement as a whole.

This was, indeed, the social profile of the movement. We can easily demonstrate this by looking at the list of the Besht's disciples and their social positions. True, we do not have an exact or complete list,[189] but for our purposes it will suffice to examine the circles closest to the Besht, who figure in the earliest Hasidic legends and the first Hasidic books. According to the information we have, most of these disciples were either preachers,[190] or schoolteachers, or meat-slaughterers,[191] or cantors and rabbis.[192] Of the last category, the rabbis, there were very few, however, among the earliest Hasidim. Similarly, among all the representatives and leaders of the movement at the time, we know of only one (R. Nahman of Kosów [Kossover]) who was an *arendar* with a whole village under his administration, and was also, as an affluent man, involved in trade.[193]

In contrast, the most important social element in the movement seems to have been "the Jews of the countryside." These were the people to whom the Besht told parables, of them he made stringent demands, they are the ones who are put up for the night at his home when they come to the city and who give him a place to stay during his travels. They accord him a respectful welcome, they pray in his prayer hall, and they turn to him in their hour of need.[194]

Not only the poorest leaseholders were closely associated with the

Besht: There were some who were quite well off, such as the *derzhavtses* of Sluck, and other wealthy people who joined later, as the movement spread. We even find among them communal bosses with close ties to the authorities, who go to complain about the rabbis to the magnate and receive the blessing of the Besht en route.[195]

This social structure—the heavy preponderance of teachers, cantors, and slaughterers and the numerous wealthy "strongmen" with political clout who also joined—is confirmed by anti-Hasidic writings of the period. According to the "regulations of the fine community of Leszno,"[196] the local leaders of the Hasidim there were "R. Leyb the schoolteacher from Tarnopol" and "the cantor of our town," whom the Hasidim called *maggid* (preacher) and who would not bow to the authority of the leading householders "as is customary in all the communities."[197] The provincial council of Szklow enacted an ordinance against "those who have divided themselves from the congregation—crude, ignorant and rash people who call themselves Hasidim ["pious"]—and build themselves a high place [altar] of their own." None of those people, it was stated, was to be permitted to serve in a public religious capacity, such as leading the prayer service, assisting as judges in civil suits, preaching, "and certainly not teaching children."[198]

Anti-Hasidic literature similarly reflects the presence among the new group of communal bosses. R. Israel Loebel stated that the Besht strove to "win over the rich people" and that the Hasidim "mingled with the company of all the strongmen, all of them forming one group." And the Gaon of Vilna, too, in his letter of 1796–97, wrote: "There is much Jewish blood of poor folk on the hands of some among them, they support evildoers and violators, lending a hand to the officers and the wealthy and powerful ones."[199]

R. Israel of Zamość, the first *maskil* (Enlightenment thinker) to actively oppose Hasidism and subject Hasidic ways to a satiric critique, paid particular attention to the participation of town bosses who had cloaked themselves in piousness. He charged such Hasidim:

You have spread your wings like a stork *[hasidah]* before the whole congregation, and you go in your bent way along the road to the house of the Lord, where all Israel gathers, and there you seek to rouse heaven and earth with the stamping of your hooves. . . . His voice is heard as he approaches the sanctum, he sings a new song, he cries out and sighs and moans, calling mightily unto the Lord, bowing and prostrating himself. . . . And there are some who go down to drench themselves [in the *mikveh*, i.e. (ritual bath)] twice a day, till it seems that rivers flow from them and the aroma of purity wafts with them from the pit. . . . The Holy Spirit answers him and thunders against him: Out, out, man of bloodshed. Is it not enough that you mock the people, that you find it necessary to mock your God, too?! . . . Of what use are your travels through the water? All the water in the world will not suffice to douse the flames of love of gold and of oppression. . . . Do you suppose that He accepts your gift of supposed piety in compensation for your sins and wickedness? Being holier than all others, you wish also to take the property of others, to treat people as the fish in the sea [i.e., as food for entrapment] and as trees bearing fruit?!

The rest of his description proves that he is not talking merely of feigned pietism, but of actual "adherents of the new Hasidism," "ignorant boors," who believe they can "plant a limb of a tall tree [of traditional religious value] upon [the desires of] their own hearts, or rise up to the clouds to gain true knowledge of God and learn what the Lord of Zion has done. . . . They lift their wings, with the damp locks of their hair and wind in their sails, and men's hands are outstretched under them to receive blessings for their house."

Israel of Zamość is also familiar with the type of Hasidic preacher who "today ascends the mount of the Lord to chastise and rebuke from the heights of his lofty perch, he wags his hand dismissively at the rest of Joseph [the Jews], but tomorrow will come bowing down to them for the sake of a coin."[200] It is not by chance, however, that he focused his attention on the rich and the powerful.

The activities of the leaders of the movement also show the organic link between Hasidism and the social opposition, whether we look at the ways in which they influenced existing institutions in the Jewish community, or at their assumption of roles that in fact ought to have been filled by the community and its institutions but that had been neglected or abandoned. The earliest recorded public activity of the Besht consisted in his joining a local prayer quorum in the countryside composed of village Jews who "decided not to go to [use the synagogue in] town, since the *kahal* there used the villages to obtain revenue"; the villagers felt themselves to be "exploited by the *kehilla*."[201] Another legend has it that, after he had grown up "in a miraculous way," his first work was that of a teacher's aide, hiring himself out to take small children back and forth to the schoolroom and to the synagogue to say their prayers with them. Later on, however, we find him and his disciples engaged in "ransoming Jewish captives"—which meant, as the sources indicate, paying the rent of leaseholders who could not meet the payments and whose overlords not only threw them off their estate but also imprisoned them and their families.[202]

The Besht was also involved in improving the quality of religious life among rural Jews: encouraging them to spend holidays and especially Passover in town, appointing two learned men to go from house to house to prepare kitchen utensils for Passover and to supervise the baking of matzoh. He was similarly concerned about the "accusation heard on high about village Jews who cheat their gentile customers with false accounts" and profit from their labor on Sabbaths.[203]

Sometimes we read of the Besht observing from afar the doings of rabbis, meat-slaughterers, cantors, and preachers. Relying on "heavenly reports" that they were unfit for their duties, the Besht would see to it that they found other employment—usually without loss of income— and that others were sent in their place. On some occasions, the Besht personally conducted the new candidate to the particular town and installed him in his new post.[204] Thus, the Besht appears in the guise of having overall responsibility for the religious purity of the community at large, taking the matter into his own hands or delegating someone else to see that matters were put to rights. We can also point to the tendencies shown by the Besht's disciples in the social arena and the authoritativeness they showed in carrying out their missions. Solomon Maimon reported, for example, about

one young man, perhaps twenty-two years old . . . [who] traveled around Poland preaching Hasidism. . . . Anywhere he came, he immediately made inquiries about the communal arrangements there and would see to it that improprieties were removed and new regulations put into effect, which were punctiliously enforced. . . . The elders of the community, men of advanced age and of greater learning than [the young man], would tremble and quake before him.[205]

We find a similar example of this sort of forcefulness in notes added by Rabbi Aaron of Karlin to the communal tax regulations enacted in the province of Nieświez in 1769. The regulations were passed by "the assembly called for [that purpose]" chosen by "a large group of people who were concerned . . . about saving the poor from their [impossible] burden"; but it was R. Aaron of Karlin, according to his account, who first initiated the action when he "saw the poverty of our Jewish people. . . . How could I [stand idly by] and watch the misfortune, God forbid, that would befall the destitute among the children of Israel, and hear their cries of woe and pain." It seems clear that R. Aaron did not simply participate in the council along with the other rabbis, but that the initiative had been his and that he had been motivated by "fear that we not fall into the terrible sin, God forbid, of robbing the poor." His leading role would seem to be confirmed, again, by the vehemence of his words: "I therefore decree that anyone who tries to overturn these regulations and to sap the strength of the poor shall be ostracized and excommunicated with all the attendant penalties and curses." Indicative, as well, is the fact that he cited the authority vested in him by "our lord, rabbi and teacher, his soul is in Eden, may he rest in peace, the rabbi of the whole Dispersion [of Israel]," the Maggid of Miedzyrzecz, authorizing him "to clear away the obstacles from the Israel's path wherever possible." This demonstrates both the power of the Hasidic movement at the time and the social outlook that it championed.

The next notation in the same communal register is even more revealing in this regard. There, R. Aaron of Karlin decreed "that, under the strict penalty of my ban *[herem]*, no community tax *[korobka]* may be taken from schoolteachers . . . without the agreement of the regulatory committee . . . or the entire community [including] the poor and the destitute"[206]—that is, all those who had never before taken part in deciding the community's affairs.

R. Aaron's active role in public affairs is also known to us from Hasidic legend. He is depicted as following the instructions of the Maggid of Miedzyrzecz, sometimes becoming embroiled in conflicts with the local Polish authorities. For that reason he was told by the Maggid to use R. Menahem Mendl, "who speaks the Polish language," as an interpreter.[207] With this help, indeed, R. Aaron was said to have obtained "great authority" from the government.

In their local communities, Hasidim were considered to be aggressive and contentious. There are recorded complaints about "some people who are called Hasidim who have increased trouble and conflicts among us" and who "form their own separate groups"; "there are many violent ones, and they struck one of the leaders of the community." This was true not only in this particular instance, which derives from the community of Leszno. This tends to lend added credence to the charge that "with their cunning words they penetrate the hearts of the whole people all over the country."[208] It is probably true, then, that as the movement grew ("as the plague spread throughout the dispersion of Israel"), Hasidic representatives, supported by clandestine local followers, became increasingly belligerent and outspoken. Hasidism at that time was "like a secret society," and its influence so widely felt that "it is likely to impose its will on almost the entire people and to accomplish one of the greatest revolutions."[209]

This attempt to "impose the authority" of the movement on the people at large took place—judging by contemporary accounts of Hasidism's early surge forward—at three levels: supervision of the "lower clergy" (slaughterers, cantors, and preachers) and improving their fitness for their sublime tasks; attention on a constant basis to the neglected and isolated sphere of rural Jewish life, in its spiritual and material dimensions; and the defense of the "poor and destitute" of the cities against the established leaders. The methods employed in efforts to achieve hegemony were various. They ranged from working through existing institutions ("inspection of slaughtering knives," looking out for violations of the law, framing new regulations, publication of "decrees," bans, and condemnations), to placing their own trusted representatives in positions of religious responsibility (meat-slaughterers, cantors, preachers, teachers, and sometimes even rabbis), to organizational innovation ("messengers" or delegates) and the adoption of certain causes ("ransom of captives," defense of secondary tenant-leaseholders, etc.) in order to provide services that the existing communal structures either could not or did not deign to provide.

After the ban against Hasidism issued in 1772, however, when Hasidic gatherings were disrupted and local measures were taken to isolate Hasidim, when "a great outcry throughout our land" was raised against them, the movement's leadership counseled in favor of maintaining a low profile "until the hour of wrath shall have passed and the time to do the Lord's bidding would come again. . . . They have violated the commandments, and therefore take care for your lives, and do not openly resist those who rise up against you." In this atmosphere, the movement's social activity was bound to decline. This was doubly true for the period that followed the second ban, in which every community was enjoined "to burn out the thistles from God's vineyard, from all Israel, to pursue them, banish them, and vent all your wrath against them, to root them out body and soul . . . to separate them from their brothers lest they band together in a company of traitors." The Hasidim then went onto the defensive and they "sigh in pain for they can do nothing."

One must assume, further, that the participation of "members of the common crowd" in depredations against the Hasidim, and the fact that no holds were barred any longer ("permission was granted to make their lives a misery and to encroach on their sources of income"),[210] added a new dimension to the social awareness of leading figures in the Hasidic movement. Their reflections on proper leadership and on the kind of person who was fit to stand at the head of the community seem to reflect their experiences during the movement's initial "offensive" and its short-lived attempt to gain control of the entire people.[211] In warning of the dangers facing those who "raise themselves higher in some fashion over the rest of the people, claiming greater wisdom," they pointed out that those who wish to rule must recognize the ego-satisfaction involved: this is a (dubious) benefit that they derive from wielding authority over subordinates.[212]

One detects here a note of realism that is directed against those representatives of the movement who overplayed their tendency to ride the crest of popular desires. For, it was now said, it is crude to think that leadership and superiority depend on the agreement and satisfaction of the "demos," and therefore are necessary to curry favor with it. Rather, any true leadership must be conducted on a higher plane, without constant anxiety for reassurance from below. People who want to attain greatness should be warned that only those who act for the sake of heaven—not for their own sake and honor, and not in order to lord it over the public—can accomplish this. In that way they are able to uphold the law with regard to mundane communal matters (such as taxes) and they reinforce belief and faith, warding off all wickedness from the people of the city.[213] They should not think that such honor is their due, for they are no more worthy than anyone else—such a thought reflects overweening pride. Even Moses himself, after all, did not wish to undertake the mission of leading Israel, asking God to send another, even though it is a sacred calling to undertake a mission for God and to teach the Torah to the Jews. People ought to take this example more to heart and cease bickering over the chance to fulfill those religious obligations that carry with them a measure of authority and power; better to avoid such pitfalls. If they are indeed worthy of the office, then God Himself would see to it that they would reach a position of leadership through general consensus.

The leaders must at times don the cloak of dignity ("The Lord is clothed in royal majesty"), because the proper functioning of their office demands pride of this kind. But they must take extreme care lest the dignity of office become a pretext for their personal pride and benefit; it must always be directed only to the public good. This is a matter that demands constant consideration. Hasidic literature contains much discussion of the problem of how to balance the need "to don the pride and dignity of office (of which there is much need, for today there is much concern over the power of the ignorant masses and a consequent fear over the ability to govern properly)," and the individual leader's need for "inner humility"; between the recognition that "sometimes one must demonstrate authority because of the respect due to God," and the knowledge that "the essential aspect of God's presence in the human soul is the quality of humility and modesty."[214]

These issues and discussions, it seems to me, reflect the experiences in the social arena of the leaders of the movement and its representatives. As such, they provide an important key to understanding some neglected and unexplained episodes in the early history of Hasidism.

VIII. SOCIAL THEMES IN EARLY HASIDIC LITERATURE

One may arrive at a picture of the Hasidic movement's social composition and self-image especially through an examination of the social themes that are revealed in the teachings of its representatives and faithful interpreters. None of the social themes that they expressed was actually new, of course: they are the same themes pursued by *mussar* writers and preachers before them—the value of tranquility and peace and a revulsion for conflict and contention, the importance of humility and the dangers of pride, the greatness of deeds of charity and philanthropy, and the need to reinforce values of truth and faith, and so forth. However, if we check Hasidic teachings for the particular items that were singled out for emphasis and look at the realistic detail reflected in their content; if we also take note of the social class or "address" to which these teachings were directed; then we shall be utterly convinced of the link between Hasidism and the processes of ferment and disintegration, on the one hand, and the new unifying forces, on the other, that were active in Polish-Lithuanian Jewry.

In examining the social themes in early Hasidism, we may divide our analysis into three aspects: (1) descriptions that are contained in Hasidic literature and provide a running commentary on the social ills of the day, reflecting, in turn, the degree of popular concern over these issues; (2) the target audience of these writings, indicating the perceived causes and social origins of the problems discussed; and (3) the recommended changes or improvements and reforms, which indicate to us, once again, the social composition of, and driving force behind, the Hasidic movement.

Regarding the descriptive material that appears frequently in Hasidic literature, what is most interesting from our point of view is that such illustrative data are most often accompanied by value judgments. These allow us a glimpse of the authors' own attitude and, by extension, reveal some of the social concerns that lay behind the authors' particular choice of subject matter, as well as provide an indication of the writers' own social position or angle of vision. Of particular significance in this regard is the first Hasidic book, *Toledot yaaqov yosef* by R. Yaaqov Yosef of Polonne, a foremost disciple of the Besht and the most reliable recorder of his mentor's oral teachings. His rather condensed, terse, and suggestive observations are clear and concise: sharply sketched and invariably to the point, exuding a sense of the author's long and varied experience of life in the Jewish world.[215]

The author of the *Toledot* included in his book much description of the status of the learned class of his day: their inner differentiation and mutual relations among themselves, their attitude to the people at large and vice versa. Each such observation contains both factual detail and evaluation—whether he is describing new communities and the rabbis who made their way there, uninvited, to assume leadership and control; two categories of scholars—those who have little self-esteem and consequently are also abused by the public, and the high-and-mighty ones who are immediately recognized and who intimidate one and all;[216] the long night of oppression, with its internal problems of divisiveness among the Jews and external problems of persecution; the isolation of the rabbis from the people;[217] the different burdens that oppress the common folk on the one hand and the rabbis on the other; or the moral defects produced by these divisions and differences. Even when these matters seem to be phrased in the most general terms, applicable to almost any historical context, it is nevertheless fairly easy to discern those points which are directly concerned with immediate issues and to identify their particular "target audience."

Hence, for example, the many sermons on the old theme of the internal divisions among the Jews that permitted Haman to succeed in hatching his scheme against them (leading Esther to tell Mordecai, "Go assemble all the Jews and let them make peace among themselves"), take on new relevance for the preacher's generation when he adds the explanation,

Because of their divisiveness they were bereft of Torah . . . [because the function of scholars is] to go before the people and light their way with Torah, showing them the proper path to follow, but because of their coarseness of spirit the rabbis disdained to lead them.

Here the author was directing his remarks to the problem of his own day, fulminating against the lordly manner of the rabbis and the concomitant spiritual descent and ethical failings of the people at large, who have nothing but contempt for their supposed teachers. This theme, of course, is one of the most ubiquitous in early Hasidic writings.

Yaaqov Yosef returns over and over again to this theme throughout his sermons. Most of his comments are clearly directed at one prime target: the scholars and rabbis of his day. They may be referred to as "my people" or "Israel," but they are also apt to be "spiritually coarsened through too much study." They are "men of power," and the one religious imperative that they ought to take most to heart is the need to reduce their overweening pride.

He has much advice to give them in terms of their obligations to the people:

If you lend money to my people, do not act as a usurer. If you find satisfaction in serving God, then lend that to the people—give part of it to them and join with them, with the masses, who are poor in wisdom—and do not be a demanding creditor [in this either], do not find them wanting because they are not the same as you.

The Besht, himself, had directed similarly phrased admonitions to the rabbis:

Sometimes it happens that a person may say something offensive to a rabbi, and he [the rabbi] is full of anger because of the hurt to his honor, but there is nothing he can do immediately to punish that person. But when that person commits a sin or some impropriety, then his creditor [the rabbi] finds an opportunity to get his own back, to assuage his hatred through revenge. But the punishment he metes out to that person is not for the sake of heaven.[218]

The rabbis were not always the sole targets of such comments. There
are a number of warnings and criticisms that are explicitly directed to
both "sides": "I adjure you that there ought to be union between heaven
—that is, the rabbis—and earth—that is, the masses of the people—so
that one may influence the other, and so that truth and compassion may
meet."[219] "When the people at large are joined to the rabbis, who are
the men of thought, then all will benefit from wisdom in unison, and the
unity below [i.e., on earth] permits unification [of the divine elements]
above." "The righteous scholars ought not to say that they do not need
the people, for [the people] support the Torah and the fulfillment of so
many commandments depends on them; equally, if not more so, the
people should not be insolent to the rabbis just because they pay their
salaries. Indeed, it is quite the reverse, as our ancient rabbis said: The
whole world receives sustenance for the sake of [Rabbi] Hanina."

In some passages we find great stress laid on the idea that the split
between the rabbis and the uneducated people is the source of great
danger for the very survival of the Jews. "The generation of King Ahab
was one of idolatry," but when internal peace existed among them, they
were victorious, unlike the generation of King Saul, "whose hearts were
divided." R. Yaaqov Yosef's comment on Jacob's prayer—"Rescue me
from my brother's hand"—was as follows:

He was not praying only for his own sake, but for the entire people [in the time]
of this last exile . . . when hatred reigns between brothers and friends . . . and
their sin is remembered forever (like that of Esau). . . . 'I am afraid lest he come
and strike me'—they, the rabbis, against the people, for strife has spread among
the rabbis and among the people . . . and this causes people to behave as Esau,
hoping to overcome his fellow.

Sometimes he addresses the uneducated classes, especially the rich among
them, taking them severely to task over their humiliation of the scholars,
their lack of respect for them, their "joy over their misfortune" if "some
lack or fault is discovered about the faithful ones of Israel, which causes
some of the people to rejoice." Those are the people who think that "the
humiliation of the rabbis is a great achievement." These criticisms are
accompanied by the warning that, "When the people despise the scholars, then the Jews are forced to bend the knee to the unbelievers, and
vice versa, the honor that they give to the scholars allows the Jews to
transcend [the gentiles]."

It should be pointed out, however, that even when reprimanding and cautioning the people with respect to the honor due the rabbis, Hasidic literature conveys an exonerating or apologetic attitude that leaves the onus chiefly on the rabbis. Thus, "Most of the people who are not learned do venerate the rabbis,"[220] but they sometimes "hide their face" from the rabbis. This, in turn, evidently discourages the rabbis from speaking words of wisdom and moral truth to them, and that is the underlying reason why "sometimes [they] hold the rabbis in contempt." The implication here is that the rabbis must take the initiative to improve the situation. Each one must strive to remove "the obstructing veil of insensitivity": By joining themselves to the simple folk in one commonality, "the zaddikim will be able to bring the people back to the proper paths and raise them up along with them to [greater] attachment to Him, may He be blessed. This would also bring great benefit to the zaddik."

On the other hand:

I have compared you to one of the Pharaoh's horses, my beloved. Just as the chariot-horses of the Pharaoh were harnessed together as one, so, too, are the common people, who are the horse, and the sages, who are its rider. And if you do not control the people, the horse will kill you physically and spiritually.

Therefore, it is the duty of the rabbis "to pasture the flock, tend to those who are of a lower [spiritual] status, give them sustenance and guide them."[221] The greatness of the zaddik lies in this: "He adorns himself and then adorns others." This was a quality that Moses possessed. He "brought great merit to the many, and their merit was dependent on him."[222]

The early Hasidim were full of advice and suggestions for the rabbis, on how they might draw closer to the people "in order to elevate them"; and for the people, for whom this closeness was vitally important in determining their eternal destiny. This was true, they expounded, even for sinners, because by linking themselves to the righteous they would benefit from the atmosphere of understanding and goodness, and thus save themselves. As long as they bore hatred for the righteous and sinned against both God and man, their fate would be different from that of the righteous.

Thus we see in the episode of Korah, that even though he denied the truth of Moses's prophecies and denied that the Torah came from God, still he could not be punished until he irrevocably stood apart from the whole camp.

Dubnow's contention that R. Yaaqov Yosef was "a prophet of religious schism"[223] seems to me, therefore, quite mistaken. All Yaaqov

Yosef's texts and comments were directed toward the goal of unity and harmony between the people and the rabbis. All of his criticism against the rabbis revolved around one point: that they had brought about an internal rupture in the Jewish people by neglecting the common folk and by isolating themselves.

If "the world as a whole is a ladder, the great mass of people on the ground may be designated the foot of the world, and the sages, its head." By that logic, "when a man descends and stands in a pit, his head is necessarily also lower—and the opposite is the case when he climbs to the top of a mountain."

The division within Jewry was but a result of "a lapse of true knowledge": "Without true knowledge, there can be no union between the people and the men of knowledge—the rabbis—and this leads to greater oppression; but as truth is disseminated, the people and the sages join forces, and this leads to deliverance."

The desire for greater social order is also evident in the words of one preacher whose basic message was:

Stand as one, each recognizing his own worth and station—the leaders first, then the tribes, and then every man of Israel, each in his own proper place— which is impossible if everyone says, "I will do just as I wish, because I am the equal of any tribal chief."[224]

This resembles far more a call for reorganization according to a recognized hierarchy than it does "inciting the people to rebel against the rule of its old religious leaders,"[225] albeit with a certain "revolutionary" air that went beyond mere criticism of the status quo and saw the possibility of rebuilding the social order from its foundations.

In any event, we clearly observe here that even rabbis who preserved a closer affinity to the people also suffered the consequences of the negative image of the rabbinate in the popular mind, and were therefore concerned—religiously and socially—to remove this injurious factor. As long as the people would not listen to them, there was little they could achieve. "When times of trouble arrive, they will stop up their ears and refuse to listen to words of reprimand and chastisement—and [the rabbis] will have no opportunity to speak to them."[226] On the other hand, "If they will listen willingly and out of deep appreciation . . . then heaven will also" take a hand and give the preacher new words to say.

It would be incorrect, however, to say that the Hasidic movement simply chose a path of amalgamation with the people, out of social identification. R. Yaaqov Yosef found it necessary to argue against those who demanded, "Let us have a leader who will join us and be with us in everything, at mealtimes and at prayer, and never leave us."[227] Such words, he contended, were reminiscent of those of the "mixed rabble" of Moses's time, which "subtly foreshadowed [events of] our own day, [when] some people complain about those who set up small, independent prayer groups, but do not join them for every session." Behind the polemic we detect the kind of resistance that sometimes faced the Hasidic movement, based on some of the same complaints that were voiced against the rabbis generally.

The experience of the past generation of preachers—those who chose a less popular, puritanical style, breathing fire and brimstone and cutting themselves off from the people, as well as those who sought to mingle with the crowd ("I will walk among you in the marketplaces and in the streets"), neither of whom succeeded in drawing the people any closer—taught the leading figures of the day, the great rabbis, that they must not simply "adopt the standards of the people." This would not lead the people to mend their ways, "and we see with our own eyes how much trouble this causes, for our many sins." There was, indeed, a need to find common ground with the people; one ought to "speak words of peace to all His children"; the "sages should live in peace with the people at large." Only in that way would the people give up the complaint that they had been making as far back as Sinai: "We are willing to listen and abide by all that God has commanded us [but we will] not bear the burden of Your sages."

A reassessment of the common people was also desirable, even of the least worthy among them. Those were hard times, times of persecution and suffering. One had to recognize the truth of the words spoken by "one woman of the holy congregation of Nieświez, who said (in the Russian tongue): 'We chose well when we chose our God, but God also did well when He chose Israel, for look at Faybush—he may not be worth much but still he sanctifies the name of God.' "

Even so, finding "common ground" did not imply "merging" into the people, nor did it mean handing over authority and control to the masses. All those who bewailed the disastrous state of affairs in Jewish life consistently pointed to the deleterious impact of the rise to power of uneducated men, at the expense of the rabbinic intelligentsia. All the calamities were traced to the fact that "the scholars and the pious are disgraced and despised, the youth are insolent toward their elders, and the common herd, who should be last of all, have risen through the power of strong-arm manipulators." And the rise of this uncouth and violent element from the lower-status groups was deemed the consequence of a lack of true leadership. There was no real spiritual authority whose word was final, and such authority was absent because the rabbis were divided amongst themselves. Conflict among the leaders had brought about a diminished level of religious consciousness and knowledge. Utter confusion reigned, because the people no longer knew "which of the rabbis is reliable." [228]

"Little foxes wreak havoc—they are the rabbis who take the job for the sake of money, and they are immature youngsters, to boot." And the leaders of the generation who could heal the breach ("[Their] light is light, [their] blessing is blessed"), do not do so.

Thus, what we have here is not incitement to rebellion, but a yearning for effective leadership and authority, a desire for guidance in troubled and perplexing times, a wish for unity among the rabbis so that they might impose God's service on the masses. [229] The protest was about the fact that, as things stood, the demands of the rabbis for greater power were without solid foundation. On the one hand, "There are no true sages any more"; "if some more learned scholar turns up and settles in a town, he immediately assumes the prerogative of a judge, and enters into a conflict with the local judge [rabbi]"; "the greater their learning, the greater their pride, which coarsens their soul." On the other hand, "He tries to make himself popular, thinking that thereby he will earn more, especially the meals they are wont to give him; how, then, can he preach to them and criticize them? They will begin to hate him and will cease giving him presents."

There was no more unity among the rabbis than among craftsmen or tavern-keepers or shopkeepers—and for the same reason: competition over dwindling sources of income led to "senseless hatred." Every learned man "hates his fellow scholar" because "he believes that [the other fellow] is a threat to his livelihood." They rule but they do not truly govern, and they do not exert any positive influence. If anyone dares insult the rabbis, "they hound him half to death, but if he subverts them with false piety, they pretend to look the other way."

Moreover, there are even (it was said) some "scholars of wickedness,"

"Jewish devils," "impious rabbis who hate the God-fearing ones." These people sabotage the sincere efforts of the "leaders and other prominent men in each city . . . who seek to correct religious life and teach the proper way according to the Torah." No wonder, then, that "the eyes of Israel have grown dim with old age and can no longer see . . . for the leaders who should be the eyes of the congregation, who should watch over it and supervise it, not only have not watched over others—they have not even watched over themselves to make sure they do not stray from the straight path."[230]

The great value of *Toledot yaaqov yosef* lies not only in the fact that it gives us a clear picture of the social disintegration in the Jewish communities, as the early Hasidim saw it; equally important, it illustrates the special approach of Hasidism to the problem of reunifying the "house of Israel."

Along with the descriptions of social and religious conflict (which is identified as the primary reason of the ongoing oppression of Exile), we find an important secondary theme: that there is, in fact, no earthly remedy for the problem. "There is no natural way to create unity between Jew and Jew"; "this wrong cannot be righted by some preacher who might try to achieve unity, but only by God Himself, who can say, 'I will remove from you your heart of stone,' etc. [and then] the writ will be fulfilled, 'Behold, I send to you Elijah [the prophet of redemption].' "

This was not perceived as a new article of faith—the idea that God might remove baseless hatred from among the Jews and reinstate perfect civil peace and unity. It was rather self-evident: the sin of civil conflict was prolonging the Exile. Hence, its eradication was not only a prior condition to attaining redemption: it was itself part and parcel of that deliverance, the beginning of the messianic process. Thus we find it occurring as part of the liberation from Egypt, which symbolizes the fate of the nation in the future as well. Everything written in the Torah on this matter was naturally to be seen as directed at that particular generation, for the Torah was eternal and each and every teaching in it was directed to all men in every era. There would be no sense in the Torah's relating "mere" events, as it were, for their own sake. Thus,

Moses was the greatest of his generation, which was a generation full of knowledge. And thus it is in every generation, the leaders who are genuinely great are offshoots of Moses's spirit ["sparks of Moses"].

[Moreover,] Moses had said, "Would that all God's people were prophets," etc., by which he meant that he wished all of Israel might reach the spiritual stature that Moses himself had achieved. For it is not outside the realm of the possible that by free will a man might so refine his corporeal nature as to reach the degree of spirituality of a Moses. . . . [Even the special greatness of Moses] that made Moses higher than any of the prophets [for] God's Presence spoke with Moses's voice is attainable by any man in Israel once he has been sanctified by the holiness of God, may He be blessed.

The implication of this entire trend of thought was that a fundamental change was required in the current communal arrangements for Jewish society. Instead of "a multiplicity of leaders," instead of rabbis and lay community heads appointed by Polish authorities, there ought to be "one voice for the generation," appointed by God. The conclusion was that "if it can be agreed that the greatest ones of [each] generation be allowed to pursue their quest for God in Torah and in prayer, and be released from all public duties, then it will be of benefit to them and also to [the people], who will also be enabled to seek greater communion with God." This was taken as being analogous to what Jethro had told Moses: "You are all alone and the divine Presence is not with you, and the reason for that is that the entire nation rests on your shoulders, coming to you from morning to evening. And the burden of social responsibility placed upon you all day long will ultimately destroy your gift of prophecy."[231]

That wisdom was applicable once again. He who would stand at the head of the community must do as Moses did: "He would first meditate alone with the Lord to receive great blessing upon himself, and then he would radiate blessing to the whole house of Israel. Everyone should learn from his example."

When R. Yaaqov Yosef said that "Ahijah the Shilonite was one of the faithful preachers," and that he "received [his calling] from Moses, was among those who went out of Egypt and afterward was a judge in King David's court, then he was the teacher of Elijah the Prophet, and then he was my teacher's teacher [i.e, the teacher of the Besht],"[232] this is no mere fantasy of a pious enthusiast: It represents a sophisticated statement of self-perception on the part of R. Yaaqov Yosef and it establishes the claim of prophetic authority as the true basis for Hasidism's assumption of leadership of a renewed Judaism. The Besht was instructed by Ahijah the Shilonite, the faithful preacher, who was also the mentor of Elijah; the Besht, like Elijah, took up the mission of reuniting the people

—"returning the hearts of the fathers (the rabbis) unto their children (the common people)."

But, if the Besht was the Elijah of his day with respect to his mission and goal, it was Moses whom he had to emulate in terms of method and means. Frequently, R. Yaaqov Yosef's interpretations of biblical passages are no more than Hasidic "projections" onto the text—projections of the experiences of early Hasidism. Thus, Moses said, "Choose ye wise and recognized men for your tribes"; and the Hasidic gloss is: "all your intermediary men who have retained their ties with you."[233] These "intermediaries" are the "zaddikim" (the prophets), who are distinguishable and stand alone, even among the crowd, for "they cannot be at one with them." Again, for the verse "take from among yourselves a portion," the Hasidim read a particular meaning into the text: this was "a foreshadowing of the future, in which the Jews would establish a house of study for the chosen ones among them [the Hasidim]."

Thus, the "masses" were not the "proprietors" of Hasidism; rather, the Hasidim stood apart from the masses and wished to be distinguished from them. Their aim was to elevate the masses to a higher spiritual plateau, one that was within their reach, but not to require each and every one of them to be a Hasid. "The common people (likened to a beautiful woman who is imprisoned and whom you desire), and whom you draw closer to God's service, you would not call on them to take on the burdens of Hasidism [and change their nature] from one extreme to the other." Such extreme demands would more likely be "the cause of a total failure," both with respect to the individual and to the society at large. Of the common folk, all that could be asked was "complete observance of Torah and the commandments."[234]

The nature of the relationship between the scholars and the people was likened to that between body and soul: "The people who are called Jacob, they are the body, and the perfect faithful of Israel, who are called Israel, they are the soul."[235] Like the connection between body and soul, the connection between the rabbis and the people was necessary and involuntary. "As the soul enters the individual—'you had no choice but to be created, and no choice but to be born'—so, too, among the society at large the soul of necessity mingles with the people, who are called the 'body,' in order that they may influence each other." And the fulfillment of this mutual obligation means more than that the leaders should simply "see and supervise," but that they should be worthy of the title, "true children of your God"; and the people must not only "listen to the leaders" but also uphold the alliance between Issachar and Zevulon: between those who study the Torah and those who support them that they may continue to do so ("for the scholars are poor").

It is God's design that form and matter interact: the people ("matter") shall provide support for the rabbis ("form"), and the rabbis shall provide them with Torah, "for that is the providential nature of the world." That mutual relationship is what elevates the common people, so that "all your people are [may be called] righteous [zaddikim]." For "whoever makes an impact, he is called a zaddik—and the masses have an impact through monetary support; the rabbis are called zaddikim because their impact is felt through Torah and righteousness." The work of the "material" people and their influence upon the people of the spirit corresponds to the concept of charity, or "good works," which is so much stressed in early Hasidic literature. The various ways in which this concept is addressed enable us to understand the social significance of this theme.

The Hasidim point out that, "strictly speaking, justice would dictate" that everyone be equal in material terms. But God "had placed the wealth [that would have been the rightful property] of the poor into the hands of the rich . . . [and] a rich man holds the portions of several poor people." That being the case, "charity" should not be viewed as philanthropy, but as justice, for "justice demands that he give him what is rightfully his." God merely "makes it appear that he is giving out of his own pocket." This endows charity given to an individual person with great significance: everyone should give to the particular individual about whom he is concerned. The impulse to give money to that person in particular is not coincidental: It implies that what is donated to that person is actually his original property. Giving it to someone else would be tantamount to stealing. Extra cash that is not "returned" in this way to its "rightful owners" will inevitably be taken away in other forms: "Non-Jews will squeeze it out of him, or murderers will threaten him to kill him for it." If, however, the rich man parts willingly with the money that he has anyhow been slated to give up, he will be spared such terrifying ordeals. It is an accepted truism that "money stolen from a rich man is money that in reality belongs to the poor . . . [and] non-Jews have no power to take Jews' money except such funds as the wealthy have held back from the poor." In this, there is no difference in principle between the obligations of wealthy rabbis and the uneducated wealthy. "The wealthy—even if they are scholars—do not sit before the Lord's table."

Even though "there is a great difference between men of substance who lead the community and the poor among the people who are as degraded as animals," and certainly wealth translates into greater status and social standing; nevertheless, one's current status does not necessarily indicate one's ultimate fate. "Who can tell what spirit will move a man, when he rises he is swelled with pride, and when he descends, he makes himself like a beast; and the truth is: those who are up come down, and vice versa."[236]

The upshot is that giving charity is something like spiritual and financial insurance. And the Besht would constantly make the point in his talks that "God is your shadow": that is, just as one's shadow does everything a person does, so, too, God acts toward a person the way that person acts. One must, therefore, always keep the commandments of God and do works of charity, show compassion to the poor, "so that God will render goodness unto him in return."[237] The giver benefits from charity no less than the receiver. "Yours, o God, is the compassion —for He endowed people with compassion so that they might act with compassion toward their fellows, and then God can repay compassion with compassion." One's acts of mercy here below "arouse mercy on high." The rich man, "he who is the recipient of plenty, if he does not spread his wealth among others, then wealth will be removed from him, because [due to his behavior] there is no longer a proper circulation of plenty."[238] Therefore, the charity one gives should not be limited to the minimal requirements of the law. The regulations stated: "He need not pay more than a fifth part." But this was meant only for those who only gave grudgingly; he who gives willingly and derives satisfaction from that need not stay within any limit.[239] Indeed, "setting limits and prescribed sums for charity is needed only for those who observe the Torah [in the same way], never deviating from the strictness of the law . . . [but] someone who is in need of healing [should realize that] healing the soul is no less important than healing the body. Money is of no consequence, and a man should be prepared to give all he has for the sake of [saving] his life."[240]

Moreover, everyone is bound "to be anxious for his own welfare, and to spend more than he has to on food and clothing, etc. But [he should know that] the added costs come out of the money of the poor that has been entrusted to his care, so that he in effect is supporting himself on the money of the poor."[241] The [seemingly contrary] principle in the Talmud that, "your own life takes precedence, " was not intended for normal situations—only for the extreme case of "[two walking alone in the desert] and only one has a water bottle and so forth."[242] In that case, both lives are equal and the water can save the life of only one. That is not analogous at all to the situation in which a poor person requires assistance to feed his children, buy fuel to warm his house, and clothing to protect himself from the cold. In that case, the fine clothes and rich food enjoyed by the affluent and other such luxuries do not come under the heading of giving precedence to one's own life.[243] Furthermore, the value of giving charity is not diminished even if it is not done "purely for the sake of heaven," but for "some ulterior purpose."[244] "In these times, when [we believe] the day of the Messiah is approaching . . . the essence of serving God is doing justice through charity."[245] "Anyone who is spiritually sensitive and intellectually aware will readily perceive the stench that adheres to the money of those who do not give charity . . . like something [putrid] that has not been salted."[246]

This concept of charity played a significant role in the egalitarian tendency that was expressed within Hasidism. It buoyed the self-image of those who were needy and were dependent on others for assistance. It permitted them to avoid having to beg for compassion, and even gave them grounds to actually demand what was their due. This was not just a demand put to society at large, but to people they knew individually. This right gave them a type of status that compensated them socially. In the final analysis, no one in those perilous times could be quite secure in his life or possessions, even for the present, to say nothing of what the future might bring (and thus, everyone was potentially dependent on society).

For the same reason, the Hasidic leaders managed to be quite successful in their campaign to raise funds to "free captives," which meant providing a lump sum to someone who was otherwise in danger of bankruptcy. Charity, then, was conceived in a way that allowed for a sense of mutuality, a two-way type of assistance,[247] that also helped to unite the various strata that were drawn into the movement.

The social principles of Hasidism are reflected, as well, in some of its views on matters that seemingly pertained only to man's religious obligations to God. Of particular significance in this regard was the concept of faith in Providence. The concept itself, the way it was expounded, and the exemplars chosen to illustrate the idea, all point to the underlying social context of the movement and to the reasons for its growth.

The Besht's well-known homily on the phrase, "blessed is the man who trusts in God and for whom God is his security," emphasizes that such faith is absolutely fundamental. There is no need to seek any other means of assuring one's welfare and one's livelihood, because faith and trust are "the overall, underlying causal principle" in this regard. Even if man does not take practical steps or initiate business dealings on his own, God has the power to insure his welfare "through His boundless graciousness."[248] This was not just the statement of faith of a deeply believing man, but also characteristic of a social milieu in which security of the ordinary sort was scarce or nonexistent.

The social milieu emerges, as well, from details included in illustrative material used to explain the nature of faith. Such details furnish a glimpse of a grievous state of affairs: a world of instability, lack of confidence in what the morrow held in store, and of a basic fragility in all human affairs. This reality gave people the feeling that they "must rely on miracles." Faith instilled in people the sense that "it was not pure chance ["miracles"] but the will of God that determined everything."[249] Thus, the lack of security became the source of this type of faith, which is the cornerstone of religion. Belief and trust provided security.

The Torah was given to man only to activate in him the same sense that animated [the Israelites] who ate manna [in the wilderness]. They went out to the wilderness of Sinai empty-handed, without food or bread, save the cakes of matzoh that they had hastily prepared in Egypt. But because they were inspired by faith and trust in God, they received the manna. And they also honored the value of moderation: one measure sufficed for each person, the daily portion [each received], and they trusted that God would provide [the same again] the next day, so that there was no need to worry about tomorrow.

This held true not only for the generation of the exodus. Indeed, "even now, the manna has not ceased being supplied to each and every Jew, who receives his just portion for subsistance, regardless of his occupation."

There is thus no justification for that degree of "anxiety over income that gives people no peace, day or night, driving them to be constantly preoccupied with affairs of this world and thus cannot turn their attention to spiritual matters." "God, in a sense, contracts into Himself in order to create the immediate causal factors that allow Jews to earn their bread. God's Presence in the world takes the form, as it were, of these causal factors to provide every Jew with food and sustenance." All that is required in return is trust in Him.

> By his faith he ensures the continuation of his own support; fear and anxiety produce the opposite. . . . That is what is meant by, "blessed is the man who trusts in God, for whom God is his security." Overanxiousness and lack of faith are themselves enough to make our existence [seem] perilous. . . . The worst punishment is to remove from someone his sense of faith. . . . When one has faith, the flow of livelihood and plenty is vouchsafed.[250]

These maxims and others like them reflect the social reality of the time, which was pervaded by a sense of ceaseless struggle for survival for which there were no guarantees. The sense of confidence gained through faith became a crucial psychological factor in waging that struggle.

> Belief and faith in God is the first principle, and it renews the spark of life in a person, both physically and spiritually. . . . Livelihood is the product of faith: whoever has greater faith will achieve greater success. . . . If one's income begins to slacken and money is short . . . the best advice is to give charity with sincere generosity (because) this is the way to see in actual fact that one's fate is not dependent on the money one has; quite the reverse, one should place trust in God. . . . (There is thus no justification for the competition and senseless hatred that grow out of shrinking opportunities and the envy of others for what they have. Chasing after money) in our day is the root of all lust.[251] . . . No one will be able in any case to obtain what has been ordained for someone else.[252]

There is no cause for "the craftsman to hate his craft, the shopkeeper his shop and the taverner his wares, which produces the senseless hatred that caused the destruction of the second Temple." There is no reason why people should "chase after lucre day and night," which leads them to "encroach on others' livelihoods, depriving and robbing them of what is rightfully theirs."[253]

Yet, despite this characteristic "moral" that pervades early Hasidic literature, despite the organic connection it had with the social ferment in Polish-Jewish communal life (which no doubt significantly helped the movement to assert itself), these social themes cannot be identified as the organizing principle of the movement. They do not link up to any systematic approach to social issues as such. The only organizing princi-

ple there was—the perceived need to transfer control and decision-
making to a new, prophetic breed of leaders—was rooted in messianic,
not social, ideology. The drive to renew the prophetic tradition had
always been profoundly connected to the messianic worldview, ever
since the days of Judah Halevi (and before). It was an integral component of every messianic movement that ever arose in Judaism and was
nourished by the historical experience of each successive wave of messianic ferment.[254]

That drive for a new authority became, in the social-organizational
sense, a self-fulfilling prophecy. Cells of a new social structure grew up
within the communities, taking the form of *hevrot* of Hasidim, or similar
groups. Messianic tension developed within these cells, and then began
to percolate into society at large, for the Hasidic movement, as the
embodiment of the prophetic-messianic idea, aimed to capture the leadership of the entire nation.

IX. HASIDIC GROUPS AND HASIDIC LIFE BEFORE THE BESHT

Shivhei ha-Besht explicitly mentions the existence of small Hasidic circles before the public appearance of the Besht, which subsequently helped
form the new movement. They existed in Miedzyboz, in Kutów, and in
Brody. Moreover, according to the account in that book of the Besht's
public revelation, that event actually consisted of the recognition given
the Besht by "the conventicle of great pietists [*hasidim*] in that city
[Brody] . . . who made him their rabbi."[255]

Certainly, this account is somewhat tendentious: the writer wished to
argue that the Besht's authority had been confirmed by a select group
known, even in the estimation of Hasidism's opponents, as "greatly
learned in Talmud and rabbinics, extremely pious and devoted keepers
of the Torah and the commandments . . . famed for their piety, subser-
vient to God and faithful followers of the correct path . . . the remnant
of those called upon by God . . . [who] were [also] renowned for their
expertise in the mysteries of kabbala."[256] However, these stories—which
by nature conceal more than they reveal—lead us to conclude that the
emergence of the Besht as a leader must have followed a lengthy struggle
within existing groups.

The Hasidim of Miedzyboz, for example, looked askance at the Besht
because, as a popular healer *(baal shem),* his spiritual qualifications

might be in doubt. They were of the opinion that "this name he bears is not proper for a zaddik."²⁵⁷

Rabbi Nahman of Kosów, leader of a "sacred fellowship" (and who sent messages from his village to "each and every one regarding the sins that he ought to correct in order to mend the world"), stated that his disciples "spoke with discontent about the Besht." *Shivhei ha-Besht* does point out, of course, that R. Nahman was "greatly angered at his followers for doing this"; but R. Nahman's own words, when taken in context (referring to "that cause of dissension in our day"), imply that the contest over leadership was rather protracted. What R. Nahman objected to was the fact that his disciples "involved themselves in this issue [which was not their concern]," because, he said, it "is an ancient cause of division that had existed in the past between Saul and King David, and later on between Hillel and Shammai." His disciples, however, had viewed the matter too simplistically (perhaps, more realistically) and, therefore, had spoken harshly of the Besht. These same Hasidim, however, also played a decisive role in the ultimate victory of the Besht: they argued with their own rebbe when he continued to oppose the Besht, persuading him to accept the necessity for a meeting of the ways. "Why should we allow this [issue] to continue to trouble us?"²⁵⁸

Linked to this group of Hasidim were a few of the Besht's earliest disciples, including the first recognized rabbinic scholar who was recruited directly by the Besht (his "first achievement," as the author of *Shivhei ha-Besht* put it): the preacher of Polonne, R. Aryeh Loeb, author of *Qol aryeh*.²⁵⁹

From the teachings of R. Nahman of Kosów that are quoted in *Toledot yaaqov yosef* it would appear, I believe, that he endeavored to expand his original group and to attract younger adherents, as well.²⁶⁰ To them he directed the following injunction, punning on the Hebrew *ovot* and *avot*: " 'Turn ye not unto sorcerers [*ovot*],' that is—do not look [for precedent and legitimation] to the fathers [*avot*], when people say, 'Why were there no such Hasidim before, in the days of my father and my grandfather? Has the Messiah come [that we should change our ways and turn over a new leaf]?' "

Further details surrounding this matter may be gleaned from the account by R. Jacob Emden, who reported "on unimpeachable authority" about

what happened in Apt [Opatów] with Rabbi Nahman of Kosów, an ignoramus and a Sabbatian, who made himself out to be a preacher and was welcomed there with much respect because of a letter of recommendation furnished by [R. Yehezqel Landau], who will write endorsements for just about any wicked sinner. As a result, there broke out such a great dispute because of the Landaus that blood was spilt.[261]

R. Yehezqel Landau's endorsement, apparently, stemmed from the period he spent living in Brody, studying at the same study hall[262] frequented by the Hasidim there: that is, from 1735 to 1745 (corresponding to the first years of the Besht's "self-revelation"). In any event, this occurred before 1750–51, when R. Jacob Emden received the report from his reliable source.[263]

Similarly, it was said of several other leading disciples and intimates of the Besht that they were Hasidim before they joined the Besht's entourage, and that they had come to him only after his reputation had spread "far and wide." Of R. Nahman of Horodenka it was said that he had been "a prodigious Hasid" and had set himself stringent tests in order to rid himself of "impure thoughts," but had not succeeded until he admitted "the truth of the Besht's wisdom."[264] R. Nahman of Horodenka, evidently, had close ties to those groups of ascetic pietists which may be traced back to R. Judah the Pious, and which existed in various Polish-Jewish communities. (Emden reported that R. Judah the Pious and his circle had left behind them "poisonous roots.")[265] R. Nahman's first trip to the Holy Land took place during the first years of the Besht's career; and legend has it that R. Elazar of Amsterdam, himself originally a Hasid from Brody (known as "the most pious of his generation" and who traveled to the Holy Land in 1750 to serve God "in pureness of heart in the sacred land") had some connection with R. Nahman of Horodenka's journey. Both men evidently were part of the same circles.[266]

Two of the Besht's foremost disciples and his heirs—R. Yaaqov Yosef Ha-Cohen of Polonne and R. Dov Ber of Miedzyrzecz—came out of those same pietist ascetic circles of the school of R. Judah the Pious. Although it was said of the former that until meeting the Besht he "was not yet a Hasid," and was known in his town as someone who "had no truck with Hasidim"; and the latter, for all his profound knowledge in Talmud and kabbala, was after all only a humble schoolteacher and preacher who was "discovered" by the Besht; nevertheless, their spiritual approach was explicitly described in terms of the ascetic Hasidic model. The Maggid of Miedzyrzecz would fast seven or eight times a week, and was quite ill because of it. And in his famous letter to R. Yaaqov Yosef ("renowned for your piousness *[hasidut]*"), the Besht instructed him not to endanger his life in that way and to cease maintaining that "[you feel] compelled, as it were, to fast." Both men joined the new movement after the number of people undertaking pilgrimages to the Besht had swelled considerably, and after the Besht's reputation had become a subject for "wonderment."

Their recruitment, moreover, was a result of efforts by the Besht to discover "suitable vessels" from the surrounding areas who might be drawn into his circle. These two "suitable vessels" were men whose characters had been shaped long before; the Besht merely "raised up" the one and "breathed new spirit"[267] into the scholarship of the other. Still, their personal qualities and life-style were well established in the Hasidic mode before the advent of the Besht.

That style and image were part and parcel of that generation's experience and were shared by many others. Indeed, the very existence of "saintly fellowships" devoted to the "ways of the pious," that imposed on their members a regimen of special practices and obligations—a life of "following the ways of the righteous" and "straight paths," patterns of life that were not commonly shared by all Jews (for the most part, not even admired or emulated by them)—was not a latter-day phenomenon. Quite the contrary, such groups existed throughout Jewish history and were basic to the history of Judaism and to the development of the religious way of life Jews adopted, from ancient days down to the present. This phenomenon is particularly prominent in conjunction with the rise of new religious movements, the birth of sects, and the popular dissemination of their ideas.

That is why these "sacred fellowships," whatever their form, constitute a typical feature of the social landscape in times of religious ferment. Such groups accompany the history of movements and sects throughout the ages. They play a decisive role in the popularization of these new trends, familiarizing the public with new styles of religious behavior and custom, and to a large extent implanting such practices in Jewish life for some time thereafter.

Evidence for such groups in earlier times may be scarce, but the matter deserves careful study nonetheless.[268] By the time we get to the period of the Lurianic kabbala and the ascendancy of Jewish mysticism, we are in a much better position to trace the role of pietist groups. Not only is their existence documented, but we actually possess copies of some groups' regulations and bylaws,[269] as well as letters describing their activities.[270] Moreover, the prolific *mussar* literature of the day— with its common store of ideas and common format—may be regarded as the intellectual program and practical handbooks of these groups and, thus, a vital source for their history.[271] Scholars have already taken note of these sources and have described their overall character. Gershom Scholem, in particular, has demonstrated and explained the organic link between the messianic-redemptive concept underlying Lurianic kabbala and the idea of *tiqun,* or "setting the world alright again," which it taught. It was this idea, in fact, that provided the basis for *mussar* literature generally.[272]

Yet, I would venture to say that the importance of the pietist groups in the development of early Hasidism has not been fully appreciated. They were much more numerous and widespread than we might think. A number of facts are most relevant in this connection. .

1. Study of the kabbala and the pervasive extent of such study reinforced and encouraged the establishment of pietist circles. Study of kabbala became de rigueur, even for those whose intellectual caliber was not the highest. Such people were expected to focus on midrashic lore contained in the Zohar and other kabbalist books: "It is better to study the inner kernel than the outer shell."[273]

The Torah was given [to us] to study and to teach, so that everyone, young and old, should have knowledge of God, and many books of the kabbala warn of the importance of studying this wisdom [i.e., the mystical books], which everyone is obligated to learn.[274]

In this oppressive existence in Exile, no one can fully return to God unless his eyes have been opened a bit by the wisdom of the kabbala, so that he may understand [at least] what is written in the Zohar.

This was considered a great obligation, even for those who were not particularly sharp-witted, "slow of understanding or forgetful."[275] "Even he who does not understand [the Zohar], his tongue is still capable of [uttering the words and] purifying his soul, to bring it illumination and enlightenment."[276]

Not only was study of the kabbala considered mandatory, but it was thought "praiseworthy to engage [in it] in groups, young and old together." All the old restrictions and prohibitions against "delving into the true knowledge in public" were now considered to have been only "temporary."[277] Indeed, "the essential aspect of study lies in discussion with a partner *[hevruta],*"[278] for "each one must examine himself and his partner to check his mastery and that of his friend so that they may adjust what they teach each other accordingly."[279] "In kabbala study, one must not utter anything one has not already heard from someone who is a reliable authority."[280]

Regular study of kabbala was not mandated in vague, general terms; rather, the manner of study and the methods of study were spelled out in detail: "One ought always to have two texts for study—one for one's own focused inquiry, and one set text [for continuous reading]. . . . One should cover three pages a night of the Mantua edition of the Zohar, so that in one year one may read the entire book, together with the *Tiqunei ha-zohar.* . . . First study your own special selection, and then read the assigned daily portion." "It is not easy to fathom the full meaning in all its complexity, even if the words appear to be simple, for they conceal profound secrets."[281] Although "most of the mystic knowledge of the Torah, that is the kabbala and the knowledge of God, is contained within aggadic lore,"[282] not everyone is capable of reading them correctly. This is especially true of those who study "but have not been receptive to its revelation," because their souls must be properly attuned to it." Certainly there were not many who could accomplish on their own the "most important purpose of kabbala study," which was "to bring about unions of the divine spheres through study, and not to study merely for one's own benefit or advantage, God forbid."[283]

Thus, the mandate to study kabbala led inexorably to routinizing the forms and methods of study. Without two basic educational axioms, one could not even begin: First, "one's teacher must be steeped in learning"; second, "one should study with worthy partners." Hence, study of kabbala required the formation of groups, led by "a reliable authority." In this manner, two types of "learned men" emerged—"teaching fellows" and "preacher-rabbis"—both of which played key roles in the development and spread of the mystical movements of that period (including Sabbatianism in its various forms and the Hasidic movement, with its various branches).

The more affluent were able to spend money to employ a teaching fellow, it being considered spiritually meritorious to "acquire a friend and a teacher" and "to encourage him always in [the ways of] piety."[284] It was preferable to study with one fellow since increasing the number increased the wasting of time.[285] Those who could not afford a private arrangement would join groups. Pedagogical instructions conveyed in the kabbalist-oriented *mussar* books were aimed at "average people," suggesting ways to "awaken them [to the value of study] and attract their interest bit by bit. . . . Sometimes, you may reveal one thing to him, but then quickly cover it up again and run away with it like a bolt of lightning; on another occasion, you might speak obscurely, as from behind a heavy curtain, so that they will hear you but not see you; and sometimes, what you say should be thinly veiled to arouse their interest."[286] Such recommendations indicate that there was a large sector of "average people" like that.

In these groups there was a marked resistance to studying basic Talmudic and legal rabbinic texts. "Some of them are attracted mainly to aggadic lore" and avoid halachic literature,   *NB*

> the words of the living God, dearer than pearls . . . which [they] look down upon, and such is the case with all those who inquire [into mystical lore]. And people say, "Why should I expend great effort and time and get nothing in return, when the table [of esoteric knowledge] is set before me, allowing me to understand the inner meaning and sense in studying God's service."[287]

This complaint about the neglect of halachic study was hardly an isolated case. R. Hayim of Volozhin would later lament about "those days" when people "made their entire study revolve only around books of piety and *mussar*. . . . I myself saw in one particular district that this had become so widespread that in most of the study halls there were only *mussar* books, and there was not even one complete set of Talmud."[288] Similar plaints were raised about the low standard of knowledge among those who studied kabbala, who nevertheless "pride themselves on their achievements in highly esoteric realms, thinking themselves great adepts; but show them a text in the Zohar and they will give you an interpretation that the text will not bear."[289]

Likewise, accusations were leveled at the leaders of the pietist groups, "those hypocrites who pose as Hasidim . . . who think that they can fool God. . . . They think they are beloved by God and call themselves "Hasid" and fool the people, partly because people attach themselves to them and come to them with their secrets."[290] Such comments indicate the existence of the "zaddik" or "rebbe" model already in this period.

2. Kabbala study not only tended to become more important than the study of basic Talmudic texts, but also gave it a somewhat different

twist. This relates partly to the midrashic and aggadic focus of kabbala,[291] but mainly affected the status of the Mishna. The kabbalists laid
particular emphasis on its value, took care to prescribe regular study of
the Mishna, and saw a direct link between that text and kabbala:[292]

"If we want to bring the chariot to God into proper alignment, we
must first study the Mishna and only then [advanced works of] halacha,
for the Mishna is the chariot of the halacha." "Lessons in Mishna
precede everything else." "Mishna should be chanted with cantillation,
so that one's study may be more pleasant." "Mishna-study serves to
correct the fault of Adam."

These and many other maxims and allusions were made concerning
the Mishna, for "whoever studies Mishna for its own sake, to unite the
heavenly spheres," brings redemption that much closer. "It is good to
study the Mishna every day and, if possible, to cover eighteen chapters
every day, which is a recognized weapon against the evil inclination."[293]

We read of kabbalists enjoining their associates "to gather together,
the more distinguished and the more humble, the old and the young, to
study Mishna as a group." Although it was fairly usual "in some of the
communities [that people regularly] studied a set portion of Gemara or
Mishna every day in the synagogue and study halls,"[294] this phenomenon was typically linked to the spread of kabbalist ideas. Clearly, such
groups were instrumental in heightening the importance and influence of
the mystics (of whatever type), and served as a structural focus around
which people of similar inclination could coalesce.

3. The first tenet of the "code of the true [i.e., mystical] religion"
was: "Whoever wishes to delve into the true wisdom must conduct
himself with strict piety [hasidut]." That is to say, "he should conduct
himself in a sanctified manner with respect to all things that are permissible [and] to guard against sinning—even inadvertent sins—and therefore be punctilious down to the smallest detail; because God is especially
demanding of His pious ones [hasidav]."[295] "Study without implemen-
tation [of values] in practice is worthless, [for] had study without practice been a sufficient fulfillment of our religious obligation, they (Christians and Moslems [who are not obligated to practice misvot]) would
have received the Torah [instead of the Jews] purely for the sake of
study."[296] Therefore, people whose intellectual attainments are higher
have to adhere to a correspondingly higher standard in terms of religious
praxis. "The essential aim of studying Torah is to provide a throne for

God, but how can God be present if [the throne] is sullied with sin?"[297] To that end, one must go about "with fear of God on one's face," humbly, contemplating the sins of one's youth and regretting them constantly; "to be vigilant against sinning again in private, and to make confession with one's morning and evening prayers, before eating."[298]

Even this is not yet enough, however. "In everything you do, be sure your purpose is [directed heavenward] to help unite the divine spheres."[299] This applied all the more to one's studies and to fulfilling religious commandments. It was clear that "while engaged in Torah your consciousness should be directed toward God," and "you should, when engaged in study, think of yourself as standing in heaven, before God, and not in this world at all."[300]

Mussar literature describes the ways in which to reach such a level of piety. This was to be accomplished through solitary meditation and an ascetic regimen. "The root of acquiring any *misvah* (commandment) lies in introspection, for it takes a truly great effort to reach holiness." One must "love solitude and avoid the company of boors and women."[301] "The best rule of thumb is: do not attach yourself to just anyone, but only to a wise man."[302]

"Solitude" of this kind actually meant "exclusivity." One had to take care, "as a man of learning," not to be "associated with the ignorant, lest one begin to learn from their example, since the uneducated are, by and large, unworthy; therefore, have nothing at all to do with them." At the same time, it was taught that "one should strive to fulfill religious obligations in company [with others], for a *misvah* performed by many is incomparably preferable to a *misvah* performed only by a few."[303] "A *misvah* takes on greater value in a group setting, and the 'majesty of the king inheres in the multitude of his people.' " "He who wishes to attain eternal life should be constantly in the company of zaddikim and pious people *[hasidim]*, should attach himself to them and learn from their ways."[304]

Thus, the solitude demanded by the "Hasidic way" was in practice a basis for the formation of select companies and a mutual bond between Hasidim. Even if they did not formally establish an association, these pietist circles nevertheless possessed their particular identity, an aura of "special devotion to the sacred." Many of the works of *mussar* we have are but recorded, first-hand observations of what those "men of [holy] practices and men of grace and truth, the pillars of the earth, live by."[305]

(4)

4. Indeed, if we examine their "code of life," which may be recon-structed from the "proper practices" and the conduct that was deemed appropriate for anyone who wished to "live by pious precepts" (even if they were not strictly "required by law" of all Jews), we will find nearly all those "new customs" introduced by the Hasidim in the time of the Besht and his disciples, which drew such fierce criticism and opposition, along with warnings against "forming cliques." [306]

Changes introduced by the Hasidim in the customary mode of prayer prompted the Lithuanian Council to forbid "any modification at all, even of the melodies sung [in prayer]." The changes were presumably those derived from the liturgy of the Lurianic school. The Hasidim of Brody were said to have started to pray "for some years now" according to the "prayer book of the Ari [R. Isaac Luria] . . . and this custom of theirs was fully accepted by the rabbis, who never voiced reservations about this." Indeed, it was said that, "if you are of a spiritual inclination, and you sincerely wish to cling to God with love, if you wish to be one of that holy company that see the face of the king, then turn to the prayer book of the Ari and use it for your devotions." [307]

Another practice that was also later taken up by the Hasidic move-ment was the addition of Psalms to the prayer service during the month of Ellul ("The Lord is my light and my salvation . . .").[308] Likewise, it was the custom of "many among the pure ones to express their yearning for God by praying in joyful singing or in weeping, and they did not always bother to enunciate each syllable properly." [309] "Between words you should add, 'We have sinned, we have betrayed,' etc., and beat your breast with your fist, because this is a means for eliciting divine grace." [310] Although there were many who derided the superpious who "refrained from using tefillin [phylacteries] of Rabbenu Tam and were particular about mikveh (the ritual bath) . . . [which] is all new to us," nevertheless numerous communities saw to it that "there should be a mikveh of warm water so that any man, no matter how frail, might regularly derive strength from the waters of purification." Likewise, many people took to covering their heads with their tallit [shawl] [during prayer]," and who believed that "one should sleep with one's tallit katan [fringed undergarment] on," and so forth.[311]

Customs of the Sabbath that were later adopted by the Hasidic move-ment were also practiced in that period. Sabbaths were considered to be "consecrated to study of the kabbala," and it was "important to dis-cover some new insight or interpretation on the Sabbath," for "the soul will grieve if God should ask it on Saturday night, 'What new insight have you discovered?' and it will not know what to say." Here we see the origin of the zaddik's practice of "teaching Torah" ("new interpretations in kabbalist wisdom") on the Sabbath. "Kabbala belongs to the world of splendor, which has dominion on the Sabbath day."[312] In those early years it was already usual for pietists to "sit together for a festive meal, which they open and close with words of wisdom."[313] Although there was a certain amount of "concern over excessive pride" because pietists took to wearing whites on the Sabbath, ("even though some of the greatest rabbis go dressed in black"), yet this practice persisted among the pietists. We even encounter injunctions about the proper sharpening of knives for kosher slaughtering (later to become a trademark of the Hasidic movement). "Every God-fearing person . . . should make sure to ask the rabbi to check the knife used by the slaughterer, even in a great city."[314]

5. There was a feeling of intimacy among the pietists. They were bound to cultivate that feeling, if only because society at large was not particularly congenial toward them, suspecting them of self-righteous pride. It was not only *maskilim* [Enlighteners, skeptics] who ridiculed them for "spreading their stork's *[hasida]* wings for all the congregation to see"; for "walking in exaggeratedly humble fashion along the road to the house of God, when all the congregation is on the way there"; for "raising [their] voices in shouts and moans, calling upon God out loud, gesturing [their] confession and bowing like bent reeds"; for fasting and donning sackcloth.[315] Rather, contemporaries wrote that "even those touched by the fear of God . . . say of the Hasidim that they do what they do out of conceit." "Many poke fun at those who make much of their passion for God, crying and gesticulating [in prayer]."[316]

One of the most outstanding rabbinical scholars of the time, the author of *Mirkevet ha-mishna*, described a typical Hasid as one who:

has not read or studied, yet is called "sage" and "rabbi"; and whoever uses more gesticulations and bodily motions is considered the most distinguished. . . . He is a deceiver, he raises his voice, he prances and skips. He prays with much singing and always changes the tune, perhaps ten times. His behavior is strange and he decks himself out in whites.[317]

This assessment was not idiosyncratic, by any means, if we may judge from the countercomplaints of the pietists against those who jeered at them.

The superasceticism, too, which one rabbi described, was hardly likely to win much sympathy among the people at large: "There was a man who was perfect in all things—he labored and strove mightily to study Torah and he mortified his flesh, fasting and immersing himself, and followed the strictest interpretation of every law, sometimes adding restrictions of his own accord . . . [and in the end] committed suicide, [for] they found him defiled with blood, holding a knife in his hands and his throat slit."[318]

No wonder, then, that the pietists felt the need for mutual encouragement and intimacy. The injunctions to perform *misvot* in a group did not derive solely from religious sources, but also from a sense of what was socially desirable. That sense drove pietists to join already-existing *hevrot*. "I am a friend to all who [have joined to] serve You through [charitable societies devoted to] providing dowries for poor brides, ransoming prisoners, visiting the sick, burying the dead, supporting schools for the poor, providing food for circumcision feasts and clothing for the poor, keeping vigil until morning and reciting Psalms."[319]

Hence, too, the exhortations to "practice close comradeship": "As it is written, 'You should cling to him until you both cling together' ";[320] "if there is some friend who is in difficulties or sickness, or his children are, share his trouble with him and pray for him."

Such advice was not only a function of the religious precept that, before proceeding to recite one's morning prayers, one ought to fulfill the commandment to "love your neighbor as yourself . . . and [one] should make a point of loving each and every Jew as oneself." It was also a matter of "on this subject, of [relations with] our comrades, etc., there is no more that needs to be said."[321] There was no need for further explanation because aid and support for a friend in distress "is one of the sixteen things . . . that one good friend must do for another [see below], so that their relationship will provide satisfaction and be genuine, without ulterior motive."

All such references to the obligations toward one's friend and one's group are a reliable indication to us of the quality of togetherness, even in nonspiritual matters, that was fostered:

And these [rules of friendship] are: Be the first to greet him, offer him the best of what you have, [join with him] on the day of his rejoicing, keep his confidences secret, support him in his distress, visit him in prison and try to perform for him the tasks he cannot do while he is ill, participate in his burial arrangements should he die, correct your speech in his presence, forgive his transgressions against you immediately, reproach him if he has done something improper, respect him, do not deceive him in business, do for him all that you know how to do, do not lie to him, ask mercy for him and sincerely desire what is best for him.[322]

In a "holy epistle . . . sent by the sacred society in the land of Israel to the sacred society abroad" we read:

Among our number there are no arguments, God forbid, and even if by some error a misunderstanding should arise, the ranks of the sacred [society] intervene right away, lest a protracted dispute develop, and they effect an amicable return to brotherhood and friendship.[323]

It is likely that this determination to preserve peaceful "brotherhood and friendship", and the precautions taken against doing to a friend things that ought not to be done to anyone, let alone to a friend, were the cementing factors that gave the pietist groups their special elan of "beauty and perfection," which left an impression on the community as well as the individual.

6. One special type of pietist circle or society was the "midnight fellowship." These were men who undertook, "for the sake of the living God, to rise at midnight from the depths and to raise the Presence of God from the dust through studying Torah, it being known that this is a propitious hour."

The kabbalists, of course, were always well known for their midnight vigils, for "weeping and wailing each night over the exile of God's Presence [galut ha-shekhinah], for the weeping of Rachel and the destruction of the Temple," after which they would engage in study. They ordained that such sessions should last "until dawn," to "give comfort and exaltation to Rachel, to God's Presence, who stands outside." [324]

This custom became widespread, and there were many who felt that "it is obligatory to rise at midnight" because "whoever does not [by this action help to] rebuild the Temple [325] helps, as it were, to destroy part of it again." Ways were sought, therefore, to involve everyone somehow in these activities. One way was to take the view that those taking part in these groups were "priests" of the Temple, whose material needs had to be supplied by the public so that they might be freed from mundane concerns. In that case, those unable to take part personally in the nightly sessions and allied customs might still participate vicariously by helping to support those directly involved, delegating them, in effect, in act on their behalf.[326]

Likewise, we find instances of a type of Hasid who received communal support and who lived as a virtual recluse. Sometimes the community bought him his reserved place in the synagogue or study hall, "where [he] maintains his vigil day and night . . . sitting and studying, engaged in spiritual matters, or intending to go on pilgrimage to the Holy Land."[327]

It seems to me that, altogether, the history of these groups and this developing life-style justifies the conclusion that the term Hasid was already in use during the first half of the eighteenth century to denote a specific phenomenon of socioreligious reality and ideational content. That content, however, must be examined separately, against the background of religious life in which the Hasidic "way" developed. [— Translated by Eli Lederhendler.]

NOTES

1. The term occurs in the early counter-Hasidic polemical writings. Thus, "A new group has come from nowhere that was unknown to our fathers and they are called Hasidim . . . the Hasidim of our time" (*Zamir 'arisim* [first version] in Dubnow, *Chassidiana*, 1918, pub. as separate section in *He-'avar* 2 [o.s.], pp. 23, 25); "Those new-style Hasidim" (*Zamir 'arisim* [second version], edition published by Deinard, p. xxiv). Solomon Maimon also refers to this in his autobiography (first edition, 1792, p. 207; Taviov's translation, Tel Aviv, 1941, p. 96); but Maimon was incorrect in reasoning that the term was meant to distinguish the "new" Hasidim from the older, ascetic Hasidim, for even the old-style ascetics such as Judah the Hasid (i.e., the Pious) and his associates were themselves called "new Hasidim" in the polemical literature. See *Torat ha-qana'ut* (Lwów edn.), p. 56: "That sect of Hasidim of R. J[udah] are upstarts"; and on p. 55, just before that, we find: "a new sect of Hasidim in Poland"; thus, too, in a fragment about "the group of Hasidim" that Freiman published in volume 2 of *YIVO historishe shriftn*" (1937, pp. 140–144): "And the rabbis in Jerusalem banned them and the whole group of new Hasidim who made their recent appearance there" (p. 141). In fact, this term was meant to distinguish them from the kabbalist Hasidim that lived in Poland. See the Introduction (published in 1772–73) to the responsa collection *Zikhron yosef*, which argues that the "new" Hasidim would seek to identify themselves with "them" (the old-style Hasidim), "the great sages in that country." But as the new movement grew, the adjective was dropped and it was known

simply as "the Hasidim" or "the sect of Hasidim." See the famous letter of R. Avraham Katzenellenbogen of Brisk [Brześć] *(Dvir* 1 [1923], p. 304).

2. The locations referred to in *Shivhei ha-Besht* in connection with the life of the Besht and his travels, and the list of his disciples and their places of origin *(Seder ha-dorot he-hadash* and elsewhere) total about fifty (a few of them are difficult to identify); of these, over thirty are in Podolia (15–16) and Volhynia (17), more than ten are in Eastern Galicia, and four or five are in White Russia.

3. Dubnow, *Toledot ha-hasidut* (Tel Aviv, 1943), p. 60; the Besht's letter to his brother-in-law, R. Avraham Gershon of Kutow, dates from 1750–51, and includes an account of an "ascent of the soul" experienced by the Besht on Rosh Hashanah of 1746: i.e., the movement originated in the 1740s, or perhaps even before that. The remarks of R. Jacob Emden about the "new sect of Hasidim in Volhynia and Podolia" that "has sprung up" *(Mitpahat ha-sefarim,* 31) actually date from the end of the 1750s (the book was published in 1768, but was written by the late 1750s: it is included in the list of Emden's writings in *Megillat sefer,* p. 203, which also includes among the manuscripts list *She'ilat ya'aves,* which was published in 1758–59, and in the list of published works, *Sefer ha-shimush* which was perhaps published as early as 1757–58). Evidence from R. Shlomo of Chelm (introduction to *Mirkevet ha-mishna,* pt. 1) dates from 1749–50; *Nazad ha-dem'a* by R. Israel of Zamość only appeared in 1762–63, it is true (in Dyhrenfürth), and was published posthumously (and is not mentioned in Ben-Jacob's bibliography), but there is no doubt that the book was written soon after Zamość's arrival in Berlin. Graetz (in his *Geschichte der Juden* [1853–76] vol. 11, p. 8, n. 1: in the Hebrew translation, *Divrei yemei Yisrael* (Warsaw, 1890–1902) p. 15) assumes that the work was intended for publication in *Kehillat mussar,* that is, in 1749–50. But the style and the aggressive tone in which it was written indicate to me that the author was still caught up in Polish life, which would put it in the early 1740s, soon after his departure from Poland. (In 1740–41 he published in Frankfurt on the Main his work, *Nesah yisrael,* which is filled with the desire to spread Enlightenment.) See also Solomon Maimon's autobiography, the German version (1792), pt. 2, pp. 168–169 (and in the Baruch translation, p. 183).

4. According to R. Israel Loebel (in *Schulamith* 2 [1807], p. 307, and in Deinard's translation, *Herev hadah,* p. 3), the Besht succeeded during less than ten years at the outset of his career in attracting a following of about ten thousand people, and five years later—i.e., fifteen years after the sect was founded—the number of followers had increased to forty thousand. Compare Graetz's assessment, in his *Geschichte der Juden,* vol. 11, p. 126 (in the Hebrew edition: *Divrei yemei Yisrael,* p. 92), that before the end of the eighteenth century there were one hundred thousand. All of these figures are only estimates. Cf. Dubnow, *Toledot ha-hasidut,* p. 76. The extent of Hasidism's growth during the second half of the eighteenth

century, in the various localities, is a matter that deserves a special study in its own right, based on the rabbinic literature of the time, Hasidic literature, and other sources.

5. The position taken by some of the leading Lithuanian rabbis vis-à-vis Hasidism is quite interesting—such as that of R. Hayyim of Volozhin. See his *Nefesh ha-hayyim*, sec. 4, chap. 1; the letter (of 1803) by R. Shneur Zalman of Liady, published by Hilman in *Beit rabbi* (Berdyczew, 1902), p. 79; and ibid., Introduction, pp. 10–11.

6. Scholem, *Major Trends in Jewish Mysticism* (New York, 1941), p. 325.

7. There is no complete bibliography of Hasidic literature. Dubnow cites 194 books and short works, grouped as follows: collections of documents and polemical works (33), books of Hasidic legends (29), books on Hasidic philosophy (82), and modern scholarship about Hasidism (50). This list, however, is selective rather than comprehensive. Scholem, in his *Bibilographia kabbalistica* (1923), cites over 170 articles and books about Hasidism. *Baal shem* by R. Shimon Meir Mendel (Lodz, 1938) cites 210 books (including both works of Torah [religious learning or commentary] and legend) in the list of sources from which quotations attributed to the Besht were cited. Scholem estimates (in his bibliographical study, Introduction, p. x) that the total of such books is around three thousand—which does not strike me in the least as an exaggeration. His remarks about the great need to engage in systematic bibliographical research in this field in Eastern Europe especially and in the Near East have not, as far as I know, been taken up with any results to date. Indeed, it is to be feared that after the Second World War and the Holocaust which it brought upon East European Jewry much of that literature is "gone but not forgotten."

8. On the general interrelationship perceived between, on the one hand, the crisis that attended the failure of Sabbatianism, and Hasidism on the other, see Dubnow, *Toledot ha-hasidut*, pp. 24–34; cf. Dubnow, "Sotsial'naia i dukhovnaia zhizn' evreev v pol'she v pervoi polovine XVIII veka," *Voskhod*, Feb. 1899, pp. 54–62; I. Zinberg, in *Istoriia evreiskogo naroda*, vol. 11, chapter on "Mystical Trends" (Moscow, 1914), pp. 456–457; idem, *Di geshikhte fun der literatur bay yidn* (Wilno, 1937), pt. 7, pp. 9–14, 37; Sh.Y. Hurwitz, *Me'ayin le'ayin* (1914), p. 278; Scholem, *Major Trends*, 320–325; idem, *Ha-tenu'ah ha-shabta'it be-polin* (separate publication of essay included in *Beit yisrael be-polin*, [ed. by I. Halperin] (Jerusalem, 1948), vol. 2, pp. 36–76; Buber, "Reshit ha-hasidut," *Moznayim* 11, pp. 204–206; idem, *Be-pardes ha-hasidut* (Jerusalem 1945), pp. 9–41.

9. On the perceived connection between the crisis in Jewish self-government and the rise of Hasidism, see Dubnow, op. cit., pp. 19–23; idem, the essay in *Voskhod* cited in n. 8, pp. 49–53; S. Ginsburg, in *Istoriia evreiskogo naroda*, vol. 11, chapter on the beginnings of Hasidism, pp. 442–482; and especially the fine essays by P. Marek, "Krizis evreiskago samoupravleniia i khasidizm," and "Vnutrennaia bor'ba v evreistve v XVIII veke," both in volume 12 (1928) of *Evreiskaia starina*, pp. 45–178; cf. Marek's article in

Voskhod of June 1903, on the new and important settlement of communities in the seventeenth and eighteenth centuries.

10. Compare Balaban, *Toledot ha-tenu'ah ha-frankit* [Tel Aviv, 1934–35], pp. 63–67; Scholem, essay on Sabbatianism in Poland (cited in n. 8). We have many contemporary reports on the dissemination of Sabbatianism and its offshoots in those regions during that period, the most important being the books by Yaavetz. See: *Torat ha-qana'ut* (Lwów edn.), pp. 57, 60, 70, 120, 126; *Hitavqut*, 1a, 28a, 23b; *'Edut be-ya'aqov*, 51; *Sefer shimush*, 2b; *Petah 'einayim*, 14b, 46b, and elsewhere. Yaavetz was intimately aware of, and in close touch with, what was happening in the Polish communities. Both his older sons were living there at the time: R. Meir, son-in-law of R. Moshe, the Parnas of Lissa, was a well-known rabbi still living in Konstantin in about 1754 (see responsa *Yeri'at ha-ohel* sec. 5, no. 17, 1751 edn.); and his younger, favorite son, R. Meshullam Zalman, had lived since childhood in Poland (from 1734 to 1765), served for a while as rabbi in Podhajce, and then for the final twenty-five years served in Brody. One of Yaavetz's daughters was the daughter-in-law of the chairman of the Four Lands Council, R. Avraham of Lissa (beginning in 1757); his other daughter was married to the son of the famous *shtadlan* (communal petitioner or lobbyist) R. Borukh of Greece. Yaavetz's younger brother, R. Ephrayim, lived in Lwów, and Yaavetz's third wife (he married her in 1744) was the daughter of that brother. His other brother, R. Nathan Ashkenazi, the grandfather of R. Yaaqov of Lissa, lived in Brody; and his third brother was the rabbi and head of the yeshiva in Ostróg. Jacob Emden's three sisters lived in Poland also. One of his brothers-in-law, R. Yishaq, was the rabbi in Bialy, and the other—in Zloczow. See *Megillat sefer* (Warsaw, 1897), pp. 11, 40, 62–70, 84, 152, 154, 163–164, 177, 186, 188; I. Eisenstadt and S. Weiner, *Da'at qedoshim* (St. Petersburg, 1897–98), pp. 53–55; S. Buber, *Anshei shem* (Cracow, 1895), p. 36; M. Biber, *Mazkeret le-gedolei ostra* (Berdyczew, 1907), pp. 106–110; H. Dembitzer, *Kelilat yofi* (Cracow, 1888), pt. 1, 99–101; S. Hurwitz, *Kitvei ha-geonim* (Piotrków, 1928), pp. 123–219. The influence of Sabbatianism was strongly felt in all the places where his relatives lived, and in some cases there were active Sabbatian groups on the scene. Therefore, Emden's knowledge of the subject should be regarded as having come from first-hand and reliable sources.

11. See Dubnow, *Divrei yemei 'am 'olam* (Tel Aviv, 1958), pt. 7, pp. 76–80, 97–106; and Dinur, *Sefer ha-siyonut* (Tel Aviv, 1938), pt. 1 (*Mevasrei ha-siyonut*, pp. 148–154).

12. See Dubnow, *Toledot ha-hasidut*, pp. 24–26, the paragraph on "historical perspective."

13. Of this manifold literature—which historical, literary, and even bibliographical research have barely tapped—there are a number of books that deserve special mention in the context of our present discussion, whose authors were contemporary witnesses and who lived in those areas where

Hasidism was first disseminated. I shall cite them in chronological order: *Yesod yosef* by R. Yosef of Dubno (published Szklów, 1785, but written at the end of the seventeenth century); *Toharot ha-qodesh* by R. Binyamin Volf ben R. Matityahu (Amsterdam, 1733: the author was from Poland, evidently from the Ukraine or Eastern Galicia—see 2: 9a, "in our countries, in [central] Poland and [southeast Poland]"; 34a, "a 'spring,' called in German *kvall [Quell]* and in the Russian tongue, *krintsa*," which is actually a Ukrainian word); *Zer'a berakh shlishi* on Tractate Berakhot, by R. Berakhiah Beirakh ben R. Eliaqim Goetz of Klimontów (published, it would seem, in Frankfurt on the Oder, 1731); *Mishmeret ha-qodesh* by R. Moshe of Satanów (Żółkiew, 1746); *Ohel moshe* by R. Yaaqov ben R. Moshe Katz (Żółkiew, 1754); *Lev simhah* by R. Simhah ben R. Yehoshua of Zlozec (Żółkiew, 1757); *Beit peres* by R. Peres ben R. Moshe (Żółkiew, 1759); *'Ir dameseq eliezer* by R. Eliezer ben R. Menashe (Żółkiew, 1764); *Taqanta de-moshe* by R. Shmarya ben R. Moshe Berliner (Olexeniec, 1768: actually the first part is by his father R. Moshe ben R. Elhanan); *Nazad ha-dem'a* by R. Israel of Zamość (Dyhrenfürth, 1772); *Sha'ar ha-melekh* by R. Mordechai ben R. Shmuel of Wielkacz (Żółkiew, 1777); *Ohel rahel* by R. David Karo of Zborów (Szkłów, 1790). Among books written by authors from elsewhere in Poland, we might mention *Darkhei no'am* by R. Shmuel ben R. Eliezer of Kalwaria (Königsberg, 1764); *Beit middot* (Frankfurt on the Oder, 1777) and *Or 'olam* by R. Y. L. Margaliot (Prague, 1783); *Binyan shlomo* by R. Shlomo ben R. Avraham (Szklów, 1789); *Hillel ben shahar* by R. Hillel ben R. Ze'ev-Volf of Racki (Bialystok?, 1804); and others, to be mentioned in the proper context.

14. This genre has not yet been fully studied, although it is of tremendous value in assessing the penetration into popular Jewish culture of both kabbalist ideas and Hasidism. I believe, too, that we are in for a few bibliographical and historical "surprises" in this field, both in terms of the continuity of tradition between kabbala and Hasidism and in terms of the range and size of those movements and their modes of penetration into Jewish society. On both counts, see *Dinim ve-hanhagot adam,* attributed to R. D. Oppenheim (Jasieniec, 1747, and later editions), but which, judging by the unadorned style, was not written by him but by another author (and see the list of R. D. Oppenheim's works in *Or hayyim* by R. Hayyim Mikhl, pp. 315–318, in which the *Dinim* is not included); and *Zeh sefer mussar,* printed in Szklów in 1783, in which the printer states that "it was found in manuscript, but the name of the author is missing and cannot be established even after exhaustively checking all the pages," but whose content indicates that it was written by the same author who wrote *Zer zahav,* a Bible commentary (he quotes passages that he wrote in *Zeh sefer mussar*—see "Va-yiqra"—and in addition relates on a number of occasions his experiences while staying in Jerusalem and in communities in Turkey: sec. 46, p. 5a; sec. 77, p. 10b; sec. 85, p. 12a). See Yaari in *Qiryat sefer,* vol. 22, p. 55; and Scholem, *Qiryat sefer,* vol. 22, pp. 308–310.

15. Jost, *Geschichte der Israeliten* (1828) vol. 9, p. 44.
16. Graetz, *Geschichte der Juden*, vol. 11, p. 107 (Hebrew edition, p. 79).
17. Dubnow, *Toledot ha-hasidut*, pp. 34, 62, 329–330, 401.
18. Horodetzky, *Ha-hasidut ve-ha-hasidim* (1922), vol. 1, Introduction, pp. xiii, li, lii.
19. Buber, "Reshit ha-hasidut," p. 206 (see n. 8).
20. See *Zion*, vol. 6, pp. 89–93; vol. 7, p. 28.
21. Scholem, *Major Trends*, pp. 325–326.
22. Horodetzky, *Ha-hasidut*, pt. 4, p. 13.
23. Buber, "Reshit ha-hasidut," p. 207, and footnote.
24. Dubnow, *Toledot ha-hasidut*, p. 42.
25. The zaddik's entire life is a service to God. Even in his private life, nothing is fortuitous. Everything has symbolic significance. And if "at the moment he awakes a certain verse pops into his head, he will think about it and see that the verse was meant to reprove him or to teach him something" (*Darkhei sedeq* (1796), sec. 78). For that reason, the zaddik took care with every single action, while his Hasidim took heed and noted everything, and later related what they had seen, based on the assumption that nothing was as simple as it might look, but rather carried great symbolic meaning and hinted at "weighty things." This "symbolic" approach to surface facts no doubt influenced the character and orientation of the Hasidic tradition. But even as such, we are not dealing here with ordinary "legend," because there is a prior and deliberate idea at work here. See, for example, the tale in *Shivhei ha-Besht* about the Besht's youthful employment as a teacher's aide, escorting young children to the schoolroom and to the chapel, where he led them in prayer "with a pleasing voice" and caused "great contentment on high, like the joy produced by the Levites who sang in the ancient Temple." This is clearly a deliberate prefiguring of the Besht's later activities and his battle with Satan through the medium of prayer. Or see, as well, *Ramatayim sofim* (Warsaw, 1881), p. 32, the story about the Besht that hints at his messianic role and his resemblance to David.
26. See the Introduction to *Shivhei ha-Besht:* "And, for our many sins, faith has declined terribly. . . . And so we have decided to write of these awesome things . . . and I have recorded all this so that my children and their children might remember it and it will strengthen their faith in God and His Torah and in the zaddikim." See also *Siftei saddiqim* (1862), p. 58b: "And this is a great principle, whenever a zaddik wishes to bestow some benefit on someone, then he must infuse that person with faith that the good thing will come to him from that zaddik." On this, and on the different forms of Hasidic tales of zaddikim and their motifs, see the perceptive article by Ben-Yehezkel, "Le-mahut ha-hasidut," *Ha-shiloah* 17 (1901), pp. 226–227.
27. The period in which the collections of tales about the zaddikim were published (with the exception of *Shivhei ha-Besht* and the tales of R. Nahman of Bratslav) was the period in which Hasidic dynasties proliferated, each one with its own claim to fame. On the embellishment of the

record of the "founding fathers," see, for example, *No'am elimelekh*, "Korah"; *Derekh emunah u-ma'aseh rav* (on the "zaddik"); *Beit aharon*, selections; *'Irin qadishin, le-yom hilulah*.

28. See *Darkhei sedeq* (1796), sec. 42, p. 71. An see also: *Derekh emunah u-ma'aseh rav*, letter A, sec. 16.

29. See, e.g., *Sefer ha-middot* by R. Nahman of Bratslav, "Zaddik": "The praise one gives the zaddikim is like praising God, for through telling the good works of zaddikim one draws closer to them."

30. See Yaakov Yosef, *Sofnat peaneah*, "Teruma": " 'Find yourself a master,' this refers to greatness, for then he can struggle with the impurities *[qelip-pot]*" (Piotrkow edn., 1787, p. 186); "For (the zaddik) is entitled to dignify and elevate himself, not for that purpose as such, but so that his words might be better heeded" (ibid., p. 175); "And thus He had to descend [hidden] in a cloud to reach the level of the multitude, which is that realm of *malkhut* called the 'I'; and it is good to draw close in piety to the 'I'; and when he surrounds himself with a degree of majesty and pride, then people will be drawn to join with him" (*Kutonet passim*, "Sav"). Compare Yaakov Yosef, *Ben-porat yosef*, "Va-yaqhel": "It seems to me that the zaddik must sometimes take on unworthy qualities for the sake of heaven"; see, too, the letter of R. Mendel of Witebsk in *Pri ha-ares* (Zytomierz edn., p. 76): "Some of the great rabbis of our day are gifted with speech and are quite able to speak up for themselves." On this, see also the words of R. Pinehas of Korzec regarding "some zaddikim who have not even stopped at telling lies" (in Horodetzky, *Ha-hasidut*, vol. 1, pp. 145–147, quoted from a ms). See also *Zikhron tov*, p. 18 (section 26).

31. The custom of the zaddik who tells stories about himself goes back to the days of the Besht. See *Degel mahaneh efrayim*, "Balaq," and elsewhere. It was accepted practice among later generations, too. See, e.g., *Ramatayim sofim*, pt. 1, pp. 168, 228, 247; pt. 2, pp. 21, 29, 34; and *Zikhron tov*, p. 20 (sec. 38). It is mentioned in other sources as well.

32. Compare: *Degel mahaneh efrayim*, liqutim, "Tesaveh," citing the Besht, "sometimes the Torah must be clothed in outer layers in order for it to penetrate the hearts of the people"; and "the zaddik, no matter what worldly stories are told or related to him, always looks at the inner holy essence of the way they are told," etc. (ibid., "Va-yera"). "Thus I heard it [said] of my great grandfather—may his memory in the next world be everlasting—who told stories of external [i.e., profane] matters and in this way he serves God with his pure wisdom" (ibid., "Va-yeshev"); "And as we know, there are some people whose [spirituality] must be awakened through stories" (ibid., "Ki tissa").

33. This is the method, I believe, that should guide historical inquiry into Hasidic legends and stories, if we wish to establish—not merely guess at —their historical value. This approach is applied in the general study of hagiography: see Delahaye, *Les légendes hagiographiques* (Brussels, 1906).

34. Scholem (*Major Trends*, p. 322) correctly points to the importance of "the

Hasidic writers' penchant for epigrammatic maxims" for the popularization of Hasidic teachings. But these literary forms, along with their "almost
modern style," are not purely literary, because of the fact that Hasidic
"Torah" was fundamentally an oral tradition and it was meant for the
spiritual guidance of the individual. This is also related to the prophetic
nature of Hasidism, as will be explained below. On the language of Hasidism, see also: Gulkowitsch, *Das kulturhistorische Bild d. Chassidismus*
(Tartu, 1938), pp. 88–95.

35. Dubnow, *Toledot ha-hasidut*, p. 21.

36. Wettstein (*Qadmoniyot mi-pinqasaot yeshanim*, p. 10) contends that according to regulations from Cracow in 1595, "the wardens shall cast
ballots from among the names of all those who pay taxes for the upkeep
of the community"—that is, the first round of electors, those who would
choose a panel of five to appoint all the communal officials, were selected
from among the pool of all taxpayers. This understanding of the first stage
of the election process has been the accepted view among historians:
Dubnow (*Voskhod* 2 (1894), p. 93, in his essay on communal regulatiofis),
Balaban (in his essay on the *kahal* in *Istoriia evreiskago naroda* [Moscow,
1914], Vol. 11, p. 143), and many others. Schorr (*Organizacya Żydów w
Polsce*] [1899], p. 21) concluded that "selection of the rabbi and *kahal*
chairmen was carried out by the members of the community "[pospólstwo
gminne]". On this term and its use, see Halperin in *Qiryat sefer* 19, p. 96.
But the Cracow regulations of 1595 which Balaban published (in *Jahrbuch
d. jued.-liter. Gesellschaft* 10 [1912]), where the voting system is discussed
(pp. 315–316), explicitly state that "This is how selection is to take place:
chairmen and *tovim* [leading members] and board members *[kahal]* may
each cast one vote for someone who is unrelated to them . . . [including]
one who may be from outside *kahal* ranks." Clearly, then, the number of
ballots from which the wardens would choose the nine appointees must
correspond to the number of "chairmen, *tovim* and *kahal*"—i.e., twenty-
three (four chairmen, five *tovim*, and fourteen chosen as the *'edah* (council)
of the *kahal*). A candidate from outside the ranks of the existing board
could only be nominated by someone who was himself a member of the
board. See also: Dubnow, *Divrei yemei 'am 'olam*, pt. 6, p. 189, who notes
that the chairmen "were elected once a year, during the intermediate days
of Passover, by electors who were chosen by lot," and adds that "in
Cracow elections were organized in a three-tiered system . . . [under which]
the initial electors inscribed on their ballots the name of one of the respected members of the community . . . [and] the first nine names taken
out of the ballot box were the appointed electors." But Dubnow did not
point out that this first group of voters were the *kahal* board itself, and
that this system was followed not only in Cracow but elsewhere as well.
On this, see also Balaban, "Ustrój Kahalu w Polsce," in the Polish-Jewish
historical quarterly, *Kwartalnik* 1, no. 2 (1912), pp. 30–32, where he
discusses the voting systems in various communities, and argues that there

was no substantial distinction in this between the Poznań community and others. In fact, "the electors chose as officials only close associates and relatives," so that "no new candidate was ever given a post" (Balaban, *Lublin (1919)*, pp. 68–69). The voting system insured that "only rarely" was a new man (homo novus) able to reach the ranks of *kahal* leadership, because the two- or three-tiered system guaranteed that only the few leading families could obtain the vacant post (Balaban, "Ustrój gminy Żydowskiej w Polsce w XVI–XX wieku," in *Głos gminy Żydowskiej* [Feb. 1938], p. 30). But even here the main point was not emphasized, namely, that the selection of the electors themselves was carried out by the same ruling clique. Compare: Balaban, "Ma'amadam ha-huqi shel ha-yehudim ve-irgunam," in *Beit yisrael be-polin,* ed. by Halperin (1948), vol. 1, pp. 46–48; see also I. Halperin, "Mivneh ha-va'adim be-eiropah ha-mizrahit ve-ha-merkazit ba-meiot ha-17 ve-ha-18," *World Congress of Jewish Studies* (Jerusalem, 1946), vol. 1, pp. 439–443.

37. According to the Cracow rules of 1595, and also according to those of Żółkiew (the compromise of 1690); see S. Buber, *Qiryah nisgavah* (1903), p. 102 (app. 20, par. 1).

38. See par. 7 of the Dubno communal regulations of 1 Sivan 1717 (published in *YIVO historishe shriftn,* (1937), vol. 2, p. 86, by I. Levitats): "The following are eligible for the balloting . . . and also anyone who has held office, within two years of having left that post." Compare Buber, *Qiryah nisgavah,,* p. 103 (app., sec. 6, par. 6), on the co-opting of "those who left office in that year" onto the group involved in choosing the rabbi. See also Brafman, *Kniga kagala,* doc. 112 (1799), on the decision to give voting privileges to three men who had been chairmen but who were not members of the assembly. Not everyone who had been a chairman was automatically able to vote. See Brafman, ibid., p. 234 (1802), on the decision of the community "to elevate R. Faytl son of R. Yishaq . . . to the rank of one who has been a chairman" for all public matters. The decision was adopted unanimously and "according to all the rules and regulations."

39. See the regulations of Petrowic (Mohylew prov.) of 1777 (cited by Dubnow in *Voskhod* 2 [1894], p. 100), par. 2, according to which the right to vote was also extended to wealthy taxpayers (paying a rate of 4 zloty per hundred) and householders, even if they had held no *kahal* position. But this was explicitly said to be a provisional arrangement, to last for five years; after that period, this right would not be extended any more to those who in the interim period had not been appointed to any official post. See also the regulations of Krotoszyn of 1728 (in the article by Berger on the Jews of Krotoszyn in *Monatsschrift für Geschichte und Wissenschaft des Judentums (MGWJ)* [1907], p. 362), according to which the right to vote was given to those paying a tax of 90 zloty per annum and who had paid it regularly for four consecutive years. The correspondence between the electors and *kahal* is reflected in the way these regulations were phrased. See *Pinqas medinat lita,* p. 181 (regulations of the council of 1679): "An elector is not entitled to nominate himself for any office that

he has not held previously; rather, he must stay with his previous position."
See also the Żółkiew regulations of 1626 (Buber, *Qiryah nisgavah*, p. 87):
"There shall be no more than three chairmen among the electors"; and
from the same community, in regulations passed in 1694 (section 13: ibid.,
p. 93); "The electors may not divide all the honors among themselves,
appointing themselves as leaders." Compare, too, the regulations of Zablu-
dowa passed in 1750 (S. Assaf, in *Qiryat sefer*, vol. 1 (1924–5), p. 314):
"The electors may not choose for themselves any post that they did not
hold previously."

40. See *Pinqas medinat lita,* regulations of the council of 1695, no. 499: "The
electors must appoint five leaders who have adequate means, etc., and
anyone who holds a yeshiva even though he does not have such means, is
counted as having such." See also ibid., regulations of 1761, no. 1015:
"Whoever has been a judge and is esteemed for his learning, even if he
pays only ten parts of a zloty per week, is entitled to be an elector or an
assessor." Such consideration and allowances for scholars were the norm
in all communities.

41. See *Pinqas medinat lita,* no. 519 (1720): "The assembly shall number no
more than thirty-three members." And if "in large communities there were
about forty chairmen and in the medium and small communities between
ten and twenty" (Dubnow, *Divrei yemei 'am 'olam,* pt. 6, p. 189), then in
the large communities the initial group of electors was even smaller than
the number of board members: i.e., not even all members of the communal
leadership had the right to participate in the electoral assembly; and in
small and medium-size communities, assembly members included those
who already constituted the leadership, with the addition of the distin
guished and the wealthy (those who held the degree "morenu," etc.).
Compare: Cohn, *Geschichte d. jued. Gemeinde* (Rawitsch, 1915), p. 29.

42. Compare: Israel Klausner, *Toledot ha-kehillah ha-'ivrit be-vilna* (Vilna,
1938), p. 90; and see *Pinqas medinat lita,* no. 29 (1761), p. 268, which
states that each community may "enact regulations limiting the balloting
to fifty-one slips." This retroactively validated local regulations limiting
the ballots; the aim was to block any attempt by the "nouveaux riches" to
enlarge the number of voters, an observable trend in the communities of
that time. The council fought this trend, not always with success. Thus,
note the increased ceiling of fifty-one, up from the figure of thirty-three
cited in the regulations of 1720, p. 244.

43. Compare: *Pinqas medinat lita,* regulations of the council held in Sluck,
1761, no. 57 (p. 268); preceded by local regulations, see e.g., Witebsk
regulations of 1730 (cited in translation from the ms in the essay by
Marek, "Krizis evreiskago", in *Evreiskaia starina* 12, p. 83: "From today
on, no artisan is to be admitted to the balloting." The council of 1761
only made artisans ineligible to vote in the larger communities, but this
served as a precedent for smaller communities, too. See the regulations of
Suchoraj (Mohylew prov.) of 1781: P. Marek, ibid.

44. See Klausner, *Toledot ha-kehillah,* pp. 90–93.

45. See *Taqanta de-moshe,* no. 58: "For our many sins, in our time people spare neither their wealth nor their own persons, and instead spend all their money and commit wrongdoing just in order to stand among the great ones at the top of a fragile ladder, on which the best are at the bottom and the worst are on top." See also: *Darkhei no'am,* p. 102: "Now, in recent times, people pursue high office with all their might, even those who are unworthy." See also the letter of complaint of the leaders of Minsk against "artisans wishing to make themselves heads of the *kahal*" (*Yivo historishe shriftn,* vol. 2, p. 611).

46. Compare the decision of the Dubno community, summer 1795, pronouncing a ban *(herem)* against anyone supporting the common artisans who "were first organized under a charter from our overlord the prince—and who would question the prince? But now he has changed his mind and abolished those associations, which from now on will never be mentioned or referred to again, nor may new associations be formed." The granting of a charter and its withdrawal, as well as the *herem,* are links in a process of internal struggle within the communities and the attempts by the artisans to make their weight felt in this struggle. See also the charter granted by Potocki in 1783 for the establishment of one general trades' association for all the Jewish artisans in Wladnyk, according to which all disputes among artisans were to be brought before the association, "so that they need not go to the *kahal* or the rabbi." If the verdict of the association proved unsatisfying, members were entitled to appeal to the estate owner (*Regesty i nadpisi,* vol. 3, no. 2300).

47. Compare: *Yesod yosef,* chap. 35: "He who curses the public at large ["the majority"] and defies Israel—that is, he speaks ill of the *kahal* and the *'edah,* finding fault and never looking at the good things they do—in the manner of the common people who dare to speak against them and curse them and question their decisions . . ." See also: *Pinqas medinat lita,* council of 1670 (p. 187), regulations regarding "conspirators and plotters against the *kahal* or actions of the *kahal,* including tale-bearing gossipers, etc." On the involvement of artisans in such "conspiracies," see the promise of the Witebsk artisans (11 Adar 1783) not to conspire or rebel against the *kahal* (Marek, "Krizis evreiskago," p. 88); and the order issued by the Minsk *kahal* (28 Nisan 1803) "to all the artisan associations, not to convene their assemblies except in the presence of one of the communal officials (that is, a member of the *kahal*), in accordance with the time-honored practice" (Brafman, *Kniga kagala,* pt. 2, doc. 385). See also Bershadsky, *Litovskie evreii,* pp. 46–48.

48. See the Witebsk enactment of 1730 (cited by Marek, "Krizis evreiskago," p. 83): "Because there were no previous rules to this effect, the *kahal* head may allow those artisans who already have participated in the balloting to continue to do so, but no one may place any new person of the artisan class into the assembly." Similarly, it was now forbidden to lease any form of leasehold to an artisan, the purpose of which, again, was to block

artisans' aspirations to bolster their voice in communal affairs: by becoming leaseholders, artisans could compete with the wealthy leaders.

49. Dubnow, *Toledot ha-hasidut*, p. 21; idem., *Divrei yemei 'am 'olam*, vol. 7, pp. 76–80, 101–102.

50. Marek, "Krizis evreiskago," p. 95.

51. See the memorandum of Avraham Hirszowicz on the changed needed to reform Jewish life ("Projekt do reformy i poprawy obyczajów starozakonnych mieszkanców Królestwa polskiego," published in the book by Smolenski, *Ostani rok sejmu wielkiego* [1897], pp. 446–451), in which Hirszowicz states: "Indeed, there is not one city that is properly run on a sound footing, and funds collected from the inhabitants are simply wasted to no purpose. No one questions the fact, but the Jews themselves lack the power to institute the required reforms, for they cannot reach any mutual agreement among themselves" (p. 450).

52. See also, for example, my essay, " 'Aliyato shel r. yehuda ha-levi le-eres yisrael," in *Minhah le-david*, pp. 161–162, on daily life as reflected in liturgical poetry, and its historical value.

53. For Jewish historiography, in which literary sources constitute the main primary documents—sometimes the only ones—for the internal life of the Jews over many centuries, it is especially important to explore and illuminate these methodological issues which, even in general history, still represent a virgin territory. In our field they have not even been touched upon.

54. I. Sosis, in "Tsu der sotsyaler geshikhte fun yidn in lite un vaysrusland," *Tsaytshrift far yidishe geshikhte demografye un ekonomik* 1 (1926), pp. 14–25, discusses social history and *mussar* from the sixteenth to the eighteenth centuries. He deals with literature in Yiddish and its sympathetic approach to the lower classes, dwelling in particular on *Yesod yosef* and *Qav ha-yashar*, but does not touch on this question.

55. Traces of the sermonic form may be found in every selection. The great majority of these authors were, in fact, preachers (see the introductions to their books and the rabbinical endorsements). It should be added that because *mussar* literature was intended to instruct and teach people, the authors were always mindful of the target audience, the living reader. This is reflected even in stylistic details. The exhortatory and castigating sections in these books are written in very simple Hebrew, whereas scholarly insights are written in a heavier, rabbinic-Talmudic and philosophical style.

56. See also: B. Groethuysen, *Die Entstehung der buergerlichen Welt- und Lebensanschauung in Frankreich* (1927), which made extensive use of Jesuit sermonic and instructional materials as historical sources. He also stressed (vol. 1, p. 241) that "the specific mode of expressing" an idea is far more important in illuminating historical reality than is "the overall approach."

57. *Toharot ha-qodesh*, pt. 1, p. 22.

58. Compare: *Taqanta de-moshe*, no. 24: "*Maror*—this is an acronym mean-

ing, 'from head to foot, it is devoid of innocence.' " This is a regular theme in the *mussar* literature of the time.

59. *Ohel rahel*, p. 15b.
60. *Yesod yosef*, chap. 36.
61. *Zer'a berakh shlishi*, commentary to Tractate Berakhot, p. 14a.
62. *Mishmeret ha-qodesh:* "hilkhot ribbit."
63. *Toharot ha-qodesh*, pt. 1, p. 22b, and Introduction.
64. Maharshal, *Responsa*, no. 28.
65. Maharam, *Responsa*, no. 120.
66. *Toharot ha-qodesh*, Introduction.
67. See also, e.g., *Pinqas medinat lita*, no. 508 (1700), regarding "heads of the community of Minsk" accused of "such a case of informing that has never been heard of in all Israel."
68. *Toharot ha-qodesh*, pt. 1, pp. 22a, 34b, and Introduction.
69. *Yesod yosef*, chap. 36.
70. *Taqanta de-moshe*, nos. 48, 54. Compare *Yesod yosef*, chap. 6: " 'He shall pay with his life for his bread'—that is, he jeopardizes himself through actions that border on fraud and stealing in order to support himself."
71. *Yesod yosef*, chap. 8.
72. *Taqanta de-moshe*, no. 50. Compare, *Nazad ha-dem'a*, p. 1a; "The wicked tells himself: God will not count it against us. We do it in order to serve God joyfully." *Mishmeret ha-qodesh*, Introduction: *Taqanta de-moshe*, nos. 63, 68; the "popular sayings of the time" cited by the author give us important clues as to the social history of the day.
73. *Nazad ha-dem'a*, p. 1a.
74. *Taqanta de-moshe*, no. 23.
75. *Mishmeret ha-qodesh*. As is evident from what is said there, many people engaged in this practice: "For the most part, business suffers because of this, even if people make profits . . . and of them it is said that anger is better than laughter." Speculation was apparently widespread in such a vital commodity as salt, "a necessity for everyone." See also *Pinqas medinat lita*, nos. 70, 94, citing regulations passed in 1623 against speculating, because of the artificial inflation of prices, and see laws of interest, ibid. Compare *Zer'a berakh shlishi*, p. 14b.
76. See *Pinqas medinat lita*, pp. 308–311: verdict on money changers (1761). This may be regarded as an attempt to impose public supervision in that area in which many people were engaged "even when they did not have a communal license," merely because "they want to take up this business." From the various restrictions and conditions we learn about the widespread speculation and exploitation that were the norm in that business, and about the sanctions threatened against violators (apart from "barring him from his business" and "loss of his residence permit," these included loss of membership in the communal assembly, removal of the privilege of being addressed as *morenu* (our teacher), and loss of membership in all sacred societies). These imply that those involved in money changing in-

cluded respected members of society. A regulation had been on record since 1623 against "trading in currency" (no. 92), but had lost any force of law by this time (1761). The council tried merely to contain as far as possible the damage and the losses anticipated from the concentration of this business in artisans' hands, and to that end set up a monitoring system.

77. See *Pinqas medinat lita,* regulations of 1667, no. 605; compare *Toharot ha-qodesh,* pt. 2, p. 36b: "as it is well known how many lenders take interest twice the amount of the principal." See also *'Ateret sevi* by R. Sevi-Hirsh of Vilna (R. Sevi-Hirsh "Harif") [Jasieniec, 1722], pt. 2, responsum no. 74: "In our area it is the custom to lend money for a year and to take profits of about twenty percent. . . . If someone borrows for a year and at some point chooses to repay the loan [before the end of its term], the lender takes a half a zloty per week for every hundred zloty, that is, twenty-five percent." True, the term "about" shows that the figures cited are not necessarily precise, but the lack of precision leans far in the direction of underestimation, relative to what was the actual practice.

78. *Pinqas medinat lita,* no. 680 (1673), lowered the rate to 43 percent per annum; no. 713 (1676) reduced it further to 35 percent; no. 782 (1684) again reduced it, to 31 percent. See also Sosis, "Der yidisher seym in lite un vaysrusland," *Tsaytshrift far yidishe geshikhte, demografye un ekonomik* 2–3 (1928), pp. 32–33. Sosis points out that, in addition, the council had an interest in conserving the financial means of communal taxpayers, so that tax assessments could be met. As a debtor body itself, the council also sought a general reduction in credit rates.

79. *Pinqas medinat lita,* no. 671 (1670); no. 711 (1676): "according to what obtains among merchants and prices in their communities"; no. 966 (1720); no. 1013 (1761): on "a debtor who has fled."

80. *Zer'a berakh shlishi,* p. 14b; *Mishmeret ha-qodesh,* "Hanhagat masa u-matan"; Y. L. Margaliot *Hibburei liqutim* (Venice, 1715), author's Introuction; *Ohel rahel,* "Yeted ha-din," p. 16a; *Toharot ha-qodesh,* pt. 2, p. 7b: discussing schoolteachers, some of whom also lent money on interest. Compare Responsa, *Meqom shmuel* (1737), no. 1. It should be noted that, apart from the rabbis themselves, there was practically an entire separate class of educated people "who are Torah scholars and moneylenders." See, e.g., Margaliot, *'Ir dubna,* p. 104; *Pinqas medinat lita,* nos. 233, 607, 783, 778—regulations regarding reduction of their tax burden. Cf. *Darkhei no'am,* p. 49b; Responsa, *Nod'a biyhuda,* Tinyana, "Yoreh de'ah," 42; *Mishmeret ha-qodesh,* opening of the book; *Darkhei no'am,* p. 86b.

81. *Ohel rahel,* p. 19b. References to such "protected Jews" appear in non-Jewish sources as well. See, e.g., *Regesty i nadpisi,* vol. 3, p. 55 (no. 1956), instructions of the Braclaw gentry to their Sejm delegates in 1748, asking that they lodge a complaint against Prince Martin Radziwill who, while he was under the influence of a certain Jew, Szymon Bulzowicz, robbed their money. They therefore wished to see "this man [the prince] restrained" and "the Jew . . . who is the instigator . . . condemned to death."

82. *Toharot ha-qodesh,* Introduction.

83. *Ohel ya'aqov,* by R. Ya'aqov Krantz, "Bereishit."

84. *Ohel rahel,* pp. 9b, 22b.

85. See: Charewiczowa, *Dzieje miasta Zloczowa* (1929), pp. 62–63. The author's contention that the appointment was the result of misinformation is naive. The practice was as routine as the (analogous) confirmation of a charter for the artisans' associations in Dubno and in Siauliai (see n. 12 above), and so forth.

86. This, too, was fairly routine, a form of extortion that had always been practiced. See responsa of R. Moses Isserles (Rama), no. 123: "But if the ruler appointed him and the *kahal* accepted him accordingly, then it is valid." See also the very first charter granted to the Jews of Lublin (1556), which promised the Jews the right to choose their own leader, without interference by the authorities: J. Riabinin, *Materialy do historii miasta Lublina* (1938), p. 75, no. 218; M. Balaban, *Die Judenstadt von Lublin* (1919), p. 20. In each instance, intervention by the authorities ending with the community's "acceptance" was nothing but a way of extorting funds from the Jewish community.

87. Responsa, *Neot desheh,* by R. S. Eybeschütz, no. 26; *Yesod yosef,* chap. 17.

88. Dubnow, *Divrei yemei 'am 'olam,* pt. 7, pp. 76–80. Contemporary literature (responsa, *mussar,* sermons) is rich in descriptions of this, detailing various oppressive measures of particular fiendishness, such as prohibitions against the sale of *hames* (non-Passover food supplies) over Passover (Responsa, *Giv'at shaul,* no. 104), forced closure of synagogues on holy days (e.g., in Husiatyn, see *Regesty i nadpisi,* vol. 3, no. 1810), and violence, as well as Jewish ingenuity in coping with a never-ending struggle (see, e.g., *Yesod yosef,* chap. 77).

89. *Neot desheh,* no. 26.

90. *Taqanta de-moshe,* no. 13; *Or 'olam* by Y. L. Margaliot, second Introduction (Prague, 1783); *Zer'a berakh shlishi,* p. 29b. Here the preacher expressed his amazement that King Ahasuerus had not simply appointed rabbis for the Jewish communities of Persia, rather than authorize their wholesale destruction, for the former would have brought him greater revenue than Haman's plan would have. This sermon is very instructive about the spirit of protest that animated not just the preacher who spoke these words, but his audience as well. See also I. A. Kleinman, "Propovednik-buntovnik XVIII veka," *Evreiskaia starina* 12 (1928), pp. 179–188.

91. Hirszowicz's memorandum in Smolenski, *Ostatni rok,* p. 449; he proposed that "rabbis be appointed only in the large cities so that the small communities might be spared the rabbis' extortions and exploitation." See also: *Ohel rahel,* "Yeted ha-din," p. 15b.

92. Responsa, *Panim meirot,* pt. 2, no. 152; Responsa, *Giv'at shaul,* Introduction (1775 edn.). See also the letter from the community of Leszno (1759), published in the supplement to the journal, *Ha-melis* (St. Petersburg, 1902),

pp. 160–169, which dealt with the rabbinate in Little Poland: "It is their practice to purchase their post for money from the lords of the land"; *Toharot ha-qodesh*, pt. 2, pp. 8b, 9b.

93. *Taqanta de-moshe*, no. 27; *Siftei saddiqim, liqutim*, p. 71b; see also *Mishmeret ha-qodesh*, "Middot yesharot" ("practices for Thursday"); *Zer'a berakh shlishi*, p. 14b.

94. Emden, *Sefer ha-hitavqut*, p. 11.

95. See Asaf, "Le-qorot ha-rabbanut," *Reshumot* 3, pp. 216–271: section 10, on rabbinical appointments by governmental authorities and estate owners; see also Harkavy, "Hadashim gam yeshanim" (appendix to Graetz-S. P. Rabbinowitz, *Divrei yemei Yisrael*, vol. 7), p. 13, communal regulations from Tyszewicz of 1583. They were confirmed in 1587 and 1590, and were cited in general form in the regulations adopted in Cracow in 1595. See *Jahrbuch d. jued.-liter. Gesellschaft* 10 (1912), p. 309. Later, they were again reconfirmed at the Jaroslaw fair [conference] of 1640, on the recommendation of R. Yom Tov Lipmann Heller. The regulation was reissued several times with a public declaration (see *Pinqas pozna*).

96. Maharsha, *Hiddushei aggadot*, Sanhedrin 7b: "For gold and silver . . ."; ibid., Shabbat 119b: "Rava said . . ."; ibid., Sotah 40a.

97. In the eighteenth century (toward mid-century), the Ginzburg clan supplied some of the major communities (Pinsk, Vilna, Mohylew, Witebsk, Mir, Wizin, etc.) with eleven chief rabbis *[av bet din]*, three rabbis and rabbinical judges, and other communal functionaries. In Poland, around the same time (e.g., in Lublin, Opatów, Pinczów) and in the Ukraine and Galicia (Ostróg, Brody, and Żółkiew), the Halperins supplied about fifteen chief rabbis, almost ten leaders of the Four Lands Council, and several other rabbis, judges, etc. The same applies to other prominent families, such as the Katzenellenbogens, Hurwitzes, Rapoports, etc. See *Da'at qedoshim*, pp. 57–76, 198–213. These lists, moreover, are incomplete (as a matter of course). See the regulations of the council of 1720 (no. 913), *Pinqas medinat lita*, against the appointment of "any rabbi of a community *[av bet din]* out of marital [family] considerations or the exchange of rabbinical posts." This was directed, in part, against the prominent clans. Cf. Marek, "Krizis evreiskago," p. 50.

98. See *Pinqas medinat lita*, no. 912 (1720): "No rabbi is to be appointed unless he has been married [at least] twelve years"; ibid., no. 971, on the minimum age requirement for communal lay leaders in major cities. See also *Toharot ha-qodesh*, pt. 2, p. 9a: "Every wealthy man who has a son, even if he is a mere twenty years of age, strives to win a rabbinical post for him right away. Even more does this apply to the great rabbis who serve in the communal leadership, who, without exerting themselves very much, or sometimes through using their influence and power [act in like manner] and they [lay board members considering candidates for rabbinical posts], out of deference, must bow to the eminent rabbis' wishes." See also *Pinqas medinat lita*, regulation of 1761: "It is forbidden to appoint a rabbi or

teacher of the law who is under the age of twenty." The lower minimum age here reflects yet another victory for the leading families and powerful figures.

99. See *Toharot ha-qodesh,* pt. 2, p. 9a, on "the devious machinations" of those rabbis "whose entire knowledge consists of what their bundles of books tell them, and who, when they preach, find that their words are not easily accepted, for they are not terribly well-versed [in rabbinics]." See also: *Ohel rahel,* p. 16b: "Those teachers who take up [their posts] for the sake of money alone are unable to preach on the holy days . . . for they cheated their way into their positions or occupy them only temporarily."

100. Yaavetz, *Megillat sefer,* p. 123, characterizes R. Yehezqel Katzenellenbogen in a classic description that fits so many Polish rabbis of that time: "The rabbi is well-regarded by the important members of the community, and his modesty is widely praised; but woe to such false modesty, which is nothing but a mask for flattering the rich and the powerful, that they may have a free hand in enslaving people as they wish, and to his direct benefit." See also: *Tal orot,* pp. 71–72: "They prefer to choose one of their own kind for rabbi. They can be secure in the knowledge that [such rabbis] will not raise a hue and cry against the criminals, for his associates would retort, 'We have seen you behave as we do.' "

101. See *Pinqas medinat lita,* no. 925 (1720): "The kahal is forbidden to intervene in civil suits, and the community chairmen—and certainly the judges and bailiffs—are strictly forbidden to follow the will of the kahal in such a case, under penalty of the ban." This prohibition was repeated in 1761 (ibid., no. 987), and the threatened sanctions ("whoever interferes [in such matters] will have to pay [the damages] and he will be deposed from office") imply that such cases occurred in reality. And the addendum that "the court may co-opt two leaders [from the *kahal*] in case of need" in fact indicates a victory for the communal establishment. See ibid., no. 888 (1695); and *She'elot u-teshuvot geonei batrai,* no. 90 (responsum of the BaH), regarding three lay judges who found in favor of the claimant, from which we see how the kahal attempted to assume the authority of the court. See also: *Pinqas medinat lita,* no. 394, from the same period (1634), that prohibits the *kahal* from interfering in civil suits. See also: *Yesod yosef,* chap. 42: "This warning is doubly appropriate for the communal leaders who sit in judgment, and in this they violate the teaching of the law. They pass judgment according to rough criteria, according to their own inclinations and unfair biases. For as a matter of course the verdicts of householders [lay arbiters] and of [trained] judges are poles apart: the innocent are judged guilty and the guilty, innocent." See also *She'elot u-teshuvot geonei batrai,* no. 48, on the relationship between court verdicts and out-of-court settlements, where the judge in question was able to charge a higher fee for arbitrating a compromise settlement than for a formal court hearing. See also *Pinqas medinat lita,* no. 985; compare P. Marek, in *Evreiskaia starina* 1, pp. 161–174, on tax assessors in Lithuanian communities in the seventeenth and eighteenth centuries.

102. See *Pinqas medinat lita,* no. 925: "And it is also forbidden for the kahal to interfere in setting tax assessments."

103. The passages quoted here come from the following sources (in order of citation): *Taqanta de-moshe; Or 'olam,* by Rabbi Y. Margolis (1783); *Toharot ha-qodesh,* pt. 2, p. 6b; *Darkhei no'am,* p. 102; *Beit middot,* p. 38; *Ohel rahel,* p. 27a; *Zer'a berakh shlishi,* p. 15a.

104. *Rish'ei ares:* "wicked of the earth"; in *mussar* literature this is an allusion to *rashei ares:* "leaders of the land," i.e., the communal or provincial and national leadership.

105. The phrases quoted here are taken, in order, from: *Hillel ben shahar,* Introduction; *Nazad ha-dem'a,* pt. 1, p. 1; *Yesod yosef,* chap. 9; *Tal orot,* p. 30b.

106. *Taqanta de-moshe,* no. 68. See also *Toledot shlomo maimon,* chap. 2: The precocious young Solomon Maimon, deriding the patriarch Jacob for having foolishly rejected supremacy in the material world [which he left to Esau so that he, Jacob, might hold sway in the spiritual realm], expressed not just Maimon's incisive individual perceptivity but also the spirit of the age.

107. *Qav ha-yashar,* chap. 2.

108. Responsa, *Yad eliyahu,* no. 48.

109. *Yesod yosef,* chap. 36; ibid., chap. 11; compare chap. 64: "One must take special care [with this], and even he who is highly respected and a scholar must show respect to all men."

110. The views cited here come from the following sources, in order of citation: *Qav ha-yashar,* chap. 65; *Yesod yosef,* chap. 83; *Qav ha-yashar,* chap. 82; *Taqanta de-moshe,* no. 15, par. 14; *Yesod yosef,* chap. 36; *Ohel rahel,* p. 24a. Compare *Ohel rahel,* p. 27a: "Those who 'turned the hearts' of these tyrants . . . will be held accountable . . . down the generations . . . for their sins, without benefit of mercy or compassion."

111. *Taqanta de-moshe,* no. 29. Compare Hirszowicz's memorandum (Smolenski, op. cit.), p. 449: "What is the need for the satins, velvets and expensive furs that Jews deck themselves out in? Or the pearls, precious stones and headdresses that their wives preen themselves with? The lust for luxury destroys them, drives them to the brink of poverty, burdens them with debts and ultimately ruins them completely."

112. For the economic rationale for sumptuary laws, see the additional restrictions relating to "[someone] marrying off a daughter and receiving [for the purpose] charitable assistance or help from family" (*Pinqas medinat lita,* nos. 185, 314); and the definition of a class of well-to-do people not included under the terms stated in the regulation (ibid., nos. 184, 313, 339); for considerations of gentile opinion ("jealousy") and public grief in the wake of the persecutions of 1648–49, see ibid., nos. 511, 1026; also local regulations to this effect: *Dubna rabbati,* p. 58: "Lest they become a cause of envy, because of their conspicuousness, in the eyes of the nations amid whom we dwell in this bitter exile" (regulation of 1747).

According to the regulation of the council, each community was to supervise and strictly enforce the provisions regarding clothing and jewelry (*Pinqas medinat lita,* nos. 468 [1646], 499 [1652], 724 [1674]), "in accord with local conditions amid the temper of the times." See also A. Frenk, in the anthology *Istoriia evreiskogo naroda* (Moscow, 1914), vol. 11, p. 259, who cites several local minute-books to the effect that luxurious clothing and jewelry "are ruining both communities and individuals, and arouse the envy of the gentiles." Economic considerations prompted the enactment of "permanent regulations" regarding celebrations (*Dubna rabbati,* p. 109; *Pinqas medinat lita,* nos. 327, 408). After 1648 closer attention was devoted to this; see ibid., nos. 603, 669–674.

113. See the letters of the Russian ambassador in Poland (Bulgakov, 1792), reporting rumors in Warsaw regarding the collapse of plans to expel the Jews from Poland, once it was determined that Jews owed Poles more than the market value of their property. Jews, like the Polish upper class, lived beyond their means (*Regesty i nadpisi,* vol. 3, no. 1938).

114. "Through gentile courts": the abbreviation used here in the text also alludes to the analogous "through the laws of the nations." The rest of the statement bears out the parallelism by speaking of "the laws of Israel." *Dubna rabbati,* pp. 121–122. The date of the oath is 1779.

115. *Toharot ha-qodesh,* pt. 2, p. 10b; see also Weinryb, "Mi-pinqasei ha-kahal be-kraka," *Tarbiz* 8, p. 205: "The act committed by the board chairman . . . who forged with his own hand a [fraudulent] transaction worth two thousand and stole it from the gentiles . . ." (document dating from 1728).

116. *Dubna rabbati,* pp. 97–103. The verdict dates from 1766. R. Meir, as the verdict indicates, was president of the Four Lands Council. He did not appear before the judges, nor did "the honorable Mr. Hayyim of Kremenetz [Krzemieniec] who was found to have received travel expenses for fictitious trips, for which he did not return the funds." A week after the verdict, "the president . . . reached a settlement with the kahal" which was noted (without specifying the terms!) "for posterity" in the communal records.

117. *Zer'a berakh shlishi,* p. 15a; on the relations between the lay leadership and this preacher, see the author's Introduction.

118. Responsa, *Beit ya'aqov,* no. 33; *'Edut be-ya'aqov* p. 68b; this occurred during the course of the controversy between Jacob Emden and Jonathan Eybeschütz. The case of attempted bribery relates to R. Nahman Syrkin of Brisk [Brześć]: *'Ir tehilah,* p. 29.

119. I. Schiper, "Poylishe regesten tsu der geshikhte funem vad arba arotsoys, in *"Yivo Historishe shriftn,* vol. 1, p. 88.

120. *Nazad ha-dem'a,* pt. 1, p. 1.

121. "When a man of middling rank offers a greeting to a wealthy man, the wealthy one turns away. And if a poor man greets him, all the more . . . does he pretend not to notice" (*Qav ha-yashar,* chap. 84). This is a stock theme in contemporary sermons.

122. Memorandum of Hirszowicz, in Smolenski, *Ostatni rok sejmu wielkiego*

(1897), p. 448. Dr. Moshe Marcuse in *Sefer ha-refuot:* see Zalman Reisen, *Fun mendelson biz mendele* (Warsaw, 1923), p. 97.

123. See the regulation of the Council of 1670 (*Pinqas medinat lita,* no. 674): "If someone tries to come and settle in our district, he will be locked out of the city and will no receive a residence permit, even temporarily."

124. See Shatzky, *Gzeyres ta"kh* (Wilno, 1938), p. 92.

125. Passages about the poor quoted here are taken from Hirszowicz's memorandum (see n. 122), p. 448; the views expressed by Dohm (C. W. Dohm, *Ueber die buergerliche Verbesserung d. Juden,* [1781], section 1, 88); *Sefer ha-refuot* by Moshe Marcuse (cited by Reisen, *Fun mendelson biz mendele,* p. 97); Responsa, *Bat 'einai,* by R. Issachar Dov of the family of Sevi of Zloczow (Dubno, 1798), no. 4; *Dubna rabbati,* p. 111 (regulations of 1775, par. 20). The community whose poor accounted for 8 percent of the Jewish population was Zytomierz. See also Korobkov in *Evreiskaia starina* 1910 (loc. cit.), p. 377.

126. Seven percent of the inhabitants of Zytomierz. In Vilna in 1765 there were 133 listed as poor in a population of 3,174 (Klausner, *Toledot ha-kehillah ha-'ivrit be-vilna,* p. 52). This figure evidently refers to actual beggars and did not include those who lived in the community-supported hospice. This would seem to be indicated by the division by "class" which listed: "householders, tenants, servants [living with their employers] and the poor [in public shelters]."

127. See also: Zarchin, *Jews in the Province of Posen* (Philadelphia, 1939), pp. 107–108: regulations regarding servants (men and women) which clearly indicate that most of these were "strangers," people from out of town.

128. Responsa, R. Hayyim Ha-Cohen Rapoport: "Even ha-'ezer," no. 21. The place was Biała Cerkiew in the Kiev province; *Hibburei liqutim,* by R. Selig Margolis of Kalisz (Venice, 1715), author's Introduction, p. 5a. See also *Qav ha-yashar,* chap. 14. The information regarding servants is based on Responsa, *Even ha-shoham u-me'irat einayim* by R. Eliaqim Goetz ben R. Meir of Hildesheim (Dyhrenfürth, 1703). The incident took place in Poland.

129. See the table presented by Schiper in *Istoriia evreiskogo naroda,* vol. 11, p. 127, with data on "Jewish occupations in Poland, 1765–1790." According to the data, Jews in domestic service in the "Lwów district" (Lwów, Brody, Żółkiew, Zloczow, and other towns) represented 8.4 percent; in Cracow, 5.4 percent. See also Klausner, *Toledot ha-kehillah ha-ivrit be-vilna,* p. 52 (he estimates that 9 percent were employed in domestic service). Although none of these data are accurate, uniform, or reliable (and they are therefore of only limited value), they do provide a rough gauge of the place this particular class held in Jewish society. It should be noted that the Hebrew term *meshartim* sometimes denotes employed workers as well as domestic servants. See D. Weinryb, " 'Al yahasan shel ha-kehillot be-polin le-ba'alei melakhah u-po'alim," *Yediot ha-arkhiyon ve-ha-muzeyon shel tenu'at ha-'avodah* 3–4 (1938), pp. 9–22.

130. Schiper, loc. cit. The table shows that 41.7 percent of the Jews in the Lwów district were artisans; 47.8 percent in Żydaczów; 23.3 percent in Cracow. In Zolyszczyki (Podolia) servants and artisans constituted a total of 49.5 percent of the Jewish population. Wischnitzer (in "Di struktur fun yidishe tsekhn in poyln, lite un vaysrusland," *Tsaytshrift far yidishe geshikhte, demografye un ekonomik* 2–3, p. 34) estimates the artisan class as a quarter to a third of Polish Jewry, which seems quite reasonable. See also R. Mahler, "Statistik fun yidn in lubliner voyevodstvo," *Yunger historiker* 2 (1929), Table 6, according to which artisans constituted 50 percent (408 out of 808) of the Jewish urban population, but only 20 percent of the total Jewish population.

131. See Kremer, "Le-heqer ha-melakhah ve-hevrot ba'alei ha-melakhah esel yehudei polin," *Zion* 3, pp. 313–318; Wischnitzer, on Jewish artisans, in *Istoriia evreiskogo naroda*, vol. 11, pp. 210–292; Mahler, loc. cit., pp. 82–83; Klausner, *Toledot ha-kehillah ha-'ivrit be-vilna*, p. 52 (list of artisans according to trade, including about forty separate crafts). The garment crafts in particular were highly specialized, as was the food supply industry, and, to a large extent, gold- and silversmithing (all fields related in some way to religious life or which were heavily dominated by Jews).

132. Artisans' associations *[hevrot]* existed in virtually every community: "Since it is always the case, in every place, that where there are tailors they usually form a *hevrah* . . ." (Jaroslaw minute-book *[pinqas]*). We only know of specific cases from the rare contemporary documents that have survived. Known associations in the districts we have examined here were founded in 1721 (Luck), 1732 (Berdyczew), 1740 (Olyk), some time prior to 1742 (Dubno), and 1757 (Wladnyk).

133. Cited by Korobkov, loc. cit., p. 366.

134. *Sefer ha-berit*, pt. 2, "Divrei emet," article 12: "Derekh ha-qodesh," chap. 6. "I myself heard one scholar say he was angry at his parents for failing to teach him a trade while he was young, that might have supported him. [He said]: 'Father, father, why did you not teach me a trade? [Why did you] leave me dependent on others?' " Compare the status of preachers: Responsa, *Meir netivim*, pt. 1, no. 49

135. *Toledot shlomo maimon*, Introduction.

136. See Bershadsky, *Litovskie evreii*, pp. 21–22.

137. See, e.g., the reference to "rabbi to the haberdashers' association and the tailors' association" (1772), in Lewin, *Geschichte der Juden in Lissa*, p. 335; minute-book of the tailors' association in Przemyśl, regulation 3: "The rabbi, judge of this association . . ." (Schorr, *Żydzi w Przemyślu* (1903), p. 273). That was the common practice in all *hevrot*.

138. *Toledot shlomo maimon*, Introduction.

139. Descriptions are based on *Sefer ha-berit*, pt. 2, "Divrei emet," article 12: "Derekh ha-qodesh," chap. 6.

140. Descriptions from the end of the seventeenth century, based on *Hibburei liqutim*, Introduction, p. 5a, and *Qav ha-yashar* chap. 11, reported "in the name of R. Judah the Hasid of Szydlowce."

141. See also *Darkhei no'am*, p. 19; *Dubna rabbati*, pp. 80–84, 109–111, 132.
142. *Yesod yosef*, chap. 10, p. 5.
143. Sources attesting to moral decline among the people at large include responsa literature—e.g.: Responsa, R. Hayyim Ha-Cohen [Rapoport]: "Even ha-'ezer" no. 24; Responsa, *Eitan ha-ezrahi* no. 45; Responsa, *Pri tevuah*, by R. Y. L. Margaliot (Nowy Dwor, 1796), pt. 2, nos. 49–50; Responsa, *Gur aryeh yehuda* by R. Yehudah Aryeh Loeb Teomim (Zolkiew, 1827): "Yoreh de'ah" no. 44. In the last-mentioned, the pertinent passage is missing, but is referred to in the index.
144. Reports and references to "thieves" and "sinners" or "apostates" come from various documents and from responsa literature: see, e.g., *Regesty i nadpisi*, vol. 3, nos. 2025–2036; *Bat 'einai*, 2. See also Gelber, "Die Taufenbewegung unter den polnischen Juden im XVIII. Jahrhundert," *MGWJ* 68, p. 225. Gelber discusses conversion only in terms of official data and in connection with the Frankist heresy. See also, e.g., the 1617 document in *Regesty i nadpisi*, vol. 2, no. 1298; Responsa, *Net'a sha' ashu'im*, chap. 28: the case involves a convert who had been assistant to the *hazzan* of Lublin, and who stated explicitly that he converted because his uncle refused his request for financial assistance. See also: Responsa, *Beit ya'aqov*, no. 158; Responsa, *Penei yehoshu'a*, "Even ha-'ezer," 2.
145. Responsa, *Meir netivim*, question 32.
146. Responsa, *Gur aryeh yehuda*, "Orah hayyim" no. 142. The index gives further details that are not reported in the body of the question itself. See also Responsa, *Yeri'at ha-ohel*, no. 6; Responsa, *Pri tevuah*, nos. 32, 35; Responsa, *Meqom shmuel*, no. 32.
147. *Sha'ar ha-melekh*, pt. 2, sect. 4, p. 87; *Toharot ha-qodesh*, pt. 2, p. 34a.
148. *Pinqas medinat lita*, no. 56. Our copies of the regulations lack the word *ish* (man, person), which a copyist probably left out in error; cf. ibid., no. 59.
149. *Yesod yosef*, chaps. 6 and 35; see also chaps. 3 and 8.
150. *Pinqas medinat lita*, no. 59.
151. Regulations of Żółkiew community, 1620, in: *Qiryah nisgavah*, p. 83.
152. *Pinqas medinat lita*, nos. 373 (1639), 646 (1670).
153. Regulation enacted at the Lublin council in 1671, cited from the Tykocin (Tiktin) *pinqas*: Dubnow, in *Evreiskaia starina* (1912), p. 82.
154. *Pinqas medinat lita*, no. 56 (1623); see also the Lublin regulation of 1671, cited in n. 153, threatening sanctions of such severity that "they will make people's ears ring," against anyone daring "to complain to the Four Lands Council against his [community] heads and leaders"; *Pinqas medinat lita*, no. 113 (1627), restricting the right of appeal by individuals or groups against rules adopted with rabbinical confirmation, by the community board; ibid., no. 114, abolishing the right of appeal against verdicts of the *kahal* court; ibid., no. 389 (1639): regulation of the Brześć community prohibiting any appeal to the council against the *kahal*; ibid., no. 122, reinforcing the authority of the provincial councilmen vis-à-vis the individual communities; ibid., no. 152, sanctions imposed against those held in

contempt of the rabbi or one of the lay board members or a judge (1628); ibid., no. 199 (1628), prohibiting even lay leaders to discuss communal affairs outside formal board sessions. At the council of 1631 it was deemed necessary to formally *permit* lay leaders to seek the advice of a fellow board member (no. 240).

155. *Pinqas medinat lita,* nos. 446 (1647), 656 (1670), 754 (1679), 813 (1687), 830 (1691); also nos. 130 (1628): strict, collective supervision and regulation of the license to preach in public; 373 (1639): including reference to those "who secretly draw up petitions or conspire for some secret purpose"; 476 (1646): *herem* (ban) against conspiracies and plots against communal elders and rabbis; 546 (1662): against those who show contempt for the *herem* and who force their way into the synagogue; 596 (1667): blanket prohibition against preaching without the permission of the *kahal* and its officers; 714 (1676): broader prohibition against clandestinely organized letters; 767 (1679): prohibition against individuals seeking to present their views in writing to the *kahal,* out of fear of "conspiratorial letters" (the *herem* applied to communities, too, barred from such actions in their intercommunal dealings or at the district councils); 936 (1720): prohibition against joint business affairs being conducted by "people associated with conspiracies," or their involvement together in tax assessment, in court decisions, etc.

156. Ibid., no. 813 (1687): *herem* against "conspirators and informers"; see also no. 816, broadening the terms of the ban to include any form of attack against the communal regime, within and between communities, and between communities or district councils and their chief rabbis. See also no. 430: proclamation of the council of 1691, and no. 983 (cited by the council in 1761), restricting artisans' rights.

157. *Toharot ha-qodesh,* Introduction.

158. *Ohel rahel,* p. 26b.

159. *Mishneh torah:* "Teshuvah," 4:2. Maimonides merely incorporated into the corpus of Jewish law what was in fact a long-standing custom. See also *Sefer ha-shtarot,* by R. Judah ben R. Barzilai of Barcelona, pp. 7–8, on a "trusteeship" that was actually a writ of appointment of "[one who is] learned, wise and pious, of high financial status but eschewing greed," to teach the community "the ways of Israel," and the community's undertaking "under oath . . . that neither we nor our children will waver from his teachings." On the beginnings of such appointments of preachers, see also my sourcebook, *Yisrael ba-golah,* pt. 1, p. 151, n. 1. See also *Ohel rahel,* p. 26b.

160. The obligations of preachers cited here come from *Sha'ar ha-melekh,* pt. 1, sect. 3, p. 85. See also *Magen avraham,* "Orah hayyim,' nos. 585 and 290; *Hanhagot ha-ram'a,* loc. cit.

161. The quoted statements come, respectively, from: *Qenei hokhmah,* by R. Judah Loeb Pokhowitzer (1681), Introduction; ibid., first sermon, "Derush ha-'aravut," p. 4b; ibid., pp 8a, 9a; idem, *Kevod hakhamim* (1700), pp. 49b and 9b.

162. *Darkhei no'am*, pp. 25b, 59a; see also, e.g., *Pinqas medinat lita*, no. 51.

163. *'Ir dameseq eli'ezer*, by R. Eliezer ben R. Menashe (Zolkiew, 1764), pt. 2, p. 2b. See also *Ohel moshe*, by R. Ya'aqov Moshe Katz (Zolkiew, 1754), "Be-shalah," p. 27b: "They have not only ceased learning, but have also ceased supporting Torah scholars."

164. *Zer'a berakh shlishi*, p. 30a.

165. *Darkhei no'am*, pp. 25b, 59a.

166. *Yesod yosef*, chap. 35.

167. *Zer'a berakh shlishi*, p. 22b.

168. *Sha'ar ha-melekh*, pt. 1, sect. 3, p. 88.

169. These details are furnished by the charter of the Jewish tailors' association in Berdyczew (*Regesty i nadpisi*, no. 1742), dated 1732, and the charter of the artisans' association in Wladnyk (ibid., vol. 3, no. 2300, dated 1783).

170. See: M. Schorr, *Żydzi w Przemyślu* (1903), p. 272; Wischnitzer, *Yidishe tsekhn in poyln un lite* (1922), p. 12.

171. The associations' insistence on supervising their members' attendance at prayers necessitated holding their own prayer quorums, just as the desire to form their own groups led to the adoption of broader functions, in order to justify their existence in the face of the constant opposition of the *kahal*.

172. See Responsa, *Giv'at shaul*, no. 84; Buber, *Qiryah nisgavah*, pp. 115–116: the prohibition against holding separate prayer quorums is here directed against the tailors, too.

173. *Ohel rahel*, p. 25b.

174. See the regulation in this regard enacted by the Zolkiew community in 1765: Buber, *Qiryah nisgavah*, pp. 115–116.

175. *Pinqas medinat lita*, no. 977 (1761).

176. *Mishmeret ha-qodesh*, "Halvaat hen," in the course of which we find the statement: "In our city, too, the householders eagerly joined together for this sacred purpose."

177. *Yevein mesulah*, toward the end of the book. A full description of the various types of *hevrot*, their form of organization, and functions in Polish-Lithuanian Jewry is vital for the history of East European Jewry and would shed considerable light on the processes which helped the dissemination of kabbala, Sabbatianism, Hasidism, and the Enlightenment in East European society.

178. *Pinqas medinat lita*, nos. 641 (1670), 816.

179. *Yesod yosef*, chap. 36.

180. Margolis, *Dubna rabbati*, p. 90; Biber, *Mazkeret le-gedolei ostra*, p. 13: relating to the burial society; and see ibid., "The problem is great, for more and more [people] seek to enter the society. Whoever gives a contribution thinks he can join and thus spoils the society." The records of the tailors' association in Przemyśl, entry dated Nisan 5449 (1689)—in Schorr, *Zydzi w Przemyślu*, p. 274. The wording implies the existence of a general practice in all the *hevrot* that barred wardens of the association from serving as electors ("this rule has been the case in all the other *hevrot* in

our community"). This precedent, meant to guard against a takeover by the wardens, served as the basis for further amendments to restrict the rights of rank-and-file members.

181. *Qenei hokhmah,* "Derush ha-'aravut," p. 8b.

182. *Rafduni be-tapuhim,* by R. Eliaqim Goetz (Dyhrenfürth, 1674), "Introduction and apologia by the learned author and some good reasons for reading this book." The author was raised in Poland. *Darkhei no'am,* p. 59a; *Rafduni be-tapuhim,* p. 5a; *Kevod hakhamim,* chap. 28.

183. *Toledot ya'aqov yosef,* "Nisavim," beginning; *ibid.,* "Va-yeshev"; *ibid.,* "Va-vishlah."

184. The legends about the Besht (in *Shivhei ha-Besht* and in *Qehal hasidim* (Lwów, 1866) and *'Adat zaddikim* (Lwów, 1865) are the earliest of the Hasidic legends. See Dubnow, *Toledot ha-hasidut,* pp. 411–416 and the appendices to *Shivhei ha-Besht.* See also *Qehal hasidim* and *'Adat zaddikim,* for the story of R. Yaaqov, the Besht's assistant. After the death of the Besht he earned his keep by telling stories about the life of the Besht. The early legends reflect the conditions of the early part of the second half of the eighteenth century, or the third quarter of the century. Dubnow was right when he said that "the times of the Besht are clearly reflected in the stories about him" (p. 415). This is expressed not only through factual references and the mention of contemporary incidents, but also through the general character of the social conditions described. Thus, we have a statement, attributed to the Besht, that "everyone is bound to be imprisoned sometime" (*Shivhei ha-Besht,* Horodetzky's edn., p. 90); and "people fear that they will be informed against" (ibid., p. 92). Thus, too, "noblemen . . . do not want any Jews to live in their villages" (ibid., p. 105). Such reflections of the times may help us to date Hasidic legends as well as assess their historical value.

The method adopted by L. Holmstock (under the guidance of I. Sosis) in his thesis, "Der yidisher lebenshteyger in 18-tn yorhundert" (Belorussian Academy of Sciences, Jewish Section—in *Tsaytshrift* 4, pp. 85–120), in which he grouped together all Hasidic legends in a single corpus, ascribing it all to the eighteenth century, is incorrect. Even a cursory examination of the material demonstrates that it contains much that has a later derivation. See, e.g., the two tales about faith in providence (*Qehal hasidim,* pp. 9a and 28a): the one tells about the tax farmer in the village and the other about the wealthy merchant in Berdyczew).

185. *Shivhei ha-Besht* (Horodetzky edn.), p. 110. On the overall attitude toward wealthy arendars and tax farmers, see also *Toledot ya'aqov yosef,* "Bo": "People say, 'Where did that person go ["walk"]? He went ["walked"] to the synagogue.' But when he goes to the castle, they say, 'He ran.' That is why it is written that 'Their feet run to do wickedness.' " See ibid., pp. 87, 89–90, 108, 23, 25.

186. Facts and descriptions cited here come from *Shivhei ha-Besht* (Horodetzky edn.), pp. 105–106, 94, 91, 52, 53, 90, 101, 115, 25, 23, 81, 30, 94, 113;

THE ORIGINS OF HASIDISM 197

see also ibid., pp. 74–75: the detailed account of the washing of wool and
the attendant working conditions. See also *Qehal hasidim he-hadash* (Lwów,
1906), p. 15; *Toledot ya'aqov yosef*, "Lekh lekha": "After he went to the
castle to add his bid for the arenda, higher than that of his friend . . . and
the nobleman rebuked him [asking] how he could cause willful injury to
his friend. . . ." See also ibid., "Sav," on rabbis traveling the countryside
to "supervise villagers' affairs" and those who go "only to receive gifts"
(Warsaw edn., 1881, pp. 172–173). On artisans, see *Shivhei ha-Besht*, pp.
51–52, 73, 112, 93, 108, 82, 102, 103.

187. On the Besht's parents, see: *Shivhei ha-Besht*, p. 11; *Qehal hasidim he-
hadash*, p. 25. The information that his father was an *arendar* is probably
the one realistic fact on which the stories about him were based.

188. For the life of the Besht before his public career began, see: *Shivhei ha-
Besht*, pp. 13, 16, 19–20; *Qehal hasidim he-hadash*, pp. 1, 14–19; *Ramatayim sofim*, by R. Shmuel of Sicniawa, p. 166.

189. What we have received as the "genealogy" of the Besht's disciples is based
primarily on *Shivhei ha-Besht;* a full and accurate list of the Besht's disciples and close associates based on contemporary sources has never been
compiled.

190. R. Ber of Miedzyrzecz was a preacher (*Zikhron kehunah*, p. 3b; *Darkehi
yesharim*, by R. Mendel of Przemyslany) as well as a village teacher
(*Shivhei ha-Besht*, p. 37; *Or meir*, by R. Ze'ev Wolf of Żytomierz: "Hayyei
sarah"). R. David Firkes was a preacher in Miedzyboz—*Shivhei ha-Besht*,
p. 117; cf. *Toledot ya'aqov yosef*, "Yitro": "the rabbi and preacher from
Miedzyboz", as well as a slaughterer in Tulczyn (*Shivhei ha-Besht*, p. 63).
R. David of Kolomaj was a preacher (ibid., p. 24). R. Yishaq of Drohobycz
was also a preacher (*Qehal hasidim he-hadash*, pp. 52, 13; *Shivhei ha-
Besht*, p. 52) as was his son, R. Mikhl of Zloczów (ibid., p. 42). R. Aryeh
Loeb was the Preacher of Polonne, and author of *Qol aryeh* (*Shivhei ha-
Besht*, pp. 21, 37, 107, 123; *Toledot ya'aqov yosef*, "Va-yesei"). R. Men-
del was the Maggid of Bar (*Toledot ya'aqov yosef*, "Shemot," "Tazri'a").
R. Avraham Podlisker was a preacher in Biała Cerkiew (*Shivhei ha-Besht*,
p. 68). Note also: R. Yaaqov the preacher of Miedzyboz (p. 118); R.
Yosef, the preacher (p. 124); R. Moshe of Raszków (p. 126); R. Joel, the
preacher of Niemirów (p. 29), and others. See also the will of R. David
Halperin (in Biber *Mazkeret le-gedolei ostra*, p. 339), of 1765, in which he
bequeathed "to the rabbi, the preacher of this community, 100 zlotys, to
the rabbi, the preacher of Polonne, and the rabbi, the preacher of Miedzyrzecz, and to the rabbi, the preacher of Zloczow and to the rabbi, R. Pinhas
of Korzec—each of them is to receive 150 zlotys. . . . And to the rabbi, the
preacher of Bar, 100 zlotys." This demonstrates that they all retained their
positions as preachers even after they rose to prominence as disciples of
the Besht.

191. See *Shivhei ha-Besht*, pp. 22, 35, 40, 56, 57, 58, 74, 76, 81. See also pp.
22, 56, 63, 65.

192. R. Yaaqov Yosef Ha-Cohen served as rabbi in Szarogrod before he made the acquaintance of the Besht (*Shivhei ha-Besht*, p. 29); R. David Halperin, the rabbi in Ostróg, in whose home the Besht used to stay overnight (ibid., pp. 78, 79); R. Meir Margaliot (*Sod yakhin u-bo'az*, p. 62); R. Moshe of Kutów (*Shivhei ha-Besht*, p. 22; *Toledot ya'aqov yosef*, "Tazri'a").

193. *Shivhei ha-Besht*, pp. 56, 57.

194. *Shivhei ha-Besht*, pp. 9, 88, 110, 103, 111; *Qehal hasidim he-hadash*, p. 18.

195. *Shivhei ha-Besht*, pp. 87, 89, 76, 77. See also ibid., the story of the Preacher of Polonne, who delivered a eulogy on the occasion of the death of an informer who had terrorized the community: the Besht said that the Preacher, by berating the informer after his death, had succeeded in winning the man a reprieve from everlasting punishment. The Preacher's comment is also noteworthy: "If only the informer were alive now, he would become part of the pious sect [Hasidim] in league against the wicked ones."

196. A small Galician town close to Volhynia. See Dubnow, "Chassidiana," *He-'avar* 2, p. 17.

197. Dubnow, "Chassidiana," Lesznow regulations, no. 5. It would appear that the other teachers were suspected of sympathy for the movement: see ibid., no. 6: "Those people shall not go seeking contributions, only such teachers as are appointed by the rabbi."

198. Dated 1787. See Deinard, *Miflagot be-yisrael* (New York, 1899), pp. 21, 22: see no. 8 (p. 22), on "the formulation of the provincial regulation."

199. In his essay in *Schulamith* 2, p. 311; *Herev hadah*, p. 2; *Sefer ha-vikuah*, Introduction, and p. 69.

200. *Nazad ha-dem'a*, sec. 1, pp. 5–7 and sec. 2, p. 9.

201. *Qehal hasidim he-hadash*, no. 20. The way the story is told indicates that the Besht, then working as a "schoolteacher in the village [who was] hiding his greatness, and helped lead [the children] in their prayers" was punished "because of the great waste [of his gifts]."

202. *Shivhei ha-Besht*, pp. 13, 45, 46, 86, 87; *Qehal hasidim*, no. 31; *Shivhei ha-Besht*, pp. 90, 126, 87: "He sought to earn a living from redeemed customs notes."

203. *Shivhei ha-Besht*, pp. 109, 110, 126 (the complaint against "a certain villager . . . who studies regularly and gives to charity [but who] has lived in the village several years and each year has robbed his non-Jews.") See also ibid., p. 95.

204. *Shivhei ha-Besht*, pp. 82, 83, 73. See also *Toledot ya'aqov yosef*, "Neso," regarding the activity of early Hasidic leaders in this sphere:

> For the evil inclination has found a subtle way to work: it need not go and tempt and entrap each individual separately, but only that one person who is the source of the undoing of many others. He is the one who appoints a slaughterer who is ruled by demonic powers and so feeds a whole town on non-kosher meat, etc. Also [this applies to] a [flawed] prayer-leader, who ought to stand between God and Israel and

must fulfill the devotional obligations of a whole community—and our earliest rabbis were strict in warning that a prayer-leader must be chosen only from among the best —but now this is not the case, for they are chosen from among the worst.

See also *Shivhei ha-Besht*, pp. 82, 22, 73.

205. *Hayyei shlomo maimon*, p. 141n.

206. Dubnow, *Toledot ha-hasidut*, pp. 478, 479. It would appear that the committee that framed these regulations was newly chosen (from among the Hasidim) and R. Aaron of Karlin gave them executive power to alter the rules, along with "all the people of the town, including all the poor and indigent."

207. *Shivhei ha-Besht*, p. 38. See also, ibid.: "When they arrived in town the ruler of the place would immediately provide guards to conduct them into his presence."

208. *Zamir 'arisim*, end; Dubnow, "Chassidiana," p. 22; ibid., p. 11, letter of 1772 from the Vilna *kahal*.

209. An open letter published in Vilna in 1781, in which it was noted: "Especially in the Ukraine, there are tens of thousands of such impure ones." Dubnow, *Toledot ha-hasidut*, p. 142; *Hayyei shlomo maimon*, chap. 19 (trans. Y. L. Barukh), p. 148. See also the aforementioned Vilna letter: "Those who support them and testify for them and protect them . . ." (Dubnow, *Toledot ha-hasidut*).

210. The quotations are from *Hayyei shlomo maimon*, p. 149; the letter from R. Shneur Zalman to his followers "who live in the holy community of Ushats," in *Beit rabbi*, p. 17a (undated, but the editor placed the letter as written in 1780; from internal evidence, too, the letter fits the period between the *herem* of 1772 and that of 1781); open letter from Vilna, 1781 (5th of Av); Eliezer Zweifel, *Shalom 'al yisrael*, pt. 2, p. 38; letter of R. Menahem Mendel of Witebsk sent from Eres Israel in 1783 (*Beit rabbi*, p. 36). See also the letter of R. Shneur Zalman of 1797, relating to earlier events—see *Beit rabbi*, p. 50.

211. See R. Aaron of Karlin's notation in the record book of Nieświez, cited earlier.

212. *Maggid devarav le-ya'aqov* (Lwów, 1863 edn.), p. 10a.

213. *No'am meggidim*, by R. Eliezer of Tarnogrod, "Sav," and "Tissa."

214. The quotations are from the following sources: *Liqutei yeqarim* (Lwów, 1857), p. 24b; *Kutonet passim* by R. Yaaqov Yosef, "Sav"; *Sofnat peaneah* by R. Yaaqov Yosef, p. 22b; *Savaat ha-ribash*, p. 13b; *Meor 'einayim*, "Bereishit."

215. *Toledot ya'aqov yosef* was published, of course, in 1781; however a large part of it was certainly written earlier, some of it during the lifetime of the Besht. See the section on "Sav": "He (Samael the accuser, Esau's champion) brought trouble to the holy ones of the land, some of whom died, for our many sins, during the year of 1753 in the Ukraine." And see also *Regesty i nadpisi*, vol. 3, nos. 2014–2023; and the documents regarding "the Haidamaks who recently appeared" (in 1751–52). R. Yaaqov Yosef's sermons

and interpretations reflect his times, as he said (*Toledot ya'aqov yosef,* "Aharei"): "Every seemingly superfluous letter is there to teach us a lesson, each of us in his own time." Apart from those statements and interpretations that R. Ya'aqov Yosef explicitly attributes to his master, there are many citations of "what I heard" that, in other works, are attributed to the Besht. Many times his writings afford us a sense of the social conditions in Poland. See, e.g., his many comments about the rash of new "leaders" who are a burden on the public and "cost everyone else their livelihood." *Toledot ya'aqov yosef,* "Bo"; *Sofnat peaneah* (Piotrkow edn.), pp. 6–8. Some of his ideas show a direct influence of medieval *mussar* literature (the works of Ha-Ran, Abravanel, *'Olelot efrayim, Kli yaqar,* etc.), but the themes are illustrated by contemporary details.

216. *Toledot ya'aqov yosef,* "Shoftim": "When a new country is settled and you determine to choose yourself a king, see that you choose one before someone else makes himself your ruler."

217. The quoted passages from *Toledot ya'aqov yosef* referring to the alienation between rabbinical scholars and the people at large are taken, in order, from the following sections: "Va-yishlah" ("the long night of exile in which everyone thinks he is important and seeks to raise himself higher than others, saying 'I am the better scholar' "; " 'And he saw he could not best him,' for this could cause division and rupture, whereas Torah authorities [of our day] would argue against each other and show contempt for one another and become themselves contemptible in the eyes of the unlearned, and the wealthy only conclude that they cannot rely on [the rabbis]"); "Devarim" (" 'Alas! Lonely sits the city'; that is, the people of the city who were left without any contact with the righteous ones in their midst"; there are two types of people in this unfortunate period of the Exile—"those who are drunk with the burden of Exile, because of all the taxes and other payments, and those, the scholars, who are exempt from the tax"); "Bereishit" ("The scholars and the people stand at opposite poles and have no real point of contact"). See also: "Noah," "Shemot"; "Qedoshim"—"Israel (the scholars) came to Egypt, to the strait place [a play on Egypt = *misrayim* and straits = *mesarim*] to leave behind them the way of Torah and to seek to attain the status won by Joseph, that is, the wealthy ones who abandon Torah to follow their own dictates, they behave cunningly and they succeed, so they begin to say, 'It is useless to serve God'; they envy the sinner and do as he does." See also "Bereishit": "Scholars are called 'my people,' as in the verse, 'Tell my people what is their sin.' These are the scholars and these are called Israel, they are apt to be spiritually coarsened due to overattention to book learning. . . . 'Israel' are the powerful ones [*ba'alei serarah*—a pun on the name Israel], who should pay heed to the commandment, 'This month shall be for you . . . etc.,' that you may serve as an example, like the moon that at first is small but later is fulfilled—that is how Israel should be . . ." See also "Mishpatim."

218. *Imtahat binyamin,* by R. Benjamin of Zlozec, p. 32a. The author attributes

the statement to the Besht: "I heard it said in the old one's name, the man of God, R. I[srael] Ba'al Shem."

219. The quoted passages on the people and the rabbis are from the following sections in *Toledot ya'aqov yosef:* "Noah," "Bereishit," "Ki tissa," "Va-yishlah," "Va-yigash," "Yitro," and "Bo." Warnings against contempt for rabbis also appear in "Va-et'hanan," and elsewhere.

220. Statements of R. Yaaqov Yosef quoted here come from *Toledot ya'aqov yosef,* "Shoftim," "Noah," "Neso," and "Tesaveh."

221. *Ahavat dodim,* by R. Benjamin of Zlozec, p. 17a; p. 15a. The author preserved traditions of utmost importance to our understanding of Hasidism's first generation. He is unique in the way he quotes the Besht and other founders of the movement. See I. Werfel, *Ha-hasidut ve-eres yisrael* (Jerusalem, 1940), pp. 39–42.

222. *Toledot ya'aqov yosef,* "Lekh lekha." The following statement regarding association with zaddikim is from "Nisavim" (ibid.).

223. Dubnow, *Toledot ha-hasidut,* p. 98.

224. *Toledot ya'aqov yosef,* "Va-yeseh," "Shelah lekha," and "Nisavim."

225. Dubnow, *Toledot ha-hasidut,* p. 140.

226. *Toledot ya'aqov yosef,* "Noah."

227. Quoted from *Toledot ya'aqov yosef,* "Neso," "Emor," "Bo," and "Hayyei sarah" (for his attitude to the people at large); and see also *Sofnat peaneah,* "Terumah," and *Kutonet passim,* "va-yiqra."

228. The statements on conflicts between scholars come from *Toledot ya'aqov yosef,* "Aharei," "Shoftim," and "Bo."

229. *Ahavat dodim,* p. 42b.

230. *Toledot ya'aqov yosef,* "Qedoshim," "Va-yera," "Bereishit," "Emor," "Qedoshim," "Bo," "Va-yishlah," "Va-yeshev," and "Bo."

231. The statements about conflict and contention, and the ways to improve the situation, are from *Toledot ya'aqov yosef,* "Sav," "Bo" (the verse, "Behold I will send Elijah to you . . . and he will return the hearts of the fathers unto their sons"), "Masa'ei," "Aharei," "Neso," "Mi-qes," and "Va-yaqhel"; see also "Be-shalah," "Berakhah," and "Yitro."

232. Ibid., "Berakhah," and "Neso"; see also "Noah": "My teacher taught this in the name of his teacher." On the importance of this theme, see the discussion below, on the messianic foundations of Hasidism.

233. *Ibid.,* "Devarim." The "in-between" group here are not the zaddikim but the Hasidim, who serve to link the people with the zaddikim, just as Moses selected head men for the purpose of a link between himself and the people. The interpretation below of "Take an offering from amongst you" is from "Neso"; that on "a beautiful woman" is from "Teseh."

234. Ibid. We may have here, in a way, a summation of Hasidism's experience in its early, aggressive stage, which evoked such pronounced resistance, during the course of which many early adherents left the movement.

235. Ibid., "Shemot," citing the Besht. See also the explanation of the names of the children of Israel, which offers a veritable program: "Reuben—that

they [the leaders of the people] should 'see' [a pun on Reuben] and take care of their own behavior, so as to merit the title 'son' [again, Reu-ben]; the people itself should 'listen' [a pun on Shim'on] and be 'close to' [punning on Levi] the leaders, etc." See also ibid., "Ki tissa."

236. The citations on parity between the rich and the poor and on charity as something that the rich owe the needy are from *Toledot ya'aqov yosef,* "Bereishit," and from *Imtahat binyamin,* by R. Benjamin of Zlozec (1796), chap. 9 (compare *Toledot ya'aqov yosef,* "Ba-har"), pp. 54b, 55a, 83b; chap. 6, pp. 1a, 33b. Some of these ideas, albeit in more moderate form, may be found in the *mussar* literature of sixteenth- and seventeenth-century kabbalists. See, e.g., *Divrei hakhamim,* by R. Y. L. Pochowitzer (Hamburg, 1692), pt. 3, chap. 14; *Torat moshe,* by R. Moshe Alshekh, "Va-yiqra" 25:36.

237. *Qedushat levi,* by R. Levi Yishaq of Berdyczew, "Neso." See also *Osar ha-hayyim,* by R. Yishaq Ayzik of Komarno, "Yitro": "Every good deed down here provokes the upper spheres of heaven to a commensurate deed . . . as our holy teacher the Besht said." See also *Mevasser sedeq,* "Pinhas."

238. *Toledot ya'aqov yosef,* "Va-yiqra," "Ki tissa." See also *Ben porat yosef,* "Toledot."

239. *Ve-siva ha-cohen,* by R. Aaron Shmuel (Biala Cerkiew, 1783), chap. 15, statement attributed to the Besht. Cited also in *Orah la-hayyim,* by R. Abraham Hayyim of Zloczow (Zolkiew, 1816), "Terumah."

240. R. Shneur Zalman of Liady, *Iggeret qodesh* (Zulzbach edn.), p. 9a–b.

241. *Or ha-meir,* by R. Ze'ev Wolf of Zytomierz (a disciple of the Maggid of Miedzyrzecz), sermon for Rosh Hashanah (Korzec, 1795), p. 22b. See also *Panim yafot,* by R. Pinhas Ha-Levi Hurewitz, "Mishpatim."

242. Babylonian Talmud, Bava Mesia 62a.

243. R. Shneur Zalman of Liady, *Iggeret qodesh,* p. 14a. See also Rav Yeivi, *Hiddushei tehillim,* 49, 56.

244. *Teshuot hen,* by R. Gedaliah of Luniniec, "Terumah," cited in the name of R. Sh. of Kamenka, who told it to the Besht. See also *Torei zahav,* by R. Benjamin of Zlozec (Mohylew, 1816), "Re'eh," citing the Besht.

245. *Iggeret qodesh,* p. 8b.

246. *Meor 'einayim,* by R. Nahum of Czernobyl, "Mattot" (Slavita, 1792), p. 97a. The explanation is based on a parable in the Jerusalem Talmud, Ketubot 66b.

247. *Toledot ya'aqov yosef,* "Noah."

248. *Degel mahaneh efrayim,* by R. Moshe Hayyim Ephrayim of Sudylkow, a grandson of the Besht, "Be-shalah." See also *Or ha-meir* "Be-ha'alotekha."

249. *Qedushat levi,* "Be-shalah."

250. The deprecating statements about preoccupation with one's livelihood and prescribing faith in providence are cited from (in order): *Toledot ya'aqov yosef,* "Yitro"; *Or ha-meir,* "Be-shalah"; see also *Kutonet passim,* chap. 8: "It is possible that manna will always fall for Israel because of their faith and trust [in God]." See also *Toledot ya'aqov yosef,* "Noah"; *Meor*

'einayim, "Be-shalah"; Mevasser sedeq, "Toledot"; Pri ha-ares, letter of R. Mendel of Witebsk, p. 88 (Zytomierz edn.), section on "concern for one's livelihood." The source for all of these is the Besht's opinion on the matter: see Panim yafot, "Va-yishlah"; Toledot ya'aqov yosef, "Mishpatim"; Degel mahaneh efrayim, " 'Eqev."

251. The statements on trust in providence, in order cited, are from: R. Levi Yishaq of Berdyczew, Geulat yisrael, nofet sufim, pt. 2, p. 7b; Rav yeivi, by R. Ya'aqov Yosef of Ostróg; "Hiddushei tehillim," chap. 14; Qedushat levi, "Perushei aggadot rabi bar bar hana"; Toledot ya'aqov yosef, "Bo"; Meir 'einayim, "Mattot"; and see ibid., "Va-yesei."

252. Babylonian Talmud, Yoma 38a–b. Also in Tosefta and Jerusalem Talmud. Rashi had interpreted the verse "by your name he will call you" as follows: "No one will bother to say, 'a certain nameless someone deprived me of income.' " Meor 'einayim, "Va-et'hanan."

253. Toledot ya'aqov yosef, "Bo"; Meor 'einayim, "Bo."

254. See chap. 4 of my essay, " ' 'Aliyato shel rabi yehuda ha-levi le-eres yisrael," in Minha le-david, pp. 175–182; and my essay, "Ha-yesodot ha-ideologiim shel ha-'aliyot le-eres yisrael," in my anthology, Be-mifneh ha-dorot [1972]; and see my book Mevasrei ha-siyyonut, pt. 1, pp. 6–8.

255. Shivhei ha-Besht (Horodetzky edn.), pp. 25, 23, 123, 21.

256. From the ban against the Hasidim by the Brody kahal (summer 1772), in Zamir 'arisim, published by Dubnow in his "Chassidiana," p. 14 (He-'avar 2).

257. Shivhei ha-Besht, p. 25.

258. Details on R. Nahman of Kosów and on his relations with the Besht come from Shivhei ha-Besht, pp. 54–56: "Once the Besht said, our rabbi, R. Nahman, 'pursues me to kill me.' "

259. On the circle around R. Nahman of Kosów, see Shivhei ha-Besht, pp. 29, 56. The preacher had previously been a tutor in R. Nahman's home.

260. See Toledot ya'aqov yosef, "Balaq": "And Moav was aroused before the Children of Israel, for he was not yet completely sunk in sin. Thus I heard it taught in the name of the late pious rabbi, R. Nahman of Kosow, who told one young man: 'You have not yet entirely forgotten the ways of the heavenly world [from which your soul has come]; at any rate, do not look to the deeds of the fathers [avot].' " See also ibid., "Bo."

261. Emden normally referred to R. Yehezqel Landau (author of Nod'a biyhuda and the rabbi of Prague), who was a Levite, as "Korah"—a name he extended to Landau's family as well. This hinted at the family's great wealth, its disposition for controversy, and its overweaning power ("they cast their eyes at things they were unworthy of"). See Babylonian Talmud, Sota 9b, 42a; Sifrei, "Re'eh"; Shevirat luhot ha-'avon, p. 50b; Hitavqut, 11, p. 80b. Dubnow's explanation (Toledot ha-hasidut, p. 102) that "the 'Korah clan' was a reference to the Sabbatian sect seems to me incorrect. The Landaus were very powerful in Opatów and supplied numerous rabbis, judges, and kahal chairmen to the local community. See also Eisenstadt

and Wiener, *Da'at qedoshim,* pp. 111, 118–120, 126–127; Emden, *Petah 'einayim,* p. 14b.

262. See the introduction by R. Yaaqov Landau to *Nod'a biyhuda* (1751 edn.), in which he explicitly speaks of "the well-known and Godly scholar of the kabbala, the late rabbi, R. Hayyim of Sanz, who was—as everyone knew —his friend and guide in mystical learning." See also, in the edition of 1781, "Even ha-'ezer" no. 73, the famous response to R. Avraham Gershon of Kutów (the Besht's brother-in-law), that similarly testifies to his close association with this group. See also ibid., no. 74.

263. See R. Avraham Gershon's letters from Jerusalem, and those of members of his circle, in 1757 and 1763 (the latter, after the death of R. Avraham Gershon himself). One of the signatures is that of "Ari Yehuda, son of the late R. Alexander of Opatów, grandson of the *gaon,* R. Loeb the Pious of blessed memory, who was rabbi of Lwów" (*Yerushalayim,* vol. 2 (1887), pp. 151, 155). One of the letters also mentions his last name: Meisels. We find members of this family as old Hasidim (R. Uziel Meisels, a disciple of the Maggid of Miedzyrzecz, and his brother). See the introduction by R. Yishaq Meisels to *Kerem shlomo ve-tiferet sevi* (Zolkiew, 1803), who also quotes teachings of R. Nahman of Kosow (citing *Tiferet 'uziel*). It is likely, therefore, that he, too, was connected to the group around R. Nahman in Opatów. The practices of R. Nahman as a zaddik, during the Besht's lifetime, are reflected in *Degel mahaneh efrayim,* "Ba-midbar." The reference there is to R. Nahman of Kosow, for R. Nahman of Horodenka is always named as such (see "Lekh lekha," "Mishpatim," "Be-ha'alotekha") or "my in-law, the venerable R. Nahman of Horodenka, of blessed memory" ("Mattot," "Ha'azinu"). Taking the references to R. Nahman's teachings that we find in early Hasidic books (*Toledot ya'aqov yosef, Degel mahaneh efrayim, Tiferet 'uziel, Turei zahav, Ohel yisrael,* etc.) together with legends and vague reports about him (see *Shivhei ha-Besht,* p. 56, "the mad Nahman"), we can reconstruct a fairly clear picture of this rival of the Besht. For our purposes, however, the critical point is simply that this rivalry within the Hasidic movement existed. See Yosef Weiss, "Reshit semihatah shel ha-derekh ha-hasidit," *Zion* 16, pp. 60–69.

264. *Shivhei ha-Besht,* p. 46.

265. *Torat ha-qana'ut* (Lwów edn.), p. 57.

266. On the emergence of R. Nahman of Horodenka and that of R. Elazar of Amsterdam, see *Shivhei ha-Besht,* p. 46; Jacob Emden, *She'ilat ya'aves,* no. 170; *She'erit yisrael* (Amsterdam, 1740).

267. The tales about R. Yosef Ha-Cohen are in *Shivhei ha-Besht,* p. 29. Here R. Yaaqov Yosef is portrayed as an opponent of Hasidic ways (e.g., pilgrimage to the zaddik, the special final Sabbath meal, etc.). The Besht's letter to him is in *Shivhei ha-Besht,* p. 30. On the Maggid of Miedzyrzecz, see ibid., pp. 36–38; see also *Keter shem tov,* pt. 2 (Lwów, 1857), p. 29.

268. The method used by Baer in his study of "social and religious ideology in *Sefer hasidim*" (*Zion* 3) and of "the historical background of the *Raya mehemna*" (*Zion* 5).

269. See *Sefer haredim,* by R. Eliezer Azikri, Introduction: "We named the sacred society 'Sukkat shalom,' founded here in Safed." See also *Shnei luhot ha-berit,* "Yoma": "Derekh hayyim ve-tokhehat mussar" (Warsaw edn., 1853), p. 64a, on a "fellowship of Hasidim who have joined together in purity and piety and formed a Godly congregation of ten"; and see also *Yesod yosef,* chap. 24: "Take now the sainted epistle I have found, sent from the sacred fellowship abroad." See also Responsa, *Torat hayyim,* by R. Hayyim Shabbetai, pt. 3 (Saloniki, 1723), no. 25: "Several wealthy people of . . . wanted to form their own congregation." On the regulations enacted, compare those adopted by the circle around R. Moshe Cordovero and the leaders of Franco-German Hasidism, in Schechter, *Studies in Judaism* (1908), pt. 2, pp. 212–219. See also D. Kahana, *Toledot ha-mequbbalim, ha-shabbetaim ve-ha-hasidim* (Tel Aviv, 1927), vol. 1, pp. 50–52; Ze'ev Rabinowitz, "Min ha-geniza ha-stolinit" (letter of the disciples of the Ari [R. Isaac Luria] to R. Hayyim Vital), in *Zion* 5 (1940), pp. 125–126; G. Scholem, on this letter, *Zion* 5, pp. 133–160; the regulations of the yeshiva of R. Moshe Hayyim Luzzatto (S. Ginsburg, *Ramhal u-venei doro* (Tel Aviv, 1937), pt. 1, pp. 8–13); "Taqanot mishel havurot yerushalayim," in Frumkin and Rivlin, *Toledot hakhmei yerushalayim,* pt. 3, pp. 37–47; Barukh David Kahana, *Birkat ha-ares;* E. Tcherikover, "Di komuna fun yerushalmer mekubolim 'ahavas sholem,' " Yivo *Historishe shriftn,* pp. 133–135.
270. See the letter of R. Shlomo Shlomil from Safed (Kahana, *Sifrut ha-historiah ha-yisraelit,* pt. 2, pp. 213–215, 218, and elsewhere); and the fourth letter, published by S. Assaf, in *Qoves 'al yad* (new series) 3, no. 1, pp. 120–123; letter of R. Moshe Hayyim Luzzatto (in *Ramhal u-venei doro,* pt. 2, pp. 240–241); *Yesod yosef,* chap. 24; *Toharot ha-qodesh,* pt. 1, p. 34b.
271. It is mainly composed of lore of penitence and self-improvement, mostly of a practical, "applied," nature, arranged according to a daily or weekly schedule, or according to the order of daily prayers, or according to the monthly progression of Sabbaths. See also, e.g., R. Yaaqov Hayyim Semah, *Naggid u-misva,* Introduction: "The practice [of it] went according to the Torah reading, set out in six sections corresponding to the six days of Creation, using the simple text, and then for the Sabbath, using the esoteric meaning." This method was used in several books, such as *Sefer ha-mussar* (appeared under different titles in various editions, e.g., *Sefer ha-yirah* [Lwów, 1808], *Hanhagot yesharot me-ha-ari ha-qadosh* [Lwów, 1858]), *Sefer ha-gan ve-derekh moshe, Mishmeret ha-qodesh,* etc.
272. See Scholem, *Major Trends,* pp. 240–247.
273. Citing R. Isaac Luria, in *Sefer sha'arei siyyon,* by R. Nathan Hanover, p. 22a (Vienna, 1804).
274. *Toharot ha-qodesh,* pt. 1, p. 54a.
275. *Mishmeret ha-qodesh,* "Mussar le-seder ha-limud," exercises for Sundays. R. Shneur Zalman of Liady, in his *Shulhan 'arukh,* prescribed that, for studying Torah (*halakha* 9, chap. 2, pt. 5) "whoever has not reached this level of study [of the necessary laws of behavior] shall study the *mussar*

books that are based on *midrash* and *aggadah* and the Zohar." This, too, is the intent of R. Shabbetai of Raszkow, in his prayer book (Lemberg, 1866), p. 129b.

276. Order of study, in the prayer book *Qol ya'aqov*, by R. Yaaqov Kopl Lifschitz, the kabbalist preacher of Miedzyrzecz (Slavita edn.), p. 16a. See Shneur Zalman of Liady, *Shulhan 'arukh*, pt. 5, "rules for studying Torah," chap. 1, par. 4.

277. R. Avraham Azulai, Introduction, in *Or ha-hamah* (commentary to the Zohar: Jerusalem, 1876); see also Scholem, *Major Trends*, pp. 246, 401.

278. *Mishmeret ha-qodesh* (see n. 275); study of "this wisdom" is based on "the writings of the Ari and his disciples."

279. *Toharot ha-qodesh*, pt. 1, p. 54b.

280. *Or ha-yashar*, by R. Meir Papers, " 'Amud ha-torah," chap. 14, no. 16. See also "Order of study," in *Qol ya'aqov*, p. 16a: "He who wishes to study true wisdom should never utter anything he has not heard from a reliable person of integrity."

281. *Qol ya'aqov*, ibid.

282. *Shulhan 'arukh* of R. Shneur Zalman, "rules for studying Torah," chap. 2, no. 62.

283. *Rafduni be-tapuhim*, by R. Eliaqim Goetz (1679), p. 14b.

284. *Or ha-yashar*, chap. 15; see also *Naggid u-misvah*, p. 25a, which states that the intent of the Torah, in essence, is that "one should endeavor to bind oneself and cleave with all one's soul to the spiritual source of Torah." And see ibid., par. 39; ibid., "Hilkhot derekh eres," no. 91. See also *Mishmeret ha-qodesh*, rules for Sundays: "Do not begrudge the expense of studying (kabbala)."

285. *Mishmeret ha-qodesh* (Sundays): "purity of thought." See also the list of conditions a student of kabbala was expected to impose on himself in order to "drive away impurity."

286. *Toharat ha-qodesh*, pt. 1, p. 41a–b.

287. R. Shlomo son of R. Moshe Chelma of Lwów, Introduction to *Mirkevet ha-mishna*, commentary on Maimonides (Frankfurt on the Oder, 1751).

288. *Nefesh hayyim*, by R. Hayyim of Volozhin, pt. 4, chap. 1.

289. *Qol aryeh*, by the Preacher of Polonne, "Mishlei."

290. *Toharot ha-qodesh*, pt. 2, p. 51.

291. See, e.g., *Yesod ve-shoresh ha-'avodah*, by R. A. Z. of Grodno, pt. 6, chap. 3: "After assigning himself a portion to study in Gemara and codes, he should set aside a portion of kabbala to study, and he should arrange this in such a way as to complete a full cycle of the Zohar and *Tiqunei ha-zohar* each year, etc.; following the study of kabbala, he should assign himself a portion to study in *midrash* and *aggadah*, etc." See also ibid., chap. 5, referring to "purposes of study."

292. See the teachings attributed to the Ari in *Naggid u-misvah*, pp. 25, 31, and in *Sha'ar ha-melekh*, pt. 1, chap. 4, based on the Zohar ("Bereishit," 42a) and in particular on *Tiqunei ha-zohar* in the Introduction.

293. The sources quoted on the importance of studying Mishna are: *Sha'ar ha-melekh*, pt. 1, chap. 4; *Qol ya'aqov*, p. 15b; *Zer'a berakh shlishi*, "Berakhot," p. 1a; *Ma'aseh rokah 'al ha-mishnayot*, Introduction; *Or ha-yashar*, chap. 15, no. 12.

294. Details on the Mishna study circles *(hevrot)* and the like are cited from *Sha'ar ha-melekh*, pt. 1, chap. 4; Responsa, *Even ha-shoham u-me'irat einayim*, question nos. 19 and 20.

295. *Naggid u-misvah* (Zolkiew, 1793), pp. 3b, 4b.

296. *Zer'a yishaq*, by R. Yishaq Hayyut (1732), p. 77a, citing a teaching of R. Loeb the Pious.

297. *Qol ya'aqov*, "Kavvanat ha-limud," p. 117b.

298. *Sefer mussar*, "For Sundays," nos. 4 and 6.

299. That was the interpretation of "All your deeds should be for the sake of Heaven" (Avot 2:12). The teaching is that of R. Yossi ha-Cohen, disciple of R. Yohanan ben Zakkai, who praised his disciple as a true "Hasid"—ibid, v. 18). Cf. *Zer'a yishaq*, p. 6a.

300. The order of study prescribed in *Qol ya'aqov*, by R. Yaaqov Koppel of Miedzyrzecz, p. 15a.

301. *Or ha-yashar*, chap. 15, nos. 3 and 13.

302. *Sefer mussar*, nos. 11, 34.

303. *Or ha-yashar*, " 'Amud ha-torah," chap. 8; ibid., "Hilkhot derekh eres," no. 6.

304. *Toharat ha-qodesh*, p. 17a. Cf. *Hanhagot ha-adam* attributed to R. D. Oppenheim: "He should do so in company with others in order to benefit the others." The statement on the importance of attaching oneself to "zaddikim and hasidim" comes from *Shenei luhot ha-berit*, " 'Asarah hillulim," on repentance.

305. *Toharat ha-qodesh*, pt. 2, p. 1b.

306. On the "way of the Hasid," see *Naggid u-misvah*, p. 3b. On the charges of "creating separate groups," see *Zamir 'arisim* (Dubnow in "Chassidiana," *He-'avar* 2), pp. 14–15 (the open letter of the Brody, *kahal*, 1772).

307. Details about liturgical change come from *Pinqas medinat lita*, council regulations of 1667, no. 602; *Zamir 'arisim*, p. 14 (loc. cit.); *Toharat ha-qodesh*, pt. 1, p. 1.

308. *Sha'ar ha-melekh*, pt. 1, chap. 8; *ibid.*, pt. 5, chap. 5: "It is widely done today to read that passage *(mizmor shir hanukkat)* every day during the morning prayers, prior to *barukh she-amar*."

309. *Mishmeret ha-qodesh*, "Hanhagat tefillin."

310. *Naggid u-misvah*, p. 22a.

311. Testimony on these Hasidic practices come from: *Toharat ha-qodesh*, p. 39b; *Yesod ve-shoresh ha-'avodah*, "Ha-kotel," chap. 9. These reports refer to the previous generation ("It has always been thus"). See also *Naggid u-misvah*, pp. 10b and 11a.

312. *Dinim ve-hanhagot ha-adam*, chap. 23; *Naggid u-misvah* p. 44b.

313. *Mishmeret ha-qodesh*, "Tefillat ha-minhah ve-se'udah shlishit."

314. Responsa, *Panim meirot*, pt. 2, no. 152; *Mishmeret ha-qodesh*, "Dinei leil shabbat"; *Dinei hanhagat ha-adam*, chap. 20. I have not cited all the Hasidic customs here, only the ones that are attested to in the sources and were generally widespread.

315. *Nazad ha-dem'a*, chap. 1.

316. *Mishmeret ha-qodesh*, "Hanhagat ha-tefillah."

317. *Mirkevet ha-mishna*, Introduction.

318. Responsa, *Even ha-shoham u-me'irat einayim*, question 44.

319. *Or ha-yashar*, "Hilkhot derekh eres," no. 95.

320. *Mishmeret ha-qodesh*, "Tefillat ha-minhah ve-se'udah shlishit."

321. *Naggid u-misvah*, p. 13b.

322. *Reshit hokhmah*, "Ha-'anavah," chap. 4.

323. *Yesod yosef*, chap. 24.

324. Sources for the "midnight circles" and midnight customs are: *Toharat ha-qodesh*, p. 1a; Responsa, *Even ha-shoham u-me'irat einayim*, question 22; *Naggid u-misvah*, pp. 4b and 5a.

325. The original version of this teaching (Yerushalmi: Yoma 1) is: Each generation that does not rebuild [the Temple] is considered to have helped destroyed it.

326. *'Ir damesek eli'ezer*, pt. 2, "Sha'arei damesek," p. 3a.

327. *Ohel moshe* (Amsterdam, 1759), Introduction and endorsements.

5

Miedzyboz and Rabbi Israel Baal Shem Tov

Murray Jay Rosman

Few topics in Jewish history or Jewish thought have received the attention that scholars have devoted to Hasidism—especially its early phases. Rabbi Israel Baal Shem Tov and the movement that arose in his wake have been studied and discussed dozens of times, from varying perspectives and a variety of methodological approaches.[1] Yet, in this entire scholarly corpus one element is virtually absent: the perspective on the Besht that non-Jewish sources provide.

This lacuna is keenly felt. For one thing, we know from *Shivhei ha-Besht* that the Baal Shem Tov had dealings with Christians in his capacity as healer, wonder-worker, competitor, and employer.[2] It is not impossible, therefore, that some aspect of his life left a lasting impression on someone who may have recorded the particular instance or experience. There is no intrinsic reason why such sources ought to be considered less valuable than any other. Second, tangible details about R. Israel and his coterie, or about the time and place in which they lived, are hard to come by in the known Jewish sources. Therefore, information from any other source either about them or their milieu would assist us to better understand the Jewish sources.[3]

One may illustrate the potential value of Polish sources in this regard with just a few simple examples. *Shivhei ha-Besht* twice mentions a person by the name of R. Yosef, the Preacher, of Miedzyboz, for whom the Baal Shem Tov apparently retained an abiding respect, even after his

Reprinted by permission of the Historical Society of Israel from *Zion* 52, no. 2 (1987): 177–89.

death.[4] According to Polish sources (which I will describe presently), the salaried preacher in Miedzyboz in 1743 was a certain Jos Jampolski[5] that is, Josef/Yosef of Jampol. It is quite plausible that this person and R. Yosef, the Preacher, are one and the same. The stories in *Shivhei ha-Besht* in which he is mentioned (both times, dealing with the period after his death) thus provide independent corroboration of the man's existence and, in addition, a terminus a quo for the events described.

A second example relates to the tale in which it is stated: "And he had a singer, who is called 'Bas,' who was a great fornicator, and his songs were aimed at pleasing the womenfolk."[6] According to the financial records of the Jewish communal board of Miedzyboz, there was a *Basista*, or bass singer, who was paid three zloty a week by the *kahal*.[7] Thus, the historicity of another individual character is confirmed.

In addition to details of identification and dating, information from Polish sources furnishes the tools with which we can evaluate material containing monetary data. *Shivhei ha-Besht* mentions, for example, that a certain Polish nobleman owed the Besht 200 zloty, and in order to repay the debt, he gave the Besht's assistant, R. Leyb, eleven czerwone zloty,[8] "and told R. Leyb that he owed the Besht another two zloty." That is, eleven czerwone zloty equalled 190 zloty, or eighteen zloty apiece. Now, we know from Polish sources that in 1702 the rate of conversion for these coins had been set at eighteen zloty, and that this rate obtained in most parts of the country until at least the 1740s.[9] This realistic detail allows us to surmise that the story records an actual event, and permits us to date it as well. Moreover, it attests to the accurate attention to detail with which such stories of the Besht were handed down.

This is but one small sample of how the juxtaposition of Polish and Jewish sources can help establish the veracity of such stories, help pin down the date of their occurrence, and flesh out our knowledge of the material culture of Polish-Jewish society.[10] Indeed, apart from the corroboration of details and an amplified comprehension of the Jewish source material, Polish sources sometimes furnish new data which can sharpen or even alter our image of the Besht and his associates.

A collection of documents from Miedzyboz—the city where the Besht lived for most of the period from 1740 (after emerging publicly in 1736) until his death in 1760—can shed some light on important issues in the study of Hasidism. Such topics include the social and economic situation in Miedzyboz and the nature of the Besht's activities there. The collection is now in the Biblioteka Czartoryskich in Cracow, which houses the archives of the Czartoryski family, the magnates who owned Miedzyboz at the time. Much of the material relates to the eighteenth century, particularly to the 1730s and 1740s. Among the documents are financial records, such as income and expenditure reports of the Miedzyboz *kahal,* the local tax rolls, and contracts. In addition, there are petitions submitted by individuals and institutions to the estate owners and their agents, correspondence between these agents, and some Polish translations of entries from the minute-book *(pinqas)* of the Jewish communal board (which is no longer extant). I also found three documents in the original Hebrew or Yiddish.

A number of scholars have stressed the importance of examining the socioeconomic context in which Hasidism arose, and in describing that context have focused on conditions in Poland generally, and in Podolia in particular.[11] However fruitful this approach has been, one question has not been raised that ought to be central to our understanding of the socioeconomic background underlying the birth and growth of Hasidism: namely, the situation in Miedzyboz itself, where the Besht lived. Was Miedzyboz a backwoods hamlet, an average town, or a city? What was the size of its population and what percentage was Jewish? When the Besht settled there, was there a stable, a declining, or a growing populace? What was its economic base? What was the security situation like?

Answers to these questions may furnish significant data with which we can determine what changes took place in Miedzyboz during the Besht's time and which may help us to judge the extent of his impact. One theory, for example, posits that the Besht was rather successful because his teachings offered religious support to the masses of poor Jews who were oppressed by prevailing conditions in the declining Polish economy and by increasing Polish hostility.[12] This theory—together with the evidence of *Shivhei ha-Besht,* in which people from Miedzyboz are said to have identified themselves as coming from the nearby city of Bar[13]—has fostered the impression that Miedzyboz was a small, insignificant town, mired in poverty until the advent of the Besht began to attract large numbers of Jews. Here, we must turn to the Polish sources for a convincing answer.

Even more crucial to research on the Besht and his entourage is the need to understand the dynamics in the Jewish community of Miedzyboz when the Baal Shem Tov settled there. Who had the financial means and who had the say-so, and what was their attitude toward the Besht? How was the community organized, and did the Besht have a formal role in any communal institutions? What sort of problems faced the Jews in Miedzyboz and what part did the Besht play in attempts to find solutions?

My research to date does not allow me to answer all of these questions conclusively, but I would like to make some interim remarks that will, nevertheless, indicate the general trend of the evidence. Contrary to the implication of the *Shivhei ha-Besht* material referring to Bar, Miedzyboz was the larger community—by almost 50 percent—and was in fact one of the largest and most important cities in the Ukraine.[14] Merchants from western Poland came there to buy merchandise and to arrange caravans (for safety's sake) for the onward journey through Volhynia to Kiev.[15] The city had a fortress and a garrison to protect it and the main trade routes, which made possible a lively commercial life.[16] Miedzyboz merchants, especially the Jews among them, maintained close ties with Kiev to the east and with Silesian and German cities to the west. They were active in the export of livestock and other produce to the west, and imported luxury goods such as French cloth and silk. Some of them traveled to Germany four times a year, spending up to 20,000 zloty each time.[17] At the beginning of the 1740s, restoration work gave Miedzyboz a new Catholic church, and the foundations were laid for a new Orthodox church. Likewise, the old Jewish study hall *(beit midrash)* underwent restoration and a new study hall (or second synagogue) was built.[18] These facts seem to indicate a rather flourishing community, an impression that is borne out by demographic data.

Miedzyboz had been destroyed during the [Cossack rebellion and the] massacres of 1648–49. Seventy-five years later, however, it was once again inhabited and, in fact, growing (see Table 1). The non-Jewish population increased by some 44 percent, and the Jewish population by 67 percent, between 1722 and 1740. Growth of this magnitude in the number of taxpayers is rather impressive, and it is a good indication of in-migration, itself, the sign of prosperous town. In the next period, from 1740 to 1760, the rate of growth was slower. This has certain implications for us: it would seem that growth was far more rapid in the period *before* the Besht came to Miedzyboz than in the years thereafter.

Table 1
Taxpayers (including those exempted)

	Christians		Jews	
Year	Number	% of increase	Number	% of increase
1722	379	—	131	—
1740	545	44	219	67
1760	565	4	282	29

Sources: Biblioteka Czartoryskich 4039 (1722); Biblioteka Czartoryskich 4078 (1740); Biblioteka Czartoryskich, Gospodarczne 308 (1760).

As for the Jewish community, not only did it experience rapid growth, but it was also considered a relatively large community for that time and place. The census of 1765 listed a Jewish population of 2,039 persons.[19] That would put Miedzyboz among the top fifteen Jewish communities in all of Poland-Lithuania.[20] From the economic standpoint (as already mentioned), there were quite a number of well-to-do merchants. Apart from that, the community was able, during the 1740s, to afford salaries for a rabbi, a cantor and cantor's assistant, a beadle, a bath attendant, a preacher, and meat-slaughterers. The number of livestock slaughtered for meat consumption in 1743, for example, averaged two heavy animals per family or about four kilograms of meat a week, not counting fowl. In addition, we know that the community supported quite a number of scholars as well as unemployed and destitute individuals, and was visited by an endless stream of cantors, preachers, and Betteljuden.[21] Contrary to the stereotypical image of Podolian towns that emerges from the historical literature,[22] the Jews of Miedzyboz did not labor under an unbearable burden of communal debt. According to the expenditures listed by the Jewish tax lessee in 1743, representing funds paid out in the name of the Jewish community, the kahal paid 2,100 zloty in capitation tax to the royal treasury, 1,206 zloty in salary to its own employees, and only 850 zloty in interest for various loans.[23]

Jewish affairs in Meidzyboz were handled by the kahal, composed of chairmen, secretaries, trustees, and electors, as in any other Polish-Jewish community. A small group of families dominated public life as well as economic affairs.[24] But not everything in Miedzyboz was under the control of the kahal. There was another entity, known in Polish as pospólstwo (a literal translation of the Hebrew term hamon, "the people"). One Hebrew document uses the term yehidei segulah (select individuals), a better translation of *pospólstwo*.[25] This term appears in other Jewish communities, too, and Israel Halpern defined it as, "prominent members of the community who held no *kahal* office." In his description, these were in fact a small number of individuals who, at times, were co-opted by the communal leaders as a way of reinforcing their important decisions.[26]

However, the Miedzyboz documents indicate that these *yehidei segulah* or *pospólstwo* actually constituted an organized body that existed alongside—at times, in opposition to—the *kahal*. For example, in 1715 thirty-six members of the *pospólstwo* filed a complaint against "the new *kahal*" for alleged mismanagement. Among other charges, it was stated that, "they do not invite us, as *pospólstwo*, to the general assembly to help choose the officers."[27] In a Hebrew-Yiddish document of 1716, forty-four *yehidei segulah* warned the "chiefs and leaders"—that is, the *kahal*—not to impose new taxes or contract new debts. Should the *kahal* fail to heed this demand, they would take their complaint to the overlord.[28] In 1726 the overlord decided that, to protect the *pospólstwo* from excessive taxation, *kahal* officials were thenceforth forbidden to serve two consecutive terms of office. It was noted, in passing, that disputes between the *pospólstwo* and the *kahal* sometimes led to instability in the community.[29]

In a later period, we find delegates of the *pospólstwo* taking part in important communal decisions alongside the *kahal*, not as a mere rubber stamp, but in the role of independent examiners. For example, the contract drawn up in 1740 between the community and its tax lessees is signed by eight representatives of the *kahal* and seven representatives of the *pospólstwo*.[30] In the 1740s, when these lessees were issued receipts on payment of their debt to the community, the release was signed by two *kahal* board men, one trustee, and one member of the *pospólstwo*.[31] A fine imposed by the *kahal* court on any individual had to be decided upon by a bench made up of the rabbi and an equal number of *kahal* and *pospólstwo* members.[32]

These joint actions are significant in terms of the Jewish communal structure in Poland. Under the voting system used by the Jewish communities—a combination of a lottery system and appointment by a small committee—public offices remained the preserve of a select group.[33] But this oligarchy was not allowed to rule in Miedzyboz with a completely free hand. The *pospólstwo*, the *yehidei segulah*, possessed the necessary prestige, in the estimation of both Jews and Poles, to act as a watchdog committee, to prevent the *kahal* from acting arbitrarily, and to ensure that it would act in the wider public interest. I think we are entitled to see in this group the "congregation *['edah]*" or the "assembly *[asefah]*"—words that best express the true meaning of *pospólstwo*— terms known to us from other communities.[34] If this identification is correct, then the group was composed of well-to-do taxpayers ("men of means") who were in principle eligible to participate in the political process (voting and holding elective office), but who were not in the dominant office-holding group.[35] The archival material from Miedzyboz demonstrates the kind of rights and limited functions that they, as a group, were able to have.

Disputes between the *kahal* and the *pospólstwo* were not the only source of social tension:

There were a number of trades associations *[hevrot]* in the community. In 1741 the strongest and most influential of them, the butchers' association, lodged a complaint against the *kahal* chairmen, accusing them of discriminatory practices in the fixing of tax assessments and other imposts. This arbitrary behavior, they charged, had been taken to an extreme when the *kahal* had seized possession of their synagogue.[36]

The rabbi of Miedzyboz in the early 1740s was Hirsh Leibowicz. When, in 1744, the *kahal* attempted to oust him from his post, he appealed for support to the Polish overlord against the *kahal*.[37]

In 1743, Czartoryski's representative ordered the *kahal* to establish a committee to solve, once and for all, the vexing problem of newcomers' having grabbed the older residents' assigned spots in the synagogue. The committee was to draw up a list of people with established residence rights in the community; anyone not on the list would be subject to expulsion from the city.[38]

In 1742 the lessee of the Czartoryskis' income from Miedzyboz demanded (among other things) an exclusive license to sell liquor in the city on Saturdays. The *kahal* and the *pospólstwo* responded with a petition stating that without the right to continue selling liquor on Saturdays, small taverns [run by Jews] would not earn sufficient income, and the revenues of the *kahal* and of the overlord would suffer in consequence.[39]

In 1741 a Jew by the name of Asher ben Moshe began assembling a private prayer quorum in his home. He faced resistance from the *kahal* as well as from non-Jews.[40] Further instances of social friction might be cited from the history of Miedzyboz in the 1730s and 1740s.[41]

Some of these conflicts are typical of what previous historians have identified as the breeding ground for an emergent, new (Hasidic) leadership, an antiestablishment opposition that took up the cause of Jewish society's weakest strata.[42] From the documents that have come to light from Miedzyboz, however, it does not appear that R. Israel Baal Shem Tov was involved in any of the local disputes; nor was anyone else known to belong to his entourage involved, either as a direct party to a dispute, as a go-between, or as a defender of one side against the other. The important actors in the public arena were: the *kahal,* the *pospól-stwo,* the major *arendars* , the *faktor*—Wolf Abramowicz (who was connected with the Czartoryskis' estate management)—the rabbi, and the trades associations. There is no indication at all of the Baal Shem Tov's involvement.[43] (It should be noted, however, that the relevant material in the Czartoryski archive only goes up to about 1746.) Interestingly, none of the local conflicts in Miedzyboz figures in *Shivhei ha-Besht,* either. Immanuel Etkes has pointed out[44] that the activities of the Besht in Miedzyboz that are described in *Shivhei ha-Besht* are those dealing with the problems of individuals; he evidently did not take a position on social issues. Chone Shmeruk, too, has argued against the proposition that "the explicit goal of Hasidism was to defend the masses against the exploitation of the *kahal.*"[45]

If the Besht did not emerge here, in a community that in many ways typified eighteenth-century Polish-Jewish society, in the role of a social or political activist (and that is the conclusion indicated by both Jewish and Polish sources, at least for the first six years he spent in Miedzyboz), what exactly was his role? Where did his party fit in socially? On this, the Polish sources are not nearly as helpful to us as they are regarding the general social patterns in Miedzyboz and in its Jewish community. The material relating to the Besht and his entourage is rather "dry" and technical: tax lists and budget records. What, nevertheless, can be gleaned from them?

In Miedzyboz, as in every city, the householders (Jews and Christians alike) had to pay the *czynsz*—a kind of municipal tax—for their property. For the period that interests us, the Czartoryski archive contains records of taxpayers in Miedzyboz in the following years: 1739–42, 1744, 1752–53, 1755, 1758, 1760, and 1763.[46] Generally, Jews and

Christians were listed separately. The tax officials noted the name of the property owner along with the amount of tax paid, in sequence according to the houses' location along each street. They sometimes added a note about the type of dwelling or about the presence of a tenant other than the owner.

The *kahal* owned a house in the vicinity of the synagogue. Because of the *kahal*'s ownership, the tenant was exempt from paying the *czynsz*, and the tax officials did not always bother to register the name of the tenant or include the house on their list. In the documentation available for our period, the tenants' names were noted on six occasions:

1739—Dom kahalski wnim Moszko duchowny;[47] 1740—Dom kahalski seu kantorski wnim kabalista;[48] 1742—Balsem w domu kahalskim;[49] 1758—Balsam;[50] 1760—Balszam Doktor liber;[51] 1763—Herszko w domie kahalnym.[52]

While the tenant of the *kahal*'s house was not always registered, his neighbors certainly were. In the 1750s and 1760s the following people are identified: Ichel ziec Balszema (Yehiel Ashkenazi, the Baal Shem's son-in-law);[53] Herszko Pisarz Balszema Pargaminnik (Sevi Hirsh, the Baal Shem's scribe, and parchment-maker);[54] Szmuylo Pasierb Balszemów (Shmuel, stepson of the Baal Shem).[55]

These scant details do tell us something about the Baal Shem Tov's status in Miedzyboz. In 1739, the *kahal*'s house was occupied by a certain "Moszko duchowny"—that is, "a man of religion." This term is equivalent to the English, "clergyman," and the Polish official evidently used it to identify someone who was some sort of scholar or kabbalist but who held no official title (rabbi, cantor, teacher, or preacher). He was supported by the community in that he was given a place to live. It is well known that Polish-Jewish communities did this sort of thing, supporting scholars or mystics "in residence."[56] The financial records of Miedzyboz from 1739 also include an item relating to payment for "our poor scholar."[57] Perhaps we may view this person as the type of "servant of God," referred to by Yaaqov Hisdai, common in the generation of the founders of Hasidism.[58]

In 1740, for whatever reason, Moszko vacated the *kahal* house and in his place was installed a man whom the tax official did not know by name, but whose occupation was "kabbalist"—a mystic. A year later the registrar already knew to refer to him as the local Jews did: "the Baal Shem." In 1760 this name was supplemented by the title, "Doktor,"[59] possibly because, after twenty years in the city, the Baal Shem had acquired a measure of respect and standing in Polish eyes. They already knew that, in addition to being a kabbalist (and probably, as they must have believed, *because* he was a mystic), he was also a healer, someone to whom even Christians went for his services—as we know from *Shivhei ha-Besht*.[60] His reputation, at least among Poles, was based on his medicinal work, rather than on any other facet of his public activity. Finally, in 1763 the tenant of the *kahal* house behind the synagogue is listed as Hersz (Zvi).

The presence of the names of the Besht's son-in-law and his scribe, known to us from Jewish sources, permits us to confirm that the kabbalist who arrived in Miedzyboz and moved into the *kahal* house in 1740, staying there until 1760, was none other than Rabbi Israel Baal Shem Tov. Likewise, it is very likely that the Herszko who lived in that house in 1763 was the Besht's son, who remained there after his father's death, apparently on the strength of his father's status in the community. The matter of the stepson is a bit more complicated, for until now we did not know of his existence. I believe there are two possibilities. The Besht's wife may have been a divorcee, and Shmuel, then, would be her son from her first marriage. Alternatively, there is a story in *Shivhei ha-Besht* about Ze'ev Kitzes, a Hasid of the Besht, who raised an orphan boy in his home; the Besht, for his part, raised an orphan girl. When the time came, a match was made between the two. Perhaps Shmuel, the Baal Shem Tov's stepson, was that orphan lad—or even a different orphan altogether—who came to live with the Besht.[61] If our interpretation of the documents is correct, then what we have before us is the first external testimony regarding the life and career of R. Israel Baal Shem Tov,[62] and it appears to suggest certain conclusions. First, it would seem clear that those historians were correct who dated the Besht's period in Miedzyboz, on the basis of Jewish sources, from 1740 to 1760.[63] Similarly, the Polish terms "kabbalista" and "doktor" imply that the Besht's main activity focused on kabbala and on healing. The implication, then, is that the *kahal* of Miedzyboz did regard the Besht as an uneducated, coarse man of "the masses." On the contrary, when the Besht arrived in Miedzyboz from Tluste he was sufficiently respected to warrant giving him a place to live at the community's expense. This would tend to reinforce M. Piekarz's argument, that the Baal Shem Tov was not necessarily categorized as a member of the lowest strata of the social and intellectual order.[64] Moreover, he was clearly not perceived as a threat to the establishment. He did not represent a new type of leadership; rather, he fit right into the existing communal structure. There was a place in Miedzyboz for him: he enjoyed the patronage of the establishment until the end of his life, and his privileges were passed on to his son.

Not only the Besht, but others close to him, too, benefited from the community's largesse. The list of expenditures of the Miedzyboz *kahal* in 1743, as ratified by the Polish lord, Wilenski, records the names of "five poor Jews living in Miedzyboz who have received the recognition of the *kahal* and are approved for this year only." Three of them received one zloty per week from the community, and two received a sum of two zloty per week. We cannot determine the names of the first three from Jewish documentation, but the second two were: "Wulff Kucego Ziec" —that is, Ze'ev, the son-in-law of Kutz, or perhaps Kucz, known in *Shivhei ha-Besht* by the name Ze'ev Kitzes; and "Dawidko Purków"— that is, David Purkes.[65] Both of them were among the Besht's leading followers in Miedzyboz. This information about them tells us that the leaders of the Miedzyboz community were prepared to give their support to people who, according to *Shivhei ha-Besht,* called themselves "Hasidim" and were devotees of kabbala.[66]

We should perhaps reemphasize one point: that this group was not active on the social front. Its role seems to have been to study Torah or kabbala. In that it would have resembled—on a smaller scale—the coterie of kabbalists in Brody who used to gather at the study hall, founded no later than 1736 (as Elhanan Reiner has established in an as-yet unpublished article). They, too, were supported by the local community and they, too, kept mainly to themselves. It is likely that the leaders of Miedzyboz, like those in Brody, saw their support of such groups as a matter of obligation and added prestige for their community. It should be recalled that the Besht had high regard for those "great Hasidim" of the Brody circle,[67] and it is not implausible that he originally intended to establish his own local equivalent or to join a similar group.

The Polish documentation contains one more item that, perhaps, relates to the beginnings of Hasidism. I referred earlier to the problem of newcomers to Miedzyboz in the early 1740s, because of whom disputes broke out in the synagogue and who were subsequently expelled from the city. The list of those slated to be expelled includes thirty names, in addition to some people called *sasiedzi*—that is, neighbors or tenants in someone else's house—but who were not identified by name. The list of names also includes "tenants in the house of Ze'ev Kitzes."[68] It is possible that these tenants (by definition, a small group) arrived in Miedzyboz in order to make their own assessment of the Baal Shem Tov, and stayed at the home of the leading Hasid of the Besht at the time, Ze'ev Kitzes. However, even if this were the case, it is impossible to say whether these people had come to benefit from the mystical and medicinal powers of the Besht or to join his circle.

In any event, the material I have presented confirms what Etkes has already demonstrated on the basis of Jewish sources: namely, that one cannot speak of an actual *movement* led by the Baal Shem Tov in Miedzyboz—at least in the 1740s. Neither can it be assumed that he appealed to the *hamon* (the masses), as so many historians have argued. From the numerical standpoint, the Besht's circle was rather small. We find no evidence of a wide-ranging social activity, apart from healing the sick. As Shmuel Ettinger has contended, the Baal Shem Tov did not attempt to form a unified opposition against the establishment.[69] The opposite is actually the case: the establishment supported him.

As to Miedzyboz itself, it is not true that the Besht put it on the map, as it were, and used it as a base from which to rally the oppressed Jews of Poland. The city was flourishing for years before he arrived there, and the pace of growth actually declined during the years he lived there.[70] The Besht moved to Miedzyboz, the largest community in the area, from Tluste, a small town. Probably he, like so many others, was attracted to a central location that offered economic opportunities—a form of employment by the community, and a large population in need of his medicinal and kabbalistic services; and spiritual opportunities—the company of men such as Ze'ev Kitzes and David Purkes, who were willing to join him in his spiritual quest as he embarked upon the attempt to formulate a new religious path.

In his book, *The Birth of Hasidism,* Piekarz states:

Our knowledge of the genesis of Beshtian Hasidism is meager indeed, and we turn to legendary materials in an almost vain attempt to extract historical facts, particularly from that hagiographic collection, *Shivhei ha-Besht,* a book which, in my humble opinion, contains a number of pitfalls for the historian, both with respect to the life and activity of the main character and with respect to his party and his milieu.[71]

From the findings presented here, we see how Polish documentation can enable us to wean ourselves from an exclusive reliance on legend in our attempts to examine the history of the Besht, his immediate circle, and his milieu; and to avoid some of the pitfalls that await the historical interpreter of the traditional sources. [—Translated by Eli Lederhendler.]

NOTES

I would like to thank Professors Shmuel Ettinger, Chone Shmeruk, Immanuel Etkes, Dr. Israel Bartal, and Dr. Shaul Stampfer for their helpful comments on earlier drafts of this essay.

The following abbreviations are used in the notes: *Shivhei ha-Besht*—*Shivhei ha-Besht* (Kapust, 1815); AGAD—Archiwum Główne Akt Dawnych; BC —Biblioteka Czartoryskich; EW—Ewidencja; GOSP—Gospodarczne.

1. A select bibliography, correct up until the late 1960s, appears in *Encyclopedia Judaica* (Jerusalem, 1971), vol. 7, cols. 1426–1427. A collection of basic essays on Hasidism was edited by A. Rubeinstein, *Peraqim be-toledot ha-hasidut u-ve-toledoteha* (Jerusalem, 1978).

2. *Shivhei ha-Besht,* for example, p. 3c–d: the Besht and the robbers; p. 5a: the Besht brings rain; p. 6a: the Besht employs a non-Jew; p. 15a: the Besht and the witch; pp. 18d–19a: the Besht and the priest; p. 35c: a noblewoman recognizes the Besht's expertise as a healer.

3. I. Bartal has demonstrated this point in his analysis, based on new sources, of the story of Rabbi Elazar of Brody who appears in *Shivhei ha-Besht:* " 'Aliyat r. el'azar me-amsterdam le-eres yisrael bi-shnat 5501 (1740); *"Mehqarim 'al toledot yahadut holand* 4 (Jerusalem, 1985), pp. 7–25.

4. *Shivhei ha-Besht,* pp. 15c–27a.

5. BC EW 41: record of expenses of the *kahal* paid by the tax lessee (Akcyzniki) in 1743. The payment to Jos, in the sum of 100 zloty, appears in a list of various payments to the rabbi, the cantor, the beadle, and other employees of the community. Jos is here called *przedpowiedacz* (seer). However, in similar records from 1739 (EW 40), 1740, and 1744 (EW 41), instead of *przedpowiedacz* we find *kaznodzieia* (preacher); and in BC 4080 no. 86 the same Jos Jampolski is explicitly referred to as *kaznodzieia*. I assume that the terms are interchangeable and their significance identical. Many preachers were students of kabbala, and some of them gained reputations for possessing supernatural powers. See, e.g., the story about R. Ishaq Drobizer, a preacher, in *Shivhei ha-Besht,* pp. 9d–10a.

6. *Shivhei ha-Besht,* p. 12d.

7. EW 40, 41.

8. *Shivhei ha-Besht,* p. 18a–b.

9. C. Kamiński and J. Zukowski, *Katalog monet polskich* (Warsaw, 1980), p. 18; A. Popiol-Szymanska, *Poglady monetarne w Polsce od XV do XVIII wieku* (Poznań, 19780, pp. 108–109.

10. I intend to deal with this issue in a separate essay.

11. See, e.g., S. Dubnow, *Toledot ha-hasidut* (Tel-Aviv, 1975), pp. 8–24; B. Z. Dinur, *Be-mifne ha-dorot* (Jerusalem, 1972), pp. 83–139; I. Halpern, *Yehudim ve-yahadut be-mizrah eiropa* (Jerusalem, 1969), pp. 30–33; J. Katz, *Masoret u-mashber* (Jerusalem, 1958), pp. 266–269.

12. Dubnow, op. cit., p. 36; R. M. Seltzer, "The Secular Appropriation of Hasidism by an East European Jewish Intellectual: Dubnow, Renan and the Besht," *Polin* 1 (1986), pp. 155–156.

13. *Shivhei ha-Besht,* p. 13c.

14. S. Stampfer, "The 1764 Census of Polish Jewry," *Bar-Ilan* 24–25 (1989), 135–136. According to the census, in 1764 there were 1,477 Jews in Bar and 2,039 in Miedzyboz.

15. BC 5881 1.23400 23412 13.5.1744, 14.2.1745; BC 5796 1.8515 10.5.1709; BC 5758 1.481 12.11.1745.

16. BC 5758 1.476 27.2.1745; BC 5795 1.8467 4.8.1735; BC 5796 1.8503 8.8.1708, 1.8566 17.6.1728; BC 5987 1.48200 19.7.1739; BC 5825 1.13517 (n.d.).

17. See the petitions of: Manaszko Dubieński, Józef Moskowicz, Newach Morduchowicz, Ela Leybowicz (EW 87); BC 5825 1.13527 (n.d.).

18. BC 5775 1.4816 1.4818 11.4.1737, 11.1.1738, *Tygodnik Illustrowany,* Warsaw, vol. 15, no. 382 19.1.1867 str. 31; BC 5788 1.7170–73 22.4.1744, 15.12.1745, 3.1.1746, 12.12.1745. Compare the letter of Dessier, expressing pride in the new buildings and the growth of the population: BC 5796 1. 8495 1.8556 30.12.1730, 29.1.1731.

19. Stampfer, op. cit. (see n. 14).

20. R. Mahler, *Toledot ha-yehudim be-polin* (Merhavia, 1946), p. 244.

21. See the records of the *kahal*'s expenses in EW 40, 41.

22. Halpern (n. 11), p. 32; Mahler (n. 20), pp. 324–327; M. Balaban, "Ma-'amadam ha-homri shel qehillot yisrael," in I. Halpern (ed.), *Beit yisrael be-polin* (Jerusalem, 1948), vol. 1, pp. 98–99.

23. EW 41.

24. See the lists of those chosen for *kahal* positions, contained in EW 41, and compare the lists of taxpayers in the files noted below, n. 46, and the petitions in EW 41 and EW 87. In a book on Miedzyboz at the time of the Besht that I am writing, I intend to analyze these lists and describe the social and economic structure of the community. At this point it is possible to state that the following families figured among the elite of the community: Zalman, Moszko Haritun, Leyzer Monasterny, Wolf Abramowicz, and Baruch Czarny.

25. The term occurs in the declaration of the *pospólstwo* of 1716, in EW 41.

26. I. Halpern (ed.), *Pinqas va'ad arb'a arasot* (Jerusalem, 1945), p. 542.

27. EW 87: "Nas iako pospólstwo do consilium generalnego nieproszona dla uchwaly panów kwartalnych."

28. EW 41.
29. "Wedlug zadania pospulstwa . . .", a constitution first promulgated in 1726 by Elżbieta Sieniawksa, owner of Miedzyboz, and renewed on 25.4.1737.
30. EW 41; the contract is dated: "23 Chesfin [Heshvan] alias po polska Novemb." Four people referred to as *kwartalny* (chairmen) signed in the name of the *kahal:* three are called *lawnik*, that is, member of the *kahal* board, and one is the *starszy ziemski*, or chairman of the provincial council. The representatives of the *pospólstwo* are not described in terms of function or title.
31. EW 41: tax-lease contract of 1744.
32. EW 41: see n. 29.
33. See: H. H. Ben-Sasson, *Hagut ve-hanhagah* (Jerusalem, 1959), pp. 135–139; Halpern (n. 11), pp. 55–58; and compare the voting system used in Cracow at the end of the sixteenth century, described by M. Balaban, "Die Krakauer Judengemeinde-Ordnung von 1595," *Jahrbuch der jüdisch-literarischen Gesellschaft* 10 (1912), pp. 314–318.
34. See: B. Weinryb, *Te'udot le-toledot ha-qehillot ha-yehudiyot be-polin* (New York, 1951), pp. 5–7 ('edah), 223, (asefah).
35. Compare: Weinryb (ibid.), p. 186, doc. 10 (from the year 1728), which begins: "The leaders of this holy community of Cracow, the chiefs and appointed heads *and the remaining yehidei segulah* . . ." (emphasis added). It would appear that the latter term refers to those who had voting rights but who held no office in the community. Likewise, it seems that in Miedzyboz the combined form, "the *kahal* and the *pospólstwo* (or *yehidei segulah*)" is analogous to the Polish town's *urzad miejskie i pospòlstwo*.
36. EW 41: "Punkta Ccchu Rzcznikórw. . . ."
37. BC 5870 1.21168–69 2.4.1744, 21.12.1744.
38. EW 41: order of Wolinski dated 28.3.1743, and list of those subject to expulsion (Specifikatia . . .).
39. EW 87; compare, H. H. Ben-Sasson, "Taqannot isurei shabbat shel polin u-mashma'utan ha-hevratit ve-ha-kalkalit," *Zion* 21 (1955), pp. 188–190, 199–200.
40. EW 80/1 Dekret 1741: "prywatny nabożienstwo."
41. See my essay, "An Exploitative Regime and the Opposition to it in Miedzyboz *ca.* 1730," in S. Almog *et al.* (eds.), *Sefer ha-yovel likhvod profesor Shmuel Ettinger* (Jerusalem, 1987).
42. Dinur (n. 11): on artisans' trade associations in opposition to the *kahal* and on separate prayer quorums (pp. 136–139); on rabbis appointed by Polish authorities (pp. 106–107); and on settlement of Jews without residence permits (pp. 113–116).
43. See petitions in EW 41, 87, and cf. BC 5905 1.28043 26.6.1745, BC 5959 1.33449 (n.d.).
44. I. Etkes, "Hasidism as a Movement—The First Stage," in B. Safran (ed.), *Hasidism: Continuity or Innovation* (Cambridge, Mass., 1988), 1–26.
45. Chone Shmeruk, "Mashma'uta ha-hevratit shel ha-shehita ha-hasidit," *Zion* 20 (1955), p. 72.

46. BC 4067, BC 4078, BC 4080, BC 4085, BC 4101, BC 4111, BC 4114, BC 4117, BC 4121, BC GOSP 308, BC 4127.

47. BC 4067, p. 9a.

48. BC 4079, no. 81.

49. BC 4085, p. 12a.

50. BC 4121, no. 95.

51. BC GOSP, no. 93.

52. BC 4127, no. 110. Hyrszko Balszemowicz also appears in BC 4131, no. 96 (1766), and as the owner of a shop, in no. 23 and in the census of 1764: AGAD (Warszawa) Rewizya Miasta: Arch. Potockich z Lancuta 168 [Also on microfilm in Jerusalem, Central Archives for the History of the Jewish People, HM3660], Miedzyboz, December 25, 1764, p. 124, no. 96.

53. BC 4111 (1752), no. 88; BC 4114 (1753), no. 91; BC 4117 (1755), no. 92; BC 4121 (1758), no. 94; BC GOSP 308 (1760), no. 92; BC 4127 (1763), no. 109; he appears also in later lists, and in the 1764 census, op. cit., p. 124, no. 95.

54. BC 4114 (1753), no. 107; BC 4117 (1755), no. 107; BC 4121 (1758), no. 123; BC GOSP 308 (1760), no. 122; BC 4127, no. 139; in the census, op. cit., p. 125, no. 108.

55. BC 4117 (1755), no. 101; BC 4121 (1758), no. 107; BC GOSP 308 (1760), no. 103; BC 4127 (1763), no. 122; in the census, op. cit., p. 123, no. 80. In sources dating from 1760 we find a person identified as Jankiel Balszamów Ayzykowicz.

56. Dinur (n. 11), p. 170.

57. EW 41: "skolarz ubogi nasz."

58. *Zion* 47 (1982), pp. 258–272.

59. Both in correspondence of Polish officials (BC 5965 1.42850) and in *Shivhei ha-Besht* (pp. 5c, 8c–d, 22d, and 35c) the sense of the words "dokter," "Doktor," is that of a medical doctor. In contrast, every rabbi mentioned in the Polish documents from Miedzyboz is referred to as "Rabin." Other Jewish clergy are referred to according to specific function: "szkolnik," "bakalarz," "kantor," etc. "Men of the cloth" without specific function (including scholars who were not rabbis) are referred to as "duchowny" (see above, re: Moszko duchowny). There is even one document in which "doktor" appears together with "duchowny." The petition of a certain Sheyne, from ca. 1730 (EW 86), relates that she went to the "Doktor" to seek healing, while her adversary, Icko Oganisti, is said to have sworn "do duchownych kahalskich," that is, before the clergymen (judges of the kahal court?). See my essay (n. 41).

60. *Shivhei ha-Besht*, pp. 15d, 35c.

61. Ibid., p. 18a.

62. Gershom Scholem, "Demuto ha-historit shel r. Israel baal shem tov," *Molad* 18 (1960), pp. 339–347.

63. Dunbow (n. 11), pp. 51, 69; Scholem, op. cit., pp. 337, 342.

64. M. Piekarz, *Bi-yemei semihat ha-hasidut* (Jerusalem, 1978), pp. 136–137.

65. EW 41: "Ubogim Zydom w Miedzybozu mieszkaiacym których kahal tute-yszy uznal y przezemnie na ten tylko rok sa approbowani. . . ."
66. Compare: *Shivhei ha-Besht*, p. 22b.
67. Ibid., p. 24d.
68. EW 41: Specifikatia . . . ; "Sasiedzi w domu Wolfa Kucego."
69. Shmuel Ettinger, "Ha-hanhaga ha-hasidit be-'isuvah," in *Dat ve-hevrah be-toledot yisrael ve-he-'amim* (Jerusalem, 1965), pp. 122–123.
70. See Table 1.
71. Piekarz (n. 64), p. 136.

6

The Hasidic Movement—Reality and Ideals

Shmuel Ettinger

The Hasidic movement appeared among the Jewish people in Europe on the brink of a decisive change in their history, at a time when the Jews were beginning to take part in the social and cultural world that surrounded them. The Jewish community as a religious-social corporation, the thousand-year-old corporate framework to which individual Jews had a duty to belong, was beginning to collapse under pressures from within and from without. Outside, jurists were claiming in the name of absolutist principles that all corporations injured the authority of the ruler, and that the extensive autonomy of the Jewish community was making it a "state within the state." While inside, "enlightened" Jews were complaining that the strict communal corporate regime gave the upper hand to an oligarchy, which exploited the ordinary members of the community and deliberately kept them from closer ties with the Christian environment.

The difference in general political trends between the countries of Central and Western Europe and those of Eastern Europe, especially the difference in the situation of the Jewish populations of these two regions, led to a contrast in development between eastern and western Jewry, a contrast which grew so sharp that by the middle of the nineteenth century their ways seemed to have parted completely.

In the west the Jewish community was undermined. One reason was that the authorities withdrew their support. A more important reason

Reprinted by permission of UNESCO from *Journal of World History* 11, nos. 1–2. Copyright © UNESCO 1968.

was that the socially and politically active Jews, who were able to achieve some standing and influence in the society around them, began to despise the "narrow" Jewish society with its struggles and its honours and titles and at most were prepared to regard it as a voluntary association for the organisation of religious life. The centre of gravity of these Jews' lives was outside and beyond the community. Their language, their culture, their ambitions were those of their Christian environment. Whereas in Eastern Europe the authorities continued substantially to support the Jewish corporation. The few "educated" Jews there who called for a merger with the life outside were regarded as rebels, or even traitors to their people, and the formal cohesion of Jewish society grew.

The Hasidic movement, that was to be the chief cause and main bearer of these trends peculiar to Eastern Europe, appeared in Podolia, a distant province of south-east Poland, at a period of decline and disintegration in that country. Jewish society there was split from within, and in the grip of violent ferments. In Polish society the upper hand was gained by those opposed to the status of the central institutions of the autonomous Jewish organisation. They claimed that continuation of the recognition of those Jewish institutions was a further proof of weakness of the central government. The result of this criticism was that government recognition of the autonomous institutions was cancelled and in 1764 they were dispersed. There is not the slightest doubt that the Hasidic movement helped to unify Jewish society in Eastern Europe from the organizational point of view and that in religion and ideas it was a revival.

Hasidism means devout piety, communion with God, special devotion by man to the service of his Creator. Even before the eighteenth century several movements or circles had been named Hasidic. The best-known were the groups of Hasidim faithful to Judaism in the days of persecution by Antiochus Epiphanes in the second century B.C., and the Ashkenazi Hassidim of the twelfth–thirteenth centuries. The new Hasidism we are considering here is known as the Beshtian Hasidism, after its originator. Rabbi Israel Baal-Shem-Tov (the Besht for short) was born in Podolia in or about 1700, apparently of humble origins and in early life worked at a variety of unskilled trades. He then became locally famous as a faith-healer, who knew how to heal the sick with magic formulae and amulets (hence the appellation Baal-Shem-Tov—Master of the good name). He gave up seclusion and took on the mantle of leader at the end

of the 1730s, and in the 1740s gathered around him a group of supporters and admirers who took up his way of serving God. His personality is
veiled from us by a haze of legends; one of the few surviving authentic
documents on him is the letter he wrote to his brother-in-law Eretz Israel
in 1750 describing his mystical experience—how his soul rose up to
Heaven, and how he met the Messiah there. On that occasion the Besht
asked the Messiah when he would come and received the famous answer: "When your streams spread out", that is to say when the Hasidic
teachings of the Besht spread among the people.

When the Besht died in 1760 he left behind him a genuine movement,
although it is hard to estimate its size at that time. At its head was placed
not the Besht's chief disciple, who preserved the Besht's words and wrote
down his teaching, Rabbi Jacob Joseph of Polonne, the man who had
been closest to the late leader for many years, but a relatively new man,
Rabbi Dov-Ber of Miedzyrzecz (the "Great Maggid"[1] of the Hasidim).
During the Great Maggid's leadership (1760–1772), Hasidism spread
over the wide areas of Eastern Europe, became a real public force, and
came to its first big clash with the existing Jewish leadership in Poland-
Lithuania.

There is something novel in the rapid spread of the Hasidic movement
and especially in the fact that it remained a legitimate part of a society
so tradition-bound and conservative as the Jewish, whose leaders at that
time waged war against it. No wonder so many scholars have tried to
explain the phenomenon. The first serious student of Hasidism, Simon
Dubnow,[2] suggested that "by an immense psychic influence, Hasidism
created a type of believer to whom feeling was more important than
external observance"—as opposed to what had hitherto been the order
of importance in Jewish communities. In addition, "Hasidism was the
answer to the stress and sorrow of Jewish public life, for although it
could not change the objective conditions of hardship in which the Jews
lived, it created an ideal world for them, a world in which the despised
Jew was master". In Dubnow's view Hasidism also answered the spiritual needs of the individual believer and the aspirations of the generation
by transferring the solution of its problems to the world of the imagination.

Ben-Zion Dinur[3] opposes this view which tries to explain the success
of Hasidism by saying that "history answered the needs of the generation," and he regards it as a simplification. His method is to study the

historic circumstances in which Hasidism was created, and to examine the moralistic literature and its social criticism in eighteenth-century Poland. His main emphasis, however, is laid upon a question: "What were the social forces in Jewish eighteenth-century society that bore up the Hasidic movement, that gave shape to its public essence and set up its organisation?"[4] He also investigates "the contribution of Hasidism to the solution of social crises," and stresses that the Hasidic movement belonged organically to the social opposition in the communities.[5] And he comes to the conclusion that its torchbearers were religious functionaries of lower rank, "teachers, cantors" and the like who formed "the social opposition" of Jewish society.

Using Dinur's studies as a point of departure, developing them to an extreme degree and comparing the Hasidim to members of the Sabbatian sects, Joseph Weiss tries[6] to portray the nature of the Hasidic leadership at the outset of the movement. His hard-hitting descriptions bring before us the personality of the wandering preacher—a "miserable type," according to Weiss, who "sells his teaching for alms" and "a smell of money-grubbing rises from the grubbing of these poor wretches for a living—even a smell of Sabbatian heresy."[7] Despite this pungent description, there is, however, no evidence that the Besht's immediate circle were mainly "wandering preachers"; we know definitely that some of them were not, nor were they other representatives of "secondary intelligentsia" (to use a currently fashionable phrase for religious functionaries other than rabbis). The outstanding example of R. Jacob Joseph of Polonne, author of the Hasidic classic "Toledot Yaaqov Yosef" (Toledot), teaches us that in the Besht's circle there were people of relatively stable social position, who were ready to endanger their position for their ideas. On the other hand, some wandering preachers known to us by name from that time were not members of the movement at its outset; or even against it. What is more, a look at the histories of some of them, the author of "Zera Beyrakh Shlishi,"[8] for example, shows how doubtful it is that there was any such fixed social category as "wandering preacher": the demarcation line proposed to distinguish between the itinerant preacher and the one set up in a fixed community position was very often crossed over in reality. But it is certainly true that preachers, fixed or wandering, played an important part in the introduction and spread of new ideas, thanks to their close contacts with the people; it is also true that they sometimes took to the road out of devotion to their ideas. This may explain the decisive part played in the crystallization of Hasidic ideas and the organization of the movement by such Maggidim (preachers) as the "Mokhiah" ('rebuker') of Polonne, the "Great Maggid" of Miedzyrzecz, R. Yehiel-Michal of Zloczow, or R. Hayyim, the Maggid of Vilna. But the chief fighters against Hasidic ideas were also Maggidim—R. Israel Loebel, the Maggid of Nowogrodek; R. Jacob Israel of Kremenetz; and R. David of Makow. And as Gershom Scholem has shown in his study of R. Israel Loebel,[9] even in the sphere of ideas there were no clearly defined "fronts." The sharp social dividing line between the "upper echelon intelligentsia," i.e. the rabbis, and the "secondary intelligentsia" in eighteenth-century Poland is completely without basis in fact. Many rabbis were dependent on the community leaders while among the rabbis and the ritual slaughterers and the wandering preachers, some were connected with the ruling group and some were against it. In all, it is hard, even at the dawn of Hasidism, to define the movement socially.

It is far harder, as scholars have shown, to find grounds for the popular assumption that the radical social teaching of Hasidism conquered the hearts of the masses and answered their deepest needs. In fact, social matters had very little weight in Hasidic teaching: in all questions of livelihood and economy, the Lord would provide. In the words of R. Jacob Joseph: "Let not the poor man envy the rich, for man does not touch what is prepared for his fellow, and let not the craftsman hate his fellow-craftsman, nor the shopkeeper the shopkeeper, nor the publican the publican, nor the scholar the scholar" (*Toledot,* Bo). Even where we find some sort of "social rules for the benefit of the poor and humble" like those R. Aaron of Karlin added to the communal ordinances of taxation in Nieswiez, Israel Heilpern[10] has proved that the rules are essentially the same in spirit as those commonly accepted in the communities of the time. Nor is this all. Dinur in his comprehensive study has collected a wide range of violent social criticism from the moral literature of Poland before the rise of Hasidism, and from the days when the movement was taking shape. A painstaking comparison between parts of that literature and the first Hasidic sermons[11] shows that compared with the extent and acuteness of non-Hasidic social criticism, the Hasidic literature has very little to say on these subjects and that little is moderate in tone. The very fact that there were so many moralistic books in eighteenth-century Poland shows that the public was receptive, and the paleness and scantiness of the social morality preached by the Hasidim tells us that the source of their strength was not here.

The success of Hasidism sprang from the fact that it brought mysticism to the "intelligentsia" of the time in a form they could accept. It particularly appealed to young students and religious functionaries. On the other hand it found an echo among the masses, for instead of the ideal personality of the pre-Hasidic generation, the remote, self-mortifying mystic, Hasidism idealised the mystic who leads the people and lives among them.

The seeds of this change lay in a religious ferment that had not subsided in Polish Jewry since the failure of the Sabbatian movement,[12] and from the unceasing activities of diverse religious groups. Some of these groups were extremely radical in religious matters, and when they left the strict path of orthodoxy there is no doubt at all that they aroused opposition among the people. We seem to find an echo of this in "Shivhei Habesht" (Praises of the Besht), a collection of traditions and legends on the Besht that was partially written down in his lifetime and printed at the beginning of the nineteenth century. In this work the story is told of R. Nahman of Kosow, one of the Besht's inner circle, who came by chance to a place and prayed in a changed form of prayer: "When he finished his prayers all the people of the Beth Hamidrash (prayer house) pounced on him and asked him how he could stand before the Ark without leave and change the prayers into a version prayed neither by our fathers nor by our forefathers who were great in their generation. He answered: 'And who shall say that they are in Paradise?' "—that is to say, he cast doubt upon all the accepted religious tradition. Or there is the saying of R. Pinhas of Korzec: "In this generation people do not occupy themselves with the [study of] Torah as in early days, for now there has spread a great fear [of God] throughout the world, and in the early days there was not such fear, wherefore they used to occupy themselves with Torah. There are few places [now] where they study; there there is no fear." [13] This saying emphasizes the essential antagonism between the way of the Hasid and the way of the non-Hasid, for in Jewish society at that period the scholar, the man devoted wholly to study, was the ideal, and study of the Torah the commandment that outweighed all others. We note the behaviour of the followers of R. Abraham of Kalisk (Kałusz) a disciple of the Great Maggid, "joking and mocking at the scholars"—a practice severely rebuked by the Maggid of

Miedzyrzecz.[14] But this was not the way of the movement as a whole, which usually shunned controversy and emphasized its faithfulness to tradition in every field of life. It was, in fact, this moderation—even in times of persecution—that enabled the movement to hold out within the Jewish communities, and not to be pushed into the position of a seceding sect.

In his article on communion with God *(devekut)*, Gershom Scholem [15] noted that at the beginning of the Hasidic way of life the extreme demand for maximum communion with God was put forward as a general ideal, for every person equally. But as the movement took shape this ideal was set before the zaddikim, the leaders, alone. And even of them it was not demanded in its pristine form. For the ordinary Hasid a broad formula was found of "adhere to your sage", i.e. the Hasid should attach himself to a rabbi, his zaddik. The leaders of the movement also softened the rigorous demands that many preachers made of the public; as R. Jacob Joseph tells us, from so many threats, the public had begun to lose faith in them: "In the words of the masses: it is impossible that things can ever be as bad as they make out in moralistic books just to threaten people" (*Toledot*, Nisavim). This approach was not mere opportunism on the part of a growing movement; it seems to have been part of the Besht's own fundamental approach. In "Praises of the Besht" we are told of "a sermon by a visiting preacher," whom the Besht defined as an "informer," "speaking ill of the people of Israel," i.e. the Besht considered preaching morals and religion to the public after the manner of the maggidim an evil thing. "The Besht jumped up from his place and tears splashed from his eyes and he said: 'Know that a son of Israel goes all day in the market; at evening when he is sad he grows anxious and says "woe to me if I let pass the hour of evening prayer," and he goes into a house and prays the evening prayer and does not know what he is saying, and even so seraphim and angels are very moved at this.' " And R. Nahman of Horodenka interpreted the Besht's meaning thus: "That by fasting and mortification and persistence in study sadness grows and his way casts blame on his fellow man that none does as he did for they forsake eternal life for the temptation of transitory matters" (*Toledot*, "Things I heard from my Teacher"). And this is how the author of *Toledot* interpreted it in the name of his teacher "of whom is said: and the Lord sent fiery serpents among the people—preachers who awaken judgment on the world" (*Toledot*, Qedoshim). That is to say, extreme demands from the public, or even severe self-mortification by the righteous themselves, would not only fail to help the people but would awaken judgment (i.e., would emphasize the distance between the ideal of communion with God and the behaviour of man in the market-place) and thus put off redemption.

The reservations about severe self-mortifying piety, in order not "to awaken judgment in the world," spring from another basic part of the same circle's outlook, namely seeing the organic bond between all sections of the people, seeing the people as one body. This motif recurs again and again in the sayings of R. Jacob Joseph: "For all the world together is called one figure and the masses of the people are the legs of the figure and the righteous are the eyes of the community etc., and this is the meaning of the saying that the whole world is like a ladder, that the masses of the people are arrayed on the ground, that may be called the feet of the world, and the scholars are the head, and this means 'its top reaches to Heaven'; that if the generation acts rightly, the heads of the generation rise up a degree more . . . and when the converse is true, they go down, as our sages said of Samuel ha-kattan (one of the early Tannaim)—he was worthy the Holy spirit should shine on him, but his generation was not worthy of it . . . for when the legs of man descend into the pit, the head too is brought low" (*Toledot,* Vayese). From this organic bond, from mutual dependence, springs the responsibility of the righteous man or leader, the zaddik, towards the whole community, and this attitude is based on a particular mystical principle. There is obviously nothing "democratic" or egalitarian in it. The crowd is not regarded as equal in value to the zaddik. The difference between them is a difference in kind: the righteous man, "the man of form," is the active element, while the masses, "the people of matter," are passive. But from this springs the demand the righteous man should take responsibility for the public. And as the movement establishes itself, we find the idea recurring and being reemphasized that the righteous man must not justify himself by the decline of the generation. The essence of the bond is that the existence of one has no meaning without the other; in the words put into the mouth of Moses when he spoke to the Lord: "If Thou hast killed them (i.e. Israel in the desert) all at once, what need has the world for me? and what am I without them?" (*Toledot,* Huqat).

In order to lead the crowd, the righteous man must step down from his rank, his high degree, to the material world. This is the celebrated principle of the "descent of the righteous" in Hassidism. Whatever may be the mystic roots of the theory, it is the *raison d'être* of the Zaddik as a leader. As R. Levi Yishaq of Berdyczew put it: "Why did the Holy Name set up that the zaddik should step down from his rank? For it would seem better that the zaddik should always stand on his place, to serve the Holy Name with great sense and love Him with perfect love. This is the saying of the Besht and my righteous teacher Dov-Ber: that in the fall of the zaddik and his strengthening himself to return to his place, from this souls were created, and he is like one who would raise up his fellow from slime and rubbish—he too must go down near the slime and rubbish to raise him up" (*Qedushat levi,* on the Song of Songs). A doctrine like this not only does not deny "any justification" from "the masses" so long as they "remained without a leader,"[16] but it puts the masses in the centre of the righteous man's interests and activity—and no doubt accounts for the immense following of the Hassidic leaders. The real test of both theory and movement came in the generation of the Maggid's disciples, the period when the movement took shape and spread; and it stood the test of time. The more the zaddik stressed his responsibility to the public and his willingness to care for them, the more his popularity grew.

It should not be concluded from this that the Hasidic leaders were not aware of the gap between the two sides of their doctrine; they were torn between two duties—that of the mystic, owing perpetual allegiance to the world above, and as it were sinning if he left off communion with God; and the duty of a leader to care for his people, one and all in body and soul. It seems that a certain amount of mystical contemplation had to be sacrificed for the sake of spreading the movement. R. Elimelekh of Lezajsk, according to Dubnow, was the founder of "practical Zaddikism," and the historian regarded it as a basic condition of his work "that they should support him lavishly and supply all his material needs."[17] Yet it is R. Elimelekh who brings out the peculiar tragedy of the torn soul of the zaddik:

It is hard to know why Moses our Teacher, peace be upon him, was punished at the waters of Meribah when he smote the rock; after all the Holy One Blessed Be He agreed with him, for it is written: "and water came forth abundantly." Now since he did what was not right, the rock should not have given forth water abundantly . . . but it appears—(of course a man of God is forbidden not to do the will of the Creator, Blessed Be He)—that the way of the righteous man is always to pursue the good of Israel, and even if in following this duty he has to do something with an element of sin to it, he will do it for the good of Israel; he will even take hell upon himself for them, for all his desire is to do them good. (Noam elimelekh, Balaq)

R. Levi Yishaq too knows that the secluded mystic has greater personal righteousness because of his perpetual communion with the Divine; nonetheless, it is better to be a righteous man who breaks off his communion and looks after the needs of the people:

Let it be clear that we see that there are zaddikim who achieve through their prayers as they want, and there are righteous men who do not achieve. The matter is thus, that the great zaddik is he who comes to the garden courtyard of the king's palace, the king of the world, and recognizes that he is in the presence of the king—he forgets what he had to ask in matters of this world and asks only that he should always cleave to the king; for what is pleasant to him but to be a servant of the Creator and to be a servant of the king? and he forgets all his business. Not thus are the zaddikim who are not of this degree, even though they stand before the king, he remembers his petition, that he wishes to ask; and most of all the zaddik (i.e. the great one)—when he comes before the king he does not remember the petition about the matter of this world that he wishes to ask, so he does not achieve; and the lesser zaddik then is he who remembers his petition as he stands before the king and makes the request of him: he therefore achieves. (Qedushat Levi, on the Song of Songs)

In actual fact, it was not these late zaddikim who laid down the doctrine of the zaddik through whom plenty comes to the world; the Besht had already preached "Hanina my son (i.e. the zaddik) is a path and a pipe to continue plenty in the world" (*Ben Porath*, Veyehi), intending both the spiritual and the material plenty that the zaddik rains on the world by his influence. But gradually the material side of plenty became more important, until by the time we come to the disciples of the disciples of the Great Maggid, the ability to provide for material needs in practice is the recognized evidence of qualification for leadership:

The Rabbi of Lublin prided himself that he had been ordained by the Maggid of Rowno (the Great Maggid) to be a zaddik for a Hasidic group. For a rustic came to complain that someone had trespassed on him to take away his 'arenda,'[18] and the Maggid lay in bed and told him to go to the Beth Hamidrash [prayer house] and call someone to issue summons [to the trespasser]. And the Rabbi of Lublin was walking up and down in the Beth Hamidrash, and the rustic called him and he wrote an invitation and offered it to the Maggid to sign. And he [the

Maggid] answered him: You sign it, and they will obey you as they obey me. You have no greater authority than this. (Niflaot harabbi, 187)

The grandson of the Besht, R. Moses Haim Ephraim of Sudylków, even signed an explicit treaty in 1798 with "the chiefs of the holders of arenda in the neighbouring villages": they would "submit to his authority in all that he might say" and he would "help them with his teaching [Torah] and his prayer which effectively aids all who cleave to him," in return for 6 guildens of every thousand of their income.[19]

Despite the moderation of the new movement as a whole, sooner or later it was bound to clash with the leadership of the communities over wider areas. The movement was saved from the fate of other religious sects in similar circumstances by the fact that it refused to declare war on the whole from which it sprang. It did not regard itself as a band of saints and the rest of Israel as a "kingdom of evil"; thus it did not turn into what its opponents wanted to make it; a seceding sect cut off by both choice and necessity. Elements of religious radicalism appear in Hasidism as extraneous adjuncts. Scholars see radical elements in some of the central figures of the movement, but these tendencies found no public expression because of the view accepted in those circles that there were two separate moral systems—that of the zaddik and that of the public as a whole. Insofar as radical elements existed, they were veiled in the clouds of the first system, in which much was mysterious and obscure. As a public movement, Hasidism proclaimed and emphasized its adherence to tradition; it rejected all radical tendencies in religion, stressing chiefly the basic teachings of unity and mutual responsibility between all parts of the nation, even including the wickedest of the wicked. As R. Aryeh Leib the "rebuker of Polonne" used to say: "A little zaddik likes little sinners and a great zaddik likes and stands up for even hardened sinners." Such teachings prevented separatism.

The description of the struggle against Hasidism needs also careful examination. As is well known, relations became very strained indeed in Lithuania and White Russia, but in the Ukraine, in the sixties and seventies of the eighteenth century, i.e. before and even after the Ban of Brody,[20] there was cooperation between the heads of communities and the leaders of Hasidism.[21] In 1767 a religious court judge (Av-Beth-Din) of Rowno and his court rely on a ban in the matter of usufruct that had been proclaimed by the Maggid of Miedzyrzecz, and the signed verdict of his court is validated by the famous Hassidic leader R. Yehiel-Mikhal of Zloczow. In 1778 the heads of the important community of Dubno make an agreement with "the honoured rabbi, head of the religious court of the holy community of Polonne and his adherents," this being R. Jacob Joseph, the disciple of the Besht, for joint action in "the ransoming of prisoners," i.e. the freeing of a leaseholder seized by his overlord. These communal leaders seem to cooperate with the heads of Hasidism in order to get their help in matters beyond the reach of communal organization; while the authority and the ban of the zaddik had great force in that section of the public.

The main principle at issue in the clash between Hasidim and Mitnaggedim ("opponents") was the problem of authority which is to say, that in most disputes the Hasidim would be asked—: where did they get the authority "to change the coin that the sages had minted?"[22] But such objections did not rest mainly on the assumption that it was forbidden to alter what heads of communities had uttered. These heads, even in Vilna, did not themselves tend to be extreme in persecuting the Hasidim. The authority and validity for heads of communities to persecute and oppress the Hasidim came from a man who held no official position at all and had not been chosen by "rational choice," the Gaon of Vilna "Man of God . . . Rabbi Elijah Hasid, may his light shine." This was the man who "sent for the dignitaries [heads of the community in Vilna] and asked them angrily why they had dealt lightly with them [the Hasidim]. Were it in my power I would do to them what Elijah the prophet did to the prophets of Baal."[23]

It is an error to suppose that the struggle between the Hasidim and the Mitnaggedim, their opponents, was a clash between establishment and charisma. The Gaon certainly had the authority belonging to a great scholar, but despite this (or rather because of it) his main influence was charismatic. None other than his own pupil, R. Hayyim of Volozhin, attested that the Gaon had had a "revelation of Elijah" (i.e. prophetic visions). There are no doubt degrees of charism, but the clash here was between two forms and two sources of charismatic leadership.[24] An added proof is that R. Hayyim, the faithful disciple, had an approach to Hasidim completely different from that of his teacher. It cannot be merely assumed that the difference in time was responsible for the change, i.e. that Hasidism was well established by R. Hayyim's time. It seems more likely that Elijah the Gaon's personality, with its charismatic power, shaped the struggle he headed.

The main authority of the Hasidic leader came from his direct connection with supernatural powers—powers that he brought to the aid of the individual and the public. But the way the Hasidim were organized also played its part, in the Hasidic group ('Eda'), that clustered around the zaddik. The open nature of this group did not bridge the gap between Hasidim and their opponents, but it did serve to exorcize the suspicion that the Hasidim have downright heretical tendencies, for these groups were open to all and exposed to the eyes of all.

The transformation from the small group to the wide movement, as is well known, was the work of the Maggid of Miedzyrzecz. He transferred the centre from out-of-the-way Podolia to Volhynia, which was much more in the centre of the Polish kingdom, and sent emissaries to spread his doctrine far and wide to White Russia, to Lithuania, and to central Poland. His disciples, who have no specific social distinguishing marks, came from various social strata, and were learned in equally differing degrees.

We now encounter a paradoxical element in the formation of the movement: Rabbi Dov Ber of Miedzyrzecz, the Great Maggid, the well-known figure called by his disciples the "Rabbi of all the sons of the Diaspora," was a leader of authoritarian views, and yet directed the movement into ways of decentralization. He set up group after group with a pupil of his at the head of almost every one, with the result that after his death there was no single agreed leader of the movement. The tradition of autonomous activity in the local Jewish communities must have assisted the decentralizing tendency in the movement. But this certainly does not imply identity between any Hasidic group and a particular community. On the contrary, the zaddik, the righteous man, had followers (Hasidim) in various places, and his influence was sometimes spread over wide areas and large communities, while he himself lived in some small remote township. But it should be emphasized that the decentralizing tradition of communal organisation was able to assist the splitting of the Hasidic leadership, in which every zaddik and group had a great and growing degree of independence.

This process by which the Hasidic leadership grew did not lack internal stress and struggle. Few of the Besht's disciples were among the disciples of the Maggid. Even in the Maggid's lifetime there was no general agreement with his ways. Some disagreed with his ideas; others, apparently, with his new methods of organization in the movement. We seem to hear an echo of the latter criticism in the severe words of the author of *Toledot:*

Now we have to interpret the rest of the plagues [of Egypt] up to the plague of locusts ... a multiplication of locusts. ... The matter is the multiplication of leaders, that there is no [single] spokesman for the generation; just the opposite, they are all heads and spokesmen; as I heard, that was the blessing [i.e. curse] of Elijah on a town that they should all be leaders etc. And then spokesman *[dabar]* becomes murrain *[dever]* or hail, and by its force "he covered the eye of the land." He who is the eye of the land, like the eyes of the flock, who was worthy to keep watch over the land, has become many leaders "has covered the eye of the land" so that they cannot see the land, to keep watch over them. And this is the significance of "and he consumed the remnant that was left ye from the hail": when there was one spokesman for the generation it was a blessing, and when it was changed and became many leaders it was like hail and that causes destruction to the remnant of the community. (*Toledot,* Bo)

Perhaps the author of *Toledot* had hoped that the descendants of the Besht would produce "one spokesman for the generation." At all events R. Barukh, the Besht's grandson through his daughter, who grew up in the house of R. Pinhas of Korzec, an opponent of the Maggid's way, based his pretension to be the single leader of Hasidism on his illustrious descent. "The Holy Rabbi of Polonne," he says, "loved me very much and out of respect (for I was tender in years and he was well aged), I did not wish to sit in his presence and he likewise did not wish to sit in mine. I was forced to be seated that he might sit. And I took my box to sniff snuff before him, and he said to me: 'Boruchl, I heard from your grand-father the Besht that you will be his successor; can you take snuff like the Besht? For the Besht when he wanted to go to the worlds above would take snuff ...'" (*Bosina de-nahora ha-shalem* p. 5). Whatever the truth of the words attributed to the author of *Toledot* in this story, it is clear that R. Barukh had claims to become "the spokesman of the generation" by virtue of his pedigree. There is therefore a certain interest in his conversation with R. Shneur Zalman of Lyady, one of the chief disciples of the Maggid of Miedzyrzecz and the founder of Habad Hasidism. After a very sharp conversation, reported by R. Shneur Zalman, R. Barukh proclaimed: "I am the grandson of the Besht and I must be respected". To which Rabbi Shneur Zalman replied: "I too am the Besht's grandson in spirit, for the Great Maggid was the chief disciple of the Besht and I am the disciple of the Maggid" (ibid).

This controversy touched the roots of a problem of great importance

to Hasidism—and to all movements with a charismatic leadership—
namely, how to transfer authority. Should it be from father to son, or
from teacher to disciple? Among the disciples of the Maggid, unlike the
descendants of the Besht, the latter version appears to have been the
accepted one. As R. Elimelekh of Lezajsk stated:

There are here two types of zaddikim. There are zaddikim sanctified by their
fathers who were holy and perfect and godfearing and "the Torah returns to its
lodgings," and there are zaddikim called "nazirites" because they set themselves
apart, although they are sons of common people. And these zaddikim [i.e. the
ones who are not the sons of zaddikim] cannot quickly fall from their sacred
rank, for they have nothing to rely on, and they stay humble and watch themselves with open eyes perpetually. But the zaddikim sons of saints, even be they
full of Torah and commandments, by virtue of their fathers helping them sometimes—there can arise from that divergence on the one hand and loftiness on
the other (i.e. they will become full of pride) and they will fall quickly from their
rank. And this is "say to the priests the sons of Aaron" here he hinted at the
zaddikim who are sons of zaddikim, and are called "priests sons of Aaron,"
warning them strictly that they should not presume to think at all of the lineage
of their fathers . . . and choose the best way for themselves. (Noam elimelekh,
Emor)

Indeed, he himself acted on the principle of transferring authority to a
disciple: there is a tradition that "the rabbi Rabbi Melekh in his old age
ordered all who were sick or embittered to come to his disciple R. Itzikel
of Lancut (the "seer" of Lublin). Until he accustomed everyone to come
to Lancut. And they ceased to come to him. Then he waxed very wroth"
(*Ohel elimelekh*, 165). If our hypothesis of the clash between two systems of inheriting authority is correct, there is a certain historic irony in
the fact that it was from the descendants of the Maggid himself and his
best disciples that the great Hassidic dynasties arose. Departing from
this tendency—possibly in reaction against it—a Hasidic group grew up
around the great-grandson of the Besht, R. Nahman of Bratslav. To this
day it is the only Hasidic group that has no living leader: it remains
faithful to the memory of R. Nahman "the dead Rabbi." And there is
no doubt that R. Nahman believed himself to be the leading zaddik of
his generation, and perhaps had claims to be "the spokesman of the
generation" according to his family's tradition.

Many writers on Hasidism have dwelt on the difference between
"theoretical Hasidism" in its pure and pristine form, and "practical
zaddikism" which came later. Dubnow writes on R. Elimelekh of Le-

zajsk: "While R. Elimelekh did not innovate at all in the theoretical teachings of the Besht and the Maggid, he added much to the system of practical zaddikism, by making it a system founded in the essence of Hasidism."[25] In his opinion, that is to say, this evil in Hasidism stemmed from R. Elimelekh. It is doubtful if there is any ground for the distinction between late "practical zaddikism" and the earlier "purer" kind. Why does not Dubnow complain that the Besht took payment for writing amulets—which is a kind of payment for service—whereas he condemns as corruption and exploitation the money paid to the latter-day zaddik for leading his flock? From a historical standpoint, the main problem is not the payment and its justification but the task of leadership and the way it was carried out: Did the Hasidic leadership have an influence that was destructive and corrupting on Jewish society, as many have claimed, especially those swayed by the attitude of the Haskalah writers?

It seems that the reverse is true. Where Hasidism ruled, Jewish society was less torn by conflicts and more stable than in the period before the movement took over. It is important to remember that in earlier days much of the internal stability of Jewish society and the authority of its leaders came from the support of the government. Whereas from the beginning of the nineteenth century the governments both of Austria and Russia developed hostility to Jewish autonomy, and the unifying of Jewish society had to be achieved without the support of the government —in fact actually against it.

It is, however, true that the Hasidic group was a framework separate from the community (though not against it and certainly not a substitute for it), and the very existence of such a framework, the fact that the authority of its head, the zaddik, was higher in the eyes of its members than the authority of the communal heads, meant that the comprehensiveness of communal leadership was weakened in Jewish life. Yet this development did not break down Jewish society, and after a bitter struggle between the two kinds of authority a *modus vivendi* began to appear. Gradually it became clear that the Hasidic leadership was capable of contributing to the strengthening of the unity of Jewish society as a whole. This was largely due to the way the Hasidic leadership was regarded by the people. The leaders of Hasidism did not make claims of principle against the authority of the community, and did not deny it; sometimes they controlled communities and sometimes they gave additional validity to community regulations and deeds, a validity that was weakened when the central autonomous institutions were abolished. The study of Shmeruk[26] has shown how the needs of communal life brought about compromise and even cooperation between Hasidim and non-Hasidim, even in regions where they had previously been at each other's throats. The way of reconciliation between the two rival camps was paved with a common effort to defend the interests, social and spiritual, of the Jewish public against the intervention of the government and against the undermining of foundations from within, by new factors such as the Enlightenment.

NOTES

1. "Maggid"—preacher to the public at large, a permanent and honoured post in communities; the Maggid was considered part of the recognised religious hierarchy.
2. Simon Dubnow, *History of Hasidism* (Heb.) (Tel-Aviv, 1930), pp. 35–36. See chapters 2 and 3 of this volume.
3. Ben-Zion Dinur, "The Beginning of Hasidism and its Social and Messianic Foundations" (Heb.), in *Bemifne Hadoroth* (Jerusalem, 1955), pp. 83–227. See chapter 4 of this volume.
4. Ibid., p. 86.
5. Ibid., p. 140.
6. Joseph Weiss, "The Dawn of Hasidism" (Heb.), *Zion*, 16, Nos. 3–4, pp. 46–105.
7. Ibid., p. 40 and 56.
8. Berakhya Berakh ben R. Eliakim Getz, preacher and moralist, fierce critic of the leaders of the time; despite this he received permission from the heads of the "Council of Lands" in Poland "to mend the breaks in the generation . . . to preach in every town without having recourse to permission from the rabbi and leader". See on him I. Heilpern, *Pinkas of the Council of Four Lands*, (Jerusalem, 1945) pp. 477–479; Y. Kleinmann, *Yevreiskaya Starina*, 12 (1928) (Russian), pp. 179–198.
9. G. Scholem, "On R. Israel Loebel and His Polemic against Hasidism," *Zion*, 20 (1956), pp. 153–162.
10. I. Heilpern, "The Attitude of R. Aharon of Karlin to Communal Rule," *Zion*, 22 (1957), pp. 86–92.
11. J. Shachar, "Social Criticism in Moralistic Literature in Poland in the 18th Century"; manuscript (Hebrew).
12. G. Scholem, "The Sabbatian Movement in Poland," in *The House of Israel in Poland*, ed. I. Heilpern (Heb.), vol. 2 (Jerusalem, 1954), pp. 36–76.

13. "Light of Israel," *Gleanings from R. Pinhas of Korzec*, 53.
14. H. B. Heilmann, "Beth Rabbi" (Heb.), 2nd ed. (Berdyczew, 1903), p. 43.
15. G. Scholem, "Devekuth, or Communion with God," *Review of Religion*, 14 (1950), pp. 115–139. See chapter 8 of this volume.
16. According to Jacob Katz, *Tradition and Crisis* (New York, 1961, 1971), p. 235.
17. S. Dubnow, op. cit., p. 182.
18. "Arenda"—is a lease of an inn or an income from agricultural activity connected with a manor. An important function of the community was to prevent competition between Jewish leaseholders. In the second half of the eighteenth century, when the authority of the communal heads weakened, the Hasidic zaddikim took this task on themselves.
19. A. Kahana, *Book of Hasidism* (Heb.) (Warsaw, 1922), p. 304.
20. This is the first known ban on the Hasidim proclaimed in the community of Brody in 1772.
21. Material on this has been collected by H. Shmeruk in a paper still in manuscript.
22. See for example the dispute between R. Abraham Katzenelbogen, the rabbi of Brisk, and R. Levi Yishaq of Berdyczew in 1781, S. Dubnow, *Chassidiana* (Heb.), *Dvir*, Part I (Berlin, 1923), pp. 293–297.
23. Ibid., "Heavar" (Petrograd, 1918), p. 26.
24. On the charismatic leadership of the Gaon of Vilna, see R. J. Z. Werblowsky, *Joseph Karo* (Oxford, 1962), App. F.
25. S. Dubnow, op. cit., p. 180.
26. H. Shmeruk, "The Social Significance of Hasidic Shehita", *Zion*, 20 (1955), pp. 47–74.

SELECTED BIBLIOGRAPHY

1. S. Schechter, "The Chassidim," in his *Studies in Judaism*, vol. 1, Philadelphia, 1896, pp. 1–46.
2. A. Z. Aescoli, *Le Hassidisme*, Paris, 1928.
3. M. Buber, *Die chassidischen Bücher*, Hellerau, 1928.
4. S. Dubnow, *Geschichte des Chassidismus*, Berlin, 1931.
5. G. Scholem, *Major Trends in Jewish Mysticism*, New York, 1961, Lecture 9.
6. M. Buber, *The Tales of the Hasidim*, New York, 1947.
7. G. Scholem, "Devekuth, or Communion with God," *Review of Religion*, 14, 1950, pp. 115–139; *The Messianic Idea in Judaism*, New York, 1971, pp. 203–226.
8. S. H. Dresner, *The Zaddik*, London-New York, 1960.
9. J. Katz, *Tradition and Crisis*, New York, 1961, 1971.

7

Hasidic-Mitnaggedic Polemics in the Jewish Communities of Eastern Europe: The Hostile Phase *

Mordecai L. Wilensky

Polish Hasidism, whose founder was Rabbi Israel Ba'al Shem Tov (BESHT),[1] encountered strong opposition on the part of the organized Jewish community as early as the second half of the eighteenth century. The conflict between the Hasidim and Mitnaggedim was confined at first to the Jewish community and manifested itself in the imposition of bans and sanctions, libelous writings, and economic and social deprivation. As the conflict continued, each of the opposing camps resorted to bringing the issue before the non-Jewish authorities.[2]

As long as these groups operated in Podolia and the Ukraine, backward provinces in terms of Torah learning, they aroused no organized opposition. Soon the center of the movement moved northward to Volhynia, and the emissaries of R. Dov Ber, the *Maggid* of Miedzyrzecz,[3] successor to the Besht, began preaching their teacher's doctrine in White Russia, Polesie, and even tried to penetrate Vilna, the center and strong-

* The polemical literature between the Hasidim and the Mitnaggedim, both printed and manuscript, is scattered. In referring to this literature, much of which is otherwise inaccessible, I have cited my two-volume collection: *Hasidim U-Mitnaggedim* (Jerusalem, Mossad Bialik, 1970). Referring to my book will also allow the reader to use the introductory and explanatory material which, of necessity, I have shortened in this article. References to the book are indicated simply by volume number and page (I, p. . ; II, p. .).
Reprinted by permission of *East European Quarterly* from *Tolerance and Movements of Religious Dissent in Eastern Europe,* edited by Bela K. Kiraly, 1975.

hold of Lithuanian Torah study; it was then that organized war against the new movement began. The heads of the Vilna community, led by Gaon R. Elijah,[4] began their overt war against Beshtian Hasidism in 1772, and continued their aggressive opposition to the movement up to the beginning of the nineteenth century.

Three waves of controversy arose during the forty years of the dispute. The first was in 1772; the second in 1781; and the third began in 1796 and extended into the early nineteenth century. All three originated in Vilna, each starting with the imposition of bans and sanctions on the new sect.[5]

Each of the three phases of the conflict had a specific cause. The first ban, in the spring of 1772, was decreed after the Hasidim succeeded in infiltrating Vilna and in establishing their own prayer house *(minyan)*. The second ban was imposed in 1781, one year after the appearance of the first Hasidic book *Toledot Yaaqov Yosef*,[6] a commentary on the Pentateuch. This book by R. Jacob Joseph of Polonne, an ardent disciple of the Besht, forced severe criticisms against contemporary Rabbis and communal leaders, and in turn aroused Vilna's Mitnaggedim from their relative inaction. The appearance in print of the book *Tanya*[7] by R. Shneur Zalman of Liozna[8] (henceforth Rashaz), head of Russia's Hasidim, and the growth of the Hasidic movement caused the third phase of hostility.[9]

As has already been mentioned, during the third altercation, the site of the conflict moved beyond the confines of the Jewish community. Each side brought his claim before the Russian government which had only recently annexed large parts of Poland. As a result of the two enemy camps having resorted to the Russian civil authorities, the government used this opportunity to reduce communal authority.[10] It should be noted that the most graceless intervention of the Russian government in the conflict was in Vilna at the end of the last decade of the eighteenth century.[11]

Contrary to accepted scholarly opinion, it was not the Mitnaggedim, but the Hasidim who first turned to the Russian government who, incidently, included some of the wealthy members of the Jewish community.[12]

In 1798, a strongly written complaint was submitted to the government by the Vilna Hasidim. This complaint claimed that the community *(Kahal)* was persecuting them, and included slanderous information about the organization of the *Kahal*.[13] While there is no justification for this act of slandering, it should be noted that it did result from extended insufferable persecution by Vilna's Mitnaggedim, which became particularly acute after the death of the Gaon. Patience to endure any more had failed. As a result of their complaint, the government allowed the Hasidim to pray in their own *minyanim* and the authority of the community was further decreased.[14]

The Vilna *Kahal* did not sit idle either and turned to the government with slander about the Hasidim. As a result, Rashaz was imprisoned in St. Petersburg at the end of 1798. His second imprisonment came in November 1800, as a result of information provided by the zealous Mitnagged Avigdor ben Hayyim, the Rabbi of Pinsk.

The Russian government's position favoring the Hasidim, which was expressed both by the exoneration of Rashaz and by the promulgation of the "Statute of 1804" by Alexander I,[15] in which the Hasidim were given legitimate status, was one of the causes of the abatement of the conflict between the two hostile camps. Although the dispute continued for many more years and its traces are discernible throughout the nineteenth century, by the first decade of the nineteenth century both sides had reached a point of peaceful coexistence in Vilna, and the rest of the communities of White Russia and Lithuania soon followed in their footsteps.[16]

Much has been written about the course taken by the dispute, I would prefer to concentrate on specific accusations made by the Mitnaggedim against the Hasidim, to deal with ideological, economic, and social causes of the conflict, and to consider the reactions of the Hasidic camp to Mitnaggedic charges.

The Mitnaggedic literature available to us from the period of conflict includes mainly: (1) declarations of sanctions, miscellaneous writings by individuals and communal authorities; (b) essays. Most of the essays were written during the 1790s by two zealous opponents of Hasidism: R. David, the *Maggid* of Makow[17] and R. Israel Loebel of Sluck, *Maggid* in various Lithuanian and White Russian communities.[18] Their essays[19] include criticisms against the new sect and its leaders.

There is a paucity of written reaction on the part of the Hasidim to the conflict. Presumably, the reason for this is that few of their number had the literary ability to express their reactions in writing. The primary Hasidic spokesman was Rashaz, who from 1772 to the abatement of the controversy continually attempted to reconcile the two camps.

In his letters, he turned to his adversaries, at times pleadingly and at times resolutely, in order to make them see their error and stop their war with the Hasidim.[20] Initially, he wrote letters to his followers, in which he prevailed upon them not to antagonize the Mitnaggedim, not to insult those who studied Torah, and to be sure to respect the *Gaon* of Vilna.[21]

Aside from Rashaz, others who attempted to actively defend the movement in its difficult days were R. Samuel (Shmelka) Horowitz[22] of Galicia, later Rabbi of Nikolsburg, and to some extent R. Elimelekh of Lezajsk[23] and Rabbi Menahem Mendel of Witebsk in his letters from Safed,[24] following his emigration to Palestine in 1777.

Despite the fact that the amount of the polemical Mitnaggedic literature is far greater than that of the Hasidim, one cannot assert the same regarding its quality. Written reaction on the part of the Hasidim is more restrained and its writers avoided being dragged into using the harsh and provocative language found in Mitnaggedic writings, including those that were penned by the *Gaon* of Vilna. The Hasidic authors and especially Rashaz concentrated on the heart of the matter and did not write on petty things as did many of the Mitnaggedic writers.

The overwhelming majority of arguments and accusations on the Hasidim by the Mitnaggedim throughout the conflict, were expressed already at the very beginning of the controversy. The first anti-Hasidic writings of 1772 were collected in the pamphlet—*Zamir arisim veharevot surim* (The Song of the Terrible Ones and Knives of Flint).[25] This pamphlet, published in 1772, includes the first bans imposed on the Hasidim and voices most of the objections made, during the entire conflict, against the new sect, except the one about the "elevation of strange throughts" during prayer.[26] The accusations against the Hasidim can be summarized: as separation by the Hasidim from the established prayer houses and founding their own private *minyanim,* in which they introduced changes in liturgy, changes in the set times of prayer according to the *Halakha,* (Jewish Law), and changes in the methods of prayer. Changes in ritual slaughter *(shehitah),* using honed knives. Neglect of Torah Study and disrespect for Torah scholars. Bizarre actions. Suspicion of Sabbatianism. Much merrymaking and partying. Greediness of Hasidic *zaddikim* (Hasidic Masters) causing waste of Jewish money. Miracle-working by Hasidic *zaddikim.* Other accusations like: change of dress, a great deal of pipe smoking, etc.

I will deal only with the accusations: changes in prayer; changes in ritual slaughter; bizarre actions; suspicion of Sabbatianism. I shall end with the accusation that most hurt the Lithuanian and White Russian Mitnaggedim, that the new sect was causing neglect of Torah study and disrespect for Torah scholars.

PRAYER

The Mitnaggedim opposed Hasidic prayer on several different grounds: the change in the liturgy from Ashkenazic to Sephardic, or, more precisely, to Lurianic rite; the separation of the Hasidim from the established prayer houses, and their establishing of special houses of worship; lack of precision regarding *halakhically* defined times of prayer; new modes of prayer, such as praying aloud, strange motions and gestures; elevation of strange thoughts during prayer.

We may assume that the Besht and his circle prayed in the Lurianic rite.[27] It was, however, the Besht's successor, R. Dov Ber of Miedzyrzecz, who provided the ideological basis for this. In brief, his reasoning was that when the people of Israel were in their own land and the Temple existed, each of the tribes would pray using its own rite and would direct its prayers to its own particular gate in the Temple. With the destruction of the Temple and the subsequent lengthy dispersion of the Jewish people, a Jew no longer knew from which tribe he came. Therefore, R. Isaac Luria (Ari—the famous Kabbalist who lived in Safed in the sixteenth century) arranged a version of the prayers, known as the Lurianic rite, which included the versions of all twelve tribes.[28]

Hasidic prayer in the Lurianic rite is an important topic which has been widely discussed. It was most recently treated in Dr. Louis Jacobs's book, *Hasidic Prayer*.[29] Here, we will consider only the debate on the change in prayer as it is seen in the polemics of the two opposing camps. The Mitnaggedim were not opposed to the Lurianic rite as a matter of principle. For example, the community of Brody in Galicia, although it forbade changes in the prayer rite in its decree against the Hasidim in 1772, did permit local Kabbalists to pray according to the Lurianic rite.[30]

Opposition to the change in rite resulted largely from the new sect's audacity in abrogating a custom which had existed for generations. R. Abraham Katzenellenbogen, Rabbi of Brześć-Litewski, in his letter to R. Levi Yishaq of Berdyczew, protested the impertinence of "Defiling the prayers of all our true and God-fearing brethren, the Children of Is-rael."[31] He maintained that the great minds of the Jewish people in recent generations also knew this form of prayer and still ". . . chose the Ashkenazic rite, and it never entered the mind of any of them to change anything."[32] The Mitnaggedim also saw this change in the rite as an attempt on the part of members of the new sect to throw off the authority of the community and to compete with it. Likewise, Mitnag-gedim saw the overt change as a kind of presumptuousness on the part of Hasidim with regard to the rest of the community which prayed in the Ashkenazic rite. In the anti-Hasidic ordinances of Leszniów, a town near Brody, this was emphasized: ". . . haughtiness had rooted itself in their hearts making them change the prayer rite."[33]

This is the source of the harsh language in the Mitnaggedic procla-mations emanating from Vilna and Brody (1772); the proclamations of Grodno and Sluck (1781); the decisions of Minsk (1797) et al. In the proclamations issued in Cracow in 1785, it was even stated that one who prayed according to a different rite "would be excommunicated and banished and . . . would be dishonorably buried."[34]

Opposition to the changed version also stemmed from the fact that it drew the Hasidim away from established synagogues, leading them to establish separate *minyanim*. In addition to the fact that this meant that the Hasidim were separating themselves from the community and deny-ing its authority, there was also an economic consideration. Separation of the Hasidim obviously reduced the number of people praying in the established synagogues and consequently reduced revenues. We find mention of this in the decisions of the Vilna *Kahal* against the Hasidim in the late 1790s.[35] It should be noted that in the generation preceding the growth of Hasidism, the organized community opposed the estab-lishment of separate places of worship for craftsmen. One source of this opposition, too, was economic.

These, then, are the reasons for the community's opposition to sepa-rate prayer houses for the sect from 1772 on. They even resorted to the imposition of sanctions. In the ban of Vilna in 1797, the sanctions are specified: it was forbidden to appoint Hasidim to office in the commu-nity or its organizations. A *rodef ne'elam* or secret prosecutor was appointed to implement this. Vilna Mitnaggedim were not above threat-ening to expel the Hasidim from the community.[36] Although we know of no instance in which they actually carried out this threat, we do know that one of Vilna's Hasidim, in whose courtyard a Hasidic *minyan* met, was publicly flogged.[37]

The Mitnaggedim saw the Hasidic lack of precision with regard to the established times of prayer as a violation of *Halakha*. We find criticism of this custom even before 1772.[38] This charge is found throughout the writings and sanctions of the Mitnaggedim. In its proclamation of 1781, the community of Sluck claims that the Hasidim allowed the *shahrit*, the morning prayer, to continue "until midday."[39] In *Zamir arisim*, R. David of Makow accuses the Hasidim of Kozienice and Lublin of praying *Minhah*, the afternoon prayer, after the stars have already appeared.[40] R. Hayyim of Volozhin in his *Nefesh Ha-Hayyim* criticizes this new custom, whereby ". . . they have almost forgotten the time for the afternoon prayers which was determined by the rabbis of blessed memory."[41] In his book *Sefer Vikuah*,[42] R. Israel Loebel maintains the Hasidim "tell stories and gossip and obscenities among themselves before prayer and consequently are late in beginning to pray."[43]

In answer to this the Hasidim argued that the most important aspect of prayer is intention *(Kavvanah)*, and that it is impossible to call up in oneself the proper intention at a specific time. Intention requires preparation. This preparation for prayer is so integral a part of prayer itself that one is rewarded for it too. He who hires someone to chop down trees for him, must also pay the woodsman for the time he spends honing his ax.[44] Preparation for prayer falls within the category of honing one's ax. R. Hayyim of Volozhin is strongly opposed to this justification and sees this as a "strategem of the evil inclination" which is liable to bring about "the destruction of the entire Torah."[45]

Because not every Hasid could arouse in himself the proper intention, despite delaying prayer for a long while, in some courts the Hasidim would be advised to transfer their thoughts to the rebbe. The Hassid should intend only that his prayer correspond to his rebbe's and that his prayer rise wherever the rebbe wanted it to, because the rebbe knows all the thoughts of his followers. We know about this transference of thoughts to the rebbe, *mesirat mahshavah la-rebbe*, as it was practiced in the court of R. Hayyim Haykel, the *zaddik* of Amdur (Indura), from evidence taken before the Vilna rabbinical court.[46] In one of his letters, R. David of Makow notes the *Gaon* of Vilna saw this as "Total idolatry."[47]

Hasidism saw the matter of "transference of thoughts to the rebbe" in a different light. The purpose was that the rebbe, in his great wisdom direct the conscious thoughts of the supplicant and raise them to their source (God), even if the individual himself did not know how to do this.

It must be noted that, after the severe criticism of the Hasidic imprecision regarding the times of prayer, some Hasidic masters began to recite the morning *Shema* (prayer) at its appointed time. In the nineteenth century, there were even those in the Hasidic camp who protested the inordinately late times of prayer.

The Mitnaggedic polemical literature is also replete with criticism and mockery of the new customs of prayer introduced by the Hasidim— praying aloud, strange movements, and gesticulations during prayer. The Mitnaggedim view these customs, not only as trespassing against the words of the Sages and deviation from tradition, but also as an arrogant attempt on the part of the new group to impress the masses, "to show themselves more sanctified and purified before God than any other Jew."[48]

As to praying aloud, the Hasidim were said to "roar like lions while praying."[49] The Mitnaggedim also saw this as a deviation from the Sages who said that "He who raises his voice in his prayers shows himself to be a man of little faith."[50] It is said of Hannah, the mother of the prophet Samuel, that when she prayed, "only her lips move, but her voice could not be heard."[51] The Hasidim, however, not only "show their voices as if they were torches, but also go mad and behave boisterously in their movements."[52]

R. Samuel Horowitz's defense of the Hasidim, that even R. Akiba moved about while praying ". . . a man would leave him in one corner and find him later in another,"[53] was met with the Mitnaggedic reply that R. Akiba behaved that way only when he prayed in private, but never during public prayer.[54] To R. Horowitz's argument that even King David danced about before the Lord,[55] R. Israel Loebel answers that this was a unique event in David's life. The Hasidim dance and gyrate all the time. Loebel adds that even R. Isaac Luria, whose prayer rite the Hasidim adopted, forbade movement during prayer. Why do the Hasidim pay no attention to his words?[56]

A rational explanation for gesticulations during prayer may be found in writings attributed to the Besht.[57] A man who is drowning in a river grimaces in order to draw the attention of those onshore so that they will come to save him. He is not to be laughed at, because he is fighting for his life. Similarly, a Hasid while praying is fighting for his soul against the forces of evil trying to drown him in a sea of impurity. Thus, he grimaces. The Hasidim also found support for movement in prayer in the erotic section included in *Savaat Ha-Ribash* (The Ethical Will of the Besht).[58]

The literature of the conflict also includes an accusation against the doctrine of "elevation of strange thoughts" during prayer. In other words, how would a Hasid react if a strange thought entered his mind while he was praying? Would he suppress it or try to elevate its source in God? The basis of this doctrine is in the Lurianic theory of *shevirat ha-keylim,* the breaking of the vessels, which was adopted by Sabbatianism and infiltrated Hasidism. Because of limitations of space, I will not discuss it here. It should be said that this doctrine is attacked only in R. David of Makow's writings,[59] and that there were those who objected to it in the Hasidic camp as well.[60]

At the end of this discussion of the controversy over prayer, it can be stated that it was not prayer aloud, nor gesticulations during prayer, nor even changes in liturgy and in the set times of prayer, which aroused the fury of the Mitnaggedim to the degree that they waged war against the Hasidim. The essence of the conflict over prayer resulted from a difference in approach to the concept of prayer, its value and importance. The Mitnaggedim opposed Hasidic elevation of prayer to the highest level of Jewish values.[61] This, the Mitnaggedim opposed in principle; hence their strong reaction.

In support of this assumption, I will close with Rashaz's reaction to the Mitnaggedic war against Hasidic prayer. We find Rashaz's reaction in a letter written to one of the moderate Mitnaggedim in Szklow, which deals with the matter of prayer. The letter is included in my book[62] and because of its importance, I have included part of it as translated by L. Jacobs.[63]

Rashaz opens by saying that the Mitnaggedic war against Hasidic prayer is "a decree of apostasy against prayer." Indeed, the text of the prayers and the three fixed daily services, Rashaz says, are of rabbinic origin; but those who say that prayer itself is of rabbinic origin "have never seen the light. ... The concept of prayer and its essential idea belong to the very foundation of the Torah, namely to know the Lord, to recognize His greatness and His glory with a serene mind, and through contemplation, to have these fixed firmly in the mind. A man must reflect on this theme until the contemplative soul is awakened to live the Lord's name, to cleave to Him and to His Torah and greatly to desire His commandments. . . ."

Rashaz deduces from this that the whole Mitnaggedic approach to prayer is different from the Hasidic one, for Mitnaggedim see prayer as a rabbinic ordinance. For this reason, they have no right to criticize the Hasidic methods of prayer. They certainly cannot force the Hasidim to pray "hurriedly and without any bodily movements or raising of the voice. . . . Anyone who has drawn near to God and has once tasted the fragrance of prayer, knows and appreciates that without prayer, no man can lift hand or foot to serve God in truth, rather than as the commands of men who learn by rote." These words are among the finest and most profound uttered during the lengthy conflict between the two camps over prayer.

SHEHITAH

Hasidim practiced ritual slaughter, *shehitah,* with sharply honed knives, and the Mitnaggedim opposed it vehemently.

The practice of *shehitah* with finely honed knives had its inception in the early period of Hasidism. Already in 1772, the first Mitnaggedic proclamations and bans included the charge that the new sect had introduced this custom. The Hasidim adopted the sharply honed knife "on the basis that only from a finely ground cutting edge could every indentation be honed away."[64]

There were various opinions about who in fact ordained the use of these sharply honed knives, but it was Rashaz who provided the legal basis:[65] According to *Halakha,* the knife used for ritual slaughter must be both sharp and smooth, but Rashaz explained that when knives were made very sharp they were not smooth. He did add that there were some skilled *shohetim* (ritual slaughterers) who could sharpen a knife that it would be both sharp and smooth, but such expertise was most rare. Furthermore, unlike the finely honed knives, sharpening unhoned knives required a great deal of time which was frequently unavailable to the *shohet;* therefore the Hasidim favor the finely honed knives.

The Mitnaggedim bitterly attacked this change in ritual slaughter. "They argued that finely ground blades were liable to become nicked upon first contact with the skin of the creature about to be slaughtered, and thus cause the animal to become *nevelah*."[66]

It should be pointed out that the prohibition against Hasidic *shehitah* had no support in Jewish Law. Consequently, in all the bans promulgated against the Hasidim by the Vilna community, this charge is absent. In the proclamations issued in Lithuanian Grodno and Pinsk too, we do not find this prohibition. R. Israel Loebel never once mentioned this Hasidic practice in his polemical essays against the Hasidim, and R. David of Makow only noted the practice in passing. From one of Rashaz's letters, we know that R. Hayyim of Volozhin recalled that the *Gaon* of Vilna admitted that Hasidic *shehitah* did not violate Jewish Law. If he, the *Gaon*, prohibited it, it was only as a means of fencing off the new sect.[67]

In this matter, not all the rabbis or lay leaders, even from Lithuania and White Russia, agreed with the *Gaon*. Rabbi Katzenellenbogen of Brześć-Litewski, the anti-Hasidic zealot who made no bones about his feelings: "It is well-known that I always have hated and persecuted these sectarians,"[68] complains that the Vilna community did not include in its published bans the prohibition against the Hasidic *shehitah*.[69] The Lithuanian community of Sluck also included this prohibition in its proclamation of 1781 against the Hasidim.[70] The ordinances of the Szklow community in White Russia, issued in 1787, contained a special section against the Hasidic *shehitah*—"What their *shohetim* kill may not be eaten, it is carrion, the dishes they use are polluted and forbidden . . ."[71] Similar action was taken in Minsk in 1799.[72] The Brody community in Galicia already in 1772 prohibited the ritual slaughter by honed knives: "They make for themselves honed *shehitah* knives [*geshleefeene*], not called for in the entire Talmud and the rabbinical authorities. Meat slaughtered by these honed knives is *nevelah* and *terefah*."[73]

This strong language is especially surprising in view of the fact, mentioned above, that the Hasidic *shehitah* does not contravene Jewish Law. Thus we may suppose that the *Halakhic* aspect did not account for this strong opposition and that there were other factors with regard to Hasidic *shehitah* which irritated the Mitnaggedim.

It may be assumed that the origin of opposition to Hasidic *shehitah* was rooted in the fear that separate *shehitah* might not be carried out properly in outlying regions lacking a high level of Jewish learning, e.g. Podolia and the Ukraine, where the first Hasidic groups were organized.

This explains why R. Samuel Horowitz in his letter to the Brody community stressed that Hasidim were careful to use God-fearing *shohetim*.[74] Possibly the fear of Sabbatianism contributed to the earliest rabbinic and communal opposition to Hasidic *shehitah*. In Podolia, the birthplace of Hasidism, Sabbatian cells still existed. Nor can it be mere chance that the first ban on Hasidic ritual slaughter was issued in Brody, in 1772, only sixteen years after that community had excommunicated those suspected of Sabbatian tendencies from serving as *shohetim*.[75]

Even after these fears were largely dissipated, other factors led to continued opposition to Hasidic ritual slaughter. The fact that Hasidim separated themselves from the community and refused to eat animals slaughtered in the Ashkenazic manner, the norm for generations, and the refusal of Hasidic *shohetim* to accept the authority of the community, undermined the establishment. The *Kahal* viewed the Hasidic action not merely as a rebellion against its authority, but also as a kind of arrogance and pretension just as it had viewed other new customs of the Hasidim "in boasting before the masses to indicate that they are especially careful in fulfilling the *misvot* [the Commandments]."[76]

R. Katzenellenbogen offered another reason for his opposition to the Hasidic practice. He declares that the finely honed knife could become too easily dented when cutting the skin and thus lead to the sale and consumption of meat which had become unkosher through improper slaughtering. He was aware that Hasidic *shohetim* did reinspect their knives after slaughtering and, if they found that the knives had been damaged, making the *shehita* improper, they would declare the animal unfit for Jewish use. Still the Rabbi from Brisk (Brześć-Litewski) disparages this, asking, "Why should they waste Jewish money for no reason?"[77]

One of the sources of opposition to the new practice was due to the fact that Hasidic *shohetim* often served as propagandists for the new movement. A Hasidic *shohet* after he had established himself in a certain settlement began to organize a Hasidic group in that place.[78]

Another factor, and apparently not the least important in the strong opposition of the communal leaders to the Hasidic *shehitah* was the economic one. *Shehitah*, through the *korobka* tax, provided a significant part of the budget of the Jewish community. Thus, communal leaders saw separate *shehitah* as a grave danger to the balancing of the communal budget. Even the Vilna community, which also received a significant percentage of its revenues from the tax on *shehitah,* joined the battle against Hasidic ritual slaughter after the death of the *Gaon.*[79] Fiscal considerations were one of the determining factors in the conflict concerning ritual slaughter, but it was also fiscal considerations which led to the working out of a modus vivendi with Hasidic *shehitah* in many communities, when Hasidism had become well entrenched at the beginning of the nineteenth century.

In concluding my deliberations about *shehitah,* I want to discuss its relationship to the belief in the transmigration of souls (metempsychosis). Kabbalistic literature discussed the transmigration of souls, especially of sinners, into inanimate, vegetable, and animal forms. It was indicated that souls which have become animals, can be purified and restored by undergoing ritual slaughter and then being consumed by a *zaddik.* With this belief, a special importance would attach itself to the knife used in ritual slaughter, for any imperfection was liable to hinder the soul's restoration.[80]

The polemical literature between the Hasidim and Mitnaggedim includes a document which discusses the relationship between metempsychosis and the Hasidic *shehitah.*[81] *Shever Posh'im* by R. David of Makow contains testimony taken at a Mitnaggedic court in 1774, and the following account is recorded: The local *shohet* slaughtered a cow and declared it kosher despite the fact that according to *Halakha,* it was forbidden to slaughter it. The *shohet* apologized, explaining that he had the approval for his action from the local Hasidic *Maggid.* When the communal supervisor of *shohetim* told the *maggid* that his cow's flesh was unkosher according to Jewish Law, the *maggid* responded, "If I said it, it must be kosher. There must be a soul in this cow and God wants Jews to eat this cow's meat and restore its soul."[82]

Although the incident did not refer to *shehitah* with a finely honed knife, there is nevertheless great significance in the story. First, the communal *shohet* consulted the Hasidic *maggid* before he slaughtered the cow. More important, is the reason adduced by the *maggid,* a reason associated with the belief in transmigration of souls. We note, too, the bitter communal opposition to the *shohet's* act and the interesting response of the communal supervisor of the *shohetim* to the *maggid:* "I do not deal in mysteries."

One may even find a hint of the connection between Hasidic *shehitah* and the belief in metempsychosis preserved in *Shivhei Ha-Besht* in the story about a certain *shohet* who was discharged by the Besht. When the *shohet* protested to the Besht, that it was forbidden to eat meat which he had inadvertently rendered unkosher in the act of *shehitah,* the Besht replied: "But this cow has requested that I eat of her."[83]

BIZARRE PRACTICES

The charge that the Hasidim introduced bizarre and disgusting practices, which deviated from the traditional Jewish framework, is mentioned in all the polemical literature under consideration. The charge was leveled at a variety of odd activities.

In one of the documents issued in 1772 in Vilna, there is testimony before the communal court, investigating the new sect, about one Hasid who was accused of homosexual behavior.[84] R. David of Makow alludes to the goings-on in the *zaddik* of Amdur's court: "They all gather at night and sleep together in a loft, and who knows what disgusting things are done there."[85] The author mentions other strange acts in R. Hayyim Haykel's court at Amdur and provides the ostensible reason for them—the elimination of sadness.[86]

There were other odd doings as well. R. Katzenellenbogen feels that R. Levi Yishaq of Berdyczew's tendency to repeat the *Tetragrammaton* two or three times during prayer is "something strange and frightening." He also asks him why "before reciting the *Shema,* he throws off his shoes."[87] R. Israel Loebel in his *Sefer Viku'ah* would use the word *af* (-even, anger) deemed uncomplimentary, since it was the first word to issue from the snake, from Pharaoh's chief baker, and from Haman.[88] According to Habad tradition,[89] Rashaz was questioned during his second imprisonment in St. Petersburg about his use of *af.* The questioning resulted from R. Avigdor's treacherous accusation to the government that both the Besht and Rashaz used the word *af* in their prayers, entreating the Almighty to rain down His *af,* His anger, on the non-Jewish rulers.[90]

The Hasidic bizarre activity most often singled out for criticism by the Mitnaggedim was their somersaulting. By 1772, the Vilna communal leaders were complaining that the Hasidim "are a topsy-turvy generation who do somersaults before the ark of God's covenant . . . their heads are downward and their feet are in the air." And the Vilna Mitnaggedim ask caustically: "Has one ever heard of or seen such license as this?"[91] R. David of Makow bitterly attacks this custom which he saw with his own eyes.[92] The *Gaon* of Vilna views this practice as idolatry, "their somersaults are fitting for Peor [a pagan Deity]."[93]

It has to be noted that only certain circles within the new movement, especially those guided by R. Abraham of Kalisk, White Russia, and R. Hayyim Haykel of Amdur, introduced the custom of somersaulting. Rabbi Abraham of Kalisk was the student of the *Maggid* of Miedzyrzecz and went to Palestine in 1777 with R. Menahem Mendel of Witebsk, whom he replaced as the head of the Hasidic community in Palestine after the latter's death in 1788. We know from reliable sources that when R. Abraham was in Russia, he and his followers used to practice somersaults. The *Maggid* of Miedzyrzecz was displeased by R. Abraham's behavior and rebuked him. Rashaz, in one of his letters to him, reminds him of the sins of his youth, among them the somersaults in the streets of Kalisk.[94]

As noted before, R. Hayyim Haykel of Amdur, also a student of the *Maggid* of Miedzyrzecz, was the target of much of the Mitnaggedic criticism because of the strange activities of his court. There, too, somersaults were customary. As we learn from testimony taken in 1772, the Amdurites would somersault in the prayer house and in the street, reciting: "For the sake of God and for the sake of the rebbe." The evidence also records the reason given for such behavior. "When a man is afflicted by pride, he must turn himself over."[95]

Though Rashaz opposed this practice, he too was criticized by R. Israel Loebel for his behaving, while dancing, like one of the common folk.[96] A Habad source tells us, approvingly of course, that when Rashaz had reached a peak of enthusiasm in prayer, "he would roll on the ground almost without consciousness."[97]

Dr. Louis Jacobs, in his *Hasidic Prayer,*[98] has pointed out that somersaults were the custom of the Shaker sect which began in England in the second half of the eighteenth century and moved over to America. We may safely assume that the Hasidic leaders neither knew of nor were influenced by the English group. Jacobs rightly ascribes these phenomena to the *Zeitgeist*.

More relevant is the mention in the polemical literature of other Christian sects and their practices. R. David of Makow criticizes the manner in which the Hasidic *zaddikim* would offer "Torah teachings" without preparation during the traditional third meal of the Sabbath, and adds that the tendency to offer teachings without preparations applies as well to Mennonites and Quakers. He discusses the patterns of worship of these groups in detail.[99] Rabbi David was acquainted with the Mennonites since many of them had settled on the border of Poland and Prussia at the beginning of the eighteenth century. By means of this comparison, the author seeks to show that Hasidic mystical practices draw upon non-Jewish sources. Even when the *Maggid* of Makow admits that the Hasidim possess good qualities, such as the practice of deeds of loving kindness, he points out that these qualities are also found among the adherents of these Christian sects and in the Masonic order. Every new sect which wants to catch souls in its net, our Mitnaggedic author comments, emphasizes the attribute of loving kindness.[100]

SUSPICION OF SABBATIANISM

I need not stress that the belief in Sabbatai Zevi and in the teachings of Nathan of Gaza did not come to an end with the supposed messiah's conversion to Islam nor even with his death. We know today from the research of Gershom Scholem and others that many Jews, among them great Torah scholars, kept faith with the Sabbatian heresy in its different manifestations throughout the eighteenth century, the era of growth of Beshtian Hasidism. Moreover, precisely at the time of Hasidism's rise, Polish Jewry was traumatized by its experiences with Jacob Frank and his followers, their bitter disputation at Kamieniec-Podolsk, and the resulting burning of the Talmud.[101]

Thus, we can understand why the Jewish establishment was suspicious of any new movement which arose in its midst and which introduced deviations from the tried and true path. And no one would dispute the contention that Hasidism was a deviation from the norm. It is, therefore, clear why the Mitnaggedic camp was particularly sensitive to Hasidism which had originated in Podolia, the Ukraine, and Galicia, regions where Sabbatian cells still functioned underground. There is no doubt that some of the bizarre customs of various Hasidic groups helped to strengthen these suspicions.

We are not concerned here with an examination of the penetration of Sabbatian thought into Hasidism or with the ways in which the Sabbatian underground influenced, directly or surreptitiously, the proto-Hasidic groups or the first students of the Besht. In dealing with Sabbatianism and Hasidism, my aim is to examine the Mitnaggedic fears that the new movement was poisoned by Sabbatianism—complete heresy to Mitnaggedim—and to cite the ways in which these fears were reflected in the polemics.

The arch-Mitnaggedic writers, R. David of Makow and R. Israel Loebel, emphasize the link between Sabbatianism and the new Hasidic sect, but they generally speak in hints and allusions. They include Hasidism among the heretical sects which have arisen during Jewish history, and whose aim was to bring destruction to the Jewish people. R. David of Makow warns that the Hasidim will, like Sabbatai Zevi, bring tragedy to the Jewish people.[102] R. Israel Loebel, in scoffing at the wonders performed by the Hasidic *zaddikim,* notes that Sabbatai Zevi performed similar wonders; the analogy is, of course, clear.[103] An anti-Hasidic pamphlet by R. Aaron Auerbach, included in R. David Makow's *Shever Posh'im,* states that "the tyrants of our generation" the new ones, i.e., the Hasidim, "act more outrageously toward us than all the earlier rebels"; among these rebels he lists Sabbatai Zevi and Jacob Frank.[104] R. David himself seems to go beyond analogy when describing the machinations of the court of the Amdur rabbi. He has heard, he tells us, that "once on the night of Tisha B'Av the Hasidim were speaking obscenities, and singing songs of passion and idolatrous hymns all night."[105] The insinuation is transparently clear. The *Maggid* of Makow also introduces the Vilna *Gaon*'s opinion of the Hasidim: "Their insides are full of heresy (absorbed) from the Sabbatian sect."[106]

The Brody community's proclamation against the Hasidim in 1772, included in the pamphlet *Zamir arisim ve-harevot surim,* also expressed the suspicion that the new sect would bring both disaster on the Polish Jewish community and the public desecration of God's name, as the Frankists did. The Brody leaders feel that the current threat is more dangerous since the Council of the Four Lands has been disbanded, and thus there was no leadership to step into the breach.[107] The editor of the pamphlet notes that he has received information from Vilna that when the Hasidim pray, they "shout out" certain words which, when their letters are reversed according to the proper codes,[108] spell out the name of Sabbatai Zevi. According to the Vilna *Gaon,* "this is a great *kelipa* [evil spirit]."[109]

As far as can be determined, only one in the Mitnaggedic camp, R. Avigdor ben Hayyim, the rabbi of Pinsk, explicitly accuses the Hasidim of being Sabbatians and Frankists. The Hasidim of Pinsk had been instrumental in removing R. Avigdor from his rabbinic post and the rabbi had sued for reinstatement in the municipal courts of Pinsk, but had lost the case. His prior ideological opposition was thus joined to his personal pique, so that instead of remaining a mere adversary of the Hasidim, he became an informer. In the spring of 1800, he submitted written accusations about the Hasidim to Czar Paul and these resulted in R. Shneur Zalman's second imprisonment in St. Petersburg.[110]

In his accusations, to which he attached selections from *Savaat Ha-Ribash*, he unfolds the tale of Sabbatai Zevi in Turkey and the Jacob Frank chapter in Poland. Sabbatai Zevi rebelled against the Sultan, and Frank and his followers were charged by the Polish government with being plotters. They, the Frankists, were expelled from the Jewish community, and thereupon, became Catholics. Three of their group, however, Israel of Miedzyboz, Berel of Miedzyrzecz, and Jacob of Polonne[111] managed to evade punishment and established for their own aims this new group, the sect of Hasidim. In short, the members of the new sect are continuing the traditions of Sabbatai Zevi and Jacob Frank, both rebels against governmental authority. And, indeed, in his charge brought against R. Shneur Zalman, R. Avigdor calls the Hasidim *"Sabbatai Zevinikes."*[112]

R. Shneur Zalman's response to most of R. Avigdor's charges, among them the Sabbatian charge, has not been preserved, but in one of his letters to his followers, we do have his response to the charge of Sabbatianism. Rashaz tells them not to be troubled by it. On the contrary, the accusation of Sabbatianism makes him happy since it is exaggerated and extreme that it will not be believed and will lead people to refuse to believe all other charges leveled by the Mitnaggedim at the Hasidim.

As far as I know, this is the only extant Hasidic reaction to this grave accusation in the polemical literature.

NEGLECT OF TORAH STUDY AND DISRESPECT OF TORAH SCHOLARS

In discussing the role of prayer in the conflict, I said that it was not the new and strange ways of prayer, nor even the changes in liturgy, which angered the Mitnaggedim enough to impose sanctions against the Hasidim. The wrath of the Mitnaggedim on the issue of Hasidic prayer resulted from their excessive emphasis on the value of prayer and its importance in the range of Jewish values. This is closely tied to the last accusation, which we will examine now,—that the new sect caused neglect of Torah study and disrespect for Torah scholars.

The Mitnaggedim, particularly those from Lithuania, were enraged by the attitude of the new movement to the primary importance of the study of Talmud and Codes of Law *(Poskim),* which had been unquestioned for many generations. The viewpoint of the Lithuanian Mitnaggedim was that a Jew is required to study Talmud, Codes of Law, and their commentaries diligently, and that anyone who wavered from this road struck at the very heart of Judaism and committed heresy.

In the light of the Mitnaggedic view, then, this argument was well-founded. The Mitnaggedim knew of the saying attributed to the Besht: "The *neshama* (Soul) told the Rav (Besht) that the reason why the supernal matters were revealed to him was not because he had studied many Talmudic tractates and Codes of Law, but because he recited his prayers with great concentration." [113] In his book *Toledot Yaaqov Yosef,* R. Jacob Joseph of Polonne censured study: "One should not habituate oneself to constant diligence of Torah Study, but should also become involved with other human beings." [114] Persistent study of Torah, the ideal of the Gaon and his followers, had reduced importance in Hasidic ideology. R. Jacob Joseph also voiced severe opposition to the swarms of Yeshivah students: "The more they weary their feet in going to Yeshivah to study, the more you add to the rebellion to go away and turn from God." [115]

The Mitnaggedim were of the opinion that the study of Torah was of high merit even it if was not done for its own sake, and even a person who studied Torah not for its own sake, would ultimately grow to do so for its own sake. The Besht and his followers placed all the emphasis on intention *(kavvanah),* not only in prayer, but also in the study of Talmud and Poskim.

In his book *Nefesh ha-hayyim,* R. Hayyim of Volozhin voices strong opposition to the approach which emphasizes the intention exclusively: "If a man pursues Torah even not for its own sake, although he has not yet reached the true high level of holiness, it is forbidden to belittle him, even in one's own mind." [116]

The Mitnaggedim thought that this "New Torah" they, the Besht's followers, were practicing was likely to influence the common people who would base their mode of behavior on this and neglect Torah study. This neglect would bring in its wake disrespect for those who studied Torah. When the leader of the Vilna Hasidim, Meir ben Rafael, was summoned by a special committee to account for his membership in the Hasidic sect, he was asked, "Why did he ridicule, insult, and belittle scholars and students of Torah?"[117]

Thus, the leaders of the Mitnaggedim realized that the new sect was making changes in the traditional hierarchy of Jewish values—a hierarchy in which the highest level was Torah learning.

Here is hidden the explanation of why the Mitnaggedim fought relentlessly against the Hasidim: floggings, prohibition of marriage with the sectarians, economic sanctions, and more. According to Mitnaggedic sources, the *Gaon* was not satisfied with the punishment dealt the leaders of the Hasidim in Vilna in 1772. In his opinion the punishment was too mild: "Had the decision been mine, I would have done to them as the prophet Elijah did to the prophets of Ba'al."[118] In his letter against the Hasidim, written the day after Yom Kippur, 1796, he writes: "No man should pity them and none should treat them mercifully."[119]

In all Mitnaggedic writings, from 1772 on, the argument that the Hasidim are fostering neglect of Torah study and denigrating scholars is raised repeatedly. This accusation is often associated with the additional fact that instead of engaging in Torah study, the Hasidim waste their time with numerous parties and celebrations. In a letter from Vilna, at the beginning of the conflict, the Hasidim are accused of saying: "Heaven forbid that they spend their days in Torah study . . . and God forbid that they be sad. There should always be laughter and gaiety."[120] "And they despise those who study the holy Torah and always [spend] the days in laughter and fun and joyous dissipation."[121] In the above-mentioned letter to R. Levi Yishaq of Berdyczew, R. Katzenellenbogen voiced strong opposition to the members of the sect "who had despised the Oral Law and who think of the Talmud commentators as nothing and are contemptuous of them."[122]

In court testimony in 1774, it was said that in a Hasidic prayer house on the night of Shemini Aseret, the Hasidim "made fun of one rabbi who was a great Torah scholar" and the Hasidic *maggid* stood upon the table and mocked a rabbi "who was not a member of their sect."[123]

The writings of the Mitnaggedic authors R. David of Makow and R. Israel Loebel are full of sharp criticisms of neglect of Torah study and the humiliation of its students in the Hasidic camp. I shall present but a few examples. In *Shever posh'im* David of Makow quotes the words of a Hasid to a Mitnagged: "I will give you good advice. Do not spend your time (studying) Gemara and Tosefot for that is unnecessary study. We have a Torah given to us by the divine man Israel Baal Shem [Tov]." [124] Elsewhere in the same essay, he cites a Hasid, Leib Cohen, who declared publicly: "I wish to do your will, Master of the Universe, but what can I do with your Torah in my gut, the Gemara is weighing on my gut; because of the Gemara I have learned I cannot fulfill the will of the Creator." [125]

In his letter to R. Shlomo Lipshitz, Rabbi of Warsaw, the aforementioned zealous *maggid* of Makow, states that the Hasidim "despise God's Torah . . . by calling the study of Gemara a mere *kelipa.*" [126] In his ethical will to his sons he says: "They [the Hasidim] make an abomination of Torah study and of those engaged in it." [127] In one of his essays, he also cites a Hasidic rite in which a Torah scholar is humiliated after death. [128]

In *Sefer viku'ah,* R. Israel Loebel complains of the new sect that precipitated a decline in Torah study, Leobel declares that the Hasidic *zaddikim* are ignorant boors. No one, says Loebel, has ever heard of a rabbi who was not learned in Torah "and you choose an illiterate for your rabbi." [129] This is not really surprising, Loebel continues, considering that the Besht, the sect's founder, whom he calls "the instigator," was himself an ignorant boor. [130]

The previously quoted statement, attributed to the Besht, that his soul told him that the reason why the supernal matters were revealed to him was not because he studied Gemara and Poskim . . . , totally infuriated Loebel: "If he is telling the truth and the soul told him that, then it lies, and if the soul does not lie but did not tell him this, then he [the Besht] is a liar." [131]

Loebel complains bitterly that in Hasidic houses of study only Hasidic books are studied ". . . but not our holy Torah, both written and oral." [132] Such accusations are made not by the most zealous Mitnaggedim alone. R. Hayyim of Volozhin, a moderate Mitnagged, also complains about the deterioration of Talmud study among the Hasidim and testifies that he himself saw that in most Hasidic Houses "There is not even one complete set of the Talmud." [133]

Comments in the writings of R. David of Makow and R. Israel Loebel indicate that they were occasionally asked why they made the target of their attacks the Hasidim, rather than the *Maskilim,* who openly opposed traditional Judaism and lured the young generation away from the study of Gemara and other rabbinic literature. R. David wishes them "a plague on both their houses."[134] Loebel makes the distinction that the Maskilim are known to have overthrown the Torah and have declared themselves to be free-thinkers, unlike the Hasidim who misrepresent themselves as faithful to Torah and *misvot* and are consequently more dangerous.[135] In his German anti-Hasidic essay,[136] he repeats this and maintains that the hatred of the Hasidim for the Mitnaggedim is also greater than the hatred of the Maskilim for faithful Jews.[137]

Hasidic authors recognized the severity of the accusation that they neglected Torah and therefore attempted to refute it. R. Samuel (Shmelka) Horowitz maintains repeatedly that there is no basis for this Mitnaggedic claim that the Hasidim threw off the yoke of Torah and said that the opposite was, in fact, true, that ". . . they drank of the waters of Torah both written and oral."[138] In a letter in the late 1780s to the community of Mohilev on the Dnieper,[139] Rashaz complains bitterly over the Mitnaggedim in Mohilev and Szklow who segregate the Hasidim from the Jewish community and call them ". . . those who belittle the words of the sages." He said that if an individual were found who "could be numbered among the belittlers," he should be punished, but it was wrong to accuse the entire body of the Hasidim. By believing in this way, the Mitnaggedim were lending a hand to the anti-Semites who also generalized from the crime of an individual Jew and ascribed it to all Jews. This was also similar to the ". . . intellectuals who had recently arisen" i.e. the Maskilim, "who lend a hand to the evildoers of the nations of the world."[140]

In his conscience Rashaz knew that there was some truth to the Mitnaggedic complaint that the Hasidim belittled Torah students and for this reason, he demanded that his followers put an end to their disgraceful habit. In one of his letters to them, he strictly warns the younger Hasidim who habitually ". . . heap insult and disgrace upon Torah scholars that if they persist, they will become estranged from him."[141] In a letter to R. Abraham of Kalisk in Tiberias, written at the beginning of the nineteenth century,[142] in which he retrospectively describes the beginnings of the conflict, Rashaz notes that even the *Maggid* of Miedzyrzecz spoke sharply to R. Abraham of Kalisk, for disrespecting scholars and belittling them. According to Rashaz, this was the determining factor in the Mitnaggedic imposition of sanctions upon the Hasidim in 1772.

It may be assumed that the vitriolic attack on the Hasidim by the Mitnaggedim regarding the neglect of Torah study was the cause of the change of attitude in the Hasidic camp to the traditional study of Torah. This change was one of the factors leading to the reconciliation of the two opposing camps.

NOTES

1. ca. 1700–1760.
2. Even during the lifetime of the Besht, criticism was voiced against the first Hasidic groups, which he headed, although his name was not explicitly mentioned. See G. Scholem's articles in *Tarbiz,* Jerusalem 1949, 228–240; *Zion,* Jerusalem 1955, 73, 81.
3. ca. 1710–1772.
4. 1720–1797.
5. At the head of the signatories of the decrees imposing these sanctions appeared the name of the *Gaon* of Vilna, a name revered in Lithuania, White Russia, throughout Poland, and beyond.
6. Korzec 1780.
7. Slavita 1796; see I, 188, note 20.
8. He settled in Liady after he left Lyozna.
9. This last controversy also had an additional cause: rumors spread by the Hasidim that the *Gaon* of Vilna had ended his opposition to them; see my article in *Bitsaron,* New York 1968, 143–148.
10. *De jure* autonomous institutions of Polish Jewry no longer existed. The Council of Four Lands and the Council of Lithuania, had been dissolved by the end of the Polish rule (1764), but the real power of Lithuanian Jewish communities had not yet faded. Regional committees, which met at intervals in order to pursue common goals, were also troublesome in the eyes of the government. These facts may explain why Lithuanian Jewry was able to succeed for a while in halting the infiltration of the new sect into its borders, and why, in the final analysis, Lithuania never turned into "Terra Hasidiana."
11. As a result of this intervention the communal organization was taken over by the Hasidic minority in Mitnaggedic Vilna on February 6, 1799. (I, 216–218).
12. I, 210–229.
13. It is noteworthy that this complaint was registered with the approval of

Rashaz and later he regretted it. Later appeals of the Hasidim to the Russian authorities, accompanied by slander, were made without Rashaz's knowledge. In fact, he protested vehemently after he became aware of it. I, 313.

14. I, 212.
15. Paragraph 53; I, 295.
16. In my recently published document concerning the controversy in the early nineteenth century, there is reflected the situation during the abatement of the controversy; see *Hagut 3*, Jerusalem 1974, 112–119.
17. Congress Poland; he was a native of Lithuania, see II, 50.
18. II, 253–254.
19. II, 57–180; 189–250; 266–342.
20. I, 161–167; 198–203.
21. I, 296–312; See also D. Z. Hillmann. *Iggerot ba'al ha-tanya*, Jerusalem 1953, 48–49.
22. I, 85–88.
23. I, 169–176.
24. I, 90–97.
25. This title is based on Isaiah 25:5 and Joshua 5:2. The word "Zamir" is ambiguous: it may mean song, referring to the custom of the new sect, attacked by the Mitnaggedim, to sing, merrymaking, and partying; it may also mean pruning hook, as a parallel to "Knives of Flint."
26. This last accusation is dealt with only by R. David of Makow.
27. *Shivhei Ha-Besht*, 13a (Zolkiew edition, 1850).
28. *Maggid devarav le-yaaqov* 16a (Lemberg edition 1796); It must be noted that not all the Masters of Hasidism agreed with the *Maggid* of Miedzyizecz's reasoning. R. Elimelekh of Lezajsk preferred the Lurianic rite but did not deny the validity of the accepted Ashkenazic rite; see *Iggereth ha-qodesh*, I, 171–172.
29. L. Jacobs, *Hasidic Prayer*, New York, 1973.
30. I, 47.
31. I, 128.
32. I, 124.
33. I, 67.
34. I, 139.
35. I, 208–209; 227–229.
36. I, 205–206.
37. I, 211; In the literature of the conflict we find no direct Hasidic reaction to the complaint of establishing separate prayer houses. Justification for separate *minyanim* appears in a book by R. Aaron of Karlin II—a book which first appeared in 1875. There he says: ". . . it is better to pray with few men where the spirit of friendship rests among them, then to pray in a large congregation with people whose hearts are elsewhere." He relies on a responsum of R. David ben Zimra, a sixteenth-century scholar, which discusses separation from an established synagogue. See A. Wertheim,

Halakhot ve-halikhot ba-hasidut, Jerusalem 1960, 71; See also Jacobs, op. cit., 43–44.

38. See above, note 2.
39. I, 118.
40. II, 214.
41. II, 348.
42. Warsaw 1797.
43. II, 273.
44. This illustration which justifies the delay of prayer, was reputedly offered by R. Mendel Morgenstern, the nineteenth-century Rebbe of Kock. See *Amud Ha-Emet,* 82.
45. II, 347.
46. *Shever Posh'im,* 58; II, 149–150.
47. David of Makow adds that *"Mezizat Mahshavah la-Rebbe",* transference of thought to the Rebbe, was also practised in the court of R. Israel Hofstein, the *zaddik* of Kozienice, II, 236.
48. I, 125.
49. II, 192.
50. *Berakhot,* Babyl. Talmud, 24b.
51. I, *Sam.* 1:13.
52. I, 62, 125; II, 87.
53. *Berakhot,* 31a.
54. I, 87, 125.
55. II *Sam.* 6:16.
56. II, 302–303.
57. *Keter shem tov,* I, 27a (Lemberg edition, 1857).
58. (Cracow edition, 1896), 14.
59. II, 146–147; 153–154; 157–160; 245–246.
60. The topic is treated by Joseph Weiss in his articles in *Zion,* 1951, 46–106; *Journal of Jewish Studies,* vol. 9, 1958, 163–192; by Tishby-Dan in *Encyclopedia Hebraica,* vol. 17; L. Jacobs, op. cit., 104–120.
61. See N. Lamm, *Torah lishma,* Jerusalem, 1972, chapters: 3, 4, 5; on the preference of Torah study over prayer, see Jacobs, op. cit., 126–127.
62. I, 299–301.
63. Ibid., 18; 58.
64. See J. Berman, *Shehitah,* New York, 1941, 78.
65. See responsum 7, appendix to Rashaz's *Shulhan arukh,* vol. 5, Juzefov, 1875.
66. carrion; see Berman op. cit.
67. I, 311.
68. I, 130.
69. I. 117.
70. I, 120.
71. I, 151–152.
72. I, 193.

73. I, 46; 48; see also the letter of R. Meshulam Igra to the Lwow community in 1794, I, 178.
74. I, 86.
75. See I. Halperin, *Pinkas vaad arba arasot,* Jerusalem 1945, 417.
76. It should be noted that Rashaz in his responsum (see note 65) stated: The use of honed knives by the Hasidic *shohetim* should not be taken to reflect upon the kashrut of meat slaughtered by shohetim who used the unhoned knife. Furthermore, in a letter to his followers in Vilna, Rashaz advised them that while participating at a religious feast together with other members of the community (Mitnaggedim) "God forbid that they should separate from them and thereby, imply that they were eaters of unkosher food. He himself did not avoid using utensils which had been in contact with meat slaughtered by the Ashkenazic method even if they had been used that very day." I, 312.
77. I, 126–127.
78. See R. Mahler, *Ha-hasidut ve ha-haskalah,* 1961, 176.
79. *Korobka* "basket-tax," imposed on consumption items, mainly on kosher meat. I, 310–311; as early as 1773, R. Horowitz in his letter to the Brody community, alluded to the role of non-*halakhic* considerations in the community's struggle against Hasidic ritual slaughtering, I, 86.
80. See C. Shmeruk's article: *The Social Significance of the Hasidic Shehitah* (Hebrew), *Zion* 1955, 58.
81. Ibid., 62–64. Shmeruk knew this document, but only cited it in passing, ibid., 64, note 71.
82. II, 138–139.
83. 15b–16a (Zolkiew edition, 1850).
84. I, 65; see also 41; 43.
85. II. 174; R. Moshe Satanow's *Mishmeret ha-qodesh* (1746), which includes criticism of the first Hasidic groups, also speaks of this base act. See G. Scholem's article in *Tarbiz* 1949, 232.
86. I, 162–163.
87. I, 126.
88. See *Genesis* 3:1; *Esther* 5:12 and *Midrash Megillat Esther,* 9.
89. *Ha-Tamim,* Warsaw 1935, 56.
90. II, 293.
91. I, 39–40.
92. II, 172.
93. I, 40; See *Num.* 25:3.
94. I, 40.
95. II, 140.
96. II, 293.
97. H. M. Hielman, *Bet rabbi,* Berdyczew 1903, 178–179; see also 31.
98. 56.
99. II, 166–167.
100. II, 169.

101. M. Balaban, *Le toledot ha tenuah ha-frankit,* Tel Aviv 1935, vol. 2, 181–192.
102. II, 180.
103. II, 321.
104. II, 104.
105. II, 174.
106. II, 179.
107. I, 46.
108. Aleph-Taf-Beth-Shin.
109. II, 178.
110. R. Avigdor's written charges have been published by S. Dubnow, along with other documents in this episode in *Evreiskaia starina,* 1910, 90–109, 253–281.
111. R. Avigdor's names for the three pillars of Hasidism: R. Israel Baal Shem Tov; R. Dov Ber, the Maggid of Miedzyrzecz; R. Jacob Joseph.
112. *Evreiskaia starina,* 266.
113. *Savaat Ha-Ribash,* 8.
114. *Vayese* (Warsaw edition 1881), 28.
115. *Vayehi,* Ibid., 39.
116. II, 346.
117. I, 223; When asked why he had joined the Hasidic sect, he answered: "In our community [Vilna], I saw no truth and there [in Lyozna, the hometown of Rashaz] I saw the truth.", ibid.
118. I, 66.
119. I, 189.
120. I, 38.
121. I, 41.
122. I, 128.
123. II, 140.
124. II, 157.
125. II, 145.
126. evil spirit; II, 235.
127. II, 244.
128. II, 155.
129. II, 320.
130. II, 290.
131. II, 307.
132. II, 309–310.
133. R. Hayyim of Volozhin does not mention the Hasidim explicitly, but there is no doubt that he was referring to them, see N. Lamm, *Torah lishma,* 222.
134. II, 226.
135. II, 286.
136. *Glaubwürdige Nachrichten von einer neuen und zahlreichen Sekte unter den Juden in Polen und Lithauen, die sich Chassidim nennt, und ihren die*

Menscheit empörenden Grundsätzen und Lehren, Frankfurt on the Oder, 1799; this essay was reprinted in *Sulamith,* I, 1807, 308–333.

137. II, 332; Despite these comments, it may be assumed that the advent of the Maskilim was a factor in reconciliation between the two camps.

138. I, 85.

139. I, 161–167.

140. I, 165.

141. I, 309; See also his letter published by Hillmann, *Iggerot ba'al ha-tanya,* 213–214.

142. I, 40.

II

TEACHINGS AND CUSTOMS

8

Devekut, or Communion with God

Gershom Scholem

I

Every discussion of Hasidic doctrine has to start with a basic question, namely: Is there a central point on which Hasidism is focused and from which its special attitude can be developed? I think there can be little doubt that there is, indeed, such a focal point, the discussion of which will take us right into the heart of the problem. This is the doctrine of *devekut,* the practical application of which has determined the spiritual physiognomy of Hasidism.

Devekut, the meaning of which I am going to analyze, is, of course, neither an exclusively Hasidic concept nor a novel invention of the Baal Shem. Exactly where the new departure in its Hasidic application is found will become clear if we proceed to consider both its "prehistory" and its position in Hasidism.

Throughout Kabbalistic literature, *devekut* is frequently mentioned as the highest ideal of the mystical life as the Kabbalists see it. This is not to be wondered at, considering the meaning of the term as used in many books. In general Hebrew usage, *devekut* only means attachment or devoutness, but, since the thirteenth century, it has been used by the mystics in the sense of close and most intimate communion with God. Whereas in Catholic mysticism, "Communion" was not the last step on the mystical way—although a book *De adhaerendo Deo (On Communion with God),* ascribed to Albert the Great but actually by the Bavarian monk Johannes of Kastl, was one of the outstanding mystical manuals of the later Middle Ages—in Kabbalism it is the last grade of ascent to God. It is not union, because union with God is denied to man even in that mystical upsurge of the soul, according to Kabbalistic theology. But it comes as near to union as a mystical interpretation of Judaism would allow. I have already spoken briefly of this Kabbalistic concept of *devekut* in my former lectures on Jewish mysticism, but I may be permitted to add some remarks on the subject. *Devekut,* or as we may also call it, communion, is characterized in Kabbalistic literature by the following three traits:

1. It is a value without eschatological connotations, i.e., it can be realized in this life, in a direct and personal way, by every individual, and has no Messianic meaning. It is a state of personal bliss which can be attained without having recourse to the vast field of eschatology, utopianism, and Messianism. Being a strictly individual attainment, it is not an experience of the group, the social community of men, as is Messianic redemption, nor is it rooted in a hope or, for that matter, an anticipation of the Hereafter, of the World-to-come. In an eschatological sense, man cannot be redeemed alone, individually. Such individual redemption or salvation carries in Judaism no Messianic meaning. It is essentially a private experience; *devekut* can be reached alone. The only exception, when *devekut* became an experience of the whole community of Israel, was—at least according to some Jewish theologians—the revelation at Mount Sinai, but even then it was more in the nature of a multiplied experience of many single individuals than of the community as an integrated whole.

2. Furthermore, such *devekut,* although attained within the framework of this world, is, for the most part, realized only by the paradoxical means of abnegation and denial of the values of this world. Moses Nahmanides, for instance, speaks of "those who abandon the affairs of this world and pay no regard to this world at all, as though they were not corporeal beings, but all their intent and purpose is fixed on their creator alone, as in the cases of Elijah and Enoch, who live on forever in body and soul, after having attained Communion of their souls with the Great Name" (on Lev. 18:4). The realization of *devekut* means, therefore, a constant being-with-God which is not dependent on death and life after death.

3. For the understanding of the new turn of the idea of *devekut* in Hasidism, however, no passage is more important than Nahmanides' commentary on Deuteronomy 11:22, "To love the Lord your God, to

walk in all His ways and to cleave unto Him." The old commentaries are divided on the question of whether this cleaving, which is *devekut,* is to be understood as a promise held out to the faithful, or as a commandment binding upon everyone. Abraham ibn Ezra is of the first opinion; Nahmanides of the second. He explains the verse as follows:

It warns man not to worship God and somebody beside Him; he is to worship God alone in his heart and his actions. And it is plausible that the meaning of "cleaving" is to remember God and His love constantly, not to divert your thought from Him in all your earthly doings. *Such a man may be talking to other people, but his heart is not with them since he is in the presence of God.* And it is further plausible that those who have attained this rank, *do, even in their earthly life, partake of the eternal life,* because they have made themselves a dwelling place of the Shekhinah.

This statement, by the way, bears a strong resemblance to a similar one by Maimonides about the highest rank of prophecy, at the end of the *Guide of the Perplexed* (III, 51). In Nahmanides' definition, there appears, for the first time, an element which has played no great part in the Kabbalistic doctrine of *devekut,* although it is mentioned often enough in quotations of this classical passage, but which was given great prominence by the Baal Shem, and even more by his followers. I am referring to the combination of earthly action and *devekut.* Of course, it was not Nahmanides' intention to say that *devekut* could be realized in social action and association too. But he clearly thought that it could be sustained even in social intercourse, although such intercourse in itself is considered rather as a hindrance which must be overcome by special effort. *Devekut* is a value of contemplative, not of active life. But Nahmanides' saying could be used to prove the possibility of the coincidence of the two spheres. A man might appear to be with other people, to talk to them and, perhaps, even to participate in their activities, but in reality he is contemplating God. This is the highest attainment in the Kabbalistic scale of values and represents a blend of action and contemplation. For Nahmanides, *devekut* has always the specific meaning of communion with the last of the ten *sefirot* or grades of divine manifestation, namely, with the Shekhinah, but this detail was not retained by other Kabbalists, who keep to the more general definitions of *devekut* given by other members of Nahmanides' circle of Gerona. His older colleague, Rabbi Ezra ben Solomon, already speaks of *devekut,* or communion with the Naught, which is certainly a much higher rank than communion with the Shekhinah, the Naught being the most hidden recess of divinity which contemplation may behold.

This idea of *devekut* as the ultimate fulfillment of the mystic's path permeates the theosophical and ethical literature of the Kabbalists. Isaiah Horovitz connects the state of *hasidut* with that of *devekut:* "Who is a Hasid? He who acts in piety towards God and gives pleasure to his Creator and all of whose intention is bent on cleaving to Him and thereby becoming a chariot for God." Characteristically, it still appears in Moses Hayim Luzzatto's *Path of the Upright* as the last stage of the Path. In the opinion of this contemporary of the Baal Shem, it is a special grace granted to the Hasid, a gift of grace for which man can only prepare himself by incessant striving for knowledge and cognition and by the sanctification of all his actions. It is at the very end of the Path that God Himself takes over his guidance and causes divine holiness to dwell on him. Only then—says Luzzatto—may man succeed in his quest for such *devekut* with God as may last forever, for he may be helped by God to what Nature withholds from him. "If a man attains such spiritual rank, even his earthly actions become actually holy matters, and this is alluded to in the biblical prescriptions on meals made of holy offerings."

Here we find two basic motifs in connection with the doctrine of *devekut* which reappear and are given prominence in the Hasidic teaching of the Baal Shem: (1) the sanctification of the profane sphere in the life of the perfect Hasid, its transformation into one single sphere of holy action which leaves no room for the concept of a separate state of "profane" action; (2) the paradigm of eating in holiness as the perfect example of this supreme state of man. What is generally considered as an earthly performance par excellence, is transformed into a holy, nay, a mystery rite. This paradigm, by the way, is by no means a late addition, nor is it a specific trait of Hasidism, as it is sometimes considered to be. It is common to the whole Kabbalistic renaissance of Safed. The transformation of the profane sphere of human activity is stressed by Luzzatto, who says that he who has attained communion lifts up the earthly things which serve his needs, and does so by the very act of using them. "He raises them up to himself, rather than descending from his rank and state of *devekut* by using them." But Luzzatto draws no social conclusion from this conception of *devekut*. With him, everything connected with it remains wholly within the sphere of contemplation. He only follows in the footsteps of the older masters of Kabbalism by insisting on retreat and withdrawal from social intercourse as the principal means of attaining such "holiness" or "communion" (to him the two terms cover the same meaning). If *devekut* is the last stage on the path of ascetic self-abnegation, it would obviously be difficult to interpret it in terms of social ethics.

Luzzatto's book cannot be considered a literary source of the new Hasidic turn, but rather the opposite. But among the books with which the Baal Shem and the old Hasidic conventicles were undoubtedly conversant, there is the *Sefer Haredim (The Book of the God-Fearing),* one of the popular classics of Kabbalistic ethics, composed before 1600 at Safed by Eliezer Azikri. The three highest values which, according to him, the "Hasidim of Israel" cultivate, are "loneliness or retreat from society, asceticism, and *devekut."* He defines the latter as the fixing of thought on God (ed. 1601, fol. 66b). When the Baal Shem's Hasidism, in the eighteenth century, said that *devekut* was more important than study, this thesis aroused considerable hostility and was quoted in all polemical writings against the movement as proof of its subversive and anti-rabbinic tendencies. But it is noteworthy, and has been overlooked, that this fundamental tenet of Hasidism is quoted by Eliezer Azikri in the name of no less an authority of Kabbalism than his teacher, Isaac Luria himself. "These three principles of conduct are seven times more useful to the soul than study," Luria is reported to have said.

The bond between the old Kabbalists of the thirteenth-century school of Gerona and latter-day Hasidism, in their evaluation and elaboration of *devekut* as a mystical state of mind, is proved conclusively by a statement of Eliezer Azikri to which no attention has been paid. This author tells us that the "Hasidim of old times" took off no less than nine hours daily from their study of the Torah

for the spiritual activities of retreat and *devekut* and used to imagine the light of the Shekhinah above their heads, as though it were flowing all around them and they were sitting in the midst of the light, and this is the way I have found it [the meaning of *devekut*] explained in an old manuscript of the ancient ascetics. And while in that [state of meditation], they are all trembling as a natural effect, but [spiritually] rejoicing in trembling.

Azikri's source, the "old manuscript," is known to us. It was my good fortune to discover it some years ago in a lengthy and extremely interesting description of the meaning of Kabbalistic meditation *(kavvanah)* whose author was none other than the great mystic Azriel of Gerona.

Through the intermediacy of the sixteenth-century moralist of Safed, this description had come down to the Baal Shem and his followers, and the description of the state of *devekut,* which I quoted in my former set of lectures from a book of one of the Great Maggid's disciples, is taken, albeit without naming the source, from Azikri's work. This little example may serve to demonstrate the hidden after life of the old Kabbalistic manuscripts, the impact of which is too easily overlooked.

II

But let us return to the crucial point which our discussion of *devekut* has now reached. The questions can now be asked: What is the difference between the old Kabbalistic idea of *devekut* and the Hasidic one? Why could Luria and Azikri, in the sixteenth century, make the statements I have quoted without being attacked, whereas the rabbinical antagonists of Hasidism lost their tempers when they found an essentially identical statement in the writings of Ber of Miedzyrzecz and Mendel of Przemyslany? Was it only a question of the different time and environment that made a perfectly orthodox statement sound wicked and heretical two hundred years later? This, of course, would by no means be impossible. The history of religion abounds in examples of such different evaluations of the same tenet under different historical conditions. But the true answer to our problem is to be found in another consideration which, in my opinion, will take us into an even deeper understanding of the essential nature of Hasidism.

It is not so much the meaning of *devekut* that has changed in Hasidism as its place, and this is a most significant change indeed. The novel element is the radical character given to *devekut* by this change. Hasidic *devekut* is no longer an extreme ideal, to be realized by some rare and sublime spirits at the end of the Path. It is no longer the last rung in the ladder of ascent, as in Kabbalism, but the first. Everything begins with man's decision to cleave to God. *Devekut* is a starting point and not the end. Everyone is able to realize it instantaneously. All he has to do is to take his montheistic faith seriously. It is, therefore, small wonder that the Baal Shem identifies *emunah* (faith) and *devekut.* "Faith," he says (*Toledot* 195b), "is the intimate communion of the soul with God." And the first, and most pointed, consequence of this identification is the frequently repeated formula that to fall away from the state of *devekut* is essentially equivalent to separation of the creature from its Creator, nay, to idolatry *(avodah zarah).* God pervades everything, or, as the old adage goes, "no place can be void of the Shekhinah." Therefore, to be aware of this real omnipresence and immanence of God is already the realization of a state of *devekut.* In the opinion of the Baal Shem, to be out of *devekut* is not simply a state of estrangement from God, it rather implies the negation of His oneness and all-pervading presence. This idea is not an accidental obiter dictum of no consequence. It is commonly repeated from the Baal Shem's teaching in all the early writings of Hasidim before 1790. The Baal Shem formulated it in the words of the Torah (Deut. 11:16), *ve-sartem-va-avadtem elohim aherim,* "lest you turn aside and serve other gods," meaning, "once a man turns aside from *devekut* and the fixation of his thought on God, he is considered as one who serves other gods and there is no mediating path."

This change of position in the scale of values explains, to my view, much of the attraction Hasidism has held for the "common Jew." On the one hand, there could be—and, indeed, has been—the continued stress on the mystical implications of the state of *devekut* as an extreme attainment, and Nahmanides' passages on it are frequently quoted by those who consider it ultimate. On the other hand, it could be considered the focal point in the religious life of every Jew. Even if the leaders and saints took *devekut* in its most exalted meaning, this novel turn explains why it could very quickly become externalized when put as a demand to the average man. To be sure, it was a comfort to the masses that to cleave to God was no longer a remote ideal for the few, but there is also the second aspect which cannot be overlooked: if *devekut* was demanded from everybody and, in a way, forced upon the masses, it was bound to assume rather crude and vulgar forms. Once the radical slogan, "Judaism without *devekut* is idolatry," was accepted, its very radicalism already contained the germ of decay, a dialectic typical of radical and spiritualist movements. Since not everyone was able to attain that state of mind by mere introspection and contemplation, external stimulants, even liquor, had to be employed. *Devekut* in its popular and even objectionable forms was not a phenomenon of later degeneration, but was well known from the very beginnings of the newfangled Hasidic conventicles. As Moses of Santanow tells us, *devekut* was practiced about 1740 by rather simple people, who found in it an outlet for their emotional piety.

It is important to note that the same connection between *devekut* and the state of retreat and isolation constantly emphasized in the older literature of Kabbalistic ethics continues to prevail in the writings of eighteenth-century Hasidim. In this respect, there is no difference between the old-fashioned ascetic, such as that of Moses of Satanow, and the new school of the Baal Shem. *"Devekut"* says the former, "can be mainly attained during the time one spends in solitary retreat, for it is then that the soul actually cleaves to its Creator, for the whole earth is full of His glory." The reason given here that *devekut* is possible because God is everywhere, is exactly the same advanced by the Baal Shem and the Maggid of Miedzyrzecz.

III

A closer analysis of the Baal Shem's sayings on *devekut* will enable us better to understand its two fold aspect in Hasidic teaching. We have already mentioned the connection between "faith" and *devekut,* but the authentic dicta of the Baal Shem provide us with several other elucidations which are relevant to our discussion.

As a classical illustration of the meaning of *devekut* and, incidentally, also of the way famous Hasidic dicta have traveled through Hasidic tradition, we have the daring reinterpretation of Psalm 81:10, "There shall be no strange God in thee." These words, said the Baal Shem, can be taken according to the Hebrew sequence of words to mean "God shall not be a stranger to thee." And when is God no longer a stranger to man? When man constantly fulfills the admonition of the psalmist, "I set the Lord always before me." It is the communion with God through *devekut* that makes God an intimate friend of man, instead of a forbidding and remote stranger. This saying, quoted by Gedalya of Liniec, was not, even in Hasidic circles, generally known to belong to the Baal Shem. It is frequently quoted as one of the epigrams of Rabbi Mendel of Kock, in the fourth generation after the Baal Shem, who used to translate the biblical passage in a literal manner, *Nit zol zeyn in dir Gott fremd.* The Rabbi of Kock obviously liked the saying, and it is considered by many as one of his great words. Since there was no critical examination of the old and authentic sayings, many of them have, in the course of time, come to be ascribed to later authorities who were wont to quote them.

The performance of the commands is in itself an act of *devekut,* as is shown by an etymological pun. According to the Baal Shem, *misvah* means a bond. The Talmudic adage, "each good deed brings about another one," is taken to mean that every communion with God leads to ever closer communion. *Devekut* is thus not a state but is in itself a Path comprising an infinity of ever more intimate communions.

If the essence of religious action is communion or *devekut,* it follows that leaving this state of communion is the essence of sin. Even he who "falls away from the fixation of his thought on God for a moment only" is called a sinner. But this statement, mentioned by the Baal Shem's grandson, sets such a high standard for *devekut* that it had to be qualified and mitigated, as will be shown presently.

The Maggid Rabbi Mendel of Bar used to quote the following literal translation of Psalm 32:2 in the name of his teacher, the Baal Shem, "Blessed is the man to whom not to think of God is iniquity." Here the primitive radicalism of the demand of *devekut* is somewhat mitigated. Blessed is the man who has no other sin to repent of than his falling or stepping out of *devekut.* It is a sin, but the sin of a blessed man, of the perfect Hasid who has attained a higher level than the rabbinical zaddik. It is *devekut* as the final stage on the Kabbalist's path that is reflected in this and similar statements. Incidentally, this is the only word of the Baal Shem quoted (though anonymously) in a book of an old-fashioned Hasid like Simhah of Zolozec, a contemporary of the master.

Of what does that *devekut* consist which is realized in study and prayer? The answer is given in many authentic dicta of the Baal Shem stressing that *devekut* is a spiritual or contemplative act by which a man binds himself to the spiritual element inherent in the letters of Torah and prayer. The words and their element, the letters, are the vessels which contain a priceless jewel, the light of The Boundless *En-sof. Devekut,* in the opinion of the Baal Shem, is communion with this inner light that animates the letters of the Torah or, for that matter, everything. For he accepts the Kabbalistic conception of creation as externalized speech: Everything that exists consists of letters of the divine language. Each of them is only the vessel which contains unfathomable depths of divine light, a light which is not created, but is the light of the Shekhinah herself. What is required, therefore, is to concentrate in study and prayer not on the external figures of speech, nor on the "letter," but on the "spirit" that animates it. That is what *devekut* can perform. Meir Margalioth, the Rabbi of Ostrog, says that it is this special conception of *devekut* that he learned from his master, the Baal Shem, and that he had actually observed how it was practiced by him. This definition, which occurs also in the Baal Shem's authentic letter to his brother-in-law, puts the emphasis on a definite technique of contemplation which the Baal Shem practiced and taught, and there can be no doubt that it goes far beyond the earlier definitions of *devekut* which I have discussed. I am inclined to think that the dialectic of *devekut* to which I have made reference is fully reflected in this conception: It sounds very simple and anyone might start practicing it, but it is extremely difficult to attain as a sustained state of communion. Why should not anyone be able to concentrate on the inwardness of the spiritual element in everything? As a matter of fact, it is a counsel given not to the accomplished Kabbalist at the end of his path, but repeatedly addressed to everybody. Yet, it has the unmistakable ring of a mystical practice which has its esoteric side and is by no means as easy to carry out as it appears to be.

Sometimes the letters and the holy names composed of them are identified with the light that dwells therein, the letters themselves being transformed into the spiritual element, with which communion must be established. In this connection, great interest attaches to the mystical turn the Baal Shem gave to an old Jewish saying which extols the merit of the study of the Torah for its own sake *(torah lishmah)*. Several dicta explain the new meaning infused into the old phrase. This high ideal— the Baal Shem is reported to have said—must be understood according to the precise meaning of the phrase, which is "for the sake of its name." It is the name of God, the spiritual element, which is evoked by true study and which should be aimed at in study and worship. Study of the Torah *(lishmah)* is not a principle like "art for art's sake," but reflects the longing to discover the hidden element inherent in the letters and words. There are many variations of this motif among the Baal Shem's sayings, and it is obvious that he used the idea very often. Lurianic Kabbalism knew of a parallel explanation of *lishmah,* but whereas the Lurianic idea aimed at some theosophic detail in the mechanism of the Upper Worlds, the Hasidic exegesis of the saying is of a much more general nature. It is interesting that Jacob Joseph of Polonne quotes both explanations, the Kabbalistic and the Hasidic; he senses that there is a difference between them, but he strives to efface it.

As I have said, this definition of *devekut* as man's binding himself to the core *(penimiut)* of the letters, the Torah and the commandments, instead of to their external aspects only, seems to be a new point made by the Baal Shem. He was in dead earnest about the religious implications of this thesis. How much so is shown by one of his sayings, where he infers from this definition that he who does *not* bind his thought to the "root" or core of the action which he performs, is positively sinning by introducing separation into the world of spiritual unity and by "cutting down the trees of Paradise." This is the familiar Hebrew phrase for falling into heresy. Therefore—and this idea is hammered into the readers of Jacob Joseph of Polonne's books—he who keeps the Torah in its externals only, without *devekut,* is an arch-heretic in the sense of Kabbalism: instead of binding and uniting things to God, he separates and isolates them from Him. This, of course, is a radical and essentially spiritual thesis. It is interesting to observe how early Hasidic authors strove to discover a Kabbalistic authority for it. The Rabbi of Polonne tries to read it into a statement found in Abraham Azulai's *Hesed le-Avraham* (written about 1640). But Azulai's statement is of an altogether different nature and lacks the radicalism of the Hasidic thesis. The fact that it was necessary to twist quite innocuous Kabbalistic sentences in order to extract from them his new meaning of *devekut,* tends to show that we are dealing here with a novel departure. This central thesis that the core of every true worship is *devekut* could not be held by Kabbalists as long as they placed *devekut* at the end of the Path, and, as a matter of fact, Azulai never said it. He says only that the prayer of man is heard if he succeeds in drawing out the spirituality of the supernal spheres into the letters. This is quite different from discovering them there as an ever-present reality. And, of course, no mention is made by Azulai of the absence of *devekut* constituting a sin or transgression.

Devekut, or "communion," is not "union" in the sense of the mystical union between God and man of which many mystics speak. But it leads to a state, or, rather, implies an action which in Hebrew is called *yihud,* which means unification, the realization of union. The term has not always a mystical connotation, and it is not always easy to determine what is meant by it. Sometimes it only means concentration of mind by uniting all its powers on one focal point, sometimes it means even less, namely, the acknowledgement of God's unity. This latter meaning, however, is more or less restricted to non-mystical literature, where it is frequently found, whereas Hasidic literature uses the term in the same special sense given to it by the Kabbalists. If a man binds his thought to the root of the Torah, this is called a *yihud,* both because he concentrates on it and because he breaks down the barriers and brings about unification by making into an organic whole what seemed separated and isolated. He does not become God, but he becomes "united" with Him by the process in which the core of his own being is bound up with the core of all being. There is one saying of the Baal Shem—apparently the only one—stating that the process of *yihud,* which is accomplished through *devekut,* transforms the Ego, or *ani,* into the Naught, or *ain.* This idea, which plays no central part in the Baal Shem's conceptions, was taken up with great vigor by the Maggid of Miedzyrzecz who, as a radical mystic, made it one of the cornerstones of his thought. The hidden Naught, an old Kabbalistic symbol of the depths of the Godhead, held no special attractions for the Baal Shem, but it takes on a new vitality in the teachings of Rabbi Ber and his pupils. Many of the classical writings of Hasidism overflow with lucubrations on the communion with "Nothingness" and the path by which man retraces his steps from "aught" to "naught." The strange enthusiasm which characterizes these sermons on a truly paradoxical symbolism wanes after the generation of Rabbi Ber's pupils. But for the first generation after the Baal Shem it held a fascination unequaled in Jewish literature and not easily explained. It seems to express a degree of abandonment to emotionalism that has no precedent, except for the short upsurge of Sabbatianism in 1666, and could find no adequate expression but in the most daring paradoxes of mysticism. The Baal Shem never said that *devekut* represented a state where man was able to stand within the Naught, an idea cherished by the Maggid. Of course, the new departure introduced by Rabbi Ber did not prevent him from using definitions and theses about *devekut* which he had inherited from the Baal Shem.

There is a point in connection with the Baal Shem's conception of *devekut* that deserves further attention. I am referring to the relation between Talmudic study of the Torah and the new central virtue. As far as I am aware, it has been overlooked that this the shifting of the place of *devekut* in the scale of values, and the new definition given to it, has something to do with the evaluation of Talmudic learning in early Hasidism. The old Safed school clearly already knew that the "Hasidim of old" took nine hours off their time of study in order to practice solitude and *devekut.* Now, when *devekut* was no longer considered a final stage for the few, but a demand on anybody who harkened to the voice, this was bound to hasten the clash between a purely Talmudic orientation and the new school. If you concentrate on the spiritual core of the Torah, on the mystic light shining through the letters, and if this is *devekut,* it follows that you cannot concentrate with equal fervor on the specific and concrete meaning of the words, and certainly not on the intricacies of Talmudic lore and discussion. To penetrate an intricate discussion is one thing, and to contemplate the divine light that pervades the words is another.

The Baal Shem, and still more his main disciples, were fully aware of the gulf between the understanding of the specific detail and the contemplation of the all-enveloping light which transcends human grasp and understanding. They did not think it possible to unite both of them in one and the same act. (The Baal Shem said to the Rabbi of Polonne that on Sabbath there was almost no time to study, because all of it ought to be devoted to *yihudim,* i.e., contemplation.) Hence the insistence on taking time off from study and devoting it to contemplation and meditation. The two did not go together. Mendel of Przemyslany, who counseled not to devote too much time to Talmudic study, only drew the logical conclusion from the basic demands of *devekut.* The famous warning so vehemently assailed in the struggle between the two camps is to be found in a context where special emphasis is laid on the practice of *devekut.* The radicalism of the mystics and protagonists of popular revivalism, which necessarily brought about the clash, had not yet been watered down. Later on, it would be argued, as some Kabbalists, including Moses of Satanow, had done before, that *devekut* and penetrating study were not mutually exclusive and might be practiced together. Honesty requires us to state that Hasidism, in its beginning, was far removed from such an irenic attitude. Talking about *devekut* and contemplation, it meant what it said, and meant it in an uncompromising sense. The emphasis on *devekut* had, of course, two aspects: one for the average man, to whom it opened up a new vista and, especially through the practice of fervent and ecstatic prayer, a Path to God; the other, for the learned, from whom it required a new balance between the intellectual and emotional sides of his nature. In both cases, the problem could not have arisen without the afore-mentioned shifting of the place of *devekut* into the center of man's spiritual activity.

So far, we have found in *devekut* a value which, to the Baal Shem no less than to his precursors, is connected primarily with solitary meditation and prayer. In prayer, even in communal prayer, man is alone with God, much as he may strive to bind himself spiritually to "Catholic Israel." What I said at the beginning of the characteristics of *devekut* in Nahmanides holds emphatically true for the Baal Shem's conception too, in spite of the change I have just been analyzing. The possibility of a social meaning of communion with God begins to show here and there and seems to be based on the practice of the Baal Shem. His disciple, Moses of Dolina, reports in his name that *devekut* can be sustained even in seemingly idle talk and in attending to one's business. But to accomplish this, he says, special zeal and fervor are required. The very close relation between *devekut* and *yihud* is also shown by the fact that the same saying that Moses of Dolina quotes about *devekut* is mentioned by the Baal Shem's grandson in connection with the possibility of performing *yihudim* not only by prayer and contemplation, but by every earthly performance. Even in social intercourse, in attending to business, etc., it is possible to continue the contemplative attitude by binding oneself to the spiritual core of the matter. In other words, *devekut* and *yihudim* are not concerned so much with the concrete as such, but rather with emptying it of its concrete content and discovering in it an ideal aspect that opens a vista into the hidden life which flows everywhere. *Devekut* was not preached as an active realization of the concrete, but as a contemplative realization of the immanence of God in the concrete.

In the teaching of Ber of Miedzyrzecz, the re-evaluation of *devekut* has proceeded a step further, in harmony with the general trend of his thought, which could be characterized as a transformation of Kabbalistic theosophy and its terminological apparatus into mystical anthropology. It is remarkable that the central concept of Lurianic Kabbalism, the idea of *tikkun* (restoration), plays no great part in the first Hasidic writings. Its place is taken by *devekut,* a substitution which I have found nowhere in pre-Hasidic literature, and which, indeed, could never be found there. Why? Because the idea of *tikkun* in Lurianic doctrine had a strong Messianic connotation and implication on which I have dwelt elsewhere. But *devekut* is essentially a non-Messianic and non-eschatological value. When it took the place of *tikkun* in the mending of the "broken vessels," in the restoration of harmony in the broken state of our being, it could do so only because something had fundamentally changed in the outlook of the Hasidim. About this change, namely, the neutralization of Messianism as a driving power, I shall speak at greater length later. Before this liquidation of Messianism had taken place, nobody could have thought of substituting the private and contemplative experience of *devekut* as a healing force for the broad and comprehensive action that was the essential meaning of *tikkun*. This substitution tells much about the real difference between Lurianism and Hasidism.

Rabbi Ber enumerates three factors which may induce the state of *devekut:* retreat from association with other people; the writing down of Kabbalistic mysteries on the Torah; and the practice of *yihudim,* in the sense of special meditations. No special emphasis is laid as yet on the attainment of *devekut* within the group. He does not change the basic meaning of *devekut* as a value of introspection which consists of solitary intercourse with God. It is not a social value. In his opinion, it is a high degree of perfection if a man is "sometimes" able to be alone with himself and God "even when in one room with many other people." It was left to Rabbi Ber's disciples, especially to Elimelekh of Lezajsk, to take the final step and demand the realization of *devekut* as a social value. But this could be done only at a high price, namely, by binding *devekut* to the institution of Zaddikism, a connection wholly foreign to primitive Hasidism.

Looking back on our analysis, there is one point which deserves to be amplified. It is remarkable that *devekut,* an essentially emotional value, is linked in a surprisingly large number of sayings of the Baal Shem and his various pupils or associates with a seemingly intellectual effort. *Devekut* is reached by a fixation of one's thought *(mahshavah)* or mind *(sekhel)* on God. True, there are some sayings which mention the soul as a whole, and not only its intellectual power, as the instrument of *devekut.* But the insistence on the use of mind and thought cannot be accidental, even if we concede that "thought" is sometimes used in a rather loose sense. For it does not always mean the purely intellectual and intentional act of the mind, but rather indicates in some places any intentional act of the soul, including its voluntaristic and emotional spheres. I assume, however, that the strong emotional coloring of the "thought" of man in the dicta about *devekut* has something to do with the nature of this act. In fixing all one's attention on God, thought, sunk in contemplation of the ineffable light, loses its definite content as an intellectual act. By the practice of *devekut,* thought is transformed into emotion; it is, if I may be permitted to use the expression, de-intellectualized. In other words, the insight which is won by *devekut* has no rational and intellectual content and, being of a most intimate and emotional character, cannot be translated into rational terms.

This point is very succinctly put forward by Meshullam Feibush Heller, a pupil of the Maggid of Miedzyrzecz and the Maggid of Zloczow. His classic epistle on the fundamentals of Hasidism contains pointed criticism of the contemporary study of Kabbalah. True mystery, he says, is not what can be read and studied by anybody in the printed volumes of Kabbalistic teaching, which is a purely intellectual affair, like so many other studies; there is no point in calling this an "esoteric" knowledge when it is, in truth, as exoteric as any other knowledge that can be imparted by books. The real mystery and esoteric wisdom is that of loving communion with God, *devekut ha-ahavah ba-shem yitbarakh*. It cannot be told or transmitted, and "everyone knows of it only what he has found out for himself, and no more."

It is, however, not without interest that the link between *devekut* and intellectual effort may have come down from Kabbalistic tradition. Joseph Gikatilla (about 1300) defines *devekut* as the process by which man binds his soul to God by way of intellectual thought, and he labors this intellectual view of *devekut* at some length in his book on the Kabbalistic reasons of the commandments.

IV

If Hasidic piety was focused to such a degree on *devekut,* there could be no doubt that the great demand could not be fulfilled continuously. There are two ways in which the Baal Shem dealt with this question in his sayings. Sometimes he admits the necessity of an interruption of *devekut.* The soul, too, must take a rest from the exertions and the emotional strain. By simple and unstrained activities it must gather new strength for the renewed exercises of *devekut* (*Ben porat,* fol. 34a). Seen in this light, attending to the business of daily life is a necessary interruption and preparation for the adventure of spiritual life, and therefore no reproach attaches to it. In *devekut,* man is cleaving to the spiritual life of all worlds which is the Shekhinah or the immanence of God. This vital force, which is aroused by communion, cannot operate without interruption. A "descent," a *yeridah,* from the state of *devekut* is therefore part of human nature. The Baal Shem used to apply to this the verse in Ezekiel 11:14, which he interpreted to mean, "the force of life" (*hiyut*), instead of *hayot* of the text, "runs and returns," i.e., operates not steadily but with interruptions. The meaning of all this, of course, is that the force of life, although it is there, cannot be continuously realized and made conscious. Jacob Joseph of Polonne mentions twice such a "fallen state" or *yeridah* of the Baal Shem himself when he had gone to another country; it is to be regretted that he gives no further details, but contents himself with the remark that after that he had double power of "ascent," *aliyah*.

But it must be admitted that in the light of his own pronouncements, this is not a satisfactory solution. If it is sin, or even heresy, to fall out of *devekut,* how could an explanation such as this one hold good? Out of this dilemma came a fundamental thesis of the Baal Shem, meant as a qualification of the doctrine of *devekut* and which, indeed, played a very important part in early Hasidism. This is the doctrine of *katnut* and *gadlut,* the minor and major states of man.

As a matter of fact, *katnut* and *gadlut* are not only states of man's mind or being, but, according to the Baal Shem, two basic states of every being. "Just as there exists a state of *katnut* and *gadlut* in the supernal *sefirot,* there is a similar state in every thing, even in the clothes that a man wears," his grandson quotes him as saying. We have here another striking example of the metamorphosis of Kabbalistic terms. In Lurianic Kabbalah these terms have a specific theosophic meaning, as states of the divine mind in some of its manifestations. The chapters on these states in Vital's *Es hayyim* are famous for their difficulty and their daring use of anthropomorphic symbolism. The Baal Shem takes the terms back into the human sphere and gives the theosophic idea a new turn or twist.

With him, *katnut* and *gadlut* are phases of life, everywhere and at all times, from purely natural and even artificial things up to the configuration of the divine *sefirot* where the same rhythm and the same law prevail. *Katnut,* the minor state, is the state of imperfection, even of degradation, whereas *gadlut* means the full development of a thing to its highest state. Everywhere in time, space, and the soul there is the same organic law of the two states, an idea which the Rabbi of Polonne was tireless in preaching and applying.

There is a higher and lower state in human existence and human affairs, and particularly in worship. But everything depends on the rank a man has reached in his spiritual struggle for perfection. With one, *katnut* may mean an outward and mechanical way of worship "without soul" or, as the Baal Shem was fond of putting it, "without joy." But with another class, it may mean only a lower standard than their customary one. *Katnut*, then, is the time of man's struggle with his lower instincts in order to lift himself up to *gadlut*, a state that knows of no struggle, but only of the enjoyment that comes with victory over the darker side of his nature.

The same verse in Ezekiel I, used by the Baal Shem in support of the interruption of *devekut*, is also adduced by him in connection with this rather different theory. There is a steady flow of life, up and down, and no state is void of its manifestation. There can be a modest form of *devekut* even in the minor state. It is limited and without that exuberance and exhilaration that comes to man only when joy sweeps him off *katnut*. But still, it enables him to keep some sort of communion even in that state of estrangement from God as *katnut* is frequently pictured. One saying has it that "in the time of *gadlut* man is literally cleaving to God, which cannot be said to apply in the time of *katnut*." For when man falls into this state—and there is no exception to the law that necessitates this periodic occurrence—he finds himself in melancholy sadness and estrangement. His worship contains an element of compulsion and not those high qualities of pure fear and love which characterize that worship out of an overflowing heart which is essentially what *gadlut* means. Only by constantly striving to overcome this state of separation and to attain anew the higher state, by the very struggle to get oneself out of the spiritual desert, there remains some indirect approach to God. This is the point on which the Baal Shem's defense of his behavior with simple folk is centered. *Katnut* is the time to serve God even through idle talk or story telling! For, even by this means, man can bring about the spiritual concentration which will help him to attain *devekut*. In *katnut*, man should devote himself to external action or worldly talk, but even then the true Hasid will be meditating on the spiritual side of what seems to be a purely material undertaking. Nobody may notice it, yet he transforms the lowest forms of activity into something of a higher order. It is obvious, and I need not labor the point, that this thesis can be as sublime as it may prove dangerous. The mystic content of idle talk —that is certainly a thesis full of perverse possibilities! And a very popular thesis at that. It is constantly emphasized in the doctrinal tradition of early Hasidism and must be considered as an active factor in its propaganda.

Katnut is, therefore, the time of trial through which the perfect man, no less than anybody else, must pass. There is, to be sure, a twofold aspect of *katnut:* it can be the natural relaxation after the strain of *devekut*, but it can also be an intentional descent, because of some hidden purpose. This second aspect plays an important part in Hasidic doctrine. It is connected with the motif of the falling, or stepping down, of the zaddik, a problem that had a special fascination for the Hasidim. I do not think it could have acquired this importance had it not been for the Sabbatian theories of the necessary fall of the Messiah and its later Podolian metamorphosis. Only after Sabbatianism, the problem of *nefilat ha-zaddik,* (fall or descent of the zaddik) became an acute one that needed to be discussed. Earlier Kabbalistic ethics does not know it as a pressing one. Now, from the Baal Shem's sayings till Elimelekh of Lezajsk, it takes on rather astonishing dimensions. In my view, it is a sublimation of an antinomian thesis, on a plane where it was calculated to lose its sting. The deliberate stepping down from holiness into a state of *katnut*—says the Baal Shem—is very dangerous, and there are many who have remained there and could not rise again. This sounds very much like an echo of the Sabbatian turmoil!

Another saying of the Baal Shem has it that, "if it happens to a perfect man that he cannot study or pray, he should realize that this also shows the hand of God who is pushing him back in order that he may come nearer." Here we have essentially the principle which, as far as I can see, was formulated in its final shape by Rabbi Ber of Miedzyrzecz, if not by the Baal Shem himself. The formula *yeridah sorekh aliyah,* "the descent, or stepping down, is necessary in order to ascend to a higher rank"— something perhaps best translated by the French phrase, *reculer pour mieux sauter*—recurs constantly in Rabbi Ber's sayings on the meaning of *katnut*. But he admits two kinds of "stepping down": "Sometimes," he says, "a man falls from his rank because of himself . . . and sometimes the state of the world causes him to fall, and in both cases the descent is for the sake of an ever higher ascent." *Katnut,* then, for all its personal color, is not only a matter of purely personal causation. It may depend on the surroundings of a man, his fellow men, or other factors. This explanation was very frequently used to justify the deliberate or quasi-deliberate stepping down of a perfect man, a zaddik, in the Hasidic sense of the term. If all the world is in a state of *katnut,* he should join in and associate his efforts with theirs in order to reach *gadlut.* It is in this context that Jacob Joseph of Polonne uses almost the same formula as the Maggid of Miedzyrzecz. (Incidentally, since he uses it immediately before a quotation from the Baal Shem, we may infer that the formula itself was not known to him as a saying of his master; otherwise he would have acknowledged it as such.)

We even have the prescription of the Baal Shem as to which parts of prayer should be said in a state of *katnut* in order to be able to pray the other parts in the ravishment of *devekut*. It is obvious, therefore, that a state which is considered as preparatory to *devekut* does *not* constitute a sin in the sense I have explained before. Of course, there is danger in *katnut,* namely the danger of remaining in what should be only a transitory stage. But the whole teaching of the Baal Shem is centered around this conception of a steady ebb and flow in the spiritual life of man: in *gadlut,* there is communion and even ecstasy, but in *katnut,* there is preparation for it. Understood in this right sense, no fault is to be found in such a state.

V

In the foregoing analysis of *devekut,* I have laid stress on those points which characterize the specific color and significance the term has taken on in Hasidic parlance, and particularly with the Baal Shem. They are more or less typical of the conception of *devekut* in the bulk of Hasidic literature. But there is one further point which I think should be discussed here. I have said that communion, for all its depth and importance, is not union. But is this truly so? Are there no stages of deeper contemplation, ravishment, and ecstasy where one state passes into the other? Since much has been made of the allegedly pantheistic leanings and doctrines of the Baal Shem and his early pupils, especially by S. A. Horodetzky and Jacob S. Minkin, it may be worthwhile to go into the matter. All the more so, since Horodetzky uses the term pantheism in a very loose way which tends to make pantheists of a great many inside and outside of the Hasidic camp who might never have so much as dreamed of such a faith as that venerable author ascribes to them. If Creator and Creation are essentially one, then *devekut* may indeed be union. I propose, therefore, to examine this question, if only briefly, in order to reach a better understanding of some shades of the concept of *devekut* which deserve our attention.

As to the Baal Shem himself, there is no proof, in his authentic sayings, of any doctrine which might properly be called pantheistic. In contradistinction to this absence of an identification of God and the universe, of the Creator and Creation, there is full proof of his belief in the immanence of God in every one of His creatures. It is at most what philosophers call "panentheistic" teaching—all Being *in* God, but not all Being God. This sort of teaching was current in Kabbalism, especially in Cordovero's works. If we knew for sure that the Baal Shem had studied Abraham Azulai's *Hesed le-Avraham,* which is an abstract of Cordovero's Kabbalah, we would better understand the genesis of some of his formulas as quoted in the books of the Rabbi of Polonne. For Azulai sharply accentuates the panentheistic core of Cordovero's teaching. But all we know positively is that this rabbi himself had read the book, which was printed as early as 1685. Whether his master knew it we can only guess. Azulai states, for instance, that man is "in communion with God," because "there is nothing that is separated from Him." But the reason he adduces for the latter statement is perfectly orthodox and non-pantheistic; it is the chain of cause and effect which, in the last resort, links God with His Creation. The formula of the "chain of causes" enables the mystics to reinstate God as the immanent soul or life of all being. And it is only in this quality, and not as the last and transcendent cause, that God appeals to the mind of the Baal Shem. His thinking on this score is very simple and unsophisticated. He repeats the old formulas which every Kabbalist had used before him, and, with one notable exception, without additions of his own: "Everything is full of His glory," "No place is void of Him," "Thou keepest them all alive" (Neh. 9:6), which was frequently understood to mean: Thou art the vital force, *hiyut*, of everything. To this last quotation the Baal Shem made the significant addition, of everything, even of sin, an idea which he repeated in a great many variations.

On the other hand, the Baal Shem was fond of telling a parable which recurs in several variations in the books of his disciples and apparently carries quite a different meaning.

A king had built a glorious palace full of corridors and partitions, but he himself lived in the innermost room. When the palace was completed and his servants came to pay him homage, they found that they could not approach the king because of the devious maze. While they stood and wondered, the king's son came and showed them that those were not real partitions, but only magical illusions, and that the king, in truth, was easily accessible. Push forward bravely and you shall find no obstacle.

The interpretations put on this parable in Hasidic literature differ widely. Its literal sense conveys no pantheistic meaning but rather an "acosmic" one: the world is denied real existence, reality is seen rather as a sort of "veil of Maya." The perfectly devout man, the "son of the king," discovers that there is nothing that separates him from his father. External reality is but an illusion. This is the way the parable is commented on by the Baal Shem's grandson. But others, for instance the Rabbi of Polonne, give it a pantheistic turn: "People with true insight know that all the walls and partitions, all the outward clothes and covers are in truth of His own essence, for there is no place void of Him." If the formula alone were decisive, we might safely say that there is, indeed, a pantheistic element to be found, at least in some of the Baal Shem's disciples. But the ideational content of the formula is, almost in every case, limited to a much less radical interpretation, by reading into it either the doctrine of divine immanence or that of the annihilation of reality before the contemplative mind. For if one looks closely into the context of such passages, all that remains of the high-flown formulas is always the omnipresence of the divine influxus, *shefa*, and *hiyut*, the vitalizing power, instead of that of the divine substance. I think that the numerous writers who have compared the Baal Shem's teaching to that of Spinoza have considerably overshot the mark. I, for one, am unable to find any teachings reminiscent of Spinoza in the Baal Shem's doctrinal sayings.

An excellent example of the shifting of emphasis in the use of extreme formulations is provided by a saying of Pinhas of Korzec on the subject, in his *Midrash pinhas* (1872f., 9b, 60):

If a man fulfills the commandments of the Torah, such as the commandment of the phylacteries, and says the formula prescribed by the Kabbalists, namely, "In the name of all Israel [I am doing this]" then he lifts up the whole universe to its "root" above, *for the world is really God Himself,* like the locust whose clothing is part of its own self. Therefore, he annihilates [by his action] the [outward] existence of the whole universe. And if we see that in spite of all this the world is still there, it is because the vital energy of God is always active and the world is incessantly renewed.

Here, then, we have within one sentence the different motives I have just mentioned, and this, I think, should warn us against over-stressing such formulas as "the world is really God Himself." What is particularly interesting in this view is that the performance of the *misvah* does not give more meaning and reality to the world, as modern interpretations of Hasidic theology would lead us to expect but, on the contrary, detracts from its apparently illusory reality and leads from the Aught to the verge of the Naught. For the "root" of the world is the Naught which the mystic contemplates, with which he communes and in which he longs to "stand." At their "root" the created things lose their identity as creatures, because all that can be beheld there is God alone. But we should not forget that, to reach that state, Creation as Creation must be "annihilated," which implies that Creation, in its own right, is not what pantheism would declare it to be, namely a mere mode of Infinity. We are indeed, as we may put it, dwelling in God, but we are not God. Also, it should be borne in mind that the "son of the king," who pushes through to his father, sees his father and cleaves to him, but does not become one with him.

This, then, brings us back to the point I have raised: are there, in original Hasidic teaching, more radical formulations of the central doctrine of *devekut* than those we have been considering? The answer is that there is a definite turn toward a more mystical formulation of it in the teaching of the Maggid of Miedzyrzecz and some of his pupils. The Baal Shem and Jacob Joseph of Polonne do not emphasize a "union" or "unity" *(ahdut)* between God and man, and their formulations are much more careful than those found in Rabbi Ber's sayings. This adds further weight to what I have said about the necessity of taking Jacob Joseph's allegedly pantheistic statements with not too small a grain of salt. Comparing the two most conspicuous pupils of the Baal Shem, there can be no doubt that Jacob Joseph is the relatively sober one, whereas Rabbi Ber of Miedzyrzecz has gone far on the way of what must be described as mystical intoxication. The difference between the sermons of the two, which have come down to us, is tremendous. I have mentioned the streak of soberness that characterizes the Baal Shem. In Rabbi Ber, this trait has disappeared. He is no longer the friend of God and the simple folk, who roams through the markets. He is the ascetic whose gaze is fixed on, or, I might rather say, lost in God. He is a mystic of unbridled radicalism and singularity of purpose. His predilection for the more paradoxical figures of mystical speech colors his sermons to a degree equaled by few of his predecessors in the history of Jewish mysticism. It is, therefore, not astonishing that he should use the terminology of mystical union in describing some stages of *devekut,* although here, too, it may be wise not to lose ourselves in his terminology, which is radical indeed, but to consider the context of his thought.

It will serve as an illustration of this peculiar mystical bent of Rabbi Ber if I close by summarizing his bold explanation of Numbers 10:2 which, as a description of the ultimate goal of *devekut,* goes as far as anything in early Hasidism. The rather inoffensive prescription of the Torah: "Make thee two trumpets of silver, of a whole piece shall thou make them," gives birth in Rabbi Baer's mind to the following enthusiastic explanation based on a mystical pun, the word *hasoserot,* trumpets, being taken as two words, *hasi-surot,* halves of forms. Man and God, he says, are each only a half-finished, incomplete form. Man without God is really not man, *adam,* a sublime and spiritual being, but only *dam,* blood, a biological entity. He is lacking the *a* or *alef,* which is God, *alufo shel olam,* the master of the world. Only when the *alef* and *dam,* God and man, get together, the two form a real unity, and only then does man deserve to be called *adam.* But how is such unity, *ahdut,* accomplished? By *kisuf,* which means "the constant striving for union with God." If man casts off all earthly or material elements and ascends through all the worlds and becomes one with God to the degree of losing the feeling of separate existence, then will he be rightly called *adam,* Man, "being transformed into the cosmic figure of the primordial man whose likeness upon the throne Ezekiel beheld." This, according to Ber, is the transfiguration of man which is reached through, or in, the state of *devekut:* man finds himself by losing himself in God, and by giving up his identity he discovers it on a higher plane. Here, and in many other sayings of Rabbi Ber, *devekut* is said to lead not only to communion, but to *ahdut,* union. But—this union is, in fact, not at all the pantheistic obliteration of the self within the divine mind which he likes to call the Naught, but pierces through this state on to the rediscovery of man's spiritual identity. He finds himself because he has found God. This, then, is the deepest meaning of *devekut* of which Hasidism knows, and the radical terms should not blind us to the eminently Jewish and personalistic conception of man which they still cover. After having gone through *devekut* and union, man is still man—nay, he has, in truth, only then started to be man, and it is only logical that only then will he be called upon to fulfill his destiny in the society of men.

9

God and the Zaddik as the Two Focal Points of Hasidic Worship

Ada Rapoport-Albert

It is generally accepted now that the religious ideal of *Devekut,* mystical adherence to or communion with God which was adopted by Hasidism from earlier Kabbalistic traditions, became the highest religious ideal of the movement, and it was toward the fulfillment of this ideal that every Hasid was expected to concentrate all his spiritual efforts at all times.[1] The notion that *devekut* could and should be maintained at all times is present in the earlier Kabbalistic formulations of the ideal of *devekut,* notably in Nahmanides' comment on Deuteronomy 11:22: "To love the Lord your God, to walk in all his ways and to cleave unto Him." Nahmanides interprets the last section of this verse, "and to cleave unto Him," as a command, in contrast with Ibn Ezra who sees it as the end achieved by those who fulfill the previous two commands listed in the verse. Nahmanides' comment reads as follows: "This cleaving to God may well consist of remembering God and His love always. One must not allow one's consciousness to part from Him at any time, not even when one is walking, sleeping or rising. Thus, when a man engages his mouth and tongue in conversation with his fellow men, his heart should not be occupied with them but rather it should rest before God."

This paper was read at the Conference on the Jewish Religious Tradition held at the Divinity School of the University of Chicago, April 17–20, 1977. I would like to thank Professor C. Abramsky who read an early draft of this paper and made a number of valuable comments.
Reprinted by permission of the University of Chicago Press and the author from *History of Religions* 18, no. 4 (May 1979): 296–325.

While Nahmanides is suggesting in this passage that *devekut* should be sustained even through mundane, nondevotional activities, he still considers such activities as a hindrance which the true mystic may and should overcome without renouncing worldly life but by transcending it through contemplation. Basically, his conception of the *ideal* state of communion with God is of seclusion with Him through the expulsion from one's higher consciousness, if not always from one's concrete circumstances, of all earthly material affairs. The true mystic may achieve this by applying the technique of dividing his consciousness, to enable one part of it (his mouth and tongue) to carry out mundane tasks, while the other, more elevated part (his heart), may continue to absorb itself in the contemplation of God.[2]

In Hasidism, while there are some early traditions which reflect practically no departure from this notion of maintaining *devekut* at all times, despite the inevitable need to engage also in profane activities, other traditions, especially those which are associated with the Besht, introduce a more positive evaluation of earthly activities by presenting them as a ground which is as fertile for the cultivation of *devekut* as that of spiritual activities.

If man's contact with or access to the deity is conceived of as *devekut*, then worship is that practice or activity which leads to the attainment of this state. Under the obligation to strive for *devekut* at all times, including the times of "walking, sleeping or rising" or of profane conversation with one's fellowman—namely, activities which are religiously neutral or, if this notion is to be pursued to its logical conclusion, even activities which are religiously negative—then all man's activities become potential vehicles for *devekut*. Thus, the concept of worship in Hasidism, particularly in the first generation of the movement, assumes a totality of scope which it had rarely entertained before. The request to strive for and maintain *devekut* at all times, as it was presented by the Besht and his associates, extended the arena on which devotional activities could take place beyond the traditional rabbinic boundaries of study and prayer, as well as the Kabbalistic boundaries of asceticism and solitary contemplation of God. And even though mundane occupations had been recognized previously as an obstacle which did not necessarily prevent the fulfillment of the ideal but could be removed by divorcing the contemplative consciousness from them to the enhancement of *devekut*, now such occupations were proclaimed, at least by some Hasidic masters, as a legitimate mode of worship in *devekut*. This was achieved in Hasidism by the introduction of the practice of "worship through corporeality" *(avodah be-gashmiyut)*.

In the circle of the Besht, R. Nahman of Kosow was one of the main advocates of the ideal of constant *devekut* which was to be maintained even during the pursuit of mundane tasks such as conducting commercial affairs: "I have heard it said of our master, R. Nahman Kosover, that he used to reproach people for not fulfilling [the request indicated by the verse in Ps. 16:8] 'I have set the Lord always before me' even while they are dealing in merchandise and concerned with business affairs. And if one may ask how this is possible, [the answer is that] just as a man praying in the synagogue may be thinking of various kinds of merchandise and business affairs, so it is possible to do the opposite."[3]

Notably, R. Nahman of Kosow was the only member of the Besht's circle of associates who did not earn his living by pursuing a "spiritual" profession, such as that of a teacher, preacher, or rabbi. R. Nahman was a tax farmer and a merchant.[4] The gulf between his material occupation and his spiritual activities may have heightened his sensitivity to the scope for worship which lay even in "dealing in merchandise and business affairs" under the call for constant *devekut* which was shared by the entire circle.

But while R. Nahman Kosover's formulations of this notion still allow for the continuation of contemplation and *devekut* even during commercial dealings, by means of a division of consciousness such as was suggested by Nahmanides ("the opposite" of the practice he reproaches being the conduct of business affairs while at the same time thinking only of God)[5] the following tradition, ascribed to the Besht, suggests that profane conversation may lend itself to the contemplation of God just as well as any sacred utterance: "I have heard it from my master . . . that 'acts of unification' *(yihudim)* are contained in words, either in the words of Torah and prayer or in [the words uttered during] conversation with one's fellow man in the market place. Each man according to his level may be 'joined' and uplifted, either by means of words of holiness or by means of profane words which contain the 22 letters [of the Hebrew alphabet] etc."[6] With the aid, in this case, of the Lurianic concept of *yihudim*, meditations of the various combinations of Hebrew letters yielding the divine name into which the entire range of letter combinations within the Hebrew language may be reduced, the

Besht avoids the need to divorce man's higher consciousness from mundane conversation in order to enable him to maintain *devekut* even while engaging in such conversation. On the contrary, since the profane utterance, just as the holy one, consists of the twenty-two letters of the Hebrew alphabet which offer the vehicle for ascent, man's higher consciousness should embrace, not transcend the profane utterance, in contemplation leading to *devekut*.

One qualification should, perhaps, be stressed. The profane is presented as a positive means to worship in *devekut,* not through its profanity, which is only apparent and external, but rather through the divine element which constitutes its core and which is its true reality, rendering it a part of the total unity of God who is constantly present throughout the universe. The following passage highlights the external, or even unreal, nature of profanity as it appears to manifest itself in mundane activities at the time of refraining from study and prayer, or, in the next stage down from purely spiritual pursuits, "straying thoughts" whose content is positively evil: "A teaching received from the Besht: He who cleaves to one part of the unity cleaves to the whole. And the same applies to the opposite condition: 'I sought him whom my soul loveth, I sought him, but I found him not' [Song of Sol. 3:1]. The meaning is that the Holy One Blessed be He disguises himself behind several garments and partitions, such as straying thoughts or the cessation of study and prayer. . . . But for the men of knowledge, who know that no place is empty of Him, these are not true disguises. . . ." [7]

However, there are traditions ascribed to the Besht, as well as to other members of his circle, which offer an alternative legitimation of profane activities, presenting them as a means to attaining holiness without at the same time disposing of the essential reality of their profane nature by relegating it, as in the previous examples, to the position of an external appearance. One source for this view is the following parable related in the name of the Besht:

Received from the Besht: A king had a son whom he wanted to teach various wisdoms necessary [for a prince]. He hired a number of scholars to study with him, but the prince did not learn anything. Finally, the scholars despaired of ever teaching him, and only one of them remained with the prince. One day the prince saw a young girl and desired her beauty. The scholar reported this to the king and complained. But the king said: Since he has experienced desire, even in this way, through his physical desire, he will attain all wisdoms. The king summoned the girl to court and instructed her not to submit herself to the prince until he has acquired one wisdom. The girl followed the king's instructions. On each subsequent occasion she demanded that the prince should acquire one additional wisdom, so that eventually he acquired them all. Once he became a scholar, he dismissed the girl, for he was to marry a princess of his own rank. The meaning of the parable is clear. . . . In the name of R. Saadia Gaon: It is befitting for a man to learn from his desire for physical things how to desire the service of God and his love.[8] *NB*

The reference to Saadia which concludes the passage is inappropriate, as Saadia, while he does describe intense physical desire in bold language, in fact condemns it as excessive and rejects the view (which, he states, is held, unfortunately, by some "ignorant fools"), that intense physical desire is commendable in that it teaches man how to desire God and to crave for submission to Him—precisely the view which the Besht advocates in the name of Saadia himself![9] However, even the view which is falsely attributed to Saadia by the Besht is not quite in harmony with his parable. For while Saadia allegedly presents physical desire as an allegory of the spiritual desire for God, the intensity with which it is felt serving as a measure of the intensity with which God should be desired, the parable establishes a concrete link between the two types of desire: physical desire is itself instrumental in awakening the spiritual desire for God. The girl is not an apparition, nor does she turn out in the end to be essentially spiritual and "wise." She is physical, profane to the core; and it is precisely in this capacity that she is enlisted to the service of spirituality. The satisfaction of physical desire is rendered a precondition for the spiritual desire to know God.

Similarly, the famous parable recorded by R. Jacob Joseph of Polonne in the names of both the Besht and R. Menahem Mendel, the Maggid of Bar, presents the satisfaction of a need which is irredeemably physical and profane as serving the cause of spiritual joy in God:

I have heard the following parable from my master [the Besht]: A prince was once expelled to distant lands and settled in a village inhabited by inferior men. After he had been there for a long time, a letter from his father the king reached him. The prince longed to rejoice in this letter, but he was inhibited by the villagers who might have ridiculed him, saying, what is so special about this day, and what has brought about this joy? Therefore, he summoned the villagers, bought them wine and other intoxicating drinks, so that they rejoiced in the wine and he was free to rejoice in his father.[10]

Although the parable is introduced, in almost all the instances where it occurs, to expound the request addressed to every Jew to celebrate the Sabbath with the physical joy of his body in eating and drinking as well as with the soul's spiritual joy, in every case, once the meaning is extended beyond the body and soul of the individual to cover (in R. Jacob Joseph of Polonne's language a little further on in the same passage) "the universal body and soul," namely, "men of matter" and "men of form," the ability and need to rejoice in physical pleasure is ascribed to the "vulgar," inferior villagers, while the ability to rejoice in spiritual matters is unique to the "prince," the spiritual man. Not once is it suggested that the prince himself became intoxicated with drink to induce his joy in the king's letter. However, the presence of other traditions which, unlike all the versions of this parable, do regard the satisfaction of physical needs and the ensuing satisfaction of the spirit in *devekut* as occurring in the body and spirit of one man or one category of men only,[11] eliminates the possibility that the exclusive allocation of physical satisfaction to the "villagers" and spiritual satisfaction to the "prince" in the parable is essential to its central point, namely, that the satisfaction of physical needs is a precondition for spiritual satisfaction. Most likely, this particular formulation of the idea is one of several, but inconsistent, attempts to idealize the spirituality of the "men of spirit" and to distinguish it sharply from the vulgar corporeality of "men of matter," to the point of denying the former the very awareness of their own physical and material needs while the latter are denied the capacity for spiritual yearnings.[12] What emerges clearly as the real view behind this idealized or, one might say, stylized picture is that already in the circle of the Besht men of spirit, such as the prince who acquired wisdom through satisfying his physical desire for a beautiful girl, were considered as capable of utilizing profane activities and thoughts (in which they most certainly engaged quite openly) to achieve the spiritual joy of *devekut*. Men of matter, on the other hand, enjoyed a more limited scope for worship from which were excluded all profane activities and thoughts. Paradoxically, although the men of matter were regarded as incapable of spirituality, the method of worshiping God which was prescribed for them consisted entirely of the conventional range of spiritual activities in which study, and especially prayer, featured most prominently. As for their normal pursuit of profane activities, they were expected to call a spade a spade, to accept profanity at its face value and not to attempt the impossible by investing it, as do men of spirit, with spirituality and holiness. The original version of the parable of the prince who acquired wisdom through his physical desire for the girl takes up this issue more explicitly than the abridged version of *Keter shem tov*,[13] insisting that this route to *devekut* lies entirely outside the range of "commoners," in whom the satisfaction of physical desire is plainly that; it leads them no further and is considered as the product of their evil inclination: ". . . However, all this happened only through the 'wise man,' namely, the king, who could tell the outcome of the matter in advance. For this is the quality of a wise man, who can see into the future[14] and alter human nature from evil to good. . . . But this could not apply to the 'non-wise' man, who would have remained true to his nature, susceptible to evil in all manner of deeds and transgressions. . . ."[15]

Likewise, the Besht is reported to have warned: "Received from the Besht: Each man should conduct himself according to his own rank. For, if he adopts the conduct befitting another man's rank, he fails to comply either with his own or with the other man's standard. In this connection it was said: 'Many a man had done as R. Simon bar Yohai, but failed.'[16] The meaning is that they were not of his rank, but modelled themselves on him . . . and this is why they failed."[17] And R. Jacob Joseph of Polonne, who in this case is not, apparently, recording the view of the Besht but whose own view seems to be in harmony with the Besht's, states specifically in connection with the practice of worship through corporeality:

In this way may be understood the saying "Warm thyself by the fire of the wise,"[18] meaning when they are in the state of *gadlut* ("major" state a state of fulfilling *devekut*) occupied with the fire of Torah and prayer . . , "but beware of their glowing coals" on the days when they are in *katnut* ("minor" state in which profane activities are carried out), for at such times they do not glow with inner fire but they are called a coal without inner fire. A pupil might want to emulate such a wise man when he carries out corporeal tasks. But the pupil does not know that at such times his teacher is fulfilling [the request implied in the verse] "Thy word have I hid in mine heart" [Ps. 119:11], namely, that he is occupied with corporeal things while at the same time meditating their inner, spiritual content. Thus, the pupil may emulate the external appearance of the teacher's corporeal activities, and be punished. . . .[19]

There are, it is true, quite a number of traditions which, at least by implication, address to any Jew the request to worship only in *devekut*, and even through profane activities, without distinguishing, as R. Jacob Joseph of Polonne does so often, between corporeal men of matter and the qualitatively different and superior men of spirit. Other traditions ascribed to the Besht and his associates go even further in advising every individual to address himself directly to God or to engage in battle with the forces of evil and not to trust "great men" to do this on his behalf. For example:

"Blessed is the people that knows the joyful sound" [Ps. 89:16]. The Besht interpreted this verse by the following parable: There was a country in which there lived a hero. All the inhabitants of that country relied on him [to fight for them] and did not learn the art of warfare. Eventually war broke. The hero wanted to prepare his weapons, but the enemy tricked him and stole all his weapons one by one, so that the hero had nothing with which to fight, and all the inhabitants of that country who had relied on him were captured with him. This is the meaning alluded to in the verse "Blessed is the people that knows the joyful sound," namely, when the people do not rely on the hero but they know the joyful sound of war for themselves. Then, "they shall walk, O Lord, in the light of thy countenance" [ibid.], "to meet the king" [probably 2 Sam. 19:16].[20]

Likewise, R. Jacob Joseph of Polonne, the chief exponent of the doctrine of the dichotomy between men of form and men of matter, appears to suggest that every Jew is capable of reaching the supreme level of spirituality attained by Moses:

Furthermore, no other pentateuchal portions except this one *"va-yaqhel"* [Exod. 35–38:20] and *"Qedoshim tihyu"* [Lev. 19–20] begin with a request for Moses to gather the entire nation together.[21] The matter has already been explained, for Moses, may he rest in peace, had said: "Enviest thou for my sake? Would God that all the Lord's people were prophets" [Num. 11:29], etc. Moses . . . wished the whole of Israel to attain the rank which he had attained. And this is not impossible. For man has free choice to purify his corporeality until he reaches the rank of Moses, may he rest in peace. And Moses was distinguished from all other prophets by one other quality, namely . . . that the *shekhina* (immanence of God) itself spoke through his throat. This rank also may be reached by every Israelite after he had sanctified himself with God's holiness.[22]

However, all these qualifications of the deterministic division of humanity into those few who naturally have, and the majority who cannot possibly attain, spirituality and direct access to God, do not cancel it out. They are felt to be ethically necessary so as not to discourage that vast majority who are classified as spiritual "have-not's" from birth, but there is little doubt as to which is the truly operative notion. To exemplify this, reference might be made to a zaddik, two generations later, such as R. Nahman of Bratslav. In his conception of himself as a supreme zaddik, utterly different in essence and, therefore, in his moral and religious standards of conduct, from all other men, fellow zaddikim and ordinary folk alike, this categorization of humanity found one of its most extreme formulations in the entire Hasidic movement. Surely, if he was still capable of reproaching his followers on one occasion for entertaining the thought—". . . the rank of the zaddik and his achievement derive only from the fact that he is endowed with a sublime soul. But he said that this was not so. For it derived mostly from good deeds, endeavour and works. And he said explicitly that every individual can attain to the highest rank, for this depends entirely on his free choice . . ."[23]—a statement which, if taken seriously, would undermine his most profound and essential consciousness of his own uniqueness as a zaddik, then the marginality of the age-old conflict between religious-social determinism and the doctrine of free will in Hasidism becomes blatantly obvious. Although it stressed the corporeal vulgarity of the masses time and again, early Hasidism did promise them the possibility of transcending their corporeality. Without this promise it would be hard to explain the immense success of the movement from the very start. But, with the exception of a few relatively marginal trends in the early generations as well as the singular exception of Habad,[24] the method of fulfilling this promise to the masses was not by emulating the spiritual elite but of "cleaving" to it, by setting at the focus of their inherently limited religiosity not God, but the figure of the "man of spirit" who is eventually defined institutionally as the zaddik. The true scope for exercising their free will lay, for the masses, in their choosing, or failing to choose, to "cleave" blindly and with unquestioning faith to their "spiritual man."

NB

It is important to consider all this alongside the suggestion made more than once that early, or "primitive," Hasidism not only extended the scope for worship in *devekut* to cover the full range of human experience and expression but also widened its area of application by opening up, at least implicitly, the possibility of fulfilling this new ideal for all Jews. As Professor Scholem has pointed out: "Hasidic *devekut* is no longer an extreme ideal to be realised by some rare and sublime spirits at the end of the path. It is no longer the last rung in the ladder of ascent, as in Kabbalism, but the first. Everything begins with man's decision to cleave to God. *Devekut* is the starting point and not the end. Everyone is able to realise it instantaneously."[25] However, Scholem himself senses that this is an oversimplification of the Hasidic departure from the Kabbalistic ideal and, a little further on in the same work, he injects a note of

ambivalence to his earlier observation: "It sounds very simple and anyone might start practicing it, but it is extremely difficult to attain as a
sustained state of communion. Why should not anyone be able to concentrate all the inwardness of the spiritual element in everything? As a
matter of fact, it is a counsel given not to the accomplished Kabbalist at
the end of his path, but repeatedly addressed to everybody. Yet, it has
the unmistakable ring of a mystical practice which has its esoteric side
and is by no means as easy to carry out as it appears to be."[26]

It would seem, in fact, that the ideal of *devekut,* already in the first
generation of Hasidism, was conceived of as anything but capable of
universal fulfillment or, rather, it could not be fulfilled by everyone in
the same way. But the gap between the *devekut* of ordinary people and
that of "spiritual men" was so fundamental that it would be misleading
to bridge it over by assuming a democratization of this ancient philosophical and Kabbalistic ideal to have taken place in "primitive" Hasidism. Right from the start the Besht and his contemporaries in Hasidism,
almost without exception, were perfectly conscious of this vast difference between spiritual men with whom they themselves identified and
all ordinary people, to the point, as it sometimes seems, of taking it for
granted. It is true that not all of them seem to have been as consistently
or as acutely concerned with it as R. Jacob Joseph of Polonne. But, with
all the reservations about the authenticity of the language and terminology recording traditions in their names, particularly since a considerable
number of these traditions were recorded by R. Jacob Joseph himself
(and might be suspected of imposing his own sensibilities on others'
views), they still betray quite often a shared notion of the dichotomy
between the two categories of men and of its implication regarding their
respective modes of worship. For example, the term men of form *(anshey
surah)* which is contrasted time and again with men of matter *(anshey
homer)* seems to be favored by Jacob Joseph who often drew the analogy
between these two categories and "soul" and "body," respectively. But
the juxtaposition of "vulgar masses" *(hamoney am)* with men of spirit
(anshey ha-ruhani) is ascribed with some measure of consistence to R.
Nahman of Horodenka.[27] And in the traditions recorded specifically in
the name of the Besht, the terms "men of knowledge" *(anshey daat),*
"men of understanding" *(anshey binah),* "the perfect man" *(ha-adam
ha-shalem),*[28] as well as the widely used and, as yet, institutionally
undefined "righteous man" *(zaddik),* "scholar" or "teacher" *(talmid
hakham; rav)* are all mentioned in reference to the ideal manner of

worship, distinguishing it either explicitly or implicitly from the practices and aspirations appropriate to ordinary people. To exemplify the way in which the applicability of the ideal to the distinct category of spiritual men is to be taken for granted even where it is not stated explicitly, one may return to a tradition, cited earlier on, which was recorded more than once by R. Jacob Joseph of Polonne in the name of the Besht. This was the warning directed to ordinary people against emulating the "scholars" when the latter are engaged in profane activities while in the state of *katnut*.[29] The warning appears at the end of a longer passage whose central theme is the difference between *katnut* and *gadlut,* the minor and major states of *devekut,* respectively.[30] The entire passage is presented as an explanation of the saying in Avot 2.10: "Warm thyself by the fire of the wise but beware of their glowing coals, lest thou be burnt," which opens and concludes it. The whole section in between, describing the manners of worship possible in each of the two states of *devekut,* can be read easily as intended for universal application. The subject is "man," and one of the opportunities for worship in *katnut* is thought to be idle conversation with one's "fellow man" *(sippurim she-mesapper im havero),* as if all were equal and both participants in such idle conversation were capable of rendering it a manner of worshiping God. Only the concluding paragraph, which is still part of the tradition recorded, as R. Jacob Joseph recalls, in the name of the Besht, introduces as a matter of course the restriction on the applicability of this notion and converts the situation into idle talk between scholars and ordinary men who cannot see through the scholars' apparent "corporeality" and therefore should not emulate them.[31]

Likewise, a teaching by R. Jacob Joseph of Polonne himself, pointing out the lowest starting point for the ascent to *devekut,* seems to be directed once again at "man." The passage reads as follows:

"Thus (with this) shall Aaron come into the Holy Place" [Lev. 16:3]. The meaning is that "this" is . . . the lowest rung of the ten sublime *sefirot* [i.e., *malkhut*] with which the world was created. And when *man* is at this low rung, either worshiping or engaged in the affairs of this world, such as business affairs etc., the following advice may be given to the *perfect man:* He should realise that this is the rung of "Shekhina" (God's immanence: *malkhut*). He should then pray from this low level, which is called "this," and from there he may ascend further, into the holy place. . . .[32]

Universal "man" becomes the "perfect man" almost incidentally, indicating the real address of the author's advice. Occasionally, R. Jacob

Joseph, who is without question the most insistent on the distinction, does highlight it when he interprets the somewhat less explicit traditions which he records in the name of others. He does this, for example, on one of the many occasions when he reports R. Yehudah Loeb Pistiner's interpretation of the verse (Ps. 12:2) "for the faithful fail from among the children of men": "I have already mentioned in the name of the late pious man, R. Yehuda Loeb Pistiner, the meaning of the verse . . . 'Help, Lord, for the godly man ceaseth; for the faithful fail from among the children of men' . . . etc. The verse may be interpreted in two ways, either from the beginning to the end or from the end to the beginning. Thus, because the 'godly man,' the men of form, ceases, therefore, ordinary 'children of men,' that is, the men of matter, have no faith. And vice versa: The reason why the 'pious man' ceases is that ordinary men have no faith." [33] It is quite likely that R. Jacob Joseph himself added to R. Yehuda Loeb's interpretation the identification of the "godly man" with the man of form and that of the "children of men" with ordinary men. But this addition by no means distorts the original interpretation; it only colors it with R. Jacob Joseph's own terminology.

And even where the distinction between the two categories of men and their appropriate manners of worship is missed out altogether, it is still clear that more often than not, when the ideal of communion with God is set as a target, the expectation of fulfillment is restricted to those who are spiritually endowed. For example, the following tradition is ascribed to the Besht: "Received from the Besht: One should 'adhere' *(Yadbiq)* his 'thought' to the infinite Divine Light which is contained in the letters. . . . This is an important rule to be applied to the study of Torah and to prayer. Furthermore, it enables one to cancel 'evil charges.' " [34] Similarly, another tradition which also concerns the Besht's special method of attaining *devekut* during study (and prayer) by means of "cleaving" to the letters cannot possibly have meant to apply to ordinary people, even though it does not state this explicitly: "According to a tradition received from my master [the Besht], the essence of Torah and prayer is for a man to cleave to the inner aspect and spirituality of the infinite Divine Light contained in the letters of the text of Torah and prayer. This is called 'study [of Torah] for its own sake.' Concerning this, R. Meir said (Avot 6): 'Whosoever labors in the Torah for its own sake merits many things . . . to him the secrets of the Torah are revealed' etc. This means that from the Torah he will know the future and all that will happen to him. . . ."[35] In both these cases the Besht attributes pneumatic powers to his method of study and prayer which utilizes the Hebrew letters of which such texts are made up for the ascent to *devekut*.[36] There is no doubt that such powers were thought to be supernatural. The Besht possessed them, as did a number of his immediate associates, but not everyone. Nor could just anyone acquire these powers. The promise whereby the adoption of this method would guarantee the ability to cancel "evil judgments" or to see into the future surely was not made to everyone. Those powers were thought then, by the Besht and his circle, as they seem to us now, to be capable of cultivation only by those few who are born to be receptive of them, not by ordinary people, even though through the failure to state this explicitly ordinary people appear to be welcomed to exercise clairvoyance and to cancel evil charges.

Where the distinction between the possibilities of *devekut* open to men of spirit on the one hand and to ordinary people on the other hand remained implicit and unstated in the first generation of Hasidism and, to some extent, in the second generation as well, this was so simply because it was not felt necessary to state something which was so deeply and naturally felt as to be taken for granted.[37] The reasons for this become evident when one examines, inasmuch as this is possible, the nature of the affiliation between the Besht and his associates as well as the relationship between R. Dov Ber, the Maggid of Miedzyrzecz, and his disciples in the first two generations of Hasidism.

Through the efforts of a number of distinguished scholars in the relatively recent past, the origins and organization of these early circles have become better known. B. Dinur drew attention to the existence of circles of Hasidim before and during the time of the Besht and argued that the "Beshtian" Hasidic movement must be viewed within the context of these "pre-Hasidic" circles, since some of their active members, mentioned in the works of R. Jacob Joseph of Polonne and others of his generation as well as in *Shivhey ha-Besht,* subsequently came to be seen as the Besht's disciples.[38] J. G. Weiss further contributed toward viewing the conditions from which the new Hasidic leadership arose in a correct historical perspective by portraying the Besht as a member, and not necessarily the one and only leader, of a circle whose views and activities later became associated primarily with him.[39] Finally, and most convincingly, A. J. Heschel provided abundant evidence to show that several of the Besht's early associates, who had been considered by later Hasidic biographers and historians as his devoted pupils,[40] were, in fact, independent Hasidim who, in some cases, commanded their own following and regarded the Besht as their equal, if not, indeed, as their rival or as inferior to themselves.[41] This message comes across even from *Shivhey ha-Besht* alone, which is heavily biased in favor of the Besht's supreme leadership over his circle, projecting the later organizational reality of its own time of composition onto the earlier period.[42] Clearly, the inconsistency of the terminology used in relation to "spiritual," "righteous," or even "learned," men in this period which has been pointed out often reflects the fluidity of the situations. In the first generation of Hasidism it was far from clear who was considered as a spiritual "master," in relation to whom, and who was a mere "follower." Surely R. Pinhas of Korzec, R. Aryeh-Loeb of Polonne, R. Nahman Kosover, and others cannot be fitted into the category of ordinary men of matter, totally devoid of spirituality in relation to the Besht. With some qualifications, the same can be said of the second generation under the leadership of the Maggid of Miedzyrzecz. While he was acknowledged by many as their master and teacher, some, notably R. Jacob Joseph of Polonne and R. Pinhas of Korzec, rejected his leadership,[43] while others who did accept it clearly belonged to the same, superior anthropological category to which he himself belonged and proceeded, already during his lifetime, to establish their own circles of followers and to operate as zaddikim quite independently of him.[44] However, in the new zeal to dispel the misguided notions, particularly regarding the first generation of masters whereby all were submissive disciples of the Besht and inferior to him, the scholars who so aptly stressed the virtual equality of these men with the Besht seem, to a greater or lesser extent, to have overshot their mark by drawing from this fact the conclusion, tolerated by the often inexplicit nature of the underlying division of humanity into two categories, that the circle "democratized" various mystical and ethical notions previously confined to small elitist circles of Kabbalists. This "democratization" has been presented as gaining additional weight from the fact that, although inevitably short-lived,[45] it could be distinguished, not only from the past, but also from the almost immediate future for, with the rise of institutionalized Zaddikism a generation or two later, the opening up of sublime mystical possibilities to the rank-and-file followers of Hasidism came to an abrupt conclusion.[46]

This appreciation of "primitive" Hasidism must be modified, particularly in view of the lingering currency of popular, undynamic, and less analytical designations of Beshtian Hasidism as "a religion of the people," proclaiming the dignity of common men and putting within their reach that quality of religious life which both the corrupt oligarchic regime of eighteenth-century rabbinic orthodoxy in Poland and the aristocratic practitioners of Kabbalah had made inaccessible to them. Thus we read, for example, that "the Ari (R. Isaac Luria) lifted God upwards, where He resides, remote from the lower universe of life and deeds. Then came the Besht and brought Him down, returning God to the people, to all creatures. The Besht's God is popular, even though he 'disguises' Himself. ... 'men of knowledge' know these disguises to be part of Himself ... while the Ari's God is aristocratic."[47] There is complete confusion here between the notions of God's immanence and transcendence on the one hand, and a democratic versus an aristocratic religious doctrine on the other hand. It is true that Luria's God is transcendent while the Besht's is immanent. But in effect, Luria's conception of God's accessibility is much more egalitarian than the Besht's. Ultimately, his God is equally inaccessible to all, in that He has removed Himself from this world in order to create it. For the Besht, on the other hand, God is directly accessible, but only to those who can see through His disguises. And to see through God's disguises, to experience Him directly, one has to be especially endowed. The Besht does not consider himself, nor is he considered by others, as "an average scholar and a simple man, no more."[48] He is indeed an average scholar, perhaps worse, and a simple man, but the crucial fact is that he is, and is recognized to be, much more: he has, for the lack of a better term, charisma; he can perform supernatural acts; he can see into the future; he can interfere with God's schemes and affect His decisions. What is more, as has been shown by Dinur, Weiss, and Heschel, he is not the only one. The entire circle of his associates, the early masters of Hasidism, are all endowed with these qualities. The circle reeks of the consciousness of its own collective uniqueness.[49] It does not constitute an ascetic, secluded elite after the model of the pre-Beshtian Kabbalistic circles of Hasidim, nor does it form an intellectual, wealthy elite such as the ruling classes of the traditional community, but it is all the same an elite. The novelty it represents is not in discarding the traditional elitist framework but in altering its contents, in substituting intellectuality with emotionality, asceticism with direct involvement and concern with ordinary people and the affairs of this world, etc. Far from "bringing God down to the people," Hasidism, right from the start, did precisely the opposite. It blocked entirely and a priori the direct route of ordinary people to God by placing the righteous or perfect men, the men of form, spirit, knowledge, or understanding or eventually, the zaddikim, in the middle of that route. To put the point more poignantly at the risk, perhaps, of being a little unfair, it can be said that in "primitive" Hasidism, just as in subsequent "mature" Hasidism, the majority of ordinary people could not follow the direct route to God precisely because a minority of extraordinary people were blocking it, insisting that every contact with God should be regulated, "channeled" by them. The only difference between primitive and mature Hasidism in this respect lay in the loosely defined and uninstitutional nature of the elite in the earlier stage.[50]

The collective elitist consciousness of the early circle explains the inconsistency of the imposition of restrictions on the application of the highest religious ideal. That direct communion with God and all the powers which derive from it could be attained only by the spiritually endowed was self-evident and did not need to be stated explicitly to an audience consisting of equally endowed men. In addition, the collective consciousness of an elite which characterizes the circle is in perfect harmony with the atmosphere prevalent in the pre-Beshtian Hasidic circles which, as is now acknowledged by all, were the immediate ancestors of the new Hasidic movement.[51] For these circles were pronouncedly elitist. And it is important to remember that at the very start of his career as a spiritual master the Besht could conceive of no other source of validation of his ability and uniqueness but admission into one of these elitist circles.[52] In fact, far from being the demotic figure he is so often said to have been, the Besht was an aspiring elitist and a religious social climber. He was rejected by the Brody circle at first because he did not conform with the traditional qualifications for admission, but eventually the entire circle, as *Shivhey ha-Besht* states, perhaps exaggeratedly, swung round to his style of worship while retaining—and this is the crucial point—its original elitist consciousness. Surely, without unequivocal evidence for drastic or deliberate change, it is much more natural to assume a direct continuity in this respect between the immediate precursors as well as the immediate successors of "primitive" Hasidism than it is to assume a sudden break with the traditional social framework, which was soon afterward, with the alleged "degeneration" of the cult of Zaddikism, bridged over completely to reinforce the traditional framework and even to inject it with extra vigor and rigidity.

Perhaps the best test of the extent to which the elitist framework was retained, despite the drastic changes which shook its contents, is the fate of the Lurianic Kavvanoth of prayer in early Hasidism. It has been shown that, without opposing it explicitly, the Besht abandoned the practice of these highly technical meditative aids, which had been used by generations of Kabbalists since Luria, including the circles of Kabbalistic Hasidim from whose ranks the early Hasidic leadership rose.[53] The Besht apparently substituted Luria's Kavvanoth with his own Kavvanoth of prayer whose precise nature is not quite clear. From the time of the Maggid of Miedzyrzecz on, explicit objections to the system of the Lurianic Kavvanoth were raised, mostly on the grounds that they did not enhance but rather distracted from the endeavor to fulfill the new Hasidic ideal of *devekut*. Weiss, who first observed the phasing out of Luria's Kavvanoth in Hasidism, described them as "an aristocratic art" and suggested that "The practice of the elaborate technique of the Lurianic Kavvanoth was by necessity confined to the limited number of a spiritual elite who could cope with the immense intellectual task of countless contemplative flying visits to precisely charted points of the Sephirotic Universe. ... It is very doubtful whether Israel Baalshem himself was fully qualified as a Kabbalist to become one of those initiated into the mysteries of meditative prayer life."[54] Implied in this is the misleading suggestion that, since the Lurianic Kavvanoth were beyond his grasp and might have offended his undisciplined spontaneous religiosity, the Besht devised a system which was more accessible to all those who were not members of the Kabbalistic elite. In fact, from the descriptions of the Besht's prayer which appear in *Shivhey ha-Besht* it emerges quite clearly that his method was even less accessible to the uninitiated and required greater and more unique spiritual qualities than Luria's Kavvanoth.[55] On one occasion meditative activities during his extraordinarily prolonged prayer entailed conversations with myriads of souls of the dead and the endeavor to effect *tiqunim* for all of them.[56] On a second occasion he lingered in meditation, of a distinctly non-Lurianic type, over one verse of the psalms recited during the morning service, engaging in clairvoyance with the object of averting an event threatening the life of a certain Jew.[57] Surely this cannot possibly be construed as a

Weiss

popular practice taking the place of an elitist one. In principle, the Lurianic Kavvanoth could be mastered by anyone willing to devote the time and intellectual concentration required for them. The books prescribing these Kavvanoth were available and could be consulted, which is precisely what R. Eliyahu of Sokolowka, the young man who witnessed the second demonstration of the Besht's prayer according to *Shivhey ha-Besht*, proceeded to do when he was puzzled by the Besht's lengthy meditation of the verse, assuming it to be a Lurianic Kavvanah unknown to him. But the Besht's method clearly could not be followed by the uninspired.

The most famous pronouncement on the Lurianic Kavvanoth by the Maggid of Miedzyrecz is the following: "This resembles a door which may be opened with a key. But there are thieves who open it with something which can break iron. Thus the ancients used to meditate the Kavvanah suitable for each thing. Now, however, we have no Kavvanah. Only the breaking of the heart opens [the door] to everything."[58] The Maggid also rejects the Kavvanoth of Luria, not because they are an elitist practice but because they offend his religious sensibility. As a true spiritualist for whom prayer in *devekut* entailed the total loss within God of individual self-awareness, he considered the Kavvanoth to be too restrictive, incapable of exhausting the full possibilities of *devekut*.[59] But this is not to say that his ideal of prayer in *devekut* was any easier to fulfill or more widely applicable than prayer with Kavvanoth according to Luria. On the contrary. Anyone can use a key or endeavor to obtain one. But when the key is not available, the truly ordinary, uninspired man, unless he can rely on someone else to open the door for him, simply stays out. The ingenious thief, on the other hand, who is, in his way, highly skilled, can tackle the lock and break in. Alternatively, if the dominant image is not that of the thief's ingenuity but rather that of the impatient impulsivity of the thug who smashes the door down with "something which can break iron," then the ideal is still confined to those endowed with immense spiritual force. It is quite clear that the line of demarcation between those who could fulfill this ideal and those who could not (without the intermediacy of others) was not drawn around the Hasidic movement as a whole to the exclusion of all "nonbelievers" outside the Hasidic camp. Rather, the line cut across the entire community, distinguishing the supermen from the masses with greater rigor than was applied to the division between the followers of Hasidism and those who ignored or opposed it.[60]

For the Hasidic movement was markedly not what has sometimes been called an "introversionist" sect,[61] feeding on a collective sense of its own election and discarding all outsiders as doomed for eternal damnation. Rather, its vision of society or, at least, Jewish society, was all-embracing.

Because the deterministic notion of the perfect man versus the ordinary person was more operative than the traditional commitment to the doctrine of free will, the division between those who exercised their free will badly by failing to adhere to the teachings of Hasidism and those who exercised it well by joining the movement was not felt as acutely as the division between the ideal spiritual types and the masses.

The few, and relatively marginal, exceptions to this rule (apart from Habad which, constituting a unique case, deserves special treatment and is, therefore, excluded from this discussion) confirm the general picture by their very marginality and isolation.

Thus R. Meshulam Phoebush of Zbaraz sensed the elitist undertones of the Besht's, and especially the Maggid's, notion of worship in *devekut* and rejected not only the Lurianic Kavvanoth of prayer[62] but also the Hasidic ideal of *devekut*[63] which had originally ousted the Kavvanoth, particularly *devekut* as it was to be achieved through corporeal, profane activities.[64] R. Meshulam argued that the Kavvanoth of Luria on the one hand and *devekut* on the other were applicable to, and intended for, a select group of supreme religious authorities of the past, but not for himself or for all his contemporaries. Professor Rivka Schatz-Uffenheimer rightly observed that R. Meshulam appears to have substituted an ethical ideal of his own, capable of universal application, for the more aristocratic spiritual ideal of *devekut*.[65] Notably, he contrasts the non-Hasidic study of Torah by those who have been traditionally accused in Hasidism of abusing it for self-aggrandizement not, as one would have expected, with the Besht's (and Maggid's) method of study in *devekut* by means of contemplating the letters of the alphabet constituting the text, but rather with his own ideal of study in constant "fear of sin," leading to humility of which he conceives, not in the Maggidic sense of mystical self-annihilation but in the traditional ethical sense.[66]

In summing up, it is appropriate to pose the question again: If, right from the start, Hasidism confined the possibility of direct access to God to a specific class of supreme spiritual men, and denied it to the ordinary person, what did it offer the ordinary person that seemed so attractive to vast sections of Eastern European Jewry of the time as to account for its rapidly increasing popularity? As was suggested earlier on, while it denied him direct access, it guaranteed access to God to the ordinary person by means of his adherence to those who enjoyed it directly. It may be argued that the present discussion so far has been inclined to overlook the importance of this point. Indeed, from the viewpoint of the potential convert, does it matter very much whether one is guaranteed that he may "cleave" to God directly or through the intermediacy of a direct recipient of divine grace? Whatever admissions of his inherent imperfection it required of the ordinary person a priori, it is clear that the doctrine was effective in injecting him with the sense of his own communion with God.

Of the way in which this worked, we read in the writings of R. Jacob Joseph of Polonne: "There are two kinds of *devekut*. One is that of the learned who cleaves to God directly, and the other is that of the common people who do not know how to cleave to the Lord directly. Therefore, the Torah commands them, 'thou shalt cleave unto him' (Deuteronomy 10.20), meaning, to cleave to the learned, which is like cleaving to God."[67] There is no need here to expound this important doctrine further. With regard to the writings of R. Jacob Joseph of Polonne, this topic has been given an excellent and exhaustive coverage by S. Dresner in his work *The Zaddik*.[68] As for the Maggid of Miedzyrzecz, it is regrettable that such an analysis of his teachings has not yet been produced. However, owing to the conspicuous absence from the compilations of his sermons of the doctrine of the descent of the zaddik or his mission on behalf of all ordinary people, a notion which is so prominent in the writings of R. Jacob Joseph of Polonne (and inasmuch as this is possible to ascertain, also in the original teachings of the Besht), it has been suggested that "no activity which he [the Maggid] attributes to the zaddik is unique to the zaddik. These activities which are attributed to the zaddik in the teachings of the Maggid are in fact the duty of every Jew. The only difference is that the zaddik is certain to be more successful in carrying them out than anyone else. In other words: the zaddik appears here as an ideal figure, the model for everyone's behaviour. What the zaddik does, anyone can and should do. The Maggid renounces in principle the unique religious status of the zaddik."[69] This representation of the Maggid's position seems far too extreme. The absence from his teachings of the social dimension of the zaddik's role seems more easily attributable to his lack of interest in this dimension, which is so marked by contrast in the writings of R. Jacob Joseph of Polonne, than it is due to any conscious renunciation on his part of the unique quality of the zaddik. The difference between his religious temperament and that of R. Jacob Joseph of Polonne entirely accounts for his complete lack of interest in the structure of society or the responsibility toward the community of the spiritually gifted man. For him, the responsibility of the true mystic was toward himself in God; namely, it was his duty to abandon his own individuality in the divine "nothingness," to merge with it completely. It is difficult to imagine that he was so out of touch with reality as to imagine everyone to be capable of achieving this. More likely, surrounded by a considerable number of people who were his intimate associates and who clearly belonged to his class of spiritual men, he did not feel the need to dwell on the exclusion of others from the practices advocated within his circle. As Weiss himself noted, the doctrine of the descent of the zaddik, which was obviously not taught in the school of the Maggid, was instantly and enthusiastically adopted by that school after his death. It was incorporated into its main body of teachings as soon as it became known through the publication in 1780–81 of the works of R. Jacob Joseph of Polonne, where it was featured so prominently.[70] Surely if this doctrine, which was based entirely on the supposition that ordinary people were incapable of fulfilling the ideal for themselves, had been out of tune with the Maggid's own system of thought, it would not have been integrated so smoothly and unapologetically into the teachings of the majority of his disciples.

It seems, then, that right from the start, and more unequivocally so with the institutionalization of the leadership of Hasidism, it was the duty of a minority of spiritually endowed men to "cleave" to God, while it was the duty of the majority of ordinary people to "cleave" to their leaders. It is not by accident that the same weighty term, to cleave, is used to describe the nature of the affiliation in both cases. The ordinary person stands in relation to the zaddik as the zaddik stands in relation to God. Just as God is the focus of the zaddik's religious life, so the zaddik is the focus of the ordinary person's religiosity. To convey the concrete dimension of the ordinary person's cleaving to the zaddik as his only point of access to the deity, the following passage may be quoted, advising on how to perfect the "cleaving" (in this case the term *hitqash-erut* is used, which is synonymous to *devekut*) at the time of prayer: "Even though he cannot pray with awe and love, his prayer may be uplifted by means of his connecting himself *(hitqasherut)*, when he says: I hereby undertake to fulfill the positive commandment of 'Love your fellow man as you love yourself' (T. Y. Nedarim 9d). With perfect love, he should include himself in the holy souls [of] those righteous men *(zaddikim)* of the generation with whose physiognomy he is familiar. At such times he should visualise their physiognomy in his mind. This is of great and special benefit. . . ."[71] At times of prayer, the man who cannot pray with true "awe and love" of God is advised to contemplate the familiar face of the zaddik.

There is little wonder, therefore, that the Hasidim were so fond of such turns of phrase as allowed them, on the one hand, to present the figure of the zaddik as parallel with God and, on the other hand, to depict the zaddikim as partaking of God's tasks, all within the perfectly legitimate tradition of rabbinic and Kabbalistic literature.[72] One such example is the depiction of the zaddik as creator of the world. Rabbinic tradition bestows the title of "God's partner in Creation" on individuals who distinguish themselves in righteousness and piety.[73] The *Zohar* attributes to the righteous the ability to create new worlds by their wise utterances, an ability which is portrayed as analogous with God's creation of the world by means of His Utterances of Creation.[74] In Hasidic literature the motif recurs often. The Maggid of Miedzyrzecz, for example, echoing all these earlier traditions, taught:

"Unto thee, O Lord, belongeth mercy; for thou renderest to every man according to his work." [Ps. 63:13] This may be understood by way of comparison with a craftsman who works for an employer. What reward does he receive if not a wage for his labour. For, surely, the employer does not award him the full value of his labour. Similarly, a comparison may be drawn with a country which appoints a king over it. The king rewards the princes [who had appointed him] and pays each one according to the value [of his effort]. But he cannot reward them by bestowing the crown of kingship on any one of them, as they had done for him. By distinction, the Holy One Blessed be He rewards, measure for measure: Who declares God as king, God makes him king over all the universes; God decrees and he cancels the decree . . . and the righteous create worlds[75] (and resurrect the dead and call upon infertile women). . . .[76]

R. Elimelekh of Lezajsk, a disciple of the Maggid of Miedzyrzecz and the man who is often described as the chief theoretician of institutionalised Zaddikism, employs the notion of the zaddik as creator to explain the means by which he can, according to rabbinic tradition, cancel the decrees of God:

For God created and made His world, and He does with it as He pleases. On the other hand, God created the zaddik who is able to cancel his decrees. How is it possible that he [the zaddik] is able to cancel the decrees which had been decreed in Heaven, in the upper worlds? This may be explained . . . by the verse [Ps. 33:6], "By the word of the Lord were the heavens made, " namely, by means of the zaddik's pursuit of the Torah [i.e., the word of God] for its own sake, and by his new interpretations of it, new heavens are created, and he performs the act of Creation. The decrees are thus canceled of themselves (mimeyla), for they are not included in those newly created worlds.[77]

The same author returns to this subject, in an attempt once again to explain the zaddik's ability to cancel God's decrees. He portrays him as a partner, with God and the *shekhina,* in the creation of man: "The Talmud says [Kiddushin 30]: 'There are three partners in [the creation of] each human being: The Holy One Blessed be He, his father and his mother.' this means that the Zaddik is his father, for he is called 'father,' as [in the case of] Elisha who said to Elijah [2 Kings 2:12]: 'My father, my father, the chariot of Israel. . . .' And his mother, that is to say, *Knesset Israel* (the people of Israel) is the *Shekhina.* 'His father ejaculates the white semen,' namely, the zaddik white washes transgressions and converts judgements into mercy. . . ."[78] L. Jacobs, who refers to this passage in his book on Hasidic prayer,[79] describes "R. Elimelekh's zeal for Zaddikism" as "bordering on the blasphemous." Indeed, R. Elimelekh, as all others within the movement who sensed the zaddik to be the real focus of religious life, bordered on blasphemy without ever quite falling into it. The zaddik was never deified; he never became the object of worship in his own right. It is not impossible that attempts to worship Hasidic masters even after their death rather than to seek immediately another living zaddik to adhere to were curtailed with at least an unconscious awareness of the possible degeneration into a cult of living deities, which the zaddikim fell decidedly, but not by far, short of becoming. The following tradition may be mentioned in this connection: After the death of Jacob Isaac, "the Jew" of Przysucha, R. Mendel of Kock was anxious to find a new teacher. "The Jew" appeared to him in a dream and offered to remain his teacher even after death. R. Mendel replied: "I do not wish for a teacher from the World to Come."[80] Whether or not this late story is authentic it reflects a clear orientation toward personal contact with a zaddik who is a living man and away from spiritual contact with a dead zaddik who is, uncomfortably, a little too proximate to God in Heaven.

see below p. 322

It is not a coincidence that the one Hasidic circle in whose writings the formal analogy between the zaddik and God is most rigorously and frequently stated is also the circle which, alone in the entire Hasidic camp and unpopularly so, still continues to worship its dead founder, R. Nahman of Bratslav. In the teachings of R. Nahman, as well as in the works of subsequent Bratslav authors, the Lurianic myth of God's withdrawal from this world *(simsum)* and His modes of self-revelation were applied wholesale to the zaddik—R. Nahman.[81] The parallel between God and R. Nahman was perceived so vividly that, as it would appear in some instances, God ceased to be the original whose human replica R. Nahman was and became Himself a divine replica of the original, R. Nahman. Thus, for example, a certain feature of R. Nahman's biography, namely, his controversy with R. Arieh Loeb of Shpola, was interpreted as a manifestation of *simsum* and projected onto God's biography according to Luria.[82] R. Nahman sensed God's transcendence in relation to this world with the full severity of the literal meaning of Luria's notion of *simsum,* and he recognized the clash between this and the general Hasidic commitment to the view of God's immanence. He did not believe that this contradiction may be harmonized, that is, the God's immanence would become apparent despite his strong sensation of His transcendence, except at the end of days, in the messianic era.[83] He projected this notion of God's inaccessibility onto himself, who likewise underwent *simsum* and was capable of manifesting himself to his followers only by means of withdrawal apparently beyond their reach.[84] It is not surprising that his death was seen by his followers as one such act of "withdrawal," by which he alone could reveal himself to them, until the time when the Messiah will come. *Liqutey tefilot,* the collection of new prayers composed by R. Nahman's disciple and scribe, Nathan Sternharz, after the death of R. Nahman and by direct inspiration from his recorded teachings as they appeared in *Liqutey moharan,* contains adaptations into prayer form of the majority of these *"torot"*—a unique type of composition for which R. Nathan was attacked by Bratslav's Hasidic opponents.[85] It is interesting to compare R. Nahman's teaching on *simsum* in *Liqutey moharan* with the prayer in *Liqutey tefilot* which is modeled on it. The teaching begins with a stark statement of the *Peshat* (simple meaning) of the Lurianic concept of God's transcendence through *simsum:* "For God created the world out of his compassion, which he wanted to reveal. Had he not created the world, to whom

see 32?!

would he have revealed his compassion? . . . And when God wanted to create the world, there was no space in which to create it, for everywhere there was infinity. Therefore, God withdrew *(simsum)* the light sideways, and by means of this withdrawal the empty space was formed. In this empty space . . . was Creation. . . .";[86] *Liqutey tefilot,* which often adheres to the text of *Liqutey moharan* quite closely, simply converting statements into supplications, digresses from it in this case by introducing the prayer corresponding to this teaching with an unequivocal statement of the general Hasidic principle of God's immanence: " 'which does great things past finding out; yea, and wonders without number' (Job 9,10) Master of all, 'above all things, and nothing is above you,' 'He who fills all the universes and surrounds them'; 'He who is above all universes and below them and in between them.' 'There is no place empty of you.' "[87] One has the impression that in this case as, indeed, throughout the book *Liqutey tefilot,* the dominant perception (of necessity, since the book, after all, is a book of prayers to God) is of God's immanence and accessibility rather than, as in *Liqutey moharan,* of His transcendence and ultimate inaccessibility. The focus for all sense of transcendence seems to have shifted from God to R. Nahman who, already in his lifetime, but certainly now after his death, has "withdrawn his light" which will be revealed only in the World to Come.

But a full account of R. Nahman's peculiar position within his circle, both before and after his death, is a subject for a separate discussion.

NOTES

1. See G. Scholem, "Devekut, or Communion with God," in his *The Messianic Idea in Judaism* (London, 1971), pp. 203–27. And see Ch. 8 in this volume.
2. See ibid., p. 205; J. G. Weiss, "The Beginnings of Hasidism" (Heb.), *Zion* 16 (1951): 63.
3. Jacob Joseph of Polonne, *Toledot yaaqov yosef* (Korzec, 1780), p. 17b, quoted by Weiss, p. 61.
4. See B. Dinur, *Be-mifneh ha-dorot* (Jerusalem, 1955), pp. 141–42; A. J. Heschel, "Rabbi Nahman mi-Kosov, Havero shel ha-Besht," in *Sefer ha-Yovel li-khevod Sevi Wolfson,* Heb. (Jerusalem, 1965), pp. 117–18.
5. Cf. Jacob Joseph of Polonne, *Sofnat pa'ane'ah* (New York, 1954), p. 31b (Korzec ed. [1782], p. 24b): " 'Thy word have I hid in mine heart' (Ps. 119:11), while outwardly he carries out material affairs."
6. Ibid., p. 76a (Korzec ed., p. 60a), quoted by Weiss, p. 64.

7. *Keter shem tov* (Jerusalem, 1968), p. 15. For the numerous parallels in the writing of R. Jacob Joseph and in *Degel mahaneh ephrayim,* see Weiss, pp. 97–99.

8. *Keter shem tov,* pp. 14–15. For the original version of the parable in the writing of R. Jacob Joseph, see his *Ben Porat Yoseph* (New York, 1954), p. 85a (Korzec ed. [1781], p. 66b).

9. See *Emunot ve-de'ot,* ed. Slucki (Leipzig, 1864), chap. 10, sec. 4, p. 150. G. Scholem in his book *Major Trends in Jewish Mysticism* (New York, 1961), p. 96, and in the notes, p. 372, quotes the passage in which the Besht ascribes this view to Saadia, implying, particularly in the note, that Saadia was indeed the Besht's source for "such erotic imagery for Israel's love for God." Following him, Weiss (p. 101), who likewise quoted the passage, referred the reader to Scholem's genealogy of the idea. As he himself testifies, Scholem quotes the passage, not directly from its origin in the books of R. Jacob Joseph of Polonne nor from the anthology *Keter shem tov* which reproduced it shortly after the publication of R. Jacob Joseph's works, but rather from a relatively late source, M. L. Rodkinsohn's *Toledot Ba'aley Shem Tov* (Koenigsberg, 1876). Although in a subsequent Hebrew work ("Demuto ha-historit shel ha-Besht," in his *Devarim be-go* [Tel-Aviv, 1975], p. 321 or in *Molad* 144–5, 1960, p. 355) he does clarify this point, Scholem does not note here, first, that Saadia's vivid description of physical desire is not an allegory of Israel's love for God but a strong denunciation of physical desire as such, which Saadia considers to be devoid of any merit, physical or spiritual, and an impediment to, rather than an enhancement of, man's spiritual love for God. Second, Scholem does not mention the fact that Rodkinsohn himself, having paraphrased (not quoted) the passage from *Keter shem tov,* pointed out the discrepancy between Saadia's actual view and the one ascribed to him by the Besht. Rodkinsohn noted that the question was first raised by "R. E. Katz" (Eliezer Zvi ha-Kohen Zweifel) who searched in vain for such a view in Saadia's writings and finally resolved the difficulty by admitting that the Besht must have been so inspired by Saadia's lively description of physical desire that he himself drew the analogy between it and spiritual passion for God (see M. L. Rodkinsohn [Frumkin], pt. 1, *Or Israel,* pp. 96–99; E. Z. ha-Kohen Zweifel, *Shalom 'al yisrael,* pt. 1 [Jerusalem, 1972; 1st ed., Zhitomir, 1868–73], 1:110–13).

10. *Toledot yaaqov yosef,* p. 195b, quoted by Weiss, pp. 66–68, with several parallels.

11. Cf., for example, Weiss, p. 51.

12. Cf., for example, *Sofnat pa'ane'ah,* p. 29a (Korzec ed., p. 22a).

13. Quoted above.

14. T. B. Tamid 32a.

15. *Ben porat yosef,* p. 85a (Korzec ed., p. 66b).

16. T. B. Berachot 35b.

17. *Keter shem tov,* p. 5.

18. M. Avot, 2.10.

19. *Sofnat pa'ane'ah*, p. 32a (Korzec ed., p. 24b–c); cf. *Ben porat yosef* at the end, p. 127a.
20. *Keter shem tov*, p. 29; cf. pp. 10, 59.
21. Cf. *Midrash va-yikra rabba*, 24:5.
22. *Toledot yaaqov yosef*, p. 67a.
23. *Shivhey haran* (with *Sihot haran*), (Lemberg, 1901), p. 6b, no. 26; cf. pp. 60b, no. 165; 61a, no. 170.
24. See below.
25. Scholem, "Devekut," p. 208. [Above Ch. 8]
26. Ibid., p. 212.
27. See Weiss, p. 51.
28. See *Keter shem tov*, pp. 15, 21, 22.
29. Cf. above.
30. For these two qualifications of the state of *Devekut*, see Scholem, "Devekut," pp. 218–22.
31. See *Sofnat pa'ane'ah*, p. 32a (Korzec ed., p. 24b–c); cf.parallel at the end of *Ben porat yosef.*
32. *Toledot yaaqov yosef*, p. 78c.
33. Ibid., p. 56c.
34. *Keter shem tov*, p. 22.
35. *Toledot yaaqov yosef*, p. 25a.
36. For the Besht's method of study "for its own sake," see J. G. Weiss, "Talmud Torah le-shitat R. Israel Besht," in *Israel Brody Jubilee Volume* (London, 1967), pp. 155–56, 163–64, 167.
37. Sharing the view that the ideal of *devekut* in early Hasidism was open for all to fulfill, while at the same time drawing attention to the frequently asserted distinction between the "spiritual" and "corporeal" human categories in early Hasidic writings, Weiss ("The Beginnings of Hasidism," pp. 84–85) rightly raised the question of the historical origins of this notion of society.
38. See Dinur, *Be-mifneh ha-dorot*, pp. 159–70.
39. See Weiss, "Beginnings of Hasidism," pp. 46–49 and passim, and "A Circle of Pneumatics in Pre-Hasidism," *Journal of Jewish Studies* 8, nos. 3–4 (1957): 192–213.
40. See, for example, *Shem ha-gedolim he-hadash* (Warsaw, 1869), pp. 35 (sec. 234), 65 (original, p. 25); *Seder ha-dorot mi-talmidey ha-Besht zal* (Lublin, 1927), pp. 12–13; Rodkinsohn (n. 9 above), pp. 30, 35, 38, 43; S. A. Horodecky, *Ha-hasidut ve-ha-hasidim* (Tel Aviv, 1927), vol. 1, passim; S. Dubnow, *Toledot ha-hasidut* (Tel Aviv, 1960), pp. 59, 63.
41. See A. J. Heschel, "Le-toledot R. Pinhas mi-korez," in *Aley Ayin* (Jerusalem, 1948–52), pp. 218–20, idem., "R. Yishaq of Drobitz," in the *Hadoar Jubilee Volume* (New York, 1957), pp. 89–91, and idem., "Rabbi Nahman mi- Kosov" (n. 4 above), pp. 113–16, 118–19, 123, 136–37.
42. See, for example, *Shivhey ha-Besht*, ed. S. A. Horodecky (Tel Aviv, 1960) pp. 92, 93, 89–90, 61.

43. See Heschel, "Le-toledot R. Pinhas," p. 221.
44. For the activities of R. Aaron of Karlin in Lithuania during the lifetime of the Maggid, see W. Rabinowitsch, *Lithuanian Hasidism* (Heb.) (Jerusalem, 1961), p. 11. For the equal status of Karlin to Miedzyrzecz as a Hasidic center during this period, see Solomon Maimon, *Lebensgeschichte*, Hebrew translation, *Hayey Shlomo Maimon* (Tel Aviv, 1942) p. 135 [see above Ch. 1]. As an echo of the fluidity of the situation, and the relativity of the titles "leader" and "follower," the following tradition may be quoted, received in the name of R. Yehiel Mikhal of Zloczów, a disciple of the Maggid of Miedzyrzecz: . . . indeed, I have heard from . . . R. Yehiel Mikhal, of blessed memory, that he said: Before the start of each prayer I connect myself [*mitqasher*—synonymous with 'cleave'—*daveq*] to the entire nation of Israel, both to those who are superior to me and to those who are my inferiors. For the benefit of connecting myself to my superiors lies in that, through this my thought may be uplifted. And the benefit of connecting myself to my inferiors lies in that through this, they may be uplifted" (Meshulam Phoebush of Zbaraz, *Derekh ha-emet (Yosher divrey emet)* [Jerusalem, n.d.]), p. 42. R. Yehiel Mikhal was a disciple of the Maggid of Miedzyrzecz who became himself a Hasidic master commanding a following of his own.
45. Scholem, who points out that it was virtually impossible to expect everyone to fulfill the highest ideal of *devekut* even though this was demanded or "in a way, forced upon the masses," concludes, therefore, that "it was bound to assume rather crude and vulgar forms. Once the radical slogan 'Judaism without *devekut* is idolatry' was accepted, its very radicalism already contained the germ of decay, a dialectic typical of radical and spiritualist movements. Since not everyone was able to attain that state of mind by introspection and contemplation, external stimulants, even liquor, had to be employed" ("Devekut" [n. 1 above], p. 209).
46. For this view, see, for example, Weiss, "The Beginnings of Hasidism," pp. 64–65, n. 61; Dubnow, p. 59.
47. Horodecky, 4:22.
48. Ibid., p. 48.
49. A possible exception is R. Menahem Mendel of Przemyslany whose pamphlet *Darkhey yesharim* (Zhitomir, 1805) does appear to request direct *devekut* from everyone. There is not a single reference in the pamphlet to the division, so often stated by R. Jacob Joseph of Polonne and others, between ordinary "corporeal" people and the supreme group of "spiritual men." On the contrary, R. Menahem Mendel seems to advocate the complete equality in *devekut* of all creatures before God: "And let not a man say to himself that he is greater than his fellow man. since he can worship in greater *devekut*. For he, as all other creatures, was created in order to worship God. Has God not given his fellow a mind such as he gave to him? By what is he more important than a mere worm? For the worm also worships God with all its might and mind, and man likewise is a worm . . ."

(*Darkhey yesharim*, p. 9a). R. Menahem Mendel acknowledges that it is very difficult to maintain his own extreme version of the ideal of *devekut*, and, therefore, he advises everyone to refrain as much as possible from all activities which are not directly conducive to it. Notably, unlike the Besht, he considers study, and sometimes even prayer, as a hindrance, not a potential vehicle, for *devekut* which can be achieved in total silence and seclusion. (For his attitude to study, see Weiss, "Talmud Torah," pp. 158–62.)

50. With this in mind, it would be appropriate to examine the question of the representation of Beshtian traditions in the writings of his grandson, R. Ephrayim of Sudylków, as it was raised by Weiss. Weiss compares two parallel traditions in the name of the Besht, one recorded by R. Jacob Joseph in *Sofnat pa'ane'ah* and the other by R. Ephrayim of Sudylków in his *Degel mahaneh ephrayim*. He recognizes in the latter a paraphrase of the former ". . . into which R. Ephrayim had inserted a few words to sharpen the general idea of the Besht by confining it to the activities of the zaddik only. . . . The appropriate historical position of this passage is not in the Beshtian stage but in a later development in the history of Hasidic ideas, at which the tendency came to prevail of confining to the zaddik that which was everyone's right according to the teachings of the Besht. . . ." ("Beginnings of Hasidism," pp. 64–65). However, a careful examination of the two texts would show that R. Ephrayim did not depart from the Besht's idea, as recorded by R. Jacob Joseph, in any other way but in the introduction of the term zaddik, which for him has a clear, institutional meaning, and possibly, in emphasizing something which his grandfather may not have felt the need to emphasize, namely, that only the zaddik could fulfill the ideal. But the clear division between the man who can "raise" and the man who may be "raised" is present in the original version in *Sofnat pa'ane'ah*. The Besht himself clearly identifies with the man who can "raise," and there is no question of the two distinct roles being interchangeable.

51. See, for example, Weiss, "A Circle of Pneumatics in Pre-Hasidism," n. 39 above.

52. For the attempt by the Besht to gain recognition by the circle of the "great Hasidim" in Brody, see *Shivhey ha-Besht*, p. 51.

53. See. J. G. Weiss, "The Kavvanoth of Prayer in Early Hasidism," *Journal of Jewish Studies* 9 (1958): 163–92; Rivka Schatz-Uffenheimer, *Quietistic Elements in 18th Century Hasidic Thought* (Heb.) (Jerusalem, 1968), pp. 129–47; L. Jacobs, *Hasidic Prayer* (London, 1972), pp. 74–81.

54. Weiss, "The Kavvanoth," p. 168.

55. See *Shivhey ha-Besht*, pp. 104–5, 148.

56. See ibid., p. 105.

57. See ibid, p. 148.

58. *Or ha-Emet*, p. 14b, quoted by Weiss (with a slight omission) in "The Kavvanoth," p. 177.

59. See *Or ha-Emet*, p. 64a; Weiss, "The Kavvanoth," p. 178.

60. This, of course, was particularly true of the first and second generations of Hasidism, before the start of the organized campaign against the movement by its opponents. But even subsequently, while the opponents regarded Hasidism as a deviating sect and attempted to sever it from the main body of Judaism, the Hasidic response was remarkably harmonistic, stressing the sense of belonging to the community and conforming with its values, rather than breaking away from it (see, for example, M. Wilensky, *Hasidim u-mitnaggedim* [Jerusalem, 1970], 1:84–100, 161–76, 296–313).

61. See, for example, B. R. Wilson, "A Typology of Sects," in *Sociology of Religion*, ed. R. Robertson (London, 1969), pp. 366–67.

62. See Weiss, "The Kavvanoth," pp. 185–92.

63. See Schatz-Uffenheimer, pp. 138, 145–47.

64. For his rejection specifically of *devekut* in corporeality as inapplicable to "our generation," see *Derekh emet (Yosher divrey emet)* (Jerusalem, n.d.), pp. 61, 66.

65. See Schatz-Uffenheimer, pp. 138, 146.

66. See *Derekh emet*, pp. 76–77, but cf. pp. 49–50.

67. *Sofnat pa'ane'ah* (Korzec ed.), p. 30b, quoted by S. H. Dresner, *The Zaddik* (New York-Tornoto-London, 1960), p. 129.

68. For the cleaving of the common people to their spiritual leader rather than directly to God, see Dresner, pp. 113–41. Dresner, however, argues that the Baal Shem Tov and R. Jacob Joseph did not advocate the complete dependence of the ordinary person on the zaddik, and that in this one can detect "a difference in attitude towards the zaddik between the earlier and later generations of Hasidism" (pp. 133–36). But the sources he quotes for this are not entirely convincing and could easily be explained as a token acknowledgment of the doctrine of free will and an awareness of the obligation not to discourage anyone from attempting his best (cf. above). Significantly, the most powerful insistence on the limitation of the dependence of ordinary people on the zaddik which Dresner quotes in this connection is not taken from any Hasidic text but from Martin Buber's interpretation of these texts (see Dresner, pp. 134–36).

69. J. W. Weiss, *Studies in Bratslav Hasidism* (Heb.) (Jerusalem, 1974), p. 104.

70. See ibid., pp. 105–7.

71. *Derekh emet*, p. 42. For a similar recommendation, see *Va-yaqhel moshe* (Lemberg, 1863), in the comment on Psalm 16, p. 4a (quoted by G. Nigal in *Mishnat ha-hasidut be-kitvey Rabbi Elimelekh mi-Lizensk u-veney doro*, [doctoral diss., Hebrew University, Jerusalem, 1972], pp. 200–201). In *Derekh emet*, R. Meshulam Phoebush refers the reader, at the end of the passage quoted above, to the book *Hesed le-avraham* as a source in which the matter is explained further. Indeed, in *Hesed le-avraham* (Amsterdam, 1685) Ma'ayan II, Eyn ha-qore, nahar 33, p. 18a–b, R. Abraham Azulai writes: ". . . It is forbidden to look at idols, for that shape damages the mind. And this is the secret meaning of the prohibition on looking at the face of a wicked man. Conversely, if the form of an honorable man is drawn up in a man's mind, he may reach a great and wonderful eminence. . . ."

However, when he speaks there of the man who achieves the status of someone much closer to God than himself, Azulai, using the example of Elisha and Elijah, prescribes a somewhat different technique whereby the lesser man, Elisha, causes his own form to be drawn up in the mind of the greater man, Elijah, and thus himself "coming to stand before God," like Elijah. Altogether, Azulai's ideas in this connection are somewhat less striking in that they are free from the Hasidic context of the zaddik as a focus of the ordinary person's devotion.

72. See, for example, T. B. Baba Batra 75b; Pesahim 68a, Moed Katan 16b, Shabbat 63a; *Midrash Shir ha-Shirim rabba,* 1.31, *Zohar* 1.45, 114, 135.

73. *Midrash tanhuma,* ed. Buber, Toledot 11.

74. *Zohar,* introduction, p. 5.

75. This is clearly an allusion to the *Zohar* text referred to above in n. 74, just as the attribution to the zaddikim of the power to resurrect the dead and to cure the infertility of women is based on the rabbinic sources referred to in n. 72.

76. *Maggid devarav le-yaaqov,* ed. R. Schatz-Uffenheimer (Jerusalem, 1976), no. 165, p. 285.

77. *Noam elimelekh* (Jerusalem, n.d.), "Tesze," p. 144.

78. Ibid., "Devarim," p. 133.

79. Jacobs, *Hasidic Prayer,* p. 131.

80. Adapted by M. Buber from *Nifle'ot ha-yehudi* in his *Or ha-ganuz* (Tel Aviv, 1976), p. 429 (English ed., *Tales of the Hasidim, The Late Masters,* pp. 271–72). For an account of a Jew who remained loyal to the Besht even after his death and refused to accept another master, see A. Kahana, *Sefer ha-hasidut* (Warsaw, 1922), p. 24.

81. For preliminary comments on this, see Weiss, *Studies in Bratslav Hasidism,* pp. 152–54; see also M. Piekarz, *Studies in Bratslav Hasidism* (Heb.) (Jerusalem, 1972), pp. 112–17.

82. See *Liqutey moharan,* pt. 1, torah 64, sec. 4. Here, too, the passage from the introduction to the *Zohar* which was referred to above, depicting the righteous as creators, is the source for the attribution of this power to the zaddikim.

83. See ibid., sec 1.

84. See, for example, ibid., torah 63, where the Zaddik's mode of self-revelation is, paradoxically, concealment and disguise "in small things," since his full, undisguised "mind" cannot be revealed at all. This is a clear echo of the classic Hasidic interpretations of the Lurianic *simsum* with regard to God who, equally paradoxically, conceals or disguises himself because this is the only way in which he can reveal himself to the world (see also, torah 140).

85. See, *Yemey moharnat* (Beney Brak, 1956), pt. 2, sec. 5, p. 85.

86. *Liqutey moharan,* pt. 1, torah 64, the beginning of sec. 1.

87. *Liqutey tefilot,* pt. 1, prayer no. 64, the beginning of sec. 1. The entire first section of the prayer is made up of a string of immanentist slogans of Hasidism.

10

Hasidic Prayer

Louis Jacobs

THE NATURE OF HASIDIC PRAYER

An early Hasidic text,[1] speaking of the dialogue of the Baal Shem Tov
(d. 1760), the founder of the Hasidic movement, with his own soul,
remarks:

The soul declared to the rabbi, may his memory be for a blessing for the life of
the world to come, that the reason why the supernal matters were revealed to
him was not because he had studied many Talmudic tractates and Codes of Law
but because of his prayer. For at all times he recited his prayers with great
concentration. It was as a result of this that he attained to an elevated state.

There is no doubt whatsoever that prayer occupied a central place in
early Hasidic life and has continued to to do down to the present.
Speaking of the doctrines of the Maggid of Miedzyrzecz, the disciple of
the Baal Shem Tov, Rivka Schatz[2] rightly observes:

Contemplative prayer became the spiritual message *par excellence* of Hasidism.
A Hasid who did not pray with the aim of divesting himself of corporeality,
detaching himself from this world, and rising above nature and time in order to
attain complete union with the divine "Nothing," had not really achieved anything of spiritual value.

She is not, however, correct when she goes on to say[3] that Hasidism has
assigned an exclusive role to prayer "giving it—*in keeping with the
Jewish tradition*—pride of place in the religious life (italics mine). The

Hasidic elevation of prayer over other religious duties, even over that of study of the Torah, is not in keeping with the Jewish tradition. The Hasidim here were innovators. In the rabbinic tradition the obligation to pray is rabbinic, not biblical.[4] In the Talmud[5] one rabbi can rebuke another who prolongs his prayers unduly by protesting "they leave aside eternal life [= the Torah] to engage in temporal existence" [= prayer]. Scholars like R. Simeon b. Yohai, we are told, whose sole occupation was study of the Torah, would not interrupt their studies in order to pray.[6]

The Hasidic teachers were not unaware that their elevation of prayer over all other duties was a departure from what, at least, was held to be the tradition and they sought to justify their innovation by seeking to demonstrate, as religious innovators are wont to do, that the tradition, rightly understood, was really in line with their attitude. Thus R. Shneur Zalman of Liady (1747–1813), founder of the Habad group in Hasidism, in a letter addressed to Alexander of Szklow,[7] makes the point explicitly:

Those who argue that prayer is only binding by Rabbinic law have never seen the light. It is true that the forms of the prayers are Rabbinic, and that prayers must be recited three times a day, but the concept of prayer and its essential idea belong to the very foundation of the Torah, namely, to know the Lord, to recognise His greatness and His glory with a serene mind, and, through contemplation, to have these fixed firmly in the mind. A man must reflect on this theme until the contemplative soul is awakened to love the Lord's name, to cleave to Him and to His Torah and greatly to desire His commandments. Nowadays, all this can only be achieved by reciting the verses of praise and the benedictions before and after the Shema with clear diction and in a loud voice so as to awaken the powers of concentration. All this and then perhaps! It was otherwise with regard to R. Simeon b. Yohai and his colleagues. For them the recitation of the Shema alone was sufficient for them to attain all this. It was all achieved in a blink of the eye, so humble was their heart in its convenantal loyalty. But, nowadays, anyone who has drawn near to God and has once tasted the fragrance of prayer, knows and appreciates that without prayer no man can lift hand or foot to serve God in truth, rather than as the commands of men who learn by rote.

Similarly, R. Kalonymus Kalman Epstein of Cracow (d. 1827) writes:[8]

When the Jew draws near to the form of worship that is prayer it is to the greatest thing in the whole world that he draws near, as the holy book tell us. The Talmud states explicitly that prayer is greater than good deeds.[9] In our generation, especially, the chief method by means of which a man can refine his character, so as to approach the divine and serve God, is prayer. From the time of his coming, the holy Baal Shem Tov, may the memory of the holy and saintly be for a blessing, caused the tremendous sanctity of prayer to illumine the world for whoever wishes to draw near to God's service. However, in order for a man to attain to pure prayer it is necessary for him to engage in much service of the sages, to labour long, night and day, in the study of the Torah and in performance of good deeds so that, as a result, he may learn how truly to pray with fear and great love, as those who have discernment know full well.

Here we clearly see how an influential Hasidic author strives to reconcile the traditional view of the supremacy of Torah study with the new Hasidic emphasis on the supremacy of prayer. His solution is that, indeed, the study of the Torah and the performance of good deeds are essential and that without them prayer is futile. But—and a complete transvaluation is involved in the qualification—these are essential as aids to prayer. They are the guarantee that the worshipper will be capable of offering his prayers "with fear and great love." In another passage [10] R. Kalonymus Kalman, commenting on Jacob's dream, notes that a Midrash reads homiletically that Jacob awoke from his learning (*mi-mishnato*, instead of *mi-shenato*, "his sleep"). The Midrash, of course, suggests that Jacob saw his vision of the divine because he was learned in the Torah. But R. Kalonymus Kalman boldly turns the Midrash on its head to suggest that, on the contrary, once Jacob had experienced true prayer he saw that his learning was only a dream insofar as he had imagined that by it he could come to love God. Jacob, remarks our author, had hitherto known only that man can draw near to God through the study of the Torah. When, however, he prayed to God in the place of his dream, he experienced such a powerful feeling of nearness to God that he came to realise that the true awakening of the spirit is through prayer alone. Jacob, speaking of prayer, then declared, "Surely the Lord is in this place; and I knew it not." After remarking that both Torah study and prayer are essential and that one without the other is inadequate, R. Kalonymus Kalman goes on to say that a man cannot perfect his soul by the study of the Torah alone:

There is no doubt that a man who studies the Torah for its own sake can attain to great sanctity, provided always that he studies for its own sake and attaches all his vitality, spirit and soul to the letters of the Torah. For all that, the only way he can attain to real fear and love of God, to the longing for the worship of God, and to comprehension of His divinity, is through prayer offered with self-sacrifice and burning enthusiasm. All this is well known and is stated in all the holy books.

The early Hasidic master R. Meshullam Phoebus of Zbaraz, disciple of the Maggid of Miedzyrzecz and of R. Yehiel Mikhal of Zloczow, adopts a different way of reconciling the traditional demand for the supremacy of Torah study with the new Hasidic claims for the supremacy of prayer. He declares that indeed the study of the Torah is the highest value, but argues that true Torah study is only possible if it is attended by a proper life of prayer, that is by prayer as understood by Hasidism. In his little book *Derekh emet*[11] this author accuses the learned of his day as totally lacking in real religious fervour even though they are well versed in both the "revealed" Torah and the Kabbalah. Of the scholars he attacks he remarks:

They know nothing of what attachment *[devekut]* to God means and nothing of what love and fear mean. For they imagine that their studies themselves constitute attachment to God and that these are themselves the love and fear of God. But how can this be? It is well known that many of the scholars are guilty of fornication, Heaven spare us, and they are notorious sinners. It is also true that many Gentiles study our Torah. How, then, can this be considered attachment to God? For one who is attached to God in love and fear cannot possibly commit even the slightest sin, to say nothing of a severe sin, God forbid, and to say nothing of attachment to some lust, God forbid. For, behold, God is holy and separate from all materialism. Consequently, it does not need saying that the love and fear of God are quite a different matter and they have to do with the heart, that a man's heart should be constantly in dread and awe of God and that the love of God should burn always in his heart. . . . No one can attain to this state except by virtue of the study of the Torah for its own sake. And the prior, essential condition is prayer with attachment *[devekut]*, with burning enthusiasm *[hitlahavut]* of the heart, with a coercion of all man's psychological faculties in the direction of clear and pure thoughts on God constantly, and in separation from every pleasure. It goes without saying that there must be separation from light and severe sins and that all the laws must be obeyed scrupulously and that all the limbs of the body must be clean and protected by the special kind of sanctity appropriate to each of them, as the moralistic works have recorded, and especially the author of *Reshit hokhmah* [Elijah de Vidas]. But how can there possibly be attachment *[devekut]* by means of the Torah in the way they conduct themselves in that they despise prayer? The truth is that they only learn by rote in order to be considered wise.

The Hasidic attitude towards prayer and the reason for the significance of prayer in Hasidic thought cannot be understood without reference to the basic Hasidic idea of *devekut,* attachment to God, to which R. Meshullam Phoebus alludes and which has been explored in a famous article by Gershom Scholem (see chapter 8 of this volume).[12] Briefly stated, the doctrine means that ideally man should always have God in his thoughts, seeing beneath appearances only the divine vitality which infuses all things. For Hasidism, though with varying emphases, the only true reality is God. The material world, and, for that matter, the "upper worlds" as well, only seem to enjoy reality. They are a kind of screen, which hides God from human eyes, but through which He can be seen if man's spiritual gaze is properly directed. The Hasid can learn to restore all things to their Source and to see only the infinite, divine power as this is manifested in creation. This is the Hasidic doctrine of *panentheism,* that all is in God. The Hasid is expected to attain to the state described in Hasidic thought as *bittul ha-yesh,* "the annihilation of something-ness", that is an awareness that God alone is true reality and that all finite things are, as it were, dissolved in His unity. *Bittul ha-yesh* includes the annihilation of selfhood, the soul soaring to God with the ego left behind. This attitude is especially to be cultivated at the time of prayer, so that in Hasidism prayer is essentially an exercise in world-forsaking and abandonment of self.

In a passage[13] from the work *Maggid devarav le-yaaqov* (otherwise known as *Liqute amarim*), containing the teachings of the Maggid of Miedzyrzecz, the disciple of the Baal Shem Tov, the process is described as follows:

It is stated that when a man studies the Torah or when he prays he should think to himself that he is, as it were, in the Garden of Eden, where there is neither envy not lust nor pride, and by so doing he will be spared from motives of self. But one has to understand the meaning of this. For how can a man think that this is so when he knows only too well that, in fact, he is in this world among persons he can identify? The matter is as follows. When a man studies or prays with fear and love, attaching himself and binding himself in his thoughts to the Creator, blessed be His name, and when he considers that the whole world is full of His glory and that no place is empty of Him, all being filled with the divine vitality, then all he sees in whatever he observes is the divine vitality which is drawn down into the object of perception. For example, when he sees other human beings, he observes that their appearance, their voices which he hears, their speech and their wisdom, all stem from this divine vitality. And this applies to whatever he sees or hears. For everything has that form and purpose to which it is suited. The same applies to that which he sees and that which he smells. It is all the vital power of the Creator, blessed be His name. It follows that when a man studies or prays with fear and love he gains much from it in that he becomes bound in his thought to the Creator, blessed be He. Such a worshipper sees nothing and hears nothing except the divine vitality that is in all things. For everything is from Him, blessed be His name; only it is clothed, as it were, in various garments. How, then, can motives of self, worldly desires, enter his mind, if all he sees before him is the vitality of the Creator alone and the spiritual delight that inheres in all things?

In another early Hasidic text[14] it is similarly taught:

In what way is a man better than a worm? For the worm serves God with all its might and mind, and man, too, is a worm, as it is written, "But I am a worm, and no man" [Ps. 22: 7]. If God had not endowed man with intellect he could only have worshipped Him as a worm does. Consequently, he has no more worth up above than does a worm and certainly not more than other men. He should think to himself that he and the worm and all minute creatures are all companions in this world, for all are God's creatures and have no power except that which the Creator, blessed be He, gives them. This should always be in his thoughts.

The Hasidic attitude to prayer as an exercise in self-transcendence created for the Hasidim an especially acute problem. Prayers of adoration could effectively produce the desired aim; the Hasid could, by their aid, lose himself in reflection on the divine majesty. But what of petitionary prayer? In this type of prayer man entreats God to satisfy his needs, both spiritual and material. He prays for knowledge and wisdom, for bodily health and sustenance, for forgiveness of sin and redemption. This would seem to frustrate the whole purpose of prayer, since consciousness of need implies self-awareness. If man's aim in prayer is to see only the divine vitality, how can he petition God to attend to his own needs? Far from this type of prayer leading to the desired aim of loss of self it encourages concentration on self. The logical conclusion of the Hasidic doctrine would have been to reject all petitionary prayer as a hindrance to the attainment of self-annihilation. But such a solution was not open to the Hasidim who believed, like their contemporaries, that the traditional liturgy, which contains numerous petitionary prayers, was divinely inspired and divinely ordained.

The quietistic and radical way out of the dilemma generally adopted by the early Hasidim is that petitionary prayer is not, in fact, a request to God to satisfy man's needs but to satisfy His own needs. In the language of Hasidism, petitionary prayer is for the sake of the Shekhinah

("Divine Presence"). In the Kabbalah, upon which a good deal of Hasidic teaching is based, the Shekhinah is a kind of female element in the Godhead; female because it is the passive aspect of Deity, the manifestation of the divine power which vitalises all creation. God's purpose, the Kabbalistic doctrine runs, in creating the world is to benefit His creatures. True, if there were no creatures no loss of benefit or good would be experienced by anyone, but it is the nature of the All-good to have recipients for His bounty so that, as it were, He can fulfil Himself. Moreover, since man is created in God's image, since he is the microcosm of which the universe is the macrocosm, his deeds have a cosmic effect. When man is virtuous he sends up on high spiritual impulses which help to promote harmony in the realm of the Sefirot, the various potencies in the Godhead. God's purpose of benefiting His creatures as worthy recipients of His goodness can then be fulfilled. There is harmony above and so grace and blessing can flow through all creation. Man's wickedness, on the other hand, arrests the flow of the divine grace, producing disharmony in the Sefirotic realm. This is the cause of all death and destruction, of chaos and catastrophe, of evil and man's lack of all he requires for his continued existence and well-being. The Shekhinah is one of the Ten Sefirot. It is known as Malkhut ("Sovereignty") because through it God's rule over His creatures is established. In mythological language—and the whole of the Kabbalah is highly-charged mythology—when man lacks anything the lack is in the Shekhinah since then God's purpose remains unfulfilled. The Hasid, it is therefore taught, should not ask for his needs to be satisfied because they are *his* needs but because ultimately they are the needs of the Shekhinah. Even when praying for himself his true aim is for God. Even petitionary prayer serves his aim of self-transcendence.

The whole doctrine of prayer influencing the "upperworlds" was accepted without qualification by the Hasidic teachers. R. Jacob Joseph of Polonne, disciple of the Baal Shem Tov, writes[15] that this is why the prayers have to be recited verbally and it is not sufficient for man simply to have the prayers in mind. Although God knows all thoughts, when a man gives verbal expression to his prayers he provides a "vessel" through which the divine grace can flow to the material world, otherwise it would only be capable of flowing into the spiritual "vessels" provided by thought. In his *Toledot yaaqov yosef*,[16] the first Hasidic book to be printed, R. Jacob Joseph remarks that a prayer for man to cleave to God (where the question of the divine flow of blessing is not involved and is purely spiritual) can be simply thought of in the mind and requires no verbal expression.

The theme of prayer for the sake of God—more specifically, for the sake of the Shekhinah—is treated with variations in the classical Hasidic writings, of which a few examples should be quoted here. All these are from early Hasidic works, but even at this early stage in the development of Hasidic thought there are differing emphases, so that one will look in vain for a consistent, systematic treatment acceptable to all the Hasidic masters.

R. Moses Hayim Ephraim of Sudylków, grandson of the Baal Shem Tov, reports,[17] in the name of his grandfather, a comment on the Mishnah[18] that one should serve God without conditioning for reward. In some texts the reading is "conditioning for no reward." The Baal Shem Tov is reported as saying that both versions are correct and refer to different stages in the prayer life of man. There is an ebb and flow in man's life of prayer. It is not possible for him always to have the highest motives and conduct himself on the most elevated plane. The two versions are interpreted as referring to prayer but to two different stages, one higher than the other. Both versions refer to those who pray for the sake of God, not for themselves. One worshipper declares that God's will, not his own, be done. While he acknowledges that tradition demands that he entreat God to satisfy his needs, he accepts in love that God may not answer his prayers. His service is without conditioning for reward. It is simply his duty to pray, leaving the rest to God. The second stage in the life of prayer is still higher. Here the worshipper "conditions for no reward." He, too, prays for his own needs, since he is so obligated to do by the tradition, but he does not want his request to be granted. His true desire is always to be in a state of need so that he can come again and again before God to present his petition. The particular things he needs form only the excuse he has for praying to God. What really matters for him is the joy of approaching his Maker.

This parable can be given. A man is possessed of a powerful desire to commune with the king, his heart burning in longing for it to happen. The king decreed that whoever presents his requests to him will have them answered. This man, whose desire and longing it is to converse with the king, is apprehensive that, when he comes to present his request, the king will grant it and he will then have no further excuse for conversing with the king. He prefers that the king should not grant his request so that he will have good reason for coming again to the king and having once again the joy of conversing with him.

Another report in the name of the Baal Shem Tov [19] speaks of petitionary prayer as unanswered automatically:

The main thing in prayer is the belief that God, blessed be His name, fills the whole earth with His glory. A man should also believe that his request is answered immediately as soon as he utters the formal words of the prayers. If you ask, how is it, then, that the request is not, in fact, granted? The answer is that the prayer is always answered but sometimes in a way hidden from men. For example, even though a man's particular request was for his own pain to be removed his prayer may be answered for the pain of the world to be lessened. And, in reality, it is for his own good or to cleanse him from sin and the like. For if a man has the intention of waiting for his prayers to be answered he introduces something corporeal into his prayers, whereas the proper thing is for them to be purely spiritual, for the sake of the Shekhinah and not for the sake of worldly things.

In this passage the magical power of petitionary prayer is stressed. No prayer goes unanswered but the answer is not necessarily personal. It may have an effect on the well-being of the world as a whole while, for various possible reasons, having no direct effect on the life of the petitioner himself. Since this is so, then it is futile for the worshipper always to expect a definite personal answer to his petition. Moreover, it is really undesirable for him to expect a personal answer. By so doing he introduces the note of selfhood and this frustrates the whole aim of prayer. The additional *motif* here is that the granting of the request for the world in general does not involve any catering to the ego. Consequently, petitionary prayer is not an exercise in futility and yet, at the same time, it is for the sake of God whose desire it is to benefit His creatures.

"For this let every man that is godly [*hasid*] pray" (Ps. 32: 6). This verse was used [20] to summarise the aim of Hasidic prayer. "This" (*zot*) represents the Shekhinah. Man should consider that whatever happens to him happens, as it were, to the Shekhinah. The events of the Hasid's personal life call attention to that which the Shekhinah lacks. If the Hasid finds himself to be sick in health, for example, he should reflect that God wants him to be well again, and until he recovers from his illness God's will is unfulfilled. His purpose, then, in praying for good health and a speedy recovery should be so that the Shekhinah will lack no more. The further mystical meaning of *zot* is said to be that the word represents the whole Sefirotic realm. The word *zot* is formed from the three letters *zayin, alef, tav*. Of the Ten Sefirot there are three "higher" and seven "lower." The three "higher" are: Keter ("Crown"), Hokhmah ("Wisdom"), Binah ("Understanding"). The seven "lower" are: Hesed ("Loving kindness"), Gevurah ("Power"), Tiferet ("Beauty"), Nesah ("Victory"), Hod ("Splendour"), Yesod ("Foundation") and Malkhut ("Sovereignty"). The three "higher" Sefirot have to do with the divine thought; the seven "lower" with the divine emotions, as it were, as manifesting that thought. Malkhut, or the Shekhinah, is the link between the Sefirotic realm and the worlds beneath. Into Malkhut there flows the divine grace so that, including itself, it is said in the Kabbalah to be called "Bathsheba" (= *bat sheva*, "daughter of seven") and from Malkhut the flow of blessing is transmitted to all creatures. Thus *zot*, containing the letters *zayin, alef, tav*, does not represent the Shekhinah alone but the Shekhinah in its relationship with the whole of the Sefirot realm as well as with the whole of creation. This is because the numerical value of *zayin* is seven, representing the seven "lower" Sefirot, while *alef* and *tav*, the first and last letters of the Hebrew alphabet, represent the Shekhinah as the alpha and omega of all finite being. These letters are, in the Kabbalistic scheme, not mere symbols but the form assumed here on earth by those spiritual forces on high that God uses in His creative activity. The purpose of prayer is to elevate these spiritual forces inherent in the letters, to bring them back to their Source and by so doing restore all creation to the divine "Nothing" whence it came. When this takes place all is blessed unity. Complete harmony is promoted in the Sefirotic realm and the divine grace can freely flow. The *alef* and the *tav* are united with the seven Sefirot and the Shekhinah becomes whole. "For this [*zot*] let every Hasid pray." The Hasid should have this in mind when he prays and his prayers will then be for the sake of the Shekhinah. Furthermore, he should have in mind that the letter *tav*, the final letter of the alphabet, represents the ultimate extent of the Shekhinah's influence, while the letter *zayin* represents the seven stages of the Sefirot flow. All this should be connected in the mind of the worshipper with the letter *alef* (the middle letter of the word *zot*). This represents *En Sof*, the Limitless, God as He is in Himself, the Ground of all being from which the Sefirot emanate. The letters of the word *alef (alef, lamed, pe)*, when transposed, form the word *pele*, "marvel." Thus the whole of creation is raised, as it were, to its source in *deus absconditus*, the Marvel and Mystery behind all things and in which all things have their being.

The implications of this intricate but not untypical comment are that, whatever prayers are offered, the worshipper should not be concerned at all with the personal aspects of his petition but with the power of the letters through which unity and harmony is achieved. The worshipper is engaged in assisting God's creative processes. From this way of looking at it, unlike the other descriptions of prayer for the sake of the Shekhinah, petitionary prayer is virtually rejected except for its formal letters which, in fact, mean something quite other than the plain meaning of the words formed from them. It must be repeated that early Hasidic thought is not in the nature of a complete system. More than one way of coping with the basic problems is found in the early Hasidic writings.

For all the various interpretations given to it, however, there is no reason to doubt that the basic doctrine of prayer for the sake of the Shekhinah is an authentic doctrine of the Baal Shem Tov. R. Moses Hayim Ephraim of Sudylków reports this, as we have seen, in the name of the Baal Shem Tov and he returns to the theme again and again, as do other Hasidic writers, in the name of the Baal Shem Tov. Elsewhere[21] R. Moses Hayim Ephraim writes:

The matter has to be understood on the basis of the saying of my master, my grandfather, his soul is in Eden, may his memory be for the life of the world to come, that all things derive, as it were, from the Shekhinah. A man should know that whatever he lacks is a lack in the Shekhinah, blessed be He and blessed be His name. With breadth of knowledge he [the Baal Shem Tov] illumined our eyes in this matter. Consequently, all prayer should have as its aim that the Shekhinah's lack should be filled, as it were, and man's own needs will automatically be satisfied. This is the meaning of the saying that the righteous are the deputies of the Matrona, for when the righteous experience any lack they know that, corresponding to their own, there is a lack in the Shekhinah, and they cause the Shekhinah to attain to complete unification.

This is how the Baal Shem Tov is said to have solved[22] the contradiction between two passages in the Zohar. In one passage it is said that whoever does not pray for his sustenance daily is of little faith. But in another passage scorn is poured on those who bark like dogs begging for food. The solution is that man should not beg for his food solely for his own sake. Man's experience of lack of food is due to his vital soul. Since this vitality is, in reality, that of the Shekhinah, he should pray for the pain experienced, as it were, by his vital soul, which is only another way of saying that he should pray for the sake of the Shekhinah.

A realistic note is sounded in the writings of R. Jacob Joseph of

Polonne in the name of R. Menahem Mendel of Bar.[23] A man's troubles may be so heavy that he cannot rise above them to forget himself in praying solely for the sake of the Shekhinah. At such times, rather than pretend to himself that he is indifferent to his own pain, a man should be honest enough to offer his petitionary prayers in their plain and simple meaning, that is for his own needs to be satisfied. R. Menahem Mendel of Bar was an associate of the Baal Shem Tov, evidently a member of the latter's circle, but with independent views. It seems that the doctrine of prayer for the sake of the Shekhinah was taught in the circle of the Baal Shem Tov, with each subsequent teacher interpreting the doctrine in his own way, so that in some early Hasidic writings the prayer for personal needs was ruthlessly rejected while in others some concession was made to human frailty.

The Maggid of Miedzyrzec, disciple and successor of the Baal Shem Tov, when dealing with the theme of prayer for the sake of·God, gives[24] a curious turn to the verse, "He will fulfil the desire of those who fear Him" (Ps. 145: 19). The word *yaaseh,* translated as "fulfil," can mean "He will make." The Maggid translates the verse "He will make the desire of those who fear Him" to yield the thought that the righteous have no will of their own. Selfhood is so little pronounced among the righteous that they have no desires. But since God wishes the righteous to pray to Him, He puts into their hearts a desire for worldly things which otherwise they would never have, so that they might turn to Him.

God makes those who fear Him to have a desire, for prayer is called "desire." God puts this desire to pray for something into man's heart, for of himself the God-fearing man would have no desire to pray at all to ask God for anything since "there is no want to them that fear Him" [Ps. 34: 10]. The God-fearing man says "enough" to whatever God gives him. Consequently, God puts the thought of prayer into man's heart for He desires man's prayers. Therefore, the verse concludes: "and He hears their cry and saves them" [Ps. 145: 19].

Elsewhere[25] the Maggid is reported as teaching:

Behold, when a man prays, God forbid that he should direct all his desire towards that corporeal thing for which he asks but he should rather have the following in mind. Our Rabbis say that the cow wishes to feed the calf more than the calf wishes to be fed. This means that a giver has a greater desire to give than the beneficiary of his bounty has the desire to receive. So it is with God. His delight in benefiting His creatures is greater than that of the creatures He benefits.

In other words, petitionary prayer should be to please God in His role as Giver. The worshipper, knowing that God has this desire to give, should ask but not for his own sake. The paradox of petitionary prayer is that the request is real and the satisfaction of man's needs guaranteed. But the true worshipper sees it all as the fulfilment of God's purpose. In the act of receiving, or requesting to receive, the righteous man becomes a giver because he assists God to attain His desire to be a Giver.

A further elaboration of the theme found in early Hasidic writings is that, since the righteous pray for the sake of the Shekhinah, then their prayers for different particular things such as health, sustenance and wisdom are not for the different satisfactions of their own needs but are all for the lack in the Shekhinah evidenced in their own needs. The result is that all petitionary prayer, no matter how varied in relation to its particular requests, is basically one simple prayer, that the lack in the Shekhinah be filled. R. Zeev Wolf of Zytomierz, disciple of the Maggid of Miedzyrzecz, finds this idea[26] in the verse, "One thing have I asked of the Lord" (Ps. 27: 4).

You can see that, since a man's chief aim when he pours out his speech in prayer and supplication is only for the sake of the exile of the Shekhinah, it follows that he has only one request. Even when many evil events and happenings befall him, yet the many requests for them to be eased are only a single request. This is that he experiences in all these evil happenings the clothing of the limbs of the Shekhinah. It is to this that his aim and his efforts are directed, to elevate them to their source, and he senses nothing of his own needs. It is otherwise when a man senses his own physical sorrows in all the many details of the events and happenings which befall him. His requests are numerous in proportion to the different kinds of sorrow he experiences all the time.

Reference must here be made to the valuable analysis of this theme of prayer for the sake of the Shekhinah by Rivka Schatz-Uffenheimer.[27] She rightly sees in the doctrine the strong element of quietism in early Hasidic thought and she points to similar ideas in Christian quietism. Father Ronald Knox, for instance, in a chapter on quietism, describes the very same problem: [28]

But it is more important to ask, in view of the Quietist controversy, what is the attitude of the mystics towards the prayer which asks favours, temporal or spiritual, for ourselves? Here a new principle emerges. The prayer of petition does, in any case, tend to disappear, or rather to be merged in the stream of contemplation. But, more than that—in proportion as the soul becomes united to God, its will becomes united to his, and the objects of ambition (spiritual, no less than temporal) are seen rather as something that must be left to him by an exercise of holy indifference than as something we must secure from him at all costs.

The passivity of the mystic appears to be a universal tendency, but the Hasidim were Orthodox Jews and traditionally Judaism is activist and, as we have noted, petitionary prayer occupies an important place in the traditional liturgy. That is why there is so much tension in the matter among the Hasidic masters, the ideal of mystical contemplation and loss of selfhood pulling one way, the demands of the tradition pulling the other.

Rivka Schatz-Uffenheimer sees the most extreme attitude of quietism in the Maggid of Miedzyrzecz. Although, as we have seen, many of the early Hasidic masters favour the doctrine of prayer for the sake of the Shekhinah, nowhere is personal need more negated than in the teachings attributed to the Maggid, even though some of his disciples tend to soften his rigours. The fact is that nowhere in the works containing the teachings of the Maggid himself do we find any leniency. It is simply forbidden for a man to ask for his own needs, only for the needs of the Shekhinah. Nowhere in the works of the Maggid do we find the kind of distinction made by R. Jacob Joseph of Polonne that when a man is weighed down with sufferings he should have his own personal needs in mind when he prays.

The Hasidic ideal then is contemplative prayer in which the Hasid practises self-annihilation. Petitionary prayer is not only accepted but is binding by the tradition. Yet this aspect of prayer is so interpreted by many teachers that it, too, is an important part of contemplative prayer. On this they are virtually all agreed. Where they differ is in the extent to which selfhood can and should be transcended in the prayer of petition.

Thus far we have been examining early Hasidic thought on prayer. In later Hasidism all these ideas are somewhat softened or even overlooked entirely. There is no longer any detailed consideration of whether prayer should be active or passive, with selfhood or without it. The later Hasidic teachers were familiar with the ideas presented in the classical Hasidic texts, but tended to suggest that many of these were only intended for the spiritual supermen of "those times," not for the spiritual pygmies of "our day." But purity of intention is still insisted upon even in the much later Hasidic works and the ideal of self-annihilation in prayer is never completely abandoned.

In the interesting document *Sav ve-ziruz,* compiled by R. Kalonymus Kalman Spira of Piatzina, a Hasidic master who flourished in prewar Poland and who was murdered by the Nazis, the rabbi gives his young followers advice on how to purify their hearts for God's worship. He advises them to offer, from time to time, a private prayer to God to assist them in their task. While he is averse to writing such private devotions for them, he gives the following as an example.[29] In his private devotion we have as good an example as any of how the ideal of prayer finds its expression in more or less contemporary Hasidism.

Sovereign of the universe! Thou hast created me out of nothing and Thou hast formed all my body, my spirit and my soul. Thou seest how great is my longing to stand in Thy presence with a pure and refined soul which senses Thy will and meditates on Thy thoughts. In the innermost recesses of her heart Thy voice is heard. But how great is the sickness of my heart within me because of her coarseness. She experiences foreign sensations and desires gross things. Instead of becoming a golden bell whose sound is heard on entering the holy place, the voice of a wicked man is heard in her, towards which she rises and bestirs herself. Even when I rise and strengthen myself to drive away every unworthy sensation and desire and to silence the voice of the wicked which springs out to call, it is only from my mind and my heart that I succeed in driving them away, but they remain in my soul.

Sovereign of the universe! Pure and Purifying! How exceedingly does my heart melt within me when I consider that if it is only his house or his courtyard that a man cleanses yet does he throw out the rubbish and places it far away from where he resides. Yet when I try to purify my whole essence and being, to sate my soul with delights, to bathe her and cleanse her before the Lord of eternity, the Pure, whose ministers are pure, higher than all names and attributes, I succeed only in hiding the filth on the surface but it still pushes in to enter my innermost self. I become loathsome and filthy in my own eyes because of the ugly stock that has accumulated in my innermost self. My soul swells and is puffed out ready to burst so as to drown me, God forbid, in the waters of presumptuousness, when the time comes. Even at this moment this thought or that lust (it is proper to mention this explicitly) has bestirred itself within me. It is very bitter to me when I reflect that even though I can prevail over it, with Thy help, and refuse to allow it to achieve its aim, yet my soul has not been cleansed and it will appear again from time to time, whether as a thought or as a lust. O Lord purify my soul! Remove the evil inclination from me! Cast away the evil part of my soul to a place in which it will not be mentioned and not visit me and never enter my heart again, not now and not when I grow old. Especially when I attain to a state of greatness of soul at the time of studying the Torah and prayer and so forth, when my soul has the merit of ascending to the Throne of Thy Glory, let my soul be clean and pure to become clothed with the pure white garments provided by the light of the precepts, and to fly aloft in yearning and longing to be annihilated and embraced by the unity of the One God.

In view of all that has been said, the opinion, encouraged, unfortunately, by popular works on Hasidim, that the movement hailed the prayers of the unsophisticated offered in simple faith, needs to be drastically revised. It is true that there are Hasidic tales about the Baal Shem Tov and his followers refusing to reject the prayers of the untutored, but such tales are not peculiar to Hasidism and are found even among the Lurianic Kabbalists who certainly favoured, as we shall see later, highly sophisticated techniques of contemplation in prayer.[30] These tales mean no more than that the leaders of the movement, with their stress on inwardness and concern for the masses, believed that God accepted every true prayer even if it was confused and in error. But this was because nothing higher could have been expected from the heroes of these tales. The Hasid, if he was capable of it, was expected to rise to much higher realms in his prayers and for him the simple prayer was most emphatically not enough.

For instance, the story is told[31] of the Baal Shem Tov that it once happened that there was a severe drought. The people fasted and cried out to God, but all to no avail. The Baal Shem Tov noticed, however, that "a certain person belonging to the ignorant and the simple folk" was reciting the Shema and when he recited the verse "and He shut up the heaven, so that there shall be no rain" (Deut. 11: 17), he said it "with great concentration." The Baal Shem Tov asked him what he had in mind when reciting the verse. The man replied that he thought the verse meant "and He shall squeeze out the heaven, so that there shall be no rain (left there)." Because of this prayer all the prayers of the people were answered and the rains came.

For the Creator, blessed be His name, searches the heart and knows all its secrets and it is the heart that He wants. That is why the words of this man were so pleasant to Him since his prayers were recited with such great concentration of the heart and were so true and inwardly sincere, and his prayers were answered.

In this and in all such similar tales it is emphasised that the hero was an ignorant but devout man, one who could do no better. It is nowhere suggested that the Hasid with spiritual aspirations dare rest content with simple, untutored prayer. On the contrary, as we have seen, Hasidic prayer belongs to the group of mystical exercises of a most rigorous nature through which the self is transcended.

GESTURES AND MELODY IN PRAYER

Gestures in prayer and a special posture for prayer are known at an early period in Judaism. The biblical record refers to bending the knees while praying (1 Kgs. 8: 54; Isa. 45: 23); prostration on the face (Exod. 34: 8; Ps. 29: 2); the spreading of the hands heavenwards (1 Kgs. 8: 23; Isa. 1: 15); and, possibly, the placing of the face between the knees (1 Kgs. 18: 42). In the rabbinic period bowing the head and body was advocated at the beginning and end of the Eighteen Benedictions[32] and this became the standard practice. In another Talmudic passage[33] it is said that a layman should only bow at the places ordained but the High Priest should bow more frequently and the king more frequently still, though it is doubtful whether the passage reflects historical conditions in Temple times. The idea behind the passage may be, as Rashi, the famous Talmudic commentator, suggests, that the greater the rank the more there is need for abasement before God, or, it is possible that, on the contrary, rank brought with it the privilege of bowing more frequently. Of Rabbi Akiba in the second century it was said[34] that he would cut short his prayers in public but when he prayed alone he would bow and prostrate himself so much that he would begin his prayers in one corner and finish them in another corner. This statement about Rabbi Akiba was frequently quoted by the Hasidim in defence of wild Hasidic gestures in prayer. It is quoted, for example, by the disciple of the Maggid of Miedzyrzecz, R. Shmelke of Nikolsburg (d. 1778).[35] R. Shmelke also quotes the instance of David dancing before the Lord (2 Sam. 6: 14–16).

Both the Zohar[36] and Judah Ha-Levi's Kuzari[37] refer to the Jewish practice of swaying the body while studying the Torah and it would appear that the practice was also widespread in the Middle Ages of swaying during prayer. R. Moses Isserles, in his notes to the Shulhan Arukh,[38] quotes earlier authorities who advocate swaying during prayer on the basis of the verse, "All my bones shall say, Lord, who is like unto Thee?" (Ps. 35: 10), a verse that was to be frequently quoted in Hasidic discussions of the subject. However, the Kabbalist R. Isaiah Horowitz (d. c. 1630) remarks:[39]

One who sways during his prayers causes his powers of concentration to be destroyed while to stand perfectly still without any movement at all assists concentration. As for the verse, "All my bones shall say," this applies to the recitation of the songs of praise, to the benedictions of the Shema, and to the study of the Torah, but not to prayer. If any authority has declared that it applies to prayer as well it seems to me that his view should be ignored since experience proves that to stand perfectly still during prayer is an aid to concentration. Just see for yourself! Would a man dare to offer supplication to a king of flesh and blood if his body moves as the trees of the forest in the wind?

R. Abraham Gumbiner in his notes to the Shulhan Arukh,[40] after quoting authorities who favour swaying during prayer and others who denigrate it, concludes, "It is correct to prefer either of these opinions provided that it assists concentration."

With reservations here and there, the Hasidim favoured violent movements in prayer, believing these to be an aid to concentration as well as enabling man to put the whole of himself into his worship. Very revealing is the reply attributed to the Hasidic master R. Menahem Mendel of Kock[41] to the Mitnagged who asked him why the Hasidim run about during their prayers, since the Talmud[42] rules that when a man prays his feet should be placed together. The rabbi is said to have answered that the Talmud means that a man should figuratively have both feet together when he prays, not one foot in heaven and the other in hell!

R. Elimelekh of Lezajsk, disciple of the Maggid of Miedzyrzecz, teaches that every limb and organ of the zaddik is under the control of his soul.[43] As his soul journeys in the higher realms in prayer, it influences the body to make gestures of an entirely uncontrived nature. Because of their spontaneity, the gestures of the zaddik do not appear odd or grotesque. On the contrary, so attractive do they appear that they are not infrequently copied. Naturally, such imitation of the zaddik's gestures is not authentic and invites ridicule.[44] R. Nahman of Bratslav,[45] great-grandson of the Baal Shem Tov, states that the way to set the heart on fire for God is by motion, since rapid motion generates warmth. When wax is attached to an arrow the wax melts when the arrow is released from the bow at great speed. However, R. Nahman goes on to say that he refers not to the movements of the body but to those of the soul as it speeds from one contemplative idea to the other.

Some of the early Hasidim took the notion of physical movement in prayer to absurd extremes. It is reported that the followers of R. Abraham of Kalisk and R. Hayim Haikel of Amdur (Indura) (both disciples of the

Maggid of Miedzyrzecz, though their corybantism did not meet with the Maggid's approval) used to turn somersaults in their prayers.[46] The Hasidim of the Rabbi of Amdur, we are told, used to say, while engaged in these acrobatics, *Fun Gotts vegen un fun Rebbens vegen* ("For the sake of God and for the sake of the rabbi"). It is extraordinary, but such is the mystery of the *zeitgeist*, that at approximately the same time the "Shakers" emerged in Manchester (where they were called "Shaking Quakers") and later flourished in America.[47] The Shakers practised a rolling exercise which consisted in doubling the head and feet together, and rolling over like a hoop. It would seem that the practice of turning somersaults in prayer was derived in part by the Hasidim from their doctrine of self-annihilation, to which attention was called in the first part of this chapter. The self was overturned, as it were, seeking nothing for itself and desiring only the glory of God. As part of the process the Hasid would deliver himself up completely to the zaddik through whose prayers he would be led to God.

In a book published in Altona as early as 1768, only eight years after the death of the Baal Shem Tov, the fiery R. Jacob Emden writes of the Hasidic gestures in prayer:[48]

I trembled when I heard only recently that a new sect of foolish Hasidim had arisen in Volhynia and Podolia, some of whom have come to this country, whose sole occupation is to study moral and Kabbalistic works. They prolong their prayers for half the day, far longer than the Hasidim of old who used to spend no more than an hour[49] in prayer itself. Moreover, these men perform strange movements, weird and ugly, in the prayer of the Eighteen Benedictions. They clap their hands and shake sideways with their head turned backwards and their face and eyes turned upwards, contrary to the ruling of the rabbis[50] that the eyes should be directed downwards and the heart upwards. The Tanhuma only advocates that the eyes should be directed upwards when the Kedushah is recited and even then they should be closed.[51] R. Menahem Azariah in a Responsum forbids any movement at all in prayer.[52] I stormed the battlements time and again in order to discover some compromise whereby some slight and gentle motion of the body to and fro might be permitted, and this alone is permitted in order to bestir the vital powers. The teachers of old used to recite their prayers without any physical sensation. There is a maxim, based on the Zohar, "When they stood, they let down their wings" [Ezek. 1: 24].[53] But these men make wings for themselves wherewith to fly in the heavens. Ask yourself if they would dare to do so in the presence of a king of flesh and blood. Why, he would have them thrown out so that their limbs would be shattered and their bones broken. Verily, if I ever see those who do these things, which our fathers, of blessed memory, the true Hasidim, never dreamed of doing, I shall break their legs with a bar of iron.

It is reported even of a Hasidic master like R. Shneur Zalman of Liady, founder of the intellectual movement in Hasidism known as Habad and opposed to the more bizarre antics of some of his colleagues,[54] that he used to bang his hands on the wall during his prayers so that blood would be found on his hands.[55] Eventually, the Hasidim were obliged to place soft hangings on the wall so that the rabbi would not come to harm. The letter written by the rabbi to Alexander of Szklow is interesting in this connection.[56] In the year 1787 the rabbis of Szklow issued a proclamation against the Hasidic manner of prayer, referring especially to the strange gestures in which the Hasidim indulged. Alexander of Szklow was at first a moderate Mitnagged but afterwards became a disciple of R. Shneur Zalman. He had evidently turned to the rabbi for advice after the attack on the Hasidim by the rabbis of Szklow. The letter of R. Shneur Zalman, part of which has been quoted in a previous chapter, begins:

Though I do not know you personally I have heard that the spirit of God has stirred you not to become involved in the counsel of the scoffers who pour scorn on those who desire to serve the Lord in truth in the service of the heart that is prayer.[57] Although they [the Mitnaggedim] have achieved much in the study of the Torah and through acts of mercy—would that they kept to this in truth all their days—now they have gone too far and have acted illegally when they have gathered together to attack me and to issue a decree of apostasy against prayer. They claim that we must pray as they do, that is, only hurriedly and without any bodily movements or raising of the voice just like those angels on high who have reached a stage than which there is no higher, as it is said, "When they stood, they let down their wings" [Ezek. 1: 24]. But this is only said of the highest rank of angels known as the Seraphim and it does not apply to the other ranks, as it is said,[58] "And the Ophanim and the Holy Beasts with a noise of great rushing." Even of the Seraphim it is written, "A noise of tumult like the noise of a host" [Ezek. 1: 24] and they make great movements as it is said in the Piyutim based on the Pirke Hekhalot.[59] Consequently, there is no proof from the saints of old who were greater than the ministering angels. But dare we, orphans of orphans, imagine that we can compare ourselves to them? It can only be that their heart is evilly disposed and falsehood is in their right hand.

It is interesting to find R. Shneur Zalman quoting the same verse from Ezekiel that R. Jacob Emden quotes. This can only be because it featured in the debates between the Hasidim and their opponents on the value of movement and gesture in prayer. R. Shneur Zalman is aware that the kind of violent movement and shouting aloud in prayer in which the Hasidim indulged was an innovation. He resorts to the defence that immobility and silent prayer was, indeed, once the ideal but it is an ideal only for the saints of old. For an orphaned generation, in which saintliness is lacking, the only way to awaken the powers of concentration is through gesture and strong verbal expression. R. Shneur Zalman's contemporary, R. Mordecai of Czarnobyl, similarly remarks[60] that swaying in prayer is necessary so that all man's psychological powers and all his limbs, bones and sinews should move to awaken the supernal power, the power of En Sof that is contained in the letters of the prayers. This author writes that since the nations of the world have false beliefs, their adherents have no vitality in their prayers and that is why they stand in their houses of worship "like a silent stone." Nevertheless, he concludes, the Jew should learn from them to have decorum in the synagogue, "for great is their respectful and bashful stance in their houses of prayer."

It is clear from the many references to movement and gesture in the early Hasidic writings that the practice was an integral part of Hasidic behaviour from the beginning of Hasidism. It is notoriously difficult to establish how many of the sayings attributed to Baal Shem Tov in Hasidic literature are authentic, but the fact that the early writings do attribute to him sayings in which the practice of violent movement in prayer is defended is itself significant in assessing the extent of such practice in early Hasidism. In one early source[61] it is said:

Rabbi Israel Baal Shem, on whom be peace, said: When a man is drowning in a river and gesticulates while in the water that people should save him from the waters which threaten to sweep him away, the observers will certainly not laugh at him and his gestures. So, too, one should not pour scorn on a man who makes gestures while he prays for he is trying to save himself from the waters of presumption, namely, from the "shells" and strange thoughts which attempt to prevent him from having his mind on his prayers.

The "shells" (qelipot) are, in the Kabbalah, the forces of impurity, so called because they surround the good and are nourished and sustained by it as the bark the tree and the shell the kernel of the nut. The strange thoughts, i.e. thoughts of gain and self-interest and of self in general, intrude to prevent concentration on God. They can only be driven away by physical movements of the body.

In some early Hasidic writings the defence of violent movements during prayer is expressed in crudely erotic terms to the scandal of the Mitnaggedim and the "enlightened" opponents of Hasidism, the Maskilim. The mystical prayer is here described as "copulation" (zivvug) with the Shekhinah. In two passages in particular the erotic element is pronounced. In the first[62] it is said:

This is from the Baal Shem Tov, may his memory be for a blessing, "From my own flesh I behold God."[63] Just as no child can be born as a result of physical copulation unless this is performed with a vitalised organ and with joy and desire, so it is with spiritual copulation, that is, the study of the Torah and prayer. When it is performed with a vitalised organ and with joy and delight then does it give birth.

The second statement[64] is couched in even more direct terms:

Prayer is copulation with the Shekhinah. Just as there is swaying when copulation begins so, too, a man must sway at first and then he can remain immobile and attached to the Shekhinah with great attachment. As a result of his swaying man is able to attain a powerful stage of arousal. For he will ask himself: Why do I sway my body? Presumably it is because the Shekhinah stands over against me. And as a result he will attain to a stage of great enthusiasm.

Joseph Perl, in his satire against Hasidism, *Megalleh temirin*,[65] gives these two passages, and others from the Hasidic writings, as illustrations of the alleged obscene nature of some of the Hasidic works. It is interesting that in the Hasidic anthology by Nahman of Czehryn entitled *Derekh hasidim*,[66] a bowdlerised version of the second passage is quoted with instructions to the reader to consult the work itself for further details. That man's love for God can be expressed on the analogy of erotic human love is not, of course, unknown in Jewish thought. Even so austere a thinker as Maimonides uses erotic imagery[67] and interprets the Song of Songs as a dialogue between God and the individual human soul. Scholem[68] remarks that the Zohar, on the other hand, while it frequently uses erotic symbolism to describe the relationship between the Sefirot of Tiferet and Malkhut, hardly ever uses this kind of symbolism to describe the relationship between God and man, and that the older Kabbalists never interpret the Song of Songs as a dialogue between God and the soul. This latter was left to the later Kabbalists in sixteenth-century Safed. But of Moses the Zohar[69] does say that he had intercourse with the Shekhinah! Tishby[70] has, however, shown that there are, in fact, many passages in the Zohar in which erotic symbolism is used for man's relationship with God and not only with regard to Moses. For instance, the Zohar[71] states that when a man cannot be with his wife, for example, when he is away from home, or when he is studying the Torah, or when she has her periods, then the Shekhinah is with him so that he can be "male and female." There are similar developments in the Christian mystical tradition.[72] The Hasidic passages quoted are still extraordinary in their physical emphasis. It follows from the imagery of the Shekhinah as female and the worshipper as male that women are not normally within the full scope of the Hasidic doctrines on prayer. It is no doubt true that in certain areas Hasidism improved the status of the Jewish woman but, while Hasidic women offered their prayers, they occupied no place in the detailed life of prayer as discussed in the classical Hasidic writings.[73]

Joy and enthusiasm in prayer, mentioned in the first of these passages in connection with swaying, are essential ingredients in the life of prayer as understood by Hasidism.

Prayer recited with great joy is undoubtedly significant and more acceptable to God than prayer recited in a melancholy fashion and with tears. There is a parable to illustrate the matter. When a poor man entreats and supplicates a king of flesh and blood, weeping copiously all the time, all that is given to him, in spite of his tears, is some small thing. But when a prince sings the praises of the king with great joy and, in the course of his praise, he introduces a petition, the king gives him a great gift suitable for an aristocrat.[74]

It is clearly in reaction to Hasidic stress on movements in prayer that R. Hayim of Volozhin laconically remarks,[75] "Swaying in prayer is solely for the purpose of keeping awake, as the *Shelah* observes.[76] But if one sways automatically out of powerful longing and purity of heart how good it is! Apart from this, the obligation is to put soul and sensation into the words" [i.e. and not into physical gestures].

It is not surprising to find a reaction to movement in prayer even among the Hasidim. Indeed, there is evidence of a certain ambivalence in this matter in the early sources themselves as can be seen from the following:[77]

At times one should serve God with the soul alone, that is with thought. At times a man can recite his prayers with love and fear and powerful enthusiasm and yet without any bodily movements at all so that it seems to observers that he is reciting the prayers quite simply and without attachment. A man is capable of doing this when he is greatly attached to God. Then he can serve Him with the soul alone with great and strong love. This kind of worship is better, proceeds more speedily, and becomes more attached to God than prayer that can be witnessed externally through its effect on the limbs of the body. The "shells" have no power to seize hold of such a prayer since it is all of inwardness.

In the passage about the "shells" quoted previously (from the same work!) powerful movements are necessary in order to drive away the distracting thoughts. Here the exact opposite is stated. Inward prayer is too remote from the physical universe to be affected by external distractions. To be sure, Hasidism is not unaware that a worshipper may sway in his prayers with completely sham motives, such as in order to impress others with his piety. There is a saying attributed, though with very doubtful authenticity, to the Baal Shem Tov,[78] in the form of a comment on the verse, "And when the people saw, they swayed, and stood afar off" (Exod. 20: 15). "If a man sways in prayer in order that people might see him [i.e. in order to be admired for his piety] it is a sign that he is afar off, remote from God."

One of the early Hasidic masters, R. Zeev Wolf of Zytomierz, disciple of the Maggid of Miedzyrzecz, is very critical of gestures and loud shouting in prayer, especially when such behaviour is not in accord with the Hasid's true feelings. Critical, here and elsewhere, of some of the Hasidic tendencies among his contemporaries, this author observes:[79]

We can see for ourselves that many are to be found who, at the time of Torah study or prayer, raise their voices too much so that they are heard at a distance. They smite palm to palm and make similar gestures with their limbs and dance on their feet as is the custom. Many of them are ignoramuses who imagine that the main idea of prayer depends on this. The truth is otherwise. It is proper for man to stand when praying in dread and fear. His legs should be straight, his voice should not be heard and only his lips should move. . . . In short a man is expected to weigh his actions in the balance of his mind when he raises his voice in prayer so that he should not raise it higher than the expression he needs to give to the love and fear of God that is in his inmost thoughts. For it is obvious that his heart and mouth must be in one accord, otherwise the letters he utters with his mouth have nothing of that freshness which comes from the illumination from on high that is drawn into them from preconceived thought. . . . The principle is that before a man begins to pray to God he should be filled with love and fear. He should allow the thought of the majesty and greatness of En Sof to enter his mind and then he should recite his prayers with a clear enunciation of the words and gently withal, without any movements of the limbs in order to push away strange thoughts . . .

However, it must be said that in this lengthy passage, of which we have quoted only the gist, R. Zeev Wolf acknowledges that while the ideal is for the worshipper to be so pure that he has no "strange thoughts"; if he has them, then the way to transcend them would seem to be in part by means of violent gestures and raising the voice.

The Lithuanian Hasidic master R. Abraham of Slonim (1804–1884) used to say his prayers silently and without any bodily movements whatsoever, yet, we are told, "his face burned with fire so that whoever saw him became affected with a burning enthusiasm [*hitlahavut*]." In this connection an interpretation of R. Menahem Mendel of Kock is mentioned. R. Menahem Mendel interpreted the verse, "If thou wilt return, O Israel, saith the Lord, yea return unto Me; and if thou wilt put away thy detestable things out of My sight, and will not waver" (Jer. 4: 1), to yield the thought that when a man rises above his physical nature he becomes so filled with the awe of God when he prays that he can only remain immobile in dread and he will not "waver," i.e. sway his body in prayer. It is further said that R. Elimelekh of Lezajsk said of a contemporary who remained completely immobile in prayer that he had such a great dread of God that he was unable to move any of his limbs.[80] Statements such as these demonstrate that by no means all the Hasidim imagined that gestures and bodily movements were essential in the life of prayer.

As for later Hasidism down to the present day, the majority of the Hasidim did perform gestures and movements in prayer and still do so, but some of them, especially the later masters, prepared with complete immobility. We have noted earlier in this chapter that R. Shneur Zalman of Liady, founder of the Habad group, favoured both gesture and vocal expression in prayer. His son, R. Dov Ber (1773–1827), however, adopted the opposite method. R. Shneur Zalman is reported as saying to his son,[81] "For both of us the intellect is in control of the heart but for me it controls only the external heart; but for you it controls even the inner heart." Jacob Kadanir,[82] disciple of R. Dov Ber, claims that he was an eyewitness to his master's prolonged prayer on the New Year festival and that for the three hours of its duration he made not the slightest movement of his body. Kadanir writes further that on such occasion R. Levi Yishaq of Berdyczow, while on a visit to R. Shneur Zalman, requested Dov Ber to recite the grace after meals in order to observe Dov Ber's powerful ecstasy in prayer about which he had heard so much. To R. Levi Yishaq's astonishment, Dov Ber recited the grace without any overt ecstasy at all, as if he understood no more than the bare meaning of the words. When R. Levi Yishaq expressed his surprise, R. Shneur Zalman replied that R. Dov Ber's worship was of a very high order of which he, R. Shneur Zalman, was envious. R. Dov Ber was filled with such an elevated love and fear of God that it could not be experienced at all externally. Only a lofty soul from "the world of concealment" can experience this type of worship while still in the body. The successors of

R. Dov Ber, the Hasidim of the Lubavitcher movement, to this day generally prefer immobile prayer and certainly eschew violent gestures.

It is reported of R. Menahem Mendel of Kock that he used to stand completely immobile in prayer. The only indication that he was engrossed in his prayers was his flushed face and burning eyes. So lost was he in prayer that it used to take him some time afterwards before he became aware of his surroundings.[83] On the other hand, of the Kotzker's disciple and brother-in-law, R. Yishaq Meir of Gur [Góra Kalwarija] (d. 1866), it is reported that his prayers were accompanied by loud cries and strange gestures, with his body bent double. After he had recited his prayers his clothes would be found to be bathed in perspiration. It once happened that in his burning enthusiasm he lost a tooth during his prayers and was unaware of it.[84]

Jiri Langer[85] describes his first personal encounter with prayer at the Hasidic court of Belz on a Friday evening in the second decade of this century. The old rabbi of Belz had advanced to the reading desk in order to lead the Hasidim in the recital of the psalms to welcome the sabbath.

It is as though an electric spark has suddenly entered those present. The crowd which till now has been completely quiet, almost cowed, suddenly bursts forth in a wild shout. None stays in his place. The tall black figures run hither and thither round the synagogue, flashing past the lights of the sabbath candles. Gesticulating wildly, and throwing their whole bodies about, they shout out the words of the Psalms. They knock into each other unconcernedly, for all their cares have been cast aside; everything has ceased to exist for them. They are seized by an indescribable ecstasy. . . . The old man throws himself about as though seized by convulsions. Each shudder of his powerful body, each contraction of his muscles is permeated with the glory of the Most High. Every so often he claps the palms of his hands together symbolically.

Herbert Weiner[86] describes his visit to the Hasidic centre, in the Meah Shearim district in Jerusalem, of the followers of the Hasidic master R. Arele Roth.

"Amen," shrieked the man next to me. He was doubled over, his face red, yelling at the top of his lungs, "Amen—may His great name be blessed for ever, and ever, and ever." For a moment I thought he was ill, but then I saw that all the worshippers were carrying on in the same way. The room resounded with a cacophony of shouts. My guide noticed my bewilderment. One of R. Arele's teachings is that the response, "Amen, may His great name . . ." be recited, as the Talmud suggests, in an utter abandonment of soul, as if one were willing at that moment to die in sanctification of the name.

R. Arele himself, in his ethical will, advised his followers on how to conduct themselves during their prayers.[87]

It is a fundamental principle in connection with prayer that a man should not be embarrassed, God forbid, because people laugh at it. For consider and reflect, my beloved child, that you are engaged in putting right the world, and all worlds and all angels desire every world and every utterance in which you express your nostalgia for the Creator in love and longing. Why should you be concerned with a foolish, brutish and stupid person who cannot discern between his right hand and his left! For all that, when you are among people who are unaccustomed to worship, then you must try to limit it as far as you can so as not to encourage scoffers to pour scorn. And you should not make any peculiar and crazy gestures, God forbid. All the members of our group are fully aware how strict I am about this, and this way is not our way, God forbid. What you should do is to toil with might and self-sacrifice, with the inner and outer organs, and to exercise the mind in toil, in the category of, "Nay, but for Thy sake are we killed all the day" [Ps. 44: 23], which, as is well known, refers to prayer. But as for that which cannot be limited, do not bother to look at the whole world, God forbid, to prevent your giving satisfaction to your Creator. Thus have I seen it written in the work of one of the members of the king's palace, the disciples of the Baal Shem Tov, may his merit shield us and all Israel.

R. Arele's reference to the verse in Psalms is clearly intended to call attention to the Hasidic doctrine of self-annihilation in prayer.

R. Arele's letters of spiritual counsel have been collected and published. In one of them[88] he expresses his strong disapproval of peculiar gesticulation in prayer but not of swaying or of shouting aloud in prayer.

This was the reply I gave to a certain famous man, of the great and famous, who asked me about the peculiar gestures he had observed among some of my disciples. I replied that in reality this was not my way at all but it can be attributed to one of two things. Either the disciple who behaves in this way is a tyro in God's service and then one must allow him the freedom to pursue his own way if, beforehand, he was an inferior person and a sinner, God forfend [i.e. and he behaves in this way in order to escape from his past]. Or else he is an immature disciple who left me after having stayed only for a short time. He acquired some warmth through his association with our company and so forth, but he has not learned a sense of balance so as to be able to assess accurately the type of gesture he makes. This is intelligible. But after he has spent a year or two in beginning to serve God he must then choose a circumspect and moderate way, though inwardly it should be with a spirit of real self-sacrifice, uncomplicated and true. Now I do not mean by this any spirit of indifference, God forbid, such as to cancel out self-sacrifice and toil in prayer with all one's might. This must never be given up even if the whole world protests. For it is like a railway line, from which the train must not be derailed, God forbid. For it is this which brings sanctity and purity to body and soul and which draws down godly vitality to all the limbs and muscles. I refer only to a few imbeciles who make strange noises in their prayers and shake their heads about in a way different from that of the rest of the world, I mean of the world of those who worship God with self-sacrifice. I refer to such strange conduct as glazing the eyes or making odd gestures with other parts of the body. If one notices that sometimes a certain zaddik does these things one should not copy him, for he does so at times because God's fire burns within him. However, as for swaying in the ordinary way, even with all one's strength and in a spirit of real self-sacrifice, and as for reciting the prayers in a loud voice and with effort, with regard to this it is said: "Nay, but for Thy sake are we killed all the day" (Ps. 44: 23). Now how is it possible for a man to kill himself every day? The sacred books of old explain that the verse refers to prayer in an spirit of self-sacrifice and with all one's strength. As it is said [in those books]: How far should the power of prayer reach? Until one [virtually] expires. May the Lord help us to sacrifice ourselves to Him, blessed be He, and to sanctify His name continually. Amen.

As an aid to concentration and *devekut* in prayer, the Hasidim resorted to melody. Much has been written on the general Hasidic attitude to singing and dancing.[89] But this does not apply specifically to prayer. The Hasidim would sing as they sat around the table of the zaddik, on festive occasions, or whenever the opportunity arose. We are concerned here only with the Hasidic use of melody in prayer.

The Jewish tradition knows of special melodies for the prayers. These have been handed down from generation to generation. The Hasidim used these but, in addition, composed original melodies of their own. Some of the zaddikim composed melodies for particular prayers. In Habad Hasidism, with its strong emphasis on contemplative prayer, each Hasid would hum a melody of his own as he reflected on the mysteries of the upper worlds. R. Dov Ber, to whom we have referred earlier, in his *Tract on Ecstasy* observes:[90]

One should begin by considering the subject of melody. What is the nature of melody? There is a well-known saying that the Faithful Shepherd [Moses] used to sing every kind of melody in his prayers. For his soul embraced the six hundred thousand souls of Israel and each soul can only ascend to the root of the Source whence she was hewn by means of song. This is the category we have mentioned of essential ecstasy in which the soul is rooted on high in the supernal delight. He who embraced them all was the Faithful Shepherd who therefore used to sing with every kind of melody, as we have written elsewhere. First, it is necessary to understand the nature of ecstasy produced by melody. This is in the category of spontaneous ecstasy alone, without any choice or intellectual will whatsoever. This is an ecstasy that is felt, and yet the one who experiences it is not himself aware of it, because it does not result from an intention of the self to produce ecstasy, but is produced automatically and comes of its own accord without its being known to him. Since it is as if it is not felt or known to him at that very moment, it can be said that there is a total lack of self-awareness. But, for all that, it is an experienced ecstasy.

R. Dov Ber uses the illustration of music to demonstrate the possibility of rapture in prayer without self-awareness, a contradiction on the face of it. It is possible, declares R. Dov Ber, for the self to have a profoundly ecstatic experience, as when one is moved by a melody, and yet to be so involved as to be lost in the music. The self of the Hasid can similarly experience the nearness of God to the extent that he is moved to ecstasy and yet be unaware of the self, so lost is he in God at that time. It can justifiably be inferred from this that R. Dov Ber would have favoured the use of melody as an aid to contemplation. In fact, he had in his court an expert choir and orchestra, though, of course, the latter did not play during the prayers.

R. Elimelekh of Lezajsk speaks of some zaddikim of his day who sang the sweetest spontaneous melodies as they prayed even though, normally, their voices were far from tuneful.[91] Hasidic legend tells of a visit to R. Elimelekh by the Baal Shem Tov's cantor.[92] This man when young had no voice, but once the Baal Shem Tov had "bound him to the world of melody" there was no one in the whole world who could sing so sweetly. R. Moses of Kozienice[93] reports in the name of his teacher, R. Meshullam Zusya of Annopol (d. 1800), R. Elimelekh's brother, that both worship of God with tears and weeping and worship of God with joy and song are acceptable to Him, but that worship in tears is capable of achieving only limited results while worship in joy and song can achieve results without limit. R. Meshullam Zusya paraphrases Psalm 126: 6 as, "Though he goeth on his way weeping he beareth the measure of the seed, but if he goeth with joy he shall bear his sheaves."

As we have seen, R. Dov Ber of Lubavitch devotes some of his work to the philosophy of melody in prayer. This theme is especially prominent among Habad writers. In the work *Magen Avot* by R. Solomon Zalman of Kopust (1830–1900), a great-great-grandson of R. Shneur Zalman, the founder of Habad, there are detailed theories regarding the role of melody in prayer.[94] R. Solomon Zalman observes[95] that the three colours of white, red and green can be expressed in melody. The meaning of this is that in the Kabbalah the colour white symbolises mercy (the Sefirah Hesed), red symbolises judgement (the Sefirah Gevurah), and green symbolises the harmony between the two (the Sefirah Tiferet). The three "colours" of the melody are the way in which the worshipper, as he sings in his prayers, brings his contemplation to bear on these three aspects of the Sefirotic realm. Elsewhere[96] R. Solomon Zalman remarks that, in order to bring down the divine vitality from the upper worlds, the worshipper has to so sing in his prayers that it is as if his soul were ready to expire in longing for God.

NOTES

1. *Keter shem tov* (Jerusalem, 1968), p. 22b.
2. "Contemplative Prayer in Hasidism," in *Studies in Mysticism and Religion presented to G. Scholem,* (Jerusalem, 1967), p. 209.
3. Schatz, p. 210.
4. Ber. 21a; Sukk. 38a, but see Maimonides *Yad, Tefillah* 1:1 and *Kesef Mishnah* ad loc.
5. Shabb. 10a.
6. Shabb. 11a.
7. D. Z. Hillmann, *Iggerot baal ha-tanya* (Jerusalem, 1953), no. 21, pp. 33–4.
8. *Maor va-shemesh* (Tel Aviv, 1965), *va-yehi,* to Gen. 49: 22, p. 56b.
9. Ber. 32b.
10. *Maor va-shemesh, va-yese,* to Gen. 28: 16–17, p. 30b. The Midrash quoted is in the *Yalkut* to Gen. 28: 16.
11. (n.p., n.d.), pp. 8–9.
12. "Devekut, or Communion with God" and now reprinted in his *The Messianic Idea in Judaism* (New York, 1971), pp. 203–27, and as chapter 8 in this volume.
13. Solomon of Luck, *Maggid devarav le-yaaqov* (Jerusalem, 1962), pp. 134–5, s.v. *ve-es ha-hayim be-tokh ha-gan.*
14. *Savaat ha-ribash* (Jerusalem, 1948), p. 2.
15. *Ben porat yosef* (Korzec, 1781), p. 53a, in the name of R. Nahman of Kosów but on p. 23b in the name of "R.I."? In *Toledot yaaqov yosef* (Warsaw, 1881), p. 176b, *va-ethanan,* he simply says that he "heard this." Cf. A. J. Heschel, "R. Nahman of Kosov," in Harry A. Wolfson Jubilee Volume (Jerusalem, 1965), p. 130 and *Sefer Baal Shem Tov* (Sotmar, 1943), vol. 1, p. 143, note 9.
16. *Toledot, va-ethanan* p. 176b.
17. *Degel mahane efrayim* (Jerusalem, 1963), *haftarah ki tese,* p. 253.
18. Avot 1: 3.

19. *Keter shem tov,* p. 9a.

20. Ibid., p. 14a–b.

21. *Degel mahane efrayim, toledot,* p. 34.

22. *Degel mahane efrayim,* p. 283.

23. *Tolèdot, kedoshim,* pp. 100b–101a.

24. *Maggid devarav le-yaaqov,* p. 101.

25. *Maggid devarav le-yaaqov,* p. 84.

26. *Or ha-meir* (Jerusalem, 1968), vol. 2, *derush le-rosh ha-shanah,* p. 258a. The same comment in shorter form is given in *Maggid devarav le-yaaqov,* pp. 16–17.

27. *Ha-hasidut ke-mistikah* (Jerusalem, 1968), Chapter 6, pp. 78–95. This is the same author as the Rivka Schatz quoted earlier.

28. *Enthusiasm* (Oxford, 1957), p. 254.

29. *Sav ve-ziruz* (Jerusalem, 1962), pp. 6–7.

30. See e.g. the section on this theme in R. Arele Roth's *Shomer èmunim* (Jerusalem, 1966), vol. 1, pp. 95a–98a.

31. R. Moses of Kozienice, *Beer moshe* (New York, 1964), *shemini aseret,* p. 195a.

32. Ber. 34a.

33. Ber. 34a–b.

34. Ber. 31a.

35. See the letter in defence of Hasidism by this teacher in M. Wilensky, *Hasidim u-mitnaggedim* (Jerusalem, 1970), vol. 1, pp. 84–8.

36. III, 218b–219a.

37. II, 79–80.

38. Orah Hayim 48: 1.

39. *Shelah,* part 2, *inyane tefillah,* p. 79.

40. *Magen avraham* to Orah hayim 48: 1, note 4.

41. Quoted, as a tale current among the Hasidim, by A. Wertheim, *Halakhot ve-halikhot ba-hasidut* (Jerusalem, 1960), p. 103, note 82.

42. Ber. 10b.

43. *Noam elimelekh* (Jerusalem, n.d.) to Lev. 23: 6, p. 99.

44. *Noam elimelekh* to Lev. 19: 4, p. 94; to Lev. 23: 6, p. 99; to Exod. 30: 12, pp. 78–9.

45. *Likkute maharan* (Bene Berak, 1965), no. 156, p. 105b.

46. On R. Abraham of Kalisk see the notes in my translation of *Tract on Ecstasy* by Dov Baer of Lubavitch (London, 1963), pp. 34–5. R. Shneur Zalman of Liady, in a letter to Abraham of Kalisk (D. Z. Hillmann: *Iggerot baal ha-tanya* [Jerusalem, 1953], p. 175) reminds him of the Maggid's displeasure and the Maggid's rebuke to him in 1772 precisely for the practice of turning somersaults. For R. Hayim Haikel of Amdur see S. Dubnow, *Toledot ha-hasidut* (Tel Aviv, 1967), pp. 132, 367–72. Dubnow, p. 132, quotes the saying of the Hasidim defending the practice of turning somersaults, *"Az es kumt zu menschen gadlus azoi mus er sich übervarfen"* (When a man is afflicted with pride he must turn himself over").

47. See Knox, pp. 558f.

48. *Mitpahat sefarim* (Altona, 1768), p. 31.
49. Ber. 32b.
50. Yev. 105b; Shulhan Arukh, Orah Hayim 95: 2.
51. Evidently referring to Shulhan Arukh, Orah Hayim 125:1, "One should raise the eyes on high when reciting the Kedushah," see *Ture zahav* ad loc. who quotes the Tanhuma and argues that the eyes should be closed.
52. R. Menahem Azariah of Fano, *Responsa* (Venice, n.d.), no. 113.
53. I.e. when the angels stood their wings did not move and so, too, when man stands in prayer there should be no bodily movement.
54. See note 46 above.
55. H. M. Hielmann, *Bet rabbi* (Berditchev, 1903), p. 16a, note 2.
56. Hillmann, pp. 33–4.
57. That prayer is "service of the heart" is stated in Taan. 2a.
58. In the Prayer Book, see Singer's Prayer Book, new ed. (London, 1962), p. 40.
59. The *Pirke Hekhalot* are late Midrashim on the angelic hosts and their praises. The *Piyutim* are the liturgical poems composed in the Middle Ages.
60. *Likkute torah* (Israel, n.d.), *Hadrakhah* 7, p. 8a.
61. *Keter shem tov*, p. 24a–b.
62. *Keter shem tov,* p. 3b.
63. This interpretation of Job 19: 26, that man can know God by observing his own physiological and psychological make-up and processes, was first put forward in the Middle Ages (for the details see A. Altmann, "The Delphic Maxim in Medieval Islam and Judaism," in his *Studies in Religious Philosophy and Mysticism* (London and Ithaca, 1969)) and was very popular with the Hasidim.
64. *Savaat ha-ribash* (Jerusalem, 1948), p. 7b; *Liqute yeqarim* (Lemberg, 1865), p. 1b; *Sefer shem tov* (Sotmar, 1943), vol. 1, p. 145, note 65.
65. Lemberg, 1864, p. 40a (wrongly printed as "50"), note 7.
66. Jerusalem, 1962, no. 42, p. 411.
67. *Yad, Teshuvah,* 10.
68. *Major Trends in Jewish Mysticism*, 3rd rev. ed. (New York, 1954; London, 1955), pp. 226–7.
69. I, 21b–22a.
70. *Mishnat ha-zohar*, 2nd ed. (Jerusalem, 1957), vol. 2, pp. 280–301.
71. I, 49–50a and 230a.
72. See David Knowles, *Western Mysticism*, 3rd ed. (London, 1967), pp. 110f.
73. On the position of women in Hasidism, see S. A. Horodetzsky, *Ha-hasidut ve-ha-hasidim* (Tel Aviv, 1951), vol. 4, 67–71; H. Rabinowicz, *The World of Hasidism* (London, 1970), pp. 202–10.
74. *Keter shem tov*, p. 25b.
75. *Keter rosh*, printed at end of *Siddur ishe Yisrael*, no. 29, p. 527.
76. See note 39 above.
77. *Keter shem tov*, p. 26a.
78. *Yalkut moshe*, quoted in *Sefer Baal Shem Tov*, vol. 2, p. 31a.
79. *Or ha-meir, terumah*, pp. 68b–69a.

80. For these details see M. H. Kleinmann, *Or yesharim* (Jerusalem, 1967), p. 84b.
81. Hielmann, part 2, p. 4, note 3.
82. *Sippurim noraim* (Lemberg, 1875), no pagination.
83. Alfasi, *Ha-hasidut*, pp. 141–2.
84. Alfasi, *Gur*, p. 157.
85. *Nine Gates* (London, 1961), pp. 6–8.
86. *Nine and One Half Mystics* (New York, 1969), p. 209.
87. *Shomer emunim*, vol. 2, p. 291a.
88. *Iggerot shomer emunim* (Jerusalem, 1942), no. 44, pp. 63a–64b.
89. See M. S. Geshuri, *Ha-Niggun ve-ha-riqud ba-hasidut* (Tel Aviv, 1955); T. Ysander, *Studien zum Beschtschen Hasidismus* (Uppsala, 1933), pp. 317–320; Wertheim, pp. 103–6; Rabinowicz, Chapter 20, pp. 192–201.
90. *Kunteros ha-hitpaalut*, in Hillel ben Meir of Poritch, *Liqute biurim* (Warsaw, 1865), p. 11a–b, pp. 76–7 in my translation.
91. In the letter of his son Eleazar printed at end of *Noam elimelekh* in various editions.
92. Quoted from a MS. of R. Yishaq Eisik of Komarno in R. Arele Roth's *Shomer emunim*, vol. 1, p. 33b, note 37.
93. *Beer moshe* (New York, 1964), *mishpatim*, p. 57a.
94. The remarks in this passage follow Geshuri, pp. 249–60.
95. *Magen avot, yitro*.
96. *Magen avot, va-yiqra*.

11

Traditions and Customs in Hasidism

Aaron Wertheim

THE HASIDIC WAY OF PREPARING FOR THE SABBATH
AND OBSERVING IT

The Purification Bath in Honor of the Sabbath

Immersion in the *miqveh* (ritual bath) for the purpose of spiritual purification is not mentioned in the Talmud (as far as males are concerned) except for the cleansing required after contact with the dead and after a nocturnal emission of semen. There is no reference to the ritual bath as part of the preparations to welcome the Sabbath or holidays,[1] but in kabbalistic writings of the Lurianic school we find much attention lavished on the importance of immersion not only on the eve of the Sabbath but also on the morning of the Sabbath itself.[2] This provided the inspiration for the early Hasidic leaders who were much taken with this idea. Special meditative preambles *(kavvanot)*, attributed to the Besht, were formulated for recitation upon entering the ritual bath, beginning with the words: "for the sake of observing the Sabbath in full." Immersion is called "[a step] preparatory to making oneself fit for the holiness and purity demanded for welcoming the Sabbath."[3] And, as R. Aaron of Karlin wrote,[4] "It is well worth walking a mile for the sake of performing the rite of *miqveh* on a Friday afternoon, and three miles—were that permissible—for a Sabbath morning immersion" (the distance one is permitted to walk on the Sabbath being restricted).

Reprinted by permission of Mosad Harav Kook from *Halakhot ve halikhot ba-hasidut,* by Aaron Wertheim, 1960.

The custom of Sabbath immersions constituted one more occasion for the anti-Hasidic rabbis to vent their anger against the Hasidim, for such baths could be suspect on religious grounds: Bathing on Sabbath morning might be construed as contravening Sabbath laws forbidding rubbing off hair. For that reason, Hasidim took care not to dry their hair, beard or sidelocks with a towel, but they never doubted the propriety of the immersion itself, relying as they did on the Lurianic precedent.

This was one of the customs understood as an obligatory aspect of being a Hasid. The Hasidim made much of its importance, comparing the eve of the Sabbath to the eve of Yom Kippur: "A person must review his behavior [as carefully] as on the eve of Yom Kippur." For that reason, he must "prepare himself for purity and sanctity by the *miqveh* just as on the eve of Yom Kippur."[5] Such was the importance attached to this rite, that Hasidic custom permitted even the bereaved, in the first week after suffering the loss of a member of the family, to be ritually cleansed. Citing the Ari (R. Isaac Luria) as their authority, Hasidim said: "The entire essence of [the rules of] mourning lies in honoring the dead, and the dead are certain to care if they are the cause of his [the bereaved's] violation of the sanctity of the Sabbath."[6] Likewise, Hasidim would perform the Sabbath immersions even on the eve of the solemn Sabbath preceding the Fast of the Ninth of Av and on the Sabbath morning following.

Silk Garments for Sabbath and Holidays

As early as the days of the Talmudic sages of antiquity, it was the Jewish custom to don special clothes in honor of the Sabbath and holidays.[7] Naturally, these were of finer quality than the workaday clothing worn all week long. During the long course of the Exile, when Jews were sorely pressed by the restrictions they faced in earning a decent livelihood, the Sabbath remained their only release from such burdens and their sole opportunity to indulge their spiritual as well as their bodily hunger. Many Jewish brethren took to decking themselves out in silken and embroidered finery to such an extent that they incurred the anger of their religious leaders; for such fancy luxuries were bound to arouse envy and hatred on the part of their non-Jewish neighbors, and apt to provoke rivalry and internal tensions in Jewish society as well. Each woman would attempt to outdo her neighbors. For these reasons, Jewish prohibitions aimed at such practices were enacted in various countries.[8] The Council of the Four (Polish) Lands enacted a provision several times over the course of a hundred years and more—from 1628 to 1761— stating "that no Jewish person shall wear luxurious silk, velvet or satin clothing or costly garments of white linen."[9] One enactment of the Council[10] proscribed even worn-out silk garments, except for Sabbaths and holidays. As we know, the period in which the Council became defunct [1764] coincided with the rise of Hasidism.

The earliest zaddikim maintained the custom of dressing in white for the Sabbath—white having entered kabbalist tradition as a symbol of divine virtue.[11] According to the ban against Hasidism enacted by the Jewish community of Brody (1772), the custom had been adopted by many of the Hasidic rank and file as well,[12] prompting the communal elders to decide: "No one may wear white on Sabbaths and holidays except for a few prominent persons." The custom soon fell into disuse, however, and even the zaddikim made do with "ordinary" silk. Still, special design requirements were often adhered to for Sabbath-wear: Caftans were floor-length, with button clasps reaching all the way to the neck. The trousers were white, rather than black, and long white stockings were pulled over the trouser legs, up to the knees.

This ensemble became virtually de rigueur among Hasidim, particularly in the Polish and Galician districts. Bridegrooms' marriage trousseaus normally included a silk Sabbath robe. So much importance was attached to this outfit that people would continue wearing it for Sabbath prayers regardless of the condition it was in, even when it became ragged and patched, simply because it met the condition of being made of silk. Other clothes—newer and more presentable, perhaps—would not serve as well.

There were some zaddikim who on principle[13] wore only satin or velvet, explaining this by saying that the word "satin" *(atlas)* was an acronym signifying "this indeed is fit solely for Israel" *(akh tov le-yisrael selah)*, and that velvet *(samet* or *samut)* stood for "avoid evil and do good" *(sur me-ra va'asei tov)*.

Establishing Common Domain *(Tiqqun 'eruvin)*

The prohibition barring the removal of objects on the Sabbath from one domain (private or public) to another (private) one was troublesome for neighbors living in close proximity around a single courtyard or entrance way. This had prompted the sages of the Mishnaic period (first to second century C.E.) to determine that shared access areas such as courtyards and doorways might be considered common to both neighbors' domains, and therefore did not constitute a boundary for the purposes of carrying objects on the Sabbath. In the days when Jews lived in enclosed ghettos, the ghetto itself became a single "yard" and carrying was permitted under the common-domain principle. The early sages invoked this concept when they conducted a Passover Eve ceremony that united members of the community into one symbolic household: They would bake a single piece of matzah to be shared among the townsfolk, and thus symbolically initiate a license "to carry objects from one domain to another in [common] courtyards and entranceways throughout the year."[14]

As Jews settled on the Ukrainian steppe and in the Galician countryside, their homes were more spaciously set apart than in the familiar huddle of the ghetto. There could be no question, in the new circumstances, of common entranceways. In these *shtetlakh* (hamlets) each house, with its own courtyard, constituted a separate domain unto itself. Since the old method of establishing common domain for adjoining properties was no longer applicable, other methods were introduced. These innovative methods involved a legal fiction creating a single domain out of an entire town and its streets, as if they constituted a single system of common courtyards and doorways. This dispensation made it legally possible to carry objects freely from place to place. Special efforts were required to effect this solution. At the ends of each street (leading to the edge of town) a "portal" of some sort had to be erected—two pillars supporting a crossbeam or metal wire—so that the entire town would be encompassed by partitions or beams that created one large domain with multiple entrances. Wardens responsible for certifying that these connectors remained intact were appointed. (Such arrangements were popularly termed *'eruvin* [mixing or amalgamation; sing.: *'eruv*], even though that is something of a misnomer, the Talmudic term actually referring to the bread or matzah that joined together or amalgamated properties around a single access area.)

Hasidim made extensive use of this arrangement to permit the carrying of objects on the Sabbath within a *shtetl*. The Besht is said to have claimed that the widespread establishment of the *'eruv* was one of the three principal missions he sought to accomplish, along with *zeviha* (punctilious methods in kosher slaughtering) and *miqveh*. Together, the names of these three practices formed the acronym *za'am*, recalling the word that figures in the biblical passage (Habakkuk 3: 12), "Thou dost march through the land with indignation *[za'am]*." Hence, the implication was that these three practices were the means of "marching through the land"—making the world as it ought to be.[15]

Anyone familiar with Jewish life in the small East European towns will readily appreciate the importance of the *'eruv*. In *shtetlakh* equipped with one, the flavor of the Sabbath was considerably enhanced. If a fault occurred in an *'eruv*, producing a situation in which carrying on the Sabbath had temporarily to be suspended, the nuisance and burdens this involved were immediately palpable. Men could no longer carry their *tallith* (prayer shawl) and prayer book to the synagogue, or bring wine for the after-prayers *kiddush* (wine benediction). Hasidim found the *'eruv* particularly helpful, since they habitually foregathered on late Sabbath afternoons for table fellowship *(se'udah shlishit)*. And the arrival of a zaddik in town was the occasion for an entire round of festive meals, young and old converging on the zaddik's table. Food and drinks of all kinds were taken back and forth from every house; if, God forbid, the *'eruv* was not as it should be, the entire celebration could be ruined, it being otherwise impossible to set a proper collective table.

In all the Hasidic towns special care was taken to carry out the will of the Besht by keeping the *'eruvin* in constant repair. Even in recent times, when many Jews were forced once more to take up the wanderer's staff and search for a safe haven across the sea, tens of thousands arriving in the United States of America where they helped to build the city with the greatest Jewish population in the world—New York— there, too, a scion of the Hasidic leaders[16] took it upon himself to endeavor to set up *'eruvin*. He thereby aroused deep anger against himself on the part of the rabbis there, who feared that in such an impious generation people would take improper advantage of the right to carry permissible objects and begin to carry what was impermissible on the Sabbath. Also, they feared that the people at large would fail to make the proper distinction between streets that were included in the *'eruv* area and those that were not.

Tallith on Friday Nights

Many zaddikim used to don a *tallith* on Friday nights, too,[17] even when they were not leading the prayer service.[18] Although, according to religious law, there is no need to wear a *tallith* at such times ("nighttime is not the time for *sisit* (fringes)"),[19] they followed the custom of the Ari and his disciples, who mentioned the practice in the prayer books they composed.[20]

Spices and Myrtle Branches on Friday Night

There were zaddikim who used to pronounce blessings over spices and myrtle on Fridays, before the Sabbath eve *kiddush*. The custom is originally mentioned in the Talmud, in a story about R. Simon bar Yohai,[21] who came upon a certain old man running on Sabbath eve close to twilight, holding two myrtle branches. R. Simon asked him: "For whom are these?" to which the man replied: "In honor of the Sabbath." "And isn't one enough?" to which he replied, that two were required (just as two candles must be lit), in keeping with the dual wording (*zachor*—remember—and *shamor*—observe) in the biblical commandment to observe the Sabbath. Kabbalists expounded at length on the significance of this custom, explaining it in terms of mystical teachings.[22]

Food for the Sabbath

Ever since antiquity, special Sabbath foods have been mentioned in the laws and customs governing the holy day. In Talmudic times[23] it was usual to enhance the Sabbath joy "with a dish containing spinach, large fish and garlic cloves." The sages of the Talmud devoted much attention to the importance of this mitzvah, and their tale of "Joseph who honored the Sabbath"[24] was always one of the favorite Hebrew children's stories. Over the generations it was practically assumed that both fish[25] and meat, as well as wine, should be served at the Sabbath table on Friday nights. There were some places[26] during the Middle Ages where a pudding of sorts *(kugel)* was served, meant to be reminiscent of the manna in the desert that was coated on both sides. The custom spread throughout the Jewish settlements of Germany, Poland and Ukraine. Apples, too, were associated with the Friday night observances of kabbalists,[27] who saw in the apple an allusion to the "fields of sacred apples" mentioned in a Friday night song (taken from the Zohar; the word "apple" —*tapuah*—is an acronym that refers to the revelation of the mystical knowledge of Torah).

When Hasidism arose, new significance was added to the notion of special Sabbath foods. Hasidim found reasons for the consumption of each item and even inaugurated a set number of dishes and a fixed order in which the foods were to be eaten. They refused to depart from this schedule even by one iota, and should a youngster have dared to question the need for any one of the dishes and refrain from eating it, he was immediately suspected of having absorbed some heresy, for he was questioning the very sanctity of the Sabbath itself!

Among the zaddikim, especially those who were descendants of the Besht, the Friday night meal included a cereal pudding (*farfel* in Yiddish). They claimed that the Besht had related this Sabbath observance and the heavenly decision to forgive the Sabbath-observer his sins, which were then *farfalen*—that is, nullified and forgiven.[28]

It was said in the name of R. Pinhas of Korzec that noodles were a proper food for the Sabbath, since they symbolized unity, for noodles become interwoven in one mass. Thus, they might be seen as alluding to Sabbath peace.[29]

Another Sabbath dish was cooked from cows' feet,[30] and a staple item on the Sabbath menu was onion and radish,[31] for which a specific purpose was found. And they would do as the Besht was said to do: They said *kiddush* Sabbath mornings over a sweet drink "so that the harsh judgment [of heaven] might be sweetened," and over brandy, to "burn" the force of heaven's judgment.[32]

Hasidic books warned against eating fewer dishes than required during the Sabbath daytime meal. The number was set at ten, to represent the ten "spheres" of divinity (in kabbalist lore). The pastry was of particular importance, because it was accounted as the symbolic counterpart of the "sphere" called *yesod* (the "basis" or "foundation" of all active forces in God, placed between the immanent "kingdom" (*malkhut*) of God and the "majesty" [*Hod*] of God).[33] The *yesod,* in Hasidim, was analogous to the zaddik, an idea that was related to the biblical verse (Proverbs 10:25), "The righteous is an everlasting foundation" (*zaddik yesod 'olam*).

The Twelve Challahs (Hallot)

The Hasidic leaders determined that the custom mentioned in the Lurianic books,[34] of baking twelve loaves and setting them on the table for each of the Sabbath meals, ought to be considered mandatory. The simple reason given was that these loaves were meant to recall the shewbread of the ancient Temple service, which were set each Sabbath upon the golden table. But there were additional reasons, related to kabbalistic ideas.[35]

This custom was adopted by Hasidim throughout the Ukraine and in the greater part of Poland and Galicia as well. In Ukrainian *shtetlakh* another custom developed from this: baking one large challah loaf made up of twelve parts, known in Yiddish as a *yudbeysnik* (i.e., "a twelve-nik"). This challah was meant for the first Sabbath meal, held on Friday night. But on a Sabbath on which a zaddik came to sit together with his Hasidim at table, the setting of the challahs was made in front of him, and no one else. If, however, there was a second zaddik present to whom the first one deferred, twelve challahs were set before him, too.[36]

The twelve loaves were arranged in a prescribed order.[37] After the rabbi said the blessing, the loaf would be divided among those in attendance, usually at the table fellowship held for the final Sabbath meal. This was in imitation of the way the Temple priests of old would divide the shewbread among themselves at the conclusion of the Sabbath.[38]

"Sixth" in Place of "Third"

The order of priority for calling Jews to the lectern for the reading of the weekly Torah portion was long ago established by the Talmudic sages: "A priest *[cohen]* reads first and after him a Levite, after him come scholars who hold office as communal leaders, and after them come scholars who are worthy of holding public office, after them leaders of congregations and then anyone may read."[39] This rule of placing the most important reader third was formally set down as having the force of law in the *Shulhan 'arukh* (legal code).[40] That was the universal procedure among Jews everywhere, and the most eminent person present in the synagogue would normally be called third.

But the Hasidic leaders changed the custom in accordance with kabbalistic teaching,[41] making the sixth reader the most important. All the zaddikim used to be called to the lectern as "sixth," rather than "third," and in all Hasidic houses of worship it was the most highly regarded Hasid present who was given this honor.

The Third, or Final, Sabbath Meal

The Talmudic sages made it incumbent upon all Jews to eat three full meals on the Sabbath, basing themselves on Scripture.[42] Halakhic authorities, both of the early and later Middle Ages, devoted much attention to the details involved in these three meals. In the *Tur* (law code) and in the *Shulhan 'arukh,* a separate section[43] of the law code was assigned to this matter. The section begins: "[The Jew] should be sure to eat the third meal. . . ." The kabbalistic masters, too, were of the opinion that this meal was of especial significance, and would make it the most joyous of occasions.[44] But none of the halakhic authorities make mention of turning the third meal into a public event at the study hall *(beit midrash).* This was an innovation introduced by the Hasidim, for whom the third meal was a collective one, a rite of table fellowship accompanied by spiritual songs and melodies and by words of Torah and Hasidic philosophy.[45]

At this meal, the absolute minimum of bread and fish was all that had to be consumed; meat or other dishes were generally not served.[46] Thus, the essence of the meal was in its spiritual, not material, content. For that reason, Hasidim believed that it was this meal that constituted the real *tiqqun* (mystical purpose, consecration) of their Sabbath.[47] When a Hasid would travel to the place where his rebbe resided, or when a zaddik came to town, it was to this, third meal that everyone was drawn, flocking to the zaddik's table as soon as the first hint of evening appeared. This was the time when they felt the full impact and meaning of the Sabbath's sanctity, and it was on this occasion that the zaddik would preach the core of his message. And the Hasidim believed that even souls of the departed would gather to hear the Torah spoken by the zaddik, and so they did not hurry to light any lamps, "lest the souls perceive a this-worldly luminosity and it would become dark for them."[48]

Hasidic lore tells us that the Besht:

once observed the Sabbath in a certain village, together with his prayer quorum, and when it came time for the third meal, the *arendar* of that village gathered some of the [Jewish] villagers, too, and he sat and ate and drank with them with songs of praise. The Besht—may his great merit be our shield—noted this, seeing that this was very acceptable on high, and afterward asked him why he did so, spending so much on the third meal? And he answered him: "I have heard people say, 'Let my soul depart among people of Israel,' and I heard that on the Sabbath each Jew receives an extra soul, which departs from him on the conclusion of the Sabbath, so I also said to myself, let my extra soul depart among people of Israel; therefore I gather Jews together for this meal."[49]

What beauty lies in this villager's simple understanding! The Hasidic movement recognized that quality, was able to honor it, and perpetuated the memory of it.

The *Melaveh Malka* after the Conclusion of the Sabbath

The meal on Saturday night, after the end of the Sabbath, known as *melaveh malka*—"escorting the queen"—(expressing the idea that one honors the Sabbath on its departure as a person honors a queen by conducting her out of a city at the end of a state visit) is mentioned in the Talmud[50] and in halakhic literature of the Middle Ages. In the *Shulhan 'arukh* law codes it merits its own section, "so that its importance not be demeaned."[51] Yet, it did not come fully into its own until the advent of Hasidism. They enhanced its importance considerably and celebrated it in unison, all the Hasidim of the community joining in, amid songs and melodies. They rated its value very highly and considered it certain to have a beneficial role in curing all manner of sickness and even in aiding those who had "difficulty in having children."[52]

There were some zaddikim who held this meal as long as three days after the Sabbath; it was not essential to hold it on Saturday night, but more important that it be held in the company of a group.[53]

In addition, it was the custom on Saturday night to relate one tale about the Baal Shem Tov, something that was considered to be of particular value, and "of known benefit for all matters pertaining to both body and soul" throughout the week ahead.[54]

THE HASID, THE ZADDIK, AND THEIR MUTUAL OBLIGATIONS

The Hasid and His Duties

The idea of the Hasidic zaddik and his function, and the place of the Hasid in relation to the zaddik, were first outlined in the teachings of the founder of Hasidism, the Besht. It is the duty of the simple person to attach himself to the great spirits of the age, who in turn will take the prayers of the simple man and his religious aspirations and raise them to heaven.[55] The rabbi (Yaaqov Yosef ha-Cohen) of Polonne explained this point at length:

Providing formulae for religious intent *[kavvanot]* for prayer is not for everyone, but only for the chosen few. For those [the select ones] may be considered in the category of "drunk, but not with wine" with respect to the burdens of the Exile: Like a drunkard who throws off the yoke of Torah but accepts the yoke of worldly authorities, only the reverse—the chosen few, once they take upon themselves the yoke of Torah, they are called free men with respect to the drunkenness of Exile. Therefore, to them are entrusted the consciousness and the soul of prayer. Behold how God, Blessed be He, in His desire for goodness, offered us the six hundred and thirteen commandments as the proper way. And He joined two of the commandments together: "Him shall ye serve"—that is prayer; and "Unto Him shall ye cleave"[56]—that is, cleave unto the Torah sages *[talmidei hakhamim]*. That is a great principle which the Torah tries to teach us, through implication: namely, that the body has no life unless it is linked to the soul. Therefore, it is the soul that sustains the life of the body. The opposite occurs when the soul departs from the body, and that is the case when the common masses are separated from the few great ones of each generation. This is the hidden truth to which the Ari, of blessed memory, alluded when he taught that one ought to give precedence to the commandment "love thy neighbor as thyself" over that of prayer. For when one loves in one's heart all of Israel, then one's prayer will be at one with the prayer of those of perfect faith *[shelomei emunei yisrael]*, those who know the inner meaning of prayer.[57]

בהקוב

The bond spoken of here is a mutual one, for the soul requires the body as much as the body requires the soul, and that is how the rabbi explained the meaning of the verse: "Now command the children of Israel that they bring you pure olive oil":

That is, when you, Moses—he is the zaddik—will be of one communion and one company with the children of Israel so as to raise them up to do good once more, only then will "they bring you," and you, too, will derive goodness and greatness from this.[58]

The unsophisticated Hasid must believe in his rebbe, because the "pipelines of [heavenly] influence" are in his hands, and he (the rebbe) may bring great influence to bear for the good of each person who attaches himself to him. Such benefit can accrue not only in the sense of this-worldly rewards, but also after the death, in "the next world."[59] The zaddik is granted "custodianship over all the benefits and all the means *[hashpa'ot]* that can affect the life of a Jew."[60] And "the zaddik has the power to do anything, including the power to bring the Messiah,"[61] if only the people of that generation are deserving of it. After the death of his zaddik, it is better for a Hasid to attach himself to the sons who are his heirs, rather than search for a new rebbe.[62] For the most part, Hasidim retained their loyalty to the dynasties of their own rebbes.

This form of attachment, which may be traced back to its sources in the teachings of the Besht and of his disciple, the rabbi of Polonne, is entirely of a spiritual nature and does not require money or gifts to be given by the Hasid to his rebbe. The Hasid has the ability, and may take the opportunity every day—however far he may be from his rebbe physically—to unite himself in his own mind, and for his own good, with his rebbe. "And should he require some kind of salvation or any thing, let him conjure up the image of the zaddik in his mind, and he will certainly gain the salvation he needs."[63] Over the course of time, however, this bond also took on the implication of a material obligation on the part of the Hasid to contribute to the upkeep of his rebbe's household and support his regular and irregular expenses. In general, Hasidim would pay fixed annual payments, called *ma'amadot,* and these funds were given to the *gabbaim* or collectors who came to each city. Apart from this, Hasidim would give donations to the rebbe himself, in his actual presence, such as when requesting a blessing.

Such visits to the rebbe, which took place at frequent intervals throughout the year, were also one of the duties of the Hasid. Anyone who neglected this duty soon lost status among the group, and the contrary was also true: Greater frequency enhanced the fulfillment of this obligation. Another of the duties assumed by the Hasid was to partake of the rebbe's table. Whether he was lucky enough to be seated at the table itself or was among those crowding around, he felt glad of his great fortune as a participant. When he could actually eat the food that had been sanctified by the rebbe himself, from the rebbe's plate, this was considered the height of pure joy. We shall consider these material obligations of the Hasid vis-à-vis the zaddik in a bit greater depth, as they are very important, and we shall examine their substance as well as their historical provenance.

Pilgrimage to the Rebbe

Beyond "consulting" the rebbe by mental projection, in addition to the inner sustenance that the Hasid derived from the teachings of his rebbe that were reported to him by others, and apart from the occasions on which the rebbe visited the town in which the Hasid lived, each Hasid was expected also to travel to see his rebbe at fixed times.

The source of this custom lies in a Talmudic precept: "A person must journey to see his rabbi face to face for the [three pilgrimage] festivals [Pesah, Shavuot and Sukkot]"; and not only for festivals: "he should go to him for the new moon and for Sabbaths."[64] Even before the rise of Hasidism, pious Jews would endeavor to carry out this injunction. At that time, however, there was no difficulty involved, for the only rabbi the Jew was likely to know was the rabbi of his own city, the "master of the place" *(mara d'atra)*. He would normally receive all the householders at holiday time, and on Sabbaths the members of the community would press around him in the synagogue to wish him a "good Sabbath."

The founder of Hasidism, the Besht, was wont to travel frequently to visit the small towns in Podolia, Volhynia and Galicia. As he traveled he drew new recruits to his banner, new disciples and admirers, and these would thereafter go to see him at festival time, at least, if not every new moon or every Sabbath.[65] Quite apart from this teacher-disciple aspect of the pilgrimage, however, the leaders of Hasidism assigned an additional, higher purpose to such journeys to the rabbi's place of residence, a quality that was missing from encounters which took place when the rebbe traveled to see his Hasidim.

Traveling to see the rebbe possesses great value in counteracting any coarsening of the spirit and the base corporeality of the body. For when each [Hasid] remains at home, every one holds firmly to his own place, to his substance, to each his own—whether that be his learnedness or his wealth. But by going to the rebbe he gives up his pride of place, no one can claim a place of his own in either learning or wealth, for all this is as nought when faced with the rabbi. Coarseness is as bad as idolatry *['avoda zara]*. . . . Through his bond with a Torah scholar, by listening to him speak the words of the living God, which is a divine bond . . . the preoccupation with his "substance" and the coarseness in him is negated.[66]

There is a dual mechanism at work in such a journey. "Negation of preoccupations with one's substance" is accomplished, in the first place, by leaving one's own milieu (as in the well-known adage that "distance reduces reputation").[67] In the second place, it is accomplished through contact with the zaddik, which acts to deflect the false consciousness that comes with "coarseness." The first is substantiated by the act of undertaking the journey and by gathering with thousands and tens of thousands of others at the zaddik's court periodically, year in, year out. Sitting together in a wagon as fellow pilgrims, rich and poor are not distinguishable. Even the poorest Hasid could travel to the rebbe without worrying over expenses. "His bread is given and his water is assured" out of the communal chest, that is, out of the common purse established by those traveling from the same place. The celebratory mood prevailing among the pilgrims enhanced the journey for them; this was reflected in Hasidic literature.

R. Nahman of Bratslav said: "Those who travel to see the zaddik, even if they receive no word of Torah from him, still receive reward for the journey."[68] And R. Aaron (the second) of Karlin placed great importance on the journey to the rebbe. In his book, he cites the view of the "holy one," R. Shlomo of Karlin, that "In the next world the forests and fields traversed in order to see the zaddik are reckoned in one's favor."[69] This is what he said to his Hasidim: "The important thing is faith in the zaddik, especially the zaddik whom one visits, and the spirit that he instills in one's prayer and study."[70] The zaddik R. Uri of Strelisk went so far as to say that it was well worth traveling a great distance, even if that means forgoing (communal) prayers and study,[71] for "one word of a true zaddik repairs the soul more than all the commandments."[72] The historian of Hasidism, S. Dubnow, was right when he observed:

It was not out of greedy desire for the "redemption" gifts brought by the Hasidim that this rebbe sought to broaden his circle of Hasidim and to spark their desire to visit him often. The Hasidim of Strelisk were among the poorest and could not enrich their rebbe. Rather, he felt an inner need to surround himself with Hasidim. Their presence would inspire him to greater heights in worshiping the Creator.[73]

These words are equally applicable to R. Nahman of Bratslav and R. Aaron of Karlin. Both of them were as far as could be from avarice, and both were known for being greatly involved in the lives of their Hasidim, arising early in the morning to address words of Torah and morality to their adherents. Both might be said to have personified the adage that "more than the calf wishes to drink, the cow desires to give milk,"[74] and that was what motivated them to place such a premium on pilgrimage.

Such journeys did not necessarily have a set schedule. As already mentioned, they could take place any month, any Sabbath, any holiday. But for the most part, Rosh Hashanah often served as the occasion for a pilgrimage to the rebbe,[75] as did Yom Kippur and Shavuot—the festival celebrating the revelation of the Torah at Sinai.

As zaddikism developed these customs altered, emerging differently in each place and changing over time. As already mentioned, the Besht used to travel a great deal to visit his disciples and admirers where they lived. His successor, the Maggid of Miedzyrzecz, was not a well man: He suffered from pain and had to keep his travels to a minimum. His disciples had, therefore, to travel to him, instead. During the entire twelve-year period of his "reign," we only know of two instances in which he traveled: when he moved from Miedzyrzecz to Rowno, and afterward from there to Annopol—two towns situated quite close together.

In contrast, there were other disciples of the Besht who spent virtually their entire lives traveling from city to city to spread the teachings of their master. One of these was R. Nahum of Czarnobyl, and his example was followed by his son, R. Mordechai, and, in turn, by his eight sons,[76] who became the leaders of the Hasidic movement in the Ukraine. Through making the rounds of the small towns, these rabbis greatly increased their influence in local affairs; but by the same token, they greatly reduced the number of disciples who would journey to visit them at their residences. On a normal Sabbath, the rabbi tended not to be at home, and on special days, such as new moons, holidays and such, only the closest among the zaddik's faithful tended to visit him. The majority did not do so, for they generally had seen the rebbe just recently, when he visited them.

This practice of the Ukrainian zaddikim, of roaming the countryside, drew the attention of the Russian authorities—known generally for their antipathy to Judaism and for oppression of the Jews—which issued regulations forbidding such circuit-riding by anyone known as a zaddik.[77] The rebbes now required special permits to leave their home communities even for short trips of a few hours' duration, whether it be to consult a physician or to attend the wedding of their children.

The situation was different in Poland, in Galicia and in White Russia. Such restrictions did not apply there, perhaps because the rebbes in those areas had not made a habit of extensive travel, year in and year out, to see their Hasidim. The famous zaddikim in Poland and Galicia drew their Hasidim to them, coming in droves from every direction.[78] Thousands would come from the Ukraine, too, to visit the rebbes who had fled across the border to Austrian Galicia—the family of the Zaddik of Rizhin—and many would smuggle themselves back and forth across the frontier.[79]

Even though, as time passed, the practice of pilgrimage to the rebbe became a source of income with which to enrich the opulent courts of the zaddikim, who established themselves in fine mansions and palaces, to this day the flocking of Hasidim to the seat of their leader has retained something of its beauty and grandeur. The sense of unity and the social equality that prevail among them at their rebbe's residence, regardless of class or status in their worldly lives; the collective joy; the spiritual consciousness in anticipation of the enlightenment to be spread by the rebbe; the song, dancing and passionate prayer—all these make the journey to the zaddik a profound and affecting experience for the Hasid, even today.

Pidyon ha-nefesh ("Redemption of the Soul") and Kvitl (Written Request)

One of the most important functions the zaddik performed was, as has been mentioned,[80] his involvement in the personal life of each and every one of his Hasidim: in his health and that of his family, in arranging the marriages of his sons and daughters, in decisions to move to a new place, and in financial matters. Everything that caused the Hasid to stop and consider what was the proper course to take in his life was an occasion for asking the zaddik's counsel. He would punctiliously carry out his rebbe's advice, exactly as he had received it.

In a way, this custom is rooted in the life the Jews lived ever since becoming a nation. The role of the seers of old or sometimes the priest was to deliver words of counsel and advice in times of trouble. Anyone who faced an imminent decision and did not know where to turn or how to act could approach the prophet or the priest, and he would offer guidance and pray to God on his behalf, so that the inquirer could return home with his trouble solved. When Saul and his servant went in search of the lost asses of his father, the servant said to him, "There is a man of God in that town, and the man is highly esteemed; everything that he says comes true. Let us go there; perhaps he will tell us about the errand on which we went out [I Sam. 9:6]." And when Saul refused, saying, "For the food in our bags is all gone, and there is nothing we can bring

the man of God as a present. What have we got?"—the servant responded: "I happen to have a quarter-shekel of silver. I can give that to
the man and he will tell us about our errand [ibid., 7–8]." We can fit
this description just as well to the experiences of Jews in the Ukraine,
Poland and Russia during the rise of Hasidism. If trouble came upon a
Jew, his fellow would urge him to go the zaddik to seek counsel, so that
he might know what course to take. The situations are so similar, in
fact, that it is difficult to tell that they are separated by some three
thousand years.

Even after prophecy had ceased in Israel and the priesthood had lost
its glory, other "saviors" of the people arose from among the scholars
and the "first Hasidim," to whom the people looked for aid, to whom
they came to seek remedies for illness and assistance for the needy:

Once the son of R. Gamliel fell ill. He sent two scholars to R. Hanina b. Dosa to
ask him to pray for him. When he saw them he [ben Dosa] went up to an upper
chamber and prayed for him [Gamliel's son]. When he came down he said to
them: Go, the fever has left him. They said to him [ben Dosa], are you a prophet?
He replied, I am neither a prophet nor the son of a prophet, but I learnt this
from my experience: If the prayer is fluent in my mouth, I know that he [the sick
one] is accepted; but if not, I know that he is rejected. They sat down and made
a note of the exact moment. When they came to R. Gamliel, he said to them: I
swear, your recording of the time was completely accurate. At that very moment
the fever left him and he asked for water to drink.[81]

R. Yohanan ben Zakkai, too, went to R. Hanina ben Dosa when his son
fell sick—rather than to the Temple or to the graves of his ancestors.
Ben Dosa was, he said, "like a servant before the king, who has permission to go into him anytime, and able to see the face of his king at any
time."[82]

Toward the end of the time of the Talmudic sages, the Amoraim, this
custom was renewed, and it was hoped that it would be generally
adopted. R. Pinhas ben Hama taught: "Anyone with someone at home
who is ill should go to the learned man [hakham] to seek divine compassion, for it is written [Proverbs 16:14], 'The king's wrath is a messenger
of death, but a wise man can appease it.'"[83] And Jews have many
folktales and legends about miracle workers from various historical
periods, from the poor pious man who sold Elijah the Prophet as a slave
and became rich,[84] to stories about resurrection of the dead and about
the creation of golems through the use of secret kabbalist knowledge.

It should be clear, then, that Hasidism had firm foundations on which to build its conception of the zaddik; but the structure erected by Hasidism was infinitely more elaborate than anything that existed in the past.

The "gift" brought by the Hasid to his rebbe was not only superior in form and worth to what was received by the prophet of old, it was also called something else: not a gift or a present, but "redemption of the soul" *(pidyon ha-nefesh)*. What the Hasid presented to the rebbe was essentially not considered a gift, but repayment of a debt. The Hasid willingly and gratefully offered it in the belief that by doing so he was, in a sense, "insuring" his life and that of his loved ones. Just as the father of a newborn son rejoiced at the payment of the "redemption" sum to the priest, the Hasid rejoiced upon giving his rebbe a *pidyon ha-nefesh*.

There was no fixed sum required for this payment, because it depended on what the individual could afford, the more affluent giving more, the poor giving less. There were times, however, when the Rebbe would set a particular sum based on the letter numerology involved in the request being made (for example, fifty-two coins to correspond to the numerical value—fifty-two—of the word for "son"), or on the sum produced by adding the names of the petitioner and his mother ("so-and-so son of so-and-so"). Many payments were based on multiples of the number eighteen—corresponding to the word "life." More recently, zaddikim increasingly began to charge a set "fee" for a *pidyon,* and this was a factor that markedly detracted from their stature in the public eye.

The idea behind the zaddik's role in giving succor to those who approached him, through prayer and wise counsel, and the payment of a gift in return, was not, as we have stressed, an innovation. The innovation came in the "note" or the *kvitl,* as it was known,[85] that was a characteristic part of the Hasidic custom. In this note the Hasid would record his needs or requests and those of his family. All was written down precisely, and each individual was mentioned by name and further identified by his mother's name (on the model of the verse in Psalms 116:16: "I am Your servant, the son of Your maidservant").[86] The form this letter took was well known and did not vary, and was often penned by a beadle, who was able to earn an income from such commissions. The Hasid would either present the *kvitl* himself or else send it by the hand of a messenger, together with a *pidyon* that suited his means. The zaddik would read the letter in the presence of the Hasid, at the time appointed for a personal interview. When such letters were sent by post, sometimes the beadle would read the letters to the zaddik and record the latter's answers, which he would transmit to the petitioner.

If the zaddik could not read each and every one of these letters—as might occur before Rosh Hashanah and Yom Kippur, when masses of them would accumulate—he would place them in his pockets and place his hand upon them, saying, "I bestow on all the people in the *kvitlakh* here in my pockets blessings for life, children and material sustenance, for a good year." [87]

In more recent times a custom that gained currency among Hasidim was a "blanket request" (*klolles tsetl* or "general note") sent to the zaddik for Rosh Hashanah and Yom Kippur. This would include the names of all those considered to be part of the rebbe's following. Justification for this practice was found in the words of the Shunemite woman to Elisha the Prophet, when he asked whether she wished him to speak on her behalf to the king. On Rosh Hashanah, the Day of Judgment, this would be taken to refer to the King of the Universe. The Shunemite's answer was, "I live among my own people" (II Kings 4:13) — i.e., I am content to have my name mentioned among the collective. [88]

The sources of the *kvitl* idea, its time and place of origin and the manner in which the custom spread are unclear. [89] There is a tradition among the Hasidim that attributes to the Besht himself the practice of writing such letters for his own sake, and of giving *kvitl* and *pidyon* to some of his disciple-associates. [90] This notion appears to lack solid foundation, however. In the manuscript prayer book used by the Besht [91] the margins of the pages containing the Eighteen Benedictions are marked with the names of individuals (and their mothers). It was the practice of highly esteemed Hasidim who had free access to their rebbe's prayer hall to hold his prayer book in their hands and inscribe their names on the margins of the pages, so that the zaddik would be cognizant of their names while he prayed. Evidently, this practice postdated that of the *kvitl*, and, indeed, was intended to supplement a note. There were also highly respected Hasidim who would do all that they could to squeeze into the space by the wedding canopy during the marriage of someone in the zaddik's family. The Hasid would submit his *kvitl* (even though this entailed serious risk to life and limb, as the press of humanity at that conjuncture was likely to be tremendous) so that the zaddik would remember him in the context of the joyful celebration. They believed that the hour of joy was especially propitious for the blessings they sought.[92]

In time the custom of the *kvitl* took on a regularized procedure,[93] characteristic signs, and a whole tradition of its own. People were careful, for example, not to use sand to dry the ink,[94] and it was also held to be an ill omen if the note should happen to fall down.[95] Care was taken to insure that the note was written without mistakes; mistakes that crept into a *kvitl* were thought to be the sign of evil portents.[96] It was believed, as well, that there were two ways of reading a *kvitl*: the "simple" way and a "higher" way, and not every zaddik succeeded in reading it in the higher way.[97]

The belief that lay at the basis of the *kvitl*—namely, that it was in the zaddik's power to help through the force of his prayer, to bring healing to the sick, for example—was so strongly held that Hasidim went so far as to actually violate religious law if they felt they had to get their letter to the zaddik, no matter what. They sometimes, for example, instructed Gentile messengers to ride or travel on the Sabbath in order to reach the zaddik's abode,[98] so that the zaddik would pray for the recovery of someone who was ill. Of course, the Jews of the anti-Hasidic type would cite just this sort of thing and decry the zaddikim who permitted such clear transgressions of the law.[99]

The writing of requests to a zaddik continued after his death, in which case the *kvitl* was placed on his grave. The gravesites of the zaddikim contain hundreds and thousands of such notes, and, indeed, they are usually built with special receptacles for them, situated close to the gravestone inside the tomb.

The Rebbe's Table Talk

In antiquity, the leading sages (Tannaim) of the Mishna[100] already practiced the custom of interrupting the meal to engage in learned discourse. On occasions when important guests were invited and a special meal was prepared, local dignitaries were asked to participate, too, and the guests were honored by being asked to address those assembled with words of Torah.[101] But it was never the case until the advent of Hasidism that the common meal became a fixed public-religious institution. Hasidism raised the status of the formal meal at which the zaddik presided to new, unprecedented heights. It reached the point that it seemed more important to be present at a meal with the zaddik than to attend when he prayed.[102] Many Hasidim who traveled especially to see their rebbe for a holiday—and in most cases this involved great effort and expense—were apt to forgo being with the rebbe for prayers at his house, choosing to pray beforehand in their own group, in order to be in time to find a choice place at table close to where the rebbe would sit. There they would have the incomparable privilege of hearing the rebbe's teachings literally from his own lips and to witness with their own eyes every movement and gesture the zaddik might make it the course of the meal.

There were many great zaddikim who did not engage in any learned table discourse, choosing instead to sing pious songs which were another *zemirot* form of Torah.[103] Nevertheless, their Hasidim still pressed forward, at the risk of life and limb, in order to find places close to the rebbe and "to bask in the illumination of his sainted face."

As we shall see from the words of one of the founders of the Hasidic movement, R. Yaaqov Yosef of Polonne, it was the practice in his day for students to gather for meals at the table of a renowned scholar, where they would listen to his words of wisdom and afterward would present him with gifts. The customary table discourse of this type consisted of textual amplification, to demonstrate virtuosity, rather than of preaching on the theme of piety "to make the heart surrender to greater fear of God." The rabbi of Polonne objected to this, and argued:

There are two ways of speaking Torah, either explaining the meaning [of a text] or preaching about piety. . . . And it should be asked which of these is preferable, the one or the other, or perhaps both are equally worthy, and then decide. . . . There is certainly a great message in words of piety that make the hearts surrender. . ., which is not the case with textual analysis in order to show one's virtuosity, which affects the heart mainly of the speaker with his own pride. How can he bring his listeners to a state of inner submission if he himself is full of pride? . . . And as we may testify to having seen, they do not do so [preach on pious values] but intend only to speak on the simple meaning of texts. . ., for they believe that in this way they will reap material reward, especially at the meal, for it is their custom to give presents to the scholar. And how can he preach to them words of castigation, for these will not endear him to them and they will not give him gifts.[104]

This rabbi, whose books reveal him to have been one of the keenest minds of his time in his part of the Ukraine,[105] quite above his peers, objected to the displays of intellectual agility that were customary among the educated, demanding instead that the rabbis speak plain words of exhortation that anyone could easily follow. That, in fact, was what the leaders of Hasidism and the zaddikim did: Most of their table discourses were of an exhortatory-spiritual nature and concerned the ways to achieve the proper frame of mind for the worship of God; how to escape the preoccupation with the material, this-worldly realm, negate one's pride and combat the desire and greed and other unworthy drives that interfere with loving relationships between man and his fellow-men and with doing what is right. This could be done through clinging to the Almighty Creator and to the words of those who carried out His commandments, the zaddikim, through love of God and love of Israel, through the uplifting benefits of unity and peace.[106]

The rebbe's every movement and every syllable while at table became subjects for analysis and contemplation by his Hasidim, who speculated upon the reasons behind them and thought up various explanations, some brief, some convoluted. All this derived from the simple belief that the rebbe was actually a deputy of the Lord God Himself, so that all the rebbe's actions were inspired by his thoughts of Heaven and, hence, deserved study.

As an example of the deep devotion of the Hasidim to the rites performed by the zaddik at his table, I should like to present a story that was handed down in my own family about my grandfather, R. Yossele of Radziwilów (near Brody). R. Yossele once went to see the zaddik, R. Israel of Ruzhin, and during the Sabbath meal stood behind R. Israel's chair, watching what he did and never for an instant allowing his gaze to wander from the zaddik's motions. He observed how a bowl of fish was set before the rebbe, how he carefully examined them with a fork, inspecting each piece until he found and removed the eye from the head of the fish and ate it first of all. Of course, the rebbe did nothing without a deeper purpose in mind regarding the union of the divine heavenly spheres; therefore, after giving the matter some thought, R. Yossele concluded that the reason for this particular procedure was as follows: The spiritual significance of fish is that they did not sin in the generation of the Flood, so the punishment visited upon the Earth was not directed against them.[107] And, as is well known, the beginning of sin lies in what the eye sees, as the sages said, "The eye sees and the heart desires."[108] Hence, if the fish did not sin, it must be that their sight was not corrupted, and so it is the eye of the fish that is its most important organ and ought to be eaten first. Hasidic legend adds, in concluding this story, that the Rebbe of Ruzhin, "who was able to read one's thoughts," understood what R. Yossele was thinking, turned to him and said: "Young man, that indeed is the point."

At any rate, this story should sufficiently illustrate the way that a devoted Hasid would think as he stood near his rebbe's table. Such moments provided the source of renewed strength and hope for a sagging spirit. He would consider the words of the rebbe on such an occasion as a message addressed specifically to him and no one else.[109] The rebbe's teachings, the words he used, the entire atmosphere—especially at the concluding meal of the Sabbath, as the evening dimness descended on the entire assembled congregation, amidst a perfect silence into which rose the rebbe's soft voice and his deep sighs which penetrated every heart—such experiences left with the believing Hasid a sense of grace. No wonder it was said, in the name of the zaddik, R. Hanokh of Alexander (near Lodz), that "When our sainted messiah comes, then all will see what the zaddikim accomplished with their 'tables.' "[110]

One further item about the rebbe's meal deserves special discussion: the eating of *shirayim* (remainders) of the rebbe's food.[111]

Shirayim

It is a very old custom among Jews to leave over a small portion of one's food as a symbolic "unused corner" *(peyah)*,[112] which is related to ethical considerations regarding food.[113] It was also said that whoever "does not leave behind a piece of bread on the table will never see prosperity in his life."[114] This furnished the basis for the idea that remainders were a sign of blessing. Another hint of this was discerned in the verses (Joel 2:14), "And He may leave a blessing behind"; and (Deut. 28:5), "Blessed shall be thy basket and thy *kneading trough"*—*mishartekha*, which seemed related to the word *she'erit* (remainder), and thus connected to the concept of leftover food.[115] But none of these ideas provides a direct source for importance being attached to the *consuming* of such remainders. Neither does rabbinic literature contain any mention of a distinction between the *shirayim* of a zaddik and those of an ordinary Jew.

In the Palestinian Talmud[116] it is written that "R. Yohanan would go

down to the synagogue in the morning, after the meal of the preceding
day to celebrate the new month, and he would collect crumbs of that
repast and eat them, saying, 'May I spend my life in the next world
together with those who ate here yesterday evening.' " Here we begin to
see a glimmer of the idea that consuming the crumbs of a meal with
religious significance (se'udat misva) might serve as a link with those
who partook of the meal itself, making it possible to "join" the meal, as
it were. The same concept may be found regarding the cup of wine used
for benediction, as stated in the Gemara: "He hands it to the members
of his household, for it provides blessing for his house";[117] i.e., one's
wife will be blessed in tasting the wine. Since the wine was used in
reciting the blessings for food, it was called "the cup of blessing" and
believed to portend good things for those partaking of it.[118]

From that point, it is only a mere step to the belief of Hasidim that
there is special potency in the shirayim of the rebbe. They believed, after
all, that the rebbe ate only for the sake of Heaven and that he "performs
unifications of holy spheres through every thing, great and small, even
through a drop of water that he drinks."[119] That being so, it must be
true that the Rebbe sanctifies everything that is on his plate, which
becomes permeated with blessing.

Kabbalist books provided an additional element, asserting that in the
act of eating a zaddik, who is "the perfect man," performs the task of
"extracting sparks of the divine" (birur hanisosin). Thus, the Ari is
quoted as having taught: "The point of eating and drinking is to locate
the sparks, and to locate and restore [to the proper sphere] the migratory
souls that are reincarnated in every thing that requires restoration
[tiqqun]."[120] And the Besht is quoted as having interpreted the verse in
Psalms 107:5 ("Hungry and thirsty, their soul fainted in them") as
follows: "Why did God make man feel hunger or thirst? He could, after
all, have created man without the need to eat or drink. For this reason it
is said, 'their soul fainted in them.' That is why God created man to be
hungry and to eat, or thirsty and to drink, so that he would raise the
sparks of the divine, those souls who are 'fainted' [or embodied] in the
food."[121] It should come as no surprise, then, that Hasidim venerated
the food blessed by the zaddik and left uneaten. This food, according to
their belief, had already performed the spiritual task assigned through it,
so that it was completely ready and able to radiate blessing. The shirayim thus became vested with such importance that people would jump

from their places at the table and virtually trample each other in order to grab a crumb of something from the zaddik's plate.[122]

Shirayim were held to be effective for bringing prosperity and health. As one interpretation of Exodus 23:25 ("You shall serve the Lord your God, and He will bless your bread and your water, and I will remove sickness from your midst") has it, the blessing of food in purity and sanctity is what makes possible the "removal of sickness from your midst"—"the food itself brings healing to the sick."[123] The importance of *shirayim* held true even against the prohibition against eating "soaked matzah" on Passover:[124] If it happened that a zaddik who was aged and weak could only eat softened ("soaked") matzah on Passover, even young, healthy Hasidim permitted themselves to eat the *shirayim* of the rebbe, even though the laws of Passover strictly forbade "soaked matzah."[125]

Stories Told about the Zaddikim

Hasidim were especially fond of telling stories about their zaddik, and they did so almost regularly at certain times. It was even believed that those who participated in these sessions derived mystic benefit from them.

The founder of the Hasidic movement, the Besht, was himself the initiator of this practice. He would assemble people in the streets and marketplaces and tell them stories to draw their attention to the will of their Father in Heaven.[126] He would also tell stories sometimes to his disciples. Upon reflection, they found in these tales wonderful meanings, giving them a better understanding of the worship of God and the future course of their own lives. It is told of one of the Besht's great disciples, R. Mendel of Witebsk, that during his first encounter with the Besht, the latter told him a story of an ox and a plow, in the presence of the Rabbi of Polonne and the Maggid of Miedzyrzecz. The young R. Mendel understood from the story only as much as he had already experienced; R. Yaaqov Yosef understood half the meaning of the story; and the Maggid understood its full meaning.[127] Many years later, when R. Mendel became seriously ill and his disciples stood around him crying, the sick man summoned enough strength to whisper: "Fear not, for from the story that the Besht told me I know that I am destined to go to the Land of Israel." After his recovery he indeed went to the Land of Israel, and on the way he visited the aged Rabbi of Polonne. The old man asked him, "Do you remember the story of the ox and the plow?" To this R. Mendel replied, "I remember." "And do you know what your place is there?" To this R. Mendel replied, sighing gently, "I have now deduced more than the half of it."[128]

And so, wonder-tales about the zaddikim became ritualized in the generations that followed. The mystical stories of R. Nahman of Bratslav, grandson of the Besht's daughter, are well known. The stories of his arch-rival, the "Old Man of Shpola," became the subject of intense study by Hasidim, who found in them hints of great mystical truths, in the same way that generations had done with the legends of Rabba Bar bar Hanna (of the second generation of the Amoraic sages of the Talmudic period), set down in Tractate *Bava Batra*.[129]

As we have already seen,[130] Hasidim were not especially taken with the idea of study in large groups, preferring small groups of two or three. But stories of the zaddikim were told in large groups—the larger the better.[131] They firmly believed that these stories served to strengthen faith in God and His true servants. This prompted them, in time, to set aside time on Saturday nights to tell a story about the Besht.[132]

Such was their regard for the power inherent in "recounting actual deeds" of the zaddikim that they said: "When troublesome times, God preserve us, come upon us, although we may be unable to perform the acts, the prayers or the meditations that the Besht and his disciples performed in such cases, it is enough that we tell the story of what they did, and then God, blessed be He, will help us."[133] [—Translated by Eli Lederhendler.]

NOTES

1. The custom of R. Judah ben Ilai (Tractate *Shabbat* 25b) would seem to indicate the need only to wash one's face, hands and feet in warm water before the Sabbath, not to immerse oneself in the *miqveh*.

2. See *Hemdat ha-yamim* 83b, cited in the name of R. Hayyim Vital: "One must immerse oneself on Sabbath morning even though one has already done so on the eve of the Sabbath; and there is a distinction between the particular sanctity of the Sabbath day and that of Sabbath eve. Its holiness is of the most serious nature. An analogous case is that of the priest [in the ancient Temple] who had to immerse himself on Yom Kippur between each change of his robes."

3. At the end of *Qedushat levi,* the commentary on Tractate *Avot;* and see also *Sefer ha-Besht* (Lodz, 1938), pt. 2, p. 38.

4. *Beit aharon be-liqutim,* p. 287.

5. *Taʾamei ha-minhagim,* pt. 3, p. 82, citing *Toledot aharon* on *parashat* "Tisʾa," and also citing *Sefer or la-shamayim,* "Behar," in the name of R. Elimelekh of Lezajsk.

6. *Mishmeret shalom* by R. Perlov, section 25, 28.

7. Tractate *Shabbat* 119a, "A story of Rabbi Yannai. . . ," Palestinian Talmud [*Yerushalmi*], Tractate *Peah,* chapter 8, item 7: It required two coverings, one for weekdays and one for the Sabbath.

8. See Dr. Guedemann's *Hatorah ve-ha-hayyim,* pt. 2, p. 192, and pt. 3, p. 107.

9. *He-asif* 1898, p. 171.

10. Ibid., regulation 1035–36.

11. See S. Dubnow, *Toledot ha-hasidut* (Tel Aviv, 1943), p. 85, citing S. Maimon; and see *Hemdat ha-yamim* I, p. 29, citing R. Hayyim Vital, who in turn wrote in the name of his master, the Ari: "Everyone must wear four white garments on the Sabbath eve, corresponding to the four letters of the divine Name, which represent the clothes of Creation, and these are the under- and over-garment, the girdle and the robe."

12. See *Degel mahaneh efrayim,* toward the end of *parashat Noah,* on "the sect of liars who say, let us don white, let us dress in white for the Sabbath, as if we were pure and righteous."

13. On the ban against woolens declared by Hasidic leaders for fear of violations against *sheʾatnez* (the rule against mixing linen and wool), see chapter 8 of A. Wertheim, *Halakhot ve-halikhot ba-hassidut* (Jerusalem, 1960).

14. *Tanya,* Laws and Customs [*Pisqei dinim u-minhagim*] by R. Yehiel b. R. Yekutiel (Sedilikow, 1836), section 11; see also *Mahzor Vitry,* p. 249.

15. *Beit aharon be-liqutim,* p. 289; *Birkat avraham* by the rabbi of Buczacz, *parashat* "Va-etʾhanan." And see also *Tashbes* by R. S. b. Zemah, pt. 2, section 37: "It is proper for a scholar to repair entrances, and anyone who has qualms about this, this is merely ignorance or else some heresy has entered his mind, because there is great merit in undertaking such repairs." And in more recent times, one of the great Hasidic leaders in Poland, R. Gershon Hanokh-Henekh of Radzyn, known as *Mehadesh ha-tekhelet,* published an important article on the subject of permitting ʾeruvin, "Delatot shaʾar ha-ʾir—birur halakhah la-amitah shel torah be-ʾinyan hekhsher delatot ve-ofanei ʾasiyatam la-ʾir she-i efshar le-taqnah be-surat petah."

16. This was R. Yehoshua Segal, known as the Rebbe of Sherpatz, who used to sign his name as "Rabbi of the Associated Polish Congregations *(Rav ha-kolel le-agudot qehillot anshei polin).* In 1906 he published a small work entitled, *ʾEruv ve-hosaʾa,* which was reprinted the following year with the addition of responsa by leading rabbis of the period: R. Shalom Mordechai ha-Cohen Schwadron of Brzezany, R. Aryeh Leybush Hurwitz of Stanislawów and R. Moshe Meisels of Przemyslaw.

17. See *Degel mahaneh efrayim*, "Va-yishlah" (comment on the verse, "Save me from the hand of my brother, from the hand of Esau"): "As we find in the midrash, in the future Esau would wrap himself in a *tallith* and sit among the righteous, but the Almighty pulled him out of there, etc. And it should be said that this is what happens in our world, too, for our many sins, since falsehood had multiplied in the world and everyone wants to stand high up among the pious ones of Israel, and they dress themselves in white and wear a *tallith* on Sabbath eve, saying to themselves, 'I will be like that one. . . .' "

The custom has entered Jewish folklore through one of the Galician zaddikim, the Rebbe of Dzików, who said: "One can imitate everything but a rebbe, for if a person puts on a silk robe and a *tallith* for Friday night prayers, he is not *imitating* the rebbe—he actually *is* a rebbe." This quip has been used as an illustration of the proliferation of so-called "rebbes," bereft of any special learning or gift for prayer.

18. See *Mishmeret shalom* by R. Perlov, section 27, p. 76. He provides a reason for this custom: "For on the holy Sabbath the night is as radiant as the day. And that is why we do not say, 'And it was evening and it was morning the *seventh* day,' for that day has neither evening nor night, but is daytime throughout."

19. See Tractate *Menahot* 43a; *Orah hayyim* item 18, section 1.

20. See the book by R. Kopl, *Kol yaaqov* (Lemberg/Lwów, 1859).

21. Tractate *Shabbat* 33b.

22. See *Hemdat ha-yamim*, pt. 1, p. 41c.

23 .See Tractate *Shabbat* 118b.

24. See ibid., 119a (Rashi's commentary).

25. Those who delved into letter-numerology said: fish *(dag)*, meat *(basar)* and wine *(yayin)* all may be calculated to represent the number seven—corresponding to the Sabbath day *(Osar dinim uminhagim)*.

26. *Orah hayyim*, 242n, in the name of the Maharil. Even though the Rama concludes: "There is no need to worry about this," there are late medieval legists who asserted that in their districts it was customary to eat a *kugel*. Among the Hasidim it is the custom to prepare a *kugel* for each Sabbath; if it is a New Moon or a holiday, then two or three are cooked, depending on the importance of the occasion. An important guest would receive a *kugel* of his own. The Maggid of Kozienice instituted a custom of his own, based on a particular precedent *(ma'aseh she-haya)* of eating a special Sabbath *kugel* for the Saturday morning *kiddush*, apart from the one that was served for the midday meal itself. The special *kugel* was called "the domestic-peace-*kugel*" (*Or ha-ganuz*, p. 253).

27. *Hemdat ha-yamim*, pt. 1, p. 73b.

28. Gutman, *Mi-gedolei ha-hasidut*, bk. 2, p. 30, item 129.

29. Ibid.

30. See *Ta'amei ha-minhagim*, pt. 1, p. 48, items 368–69. A reason for this is cited in the name of the Zaddik of Nadworno, who speaks of its signifi-cance as a reminder of how the lower elements (feet) are to be raised to

higher levels (the head), and that *then* the approach ("the feet" or foot-steps) of the messiah might be expected. And another reason, cited in the name of another holy man, is that lies and falsehood "have no feet" (i.e., they have not a leg to stand on), whereas the truth stands, it "has feet"; and the Sabbath is truth, and therefore we eat cows' feet.

31. *Ta'amei ha-minhagim,* ibid., item 367, cites the following reason: "Sab-bath foods retain the flavor of manna, and manna contained every flavor on earth, apart from garlic and onions — lest it harm pregnant women (*Sifrei,* "Be-ha'alotekha"); and in order to enjoy all the flavors there are, on Sabbath we add garlic and onions." But among Hasidim, onions are eaten, without garlic — they say that onions are significant because they have seven layers, one over the other, underneath the skin, and so they are eaten on the seventh day.

32. *Ta'amei ha-minhagim,* pt. 3, p. 112, citing *Sefer shearit yisrael.*

33. See *Mishmeret shalom,* section 28, par. 7, which contains a lengthy expla-nation.

34. Cited in *Be'er hetev,* comments on *Orah hayyim,* 274b. And see also *Mishmeret shalom* 28e.

35. See *Mishmeret shalom,* ibid. The anti-Hasidic camp did not agree to this custom (apparently because of the argument raised in *Mesaref 'avoda,* p. 3). On the matter of twelve challahs, the Gaon of Vilna (R. Elijah) said that this is an error, for the true meaning is twelve pieces (see *Ma'aseh ha-rav,* section 123, requiring but two challahs for each Sabbath meal, six challahs for each Sabbath, and referring to the Zohar). Among the Hasi-dim themselves, there were those who did not accept this custom, because of differences of opinion among the kabbalists, different versions of the Zohar and emendations in the text. In the Zohar, *parashat* "Pinhas," p. 245, we find, "And he said to me, 'This [*zeh:* the letters correspond numerologically to 12] is the table that is before God' and the one who has the twelve loaves has to arrange four of them on the table for each meal, making twelve for three meals." But in *Tiqqunei ha-zohar* we find that six loaves should be placed on one side, and six on the other, adding up to the number twelve found in the verse *(zeh).* These correspond to the six joints in the arms and the six joints in the legs. But there were Hasidim and kabbalists who did not maintain this custom of having twelve loaves at each meal, relying on the passage from the Zohar.

36. Karlin Hasidim who wished to invoke the high opinion that the Maggid of Miedzyrzecz held of their own rebbe, R. Aaron "the Great," told the story that when he sat at table with the great rabbi in Miedzyrzecz, twelve loaves were placed before him as well for all the Sabbath meals (*Beit aharon,* 145).

37. The arrangement of the twelve loaves was as follows: four to the right, stacked two on two, and four to the left, also two on two; two large loaves in the center stacked upon two smaller ones. This corresponds to the arrangement mentioned in *Sha'arei teshuva* 274a.

38. There is an interesting question raised in the book *'Arugot ha-bosem,*

about a Hasid who had received from his rebbe a small challah made of twelve loaves as a way to assure prosperity. The Hasid was so attached to this gift that he was unwilling to part with it, even for Passover.

39. Tractate *Gitin*, 60a.

40. *Orah hayyim*, section 136.

41. In the *Shulhan 'arukh* of the Ari we find: "The third section is greater than all the others apart from the sixth, which is greater, because the third corresponds to the divine 'sphere' of Tifereth, while the sixth corresponds to Yesod. Hence it is written in the Zohar that R. Chrospodai would not take any but the sixth [reading], for through this [sixth one] the zaddik can rise even higher (Zohar: *Shalah*, 312). And (ibid.): "Who is the greatest zaddik? The one who goes sixth, greatest of all seven." A biblical verse was used as prooftext for this idea: (Proverbs 10:25) "The righteous [*zaddik*] is an everlasting foundation [*yesod*]."

42. Tractate *Shabbat* 117b.

43. *Orah hayyim*, section 291.

44. See *Hemdat ha-yamim* I, p. 125.

45. *Hemdat ha-yamim* states that, "Those who penetrate the secrets of the divine are permitted, at this meal, to reveal the secrets of the Torah to those who are God-fearing and who delve into His Name, without fear. . . . It was the way of the first Hasidim to be joyous and happy at this meal more than at any other." I, p. 125. And perhaps the kabbalists in the Land of Israel and in Saloniki (where the anonymous author of *Hemdat ha-yamim* lived) already practiced the custom of the third meal as a public event; but it is clearly only with the Hasidim of Poland and the Ukraine that such a custom took hold in those areas.

46. R. Shneur Zalman of Liady wrote in his prayer book: "It is meet to eat fish at this meal more than at the other meals"; for the reason he gives, see *Sha'ar ha-kolel*, chap. 17, item 25. *Hemdat ha-yamim* (ibid.) gives the reason that, "it should awaken the higher vision [of Providence]," as fish are known to have their eyes always open.

47. See *Mishmeret shalom* 29, par. 2: "This meal corresponds to Jacob, who is the foremost among the Patriarchs, and this meal contains the essence of the spiritual purpose [*tiqqun*]."

48. *Ta'amei ha-minhagim* pt. 1, p. 51, item 398, citing *Shearit yisrael*.

49. *Keter shem tov*, pt. 2, p. 21.

50. Tractate *Shabbat* 119b.

51. *Orah hayyim*, section 300. The Seer of Lublin is quoted on this in *Ta'amei ha-minhagim*, pt. 3, p. 129.

52. *Ta'amei ha-minhagim*, ibid., citing *Orah hayyim*, section 300, and citing the Zaddik of Lezajsk.

53. Ibid., citing R. Simon of Jaroslaw and other zaddikim.

54. *Sefer ba'al shem tov* (Lodz, 1939), p. 32, citing *Minhat shabbat* 96, item 100–6, and citing *Beerot ha-mayyim* (Introduction).

55. The need to connect with a zaddik appears in many passages in *Toledot*

yaaqov yosef, where Yaaqov Yosef quotes the Besht, and in general is a prominent theme in Hasidic literature. See the *Toledot,* "Mishpatim" (Miedzyboz edn., p. 47), citing R. Mendel of Bar and the Besht: "This is what my teacher said regarding prayers, to raise them as well." And see *Darkhei sedeq* (Lwów, 1796), no. 39.

56. Deut. 10:20.

57. *Toledot,* "Yitro," 41b.

58. Ibid., "Tesaveh," 51b. And the Zaddik of Ruzhin said: "Just as the holy letters have no voice without the vowel points, and the vowel points alone cannot exist without the letters, so too are zaddikim and Hasidim dependent on one another. The Zaddikim are the letters and the Hasidim are the vowel points; Hasidim need the zaddikim to be able to exist and be strengthened by them, and the zaddik needs the Hasidim because they carry his voice and spread word of his works" (*Or ha-ganuz,* p. 275).

59. *Sefer ha-midot,* "Zaddik," no. 53.

60. *No'am elimelekh,* "Va-yishlah."

61. Ibid., "Mishpatim."

62. *Derekh 'edotekha* by the rabbi of Dainov; *Ta'amei ha-minhagim,* pt. 2, p. 15.

63. *Ta'amei ha-minhagim,* pt. 2, p. 13, citing the zaddik, R. Sholem of Belz.

64. Tractate *Rosh hashanah* 16b.

65. *Sefer ha-Besht,* pt. 2, p. 32, cites chapter and verse to prove that one must travel to see the zaddik in person, and not make do with studying books of ethical precepts. The prooftext comes from Exodus 17:14: "Inscribe this in a document as a reminder and read it aloud to Joshua. ...." Traveling to the zaddik is incumbent on every man, because it comes under the heading of "we will hearken." And (ibid., p. 54): "The Besht said: 'Anyone who is privileged to spend the Sabbath [with him] and partake of meals with him, he puts the life elixir into it that will enter him and be a healing and a salvation from all desires; and in the future it will influence his behavior in his own home, making it pure and sanctified." (See also n. 71, below.)

66. *Vikuha rabba,* 2: 25.

67. See Rashi's comment on Genesis 12:2.

68. *Sefer ha-midot,* "Zaddik," no. 24.

69. *Beit aharon,* p. 293.

70. Ibid., 291.

71. See *Sefer liqutei betar liqutei* on Tractate *Avot* 1, p. 88: "And it is told, in the name of the zaddik, R. Shmelke of Nikolsburg, that once he was asked by R. Y. Landau, known as the 'Nod'a biyhuda,' why he wastes such an inordinate amount of time traveling to see his rebbe in Miedzyrzecz. So he replied:

Rashi asks, in his comment on the verse *'va-yishm'a yitro,* [Jethro heard . . .]' etc. (Ex. 18:1), "What had he heard? [He heard] about the Red Sea splitting and about the war with Amalek." But these are self-evident, so what was the point of Rashi's query? The point was as follows: What did he hear? He came to [hear it in person] from the zaddik of that generation [i.e., Moses]. But could he not worship God just as well from afar? However, although he heard about the miracle of the Red Sea— a miracle about which the sages said, "There a simple maidservant could see what the Prophet Ezekiel himself could not see, and yet they soon lost their exalted consciousness, to the point that they questioned whether God was indeed in their midst, so that Amalek was sent to war against them"—this indicates that no one should rely on himself and his learning alone; rather, he must take himself to see the zaddik of his generation.

72. Dubnow, *Toledot ha-hasidut*, p. 325.

73. Ibid.

74. Tractate *Pesahim* 112a.

75. *Ta'amei ha-minhagim*, pt. 4, p. 44, citing R. Nahman's view that one must go to true zaddikim for Rosh Hashanah.

76. On the Czernobyl dynasty and the Hasidic "courts" that developed from it, see: S. A. Horodetzky, *Hasidut ve-hasidim* 3; (Berlin, 1922), bk. 3, Gutman, *Mi-gedolei ha-hasidut*, no. 3.

77. For a discussion at length, see A. Galant's article in the Ukrainian anthology, *Zbirnik prats evreiskoi istorichnoi komissii*, vol. 2, pp. 313, 344, which is based on archival materials from the state archive at Kiev.

78. This practice left its imprint in the Yiddish idiom: Ukrainian Jews did not ask, "Whose Hasid are you?" but "To whom [i.e., to which rebbe] do you travel?"

79. See *Divrei david, liqutei Torah me-ha-zaddik mi-tchortkov*, p. 6: Regarding "travel to the zaddik," there is an interesting passage which places such travel on a par with divine commandments, and, like them, "requires suitable preparation . . . and then he [the Hasid] may partake of the sanctity of the zaddik . . . and it is not, as is popularly believed, that the point of the trip is mainly to celebrate and enjoy the drinking, the singing and the dancing."

80. Wertheim, *Halakhot*, p. 155.

81. Tractate *Berakhot*, 34b.

82. Ibid.

83. Tractate *Bava batra* 116a.

84. In the *piyut*, "Ish hasid haya" sung on Saturday nights.

85. See n. 89 below regarding the source of this custom.

86. In *Me'ulefet safirim* by R. Shlomo Algazi, Tenth Day, section 22, the author cites the Zohar: "He was the son of Jesse, but why did he not mention his father? From this R. Shimon bar Yohai derived the following: that when a man should arrive before the Heavenly court of judgment, he should only state that which is beyond any possible doubt, and therefore he should say the name of his mother."

87. *Divrei david*, p. 42.

88. *Ta'amei ha-minhagim*, pt. 1, p. 82, no. 694.

89. Evidently, the custom of giving a *kvitl* to the zaddik is mentioned neither in early (pre-Lurianic) kabbalistic books nor in the works of the Ari's

disciples. It would appear to have first come into practice in the time of the
Besht and his disciples. What, however, is the source and religious basis of
this custom? R. Yekutiel Kamelhar's *Dor deʾah* (Bilgoraj, 1933) p. 37,
states that he had heard from Hasidim of Kshishai that the source is a
comment by Nahmanides (Ramban) on the verse Numbers 1:45. And
according to B. Yaushsohn, in his book *Fun unzer altn oytser,* pt. 8, p.
270: "The old Hasidic books indicate that the source for this custom is the
Ramban." Apparently, he, too, did not actually see the source in question,
for he did not cite the book by name, as was his normal practice. Therefore, it would seem that his information is secondhand. It is impossible at
this point to establish the original Hasidic source for this attribution (to
the Ramban), and whether the source (Ramban) led to the custom or was
afterward used to justify something that was already being practiced,
though it was originally based on some other source. But it seems likely to
me that the Besht was familiar with the source (Ramban) and built the
custom on it, because many of his teachings which have come down to us
through his disciple, the rabbi of Polonne, use citations from Ramban (see
Toledot, "Va-yishlah," "Va-yehi," and many other places). In addition,
Ramban was one of the most important of the early kabbalists, and it is
very likely that the Besht paid close attention to his commentaries. That
was probably the way he came upon this particular source and instituted
the practice of the *kvitl.* Ramban's comment is as follows:

> I have not understood the reason for this commandment, namely why the Holy
> One, blessed he He, commanded [that they should ascertain the number of the
> people]. For whilst there was indeed a need for them [the people] to establish their
> relationship to the [individual tribes] because of the [division of the tribes of Israel
> according to four] standards, I cannot understand why God commanded that they
> find out the number [of men in each tribe]. . . . Furthermore, he who comes before
> the father of the prophets, and his brother [Aaron], "the holy one of the Eternal"
> [Ps. 106:16] and becomes known to them by name, receives thereby a merit and life,
> because he has come "in the council of the people and in the register of the house of
> Israel" [Ezek. 13:9], and he receives a part in the merits of the community by being
> included in their numbers. Similarly, each of the people receives a special merit
> through being counted by number before Moses and Aaron, for they "will set" their
> "eyes upon them for good" [Jer. 24:6] and intercede on their behalf for mercy. . . ,
> and the shekels shall be a redemption for your souls. (Ramban, *Commentary on the
> Torah,* vol. 4: Numbers, trans. Rabbi Dr. Charles B. Chavel [New York, 1975], pp.
> 14–15)

90. See the so-called geniza pages in the edition published by "tomkhei temi-
mim" (Warsaw, 1937–38); and despite all the forgery that is present in
this collection, it does at least prove that it is a prevalent tradition among
the Hasidim.

91. The prayer book was in the possession of the Lipson family of Beltz,
Bessarabia. I heard from someone who actually saw the book that he read
the mentioned names.

92. *Taʾamei ha-minhagim,* pt. 4, p. 22, citing *Devash ha-sadeh* 1: 124.

93. Each zaddik had his own set times for these interviews and the acceptance of *kvitlakh* from his Hasidim. It was only in those hours that the Hasid could meet his rebbe face to face and present his request. The Yiddish term used for this work of the rebbe was *praven,* a word that was also used for the act of performing the Passover Seder, and it connotes an act of *tiqqun* (consecration) as in *tiqqun hasot.* Someone who had already been in to see the zaddik and had presented his *kvitl* and received his *tiqqun* was described as *opgepravet.* Habad Hasidim refer to the personal audience with the rebbe as *yehidus* (roughly: private session). When a Hasid went to visit his rebbe, and his friends did not for some reason send along their own *kvitlach* with him, they asked that he at least mention them orally to the zaddik.

94. *Taʾamei ha-minhagim,* pt. 2, p. 90.

95. Ibid.

96. *Abir ha-ro'im* (Piotrkow, 1935), p. 60.

97. Ibid.

98. *Taʾamei ha-minhagim,* pt. 3, p. 45, citing *Lev sameah.*

99. On the amulets, formulas and "protections" sometimes used by the zaddikim, see appendices to Wertheim, *Halakhot.*

100. See Tractate *Avot* 3:4: "Three who ate together and did not engage in discussion of Torah. . . ."

101. Tractate *Berakhot* 63b: "They all spoke in honor of hospitality . . ."; and Tractate *Taʾanit* 5b: "R. Nahman and R. Ishaq were sitting at a meal and R. Nahman said to R. Ishaq: 'Let the master expound something.' "

102. The importance of the meal in Hasidic religious life is also evident from this quotation from the zaddik R. Sholem of Belz (in Galicia) — one of the most prominent leaders of the movement in its middle period: "You spread a table for me" (Ps. 23:5) *[taʾarokh le-fanai shulhan],* these words have the initials tʾlʾsh, which can also stand for *tiqqun leil shavuʾot* [Shavuʾot eve vigil], and this is meant to tell us that the one is like the other: namely, that one may reach the state of consecration through love and enjoyment at the meal just as through Torah study at the vigil of Shavuʾot" (*Ta-amei ha-minhagim,* pt. 3, p. 82).

103. See Bartenura's commentary to *Avot* in this regard: "And with the after-meal blessing that they recite at the table they fulfill their obligation, and it is considered as if they had said words of Torah" (see *Tosefot yom tov* for that passage). And see also the Zohar, *parashat* "Terumah," p. 154a: "A table at which words of Torah are said is held to have a portion in God's possession . . ." (see this section generally about the great value of learned discussion at table).

104. *Toledot yaaqov yosef* "Hukat" (Miedzyboz edn.), p. 25.

105. See his discussions and responsa in his *Ben porat yosef* (Korzec, 1781).

106. *Vikuha rabba,* pt. 2, 11.

107. Tractate *Sanhedrin* 108a: "All that was on dry land perished, but not the fish in the sea."

108. *Ba-midbar rabba* 10:2; see also Palestinian Talmud, Tractate *Berakhot* 1, law 5.
109. See Dubnow, *Toledot ha-hasidut*, p. 85, the passage about Solomon Maimon (and see the chapter at the beginning of this volume—ed.).
110. *Abir ha-ro'im* (Piotrkow edn.), p. 123.
111. Dancing is also connected to the zaddik's table, for dancing generally took place around the table; but since there was dancing on other occasions as well, and meals without dancing, it therefore assumed an importance in its own right (see Wertheim, *Halakhot*, chap. 3.)
112. Tractate *'Eruvin* 53b.
113. *Orah hayyim* 170, par. 3.
114. Tractate *Sanhedrin* 92a.
115. *Sefer hasidim*, section 888.
116. Tractate *Mo'ed katan*, chap. 2, law 3.
117. Tractate *Berakhot* 51b.
118. See that passage, with the story of Yalta, wife of R. Nahman, who in her anger broke four hundred kegs of wine because he had not given her the blessing cup to taste the wine of benediction.
119. *Ma'aseh oreg*, commentary on the Mishna by R. Ishaq Yehuda Yehiel Safrin of Komarno (Introduction).
120. *Ta'amei ha-minhagim*, pt. 2, p. 23.
121. Commentary on "Praise" *(hodu)* ascribed to the Besht, which went through many printings. See also *Sefer ha-Besht* (Lodz edn., 1938), pt. 2, p. 24.
122. Compare: J. S. Minkin, *The Romance of Hasidism* New York, 1935), p. 327.
123. *Maor va-shemesh: parashat mishpatim*.
124. See below, on "soaked matzah."
125. *Ta'amei ha-minhagim*, pt. 3, p. 73, citing *Zikhron tov* by R. Sevi of Neshchiz.
126. See, e.g., the introduction to *Sefer ha-Besht* (Lodz edn.) with many sources for stories by the Besht.
127. *Qehal hasidim;* M. Buber, *Or ha-ganuz* (Jerusalem-Tel Aviv, 1947), p. 167.
128. Ibid., p. 169.
129. Pp. 73–74.
130. See Wertheim, *Halakhot ve-halikhot*, chap. 1, on study in the Hasidic world.
131. It is told that when Hasidim would sit down to study in the *beit midrash* in Liubavitch, many candles would be burning, but when they finished studying and began to tell stories of the zaddikim, they would extinguish the candles, leaving only one burning. Once, when they were telling a story of R. Mendel of Witebsk, the rebbe entered and said: You must light all the candles when you tell about that sainted zaddik, just as if you were engaged in learning Torah (Buber, *Or ha-ganuz*, p. 171).
132. *Sefer ha-Besht*, pt. p. 32, from the section *minhat shabbat*, section 96. And

see ibid., citing the view of R. Sevi of Sadegora, that telling stories about the Besht on Saturday night is a guarantee for the soul, and telling about R. Moshe Leyb of Sasow is a guarantee for prosperity; telling about the sainted rabbi of Berdyczew is a guarantee for the mitigation of punishment —even when mentioning him only by name, "the Berdyczewer [Rebbe]," rather than by his proper name, this is still effective.

133. *Knesset yisrael;* Buber, *Or ha-ganuz,* p. 302.

III

HASIDISM IN THE NINETEENTH CENTURY

12

Hasidism and the Jewish Enlightenment

Raphael Mahler

THE SOCIOPOLITICAL FOUNDATIONS OF HASIDISM IN GALICIA IN THE FIRST HALF OF THE NINETEENTH CENTURY

The Suppression of Galician Jewry

The period between 1815 and 1848, when the struggle between Haskalah and Hasidism in Galicia reached its most heated phase, was the most difficult in the history of the Jews in this province of the Austrian monarchy. The policy of brutal suppression of Galician Jewry, initiated in the era of so-called enlightened absolutism, was carried out in a more overt and shameless fashion by the Austrian government under the powerful Metternich. Not only did all previous restrictions of Jewish rights remain in effect but also new and highly oppressive edicts were issued.

As early as 1784–85, during the reign of Emperor Joseph II, Jews in the villages were forbidden to engage in trade, operate taverns or lease mills, and collect tolls; and the Edict of Toleration of 1789 banished Jews from the villages unless they were engaged in handicrafts or agriculture. Although this harsh edict was difficult to enforce, it did make life miserable for the village Jews, who lived in constant fear of being caught by the police. A Jew who was apprehended for selling liquor or for not having a special permit to reside in the village would, under this law, be returned under guard to his place of birth.[1] Jews were not allowed to reside in such towns as Żywiec, Kęty, Biała, Wadowice, Andrychów, Ciężkowice, Zakliczyn, Pilzno, Jasło, Bochnia, Wieliczka, and Mikołajów. Modern ghettos were introduced in the larger cities such as Lemberg (Lwów), Nowy Sącz, Tarnów, and Sambor, and even in the smaller ones, like Gródek Jagielloński and Jaryczów. Only individuals with an academic education or the vast fortune of thirty thousand gulden were permitted to settle outside these Jewish quarters. A Jew needed a special passport to travel from one city to another. Jews who came to Galicia had to pay the high poll tax which formerly they had paid in medieval Germany. Even for Jews involved in handicrafts there were difficulties because the Christian guilds did not admit Jews as members. Jews were forbidden to purchase either property in the cities or agricultural land from Christians, except for several hundred Jewish colonists whose number decreased from year to year due to harassment by Austrian officials.

The heaviest burden on the impoverished Jewish population in Galicia were the taxes specific to Jews which dated back to the time of Empress Maria Theresa and Emperor Joseph II. These were increased many times and new ones were frequently levied. For example, the special tax on *shehita* (ritually slaughtered meat), introduced in 1784, was so greatly increased in 1789, 1810, and 1816 that it came to three times the original levy and resulted in an increase in the price of kosher meat to twice that of nonkosher meat. Michael Stöger, a Christian scholar writing at that time, noted that "beef was either never or very seldom eaten by the poorer classes." The ignominious exploitation of the Jewish population by the pious Catholic Austrian monarchy was thus described by the well-known Viennese writer and Jewish communal leader Joseph von Wertheimer in his book, *Die Juden in Oesterreich* (On the condition of the Jews in Austria), which, due to censorship, was published in Leipzig:

Now this is not Shylock who, according to Shakespeare's slander, wanted to deprive a Christian of a pound of flesh but these are hundreds of thousands of Jews who are being deprived of substantial pounds of flesh on the ground of decrees of a Christian state.[2]

Still more invidious was the introduction in 1797 of the candle tax, which was trebled in the course of two decades. Every married Jewish woman was required to pay the candle tax of ten kreutzers on two candles to the tax lessee before the Sabbath began, whether or not she had any money to buy candles! The homes of those who could not pay promptly were raided by the tax collector on Friday night, and he was empowered to confiscate the household goods, including even the bedding. According to the reliable testimony of Wertheimer, one would often meet impoverished people on the street on Fridays begging for a few kreutzers in order to pay the candle tax.

In addition to these two imposts, the Galician Jews were burdened with a special marriage tax, a heavy residence tax, and an annual tax on *battei keneset* (houses of worship) and *minyanim* (private religious assemblies). Jews suspected of avoiding payment of any of these taxes, especially the candle tax, were required to take an oath of purgation every year, sometimes twice a year, wearing a *talit* (prayer shawl) and *kittel* (white ritual robe), in the presence of the rabbi and the district commissioner. The Austrian government also assumed the role of guardian of Jewish piety in order to increase its financial exploitation of the Jews. Thus, the eating of nonkosher meat was punishable by fine or imprisonment, and any Jewish woman who did not light Sabbath candles was subject to arrest, forced labor, and even whipping.

The institution of the *kehillah,* the autonomous administration of the Jewish community, was deeply demoralized by its being in effect handed over arbitrarily to the lessees of the candle tax. The *kehillah* became a private domain of the Jewish plutocracy. In the smaller Jewish communities, only those who regularly paid the tax on three to four candles a week were enfranchised and in the larger communities the tax was on seven candles a week. And, to be a candidate for *parnas* (trustee of the *kehillah*) or for rabbi, one had to furnish certification of regularly paid taxes on four to seven candles in the smaller communities and on eight to ten candles in the larger communities. Moreover, the candle tax lessee often issued false tax receipts for those men, including himself, whom he wanted appointed trustees. Thus, for example, in Lemberg in 1817, the candle tax lessees held four out of the five trusteeships in the *kehillah*.

In an 1818 report of the imperial chancellery, the government cynically acknowledged its financial exploitation of the Jewish masses: "The higher taxation [of the Jewish population] was maintained because a reduction of this taxation would be possible only if [the tax burden] were transferred to the rest of the population and this would create an unfavorable impression."[3]

Parallel with this economic exploitation of Galician Jews was the Austrian government's concerted attempt to germanize its Jews by attempting to eradicate their national distinctiveness, by, among other measures, destroying the Yiddish language. Having failed to germanize the Polish and the Ukrainian population, this policy was rigorously applied to the Jews, first out of sheer frustration and malice, and second in the hopes that the Jews, scattered as they were throughout the land, would serve as disseminators of the German language among the Gentiles. The closing of the German-Jewish schools is an example of an even stronger attempt to germanize the Galician Jews by legislative means. In 1806, the year the German-Jewish schools were closed, a court decree was issued requiring all officials of the larger Jewish communities to have a command of German. In 1810 the scope of this decree was broadened to require that every Jewish voter in *kehillah* elections prove his literacy in German. In 1814 an edict was issued declaring Hebrew and Yiddish documents inadmissible as evidence in the courts and invalid in government bureaus. The decree that every Jewish couple, prior to their marriage, be examined in German on the *Bnei Șion* catechism (published by the notorious school inspector Herz Homberg in 1812), was especially oppressive. The extent of the government's intention to germanize Galician Jewry is indicated in the imperial decree of January 22, 1820, which stated that, after a specified time, all synagogue services must be conducted in German or at least in the official local language.

Thus, the Jewish population of Galicia was under the double yoke of extreme poverty and governmental exploitation. According to official estimates, at least one-third of the Jewish population consisted of *luft-mentshn* (persons without a definite occupation), who subsisted on odd jobs or who had no trade and often no means of subsistence at all.[4] However, even those directly engaged in trade, approximately one-third, were primarily petty tradesmen and shopkeepers.[5] About one-fifth were engaged in crafts and small industry, of which one-half were employed in the garment industry as tailors, furriers, hatters, and shoemakers; the others were for the most part butchers, bakers, weavers, blacksmiths, goldsmiths, and watchmakers.[6] The mass of Galician Jewry lived in small towns, which at that time were still mostly the private property of the Polish nobility, as were several larger cities such as Tarnopol and Brody. Approximately one-fifth of the Jewish population lived in villages as innkeepers, tradesmen, and brokers,[7] despite all the legal restrictions, and were therefore subject to the whims of the Polish landowners and the malevolence of Austrian officials.

The extraordinary impoverishment of the Jewish population in Galicia is clearly illustrated by the fact that the government was initially forced to exempt 4,000 Jewish families from the candle tax and to reduce the tax by half for 11,000 families.[8] Since the entire Jewish population consisted of about 45,000 families (about 225,000 to 250,000 people),[9] it appears that one-third of the Jews were in such an extreme state of poverty that even the ruthless, reactionary administration had to make allowances.

The grave economic and political situation also accounts for the fact that the number of Jews in Galicia increased very little during the first half of the nineteenth century, while the gentile population approximately doubled during the same period. In 1773 the gentile population of Galicia numbered just above 2 million. Galician Jewry numbered 224,981 in 1773, and about 246,000 in 1827. Since the natural rate of increase of the Jews was certainly no less than that of the Gentiles, owing to the tradition of early marriages, it is probable that many more Galician Jews than Gentiles migrated to the neighboring provinces of Poland, the Ukraine, and Hungary.[10]

Thus, to seek solace from their grievous needs and sufferings and to express their yearning for redemption, the enslaved Jewish multitude in the small towns and villages of Galicia turned to the Hasidic movement. The nature of Hasidism in Galicia in this era of reaction (1815–48) is reflected in the Hasidic literature of the time, in official government documents, and in some of the utterances of the enemies of Hasidism, the Maskilim.

The Social Character of Hasidism

The answer to the question of which strata the adherents of Hasidism were recruited from can be found in the official acts. In the gubernatorial ordinance of July 29, 1823, regarding Hasidism, the Hasidic rebbes are described as those who exert influence on the "plebeian class" of Jews.[11] The district commissioner of Brody, in a report in 1827 to the gubernium, explains the class status of the adherents of Hasidism in the following words:

One recognizes such a Jew very easily. He goes about with a bare throat, with rolled up sleeves and usually is very dirtily and shabbily dressed. ... The commonest Jews belong to this sect. They attach themselves to no profession, are usually common tavernkeepers, swindlers and soothsayers *[Sagerer]*, for they have the firm conviction that God will provide for and help them even in the face of complete indolence.[12]

In an 1838 memorandum, the Lemberg police commissioner wrote to the gubernium:

The Hasidic leaders have discarded the outmoded and sometimes burdensome ceremonies of the Hebrew worship. The rabble hastily seized this opportunity. There are very few merchants among the Hasidim. For the most part they are idlers, drunkards and hypocritical, lazy fanatics.[13]

Although these characterizations are charged with hatred and contempt, they do state explicitly that the Galician Hasidim were a "common rabble" of tavernkeepers,[14] small shopkeepers, brokers, petty tradesmen (officially termed *Betrüger,* or swindlers), and poor, unemployed people. A similar characterization of the Hasidim is found in the casual comments in the letters of the Maskilim.

In his letter "Le yadid mithassed" of 1815, Solomon Judah Rapoport wrote that the Hasidim were lenient in interpreting the commandments "and therefore everyone of the poor people follows them."[15] A Maskil in the town of Jarosław, Ungar, described the Hasidim who came to welcome the zaddik Hersh of Żydaczów when he arrived in 1822 as a "crowd of ragged beggars."[16]

The Hasidic leader Moses of Sambor (brother of Hersh of Żydaczów) presented a similar picture of a reception for a zaddik. According to this account, "devotees hoping to catch a spark from his holy fire run to receive him. . . . As his star begins to rise the poor hasten to greet him; then the youths—like arrows from the hand of the mighty—flash by. Finally, as the noonday sun appears overhead, the princes of our generation and the leaders of the nation come to pay homage."[17]

In "Katit la-ma'or," a series of letters in *Kerem ḥemed* concerning the Rabbi Meir Ba'al ha-Nes boxes (alms boxes for the benefit of the poor in Ereṣ Yisrael that were distributed by Hasidim), Joseph Perl stated that R. Meir Ba'al ha-Nes "has no significance nor reputation at all among the great men but has been exalted by the poor people who do not understand how to differentiate between right and left." He described this as a new "custom that the ignorant and the poor are very fond of."[18] In Perl's *Megalleh temirin* (Revealer of secrets), the Hasid Reb Zaynvl of Verkhevke complains in a letter to Reb Zelig of Letitshiv that, because of the favors the Maskil "Mordecai, may his name be erased," prevailed upon the landowner to concede, "only the few poor men in our little *bet ha-midrash* [house of study] still adhere to the truth with us." [19] In *Boḥen zaddik* (The tester of the righteous), a review of his own *Megalleh Temirin*, Perl tells of his astonishment in meeting a very wealthy man in "Bitsuk" who was an adherent of "our company" and he immediately infers that this rich man probably sought esteem and honor in the eyes of the Hasidim "just to gain respect within the clique." [20]

In a letter of consolation written in 1827 by Nachman Krochmal,[21] the distinguished philosopher and leader of the Galician Haskalah, to Abraham Goldberg, a young Maskil of Mosty Wielkie, whose books had been burned by the Hasidim, Krochmal wrote that Hasidism is found only in eastern Europe:

In our province, too, they have been successful only in small towns such as the celebrated Mosty and environs, where they have made progress and taken root among the villagers dwelling on the Hungarian frontier, in the Wallachian hideouts of robbers,[22] and in the desolate Ukrainian steppes, all of them new communities recently established by refugees and exiles from the adjacent countries. The opposite is true of the old communities renowned for their learning, wisdom and large population, such as Cracow, Lemberg, Lublin, Brody, Tarnopol, Vilna, Brest, and the like. And in our areas the Maskilim leave them alone due to their insignificance and misery.

Even more characteristically, Krochmal encouraged his young friend to continue his secular studies, for "enlightenment will elevate you, will remove you from the wretched poor people and place you among the rich. The recognition and prestige bestowed upon the followers of knowledge, the genuinely enlightened, by the leaders of our people, as well as by kings and rulers, is a well-known fact." He pokes fun at the poor Hasidic rebbe who "is forced to flatter women, children and villagers . . . in order to alleviate his poverty and to satisfy his own hunger as well as that of his partisans and admiring followers. . . . The leprosy of poverty shines forth from his forehead," Krochmal writes. He wanders and begs "like those wretched gypsy families." Krochmal's letter speaks volumes not only about the social structure of the Hasidim but also about the relationship between the Haskalah, plutocracy, and ruling absolutism.

The works of the Maskilim from Poland and Volhynia also reflect their contempt for the "wretchedly poor" Hasidim. In *Teyator fun khsidim,* a play written by Ephraim Fischl Fischelsohn of Zamość,[23] the "paupers" motif appears in the opening as well as the finale. At the beginning, one of the characters, the Hasid Reb Shmuel Yerukhem of Bełz, says,

> By all means, do tell, why you don't like the Hasidim.
> What do you know! Though they're wretchedly poor
> Really naked and bare
> Without a shirt on their backs
> And indeed terrible paupers
> Still they flock to the rebbes.

Concerning the dispute between the Maskil and the Hasid, the yeshivah students conclude that Leybele the Maskil "is a fine fellow":

> And our Hasidim, those paupers,
> Are indeed vagabonds and fools. . . .

The hero of Isaac Ber Levinsohn's anti-Hasidic satire *Emeq refa'im* (Valley of ghosts)[24] relates that, when already "famous among the masses as a wonder worker," he decided to become a rebbe. He avoided settling down in the big cities, where enlightened merchants, men of keen intellect, and the very wealthy lived, in favor of a very small town where "people who, because of extreme poverty, are constantly occupied eking out a living." He did become widely known outside his own town in all the surrounding towns and villages, but he began his "rounds" in the villages. In his will, he advises his son how to find favor with "the rabble and the poor." In the satire *Divrei zaddikim* (Words of the righteous), also by Levinsohn,[25] the two protagonists, the Hasidim Reb Henekh Soyfer and Reb Hirsh Itsik, are also portrayed as indigents who lack the money to travel to their rebbe and sometimes receive alms even from Maskilim. In a letter written in 1840 by Levinsohn to Daniel Hartenstein of Radziwiłłów[26] he complains about his poverty, requests material assistance, and asks rhetorically: To whom shall I turn? Perhaps to the holy people in the land or to their gang? Or to the poor people who do not know their way about and for want of wisdom seek protection under the wings of Hasidism?

From the very beginning of Hasidism, its character was set by the middle class, which occupied the lower level of the social hierarchy vis-à-vis the Talmudists, and the merchant class, with which the Hasidim were connected. This middle class consisted of liquor franchise holders in the villages and small towns, the more prosperous innkeepers, and the brokers at the courts of the nobility. In the Polish provinces adjacent to Galicia the communal strong men and tax lessees took over. As will be shown, prior to the social transformation of Hasidism, prosperous elements from the feudal sphere joined its ranks and were a component of the movement's social structure. What all these social elements had in common was their dependence on the feudal economy within both the local community and the province at large—a feudalism weakening with the slow but steady growth of capitalism and with the increasing strength of the absolutist regime.

Thus, the wretched living conditions of the Jewish petty bourgeoisie, its concerns and hopes, dreams and ideals, are all reflected in Hasidic philosophy and practices.

Beliefs and Values of Hasidim

Hasidic doctrine is usually expressed through the exegesis of Torah passages, although comprehension of the text is not its aim. On the contrary, the Torah is merely a point of departure for homilies on conduct, consolation, assurances of imminent redemption, and the like. For example, the Exodus from Egypt provides ample material for sermons on the contemporary Exile and the promise of Redemption and the Korah story for tirades against heretics and Mitnaggedim who find no need for a rebbe. Moreover, the use of kabbalistic interpretation of the Torah (Abraham, for example, represents mercy; Isaac, judgment) always made it possible to link the Hasidic doctrine in the sermons preached at the rebbe's Sabbath table to the weekly Torah portion.[27]

The basic idea in all Hasidic doctrine of this period in Galicia is the primacy of the kabbalistic notion of *midat ha-ḥesed* (divine grace) as personified in the *sefirah Ḥesed*.[28] All the calamities of the *galut klali* (the exile of the Jewish people), as well as of the *galut prati* (the exile of the individual Jew), derive from the dominance of *midat ha-din* (stern judgment) over *midat ha-ḥesed*. This is manifested by the lack of unity in God's name; that is to say, of the four Hebrew letters which compose the tetragrammaton, the first two—the *yod* and the *he,* representing the Holy One, blessed be He—and the second two—the *vav* and the *he,* representing the *Shekhinah* (Divine Presence)—are separated. Every Jew is in a position—through fervent prayer, good deeds, and inner love of God—to restore this kabbalistic unity of God and thereby to secure the rule of *midat ha-ḥesed*. Devotion in prayer is not merely an emotion but, in a tradition that derives from the teachings of the Baal Shem Tov, is also the intention to unify the higher spheres. In this vein, Rebbe Hersh of Żydaczów explained the dictum of *Pirqei Avot* (Ethics of the Fathers) that "all your deeds should be done in the name of Heaven," instead of simply "for Heaven," as an exhortation to intend each act and word "for uniting God's names."[29] Furthermore, he claimed, the zaddik reaches the stage whereby his mere breathing achieves this unification: He exhales with the name *Elohim* (attribute of judgment) and inhales with *yod he vav he* (attribute of mercy).[30]

Thus, every Jew is responsible in his conduct not only for himself but also for the entire Jewish people. As piety, love of God, and good deeds increase, so does the abundance of God's grace that streams down upon the entire Jewish people and on each individual Jew. "However, faith is primary, for if a man believes with perfect faith that the Lord delivers the abundance of his livelihood to him every day, and truly believes in his heart in God, then this evil spirit is subjugated and is unable to rob him of that abundance."[31]

Undoubtedly, zaddikism also plays an important role in the Hasidic conception of the category of *midat ha-ḥesed*. Several Hasidic books of that period, as in the earlier works (such as the *No'am elimelekh*), constantly repeat the warning that, without the mediation of the zaddik or at least without his guidance, God's abundance cannot be attained.[32] In this respect, the conception of *midat ha-ḥesed* in Hasidism is similar to that of the dogma of God's grace in Catholicism, in which salvation cannot be imagined without the mediation of the Church, the "mediatrix of divine grace." The Hasidic teaching of divine grace and complete faith in God primarily reflects the pitiful, uncertain, and haphazard existence of the Jewish village tavernkeeper, small shopkeeper, or broker of the time who did not know in the evening if he would earn a piece of bread for himself and his family the following day.[33]

In Volhynia and Congress Poland, where because of various legal restrictions there were fewer tavernkeepers than in Galicia, smugglers *(peklmakhers)* held a significant position among the Hasidim. Rebbes are portrayed cooperating with smugglers by Levinsohn in *Emeq refa'im*, in the anonymous *Di genarte velt* (The deceived world), and by Fischelsohn in his *Teyator fun khsidim*. Abraham Ber Gottlober tells in his memoirs of knowing "such persons who call themselves Hasidim" who come over the border to Galicia to the son of Rebbe Israel of Ruzhin and whose visits are "merely coverups" for smuggling contraband on their way back home.[34]

It is not surprising that the most solid economic element among the Jewish petty bourgeoisie, the artisan, is least represented in the Hasidic stories.[35] Gottlober described the Hasidim of his youth as "particularly hating the crafts and making fun of artisans living from manual labor." Generalizing about the vocational spectrum of the Hasidim, he said, "Hardly anyone in those circles takes up a trade," but he stressed this applied to declared Hasidim and not to those who just believed in rebbes and presented them gifts, among the latter of which there were some "unlettered" artisans.[36] We may guess that these artisans were from small towns. In larger communities, they either inclined toward the Mitnaggedim or removed themselves from the controversy altogether, as the ignorant of ancient days essentially kept their distance from the Sadducee-Pharisee struggle. In *Teyator fun khsidim*, Reb Shmuel the Hasid conjoins (in the course of rhyme), of all things, "tailor's apprentices, nothing but servants" ("Shnayderyungen, same meshorim") with "such great heretics" ("Azoyne groyse apikorsim").[37]

"Children, life and daily bread" is the earthly undertone in all the consolatory teachings of the Hasidic leaders. In *Teyator fun khsidim* the Maskil, Reb Leybele, mocks the Hasidim:

You argue that a Hasid cries day and night,
Why shouldn't he, isn't he right?
How can he be happy when he thinks about his brood
And about his creditors?
What's surprising about that?[38]

The Hasidic collections of stories very often tell of people, for the most part penniless lessees and tenant innkeepers, whose deep faith remained despite their woes. Even in the second half of the nineteenth century, the folksinger Velvl of Zbaraż depicted the Hasid as a pauper whose faith never fails him for a moment.[39]

If, according to the Hasidic teachings, all the woes of the Jewish people and of each individual Jew are caused by the domination of the power of *midat ha-din,* this domination reveals itself first of all in the oppression of the Jews by the gentile nations. Almost all the Hasidic books of this period are replete with complaints about the oppressive burden of exile placed upon the Jewish people by the gentile nations.

This contrasts significantly with the position of the Maskilim of that time, who not only did not mention the oppression of the Jews, but [in their desire to gain support for their programs of reform] also preached loyalty, devotion, and gratitude to the "gracious" government.

"The holy sparks spread among the Gentiles and nourish them; they have grown up strong and are successful in their wickedness and make ever more difficult our burden of bondage and of exile," complained Naphtali of Ropczyce.[40] "On Passover today—as opposed to the Temple era—we eat bitter herbs before matzoh," explained Mendel of Rymanów a generation earlier in Napoleonic times. "Matzoh symbolizes redemption; bitter herbs, exile. In dispersion we first acknowledge the bitter, then the fervent hope for deliverance and restoration of our glory."[41]

Hersh of Żydaczów bade Jews to divide their time between studying the Kabbalah and earning a living. He justified this on the ground that "especially in our generation, with its burden of taxes and tolls and under the yoke of exile in our generation, which is the period preceding the coming of the Messiah,[42] the people of the country are becoming ever more impoverished."[43] He specifically mentioned the taxes as a tribulation of the cruel Exile; legend in fact represents him as the defender of the Jewish people against the special Jewish taxes. It is told that in keeping with an old Purim custom, Hersh's brother Kopl once disguised himself as a prince of the realm. Intoxicated and accompanied by a retinue, Kopl went to his brother Hersh, who honored him as a king and implored him to revoke the burdensome candle and kosher meat taxes. The Purim king agreed to this and even signed his name to one such edict. However, when Kopl refused his brother's request to rescind the onerous decree of military service, Hersh held it against him for some time.[44] In contrast, Rebbe Hersh, through intercession on high, was able to nullify the decree banishing Jewish tavernkeepers from the villages. He accomplished this, it was explained, because the taverns provided not only food but also prayer shawls and phylacteries for Jewish travelers.[45]

Hasidism and Germanization

In view of the Hasidim's vigilance with regard to matters of religion, the attempts of the Austrian government to germanize the Jews were considered as repressive as the taxes. Thus, the rebbes stubbornly defended the Yiddish language and the old modes of dress and customs. Mendel of Rymanów saw in the decrees concerning "new clothing" and "new languages" the work of the *qelipah gedolah,* "the shell" (i.e., the evil spirit) that precipitated the gentile nations' gaining power over the people of Israel. He cited the talmudic statement that the Jews were redeemed from slavery in Egypt because they did not change their names, their language, or their dress.[46] In this regard, Şevi Elimelekh of Dynów, a student of Hersh of Żydaczów, spoke of the edict declaring Hebrew and Yiddish documents invalid in the government bureaus and courts and the edict requiring a Jewish bride and groom to pass an examination in German as a precondition for legal marriage:

And now, because of our many sins, an unsparing, evil decree has been issued declaring that our holy tongue has become an invalid coin, God forbid. Who would have believed this about the language that has from time immemorial been regarded even among the wise men of the Gentiles as the best and most magnificent language; the language in which the world was created and that was given as a gift through divine revelation to His chosen people. Now fortune has changed through this evil decree that prohibits any document in matters of business and any bill of sale in our holy tongue. . . . The decree that a marriage cannot be performed until the couple is versed in the foreign writing and tongue.

Consequently, he demands that the Yiddish language be maintained with devotion and that it not be supplanted by German.

Therefore, my beloved brothers and friends, guard the lock on your mouth and speak to one another only in the language that was instituted by our ancestors in the Diaspora, with its admixture of the holy tongue, so that the language of Judaism should be visible as a distinct [language] from the languages of the Gentiles. Keep your children as much as possible from foreign tongues and God will bring his nation to speedy deliverance in our day as He did for our forefathers in Egypt.

The same author pours out his wrath and mockery upon "the wicked who are proud of the foreign language and consider it a disgrace to mix even a word of our holy tongue into their speech."[47]

It was not only their attachment to the Yiddish language and tradition that strengthened the Hasidim in their struggle against the attempts at germanization. The Hasidim viewed the germanizing policy as but another element in the Austrian system of oppression and fiscal exploitation of the Jews. "These were obviously our enemies," Şevi Elimelekh said of the proponents of German, namely, the Maskilim, "through denunciations, robberies and the burden of taxes."[48] The fact that Herz Homberg, the brutal germanizer of Galician Jewry, was one of the initiators of the institution of the candle tax was probably still fresh in the memory of the Hasidim.[49] The moderate Maskilim also offered the government their unqualified support. It is therefore not surprising that the Hasidim held them responsible for the anti-Jewish decrees.

The Hasidim vigorously opposed not only the study of German, but also all secular studies. Although the fear of cultural assimilation played a large part in the Hasidim's struggle against enlightenment, the principal factor was their kabbalistic Weltanschauung. According to Hersh of Żydaczów and Ṣevi Elimelekh of Dynów, every secular area of inquiry is opposed to God, as it originates in *ḥokhmah ḥiṣonit* (external science) which comes from the *sitra aḥra* (other side), and is thus essentially empty and false.

Like many of the Christian sects during the Middle Ages and the Reformation, Hasidism attacked science not only because it was hostile to enthusiastic, inwardly directed religion but also because it was closely allied to the new socioeconomic order of capitalism, which was undermining the old relationships of production and the medieval ways of life connected with them. For the occupations of the Hasidic masses were rooted in the old, essentially feudal relations of production between lord and serfs, with the small-town Jew and village Jew serving as middlemen between city and countryside, as well as between the landowner and his peasants.

Science was regarded by the Hasidim to be such a great threat to faith that even medicine was rejected by some of the rebbes. When the terrible cholera epidemic of 1831 broke out, Hersh of Żydaczów deemed it necessary to write a letter enjoining his Hasidim in Munkacs against being treated by a physician. He justified this prohibition by claiming that the true healer is the zaddik, who is the link *(qav ha-emsaʿi)* between the Jews and the Almighty, the "healer of the sick among his people, Israel." His remedy for cholera was to "recite all of Psalms every week, pledge to charity after completing each of the five books of the Psalms, recite the *ketoret* [the biblical portions concerning burning of incense in the Tabernacle] before 'May it be Thy will,' and examine the mezuzahs to insure that they are ritually fit."[50]

Rebbe Nahman of Bratslav preceded Rebbe Hersh in the absolute prohibition against physicians.[51] Rebbe Simon of Jarosław, also known as Simon of Dobromil, repeated Nachman's extreme antirationalist saying over and over, "The ultimate in wisdom is not to be wise at all."[52]

In contrast to the religious and rationalistic Christian sects which opposed superstitions as adamantly as they did secular science, the Hasidic movement was permeated by superstitions of all kinds. The Hasidim believed as much in magical remedies, amulets, exorcisms, demonic possession (dybbuks), ghosts, devils, and teasing, mischievous genies as they did in the almost unlimited heavenly power of the zaddik. Thus, the distance between the religious rationalism of most of the medieval Christian sects and the superstitious mysticism of Hasidism was in a sense as great as the socioeconomic difference between those sectarians, workers, and artisans who were directly involved in the processing of raw materials and the Jewish shopkeeper and déclassé elements who, for hundreds of years, were cut off from any direct contact with the production process.

Jew, Gentile, and the Messianic Age

The views of the Hasidim about their native land and the land of Israel, Jews and Gentiles, and the Messiah and Redemption were a direct outgrowth and development of the Weltanschauung of the Kabbalah. The Jewish people were not simply the chosen, but were the only people of God; "Israel and the Torah and the Holy One, blessed be He, are one." According to the Midrash, the whole world was created only for the sake of the Jews. The Jews are dispersed in order to gather together the holy sparks that are scattered over the earth. Consequently, their feelings of social involvement did not reach beyond their own people.

The positive expression of this attitude was the principle of the unconditional solidarity of the Jews and the idea of *ahavat yisrael* (love of the Jewish people). *Ahavat yisrael*, the leitmotif of the teachings of Levi Isaac of Berdyczew, as well as of the legends about him, is just as characteristic a motif in the stories and legends of the prominent Hasidic rebbes in the first half of the nineteenth century.[53] However, a negative attitude toward Gentiles, which took the form of contempt, was also an unavoidable consequence of this position. As Mendel of Rymanów put it, "A Gentile does not have a heart, although he has an organ that resembles the heart."[54] Simon of Jarosław asserted that the Gentiles will be held responsible not for their evil decrees—these were actually divinely inspired and had been prophesied in order to "cleanse [the Jews] of their sins"—but for their "vengefulness and revelry in the distress of the Jews."[55] The symbol for the Gentile in the Hasid's consciousness was the brutal landowner or the enslaved and boorish peasant.

In practice, however, the folk character of Hasidism caused the Hasid to relate to the [Christian] peasants with a certain sympathy. This can be inferred both from the Jewish and Ukrainian legends about the Baal Shem Tov and from the stories about Meyer of Przemyślany and other rebbes of his time. The fact that peasants would sometimes come to a rebbe for help is also related by Levinsohn in his *Emeq refa'im*.[56] In fact, the peasants were often exploited in their daily economic relations with the Jewish tradesmen and brokers, especially with the tavernkeepers, though the exploiters were themselves impoverished. But this resulted from the general phenomenon of exploitation of the village by the landowner and the city which had prevailed for hundreds of years prior to the inception of Hasidism. Only the Maskilim, who saw Hasidism as the cause of all the miserable and deceitful aspects of Jewish life, held this movement responsible even for the evils which were often an unavoidable product of the economic activities of most small-town and village Jews. In *Teyator fun khsidim*, Leybele the Maskil admonishes the Hasidim,

> The Gentile works bitter and hard.
> For all his pain, the Jew
> Comes by and steals his gain.[57]

As to the fate of the gentile nations in the Messianic Age, Hasidic books highlight two biblical positions—one positive, one negative. Even those that speak of revenge and judgment against the gentile nations[58] paint the prophetic picture of the Messianic Age, when all nations will be converted to Judaism and will devote themselves to the Torah.[59]

Just as all the nations exist, according to the Hasidim, only by virtue of the Jewish people, so the earth endures thanks only to the land of Israel because "Ereṣ Yisrael is the essence of the world and all vitality stems from it."[60] The life of the Jews in the Diaspora is considered to be a merely temporary phenomenon. Mendel of Rymanów surprisingly regards the laws permitting Jews to purchase houses as a ruse intended to bind them more closely to the lands of the Exile and subsequently to assimilate them. By way of contrast, he points to the Jews of Egypt, who lived in tents because they did not want to become permanent inhabitants in their diaspora.[61] It was not only Mendel of Rymanów, who, active in Napoleonic times when messianic expectations were heightened by the world upheaval, spoke of the Messianic Age and imminent Redemption, but also the rebbes of the later generation, such as Mendel of Kosów, Simon of Dobromil, Naphtali of Ropczyce, Hersh of Żydaczów, and his student Ṣevi Elimelekh of Dynów.[62] "The time of redemption has already arrived," writes one rebbe, "and all the predestined dates have passed and the matter depends only on great repentance."[63] The faith of the ordinary Hasidim in the imminent advent of the Messiah and the Redemption was as firm as their rebbes'. "Even though he tarries, I await him daily" was the cardinal principle of faith set forth by Maimonides and observed quite literally by the Hasidim. It is told of Rebbe Sholem Rokeakh of Bełz that, when greeted with "Next year in Jerusalem" while drawing water to bake matzoh before Passover, he replied, "Why should it be next year? We hope and pray that the water we have just drawn will be used tomorrow to bake matzoh in Jerusalem."[64]

With unwavering faith in the ancient religious tradition rooted in prophetic vision, the expositors of Hasidic doctrine taught the concept of a total redemption—both national and spiritual. Rebbe Moses of Sambor, brother of Hersh of Żydaczów, stressed a triple goal: "We seek the Kingdom of Heaven, the Kingdom of David and the rebuilding of the Temple."[65]

While these Hasidic teachings reflect the social distress and political oppression of the Jewish masses and their yearning for Redemption, the Hasidic movement did not propose any social or political programs. The healthy social instinct of self-help and self-defense did, however, thrust the Hasidic masses closer together and strengthened mutual assistance and unified resistance to the oppressive measures of the government. The spontaneity of these actions in the total absence of any social or political goals reveals even more clearly the tragic contradiction between the potential of the masses and their feeling of powerlessness. This powerlessness found expression first and foremost in greater piety and in mysticism.

Charity in Hasidic Life

Though Hasidism was a petty bourgeois movement, it never regarded wealth as a direct product of social exploitation. The Kabbalah theory of *midat ha-ḥesed* determined from the very outset that the Hasid should be resigned to the existing class differences in Jewish society. In this teaching, the rich man was the one who received a greater portion of *midat ha-ḥesed*.[66] The poor man's recourse was to increase the influx of *midat ha-ḥesed* both for himself and for all the Jews through his conduct, prayer, learning, and good deeds. The poverty of the Jewish masses was attributed to national oppression, "the bondage of the exile" caused by the sins of the Jewish people. When the Jews were worthy and the Messianic Age arrived, the disproportionately large share previously held by the gentile nations would be held by the people of Israel.

In practice, the desire to reconcile the class differences and the drive for social reform could find expression only in charity, the one possible form of self-help under the prevailing conditions. Hasidic works of that time contain numerous injunctions concerning the importance of charity. Mendel of Kosów reiterates the teachings of the Talmud[67] and the works of ethical literature[68] which oblige the prosperous Jew to regard his money as a loan from God and not as an unconditional possession. Naphtali of Ropczyce interprets the prayer of grace after meals, "Lord our God, O make us not dependent on the gifts and loans of men but rather on Thy full, open and generous hand. . . ," as saying that one should not be dependent upon those who regard the giving of charity as a gift to the poor or as a loan to God, but upon those who understand that they have received money from God's hand as a trust which was intended to be distributed to the poor.[69]

Of the three things on which the world is based — Torah, divine service, and the practice of kindliness — Meyer of Przemyślany believed the most important one to be the practice of kindliness (*gemilut ḥasadim*). In support, he cites Ps. 89:3 — *olam ḥesed yivneh* (usually translated as "forever is mercy built")—understanding *olam* as "world" instead of "forever," thus "the world is built on kindness."[70] It is on account of the poor who do not receive enough charity, says Simon of Dobromil, that misfortune is brought upon the entire Jewish people, thus causing, as it were, "dissension in Heaven."[71] The matter of charity is thus closely related to the foundations of the system of the kabbalistic-Hasidic Weltanschauung—*midat ha-ḥesed* is directly dependent upon earthly grace. If kindliness is not practiced on earth, *midat ha-din* will dominate the world.[72] Even biblical verses having no relation at all to charity were ingeniously interpreted as alluding to it.[73] Furthermore, to encourage charitableness, there was no hesitation about altering a simple interpretation of a talmudic injunction. For example, the reform of the Academy of Usha: "One who is extravagant [in alms-giving] should not squander more than one-fifth of his holdings"[74] was reinterpreted by R. Uri of Strelisk as follows: "The person for whom giving charity is the same as being robbed, should not donate more than one-fifth of his holdings; he may give more, however, if he is one who is inspired by the act of giving." This interpretation is based on the similarity between the Hebrew roots for booty *(bzh)* and squander *(bzbz)*.[75]

The Hasidic legends, even more than the rabbinic legislation, reflect the role that charity played in the Hasidic movement. There are folktales about the alms-giving and charitableness not only of the earlier generation of leaders of the Galician Hasidim, such as Moses Leyb of Sasów[76] and Mendel of Rymanów, but also of the later zaddikim, Hersh of Żydaczów, his nephew Yitskhok Ayzik of Żydaczów, and Naphtali of Ropczyce,[77] and even stories of zaddikim giving everything to the poor, for example Meyer of Przemyślany.[78] For the Hasidim, the zaddik was regarded as a kind of philanthropic administrator, receiving fees for his advice and returning them to the neediest, in the form of both cash and room and board for the steady followers at his court. In *Emeq refa'im*, even Levinsohn acknowledged that the zaddik contributed money to the poor people of his town, though he was quick to point out that those alms amounted to only a small fraction of the sum he collected during his trips to the surrounding small towns and that his true motive was to become known as a philanthropist.[79] Austrian officials of that time also attested to the fact that charity was one of the chief characteristics of Hasidism. In the 1827 report of the district chief of Stryj to the provincial presidency, we read, "They have assumed the name Hasidim, or more pious Jews, because they turn their attention to the alleviation of the misery and to the support of their unfortunate coreligionists."[80]

Hasidic Solidarity

Like charity and benevolence, unconditional solidarity was a distinctive feature of the Hasidim during that period. In a letter to his Hasidim in Drohobycz and Brody, Hersh of Żydaczów addressed them as "comrades" and emphasized repeatedly that the basis of Hasidism is love for one another and unity among them. In this letter, he added that "all poverty stems from disunity of hearts," and that it is "critical" to "join with one's fellow in love, for that is the goal of Hasidism and its source."[81] In the same vein, Uri of Strelisk preached that it is "essential to Israel that all be bound in a single unity."[82] And Moses of Sambor preached that the Jews would be able to draw compassion from heaven only when love, brotherhood, and friendship reigned among them.[83]

Solidarity was also listed in the official reports of the Austrian civil servants as one of the characteristic traits of the Hasidic movement. The commissioner of Brody wrote in his report for the year 1827: "The Hasidim are bound to each other with heart and soul."[84] The same was recorded by the district chief of Przemyśl in his report of that same year[85] and by the Lemberg chief of police in a report from 1838, in which he also pointed out the strict discipline and conspiratorial methods of the Hasidim.[86] In 1837 Levinsohn wrote to the Warsaw censor, Jacob Tugendhold, in connection with his plan to organize an association of Maskilim under the name "Zion," asking, "How much longer will we tolerate the Hasidic sect, which is united by such a strong bond and whose members help one another?"[87]

Indeed, the Hasidim responded to the oppressive policies of the Austrian government by emphasizing solidarity among themselves and the rest of the Jewish community, and by offering a form of organized passive resistance.

Thus, the village Jews could violate the governmental prohibition of the sale of liquor in the villages through the cooperation of the landowners from whom they had rented the taverns. According to an estimate of the imperial chancellery, in 1836 Jewish tavernkeepers were to be found in at least three-quarters of the Galician villages.[88] The Jewish masses likewise evaded the excessive wedding taxes and the law concerning the German language examination of all prospective bridal couples on Homberg's catechism, *Bnei Ṣion,* by dispensing with the civil regulations and merely undergoing the religious wedding ceremony. From the official statistics for the year 1826, it is apparent that the actual number of marriages among the Jews of Galicia was 1,122, while only 137 legal marriages were recorded.[89] Jews generally shunned the official government courts, resorting instead to the *bet din* (rabbinical court). Similarly, they circumvented the governmental requirement of a special permit for *minyanim* and the payment of the high tax by meeting secretly in the small *shtiblekh* (Hasidic houses of prayer). When the government outlawed the publication of Hasidic and kabbalistic works, the Hasidim established secret presses and printed false dates and places of publication. In spite of the decree of 1800 that forbade the importation of Hebrew and Yiddish books from abroad, the Jews smuggled books from Russia. Despite the prohibition on transferring money abroad without a special permit, the Hasidim succeeded in making regular collections on behalf of Jewry in Palestine and in secretly forwarding the sums there.[90] Many denunciations of the Hasidim by the Maskilim include, among their other sins, the offense of collecting money for Ereş Yisrael.[91]

To evade military service, which, under the circumstances, was considered tantamount to forced conversion, the Jews either furnished incorrect birth dates or, if possible, simply neglected altogether to register their sons. Perl, who nevertheless undoubtedly knew the true reason for this "negligence," expressed astonishment in his denunciation to the government in 1838 over the fact that the Jews "place obstacles in the way of regular registration." The Jewish masses also banded together to protect Jews from foreign lands, primarily emigrants from Russia. In the same denunciation, Perl complained that every time the police in Tarnopol arrested Russian Jews, the Jews of Tarnopol would go en masse to the prison and claim that those captured were truly native-born inhabitants. Perl further related that the officials became so confused that they were finally forced to release the imprisoned Jews.

The Hasidim and the masses offered their strongest and most organized resistance to the candle and kosher meat taxes, and they fought the lessees of those taxes by any means at their disposal. In one of the oldest denunciations against the Hasidim found on record, namely that against the local Hasidic rebbe Jacob Groynem of Tomaszów in 1824 by Hayyim Herbst of Mosty Wielkie in the district of Żółkiew, it is alleged that this rebbe lured Jews not only into "fanaticism" but also "to illegal acts that are detrimental to the imperial treasury," and that he cursed the tax lessees and put them under bans.[92] Perl justified his denunciation of 1838, in which he proposed that the government put the houses of study *(battei midrash)* under its control, with the argument that "all bans against the Jewish taxes and against the tax lessees are planned there." In a later denunciation of the same year, Perl mentioned boycotts organized by the rebbes against those tax lessees who opposed them. In such cases, "anonymous bans are proclaimed against the consumption of meat." Perl also related that the Hasidim avoided the payment of the kosher meat tax by having their *shohatim* operate secretly in the villages where there was no control, since ritual slaughter was legal only in the cities. In the 1841 denunciation of the Hasidim of Buczacz by Joseph Tepper, a Tarnopol Maskil, the offenses of the rabbi-rebbe-Halakhist Abraham David Kru, who had died the previous year, include the charge that "he used to excommunicate every tax lessee."[93] In the 1827 report of the district chief of Stryj, it is said of the Hasidim that "even the fact alone that the kosher meat [tax] lessee of the whole district has not yet been exposed to any attack can serve as evidence that the adherents of this sect have not yet slipped into the Stryj district."[94] This bureaucrat was obviously ignorant of what transpired in his domain if he concluded Hasidim were not present there. However, the struggle of the Hasidim against the tax lessees was so widely known that any region where a tax lessee had peace of mind was thought to be without Hasidim. In Lemberg the candle tax lessees were so hated that in 1808 they submitted a request to the government for permission to reside outside the Jewish quarter because of the attacks against them.[95]

Furthermore, the power of bans, particularly against the consumption of meat, was great. Even those not sympathetic to such restrictions would submit to the pressure of unified mass actions and refrain with the rest of the Jewish population from eating meat, and eat dairy dishes even on the Sabbath and holidays. When such a ban was proclaimed in a town, the district chief would send the district rabbi there to effect its repeal. Travel expenses for the rabbi came from the district chief, who later collected them from the rebellious *kehillah*. However, such "punitive expeditions" had little effect. In Lemberg, the government also attempted to counteract the bans against tax lesees by calling assemblies of the most prominent Galician rabbis. From the end of the eighteenth century there were six such rabbinical assemblies, to which several of the nineteen district rabbis and other prominent rabbis of smaller towns were invited. The last of these assemblies was convened in 1830. These assemblies issued bans against all those who "defrauded" the government by avoiding payment of the candle and kosher meat taxes. Such a ban was then printed and posted on a special black tablet in all the synagogues. Every rabbi was obliged to proclaim this ban orally in the synagogue four times a year. However, these solemn bans seldom deterred anyone. In 1830, at the very same time that a rabbinical assembly in Lemberg was issuing such a ban, leaflets were distributed there forbidding the consumption of meat under penalty of a Hasidic ban. Since the solidarity of the people was stronger than the official ban of the rabbis, the meat tax lessee was, in such instances, forced to reduce the tax.[96]

Thus, Hasidism was a significant factor in uniting the Jewish masses in Galicia to resist the oppression and fiscal exploitation of Austrian absolutism. "The nonpartisan observer who merely glances at Galician Jewry," said Perl in his anti-Hasidic denunciation of 1838, "is immediately faced with the great problem of explaining its complete disregard of almost all the state laws issued in its behalf."[97]

Social Alliances and the Roles of the Rebbes

Just as the Hasidim succeeded in gathering under their banner the greater part of Galician Jewry by their solidarity and their clandestine struggle against the oppressive decrees of the Austrian government, so Hasidism eventually became a conservative force that carried with it the Jewish middle class because of its defense of religion and tradition against the attacks of the Haskalah. Non-Hasidic Orthodoxy discerned in the Haskalah a much greater danger to the Jewish religion and to its own hegemony in Jewish life than in Hasidism, and, therefore, its struggles against Hasidism gradually gave way to the struggle against the modernization of Jewish life.

At the beginning of the nineteenth century, the borderline between the Hasidic petty bourgeoisie and the non-Hasidic Orthodox middle class in Galicia was still discernible. Mendel of Kosów, the author of *Ahavat shalom*, enumerated in his treatise four "classes" *(kitot)* among the Jews, characterizing them as follows: (1) the completely wicked; (2) the ignorant people; (3) the scholars; and (4) the Hasidim.[98] It is not difficult to infer that his "completely wicked" are the Maskilim, while the class of "ignorant people" denotes chiefly the artisans, that petty bourgeois element that was always furthest from the Hasidic movement. If the social base of the Hasidim was the petty bourgeois tradesmen, tavernkeepers, and the *lumpenproletariat*, then the class of "scholars" — i.e., Orthodox opponents *(Mitnaggedim)* of Hasidism — found its primary social support in the "respectable burghers" who constituted the Jewish middle class. I. B. Levinsohn's *Emeq refa'im* leaves no doubt that the "wealthy, the prosperous, and the merchants" were, as a rule, Mitnaggedim, adherents of the "scholars" and the "sagacious."[99] The following of the Mitnaggedim was initially much weaker than that of the Hasidim since the Jewish middle class was much smaller than the Jewish petty bourgeoisie. As early as 1837, Perl submitted a report to the Austrian government[100] in which he divided the Galician Jews, according to their religious views, into almost the same four classes as the *kitot* that Mendel of Kosów had enumerated several decades earlier. His division was: (1) "the common mass, the ignorant multitude"; (2) the Orthodox, or strictly rabbinic class; (3) fanatics, or the so-called Hasidim; (4) "the very small number of Maskilim." Perl explained that the "common mass," having no doctrine of its own on religious questions, fell under the influence of whichever group it came in close contact with. The fact that this was written at the end of the 1830s, when Perl was submitting one memorandum after another to the Austrian government, indicates that, in his view, Hasidism had already captivated the Jewish people to such an extent that there was almost nothing left to save. In his report, Perl still thought of the Orthodox class as distinct from the Hasidim. Ṣevi Elimelekh of Dynów also complained that the scholars *(baʿalei torah)* did not live in harmony with the reverent *(baʿalei yirʾah)* — the Hasidim.[101]

Thus, the oppressive measures taken by the Austrian government, together with the necessity of consolidating all conservative religious forces in the face of the Haskalah, resulted in the virtual triumph of Hasidism in Galicia by the middle of the nineteenth century. In his *Neuere Geschichte der Israeliten,* which appeared in 1847, Jost relates that according to information he received from Galicia, only about one-seventh of its Jews did not belong to the Hasidic movement.[102] The gradual process of domination of Jewish religious and communal life by the Hasidim was described by Joseph Perl in his books as well as in his memoranda to the government. The zaddikim attained such a position of power that opposing rabbis were forced out of the community (as in the case of the Rabbi of Kolne in Perl's *Megalleh temirin*). Through their unity, the Hasidim succeeded in placing their adherents in the positions of *shoḥatim,* thereby wielding considerable power, as, for example, they would pronounce meat from the ritual slaughter of other *shoḥatim* nonkosher. They used similar means to extend their influence into neighboring areas. In *Emeq refaʾim,* Levinsohn related that whenever the rebbe arrived in a town, he would summon the *shoḥet* to present his knife for inspection. If the latter did not appear, his *sheḥita* would be declared invalid.[103] This tradition stems from the early days of the movement, when *shoḥatim* were barred from showing their knives "to any but a distinguished rabbi, and then only with the knowledge of the *parnas* of that month" as in Brody in 1772.[104]

These *shoḥatim* became "the janissaries" of the Hasidic rebbes, as Perl calls them in his memorandum of 1838, and they succeeded in breaking the resistance of even the most ardent of the anti-Hasidic rabbis. The *mohalim* (ritual circumcisers), too, Perl reported, were almost all adherents of the Hasidim and used all sorts of strategems against their opponents. Levinsohn indicated that even the administration of the donations for Ereṣ Yisrael passed into the hands of the rebbes and that rabbis and highborn intending to travel to Ereṣ Yisrael had to have recourse to them.[105]

In addition to the *shoḥatim* and *mohalim,* other members of the clergy, "minor scholars" who from the beginning added a bit of intellectualism[106] to Hasidism and aided its spread, were the *maggidim* (preachers), and, especially, the cantors and the less formal prayer leaders. Gottlober, in fact, considered the prayer leaders the main factor in the movement's success. Their influence grew out of a system of mutual promotion with the rebbes: the latter drew the cantors to their side in order to promote the "Sefardic" liturgy, which in turn raised the status of the prayer leaders and drew them to the movement. Under this system, cantors whose service was both pleasant and inspiring would often become rebbes themselves.[107]

The gradual amalgamation of rabbinic orthodoxy and the Hasidic movement could not have been imagined, however, had Hasidism not gradually lost its initial character of being opposed to the social order. This amalgamation, which began in the Ukraine at the end of the eighteenth century, first appeared in Galicia and Poland in the early nineteenth century and gained momentum over the years.

The same anti-Hasidic satires that depict the Hasidim as a mass of wretchedly poor people also tell of wealthy men who come to the rebbe for advice. In *Teyator fun khsidim,* Leybele the Maskil mocks the Hasidic rebbes:

Both rich and poor flock to them
And they're taken for a ride.[108]

In *Emeq refa'im,* Levinsohn tells how the rebbe conducts his table. He personally serves the rich guests large portions, while the poor Hasidim bring their own repast from home.[109] In this satire, Levinsohn paints a portrait of such "wealthy men" as intimates of the rebbe. The rebbe advises his son, for example, not to retain the ways of the preachers of morals, not to admonish his people for their deviousness or "the rich and powerful" for robbing the poor.

To the contrary, always latch onto the strong. Honor the wealthy; show favor to the officials. Express concern for the welfare of officials like: *ratmanes* [city council members], *gemines* [town council members], communal heads, *otkuptshikes,*[110] *odavtshikes,*[111] *faktoyrim,*[112] *baley-takses,*[113] *tsekhmaysters* [guild-masters], *kvartirne komisarn*[114] and the like. Keep close to smugglers and advise them how to prosper. Do not forget the *faktoyrim*[115] either. From these you will strengthen your throne and grow rich.[116]

In short, the above are "rich men without money" who "live on businesses without substance," "on an appointment, illicit taxes, etc.," according to Levinsohn's succinct description in the well-known satire *Di hefker-velt* (The chaotic world).[117]

The famous rebbes who restricted their attention to the poor were the exception. Uri of Strelisk—called the "Seraph" for his fervor in prayer—claimed the indigent style of life of his followers was in imitation of their rebbe. Nevertheless, this did not prevent the rebbe from accepting aid in time of need from a wealthy enthusiast. At the other extreme were the cohorts of Uri's contemporary, Rebbe Hersh of Żydaczów, the majority of whom were considered "well off."[118]

The first elements of the middle class that petty bourgeois Hasidism attracted were originally involved in insubstantial trades like those of the poor brokers and smugglers, only in a higher social stratum. Both strata gave Hasidism its popular, democratic flavor.

As the middle class prospered and its merchant-scholars drew closer to Hasidism, the power, respectability, and often also the wealth of the rebbe grew, as was the case for the Rebbe of Ruzhin and his dynasty in Galicia and Bukovina. Later in the nineteenth century the social ascent increased, precipitating a more opulent style of living for the rebbes. Perl admitted in the sermon he delivered in the Tarnopol synagogue in 1838 that the rebbes of the generation of Levi Isaac of Berdyczew still "excelled in their prayer, charity and ransoming of prisoners—at that time they used to do this."[119] Dr. Nathan Horowitz, Nachman Krochmal's son-in-law, said of Perl that when he was a Hasid the rebbes were still honest, sincere people, free of sin and leading an ascetic life. He contrasted them to the rebbes of his generation (1846), who were swindlers, lacking conviction and intending to cheat "the rich and poor rabble" of its money. They undertook to heal barren women and sick people and to exorcise dybbuks, while living in palaces that glittered with gold and silver, their tables well laden.[120] This description of the rebbes' comfort and wealth, however, really reflects the conduct of the Ukrainian zaddikim and of the Sadagura dynasty that also settled in eastern Galicia. According to such witnesses as Joseph Hayyim Halberstam, Solomon Rubin, and other Hasidic sources, the generation of the rebbes Naphtali of Ropczyce, Meyer of Przemyślany, and Hersh of Żydaczów generally maintained a simple or even ascetic life, although rebbes who exploited their position in order to amass wealth and live in luxury had already begun to appear in Galicia, e.g., Hersh "the Attendant," Rebbe of Rymanów.

The struggle between the old and the new conception of the social role of the rebbes, which began in the early nineteenth century, is succinctly reflected in the following Hasidic tradition.

An old Hasid of Lublin mocked Rebbe Meyer of Przemyślany for living in hardship and want. He recited a teaching of his rebbe, Jacob Isaac of Lublin, based on the talmudic *aggadah* (*Taʿanit* 24b). "Every day a Heavenly Voice is heard declaring, the whole world draws its sustenance *bishvil* (because of) Hanina my son, and Hanina my son satisfies himself with a *qab* of carobs from one Sabbath eve to another."[121] Jacob Isaac of Lublin interpreted this *aggadah* as a rhetorical question: "How can the whole world draw its sustenance because of Hanina my son if he satisfies himself with a *qab* of carobs from one Sabbath eve to another? If the zaddik who draws abundance to the earth acts so frugally, he further explained, the whole world will obviously live in want. Meyer of Przemyślany, in an antielitist Hasidic spirit, argued that the meaning of this *aggadah* is to be understood as a conditional sentence. By dividing *bishvil* into "bi" and "shvil" ("in the path" in Hebrew), *bishvil* can be rendered "according to the conduct of." Thus, only when the zaddik is satisfied with little, like Hanina, can the world be worthy of drawing sustenance because of his merit.[122]

The Emergence of the Hasidic Reign

The struggle of the Rebbe of Tsandz (Nowy Sącz), Joseph Hayyim Halberstam, against the intemperance of the Sadagura dynasty that broke out in 1868 in connection with the "Reb Berenyu affair" was the last belated attempt to retain in zaddikism the remnants of its former folk character.

As a result of this social transformation the rebbes, as a matter of course, also lost their militancy in the clandestine struggle against Austrian government oppression. Characteristic is the fact elucidated both in the reports of the Austrian officials and in Perl's memoranda. Instead of imposing bans upon the kosher meat and candle tax lessees, the Hasidic leaders were now satisfied to obtain tax exemptions for themselves and their adherents and also the confirmation of their own appointees as *shoḥatim*. This is corroborated in Hasidic literature. In a pre-1815 letter to the tax lessees of Żurawno, Hersh of Żydaczów adjured them not to eat the meat of an opposing *shoḥet*.[123] As early as the beginning of the nineteenth century, a prominent Hasidic leader in Cracow, Berl Luxenburg, was a candle tax lessee.[124] Thus, the struggle between Hasidism and anti-Hasidic orthodoxy continually lost every vestige of ideological content, and in its last phase it was no more than a struggle for power in the Jewish community.

Along with the social transformation, Hasidic doctrine also underwent a substantial change. In many Hasidic works of the period there is not only the call to charity but also a reiterated emphasis upon peace and harmony which ought to unite both the learned and the masses (according to the author of *Toledot ya'aqov yosef*), as well as the poor and rich.[125] There was also a change in the position on the study of the Talmud and Jewish religious scholarship. Whereas originally piety was given priority over the study of the Talmud in attaining a higher spiritual plane, now the intensive study of the Talmud and its commentaries was proclaimed as an indispensable religious duty, and those who were lax in this regard were admonished.[126]

Not only had the Rebbe of Żydaczów already established a good personal relationship with the leading rabbis of his time, such as Jacob Ornstein, rabbi of Lemberg, author of *Yeshu'ot ya'aqov,* but he also promoted mutual respect between Talmudists and Kabbalists in general.[127] His contemporary, Uri of Strelisk, advocated the approach of "the Jew" *(ha-Yehudi)* of Przysucha: "Study of Torah and prayer go hand in hand." He explained, "Study leads to depth of prayer which in turn brings to greater depth of Torah study."[128]

As early as the 1830s, this new movement in Hasidism,[129] the so-called *Ḥadushim* (the new), was widespread in the land and in the course of a short time became the officially accepted tendency (as indicated by the Rebbe of Tsandz, Hayyim Halberstam, author of *Divrei ḥayyim*). The process of amalgamation with rabbinism had progressed to such an extent that most Hasidic leaders also occupied the rabbinic posts in their *kehillot*. The titles "rabbi" (rav) and "rebbe" had not yet become identical only because there still were rabbis who were not Hasidic leaders.[130] Yet Hasidism in Galicia, as in Congress Poland and the Ukraine, was, by the beginning of the nineteenth century, transformed from a popular religious movement into the reigning faith of the majority of Polish Jewry.

TWO SCHOOLS OF HASIDISM IN POLAND

The Centrality of the Zaddik

As in Galicia in the period of European reaction, Hasidism spread very swiftly through the Kingdom of Poland, albeit with differences both in its stage of development and in the conditions for its growth. On the one hand, Hasidism in central Poland was younger than its Galician counterpart, so that at the start of that epoch all the strongholds of the Mitnaggedim had not yet been captured by it, especially in the big cities, including the capital. On the other hand, this movement in Poland, at its very outset, was characterized by the faith of the simple folk in which the zaddik (the righteous one), the all-powerful helper, divinely inspired performer of wondrous deeds, figured prominently. In its early stages, a reaction set in against the vulgar element of Hasidism, and an effort was initiated to reform and dignify it.

In the first decades of the Kingdom of Poland, there still existed centers of Hasidism whose leaders, possessing little that was original, reiterated in their sermons the teachings of the zaddikim of the previous generations. They drew mainly on the teachings of the great men of the movement's golden age, the Napoleonic era in Poland. Thus, the Rabbi of Stopnica and Opatów (Apt), R. Meir Halevi Rotenberg, fostered the teachings of his master, R. Jacob Isaac, the "Seer" of Lublin, and R. Moyshele of Kozienice followed the lessons of his father, the renowned R. Israel, from whom he had also inherited the post of *maggid* (preacher) in his city.

The teachings of the Hasidic leaders of Kozienice and Opatów invariably centered on the enhancement of the zaddik's status. One of the obligations toward the zaddik, a term considered synonymous with the true scholar, was providing for his maintenance. Understandably, the material circumstances of those who were engaged professionally in the study of Torah and in prayer were greatly reduced because of the impoverishment of the Jewish population; nor could they maintain their dignity or social status while continuously exhorting their flock to support them. R. Moyshele of Kozienice chided his contemporaries for the sorry lot of the scholars by citing Ps. 19:11: "More to be desired are they than much fine gold." He explained,

the word "desired" is an allusion to the scholars and those who study, because they are constantly occupied with the holy Torah which is an esoteric delight, and it is beyond a doubt proper that they be honored by all who behold them. . . . But alas! because of our sins, they are held as naught and accounted as nothing in the eyes of the ignorant and the ordinary people. It is, alas! because of our sins, that they are without means of a livelihood and in great distress, need, and poverty. And this is the plea of the *sweet singer of Israel* in behalf of this generation which is practically in the wake of the Messiah. . . .[131] They will be full of gold and much fine gold and will wax rich in silver and gold. Then they will surely find themselves held in esteem. . . .[132]

To be sure, in consonance with Hasidic lore, the *maggid* stipulated that for the scholars to be considered zaddikim, it was necessary "that they occupy themselves with the study of the sacred Torah in the greatest measure of perfection,"[133] that is, that they act with the intent to sanctify God's name, "and that all their contemplation be directed to God, blessed by His Name." He also cited the opinion of Alshekh that when "the men of perfect faith" possess "all that is good," then also "all other men will be prompted to emulate their conduct so that they too may merit the same reward."[134]

R. Meir of Opatów repeatedly required of his Hasidim that they be among the "supporters of the Torah," namely, that they be concerned for the scholars, the zaddikim, that they provide for them. These supporters were likened to the olive leaf in the Noah episode, "for even as the leaves cover and protect the fruit, even so do those who support the Torah protect the scholars by giving in abundance to them."[135] It is an obligation to give support to the zaddik "so that he should not be burdened by mundane concerns,"[136] and thus can devote himself tranquilly to the study of Torah and the worship of God. In line with the teaching of R. Jacob Isaac of Lublin, his disciple explained that the observance of the Torah calls for a "goodly abundance" so he can observe such commandments as "to build a *sukkah* and obtain a *lulav*, *etrog* and the like."[137] Rabbi Issachar Ber of Radoszyce, known as the "Holy Grandfather" and one of the most popular Hasidic leaders in Poland, went further than his mentor, "the Seer" of Lublin. According to him, not only does the fulfillment of the commandments require a good living but even with respect to devotion to God, affluence is a beneficial factor. Accordingly, he alters the simple meaning of the scriptural verse, "Lest when thou hast eaten and art satisfied, and hast built goodly houses . . . thy silver and thy gold is multiplied—then thy heart be lifted up, and thou forget the Lord thy God"[138] to read: "If you multiply all this and your heart be lifted up, that is, that your heart will be exalted in the paths of the Lord, if Israel will have all that is good, then you will forget" [*v'shakhaḥtah* literally means "and you will forget," but in Aramaic it has another sense: ". . . then God will be with you in your heart, for the *Shekhinah* does not dwell . . . except through joy and expansiveness"].[139]

"The Holy Grandfather" also explained that giving a present to the zaddik is an essential expression of cooperation with the one who prays in his own behalf. The commandment "thou shalt surely release it with him"[140] is obligatory, according to the Gemara,[141] only when the owner of the ass which is prostrate under its burden does not refrain from participating in the effort of loading and unloading. Similarly, "when a person comes to the zaddik to pray in his behalf that person must also give aid to the zaddik . . . , and this consists in giving him money."[142] In the view of R. Meir of Opatów, this is even a matter of justice, since it is the zaddik "who causes plenty to flow from the source of all blessings, and it is fitting that he too should not lack anything, and that sustenance come to him in abundance." This is also the explanation of the commandment in the Torah that one "should not muzzle the ox while he threshes," inasmuch as "the zaddik is called *shor* [an ox], for he deems himself an ox bearing a burden."[143] R. Jacob Isaac said, "The Holy

One, blessed be He, Himself remunerated the zaddik for acting as a mediator."[144] Of course, the zaddik himself must always set before his eyes his own duty to bring abundance to his people and not just to be concerned with the perfection of his own soul "in ever rising and higher degree."[145] "The zaddik must forget his own self, all his labors being directed only toward the flowing of abundance to Israel," who will then "know no lack, but will constantly have only all that is good."[146]

But the mere provision of material assistance to the scholars and zaddikim is not enough. Faith in the zaddik is the basic article of faith, without which worship of the Creator is inconceivable. For an ordinary Jew does not have it in his power to draw close to God except by being close to a zaddik. The constant need to reiterate this principle, which had been enunciated initially by R. Elimelekh of Leżajsk, was in itself evidence of the incipient erosion of faith among the people. Obviously, the Hasidic leaders of the courts of Opatów, Kozienice, Radoszyce, and others regarded the buttressing of faith in the zaddik as the main way to strengthen religion against the peril of heresy, which had already cast its first shadows. The great-grandson of R. Issachar Ber of Radoszyce praised his "Holy Grandfather," whose wondrous deeds had checked the rise of "heresy" which had begun in many places. "Since the time he became famous . . . as a performer of deeds of salvation, even men in whom the spark of Jewishness had become extinguished, now were prompted to visit him.[147] R. Moyshele of Kozienice vented his wrath on the nonbelievers, whom he mentions in the same breath as "the wicked who devise evil decrees against Israel."[148] Undoubtedly, he had in mind the extreme assimilationists who were close to the government and who had prepared a program for the polonization of the Jewish population. R. Meir of Opatów demanded that they "be separated from the Jewish community so that they will not, God forbid, lead Israel astray." According to his interpretation of the verse "Shall one deal with our sister as with a harlot?"[149] this ostracism is a precondition for the establishment of the Shekhinah: the word hakhezonah (as with a harlot)—as he interprets it —is a compound of two words, hakh and zonah, hence, "it is incumbent upon us to strike with a fist the wicked who deny any belief in the God of the universe." They are referred to as harlots, "for he who has a false belief is called a harlot." The subsequent restoration of the Shekhinah is alluded to in the end of the verse, "He will deal with our sister."[150]

There are many ways in which the zaddik acts as intermediary between the Creator and His people, Israel.

According to R. Moyshele of Kozienice, the "light is sown for the righteous" means that the zaddik "draws light down to this world for his brethren, the children of Israel, in order to elevate them to the worship of the Blessed One,"[151] R. Meir of Opatów, expounding on the meaning of "The Holy One, blessed be He, is near to him who cleaves to the zaddik,"[152] asserted that in order "that the Torah and prayer be acceptable to the Omnipresent, blessed be He, it is necessary to participate with the zaddikim, and by means of this collaboration with the zaddikim everything one does will be clear and pure."[153] It is impossible for man to improve and illuminate his soul except by means of the zaddik, "for God has so ordained that all the integrations and emanations shall occur by means of the zaddik."[154]

The merit of those who go to the true zaddikim and gather together with them is great, for they restore the *Shekhinah,* and advance the Redemption and Ingathering of the Exiles.[155] The ordinary folk who draw close to the zaddik must thereby learn to occupy themselves with the Torah and the service of God, although they cannot attain the level at which he performs those acts. To be sure, the zaddikim can instill in these people the love of God only on condition "that they will believe in them with a strong faith, without any disparaging thoughts whatsoever concerning them."[156] For just as it is forbidden to be critical of the Torah, even with regard to certain commandments, such as that of the red heifer, "so it is forbidden to criticize the zaddik in a given generation if at times he performs vague deeds, for he is just in all his ways and his deeds are for the sake of Heaven."[157] According to the exposition of another disciple of "the Seer," R. Ezekiel of Kazimierz (Kuzmir),[158] who was also close to the Przysucha (Pshiskhe) school, if one does so he would bring about a separation between his master and himself which is like the separation between the Holy One, blessed be He, and the *Shekhinah.* Only by linking one's prayer with that of the zaddik can one attain the high virtue of reverence for God. Even when a man comes to the zaddik for help, he should first pray for the zaddik, so that he will gain God's compassion.[159]

Since the ordinary person cannot compare himself with the zaddik, he must be satisfied with his own level and must not concern himself with matters that are too great for him. "He should not do more than lies within his capacity, but act within the limits with which God favored him."[160] Only the extraordinary person knows how to cause emanations to be drawn down to the world, and the main purpose of his prayer is to restore the integrity of the upper worlds. For one who is not in this position, it is fitting that he pray even for a livelihood, provided that he believes "that the matter which he asks for also concerns the upper worlds."[161]

The role of the zaddik in the world has no measure or bounds. Creation itself was for their sake,[162] since, as the Talmud states, God desires the prayers of the zaddikim. The zaddik in each generation has the aspect, as it were, of God, and it lies within his power "to draw down a flow of great benevolence and good to the world,"[163] for by reestablishing a union with God, he causes *midat ha-ḥesed* to predominate over *midat ha-din* and thereby changes justice into mercy. The power of the zaddik extends so far "that whatever God does, it is also within the capacity of the zaddik to do."[164] The eyes of the Lord are toward the righteous" means that "though all the children of Israel are vessels for the *Shekhinah,* the eyes of the Lord mainly watch over the zaddikim, and from the blessings bestowed upon them, the rest of the nation is also blessed."[165] Angels are created from every utterance of the zaddik about Torah and in prayer.[166] It is a matter of course that all the needs of the Jewish people—spiritual and material—are fulfilled by means of the zaddik. The zaddik brings down a spiritual flow to "the holy flock, the holy people of Israel" to implant in them reverence for God so that they "will grow wise in the service of the blessed Name."[167] The zaddik does this because he grieves over "what concerns God, in that they are unable to serve Him with complete perfection; and because of the distress and exile of the holy *Shekhinah.*"[168] And by sharing in the pain of all Jews and every single Jew, he makes abundant whatever their desire. R. Moyshele, the *Maggid* of Kozienice, usually formulated this abundance as comprising: "children, life, sustenance, and healing and wealth and honor and all good for the House of Israel."[169] The zaddik spurs the holy celestial beings on to "drive away the *kelipot* [the shells; the forces of evil which veil the Light], so that they will not be able to hold back abundance from the Jews."[170] It is he who brings about the union of the Holy One, blessed be He, with the *Shekhinah,* which is at the same time His union with the people of Israel. Indeed, according to R. Meir of Opatów, it is fitting that the Holy One, blessed be He, in His love for the people of Israel, "first bestows His blessing upon His children, the Jews who are His holy people," even before that union is accomplished; this is analogous to the statement of our Sages of blessed memory [171] about the rules dealing with the interrelationships of human beings, which require that one conciliate before coming together in union.[172]

One of the principles of Hasidism was that throughout the period of Exile since the destruction of the Temple, the flow of abundance had been reversed, and this is the reason for the difficulty the Jewish people had encountered in earning a livelihood. Earlier, "during the time the Temple existed," abundance flowed mainly to the righteous, that is, to the Jews, and only from the remainder could the wicked, namely Esau, find a livelihood. This is in keeping with Isaac's blessing to Jacob: "Be a *gevir* [lord] over thy brethren," that is, be an actual *gevir*, a rich man.[173] According to R. Ezekiel of Kazimierz, improvement depends on the quality of worship of the Creator; that is, "the *very* choicest of the celestial abundance is for the most holy among the Jews." [174] This same Ezekiel explained that according to the blessing of Isaac, "Let peoples serve thee and nations bow down to thee," the Jewish people in the Diaspora also could benefit indirectly from the abundance of the nations. For even after the nations become wealthy, they will give money to the Jews so that they may serve God and study His Torah, on the analogy of Zebulon providing the sustenance for Issachar. The relationship is a mutual one: "If the nations will so contrive it" that the Jew should be free from the burden of making a living and devote himself to the service of God, "then they will also have abundance," inasmuch as abundance is brought down to the world only through the service of God.[175] But this theory of ideal symbiosis was based on a division of social functions —economic and spiritual—and was merely a reflection of the dependence of the Jews in Poland for their livelihood upon their gentile clientele, especially upon the benevolence of the Polish squires, the estate owners who paid the "court Jews" their brokers' fees from their economic abundance. Generally, it was the impoverishment of the Jewish community that was reflected in the then-current kabbalistic Hasidic doctrine concerning the sufferings in Exile, whereby the Gentiles had the preponderant share of the good things. It was the zaddik who was to reverse this situation. Indeed, R. Meir of Opatów never wearied of reiterating in his homilies that the zaddik must direct his prayer in a way that the abundance which he draws down from on high should not be squandered during its descent, and not "wander away," that is, outside, to the Gentiles, but that it mainly reach the Jews, the holy people, with

NB

only a residue flowing to the Gentiles, who are "the other side" (Satan's camp).[176]

The Message of the Zaddikim: Consolation and Approbation

The zaddik, the channel of sustenance and abundance, also has it in his power to nullify "all the harsh and evil decrees," inasmuch as "the zaddik rules in the fear of God."[177] According to R. Meir of Opatów, this power over the gentile nations is assured in the verse "The Lord brings to naught the design of the nations."[178] To be sure, it was no coincidence that what was being referred to was not the nullification of existing decrees but the bringing to naught of "the evil designs" for new decrees which were being prepared against the Jews.[179] Hasidic legend also tells of the wonders performed by the zaddikim in nullifying the plans for new decrees. Evidently, the decrees which had already been in effect for a long time were considered to be an evil connected with oppression in the Diaspora which would cease only with the coming of the Redemption. And, indeed, the bitterness of the Jewish population, which sighed and groaned under the yoke of the tyrannical absolutism of the Kingdom of Poland under the overlordship of the czar of Russia, found clear expression in the homilies of the Hasidic leaders, especially those of the school of the "Seer."

The sermons of R. Meir of Opatów reverberate with indignation at the humiliation of the Jewish nation: "The Jews are now despised and scorned in the eyes of the gentile nations."[180] He related the question asked by the sons of Jacob, "Shall one deal with our sister as with a harlot?" to the sorry status in the Diaspora, "for during the Exile the Jews must make themselves acceptable in the eyes of the princes and authorities." The reproach of the Jewish people is also, as it were, the shame of the *Shekhinah,* for it is stated that "you are My servant, in whom I will be glorified,"[181] that is, that "the main principle should be," were it not that the *Shekhinah* is in exile, that "then it would come to pass that my glory is on me, and His on Him." The question put by the sons of Jacob thus alludes to astonishment "that the upper worlds declare and state their surprise." R. Meir ended with a prayer: "Let it be His will . . . that there be a complete redemption" and the glory of Israel be restored.[182] The Redemption will be the compensation for enduring the prolonged shame: "for the zaddik lifts up Israel's desires, as well as the shame they are put to by the gentile nations, to the summit of all yearnings and draws redemption from there to Israel."[183] The Redemption is also a reward for observing the *miṣvot* even in the midst of the torment of Exile. R. Meir of Opatów interpreted the Torah's commandment "The Feast of Unleavened Bread you shall keep" as follows: "By means of the observance of the unleavened bread which Israel keeps throughout this bitter Exile in want and oppression, we will quickly merit in our own day the fulfillment of the observance of the Three Pilgrimage Festivals . . . and go up to Zion in song."[184]

R. Moyshele of Kozienice also complained about the humiliation of the nation in exile in his generation, finding solace for himself and offering the comforting thought that despite it all Israel had not ceased to be the chosen of God, His treasured people, "His delightful children." Thus he expounded on the verse, "For the Lord has called Jacob unto Himself":[185] "For Jacob, although downtrodden and humiliated as at the present time during our Exile—for we are despised and lowly—was nevertheless chosen by God."[186] He bemoaned the fate of the Jews in their "cruel and bitter Exile," saying that "each year we hope and look for redemption and salvation, but it is remote from us, and because of the multitude of our sins the yoke of Exile is protracted for us, and the burden of subjugation is beyond our capacity to endure; and time and again the yoke of servitude is made heavier upon us and the burden of the Exile grows quickly."[187] In one of his sermons for Yom Kippur, the *maggid* poured out his bitter heart against their lot: ". . . for because of our many sins we have been visited by the decrees of the gentile nations, who have made enactments against Jews in the matter of their livelihood and have laid a heavy yoke upon them through the imposition of taxes. And they have placed in particular a heavy onus upon the residents of the villages, the lessees of inns, by the amount of taxes they must pay, so that they cannot bear it."[188]

All the decrees were designed to strike at the religion of the Jews, for in depriving Jews of their bread, they were distracting them from the single-minded worship of God. This is alluded to in the words of Mordecai in the Scroll of Esther:

For our enemy oppressors confuse our minds with their evil designs, constantly devising cruel decrees against us to take from each Jew his means of sustenance, so that nothing remains to us in this bitter Exile with which to make a living and keep one's wife and children alive. And, we cannot set our thoughts in order that we be able to pray with intent as is proper, because of the great oppressive yoke of the Exile which bears down upon us so that we are unable to endure it.[189]

It goes without saying that the impoverished Jews were not able to engage in the study of the Torah.[190] Moreover, the gentile nations induced the Jews "to forsake the Jewish religion" by granting those who did so immunity "from all taxes, burdens, and persecutions."[191] The *maggid,* who understood quite well the clerical politics of the reactionary absolutism in Russia and Poland, expressed his distress over the fact that there were some individuals who did not resist temptation. But he used one set of terms for "the impious who change their religion and are tranquil and at ease without any trouble or sorrow, lacking nothing whatsoever,"[192] namely, those careerist, ambitious financial barons, and another set of terms for those "villagers who were compelled to change their religion because of their poverty."[193] But all those who forsook their people and their faith were exceptions, and the *maggid* spoke with pride of "the simple Jewish folk who proclaim themselves to bear the name of Jacob . . . [and who] are already known for the soundness of their hearts and greatness of their sincerity, for they have suffered much severe and bitter agony in order to remain within the Jewish faith." For the *maggid,* the meaning of "You shall show faithfulness to Jacob and mercy to Abraham"[194] was "that this faithfulness and great uprightness of the congregation of Jacob will abide with them forever, and then, as a matter of course, mercy will be granted to Abraham."[195]

The *maggid* R. Moyshele quite often gave vent in his sermons to his anger at those who oppressed and mocked his people. He called for vengeance like that wreaked upon Pharaoh and his servants, "so even now, as in the time of our departure from Egypt, He will show us His wondrous deeds, bringing judgment upon our enemies."[196] When the Redemption comes "He will be your God," namely, "He whose name is blessed will be manifest to you also in the aspect of *Elohim,* the aspect of strength and justice, when you will need the quality of strength to bring justice upon the enemies of Israel and be avenged of those that persecute them."[197] "Then the Holy One, blessed be He, will don a cloak of zeal and vengeance, to bring justice upon our foes and repel all our enemies before us. And he will cast them down . . . before us until there will no longer abide in them any strength to make any decrees against Israel."[198] In a sermon for Hanukkah, the *maggid* prayed that

"He whose name is blessed, grant that the great illumination and fervor enter into the hearts of our brethren, the Children of Israel, leading them to His service. Thus the kindling, the burning, and the flames which issued forth to distribute themselves [199] among the wicked Gentiles who plan evil designs against us shall bring a conflagration of God to consume them like thorns which have been cut down." [200]

In spite of all these outbursts of pent-up anger, the *maggid,* being imbued with the ethical tradition of the Bible and the Talmud, cannot disregard the doctrine of the Prophets as reflected in the passage, "I have no pleasure in the death of the wicked . . . but that he turn from his way and live." [201] Nor could he disregard the famous statement of R. Meir's wife: "Let *sins* cease out of the earth . . . does it then say *sinners?* It states rather—*sins.*" [202] Moreover, the kabbalistic-Hasidic doctrine which is based on the mystical principle of the predominance of *midat ha-ḥesed* over *midat ha-din* in both the upper and lower worlds did not hold much store in *midat ha-din,* for if it were to prevail for even a brief moment in the world there was the real danger that even the people of Israel would not be judged righteous. It is therefore not surprising that the angry cry for vengeance against the willful and evil kingdom was moderated. Thus, the *maggid*'s goal was the salvation of the Jews and not the destruction of the wicked.

It is in this light that the *maggid* interprets the verse in the Sabbath hymn, "O, continue thy loving kindness to those who know Thee, zealous and vengeful God," saying that "this in itself, which is for the good of Israel, will be a form of vengeance upon our foes, being, as it were, a matter of inflicting a blow and a healing." [203] Enlarging upon this theme, he explained that

the zaddik may desire to bring judgment upon Israel's enemies and to deal them a grievous blow. But it is not the zaddik's wont to harm any creature in the world, especially so because he does not want to arouse *midat ha-din* in the world; the zaddik therefore wraps his action in the aspect of mercy, so that it may come to help Israel to rid itself of the yoke of subjugation to the wicked. And this will, of course, compel the wicked man to turn away from his wickedness, so that he will not do any more harm to anyone among the Children of Israel.[204]

To be sure, the *maggid* could not entirely restrain his vengeful impulses; in another exposition he contended that bringing justice to the tyrannical and dominant nation would by itself bring all manner of blessings to the Jewish people: "For lo, there will descend [punishment] on Edom and a whirlwind will come down upon the heads of the wicked, and through this judgment all kinds of good will accrue to Israel."[205]

Redemption through Repentance

With all the yearning for the Day of Judgment and the Redemption, a program for satisfying the minimal daily needs of the people held an important place in Hasidic doctrine as long as the nation languished under the yoke of Exile. This program was reflected in the doctrine of the *yiḥudim* (actions designed to restore the true unity of God) and bring abundance down to the earth. It was articulated in the sermons of the disciples of the "Seer" of Lublin and the *Maggid* of Kozienice. The son of the *maggid* applied the verse, "And his king shall be higher than Agag,"[206] to the activities of the "perfect zaddik," through whom

the Kingdom of the blessed One will be elevated and exalted throughout the whole world, and all the decrees which they want to issue against the Jews will be annulled, and He whose name is blessed, in the multitude of His mercies, will implant good within the heart of kings and princes so that they will do us good with all manner of loving kindness and good that abound in the world.[207]

In another place he says that "in our own time the counsel of the nations of the world 'who devise decrees against Israel' shall fail and their designs will be thwarted," while for Israel, "He will issue decrees of beneficence, salvation, and solace." This is alluded to in the verse, "The same day came they into the Wilderness of Sinai,"[208] as well as in the passage from the Song of Songs, "Let him kiss me with the kisses of his mouth," that is, "we seek in this cruel Exile . . . to merit even now that state of delight and pleasure which prevailed at the time of the creation of the world for Israel."[209] In this theory of Hasidism, even temporary succor from the wicked lies within the power of the zaddik. As R. Moyshele of Kozienice explained, the superiority of the zaddik over the angels consisted in his power to cause children, life, and nourishment to be bestowed upon Israel, and power and justice upon those who hate the Lord, whereas each of the angels is only in charge of a particular matter—for example, Michael is responsible for grace; Gabriel, for power; and Raphael, for healing. "The sacred kingdom," the *maggid* goes on to explain, has a scale, "and that which for Israel is *midat ha-ḥesed,* is *midat ha-din* for the oppressive kingdom."[210] The zaddik "mitigates all the judgments at their very roots to convert them to mercy . . . so that they [the Children of Israel] will be able to endure the Exile—until our Messiah comes." As it is stated in the blessing of Jacob to Issachar, "And he bowed his shoulder to bear and became a servant under taskwork," that is, until the Redemption, "so that Esau will be under taskwork and we will be free men."[211]

In line with his colleague from Kozienice, R. Meir of Opatów commented on "She rises while it is yet night,"[212] saying that "Israel in Exile will be saved and rise up expansively and in comfort, and it is toward this end that we pray and this is implied in redemption."[213] But in contrast to the zaddik of Kozienice, who saw temporary deliverance mainly as the nullification of the oppressive edicts, R. Meir conceived of it in terms of "expansiveness," "sustenance in comfort," and "great wealth and much honor." It is for such a redemption in the midst of tranquillity that the zaddik prays, even though it lies within his power to annul the evil decrees against Israel, as well as being "able to exert influence that they be saved from the Wars of Gog and Magog before the complete Redemption."[214]

The fulfillment of this yearning for redemption while in a state of ease seemed to grow even more remote as the condition of the Jewish multitudes in Poland worsened. Therefore, R. Meir of Opatów added an explanation to the doctrine of salvation based on the juxtaposition of two prophecies heralding the Redemption, "Ye shall go forth with joy,"[215] and "They shall come with weeping, and with supplications will I lead them."[216] R. Meir explained that "the Redemption will no doubt proceed in the midst of joy only by virtue of the weeping of Israel out of its anguish." It is out of these tears, together with those shed by the zaddikim out of their joy in cleaving to God, that "Israel will deserve redemption."[217] From this it may be concluded that the era of expansiveness in Exile will in itself be a sign of the Redemption to come.

In full accordance with the tradition of the Prophets, and Sages of the Talmud and Kabbalah, the leaders of the Hasidim in that generation taught that complete redemption depends upon repentance. In the words of R. Ezekiel of Kazimierz, "all redemptions must come through repentance."[218] And although everything is in God's hands, and even repentance depends on His will, yet "the Lord thy God will turn thy captivity and have compassion upon thee," that is, "although He whose name is blessed will induce you to repent, He will nevertheless love you."[219] Similarly, R. Moyshele of Kozienice taught "that it is impossible that the Redemption and the advent of our righteous Messiah will come but through repentance at the end of time." It is therefore incumbent upon Israel to pray to God that "the spirit [of the Lord] be poured from on high" upon him, "to bring him near to perfect repentance," and "that He implant in our hearts to return in perfect repentance." Even the fact that servitude in Exile is ever more severe and "the yoke of the Exile is increasingly heavier" demonstrates God's intent to bring the nation to perfect repentance in order to hasten the Redemption. In the name of R. Abraham Joshua of Opatów, the author of *Ohev yisrael* (Lover of Israel), the son of the *Maggid* of Kozienice stated "that before the coming of the Messiah, the Jews will be driven out of the villages."[220] The "Holy Grandfather" of Radoszyce found support for the idea that redemption comes about through increased suffering in the verse, "And the sons of Dan: Hushim."[221] He said, "If the children are judged"— namely, if the principle of justice is dominant and evil decrees multiply —then the Redemption will come "quietly."[222]

Even according to the doctrine of the Kabbalah, repentance is an indispensable condition for Redemption, for in its view the Messianic Era depends upon the completion of the purification of the souls. It is not only that the Messiah is the last soul, whose descent from heaven is delayed as long as the souls of all Jews have not yet been purified, but also that He is "a composite of the souls of all of Israel," so that the blemish of any single Jew is also His own. R. Moyshele of Kozienice and R. Meir of Opatów found in Isaiah 53 an allusion to the idea that repentance is a *miṣvah* calling for compassion for the Messiah in that He suffers for the sins of all Israel, lovingly taking upon himself the afflictions which should have come upon the nation of Israel. This suffering of the Messiah is in itself enough to arouse "reflections of penitence in the hearts of sinners in Israel . . . to the extent that there should be no need for afflictions to beset the Messiah of God." According to the *maggid* R. Moses ben Israel, this commandment regarding both compassion and acceleration of the Redemption is alluded to in the verse "If thou at all take thy neighbor's garment to pledge, thou shalt restore it to him by the time that the sun goeth down."[223] R. Meir of Opatów infers this *miṣvah* from the verse "Thou shalt not muzzle the ox when he treadeth out the corn"[224] on the ground that "Messiah, the son of Joseph, is called *shor* [an ox]."[225]

The zaddik also served an important function in the matter of repentance. R. Moyshele of Kozienice explained that from the fervor of the penitent, "radiance is increased in the zaddik," which is the meaning of the verse, "And the angel of the Lord appeared to him in a flame of fire in the midst of a bush."[226] R. Meir of Opatów elevated the rank of the zaddik even more than any of his contemporaries. He also urged his listeners to speed the coming of the "two Messiahs," Messiah ben Joseph and Messiah ben David, by worshipping the Creator;[227] yet in his teaching, it is the repentance of the zaddik that is stressed, as in his explication of the words of Joseph "I seek my brethren. Tell me, I pray thee, where they are feeding the flock." The *maggid* said that "this is what the Holy One, blessed be He, says to the zaddik, . . . 'Speak to Me, confess your wicked deeds to Me, and do penitence in My presence in behalf of all Israel and I will accept it as if they had done penitence and I will forgive them.' "[228]

Unity of Israel: The Hasidic Path to Redemption

One of the chief ways of hastening the Redemption is the unity of Israel, a fundamental tenet of Hasidic doctrine from its beginning. R. Ezekiel of Kazimierz explained the connection between unity and redemption according to the tradition of the Talmud concerning the cause of the destruction of the Temple, "The Redemption will result mainly from the unity of the Children of Israel; for since the destruction of the Temple was caused by baseless hatred, to mend matters there must be selfless love, that is, every Jew should love his fellow Jew gratuitously, inasmuch as he worships the Lord like him, and through this means the Redemption will come to pass. Amen! May this be His will!"[229] R. Meir of Opatów chided his contemporaries who were worthy of witnessing the advent of the Messiah by dint of their knowledge but not in their "disregard for the total community of Israel." "The essential improvement is that amity, fraternity, and close attachment prevail throughout the Jewish nation."[230] When there is no union "the word of God is in exile," and conversely, "when there is union below, then there is also union on high."[231]

It can be seen from the above formulation that the unity of Israel consisted of "amity, fraternity, and close attachment," that is, a solid front against the oppression of the dominant nation, as well as mutual assistance, a quality in which—according to all official documents—the Hasidim excelled.[232] At times, the call for union even conveyed a hint of social solidarity among the classes. R. Ezekiel of Kazimierz preached not only "that every one should feel concern for the welfare of his neighbor and pray over his neighbor's distress more than over his own," but also that "when he sees good redounding to his neighbor, even if because of this he will be deprived, let him not have any misgivings whatsoever."[233] To be sure, just as the poor man is forbidden to envy one who is richer than he, a person who has attained "importance, wealth, or wisdom" must conduct himself with modesty, which is a sign that his superiority was bestowed on him by God for his good and not by Satan for his harm.[234] This Hasidic leader ascribed to the matter of unity a meaning which is both individualistic and realistic: Israel (Yisrael) may be compared to the Torah, as is demonstrated by the acronym for the phrase *yesh shishim ribo otiyot latorah* (the Torah contains 600,000 letters), which in turn is equal to the number of Israelites who went out of Egypt. Thus each man in Israel has "a root and a letter in the Torah." The levels of unity and its essence follow from this: "And just as in each scroll of the Torah there must be parchment around it so as not to touch the Torah, so must the [divine] service of each Jew be singled out unto him without touching that of his fellow. And just as no letter of a word in a Torah scroll may be far from its neighbor, so people who are close to each other must not grow far apart; and just as every Torah scroll must be stitched together in order to possess the sanctity of a Torah scroll and not that of a *Ḥumash* [a book of the Pentateuch], so must all Jews be united together . . . and the people who are closest are like one word and others like a *parashah* [a chapter] and others like a *seder* [a section] and yet others like a *sefer* [a book]."[235] This unity that does not exclude the personal way of worshipping the Creator is compounded of concentric circles, from the inner circle, of those who are closest, to the outer circle, which encompasses the whole nation of Israel.

The "Holy Grandfather" of Radoszyce gave the precept of union a Hasidic folk character, as, for example, in his assuring his devotees that the fact that "they eat a meal together leads to their associating with each other" and "then there need be no apprehension that they will not know how to pray with proper intent, because their very association is reckoned by God as equivalent to introducing all the appropriate intent in our prayers"; moreover, "through this, He will save them from their distress."[236]

It is natural that in their discourses, the Hasidic leaders did not overlook the talmudic tradition based on the prophets' views of the importance of charity for redemption. R. Meir of Opatów, particularly, taught the obligation to be charitable and gave a mystical explanation of how charity brings about salvation. He claimed that the statement in the Gemara, "Great is charity, for it brings Redemption close,"[237] was intended to indicate actual union of the (kabbalistic) Spheres, as "when a poor man comes to the door, he brings the left close to the right and the letters of *Mashiah* will be completed."[238]

It is self-evident that the significant role assigned to the zaddik by the schools of the "Seer" of Lublin and the *Maggid* of Kozienice included his mission to accelerate and actually bring about the Redemption. The son of the *Maggid* of Kozienice concluded, from the verse "Ye shall grant a redemption to the land,"[239] that the zaddik had the power to bring it about. The initial letters of the verse "Geulah titnu la-areṣ are "Gimal Lamed Tav," and the meaning of the verse is "that the true zaddik alters the combination of the letters GLT and converts it into a combination meaning *geulah* [redemption]."[240] R. Meir of Opatów, a disciple of the "Seer," taught that Redemption is dependent on the "worship of the zaddikim": they "extend the will of God to the limits of each level, and then all judgments will be mitigated and there will be a perfect Redemption." The zaddik "draws down the soul of our Messiah, the Righteous One, to the world" and by means of his *repairs* in the upper worlds he "will speed the Ingathering of the Exiles."[241]

In their sermons about the Redemption, the Hasidic leaders reflected the state of mind of the masses of Jews in Poland, "whose eyes failed" while waiting for the end of their distress and emergence into freedom. The frequency of these sermons points to the aim of the Hasidic leaders to strengthen the spirit of the nation and to encourage its hope for Redemption.

Despite the disappointment of their expectations during the epochal days of Napoleon, the disciples of the "Seer" and the *Maggid* of Kozienice remained confident that the Redemption was at hand. It was not just for rhetorical effect that R. Moyshele said, "Each year we hope and look for salvation but it is remote from us. . . ."[242] He warned his audience against accepting his explanations about the Redemption as nothing more than fine preaching; his sermon about the two Messiahs—the son of Joseph and the son of David—who, he maintained, are alluded to in the verse, "And of all thy cattle thou shalt sanctify the males, the firstlings of ox and sheep" [243] (*peter,* firstling, that is, the start of the complete Redemption; a *shor,* ox, Messiah, the son of Joseph; and *seh,* sheep, Messiah, the son of David). He concluded with the assertion, "And as Heaven is my witness, that I have come not for preaching but for action," namely to urge greater "intensity in the worship of the blessed One" and more good deeds in order to accelerate the Redemption. And he goes on to pray:

May it be pleasing before the Creator of the universe, the Lord of hosts, and may it be a time of favor from the blessed One to speed for us the hour of Redemption and salvation and, as in the days of our departure from the land of Egypt, may He show us wondrous deeds, sending us our righteous Messiah speedily in our own time. And may Judah and Jerusalem be saved before our very eyes and may He grant us everlasting Redemption so that we may live to go up to Zion in song. . . .[244]

The expounders of Hasidism were fully aware of the stringent exhortation in the Talmud "not to force the end," that is, the coming of the Messiah; the very fact that the Jews remained faithful to this exhortation, enduring persecution with forbearance, meant—as R. Moyshele of Kozienice pleaded and hoped—that the Redemption would soon come. In a discourse for Hoshana Rabba (the seventh day of Sukkot), he expounded upon the text, "she who is scattered among those who vex her" as follows:

For our Sages have stated that one of the three oaths with which God adjured Israel requires that they will not force the end.[245] And for some time now we have been fulfilling our oath and do not at all force the end, but we endure whatever is decreed, as long as we have the strength to suffer. And this is the significance of the verse in question. For now we are scattered unto every corner among wicked idolaters and heretics who are like an *akhs'a* [adder] or like vipers who sting us so very much that we no longer have strength to bear it. And it is therefore fitting and proper that you soon deliver us out of their hand.[246]

R. Meir of Opatów viewed his contemporaries as "a generation near to our righteous Messiah," as is intimated in the verse "This day ye go forth in the month Aviv," [247] as well as in the verse "And it came to pass that on the sixth day they gathered twice as much bread," [248] which is "an allusion to the sixth millennium." Consequently, there is no longer a need in his generation for many *repairs* in order to elevate "the sparks which had fallen below." In earlier generations, there had been a need for asceticism "in order to break up the shells and to set aside the curtains from the souls," whereas now it was sufficient that "they believe in the God of the universe and in their belief they shall live." Of course, "whatever in former years was corrected over a long period of time, will now be repaired . . . almost instantly in order to bring near the time of Redemption."[249]

In this view of Redemption, Ereṣ Yisrael was considered as the nation's homeland which awaited the return of its children. At times, the Hasidic leaders of this school strongly emphasized the historical right of the Jewish people to return to its land. Thus R. Moyshele of Kozienice expounded on the verse, "In the year of the jubilee the field shall return to him of whom it was bought, even to him to whom the possession of the land belongeth,"[250] saying, ". . . For everything in the heavens and on the earth is His and He gave us for our inheritance the Holy Land, and perhaps the time and season to lead us to our land has arrived and you are the one who detains it."[251] R. Ezekiel of Kazimierz went into a political and juridical discourse to prove that Ereṣ Yisrael is destined to return to the Jewish nation. The point of departure of his homily is the verse "For ye are not as yet come to the rest and the inheritance."[252] He went on to explain that since Ishmael, the son of Hagar, the maidservant of Sarah, was the servant of Israel and since, according to the law, a servant's property becomes the property of his master, then Ereṣ Yisrael, which is under the dominion of Ishmael, does not pass out of the authority of the nation of Israel. And in His kindness, God has pledged to the people of Israel "that it will yet come under the control of Israel."[253] It is likely that the zaddik heard reports of the rivalry among the great powers of Europe with regard to Turkey and its claims to Palestine by right of possession.

In addition to the political aspect of the Redemption, R. Ezekiel also gave the term *naḥalah* (inheritance, possession) the meaning of "heritage," in keeping with the well-known notion of the "little sanctuary" in the Diaspora: "A heritage unto Israel, His servant."[254] This was to teach us that "he who serves Him of the blessed name also has a heritage in his own home," that is, "in *his* dwelling he had—in a certain sense— Ereṣ Yisrael."[255]

In contrast to this school of Hasidism, the outstanding representatives of which were the disciples of the "Seer" of Lublin and the *Maggid* of Kozienice, faith was identified as casting one's burden upon the omnipotent zaddik. At the same time there was widespread throughout Poland an extreme form of folk Hasidism which brought heaven down to earth for the multitudes of devotees and also brought the zaddik down to the level of a wonder worker. While theoretical Hasidism was still being fostered in the courts of Kozienice, Opatów, and Kazimierz, the Hasidism which flourished in the courts of the "wonder workers" was exclusively practical Kabbalah.

Zaddikism Taken to Its Extreme: The "Wonder Workers"

Among the many "wonder workers" who were active in Poland in that era, the following became famous: R. Yeraḥmiel of Przysucha, the son of "the Holy Jew"; R. Joseph Barukh of Neustadt, "the Good Jew," the son of R. Kalman of Cracow and author of the commentary on the Torah *Maor va-shemesh;* R. Ḥayyim Meir Jeḥiel of Mogielnica; R. Ḥayyim David "Doktor" of Piotrków; and above all, the "Holy Grandfather," R. Issachar Ber of Radoszyce.

The biography of R. Issachar Ber, mainly a legendary account, before "he became revealed" as one of the zaddikim of the age faithfully reflects this firm belief of the multitude of Hasidim in miraculous salvation for those who trust wholeheartedly in God. The youth and early manhood of R. Issachar Ber were spent in poverty and want. Like the Baal Shem Tov, with whom his Hasidic devotees compared him, he started out as a *melamed* (elementary teacher) (after marrying a woman in Chęciny, near Kielce). Unsuccessful in this profession, he peddled small wares in the villages. But after his pious wife took upon herself the burden of earning a living, as did many wives of Hasidim, he devoted himself entirely to Torah and prayer. Yet he was like the pious man in the hymn sung on the termination of the Sabbath who had neither food nor sustenance . . . nor clothing to wear. The Hasidic legend about the Passover Seder which was prepared for him by the angels Michael and Gabriel in the likeness of two *daytshn* (German Jews) [256] later served as a basis for the story by I. L. Peretz, "Der Kuntsn-makher" (The Magician). In the meantime, he wore out his feet going to the courts of the great Hasidic leaders of his generation, such as R. Moses Leyb of Sasów, R. Abraham Joshua Heschel of Opatów, R. Jacob Isaac, the "Seer" of Lublin, R. Israel, the *Maggid* of Kozienice, and *ha-Yehudi* from Przysucha. As he himself later boasted, he succeeded in "serving and studying under one hundred twenty sages, all of them divinely inspired."[257] It is apparent that at this period in his life he was one of the vagrant wayfarers who were depicted by his biographer as "zaddikim who wandered and drifted from city to city as was then their fashion."[258] Even after he moved to Chmielnik, there was no improvement in his highly straitened circumstances, and he was still regarded by people as "Berel Batlan" (Berel the Ne'er-do-well) when he settled in Radoszyce, where he subsequently occupied the post of rabbi. In this tiny town, there were 476 Jews out of a total of 1,626 inhabitants in 1827.[259]

Various legends concerning the way the "Holy Grandfather" of Radoszyce "revealed himself" are recounted by his disciples and in turn, by their disciples.[260] The most plausible of them is the account in which he, as the central character, tells about a *melamed* without a post, who, before being revealed, eked out a meager living by healing the sick through his prayers. Once, when "all hope was fled . . . and his wife and children were crying for bread and there was none," the *melamed* tearfully poured his heart out before God: "Master of the universe, what will you lose if some sick person should be cured instantly and give me something in order to keep my soul alive? I do not mean to be presumptuous, God forbid,[261] but I am in great peril and my life hangs by a hair. Master of the universe, take pity on me and the souls of my household, for their lives are not worth living." The Zaddik of Radoszyce ended by saying that

When the *melamed* ended his prayer, God[262] helped him, and all the people of the town came running to him; this one came telling him that his wife was having difficulty giving birth, God forbid,[263] and gave him a certain sum, and this one came because his son had fainted, God forbid, and that one came because an evil spirit[264] had attached itself to his house, and the daughter of yet another . . . had disappeared, so that the poor man now had the wherewithal to supply all his needs. . . .

And as the legend has it, the Rabbi of Radoszyce had hardly ended his story when the house in which he was staying was virtually besieged by men, women, and children crying for his help in alleviating their suffering or curing the maladies besetting the members of their families or because their wives were having difficulty giving birth.[265]

One important detail about the zaddik is to be found in another story which also was reported in the name of the Zaddik of Radoszyce, but told as a true story rather than a fable. The "Holy Grandfather" tells one of his disciples that a marked change for the good in his distressed existence came when, by means of his prayer, the daughter of one of the notables of Radoszyce was healed: "Thenceforth Jews began to flock to me and reward me generously, so that I would pray in their behalf and they would be blessed for my sake."[266] These two complementary stories reflect the precarious status of local rebbes who were "zaddikim in their towns only," and who earned their meager livings by saying prayers for the sick when the opportunity offered itself. There were times when they were compelled to pray that a sick person should chance their way so that he would be delivered from his illness and they from their bitter poverty. At the same time, these stories explain how this kind of "healer of the sick" rose to the level of "wonder worker," for his reputation would spread beyond the boundaries of his town if he succeeded in performing "a great miracle" which aroused wonder and admiration.

The fame of the "Holy Grandfather" of Radoszyce after he "revealed himself" did indeed spread throughout Poland, according to the Hasidic tradition, in the course of a few weeks some four hundred sick people came to him for help.[267] Also many mentally ill people from all corners of the land were brought to him, and in two years "he exorcised some fifteen evil spirits and *dibbukim.*"[268] His method of healing the sick consisted mainly of remedies, but there were instances when it was only through physical contact. His remedies were a mixture of the sacred, the magical, and folk medicine, the "pharmacy" being made up of the

remains of jars, the residue of oil from Hanukkah lamps, the left-over wine from the Kiddush and Havdalah [benedictions ushering in the Sabbath and bidding it farewell] and of the *Afikoman* [the last morsel of matzoh eaten at the Passover seder] and of the four species [of the *lulav*] and the willows and Hoshanahs [yellow twigs held at the Hoshana prayer], the remains of myrtle leaves and the drippings from the Havdalah candles, the wax from the candles for Yom Kippur, and other such residues of objects used in performing a *miṣvah.*[269]

Besides these remedies, the wonder worker of Radoszyce also used a most simple nostrum for healing the sick: drinking water from the well in the rebbe's yard was deemed a sure cure for all kinds of ailments.

In an emergency, when the number of sick was too large for the

Zaddik of Radoszyce to give his personal attention, he would heal all of them in a group. It is reasonable to assume that he learned this collective treatment from his teacher, "the lover of Israel" from Opatów, who did not hesitate to pile all the slips, each bearing the name of a person seeking help, together and to pray for the deliverance of all of them. When about four hundred sick were assembled at the home of the Zaddik of Radoszyce, he ordered his attendant to announce in all the synagogues and inns that they should come at a specified time the following day to the well in his courtyard. At the appointed time they all assembled "and many who could not walk had to be brought there in small carts." Two strong men drew water from the well and apportioned it to the sick, telling them whether to drink it or to wash in it. The narrator ended his account by noting that all for whom waters from the "well of salvation" were drawn were healed. This strange scene brings to mind a picture of Lourdes when it first became famous as a holy spring, but there is a distinct difference. According to this account, the miracle occurred mainly by virtue of the "Holy Grandfather's" prayer: "He sweetened the waters for me for one hour, so that I would be able to heal by means of them . . . so that I would not need to spend my time and cancel my [Torah] lesson"; moreover, those who did not have faith in him and did not take water from the well were turned away.[270] The zaddik and wonder worker R. Ḥayyim David "Doktor" of Piotrków, although a skilled physician, nonetheless placed his trust in prayer. In his approach to healing the sick, he applied the verse "He creates remedies. He is revered in praises. He is the Lord of wonders."[271] If a prescribed remedy was ineffective, he would order the sick person's household to recite psalms, and if the danger was imminent, he placed his hope in the wonders of the Creator.

Aside from healing the sick, which included exorcising evil spirits (dybbuks), the Zaddik of Radoszyce was a helper in all kinds of trouble. He gave succor to lessees in the villages whose rents for their inns had been increased by the estate owners; to rich lessees in the cities who had lawsuits with the lord of the city; to moneylenders who were dunning the noblemen for the payment of debts; to artisans, such as bakers, who were troubled by gentile competitors. And it need scarcely be stated that pleas for help came to him from unfortunate *agunot* (abandoned wives). The tales about those in a predicament most frequently involved village Jews seeking vindication in lawsuits in the courts.[272] These village Jews and simple folk were the source of the wonder worker's store of abundant humor and of his knowledge of Polish expressions which served him as a basis for his puns.[273]

The "Holy Grandfather" of Radoszyce was confident that his help extended to anyone coming into contact with him, however indirectly, be it no more than touching the knob on his door. Even one traveling to him or merely intending to visit him could be helped.[274] In an unwitting confirmation of Aksenfeld's anti-Hasidic satire, the following *aggadah* (story) preserved in his family tells of his marvels: It happened that the zaddik promised rainfall to a Hasid who wanted to bathe while on the road, and some moments later he promised the opposite to a Hasid who requested that there not be any rain. When the first Hasid expressed astonishment at this contradiction, he replied: After all, he worships Him whose name is blessed, "who is all-powerful and is capable of providing for the needs of all."[275] It is true that even in boasting of his numerous miracles, which greatly exceeded the number of miracles wrought by the Baal Shem Tov, he knew "his place as one of the epigones of Hasidism." He explained the difference between himself and the Baal Shem Tov in this way: "Miracles were wrought for the Baal Shem Tov on the strength of his righteousness and holiness, whereas for me, they were wrought only because of God's compassion."[276] He also was conscious of the blessing he received from the "Seer" of Lublin, according to which his strength would lie only in wonders and not in Torah and prayer, nor in "serious matters" generally: "God will provide you with Jews who will tear you away from Torah and prayer."[277] It was in this spirit that he explained his role in Hasidism to his disciple R. Solomon of Radomsko, the author of *Tiferet shelomo* (The Grandeur of Solomon). That is, he was sent into this world to propagate the divinity of Him whose name is blessed throughout the world, but not merely "to praise and glorify His holy name."[278] R. Isaac Meir of Ger (Góra Kalwaria), the distinguished disciple of R. Mendel of Kock (Kotsk), properly defined the contrast between the two extremes in Hasidism— the refined and the vulgar. The difference is that in Kock they brought the hearts of the Jews closer to their Father in heaven, while in Radoszyce they brought their Father in heaven to dwell within the hearts of the Jews.[279]

A New Branch of Hasidism Emerges

The opposition to the Hasidism of the Lublin school broke out in the camp of Hasidim in Poland during the lifetime of the "Seer" of Lublin, and was organized at his "court" under the banner of R. Jacob Isaac of Przysucha, *ha-Yehudi* (the Jew). The counterpart in the history of the Hasidic movement in the Ukraine was the activity of R. Naḥman of Bratslav.[280] As in the Ukraine, the aim of the opposition was the regeneration of Hasidism and the refurbishing of its tarnished prestige. The common factor in both branches of Hasidism was also apparent in the content of the regeneration: Contrary to the system of miracles and assistance, the reformers—each in his respective area—called for a deepening faith in Hasidism, praising highly the virtue of absolute faith while negating every element of naturalism in its philosophy. Both the system of Bratslav and the system of Przysucha-Kock emphasized a pronounced proclivity to negate "this world" and all material concerns and to affirm the ascetic way of life. Both schools enjoined their devotees to punctiliously avoid sin and urged them to enter the road to penitence. Again, like the Hasidim of Bratslav, the Hasidim of Przysucha-Kock stood apart from the common mass of Hasidim. And just as the Hasidim of Bratslav mocked and derided R. Aryeh Leyb, "the good Jew," the savior of the masses, the "Grandfather of Shpola," the elitist Hasidim of Kock made the "Holy Grandfather" of Radoszyce the object of their scorn. In view of this similarity, it is not at all astonishing that the Hasidim of Kock esteemed, over all the Hasidic literature, the writings of the leader of the Hasidim of Bratslav.[281]

Nevertheless, with all their common elements, there was also a great difference between the two systems in both their doctrinal and their social bases. The Bratslavian Hasidism remained an isolated sect, with no marked influence among the masses of Hasidim in the Ukraine, whereas the doctrine that emerged from Przysucha struck deep roots in Hasidism in Poland and continued to exert a strong influence on later generations.

The Hasidism of Przysucha-Kock, while professing the principle of the duty to attach oneself to the zaddik, conceived of the role of the zaddik in a new light. The zaddik is, first and foremost, the guide who leads his Hasidim to a way of life of Torah and faith. The obligation of perfecting one's virtues and ascending from level to level in the service of God is incumbent not only upon the zaddik, but on every individual. In a declaration of war against all the superficiality and externality in the observance of the faith, and in the wake of the aspiration to deepen religious feeling and to purify it of all the dross and material "motives," the virtue of truth was stressed as one of the highest principles; this deepening of spiritual life was linked with the individualism that ran through the doctrine of Przysucha-Kock. This individualism reflected both the social standard of the middle-class well-to-do Hasidim of Przysucha and the self-exaltation of this class over the multitude of simple folk who were accustomed to the traditional religious practices and absorbed in the routine of daily life.

Hasidism, as established in Przysucha, was distinguished from the very start by the elevation of the study of the Gemara to a central place in the Hasid's way of life. This was carried out to such a degree that even in the time of *ha-Yehudi,* his Hasidism was defined by his Galician contemporary, Uri, the *Saraf* of Strelisk, as "the worship of the Lord through Torah and prayer together." [282] The leaders of the Hasidim were scholars who had thoroughly studied Talmud and *Poseqim* at the Yeshivot in Poland and abroad. At their meetings they would engage in casuistic interpretations of the Gemara and the commentaries, and their homilies were interlaced with their own interpretations of the Gemara. According to Hasidic tradition, R. Ḥayyim of Płońsk praised the disciples of R. Simḥah Bunem, saying, "R. Isaac of Warka is a scholar; R. Isaac Meir of Warsaw [who founded the dynasty of Ger] is brilliant; as for the R. Menaḥem Mendel of Tomaszów [who later moved to Kock], his colleagues are unable to comprehend his thoughts." [283] They also urged their Hasidim to devote themselves to the daily study of Gemara. In the name of *ha-Yehudi* of Przysucha, it was reported that in the study of the Torah every morning were encompassed all the virtues enumerated in the Talmud concerning *pat shaḥarit,* i.e., "that morning bread." [284] An allusion to this is to be found in this same tradition in that *pat* has the same numerical value as *Talmud*." [285] R. Isaac of Warka said that the desire to study Torah is a real desire only when a person does not want to do anything but study. It is reported that his last words before his death were, "The Gemara is the greatest purification." [286] The Hasidic rebbes also gave lessons in the Talmud to groups of their Hasidim. Simḥah Bunem of Przysucha required everyone in his group to develop some new interpretations of the Halakha. [287] R. Isaac of Warka studied

Mishnah and Gemara with his Hasidim.[288] The Hasidim of the Przysucha fraternity would gather in their respective cities for study sessions on the Gemara; and there were some who even shortened their prayer services on Rosh Hashanah and Yom Kippur to devote more time to the study of Gemara.[289] R. Mendel of Kock required the merchants who visited him but did not belong to his group of Hasidim "to rob themselves of at least one hour every day for the study of the Gemara."[290]

Whereas the dignity of the Talmud was elevated, that of the Kabbalah was lowered. The system of mystery in general no longer held a significant place in the doctrine of the school of Przysucha; obviously, those subjects which constituted the main preachments of the earlier Hasidic leaders, that is, the prevalence of *midat ha-ḥesed* over *midat ha-din*, reunion in the upper spheres, combinations of letters, bringing down the flow of Divine Grace, were rare or altogether absent. No wonder that the role of the zaddik as the conduit of the flow of grace and the foundation of the universe was no longer emphasized. R. Simḥah Bunem found it necessary to supply a reason for limiting one's preoccupation with the Kabbalah; namely, that in his generation there was a decline in the number of those who could grasp it properly or plumb its depth."[291] This restrained attitude toward the Kabbalah was bound up with the modification in the essence of Hasidism which took place in the school of Przysucha. With the abolition of the zaddik's function as a savior and wonder worker, and the limiting of his role to that of a guide and a teacher, it had little interest in the entire mystic apparatus, whose central prop and stay was the zaddik. The decline in the study of the Kabbalah was also a natural result of the restoration of the Talmud to its pristine status. Diligent study of the Talmud was not consistent with the study of books dealing with Kabbalah and Hasidism, the spirit of which was alien to the talmudic mode of thought sharpened by dialectic reasoning. For the same reason there was less interest in the study of the Midrash, which, in the past, had been popular with the Hasidic communities. In this respect, two *aggadot* of the Hasidim of Przysucha-Kock are characteristic. The first is about two "very sharp and keen-witted" scholars, Hasidim of Przysucha, who studied with Gaon R. Jacob of Lissa, and who "discontinued the study of GFT [Gemara, the commentary of Rashi, and *Tosafot*] and applied themselves to the study of Midrash and *Zohar*, and the Gaon of Lissa wrote a letter to Przysucha, complaining about them."[292] According to the second, R. Mendel of Kock "made a great outcry" when he learned from the Rabbi of Biała, the father of his son-in-law Abraham (who was to become famous as the Rabbi of Sochaczew), that the latter was studying a great deal of Midrash. He was apprehensive lest he become familiar "with the pious language of the Midrash," and therefore vigorously demanded that he first be imbued with a knowledge of the Gemara, and then he would also understand the Midrash in all its profundity.[293]

In the view of the Rabbi of Kock, understanding and knowledge should not only be the end but also the means of studying the Talmud. Taking exception to the original conception of Hasidism, which regarded devotion to God as the sole criterion for the study of Torah for its own sake, R. Mendel taught that of all manner of devotion to the Creator "the most proper is achieved through studying the Torah," but it is fitting to confine it to preparation alone and disengage one's mind from it while studying, lest it hinder concentration on the subject. "When a man sits at his studies, he must cleave unto God, so that he is aware before Whom he is engaged in study; but if during the time he is studying he constantly applies his thoughts to such cleaving, he will not grasp what the rabbis are saying; therefore, while learning, he should devote his thoughts to the matter being studied." He found an allusion to this in the verse (Ps. 1:2) "But his delight is in the law of the Lord," which refers to the devotion at the start of the study sessions; whereas later, during the time he is studying, the operative clause is "and in His law he doth meditate."[294]

How far the Hasidism of talmudic erudition had moved from folk Hasidism can be seen clearly in the following two *aggadot* which together reflect the contemptuous attitude of the Rabbi of Kock to the "Psalm-reciting" Hasidim. One tells of R. Mendel's early manhood, when he went for the holiday of Shavuot to his rabbi in Przysucha, R. Simḥah Bunem. At dawn he saw R. Jeraḥmiel, the son of *ha-Yehudi,* standing near the window of the *bet ba-midrash* reciting psalms, and he slapped him on the back and said derisively, "Well, Jeraḥmiel, so you are saying *Tehillim?*"[295] The second occurred after he was already a well-known rabbi in Kock. He told one of his Hasidim who was not a scholar, "My friend, someone like you need not travel to see me but ought to sit in back of the stove reciting psalms."[296]

The New Hasidism's Social Appeal and Its Relation
with Mitnaggedim

Above all, the greater emphasis on the study of Gemara marked a turning point in the social aspect of Hasidism. In contrast to Hasidism based on theoretical and practical Kabbalah, which still vexed the scholars (even though the spirit of opposition had been weakened for some time now), the exhortation to study the Torah won over new social classes (especially the scholars among them), thus bridging the rift between Hasidism and the Mitnaggedim. The revival of the study of the Torah was designed to strengthen faith, especially among those classes to whom Hasidism of the popular type could neither appeal nor satisfy spiritual needs.

One of the clear indications of this development and of the rapprochement of the Hasidism of Przysucha with the Mitnaggedim was the involvement of the rebbes in Jewish community life. Not only were the Hasidic leaders deemed worthy of entering the inner circles of the communal leadership but they were also the initiators of rabbinic enactments for the strengthening of religion as well as of interventions with the authorities to nullify decrees which were injurious to religion and tradition. R. Simḥah Bunem of Przysucha, was appointed by the government commission of the *województwo* (district) of Sandomierz as one of two fellow correspondents of that district to the Advisory Chamber of the Committee for the Affairs of Old Testament Believers. When Abbé Chiarini's project made it clear that the goal of the committee was to undermine the Jewish faith, the Hasidim, headed by the disciple of R. Simḥah Bunem, R. Isaac of Żarki (later Warka), were the most active organizers of a vigorous campaign about the imminent danger from the committee. Earlier, in 1826, it was the Hasidim who mobilized the community against the committee's plan to establish a Rabbinical School.[297]

The enactments of the rabbis in 1837 (the 19th of Ḥeshvan, 5598) for the buttressing of the faith as a remedy against repetition of "the weakness" (i.e., the plague) were signed by R. Solomon Zalman (Lifschitz), the Rabbi of Warsaw, and R. Isaac, president of the court of the community of Warka.[298] This same R. Isaac of Warka used to come to Warsaw frequently on matters relating to intercessory actions and would consult with R. Isaac Meir Alter, like himself a disciple of R. Simḥah

Bunem, and his colleague R. Mendel of Kock."[299] Both he and the Rabbi of Warsaw were signatories to an appeal at the end of December 1841 regarding agricultural settlement, and R. Isaac of Warka was a member of the delegation of eight rabbis who presented themselves before the viceroy at the end of December 1843 to request the abrogation of obligatory military service.[300] He interceded with Moses Montefiore during his visit to Poland to obtain a repeal of the royal decree against the traditional Jewish garb,[301] and according to Hasidic tradition it was he who, in consultation with R. Isaac Meir Alter, worked to nullify the strict censorship imposed on the *Ḥoshen mishpat*.[302]

A big factor in building the bridge with the Mitnaggedim was the social composition of the Przysucha Hasidim. Unlike their rival, the "Holy Grandfather" of Radoszyce, the Hasidic leaders of Przysucha were themselves members of the well-to-do and middle classes. R. Simḥah Bunem, the son of the *Maggid* of Wodzislaw, R. Ṣevi ben Judah Leyb, author of the homiletic works *Ereṣ ṣevi* and *Asarah le-meah* in his early manhood, was a businessman who mingled with merchants, served for a time as a clerk with the lessee of the consumption tax in Siedlce,[303] was a grain dealer in Danzig,[304] and later was a certified pharmacist in Przysucha. R. Mendel of Kock, the son of R. Aryeh Leybush, one of the notables of the community in Goraj, was a dealer in hides—though an unsuccessful one—after he married the daughter of one of the important men in the community of Tomaszów,[305] where he led a congregation of Hasidim before moving to Kock. His second wife, the sister of the wife of R. Isaac Meir, was the daughter of an extremely wealthy man. This brother-in-law, R. Isaac Meir, the son of the Rabbi of Magnuszew, was the proprietor of a textile shop managed by his wife; a manufacturer of prayer shawls; and later the owner of a vinegar factory until he was appointed judge in the *bet din* in Warsaw (1843). He was assisted with the necessary funds for his business dealings by his brother, a successful businessman and contractor of government projects.[306] R. Isaac of Warka was the lessee of the monopoly of tobacco in the town of Żarki and in the surrounding district before he became the rabbi and leader of the Hasidim in Warka.[307] R. Yeḥiel Meir, also the disciple of R. Mendel of Kock, was the proprietor of a tobacco shop before his appointment as Rabbi of Gostynin.[308]

These Hasidic leaders were intimates of the very rich family of Sonnenberg-Bergson in Warsaw, having ready access to their home, and some of them also received their training in the management of business enterprises as officials of their patrons' large mercantile banking firm. R. Simḥah Bunem was engaged in supervising the floating of logs to Danzig for R. Berek, the son of Tamar.[309] For some time R. Isaac of Warka managed the properties of "the wealthy lady Temerl of Warsaw,"[310] who was mother and matron to the fellowship of Hasidim of Przysucha. When she came from Warsaw, she presented each man in the fellowship who required assistance "every necessity, as was her wont."[311] In times of financial distress she appeared as a redeeming angel for R. Simḥah Bunem and his disciples.[312]

Those who "journeyed" to the rebbes of this school, as reflected in the *aggadah* of Hasidim, were people of means. Of those journeying to R. Simḥah Bunem, "a wealthy man" who brought "a sum of three silver rubles" is mentioned along with a "certain Hasid, a merchant, who was wont to stay in Leipzig a number of weeks."[313] To be sure, from the sayings transmitted in his name it may be deduced that it was primarily to middle-class Hasidim that the Rabbi of Przysucha was speaking when he foresaw that "at the time of the coming of the Redeemer" the laws of nature would be altered: "There will be scholars without knowledge of the Torah, Hasidim lacking Hasidic qualities, moneyless men of wealth, summers without warmth, winters without cold, and produce that will sprout without rain."[314] On another occasion, "as he grasped the Havdalah cup in his hand" he solemnly described what was to be anticipated "before the advent of the Redeemer": "A Jew will not make a living from his shop; everyone will be forced to have a source of livelihood on the side; my hair and my nails stand on end at this prospect."[315]

A certain *aggadah* tells of the Rabbi of Kock that "one man provided his living, for he was unwilling . . . to accept [help] from just anyone."[316] To be sure, this account is to be assigned to the period in which the Rabbi of Kock had not yet become famous as a preeminent Hasidic leader. The following highly instructive *aggadah* has been preserved concerning the inordinate demands he made upon his affluent supporters during the period of his fame: "Our master, of blessed memory, asked R. Nathan of Czyżew why R. Shmelka did not journey to Kock. And R. Nathan replied with a touch of effrontery, Because he feared you. It is said that you take money from the rich. At which our rebbe thundered, And in your opinion what else am I to do?"[317] Among his intimates were the wealthy Hirsh Leyb Kotsker[318] and Isaiah Prywes of Warsaw. The period of his self-imposed "imprisonment" (when he would isolate himself in his room) was especially hard for "wealthy merchants among his Hasidim," who were in a hurry to get back to their businesses but were compelled to wait around for a long time until the secluded rebbe was willing to give them a farewell blessing. To provide for the needs of R. Mendel's court, prominent men such as R. Wolf of Stryków would go as envoys to gather "money for Kock"—self-imposed taxes—from his Hasidim throughout the country.[319]

Those who came to the court of R. Isaac of Warka were villagers[320] as well as extremely rich men. To be sure, a number of those rich men happened to be mentioned in tales about him, but only to demonstrate the extent to which the rabbi's blessing was fulfilled, whether because of a favor they had done for him or because they had obeyed him.[321] However, the Zaddik of Warka was also on good terms with the wealthy men of Warsaw, from whom he would receive "large contributions" for the needs of the community and for the prevention of "evil decrees."[322] One of his admirers was R. Mottel of Kałuszyn, who held the "lease of Kałuszyn, including all its income from the lord of the town."[323]

The Transformation of the Hasidic Categories in Przysucha-Kock

As a consequence of the social status and the scholarly level of the new community of Hasidim, and in consonance with the new outlook on the role of the zaddik in matters of religion and faith, even the aid to his visitors in material concerns was really nothing more than good counsel, although there also was an element of blessing involved in it. This can be seen in the story of two young men who came to R. Simḥah Bunem asking his advice as to "what business to undertake and what occupation to engage in." He advised them to engage in "yokhtn," which meant tanned hides and a yoke, but the "yoke" might have referred to that of the Kingdom of Heaven.[324] At any rate, his outstanding disciple, R. Mendel of Kock, was esteemed by his Hasidim as a counselor in business matters. When he was once asked how he knew "what advice to give in all sorts of business affairs, inasmuch as he had secluded himself from worldly matters," he replied that it was precisely for that reason that he had a proper perspective, for "whoever is outside an object can look inside that object."[325] However, this did not prevent his Hasidim from pressing him, at times, to pray for anyone in trouble.[326]

Merchants would ask R. Isaac of Warka to write a deed of partnership for them,[327] and a trader in oxen from Hungary was even privileged to get from the rebbe a list of all the market days on which it was worth his while to do business.[328] His advice was sought even about whether to buy a lottery ticket.[329] Giving advice in making matches was so accepted as the rebbe's function that R. Mendel of Kock expressed astonishment at a certain Hasid who failed to turn to him for counsel in this matter. The Hasid's reply, as well as the rebbe's observation, are indicative of the new conception of the zaddik's function. The Hasid replied "that on matters of matchmaking even his rebbe is not informed," to which R. Mendel countered, "But the rebbe could, in any case, offer good counsel."[330] Indeed, this practice of turning to the rebbe as a counselor in business and family matters, which had been initiated at Przysucha-Kock, spread throughout all the reaches of Hasidism in Poland.

Although the social doctrine of the school of Przysucha was founded upon principles common to the entire Hasidic movement in that generation, the stamp of the new class which provided its base was clearly impressed upon it. R. Simḥah Bunem reiterated the idea which had already been articulated in *Toldot ya'aqov yosef*[331] concerning the obligation of the wealthy to be among the supporters of the Torah, to be near those engaged in the study of the Torah, and to provide for their sustenance.[332] He also quoted an adage of *ha-Yehudi* of Przysucha "that it is a very great service to cleave to the true zaddik and this is even harder than to be the zaddik himself."[333] Furthermore, he said that each of the classes has its own duties: the poor man, if he is learned, is obliged to occupy himself with the study of Torah and with service, which is prayer, and as for the man of wealth, "his service consists mainly in charity and benevolent deeds in order to save the poor man from those who oppress and exploit him." In his opinion, it was the ambition to ascend to an inappropriate level that was the main sin for which the Second Temple was destroyed.[334] Following in the wake of the tradition which evolved from the Talmud,[335] his disciple, R. Mendel of Kock, also taught that "God placed wealth in the world so that the glory of Heaven should be enhanced"; that is to say, the rich person is blessed with wealth not for his own benefit but in order to do the will of heaven.[336]

This doctrine of the division of social functions is to a certain extent a reflection of the Hasidic milieu, which was also preserved in the school of Przysucha-Kock. Aside from the Hasidim who journeyed to the rebbe for festivals and holidays, the rebbe was also surrounded by his "Hasidim in residence," who were engaged in the study of Torah.[337] This "congregation of Hasidim" was dependent for its livelihood, as was the zaddik, on the offerings of the benefactors "who give support to the Torah." As Hasidism spread, the number of those journeying to the rebbe from among the *baʿalei battim* (householders) class increased beyond the limited circle of the Hasidim proper. The turning point occurred when R. Isaac Meir inherited the "throne" of the Rebbe of Kock. Concerning this, an *aggadah* of Ger relates that "after the death of the holy Rabbi of Kock, with the increase in the gatherings of people, many of the *baʿalei battim* began journeying to the holy rebbe, R. Isaac Meir; and the question was asked, What need has he for such a large gathering among whom are many *baʿalei battim,* whereas the rebbe exists principally for the sake of Hasidim?" R. Isaac Meir replied with a saying from the Midrash, "A thousand enter upon the study of the Bible. . . , but only one emerges to study Mishnah."[338] In view of the continuous change in the composition of the Hasidic community, the positive view of the rebbes on the combination of Torah and commerce may easily be understood. One Hasid apologized to R. Mendel for being compelled to engage in trade, inasmuch as he was burdened with a large family and consequently no longer had any time to engage in the study of Torah and Hasidism as was his wont previously. The rebbe put his mind at ease: "One can also fulfill the Torah and the commandments through trade, by exercising care in weights and measurements, by refraining from cheating and deception, by abstaining from staring at women, and by letting one's yea be a righteous yea and one's nay be a righteous nay.[339] To be sure, the rebbe also cautioned anyone engaged in trade to devote himself to Torah and prayer as soon as he rises in the morning, otherwise it will become "very difficult to return to a state of sanctity." A young man who was being supported by his father-in-law asked R. Isaac Meir whether "it might be proper for him to engage a little in trade while being supported by his father-in-law." The rebbe jokingly cited the example of the Patriarch Jacob, who was "even a greater deceiver than Esau, and yet he engaged in the study of Torah day and night."[340]

What was new in the social doctrine of Przysucha was its individual-istic outlook on wealth and poverty and, stemming from it, the elevation of wealth to the point where it endows its possessor with merit. Accord-ing to a trustworthy Hasidic *aggadah*, R. Simḥah Bunem held "that every poor person will have to justify being poor," that is, it must be because of his sins that he became poor.[341] In a similar vein, his disciple, R. Mordecai Joseph Leiner of Izbica, taught "that God is concerned about man's bread since it affects the life of the Jew, for should he, God forbid, be lacking bread, he will then be lacking in the service of God. ... Therefore a person should reflect upon his deeds and return unto God that He may have compassion upon him." The general rule was "that when a man is more successful than his neighbor, it is because he holds within him a greater measure of worship of God and good deeds." This view was based on his kabbalistic doctrine about the dependence of the flow of spiritual and material grace on man's readiness to receive this flow. "For God does not give a blessing except in a brimming vessel; that is, provided man, for his part, prepares himself, and to the extent that he is a receptive vessel, so God fills him, and the receiving vessel is called purity, and through this vessel sanctity is received. Therefore, when one receives sanctity, one also obtains the flow of grace bearing all the good things of this world."[342]

According to R. Mordecai Joseph's master, R. Mendel of Kock, "Man's place below is his root in the upper spheres."[343] This same R. Mendel expressed his indignation that in the house of a certain zaddik (of Zaklików), the apartments were rented out to tailors, they being classed as "unworthy people."[344] This social outlook is far removed from the advocacy of the simple folk that can be seen in the doctrines and deeds of the Baʿal Shem Tov.

A rule of thumb in social conflicts was provided by R. Isaac of Warka, namely, tolerance. Thus R. Mottel of Kałuszyn, the Hasid of the Rebbe of Warka, admonished his children in his will, "Do not enter into a dispute, flee from a quarrel, and be numbered among the perse-cuted. . . ." To show that he followed these precepts he related:

At the time that I held the lease[345] of Kałuszyn, together with its various incomes, from the lord of the city, a dispute developed and the whole city conspired against me and the people . . . complained; this was the counsel of our master and teacher, the holy rabbi[346]—that we should be counted among the tolerant; and the fires of dispute died down, for he had charged me not to quarrel with them, nor to display a strong hand, for God seeks him who is persecuted. And so it came to pass that all those who rose up against me fell and even perished.[347]

No less characteristic than the counsel to refrain from "displaying a strong hand" was the rabbi's stand in support of the lessee against the men of the insurgent community. Perhaps this incident has some relation to the rebellion of the community of Kałuszyn against its rabbi in 1842, concerning which the mayor submitted a report to the Committee for Internal Affairs to the effect that on August 7, many Jews in Kałuszyn whose occupation consisted of "idleness and plotting rebellions" assembled at the synagogue. An uproar arose within the synagogue and around it, and the leaders of the insurgents extinguished the candles inside the synagogue and committed "improper acts" against the rabbi of the city.[348]

From the old social doctrine of Hasidism there remained in the school of Przysucha the glorification of the *miṣvah* of charity. R. Simḥah Bunem gave twice a fair sum as alms to a decent, needy man, the second gift following immediately upon the first. He explained it thus: The first time he gave out of a feeling of pity, but that was not enough, because we must give alms out of a sense of obligation to fulfill the Torah's commandments.[349] He also explained, with his own unique brand of witticism, the problem raised by R. Solomon ben Adret: Why is it that, unlike the other positive commandments, no blessing is required when giving alms? The reason he gave was that if a man were to make preparations, as for other commandments, by ablution, or be reciting the formula "For the sake of the sanctification," the poor man would die of hunger in the meantime.[350] In the same vein, the clever rabbi explained the reason for the absence from the Torah of a prohibition against miserliness, although it is such a reprehensible quality: "Because it is a stumbling block to all the other commandments. . . , therefore it is unnecessary to put it in writing." And he found an allusion to it in Ps. 119:165: "Great peace have they that love Thy Torah; and there is no stumbling for them."[351] R. Mendel of Kock interpreted the verse "If thou lend money to any of My people, even to the poor with thee"[352] on the basis of the saying of the talmudic Sages:"[353] "For in the hour of a man's departure, neither silver nor gold accompany him . . . but only Torah and good works." For "if a man's silver accompanies my people, you may know that it is only what you will give to the poor that you will take with you."[354] R. Isaac of Warka, a follower of Dovidl of Lelov in the quality of compassion and renowned as a charitable person[355] who dispensed justice on behalf of the poor,[356] explained that the well-known principle of the Sages, "He who wants to be liberal must not give away more than one-fifth,"[357] applies only to a squanderer and not to one "who is parsimonious as regards himself, being content with little and giving alms."[358]

The school of Przysucha-Kock also did not differ from the general Hasidic movement of its time with regard to Jewish solidarity, that is, the attachment of the individual to his people and the love of Jews. R. Simḥah Bunem also stressed the obverse; namely, the ban on association with Gentiles.[359] According to his interpretation, the commandment to love Jews obligates one to love all those who have no other virtue but the fact that they recite *Shema Yisrael*.[360] His explication of the phrase "See whether it is well with thy brethren" was that one should plead the cause of the Jews "so that he can behold them in a state of perfection and not in a defective state."[361]

In the same vein, he took the sentence of the Sages, "All Israel has a share in the world to come," to mean that "they have nothing in and of themselves except as they are within the totality of Israel."[362] His disciple, R. Mendel, interpreted the verse "Ye shall be holy" in this spirit, saying that it is only possible for the collective to be holy but not the individual.[363] He even found confirmation of this in the rearrangement of the letters of the word *sheqer* (falsehood) to read *qesher* (a tie), as if to say that he who does not tie himself to the totality of Jewry is dominated by falsehood.[364] The reward of unity, according to R. Simḥah Bunem and R. Isaac of Warka—they being in consonance with the Hasidic doctrine of the school of Lublin and Kozienice—is the acceleration of the Redemption, the coming of the end, that is, the Messianic Era, before its fixed time.[365]

The conception of Przysucha-Kock concerning the doctrine of redemption was based on the tendency to deepen religious life which distinguished this school within the Hasidism of Poland. Just as the Hasidim of Przysucha negated the miracles and wonders of the zaddik as a way to the transitory salvation of the individual, so they rejected the belief that redemption came as a consequence of a sudden miracle and not by virtue of repentance and a determined effort in the worship of the Creator. For this reason, *ha-Yehudi* of Przysucha had expressed his indignation against "those zaddikim who reveal the end of time, signaling the advent of the Messiah," even though he himself believed that the Redemption was at hand.[366]

NB

The contrast between the two schools of Hasidism in Poland in this matter grew sharpest in the atmosphere of messianic expectancy in the year 5600 (1840). This expectancy relied upon the passage in the *Zohar* that in the six-hundredth year of the sixth millennium the gates of wisdom on high and the fountains of wisdom below would be opened, and the world would prepare itself to enter the seventh century, just as a man readies himself at sunset on Friday to enter the Sabbath.[367] The masses of eastern European Jews as well as the Hasidic leaders and great scholars were all seized by this belief. It is no surprise that the "Holy Grandfather" of Radoszyce, the wonder worker, was among the zaddikim in Poland who were enthralled by this hope.[368] R. Mendel of Kock and his disciples, however, were not swept along by that flood of messianic expectation. R. Mendel himself, together with R. Isaac of Warka, brought the statement of the *Zohar* concerning the year 5600 (1840) to bear upon the revival of secular knowledge: "Except that then the Jews were undeserving of it, so science was handed over to the secularists," that is, the gentile nations. His disciple, R. Isaac Meir, explained this passage as a necessity for the repair of the blemish in the covenant.[369] However, his own disciple, R. Mordecai of Izbica, who had deviated from him, saw in it an allusion to, and thus an encouragement to reveal, precisely in that year, his kabbalistic doctrine pertaining to Hasidism.[370]

As for R. Mendel of Kock, not only did he reiterate the admonition of his teacher, *ha-Yehudi* of Przysucha, with reference to the ban against revealing the end of time, the advent of the Messianic Era,[371] but he also expressed his fear lest the disappointment would bring on the rise of a new Shabbatean movement. This is the only way one can understand his saying, which was handed down in his name by his son-in-law, R. Abraham of Sochaczew,[372] "In the period preceding the coming of the Messiah" the wearers of white robes "will need the mercy of Heaven, lest, God forbid, they fall under the influence of heresy."[373] His view, that repentance was the only way, albeit a prolonged one, to hasten Redemption was expressed in the following conversation with one of his disciples: Once, when R. Jacob David, the *dayyan* (judge) of Międzyrzecz, who was later known as the Rabbi of Kozienice, came to him, R. Mendel inquired after the welfare of his teacher, R. Hershel of Lęczna, remarking, "I love him dearly, but why does he cry out to God to send the Messiah; why doesn't he cry out that the Jews should repent? For this is what is inferred in the verse, Wherefore criest thou out to Me? Speak unto the children of Israel, that they go forward."[374]

Because he considered the improvement of the soul and character to be the main purpose of the Hasid, R. Mendel of Kock was almost indifferent to *aliyah* (immigration) to Ereṣ Yisrael. In his opinion, there was no benefit in *aliyah* if it was not preceded by an *aliyah* (ascent) in the perfection of the worship of God. On the contrary, it was bound to delude the immigrant and to assuage his conscience so that in appearance he would have discharged an obligation which in actuality was only the outer part of the commandment. To one who wanted to journey to Ereṣ Yisrael to spare himself the pain caused by the "rolling of the dead underground" (on their way to Israel for the Resurrection), R. Mendel said sarcastically, "Do you so love your body that you are afraid of bodily pains even after death?"[375] According to another Hasidic *aggadah*, he advised someone to refrain from making a trip to Ereṣ Yisrael because "it is better to travel to the Jew of the land than to the land of the Jew."[376]

R. Mendel saw no contradiction between his passivity regarding *aliyah* to Ereṣ Yisrael and his stress on the obligation of the people to be attached to their homeland. The following *aggadah* attests to R. Mendel's concern for the suffering of the people in Exile: When R. Jacob of Amshinov (Mszczonów) told him that he dreamt he saw his deceased father, R. Isaac of Warka, "standing by a river and leaning on his staff as if he were looking into the river," R. Mendel replied, "Do you know what this river is? This river consists of the tears of weeping Israel."[377] Following in the footsteps of his teacher, the *Maggid* of Kozienice, R. Israel,[378] he interpreted the verse "The land whereon thou liest, to you I have given it" as "the land with which you are inextricably bound up, I will give you,"[379] and to this interpretation he added, "and Jacob lay down in this place"—namely, that "Jacob became inextricably bound up with the land at this place."[380] His teacher, R. Simḥah Bunem, who, according to the tradition of his Hasidim, never lay down to sleep even in the daytime without placing his *talit* and *tefillin* under his head (as provision for the road, should the Messiah come), taught that abroad "there cannot be an aptitude for worship as that which prevails within the land."[381]

In keeping with his teaching that it is man's duty to ascend ever upward on the ladder of perfection, the Rabbi of Przysucha interpreted Ps. 37:34, "Wait for the Lord, and keep His way, and He will exalt thee to inherit the land," as signifying the necessity to reach an exalted state of knowledge in order to hope to inherit the land.[382] In this verse he also found support for the view that "before the land is inherited it will be good for the Jews and their glory will be enhanced ever more."[383]

With regard to the difficulties of making a living in the period preceding the advent of the Messiah, R. Simḥah Bunem explained the verse "they will mingle themselves with the nations and learn their works" (Ps. 106:35) as meaning that the gentile nations will learn from the Jews how to conduct business and thus deprive them of their livelihoods.[384] It is therefore reasonable to assume that in his doctrine regarding the End of Days he made a distinction between the period preceding the advent of the Messiah and the actual time of the Redemption, which is destined to come at a time of plenitude and ease. Similarly, his disciple, R. Isaac of Warka, on the basis of a clever combination of Ps. 147:2, "The Lord restoreth Jerusalem, he gathereth together the dispersed of Israel," with the midrashic interpretation of that verse and the law in the Gemara in reference to partners in a house and attic—distinguished between the time of the Ingathering of the Diaspora and the time of the building of the Sanctuary. "If, Heaven forbid, the Jews would not do penance, God would build up the earthly Jerusalem and have the option of not allowing them to rebuild the Temple; nevertheless, He would gather together the dispersed of Israel."[385] It appears that even the yearning expressed in the strong belief in the Redemption of the *Shekhinah* and the restoration of the Service in the Temple accorded a priority to the longing of that generation for redemption in an earthly sense, emancipation from the servitude of the Exile, the Return to Zion, and the rebuilding of the land from its desolation.

A Sustenance of Faith: Cornerstone of the New Hasidism

Faith more than any other element of the original doctrine of Hasidism was stressed in the school of Przysucha-Kock. This emphasis is sufficient in itself to indicate the tendency to combat the naturalistic outlook on the world, which already was at the threshold of middle-class consciousness. It is related that R. Simḥah Bunem, as he was strolling with his followers, lifted a grain of sand and then returned it to its place, saying, "Whoever does not believe that this grain of sand must lie precisely in this spot because it is so appointed by God, is—Heaven forbid—a skeptic."[386] He also taught, in accordance with the doctrine of his predecessors, that even in the matter of earning a livelihood man is forbidden to rely on material causes and his own efforts, but must trust in God alone.[387] R. Mendel of Kock likened to the eaters of manna those Jews who have enough for the day's needs and are not concerned about tomorrow.[388] There was a story about a man "who was very diligent at devising all manner of industrial designs, yet he was a ne'er-do-well." R. Mendel interpreted Eccles. 9:11, "The wise have no bread," as "The Holy One, blessed be He, says, 'If you are so wise, go seek out a livelihood for yourself,' " that is, he derided him for turning to all manner of schemes instead of trusting in God.[389] He also viewed "the giving of the Torah" (the Sinaitic Revelation) as closed to inquiry and as barring the comprehension of the Creator by intellectual means.[390]

All this notwithstanding, a sprinkling of rationalism is still discernible in the Hasidism of Przysucha because of the special position of the Hasidic movement of Poland. Since the Haskalah movement had no real social impact, the strong rationalist trends in Poland perforce attained some sort of expression within the most liberal wing of the devout. The rejection of the belief in miracles and wonders of the zaddik was mainly a consequence of the new mode in the worship of God. The well-known epigram was told in the name of *ha-Yehudi:* "What mastery is there in being a wonder worker? Any man of a certain achievement [in God's service] has in his power to turn heaven and earth topsy-turvy; but to be a Jew—that is really hard."[391] This view also expresses the awareness of the superiority of the new Hasidim over the masses who were addicted to superstitious beliefs. In line with this view, the Rabbi of Kock, relying on Maimonides, explained that demons do not exist at present, although they did abound before, since they are mentioned in the Gemara. He was also angry at those who prayed at the graves of the zaddikim in the Lublin cemetery, "for they are no longer there." In light of this, we can understand his well-known statement to R. Isaac of Warka when they met at the grave of their master, R. Simḥah Bunem, on the anniversary day, I am not a Jew who recites prayers at a grave [for others], I have come to see you."[392] R. Mendel of Kock even encouraged the study of the *Yad Ḥazakah,* recommended the writings of the *Maharal* (of Prague), "which provide intelligence and reason for the understanding of the Gemara and the *Poseqim*," and saw the perusal of the *Guide of the Perplexed* as beneficial to those who had alrady had their fill of studying *Shas* (the Talmud) and *Poseqim*.[393] Indeed, following in the footsteps of their masters from Przysucha and Kock, the Hasidim would study Maimonides, the *Kuzari,* the works of *Maharal* and other writings in religious philosophy. In keeping with the theosophy of the author of the *Tanya,* R. Mendel also taught "that there is not in the entire reality of the world any reality but that of God alone, for all that man sees with his eyes of the flesh is not reality at all, since only that which he beholds with the eyes of the intellect is reality."[394] His leaning toward rationalism is also reflected in his epigrams in praise of wisdom and about the reward of knowledge in matters of religion. He interpreted the talmudic aphorism "The sage is superior to the prophet"[395] to mean that intelligence *is* prophecy.[396] Similarly, he changed the simple meaning of the verse "He that increaseth knowledge increaseth sorrow" (Eccles. 1:17) to agree with his interpretation of the text: Although one increases sorrow, one should still increase knowledge; and he juxtaposed it with Hos. 4:6, "Because thou hast rejected knowledge, I will also reject thee."[397]

Despite the rationalist tendency which marked the Hasidism of Przysucha-Kock, there was a marked contrast with the Weltanschauung of the Bratslavian opposition[398] among the Hasidim of the Ukraine. Both opposition trends were far from the original Hasidism in their denial of corporeal needs and in their lack of concern for all mundane affairs. Simḥah Bunem comforted his weeping wife as he lay near death, saying, "The only purpose of my life has been to learn to die."[399] Similarly, his disciple, R. Mendel, stated, "Death is nothing at all; we transfer from one abode to another, choosing a more beautiful dwelling."[400] Displaying the same contempt for death as did Socrates, R. Naḥman of Bratslav, in the face of the approaching end, expressed his eager anticipation of being delivered from his corporeal bonds, "I yearn to remove my garment, for I cannot remain on one level." R. Mendel of Kock went to the greatest lengths in his denial of worldly life. His attitude is summed up in his well-known saying, "The entire world is not worth even one sigh."[401] No doubt the tragic circumstances of his life contributed to this pessimistic attitude, as in the case of the Zaddik of Bratslav. It is well known that R. Naḥman of Bratslav suffered from tuberculosis and died before he had even reached "the age of understanding" (forty years old); and as for the difficult personal life of the Rabbi of Kock, it is clearly marked by the fact that he lived apart from his first wife for twenty-five years.[402]

Yet in an even more pronounced manner than in the Hasidism of Bratslav, the Przysucha-Kock doctrine was interlaced with a negation of life in this world and of worldliness as a way of worship.

The doctrine that the Jewish way of life involved bearing the yoke of the Kingdom of Heaven through the study of the Torah and the strict observance of its commands was espoused by *ha-Yehudi* of Przysucha, passed to his disciples and in turn, by them to their disciples. He was wont to say—as is stated in his name by R. Isaac Meir of Ger—that he would give all of this world and the world to come "for a hairsbreadth of *Yiddishkeit*" (Jewishness).[403] Similarly, his disciple, R. Mendel, spoke of the insignificance of this world and the vanity of worldliness in his aphorisms. "A Hasid rejects the world, and he who rejects the world is a Hasid";[404] "only take heed to thyself, and keep thy soul diligently"[405] (the word "only" is a qualifying term); "give little heed to your physical self and pay great heed to your soul";[406] and "I can take a young man who is absorbed in the lusts of this world and cause him to despise them . . . to the extent that whenever he but hears of them he will spew forth his food."[407] As for "Rashi's interpretation of 'Thou shalt not commit adultery' as always referring to a married woman, this can refer only to one's own wife."[408]

This is not asceticism in the sense of corporeal mortification; it is rather inner asceticism based upon disregarding one's bad inclinations and dedicating one's life to Torah and the worship of God. This sense of asceticism he expressly stated in many of his aphorisms: "Jacob said, 'In the day the drought consumed me, and the frost by night' [Gen. 31:40] —that is, the fervor during the daytime was engendered by the frost of the night";[409] "Walking in the paths of the Torah constitutes the greatest mortification of the body";[410] and "it is easier for the body to endure all manner of mortification and torment than to bear the yoke of the Kingdom of Heaven."[411] Finding satisfaction in the Torah and the commandments does not entail any abnegation, for there is no delight comparable with spiritual delight. Accordingly, the Rabbi of Kock was astonished at the saying of the Sages, "He who enjoys the Sabbath through pleasurable acts is granted his heart's desires."[412] He responded with such aphorisms as "Since there is nothing greater than joy, what else does one lack?" and "this is the glory of royalty, for because of one's joy that he is king, he lacks for nothing."[413] He even said of himself[414] that "if it were not that he needed to speak to people, he would not find it necessary to eat, since the vitality he derived from the holy Torah would suffice for him." The delight over the fulfillment of the Torah as well as its study lasts until one gives up one's breath; moreover, it is "a great joy to be sentenced to death by the *bet din*, since this death is in accordance with the law of the Torah."[415] Consistent with this doctrine was his harsh attitude toward those Hasidim who besought him to pray for their sustenance. For example, to one who explained apologetically that he did not know how to pray "before a great and awesome king," he retorted, "If so, you have more to worry about than the worry of making a living, namely, that you do not know *how* to pray." When it was recommended that he pray on behalf of a certain Hasid who had become impoverished, he replied, "If that man is indeed a Hasid and God-fearing, he lacks for nothing."[416] As against devotion to God, all mundane affairs are as vanity of vanities, and man must even render as nothing in his heart all troubles relating to the material sphere. By giving added point to the Yiddish folk saying, R. Mendel summarized that principle in a formulation of the commentary on the verse in Ps. 37:3, "Dwell in the land and cherish faithfulness": *Lig in der erd un pashe zikh mit emune* ("No matter how dire your circumstances, find your sustenance by means of faith").[417]

This strict doctrine regarding a way of life is somewhat similar to the principles of stoicism in respect to man's overcoming his desires and schooling himself to be indifferent to all that befalls him, in order to stand firm against all of life's afflictions. The Rabbi of Kock used to say —and it is possible that therein he reiterated the words of his master, *ha-Yehudi* of Przysucha:[418] "When one snaps one's thumb at oneself,[419] one can snap it against the whole world."[420] This constant self-discipline is also related to rationalism, which marks the Weltanschauung of the Hasidim of Kock. They regarded the rule of supremacy of intellect over impulse and of purposefulness over arbitrariness as one of the principles which set them apart from the other Hasidim. As R. Mendel stated, "A Tomaszów Hasid is one who asks himself, in all things, 'What do I want in this matter?' "[421] But the main root of negation of material concerns is inherent in that goal of the reinforcement of religion and faith which required the restoration of the study of the Gemara to its original high status. With respect to the fundamental Hasidic doctrine relating to the elevation of the material world to a spiritual level, there is clearly a certain retrogressive tendency.[422] Still, the form itself of the compromise with the old philosophy of life should be viewed as a vestige of the original Hasidic trend toward ethical monism: In order to escape a dualistic conception of ethics, the Hasidim of Przysucha-Kock did not accept the notion of a struggle with the *yeṣer ha-ra*ᶜ (Evil Inclination) as regards lusts and worldliness, but of their complete negation within the mind and heart.[423]

However, in order to plumb the conceptual depth of Przysucha-Kock Hasidism, one must see both fronts on which this school fought for the regeneration and strengthening of Judaism. One front of this war of ideas was directed against the shallow miracle-working type of Hasidism, and in this struggle the old values of Judaism—the study of Torah and the rigorous way of life—were revitalized. Simultaneously, this school, with all its energy and freshness of ideas, led the battle on the second front against the petrified orthodoxy and on behalf of the liberalization of the worship of God. The impact and driving force of Przysucha-Kock Hasidism came mainly from its aggressive war on this second front.

Crystallization, Contention, and Decline: The Career of Rabbi Isaac Meir of Ger

Despite their common goals, the antagonism between the rival schools was most conspicuous and gave rise to prolonged quarrels. By the beginning of the nineteenth century, two camps of Hasidism had crystallized: that of the adherents of "the Seer" of Lublin and that of *ha-Yehudi* of Przysucha. According to an *aggadah* of the Hasidism of Kock, R. Meir of Opatów, who carried on in the ways of his Lublin master, did not refrain from cursing the Hasidism of Przysucha; and the Hasidism of Kozienice used to say that daily one should say the prayer giving thanks "that He did not make me a Hasid of Przysucha."[424] A kind of coalition of rebbes in Galicia and in the Kingdom of Poland who followed in the footsteps of the old system of Hasidism banded together against Przysucha. In order to forestall any trouble, R. Simḥah Bunem sent a delegation to the wedding in Ustilug (in Volhynia) of the grandchildren of R.

Abraham Joshua Heschel of Międzyboż (who became famous as the Rabbi of Opatów) and R. Meir of Opatów, where "four hundred rebbes wearing white *kapotes* [caftans]" were assembled. Although the astuteness of R. Isaac Meir of Warsaw—a disciple of R. Simḥah Bunem—was helpful in preventing a "holy war" against his master and his Hasidim,[425] the mutual opposition continued.

After the death of the Rabbi of Przysucha in 1827, the controversy between the Hasidim of his successor, R. Mendel of Kock, and the other Hasidic factions became sharper and the feud intensified. There are grounds for conjecture that the Hasidim of Kock were the ones who provoked the strife and their opponents were compelled to defend themselves. According to an *aggadah* of those in opposition to Kock, the Hasidim of R. Mendel did not shrink from carrying out acts of terror against them.[426] The dispute in the camp of Hasidism turned into enmity and hatred to the extent that those who had been close became distant. After R. Mendel of Kock had fallen ill with melancholia around 1840,[427] and his disciple, R. Mordecai Joseph, had left him and established his own "court" in Izbica, the Hasidim of Kock and Izbica harassed each other mercilessly. The Rabbi of Kock, in particular, could not forgive the disloyalty of his former adherents and criticized them severely.[428]

The death of R. Mendel of Kock in 1859 marked a decisive turn in the history of Hasidism in Poland. To be sure, there still existed many factions of Hasidim, almost as many as courts of the rebbes and their dynasties. The "throne" of R. Mendel was occupied by his son, R. David, and the tradition of the doctrine of Kock was ably fostered by his son-in-law, the distinguished scholar R. Abraham Bornstein, the Rabbi of Sochaczew. R. Isaac of Warka, who died in 1848, similarly had established his own dynasty in his town and in Mszczonów. Centers of Hasidism of the disciples of R. Mendel arose during the lifetime of their teacher in such sites as Ciechanów, Biała, Stryków, Gostynin, and Mogielnica. Also, the descendants of the *Maggid* of Kozienice, "the Holy Grandfather" of Radoszyce, as well as other grandchildren led communities of Hasidim in their respective "courts" who were loyal to the Hasidic schools of their forebears. But the predominant figure in the Hasidism of Poland was the disciple of the Rabbi of Kock, R. Isaac Meir (known by the initials RIM) of Warsaw, who quickly moved to the town of Ger (Góra Kalwaria) east of Warsaw. Only after his death, at the beginning of 1866, did there arise a rival court to Ger that was established in the town of Alexander, near Lódz, that of R. Yeḥiel ben Feivel Danziger, one of the disciples of R. Isaac of Warka. Most significantly, despite the rivalry among the "courts," the doctrinal division in the Hasidism of Poland came to a halt. In that era, R. Isaac Meir of Ger put his stamp on Polish Hasidism, and it was he who charted its course for the future. While his master from Kock repelled Hasidim of various schools both in his radical doctrine and in the arrogance and loftiness of his conduct, his distinguished disciple attracted them by his moderation both in doctrine and in temperament.

One of the prominent traits in the system of Ger which won over the Hasidim of Poland was the establishing of the study of the Talmud and the *Poseqim* as a fundamental way of life. In the synthesis of Torah and piety, his master from Kock stressed the element of inner perfection, while his disciple elevated the study of the Torah above all the other commandments. Indeed, he himself viewed the development of the doctrine of Przysucha as a three-stage process. "R. Simḥah Bunem led the community through love, the Rabbi of Kock led it through reverence, and I lead it through the Torah."[429] It was not for nothing that his colleague, Ḥanokh Henekh of Alexander, was wont to observe that for R. Simḥah Bunem there were "two commentaries, the first, our master and teacher of Kock; and the second, our master and teacher of Ger."[430] This goal of R. Isaac Meir indeed drew close to him the camp of constantly diminishing opponents.

The rapprochement of the camps of the Hasidim and the Mitnaggedim was facilitated by the inflexible and extreme conservatism of the Hasidism of Ger, no less than by the strengthening of the pillars of the Torah. "Anything new is forbidden by the Torah" was a saying current with the Hasidim of Ger, on the basis of the verse (Lev. 26:10) "And ye shall bring forth the old from before the new." During the lifetime of his teacher from Kock, R. Isaac Meir of Ger made every effort to oppose any modernization in the life of the people. He mobilized all the pious in the community of Warsaw against the plan of the enlightened to require the teachers in the *Hadarim* (elementary schools) to undergo an examination. In this he was very successful: even though the tests were required of all the teachers by law, only a few tried to obtain certificates. Similarly, he organized a successful opposition to the establishment of new schools for Jewish children in Warsaw, in addition to the few schools already in existence.[431] R. Isaac Meir also was the leader of those in both camps who campaigned against the decree requiring the adoption of the gentile mode of dress.

In the spring of 1846, when it became known that an edict banning the Jewish mode of dress was being prepared, R. Isaac Meir, in collaboration with his colleague R. Isaac of Warka, sought to enlist the aid of Moses Montefiore, who was then visiting Poland, but to no avail. When the decree was issued some months later, he organized an attempt to intercede with the authorities for its annulment. It is true that in 1849, when a manifesto in the name of Warsaw's rabbinate was issued urging the members of the community to obey the royal statute in the matter of the change in dress, this Hasidic leader also signed it as a member of the community's *bet din* (rabbinical court), a function he had been performing since 1843. But later he was the moving spirit in the opposition to the decree, and as a penalty for this he was arrested by the police, although he was freed the following day becaue of the popular feeling aroused by the news of his arrest. According to a Hasidic *aggadah,* it was as a result of the propaganda of R. Isaac Meir that the pious chose the Russian and not the German style of dress, for it included permission to grow a beard; moreover, the coat was longer than that in fashion in western European dress.[432]

The strong insistence and strictness of R. Isaac Meir of Warsaw regarding the preservation of the traditional Jewish mode of dress were in themselves characteristic of the development of Hasidism along conservative lines. Nor was his colleague and teacher R. Mendel of Kock—like R. Simḥah Bunem the teacher of both of them—fond of close contact between Jews and their neighbors, considering it to be dangerous to the self-preservation of the Jewish people. R. Simḥah Bunem interpreted the verse "And their laws are diverse from those of every people" (Esth. 3:8) as meaning "that this is their law that they shall be different from every other people."[433] He also commented on the verse dealing with the covenant of Abraham and Abimelech "And they two made a covenant" (Genesis 21:27), saying that "they two, and not one [means that] there shall be no unity between them, they should never be joined together to be alike in their deeds"[434] R. Mendel of Kock interpreted the prophecy of Balaam (Num. 24:14) "what this people shall do to thy people in the end of days" as relating to the days when "this people will be your people, to the extent that they will, God forbid, be alike in all their manners and customs."[435] But this same Rabbi of Kock was agi-

tated to the very depth of his being when he was told that R. Abraham
of Ciechanów, in concert with R. Isaac Meir of Warsaw, held that Jews
are obligated to risk their lives regarding the decree on the mode of
dress. Not only did he ridicule this judgment, which, in his opinion, was
not in accord with Jewish law, but also, displaying an understanding of
history, he recalled that the Jews had changed their mode of dress more
than once.[436]

The conservatism of the disciples of Kock continued to increase as the
Haskalah appeared, and also spread among Poland's backward Jewry.
R. Isaac Meir composed special poems to warn against the "plague" of
the Haskalah, which gives its devotees "the accursed waters, gall and
wormwood" to drink.[437] During the service in the synagogue, the zaddik
R. Yeḥiel Meir of Gostynin sought forgiveness from the Holy Torah
when he learned that ordinary householders and youths were reading
"books of romance" and "poems and love stories" on the Holy Sabbath,
and he moralized at great length on the desirability of reciting from the
Book of Psalms and reading from the *Qav ha-yashar* instead.[438] In the
early 1880s the son-in-law of R. Mendel of Kock, R. Abraham of
Sochaczew, issued proclamations against "those who read in the books
and periodicals of the free thinkers."[439] Thus the circle of the devout,
who viewed all social and cultural progress among the people with
hostility, became ever smaller. The refreshing and invigorating concepts
of the Hasidism of Przysucha and Kock in the period of Sturm und
Drang steadily evaporated, and nothing remained of them but memories.

NOTES

The Appendix citations refer to the appendix in the Hebrew edition of
Mahler's book, *Hasidism and the Jewish Enlightenment, Ha-hassidut ve-
ha-haskalah* (Tel Aviv, 1961).

All the documents cited here, as well as the documents published in the
above-mentioned appendices, were taken from the Polish Government
Archives (Archiwum panstwowe) in Lwów (Lemberg). For the most part
the documents cited are taken from the volume entitled *Chassiden-Juden-
sekte 1814–1838 (Acta praesidialia, Rectificatum praesidiale* 129), and
these are designated in the notes in brief as *Chassiden* with the relevant
numeration. Others are scattered in various volumes of documents pertaining to the former praesidium of the Galician provincial government *(Acta*

praesidialia). Documents from other collections are listed as "S. A., Lemberg" (State Archives, Lemberg) with the appropriate catalogue number.

1. S. A., Lemberg, *Acta Gubernialia Publ. Polit.* i/j 11 no. 8201.
2. J. Wertheimer, *Die Juden in Oesterreich* (Leipzig, 1842) 1:300–310.
3. A. F. Pribram, *Urkunden und Akten zur Geschichte der Juden in Wien* (Vienna, 1918) 2:279–306.
4. I. Schiper, "Die galizische Judenschaft in den Jahren 1772–1848 in wirtschaftsstatistischer Beleuchtung," in *Jüdische Monatshefte* 9–10 (1918): 23; cf. F. Friedmann, *Die galizischen Juden im Kampfe um ihre Gleichberechtigung* (Frankfurt, 1929), p. 9.
5. M. Stöger, *Darstellung der gesetzlichen Verfassung der galizischen Judenschaft* (Lemberg, 1833) 1:263–66. According to Stöger, only 1,172 Jews had their own commercial firms in 1826.
6. Ibid., pp. 202–8.
7. Friedmann, *Die galizischen Juden*, p. 84.
8. Wertheimer, *Juden in Oesterreich*, p. 304.
9. Schiper, "Die galizische Judenschaft," p. 23.
10. Schiper arrived at this conclusion on the basis of the figures cited (ibid., p. 229); cf. Stöger, *Darstellung*, p. 15.
11. Piller, *Galizische Provinzialgesetzsammlung*, 1823, no. 42077.
12. *Chassiden*, 18/g, 1827; cf. document 6f.
13. Ibid., 4553/838; cf. appendix: document 9c.
14. Most of the Hasidim described in Perl's satire *Megalleh temirin* (Lemberg, 1879) are tavernkeepers, whereas the wealthy merchant appears as an exemplar of the worthy Maskil.
15. Solomon Judah Rapoport, "Ner Miṣvah," in *Naḥalat Yehudah* (Cracow, 1868), p. 15.
16. This letter was published by Philip Friedman in his article "Di ershte Kamfn tsvishn haskole un khsidizm," in *Fun Noentn Over* 4 (1938): 265.
17. Moses of Sambor, *Tefilah le-Moshe* (Lemberg, 1858), Torah portion *Lekh lekha*, p. 9a.
18. *Kerem ḥemed* 2 (1836): 35.
19. Perl, *Megalleh temirin*, p. 75a, letter 101.
20. Joseph Perl, *Boḥen ṣaddik* (Prague, 1838), p. 53.
21. Published by Letteris in *Mikhtavim* (1827), letter 5; *Zikkaron ha-sefer* (Vienna, 1868), pp. 65ff.; *Kerem ḥemed* 1 (1833): 90ff. (letter is signed "Peli"); *Moreh nevukhei ha-zeman* (Lemberg, 1863), p. 24, and in Rawidowicz, ed., *Kitvei Rabbi Naḥman Krokhmal*, p. 417.
22. Perl revealed this geographical map in *Megalleh temirin*, p. 22a, letter 16 ("Among residents of Poland, Wallachia, Moldavia and part of Hungary almost all are our people").
23. Ephraim Fischl Fischelsohn, *Teyator fun khsidim*, in *Historishe shriftn fun YIVO* 1 (1929): 649–93.
24. Isaac Ber Levinsohn, *Emek refa'im* (1867), pp. 3, 4, 9.
25. Isaac Ber Levinsohn, *Divrei ṣaddikim* (1867), pp. 28, 31.

26. *Be'er Yishaq*, p. 127. A play on words in the Hebrew original: "beşel kanfei ha-ḥasidah."

27. Naphtali of Ropczyce, when once advised that his *gematria* (computation of the numerical value of letters) did not tally, replied that basically the zaddikim were worthy of hearing their teachings from heaven and the *gematriot* are no more than a hint and are subsequently sought out in the Torah; if the *gematria* did not tally, he explained, one only had to use another system of computation, such as comprehension or minor value; see his *Ohel naftali* (Warsaw, 1911), p. 138.

28. See, for example, Menahem Mendel of Kosów, *Ahavat shalom* (Czernowitz, 1883); the works of Hersh of Zydaczów; Simon of Dobromil, *Naḥalat shim'on;* Naphtali of Ropczyce, *Ayalah sheluḥah;* Abraham David of Buczacz, *Birkat david.* These words all appeared after 1848 because of the rigid Austrian censorship of Hasidic-kabbalistic books.

29. Hersh of Zydaczów, *Sur me-ra va-aseh tov* (Munkacs, 1901), p. 71.

30. Moses of Sambor, *Tefilah le-moshe, va-yeşe*, p. 18b.

31. Menahem Mendel of Kosów, *Ahavat shalom*, p. 15b.

32. Ibid., p. 88b; see also Simon of Dobromil, *Naḥalat shim'on*, on the portion *Koraḥ*.

33. Wachstein also emphasized the close relationship between the precarious existence of the majority of Galician Jewry, tradesmen, and tavernkeepers, and the Hasidic tenet of faith that in his opinion served as a means to maintain the "psychic balance" of these economically insecure masses; see B. Wachstein, *Die hebräische Publizistik in Wien* (Vienna, 1930), p. lv.

34. A. B. Gottlober, "Zikhronot mi-yemei ne'urai, "*Ha-boqer Or*, 5:24.

35. See R. Mahler, *Divrei yemei yisrael be-dorot ha-aḥaronim* (Merḥaviah, 1954) vol. 1, bk. 3, pp. 198–99; appendix 22, p. 238.

36. Gottlober (see note 34).

37. Fischelsohn, *Teyator fun khsidim*, p. 654; cf. episode mentioned in Dov Shtok (Sadan), *Zikhronot mi-mekhoz yaldut*, p. 12. The author's great-grandfather, Reb Yossi, a Hasid of Bełz, was removed from his ritual slaughterer's post in Żółkiew because "his main enemies were the artisans of the city" who forced him to sign a certificate ceding his rights to his brother, a Mitnagged.

38. Fischelsohn, *Teyator fun khsidim*, p. 651.

39. *Makkel no'am*, the satire "Der khosid mit zayn vayb um shabes."

40. Naphtali of Ropczyce, *Ayalah sheluḥah* (1903), p. 22.

41. Mendel of Rymanów, *Menaḥem şiyyon*, pp. 54–55, 185.

42. In the original: *ak'vata d'moshicha;* according to the Talmud, the impudence of the gentile nations would be intensified before the advent of the Messiah (*Sotah* 49).

43. Hersh of Żydaczów, *Sur me-ra*, p. 15a.

44. *Pe'er miqdoshim* (Lemberg, 1865), pp. 53–54. Naturally, the legend ignores the fact that the special Jewish taxes were not rescinded until the Revolution of 1848 and that Hersh of Zydaczów died during the cholera

epidemic of 1831. The historical facts presented on the following pages prove that Hersh really had a concessive attitude in relation to the government and the tax lessees regarding the Jewish taxes.

45. *Ateret zeqeinim,* referred to in Michael Braver, Ṣevi la-ṣaddiq (Vienna, 1931), p. 60.

46. Mendel of Rymanów, *Menaḥem ṣiyyon,* p. 43.

47. *Hosafot Meherṣa* (initials of Ṣevi Elimelekh) to Hersh of Żydaczów, *Sur me-ra,* p. 22.

48. Ibid.

49. On the basis of litigation which was later conducted against abuses of the tax lessees it evolved that Herz Homberg, who, as an expert, expressed his opinion that the candle tax is in accord with the Jewish religion, had previously concluded an agreement with the future tax lessees giving him 2 percent of the net income of the lease; cf. M. Balaban, *Żydzi w Galicyi* (Lemberg, 1914), p. 77.

50. Berger, *Eser qedushot* (Piotrków, 1906), pp. 38–40.

51. Cf. Mahler, *Divrei yemei yisrael,* p. 285.

52. Simon of Jaroslaw, *Imrei qedosh yisrael,* in "Ma'amar qadishin," addendum to Naphtali of Ropczyce, *Imrei shefer* (Lemberg, 1884), Torah portion *va-yaqhel,* p. 15a.

53. It is told, for example, that during the cholera epidemic of 1831, on leaving the *bet ha-midrash,* Hersh of Żydaczów put his hand on the mezuzah, saying, "I am the expiatory sacrifice for all the Jews." His brother, Moses of Sambor, allegedly stated when several hundred Hasidim arrived to celebrate the High Holidays with him, "I do not know what to do with such a large crowd ... but I take upon myself the suffering of Jewry" (Berger, *Eser qedushot,* pp. 20, 48).

54. Mendel of Rymanów, *Menaḥem ṣiyyon,* p. 37a.

55. Simon of Dobromil, *Naḥalat shimʿon,* Torah portion *Naso.*

56. Levinsohn, *Emeq refa'im,* p. 12; cf. *Dover shalom* (Przemyśl, 1910), p. 37, about Sholem Rokeakh of Bełz: "Even Gentiles came to his Holy Eminence of Bełz"; see also p. 152.

57. Fischelsohn, *Teyator fun khsidim,* p. 686.

58. Naphtali of Ropczyce, *Ayalah sheluḥah,* p. 22; Simon of Dobromil, *Naḥalat shimʿon,* Torah portion *Toledot.*

59. Simon of Dobromil, *Naḥalat shimʿon,* Torah portion *va-Yehi.*

60. Mendel of Rymanów, *Menaḥem ṣiyyon,* pp. 46–47. Yitskhok Ayzik of Żydaczów used to say that the *bet ha-midrash* of his uncle Hersh of Żydaczów stood on a strip of Ereṣ Yisrael and that all of the prayers of the Diaspora which were turned toward the land of Israel passed through this *bet ha-midrash* (Berger, *Eser qedushot,* p. 20).

61. Mendel of Rymanów, *Menaḥem ṣiyyon,* pp. 56–57.

62. Mendel of Kosów, *Ahavat shalom,* p. 9b; Hersh of Żydaczów, *Sur me-ra,* p. 1b; Naphtali of Ropczyce, *Ayalah sheluḥah,* pp. 6–7; Simon of Dobromil, *Naḥalat shimʿon,* p. 8.

63. The glosses to Hersh of Żydaczów's *Sur me-ra,* written by Ṣevi Elimelekh of Dynów, p. 4; this passage is taken from *Sanhedrin* 97b.

64. *Dover shalom,* p. 41.

65. Moses of Sambor, *Tefilah le-moshe,* Torah portion *va-etḥanan,* p. 27a.

66. Cf. Mahler, *Divrei yemei yisrael,* bk. 4, app. 28, app. 29.

67. Ibid., pp. 245, 256, the citations from the Talmud.

68. Mendel of Kosów, *Ahavat shalom,* p. 37b.

69. Naphtali of Ropczyce, *Ohel naftali,* p. 38.

70. This is related in *Seder ha-dorot le talmidei ha-Besht* (Lemberg, 1865).

71. Simon of Dobromil, *Naḥalat shimᶜon,* Torah portion *Ḥukat.*

72. *Peʾer miqdoshim,* pp. 58–60.

73. Thus, for example, Hersh of Żydaczów interpreted the verse *Maᶜaleh gerah u-mafris parsah* ("cheweth the cud and parteth the hoof"): *Maᶜaleh gerah* (he who brings up and contributes a *gerah* [coin]), and *mafris parsah* (he who breaks *[pores]* his bread for the hungry) Berger, *Eser qedushot,* p. 26); Meyer of Przemyślany interpreted the rituals of the Passover Seder, "*qadesh* (sanctify) *u-reḥaṣ* (lave) *qarpas* (greens), *yaḥaṣ* (divide)" in the following manner: If a Jew wants to sanctify himself and cleanse himself of his sins, he must share his bed and bread, *kar-pat,* with the poor (Bartfeld, *Divrei meʾir* [1909], p. 20).

74. *Babylonian Talmud, Ketubot* 50a.

75. *Imrei qadosh ha-shalem,* glosses, p. 40; a similar interpretation of the reform of the Academy in Usha was reported in the name of Rebbe Isaac of Warka.

76. Hersh of Żydaczów's account of Moses Leyb of Sasów (*Sefer maʾasei ṣaddikim im divrei ṣaddikim* [n.p., n.d.], p. 40) was adapted by I. L. Peretz in his famous short story, "If Not Still Higher"; Peretz transferred the tale to the Rebbe of Nemirov.

77. Hersh of Żydaczów gave forty orphans in marriage. Every time he married off one of his own children he would do the same for an orphaned girl and provide the couple with its keep. His nephew Yitskhok Ayzik of Żydaczów did the same (Berger, *Eser qedushot,* pp. 21, 74). It is told of Naphtali of Ropczyce that his Hanukkah menorah was pawned all year for a loan which he would take for the poor (Naphtali of Ropczyce, *Ohel naftali,* p. 135). The Rabbi of Nowy Sącz, Hayyim Halberstam, pointed out the generous philanthropy of the Rebbe of Ropczyce as an exemplar in contrast to the profligacy of the Sadagura dynasty (*Keneset ha-gedolah* [Rohatyn, 1869], p. 21).

78. See *Peʾer Miqdoshim, Seder ha-dorot, divrei Meʾir.* Solomon Rubin, one of the last Galician Maskilim, also related in his memoirs that Meyer of Przemyślany used to distribute the payments he received among the poor and he himself lived in dire need (Horodetzky, *Ha-Ḥasidut ve-ha-Ḥasidim* [Berlin, 1922], 4:110).

79. Levinsohn, *Emeq refaʾim,* p. 5.

80. Cf. appendix: document 6e.

81. Berger, *Eser qedushot* pp. 41, 44, 46; Braver, Ṣevi la-Ṣaddiq, p. 75.
82. Uri of Strelisk, *Imrei qadosh ha-shalem*, p. 29.
83. Berger, *Eser qedushot*, p. 50.
84. Cf. appendix: document 6f.
85. Cf. appendix: document 6g.
86. Ib. Chassiden, 4553/838; see appendix: document 9.
87. B. Weinryb, "le-Toledot Rival," *Tarbiz* 5 (1934): 204.
88. Friedmann, *Die galizischen Juden*, p. 93.
89. Balaban, Żydzi w Galicyi, p. 72ff.
90. The first denunciation of this activity was made against the secretary of the *kehillah* in Lemberg, Modlinger, in 1818.
91. The denunciation by Hayyim Herbst of Mosty Wielkie in 1824, by Joseph Tepper of Tarnopol against the Hasidim of Buczacz in 1841. Like Joseph Perl, Joseph Tepper accused the Hasidim of keeping the money for themselves; see appendix: documents 4, 12.
92. See appendix: document 4. The style of this denunciation (against "fanaticism") indicates that the informer was a Maskil.
93. See appendix: document 12.
94. See appendix: docuemnt 6.
95. Balaban, Żydzi w Galicyi, p. 80.
96. See M. Jost, *Neuere Geschichte der Israeliten* (Leipzig, 1828), vol. 10, pt. 3, p. 87.
97. *Chassiden*, 5611/838.
98. Mendel of Kosów, *Ahavat shalom*, p. 61b.
99. Levinsohn, *Emeq refaʾim*, p. 3.
100. Joseph Perl delivered this report in response to the government's inquiry concerning Galician Jewry's reaction to Siegfried Justus's proposal for a Jewish state. The report was published by N. M. Gelber in his book *Vorgeschichte des Zionismus* (Vienna, 1927), pp. 258–62.
101. *Hosafot meharṣa* to Hersh of Żydaczów, *Sur me-ra*, p. 35b.
102. Jost, *Neuere Geschichte*, p. 89.
103. Levinsohn, *Emeq refaʾim*, p. 4.
104. *Zemir Ariṣim ve-Ḥarvot Ṣurim* (published by Dubnow) in *Ha-avar*, vol. 2. It is well known that Hasidim used polished knives; supervision was lightened due to the appointment of persons from their own circles; cf. H. Shmeruk, "Social Implications of Hasidic Ritual Slaugher" (Hebrew), in *Zion* 20:1955.
105. Levinsohn, *Emeq refaʾim*, p. 5.
106. Concerning the role played by the low status of talmudic scholars in the intellectual deficiency of Hasidism cf. H. Graetz, *Geschichte der Juden* (Leipzig, 1870), 11:114; S. Dubnow, *Toledot ha-Ḥasidut* (Tel Aviv, 1943), sect. 12; B. Dinur, "Reishitah shel ha-Ḥasidut," *Be-mifneh ha-dorot* (Jerusalem, 1955), pp. 139–47; Mahler, *Divrei yemei yisrael*, n. 107.
107. Gottlober, *Zikhronot mi-yemei*, pp. 1035–36.
108. Fischelsohn, *Teyator fun khsidim*, p. 685.
109. Levinsohn, *Emeq refaʾim*, p. 15.

110. This refers to tax lessees for community revenue, e.g., the meat tax.
111. Those who furnished the Russian government with military recruits.
112. Brokers, "Faktoyrim" specifically refers to those in the steady employ of the nobility.
113. Tax lessee for indirect communal taxes, especially for the tax on kosher meat, known as the *Korobka*.
114. Officials in charge of quartering soldiers in civilian homes.
115. Cf. n. 33.
116. Levinsohn, *Emeq refa'im*, p. 10.
117. I. B. Levinsohn, *Di hefker-velt* (Warsaw, 1902), p. 36.
118. *Imrei qadosh*. "Kuntres Or Olam," pp. 12–13; Braver, Ṣevi la-Ṣaddiq, p. 32.
119. I. Weinlös's introduction to *Yoysef Perls yiddishe ksovim* (Vilna, 1937), p. lix.
120. N. Horowitz, in "Joseph Perl," *Kalender und Jahrbuch der Israeliten* 5 (1846): 214.
121. The same *aggadah* is also used in later Hasidic works in order to substantiate the position of the zaddik as a mediator of abundance; see, for example, Simon of Dobromil, *Naḥalat shim'on* on the biblical portion *beshalah*.
122. *Divrei me'ir*, p. 23a.
123. Berger, *Eser qedushot*, pp. 152–53. His letters to the Rabbi of Bóbrka, treat the same matter. S. J. Rapoport told S. D. Luzzatto in a letter written at the end of 1833 that he had a difficult struggle with the lessees of the meat tax until they reinstated him in his office as secretary. He explained their opposition to him on the grounds that "they sided with the wicked Hasidic sect" (B. Dinaburg, *Iggerot Shir*, collection 1–2 [Jerusalem, 1927], p. 49, quoted by Joseph Klausner, *Historyah shel ha-sifrut ha-ivrit ha-ḥadashah* [Jerusalem, 1937] 2:233).
124. M. Balaban, *Historja Żydów w Krakowie* (1936) 2:566–72.
125. Cf., for example, Mendel of Kosów, *Ahavat shalom*, pp. 2b, 29b; Simon of Dobromil, *Naḥalat shim'on*, Torah portion Ḥukat.
126. *Hosafot Meharṣa* to Hersh of Żydaczów *Sur me-ra*, pp. 4, 16.
127. According to Hasidic tradition, Hersh of Żydaczów came together with R. Jacob of Lissa in Kałusz. After the Hasidic rebbe offered a legalistic talmudic discourse the rabbi spoke on Kabbalah. This brought Hersh to comment that the two men "made peace in the world." He had proved that Hasidim are "well grounded in *GeFet*"—a Hebrew acronym for Talmud and the commentaries of Rashi and the Tosafists—and his partner-in-dialogue that scholars are also well versed in Kabbalah: cf. Ṣevi la-Ṣaddiq, p. 47.
128. *Imrei qadosh ha-shalem*, pp. 29, 34. Nevertheless, in contrast to Przysucha-Kock, Uri stressed the prayer in "Torah and Prayer" (ibid., p. 41). It was no mere coincidence that Uri also expressed individualistic ideas in the spirit of Przysucha-Kock (cf. ibid., pp. 9, 32).
129. The "Ḥadushim" are also mentioned in the memorandum of the Lemberg

police directorate of 1838 regarding Hasidism (*Chassiden*, 4553/838); see appendix: document 9e.

130. Participating in the rabbinical assembly which was convoked in Lemberg in 1830 to excommunicate those who evaded payment of the meat and candle taxes, in addition to the Orthodox rabbis like Jacob Ornstein of Lemberg. Ṣevi Hirsh Chajes of Żółkiew, Jacob of Lissa, and Landau of Brody, was the same Hersh of Żydaczów who in his books bemoaned the heavy burden of the Jewish taxes and who himself had suffered persecution by the Austrian police in past years. Among the matters about which the Galician administration solicited the opinion of the district rabbi of Żółkiew, Ṣevi Hirsh Chajes, is the folowing question: "Should the Hasidic rebbes be called in to participate in the renewal of the bans regarding the evasion of taxes [on kosher meat and candle-lighting]?" See Jost, *Neuere Geschichte*, p. 81.

131. The reference here is to the popular talmudic saying: "In the Messianic era insolence will prevail" (*Sotah* 49b; *Sanhedrin* 97a); with a slight modification, "impudence will increase."

132. *Be'er moshe* (Jozefów, 1883), p. 390 (*Liqutim*).

133. Ibid., p. 4.

134. Ibid., *Toledot*, pp. 20–21.

135. R. Meir of Opatów, *Or la-shamayim*, undated (the statements of approval are from the year 1849), p. 13a; cf. also *Vayelekh, Ha-azinu*, p. 62a.

136. Ibid., p. 6a.

137. Ibid., p. 8a.

138. Deut. 8:12–14.

139. Reuben Ḥayyim Alexander Cherniḥa, *Niflaot ha-saba qadisha* (Piotrków, 1929), p. 93.

140. Exod. 23:5.

141. *Baba Meṣia* 32a.

142. Cherniḥa, *Niflaot ha-saba qadisha*, p. 97.

143. R. Meir of Opatów, *Or la-shamayim*, p. 60a.

144. Ibid., pp. 35a, 45a.

145. Ibid., *Mishpatim*, p. 31a.

146. Ibid., *Bamidbar*, p. 42a.

147. Cherniḥa, *Niflaot ha-saba qadisha*, p. 117.

148. *Be'er moshe, Mishpatim*, p. 110, *Liqutim*, p. 392.

149. Gen. 34:31.

150. R. Meir of Opatów, *Or la-shamayim, Vayishlaḥ*, p. 15a.

151. *Be'er moshe, Toledot*, p. 23.

152. R. Meir of Opatów, *Or la-shamayim, Yitro*, p. 29.

153. Ibid., *Vayiqra*, p. 33a.

154. Ibid., *Meṣora*, p. 35a.

155. Ibid., *Bamidbar*, p. 42b; *Niṣavim*, p. 61b.

156. *Qohelet moshe* (Lublin, 1924), p. 72; *Be'er moshe,*, pp. 4, 10.

157. R. Meir of Opatów, *Or la-shamayim, Ḥuqat*, p. 48a.

158. R. Ezekiel of Kazimierz, *Neḥemad Mizahav* (Piotrków, 1909), p. 29.
159. R. Meir of Opatów, *Or la-shamayim*, p. 9b, 32a.
160. Ibid., *Shemot*, p. 20b.
161. Ibid., *Vayiqra*, p. 33b.
162. *Qoḥelet moshe, Vayeḥi*, p. 48.
163. *Be'er moshe, Vayishlaḥ*, p. 40; cf. also R. Meir of Opatów, *Or la-shamayim*, p. 20a *(Shemot):* "And Elokim is an appellation of the zaddik who holds sway by reason of his reverence for God."
164. *Be'er moshe, Vayeshev*, p. 48.
165. *Qoḥelet moshe*, p. 43.
166. *Be'er moshe, Vayishlaḥ*, p. 34.
167. *Be'er moshe, Vayeṣe*, p. 27.
168. *Be'er moshe, Toledot*, p. 19.
169. *Be'er moshe, Bo*, p. 95 passim; cf. a similar version by R. Meir of Opatów: "Abundance of blessing and prosperity and health, children, life and sustenance, healing and deliverance for all Jews" (R. Meir of Opatów, *Or la-shamayim, Aḥare*, p. 35b).
170. R. Meir of Opatów, *Or la-shamayim, Vayaqhel*.
171. *Erubin* 100b.
172. R. Meir of Opatów, *Or la-shamayim, Vayiqra*, p. 33b.
173. *Be'er moshe, Toledot*, p. 23.
174. R. Ezekiel of Kazimierz, *Neḥemad mizahav, Qoraḥ*, p. 64.
175. Ibid., *Toledot*, p. 36.
176. R. Meir of Opatów, *Or la-shamayim, Noaḥ, p. 6a; Beshalaḥ*, p. 28b; *Yitro*, p. 29a; *Mishpatim*, p. 30b; *Behar*, p. 39b.
177. 2 Sam. 23:3; *Be'er moshe, Vayishlaḥ, p. 37.*
178. R. Meir of Opatów, *Or la-shamayim, Emor*, p. 38b; the cited verse is Ps. 33:10; *Balaq*, p. 3b.
179. *Be'er moshe, Yitro*, p. 104; *Balaq*, p. 290.
180. R. Meir of Opatów, *Or la-shamayim, Bereshit*, p. 5a.
181. Isa. 49:3.
182. R. Meir of Opatów, *Or la-shamayim, Vayishlaḥ*, p. 15a.
183. Ibid., *Bamidbar*, p. 42b.
184. Ibid., *Mishpatim*, p. 30b.
185. Ps. 135:4.
186. *Qoḥelet moshe, Shemot*, p. 54; cf. also *Be'er moshe*, p. 385: "Your splendid abode, for inasmuch as we are in the bitter exile in great poverty, actually like trodden down rubbish. . . ."
187. *Be'er moshe, Liqutim*, p. 392.
188. Ibid., *Liqutim*, Omission for Yom Kippur, p. 394.
189. Ibid., Sermon for Yom Kippur, p. 373.
190. Ibid., pp. 381, 382 (Sermon for *Hoshannah Rabbah*), *Shemini*, p. 181; *Qoḥelet moshe, Shemot*, p. 61.
191. *Be'er moshe*, p. 383; cf. ibid., *Vaera*, p. 85.
192. *Be'er moshe, Vaera*, p. 85.

193. Ibid., p. 394.
194. Mic. 7:20.
195. *Be'er moshe*, p. 385.
196. Ibid., *Shemini*, p. 180.
197. Ibid., *Ki Teṣe*, p. 329.
198. Ibid., Sermon for Yom Kippur, p. 373.
199. A play on words according to the *halakhah* of R. Nathan in an interpretation of the verse "Ye shall kindle no fire": 'The law about kindling a fire on the Sabbath is specified to intimate that each transgression involved in the kindling *was* to be atoned for separately." (Thus in *Yebamot* 7b, in *Sanhedrin* 35b, the version is given in the present tense: *is* to be, etc.)
200. *Be'er moshe*, Sermons for Hanukkah, p. 59; *Vayeshev*, p. 41.
201. Ezek. 18:23, 32; 33:11.
202. *Berakhot* 10a.
203. *Qohelet moshe*, p. 232 *(Liqutim)*; the verse in the Sabbath hymn is a combination of fragments of Ps. 36:11 and Naḥ. 1:2.
204. *Be'er moshe*, *Shermot*, p. 83.
205. *Qohelet moshe*, Ḥuqat, p. 179 (in an explanation of the verse [Num. 21:19] "and from *Mattanah* to *Naḥaliel;* and from *Naḥaliel* to *Bamoth*").
206. Num. 24:7.
207. *Be'er moshe*, Balaq, p. 290.
208. Ibid., *Yitro* (Exod. 19:1), p. 104.
209. Ibid., *Rimzei shir ha-shirim*, p. 164.
210. *Qohelet moshe*, Balaq, p. 180.
211. Ibid., *Vayeḥi*, p. 48.
212. Prov. 31:15.
213. R. Meir of Opatów, *Or la-shamayim*, Beḥuqotai, p. 41a.
214. Ibid., *Behaalotekha*, p. 44b; Ḥuqat, p. 49a; Balaq, p. 50b; *Vayaqhel*.
215. Isa. 55:12.
216. Jer. 31:8.
217. R. Meir of Opatów, *Or la-shamayim*, Emor, p. 37b; in the course of the statement a really erotic and sexual interpretation is given to the opinion that the sufferings of the Jewish people and the weeping are likely to increase God's love for His people.
218. R. Ezekiel of Kazimierz, *Nehemad mizahav*, Toledot, p. 37.
219. Ibid., p. 73, a sermon on Nisavim, Deut. 30:3.
220. *Be'er moshe*, Parashat Ki 'Teṣe, p. 329; ibid., p. 392 *(Liqutim)*, *Qohelet moshe*, p. 235 *(Liqutim)*.
221. Gen. 46:23.
222. Cherniḥa, *Niflaot ha-saba qadisha*, p. 97.
223. Exod. 22:25.
224. Deut. 24:4.
225. *Be'er moshe*, Mishpatim, p. 112; R. Meir of Opatów, *Or la-shamayim*, Ki Teṣe, p. 80a.
226. *Qohelet moshe*, Shemot, p. 61.

227. R. Meir of Opatów, *Or la-shamayim, Behuqotai*, p. 40b: a comment on the verse "and keep My commandments and do them."
228. Ibid., *Vayeshev* (Gen. 37:16), p. 16a.
229. R. Ezekiel of Kazimierz, *Nehemad mizahav*, p. 77 (sermons on the Psalms).
230. R. Meir of Opatów, *Or la-shamayim, Eqev*, p. 55a.
231. Ibid., *Vaera*, p. 20b.
232. Cf. the first section of this chapter.
233. R. Ezekiel of Kazimierz, *Nehemad mizahav, Vayigash*, p. 41.
234. Ibid., *Beshalah*, p. 46.
235. Ibid., *Bamidbar*, pp. 61–62.
236. Cherniha, *Niflaot ha-saba qadisha*, p. 97: As a scriptural proof, R. Issachar Ber interpreted the verse "I pray you, my brethren, do not so wickedly" by means of his own peculiar analysis: "Do not" (namely, "if they cannot pray and achieve by means of the prayers") "my brethren *become companionable*." . . . "It is advisable . . . to join in friendly fellowship and take a repast together—in love and fraternity." In similar fashion he expounded: "And they journeyed from *Haradah*, and pitched in Makhelot" (Num. 33:25): "If a person is seized with a trembling of the heart because of the troubles which, Heaven forbid, beset him, then it is good counsel to pitch in *Makhelot*, that is, to join together with his companions in fellowship."
237. *Baba Batra* 10a, with reference to Isa. 56:1: "Thus saith the Lord, Keep ye justice and do righteousness; for My salvation is near to come, and My favor to be revealed"; *Sedaqah*, having the sense of righteousness and justice, is here given the meaning of aid to the poor.
238. R. Meir of Opatów, *Or la-shamayim*, p. 63a (selected passages); cf. there also pp. 19b *(Shemot)*, 31a *(Terumah)*, 37b *(Emor)*; Sermons of R. Moshe of Kozienice on the role of *Sedaqah* in bringing down to earth the flow of grace from on high; *Be'er moshe, Vayese*, p. 28, *Bo*, p. 95.
239. Lev. 25:24.
240. *Be'er moshe, Behar*, p. 222.
241. R. Meir of Opatów, *Or la-shamayim, Vaera*, 20b; *Ki Tisa; Shelah*, 46b.
242. Cf. pp. 252–55.
243. Exod. 34:19.
244. *Be'er moshe, Ki Tisa*, pp. 128–29.
245. *Ketubot* 111a.
246. *Be'er moshe*, Sermon for *Hoshannah Rabbah*, p. 387.
247. Exod. 13:4.
248. Exod. 16:22.
249. R. Meir of Opatów, *Or la-shamayim, Bo*, p. 22b; *Beshalah*, p. 28b.
250. Lev. 27:24.
251. *Qohelet moshe, Behuqotai*, p. 157.
252. Deut. 12:9.
253. R. Ezekiel of Kazimierz, *Nehemad mizahav, Re'eh*, p. 71.
254. Ps. 136:22.
255. R. Ezekiel of Kazimierz, *Nehemad mizahav, Re'eh*, p. 71.

256. Cherniḥa, *Niflaot ha-saba qadisha,* p. 5.

257. Ibid., p. 3.

258. Ibid., p. 50.

259. B. Wasiutynski, *Ludność żydówska w Polsce w wiekach 19 i 20* (Warsaw, 1930), p. 56.

260. A number of these legends are cited by I. Alfasi in his book *Ha-saba ha-qadosh me-radoszyce* (Tel Aviv, 1956), chap. 3 of Solomon Gabriel Rosenthal, *Hitgalut ha-Ṣaddiqim* (Warsaw, 1927), pp. 69–77.

261. *Ḥas veshalom* (God forbid).

262. *Ha-Shem Yitbarekh* (He whose Name is blessed).

263. *Raḥamana lişlan* (May the merciful One save us).

264. *Ruaḥ Ra'ah* (an evil spirit).

265. Cherniḥa, *Niflaot ha-saba qadisha,* p. 14.

266. Rosenthal, *Hitgalut,* p. 35; quoted by Alfasi, *Ha-saba,* p. 72.

267. Cherniḥa, *Niflaot ha-saba qadisha,* p. 45.

268. Ibid., p. 78; see also p. 117.

269. Ibid., pp. 15, 23, 31.

270. Ibid., pp. 45–46.

271. Yoes Qim Qadish Rakocz, *Siaḥ sarfei qodesh* (Lódz, 1927) vol. 2, no. 233, p. 72; concerning him cf. also Cherniḥa, *Niflaot ha-saba qadisha,* pp. 53–54.

272. Cherniḥa, *Niflaot ha-saba qadisha,* pp. 39–40, 42, 47–50, 57, 65, 70–71, 82, 115.

273. Cf. ibid., p. 109: On Purim at the *Maggid*'s place in Kozienice, he would strike with an axe upon stubble for a long time, until he would be covered with sweat; he explained: "I wanted to break up and render null the falsehood which exists in the world" (axe in Polish is *siekiera,* which somewhat resembles the sound of the Hebrew term for "falsehood" — *sheqer*); ibid., p. 113; he gives the reason for eating honey on Rosh Hashanah, because *devash* (the Hebrew word for "honey") has the initial letters for *Daj Boze szczescie* (a Polish phrase meaning "God give good luck," which is a benediction bestowed by the wayfarer on those who toil in the field).

274. Ibid., p. 78.

275. Ibid., p. 85.

276. Ibid., pp. 87–88.

277. Ibid., p. 16.

278. Ibid., p. 74.

279. Ibid., p. 43.

280. Cf. Mahler, *Divrei yemei yisrael,* 3:121; *"Ha-yehudi" mi-Pshiskha v-shitat ha-ḥasidut ha-metuqenet,* pp. 304–7.

281. Cf. Aaron Marcus, *Ha-Ḥasidut* (Tel Aviv, 1957), p. 160; cf. also Moses Menaḥem Walden, *Ohel Yiṣḥaq* (Piotrków, 1914) 173:68: On the day that R. Isaac of Warka received the book *Liqutei moharan,* "it was as though it were a festival day for him because of his great joy."

282. R. Uri of Strelisk, *Imrei qadosh ha-shalem* (Lemberg, n.d.) no. 68, p. 34.

283. *Siaḥ sarfei qodesh,* (Piotrków, 1923; Lódz, 1927) vol. 1, no. 276, p. 60.
284. *Baba Meṣia* 107b.
285. *Siaḥ sarfei qodesh* (Lódz, 1927) vol. 2, no. 253, p. 78.
286. M. Walden, *Ohel Yisḥaq* no. 211: p. 92; no. 259: p. 107.
287. Ibid., no. 164: p. 64; also cf. Z. M. Rabinowicz, *Rabbi Simḥah Bunem mi-Pshiskhah* (Tel Aviv), p. 37.
288. M. Walden, *Ohel Yisḥaq,* no. 88, p. 37.
289. A. Marcus, *Ha-Ḥasidut,* p. 133; Rabinowicz, *Rabbi Simḥah Bunem,* p. 69.
290. *Siaḥ sarfei qodesh* vol. 4, no. 110.
291. Shmuel of Shinavi, *Ramatayim ṣofim,* commentary upon *Tanna de-bei eliyahu* (Warsaw, 1881), p. 227; also cited in Rabinowicz, *Rabbi Simḥah Bunem,* p. 47.
292. Shmuel of Shinavi, *Ramatayim ṣofim,* p. 195.
293. Ṣevi Yehudah Mamlak, *Abir ha-ro'im* (Piotrków, 1935) 1:23; also cf. there R. Mendel's complaint to his daughter's father-in-law, that his son-in-law Abraham "prays overmuch"; he therefore fears lest this bring harm to "his mental powers."
294. Aaron Walden, *Miqdash me'at* (Warsaw, 1890), p. 27; *Siaḥ sarfei qodesh* vol. 3, no. 18, p. 25.
295. A. Marcus (Verus), *Der Chasidismus* (the original edition, in German) (Pleschen, 1901), pp. 300–301.
296. *Siaḥ sarfei qodesh* 3:18.
297. D. Kandel, "Komitet Starozakonnych," *Kwartalnik . . . Żydów w Polsce* vol. 1, no. 2, (1912), p. 89, 95–96, 100–103.
298. The appeal was published in full in M. Walden, *Ohel Yisḥaq* pp. 93–97.
299. Ibid., p. 79.
300. See A. N. Frenk, "Tsu der geshikhte fun yidisher kolonizatsye in Kongres-Poyln, "*Bleter far Yidisher Demografye, Statistik un Ekonomye* 5 (Berlin, 1925) 17–27.
301. M. Walden, *Ohel yisḥaq* pp. 14, 97; *Siaḥ sarfei qodesh* vol. 1, pp. 31–32.
302. M. Walden, *Ohel yisḥaq* pp. 7, 79.
303. *Siaḥ sarfei qodesh* vol. 4, p. 15.
304. Ibid., vol. 1, p. 33.
305. Ibid., vol. 1, no. 271, p. 59.
306. Abraham Issachar Alter, *Meir einei ha-golah* (Tel Aviv, 1954), 1:38–39, 125; 2:83–84.
307. M. Walden, *Ohel yisḥaq* 130:54.
308. *Siaḥ sarfei qodesh* vol. 1, p. 41.
309. Ibid., vol. 2, no. 24, p. 15; see Jonathan ha-Levi Eibeschütz, *Ḥedvat simḥah* (Warsaw, 1930), p. iii.
310. M. Walden, *Ohel yisḥaq* no. 16, p. 10; no. 56, p. 25.
311. *Siaḥ sarfei qodesh* vol. 4, p. 73.
312. M. Walden, *Ohel yisḥaq* no. 293, p. 125; according to that story Temerl "herself, in person, washed their shirts."
313. Shmuel of Shinavi, *Ramatayim ṣofim,* pp. 68, 215.

314. *Siah sarfei qodesh*, vol. 1, no. 653; the rhyme in the original in Yiddish (*Negidim on gelt . . . vinter on kelt* [plutocrats without money . . . winter without cold] is a trustworthy mark of the antiquity of the adage which may, perhaps, even have been culled by R. Simhah Bunem from current folklore.

315. Ibid., no. 654.

316. Ibid., no. 384, p. 74; also cf. there, vol. 3, p. 9.

317. Ibid., no. 662.

318. *Siah sarfei qodesh* vol. 2, no. 321, p. 93; *Emet ve-emunah*, no. 745; Alter, *Meir einei ha-golah* 1:78.

319. *Siah sarfei qodesh*, vol. 4, p. 33.

320. M. Walden, *Ohel yishaq* vol. 146, p. 59; no. 189, p. 79.

321. Cf. ibid., no. 18, p. 11; no. 145, p. 59: It is told of Reb Itchi Blass that at a time when the Rabbi of Warka was in straitened circumstances, he presented him with money, "and from then on he was successful insomuch that he was one of the few wealthy men of Poland"; ibid., no. 146: It is told of a Jewish villager that he treated the rebbe with a great measure of hospitality and was blessed "with very much wealth"; ibid., no. 96: It is told of one who became wealthy in virtue of having made a concession in the matter of a debt which he was to have collected in Warsaw.

322. Ibid., no. 128, p. 53.

323. Ibid., no. 25, p. 14.

324. *Siah sarfei qodesh*, vol. 4, p. 90.

325. *Emet ve-emunah*, no. 734.

326. Ibid., no. 731.

327. *Siah sarfei qodesh* vol. 2, no. 248, p. 75.

328. M. Walden, *Ohel yishaq* vol. 85, p. 36.

329. *Siah sarfei qodesh* vol. 3, no. 7, p. 24.

330. *Emet ve-emunah* vol. 91, p. 17.

331. Cf. R. Mahler, *Divrei Yemei Yisrael* no. 3, p. 226.

332. Shmuel of Shinavi, *Ramatayim sofim*, p. 61 and elsewhere.

333. Ibid., p. 61.

334. *Siah sarfei qodesh* vol. 1, no. 434, p. 50; also cf. *Qol simhah, Parashat Hayei Sarah, Matot, Masaei*; M. Walden, *Ohel yishaq* no. 186, p. 77 (R. Isaac of Warka in the name of R. Simhah Bunem).

335. *Baba Batra* 10a.

336. *Emet ve-emunah* 479:75.

337. Cf. ibid., no. 664.

338. *Siah sarfei qodesh* vol. 1, p. 96; in the midrashic source (*Koh. Rab.* 7:49): one thousand people enter upon the study of *Miqra* (Scripture), of whom one hundred go on to the study of the Mishnah; of these, ten continue on to the study of Talmud; of these, one emerges to be a religious teacher (i.e., one qualified to decide questions of law).

339. *Siah sarfei qodesh* 3:12, 26; a similar opinion on the observance of the Torah in the course of conducting business transactions had already been

voiced by R. Levi Yiṣḥaq of Berdyczew; cf. *Qedushat levi* (Berdyczew, 1908), p. 209 *(Liqutim)* on the *Avot*.

340. *Siaḥ sarfei qodesh* vol. 1, no. 666, p. 131.

341. *Shem mi-shemuel, Sefer Vayiqra* (Tel Aviv, 1957), *parashat be-har*, pp. 343–44; the author is the son of the son-in-law of R. Mendel of Kock, R. Abraham of Sochaczew; also cf. *Qol simḥah, parashat matot*, p. 51b.

342. *Mei ha-shiloaḥ* (Lublin, 1922), pt. 2, *Vayese*, p. 14; ibid., *Lekh-Lekha*, p. 10; ibid., *Be-Har*, p. 141 (supplements).

343. *Shem mi-shemuel, Sefer bereshit* (Tel Aviv, 1949), *Vayishlah*, p. 52; cf. also *Emet ve-emunah*, no. 180: man needs three things: good birth, personality, and help from God.

344. *Siaḥ sarfei qodesh* vol. 1: no. 272, p. 59; to be sure, there has also been preserved a tradition, according to which R. Mendel ordered a fiddler to "play at weddings," explaining that "whoever benefits from the toil of his own hands is an eminent Hasid"; cf. *Siaḥ sarfei qodesh* vol. 3, p. 12.

345. In Polish, "leasing."

346. R. Isaac of Warka.

347. M. Walden, *Ohel yiṣḥaq* no. 25, p. 13.

348. Warsaw, Archiwum Główne Akt Dawnych, Komisya Rzadowa Spraw Wewnetrznych, 6636, pp. 134–35; cf. appendix: document 20.

349. Shmuel of Shinavi, *Ramatayim ṣofim*, a commentary on *Eliyahu zuta*, p. 4; also cited in *Siaḥ sarfei qodesh*, vol. 2, no. 279; p. 84.

350. *Siaḥ sarfei qodesh* vol. 1, no. 657.

351. Ibid., no. 253.

352. Exod. 22:24.

353. *Avot* 6. 9.

354. *Emet ve-emunah*, no. 391.

355. M. Walden, *Ohel yiṣḥaq*, no. 56: because of his generosity in philanthropy, he owed R. Hirsh Leyb Friedman of his city, his future relative by marriage, 10,000 zlotys.

356. Ibid., no. 144: To those who argued that it was forbidden to take pity on a licentious woman who claimed the wages of her deceased husband, he replied, "If such is the case, that she became so impoverished as to be compelled to become licentious, it is surely all the more reason to take more pity on her"; in like manner, he showed mercy to the thief who had broken into his son's shop because he had not slept for two nights (ibid., no. 142).

357. *Ketubot* 50a.

358. M. Walden, *Ohel yiṣḥaq*, no. 286; an explanation similar to that kind of restriction on philanthropy was transmitted in the name of R. Uri of Strelisk, "the *Saraf*"; cf. *Imrei qadosh ha-shalem*," supplements, p. 40. According to another explanation of that principle in the Gemara, *ha-Yehudi* of Przysucha permitted a man who wanted to atone for his sins even to distribute all his money to the poor; cf. *Tiferet ha-Yehudi* (Warsaw, n.d.), p. 3.

359. *Siaḥ sarfei qodesh* 3:11, 46.
360. Shmuel of Shinavi, *Ramatayim Ṣofim*, p. 49.
361. *Kol simḥah, Vayeshev*, p. 20a.
362. Shmuel of Shinavi, *Ramatayim Ṣofim*, p. 127.
363. *Shem mi-shemuel, Vayiqra, Qedoshim*, p. 277; cf. A. D. Zigelman, *Ohel Torah* (Lublin, 1909), p. 30: Each and every person must perform all sacred acts in association with the entire community of Israel.
364. *Siaḥ sarfei qodesh* 4:171; 109.
365. *Ḥedvat simḥah, Vayeḥi*, commentary on the verse "Gather yourselves together, that I may tell you," pp. 87–88; M. Walden, *Ohel yiṣḥaq* 170:67.
366. *Tiferet ha-Yehudi*, p. 40.
367. *Zohar, Vaera*, p. 117; the Hebrew translation is by the author.
368. Alfasi, *Ha-saba* pp. 86–91.
369. See ibid., p. 88, concerning R. Isaac Meir; concerning the opinion of R. Isaac of Warka and R. Mendel, cf. *Emet ve-emunah*, no. 263.
370. *Mei ha-shiloaḥ* 2:5, introduction.
371. *Siaḥ sarfei qodesh* 1:636; 125.
372. Ibid., 4:106.
373. An epithet containing an element of ridicule, directed against the zaddikim, who wear white garments.
374. Exod. 14:15; cf. *Siaḥ sarfei qodesh* 3:285; Yeḥiel Moshe of Jadimów, *Niflaot Ḥadashot, Parashat Be-shalah* (Piotrków, 1897), p. 35.
375. *Emet ve-emunah*, no. 126.
376. *Siaḥ sarfei qodesh* 1:356:71.
377. Ibid., 3:73:227.
378. R. Hanokh Henekh of Alexander, *Ḥoshvah le-tovah* (Piotrków, 1929), p. 10; cf. Z. M. Rabinowicz, *Ha-maggid mi-koznitz* (Tel Aviv, 1947), p. 134.
379. In the Yiddish: *farleygn*—to seize hold of something and not let go.
380. *Emet ve-emunah*, no. 420.
381. *Qol simḥah, Vayishlaḥ*, p. 18a.
382. Ibid., *Liqutim*, p. 56a; also cf. *Siaḥ sarfei qodesh* 2:282:85.
383. Ibid., 27:16.
384. Ibid., 350:98.
385. M. Walden, *Ohel yiṣḥaq* p. 97.
386. *Siaḥ sarfei qodesh* 1:234:50; this same statement is also cited in the name of R. Mendel of Kock; cf. *Emet ve-emunah*, no. 801.
387. *Ḥedvat simḥah, mi-qeṣ*, pp. 77–78; this doctrine is also handed down in the name of his disciple, R. Mendel; cf. *Emet ve-emunah*, no. 769; R. Isaac of Warka was also of the opinion that Joseph the Righteous was punished, "even though he was a person who put great trust [in God], but held that . . . some action should be taken and therefore spoke to the butler"; cf. M. Walden, *Ohel yiṣḥaq*, 271.
388. *Emet ve-emunah*, no. 625.
389. The end of the anecdote: The man remained—"may it not befall us"—a pauper, that is, he was punished for his lack of faith in God; ibid., no. 617.

390. Yehiel Moshe of Jadimów, *Niflaot Hadashot,* p. 90.

391. *Siah sarfei qodesh* 4:17:67.

392. *Emet ve-emunah,* nos. 123, 670; *Siah sarfei qodesh* 3:430:118.

393. *Emet ve-emunah,* nos. 710, 762, 819; to be sure, his master, R. Simhah Bunem, did not allow the *Moreh nebukhim* to be read consistently, but it was to be perused intermittently, in order to find an answer before the question arose, for "the moment the question precedes the answer, it follows that for that moment he is not a Jew. . . ."; cf. Shmuel of Shinavi, *Ramatayim sofim,* p. 134.

394. *Emet ve-emunah,* no. 486.

395. *Baba Batra* 12a.

396. *Siah sarfei qodesh* 2:325:93.

397. Shmuel of Shinavi, *Ramatayim sofim,* p. 99.

398. R. Nahman of Bratslav, in his doctrine of perfect faith—"without any speculation whatsoever"—reached the point of admonishing against any study, not only of the *Moreh nebukhim* but even of *Hilkhot deot* (laws relating to the knowledge of God) and *Hilkhot yesodei ha-Torah* (laws relating to the fundamentals of the Torah) in the *Yad ha-hazaqah* (Maimonides' *Mishneh Torah*); cf. *Shivhei moharan,* p. 13a.

399. Shmuel of Shinavi, *Ramatayim sofim,* pp. 243, 246.

400. *Siah sarfei qodesh* 2:326:94.

401. *Emet ve-emunah,* no. 337.

402. Ibid., no. 708.

403. *Siah sarfei qodesh* 1:46:14–15.

404. Ibid., 390:67.

405. Deut. 4:9.

406. *Emet ve-emunah,* no. 484; cf. ibid., no. 887: "He said to his entourage, 'I ask no more of you than this—that you abhor the body as Reb Moishele of Lutomiersk abhors it.' "

407. Ibid., no. 666.

408. Ibid., no. 612.

409. Ibid., no. 302.

410. Ibid., no. 51.

411. *Shem mi-shemuel, Sefer Vayiqra, Sav,* p. 89.

412. *Shabbat* 118b.

413. *Shem mi-shemuel, Sefer Bereshit, Vayera,* pp. 152, 166.

414. In a conversation with the Rebbe of Alexander; cf. *Emet ve-emunah,* no. 286.

415. *Siah sarfei qodesh* 1:671:132.

416. Yehiel Moshe of Jadimów, *Niflaot hadashot,* p. 92; *Emet ve-emunah,* no. 731.

417. *Siah sarfei qodesh* 3:342:69; in the book of Yehiel Moshe of Jadimów, *Niflaot hadashot* (p. 82, *Tehillim*), this saying is cited in the name of R. Simhah Bunem.

418. *Tiferet ha-yehudi,* the letter *ayin-vav.*

419. In Yiddish, a "fig"; a *fico*.

420. *Siah sarfei qodesh* 3:12.

421. R. Ḥanokh Henekh of Alexander, *Ḥoshvah le-tovah*, pp. 56, 61.

422. Cf. Rabinowicz (*Rabbi Simḥah Bunem*, p. 64), who rightly points out that the way of lifting up "alien thoughts" seemed to the School of Przysucha a dangerous one; however, the author had not grasped the social nature of this new tendency, the significance of its retreat from the ethical monism of original Hasidism, and its compromise with the Mitnaggedic system of ethics.

423. The "annulment" or effacement of alien thoughts is expressly discussed in the teaching of R. Simḥah Bunem; cf. the quotation in Rabinowicz, *Rabbi Simḥa Bunem* (p. 64). In the name of R. Mendel of Kock a remark on this matter has been related with some variation. It is precisely the verse "In all the ways acknowledge Him" (Prov. 3:6), which had become a prop for the doctrine of the Baal Shem Tov concerning the worship of God even in a material way, that he interprets, "even in a matter of transgression, for in virtue of one's knowledge of the name of God . . . will arise the ardor to separate oneself from a transgression." See *Siah sarfei qodesh* 2:291. In contrast, R. Mendel also spoke of the negation of existence ("that one should forget one's own essence and be null and void in actuality, insomuch that there will be fulfilled in one that the Lord God is Truth" (ibid., 1:328).

To be sure, as against the doctrine of the nullification of transgressive thoughts, there has been handed down in the name of R. Simḥah Bunem a tenet that one must be incessantly on the defense against the evil inclination: "Against the evil inclination," he stated, "one must always imagine it to be as if a man stood opposite one, holding an axe in his hand to decapitate one; and if he does not have this in his mind, it is a sign that one's head was already cut off" (*Siah sarfei qodesh* 1:214:46).

424. *Siah sarfei qodesh*, vol. 3, no. 309, p. 93; Alter, *Meir einei ha-golah* no. 89, p. 24.

425. *Siah sarfei qodesh* no. 403, p. 112.

426. Cf. Cherniḥa. *Niflaot ha-saba qadisha*, p. 14: There is a tale about the son of *ha-Yehudi* of Przysucha, Reb Jeraḥme'el, who tarried in Tomaszów in the course of his journey; in the evening the Hasidim of Kock congregated around his inn, smashed the windows, flung stones through the broken windows "and cut off his beard."

427. Cf. Y. Elzet, *Le-qorot ha-hasidut;* H. Adelbaum, "R. Mendel of Kock." *Ha-Olam* (1927), p. 79; both of them fix 1839 as the year of crisis for R. Mendel, but according to an *aggadah* of Ger, the incident occurred "circa 1841"; cf. Alter, *Meir einei ha-Golah*, vol. 1, no. 360, p. 113. According to the tradition of Izbica, their rebbe began to reveal his doctrine in 1840 (cf. introduction to *Mei ha-shiloaḥ*, pt. 2, p. 5) in consonance with a prediction in the *Zohar* regarding the revelation of the wisdom in that year.

428. *Siaḥ sarfei qodesh* vol. 3, no. 378, pp. 15, 108; vol. 4, no. 29, p. 69.

429. Alter, *Meir einei ha-golah*, p. 26, no. 483.

430. Ibid., no. 481.

431. Ibid.,, pp. 65–66; J. Shatzky, *Geshikhte fun Yidn in Varshe* (New York, 1947) 2:101–10.

432. Shatzky, *Yidn in Varshe* 2:81–97, 284–85 (the proclamation of the rabbinate for the year 1849 was copied from the periodical *Izraelita* no. 18[1871]); Alter, *Meir einei ha-golah* 1:121–31; *Kwartalnik Zydów w Polsce* vol. 1, no. 2, pp. 131–36.

433. *Siaḥ sarfei qodesh* vol. 1, no. 18, p. 11.

434. Ibid., no. 215, p. 46.

435. Ibid., no. 366, p. 72.

436. Alter, *Meir einei ha-golah*, p. 128; *Emet ve-emunah*, nos. 140, 270: "He said to them: in the beginning the Jews wore Brandenburg-kaftan and fringes and they began to change [their mode of dress] but there is no need to let oneself be martyred over this."

437. Alter, *Meir einei ha-golah* vol. 2, p. 89.

438. *Siaḥ sarfei qodesh* vol. 1, p. 40.

439. Mamlak, *Abir ha-ro'im*, vol. 1, p. 118; cf. also vol. 2, p. 43.

IV

HASIDISM IN THE TWENTIETH CENTURY

13

My Way to Hasidism

Martin Buber

The Hebrew word "Hasid" means a pious man. There have again and again been communities in post-exilic Judaism that bore the name Hasidim, the pious: from those about which the first Book of Maccabees reports—a band remaining faithful to the teaching and fighting for it, and those, of whom the Mishna declares, "He who says, What is mine is thine, and what is thine is thine," i.e., he who claims for himself no possessions, "is a Hasid," up to those "Hasidim" whose other half thousand in the year 1700 journeyed under continual chastisements to the Holy Land in order to bring forth the messianic kingdom, and there perished. Finally there arose the community founded by Israel ben Eliezer, the Baal-Shem, around the middle of the eighteenth century, which fell into decay after a short period of flowering rich in memorable forms, but today,[1] still embraces a large part of Eastern Jewry. What is common to all of them is that they wanted to take seriously their piety, their relation to the divine in earthly life; that they did not content themselves with the preaching of divine teaching and the practice of divine rituals, but sought to erect men's life-together on the foundation of divine truth. This is especially clear in the last-named community, with which I am here concerned.

The Jewish historian Graetz, partially under the influence of the views of the Jewish Enlightenment, cannot say anything of this "New Hasidism" other than that it is "wildest superstition." But a contemporary

Reprinted by permission of the Estate of Martin Buber and The Balkin Agency, Inc., from *Hasidism and Modern Man,* by Martin Buber, 1966.

and friend of Graetz, Moses Hess, the founder of modern Zionism, made the deeply understanding statement that Hasidism forms within the living Jewish spirit the transition "from medieval Judaism to a regenerated Judaism which is only in formation"; its consequences are "incalculable when the national movement takes possession of it."

In fact, nowhere in the last centuries has the soul-force of Judaism so manifested itself as in Hasidism. The old power lives in it that once held the immortal fast to earth, as Jacob the angel, in order that it might fulfill itself in mortal life. But at the same time a new freedom announces itself therein. Without an iota being altered in the law, in the ritual, in the traditional life-norms, the long-accustomed arose in a fresh light and meaning. Still bound to the medieval in its outward appearance, Hasidic Judaism is already open to regeneration in its inner truth, and the degeneration of this great religious movement can only halt but not stop entirely the process in the history of the spirit that began with it.

This is not the place to present the teachings of Hasidism. They can be summoned up in a single sentence: God can be beheld in each thing and reached through each pure deed. But this insight is by no means to be equated with a pantheistic world view, as some have thought. In the Hasidic teaching, the whole world is only a word out of the mouth of God. Nonetheless, the least thing in the world is worthy that through it God should reveal Himself to the man who truly seeks Him; for no thing can exist without a divine spark, and each person can uncover and redeem this spark at each time and through each action, even the most ordinary, if only he performs it in purity, wholly directed to God and concentrated in Him. Therefore, it will not do to serve God only in isolated hours and with set words and gestures. One must serve God with one's whole life, with the whole of the everyday, with the whole of reality. The salvation of man does not lie in his holding himself far removed from the worldly, but in consecrating it to holy, to divine meaning: his work and his food, his rest and his wandering, the structure of the family and the structure of society. It lies in his preserving the great love of God for all creatures, yes, for all things. Hasidism took the social form of a great popular community—not an order of the secluded, not a brotherhood of the select, but a popular community in all its medley, in all its spiritual and social multiplicity. Never yet in Europe has such a community thus established the whole of life as a unity on the basis of the inwardly known. Here is no separation between faith and work, between truth and verification, or, in the language of today, between morality and politics; here all is one kingdom, one spirit, one reality.

In my childhood (at a very early age I came from Vienna, where I was born, to Galicia and grew up there with my grandparents) I spent every summer on an estate in Bukovina. There my father took me with him at times to the nearby village of Sadegora. Sadegora is the seat of a dynasty of "zaddikim" (*zaddik* means righteous, proven, completed), that is, of Hasidic rabbis. The "cultured" speak of "wonder rabbis" and believe they know about them. But, as is usual with the "cultured" in such matters, they possess only the most superficial information. The legendary greatness of the grandfathers has certainly disappeared in the grandsons and many are at pains to preserve their power through all kinds of petty magic; but all their carryings on cannot darken the inborn shining of their foreheads, cannot destroy the inborn sublimity of their figure: their unarbitrary nobility speaks more compellingly than all their arbitrariness. And certainly there no longer lives in the present-day community that high faith of the first hasidim, that fervent devotion which honored in the zaddik the perfected man in whom the immortal finds its mortal fulfillment. Rather the present-day Hasidim turn to the zaddik above all as the mediator through whose intercession they hope to attain the satisfaction of their needs. But far removed from their lower wills, a shudder of profoundest reverence seizes them ever again when the *rebbe* stands in silent prayer or interprets the mystery of the Torah in hesitating speech at the third Sabbath meal. Even in these degenerate Hasidim there still continues to glow, in the unknown ground of their souls, the word of Rabbi Eliezer that the world was created for the sake of the perfected man (the zaddik), even though there should be only one; "for it says, 'And God saw the light, that it was good'; but 'good' means nothing other than the perfected man" (Talmud Babli, Yoma 38b).

This I realized at that time, as a child, in the dirty village of Sadegora from the "dark" Hasidic crowd that I watched—as a child realizes such things, not as thought, but as image and feeling—that the world needs the perfected man and that the perfected man is none other than the true helper. Certainly, the zaddik is now essentially approached for help in quite earthly needs. But is he not still what he once was imagined and appointed to be: the helper in spirit, the teacher of world-meaning, the conveyor to the divine speaks? Certainly, the power entrusted to him has been misinterpreted by the faithful, has been misused by himself. But is it not at base a legitimate, *the* legitimate power, this power of the helping soul over the needy? Does there not lie in it the seed of future social orders?

At any rate, in a childish fashion, these questions already dawned on me at that time. And I could compare: on the one hand was the head man of the province whose power rested on nothing but habitual compulsion; on the other was the rabbi, who was an honest and God-fearing man, but an employee of the "directorship of the cult." Here, however, was another, an incomparable; here was, debased yet uninjured, the living double kernel of humanity: genuine *community* and genuine *leadership*. Ancient past, farthest future were here, lost, longed for, returned.

The palace of the rebbe, in its showy splendor, repelled me. The prayer house of the Hasidim with its enraptured worshippers seemed strange to me. But when I saw the rebbe striding through the rows of the waiting, I felt, "leader," and when I saw the Hasidim dance with the Torah, I felt, "community." At that time there rose in me a presentiment of the fact that common reverence and common joy of soul are the foundations of genuine human community.

In boyhood this early presentiment began to slip away from me into the unconscious. I now spent the summers in another province and was finally close to forgetting the Hasidic impressions of my childhood. Then I came after many years to a newly inherited estate of my father, in the neighborhood of Czortkow, a village which is the place of residence of a collateral line of the same dynasty of zaddikim. As there still lives in Sadegora the memory, handed down by generations, of the great "Rishiner" (so called because he had to flee out of Ruzhin in Berdyczew, under suspicion by the Russian government of being "King of the Jews," and after many wanderings settled in Sadegora), so in Czortkow there still lives today the direct recollection of his son David Moshe. Unfortunately I received nothing from him at that time. In any case, my impressions this time were paler and more fleeting. That might be caused by the fact that meanwhile I had been seized by the fermenting intellectuality which is often characteristic of the decisive years of youth and which puts an end to the natural seeing and experiencing of the child. Through this intellectuality I had become alienated from the Hasidim; it robbed me of my naive affinity with their being. By virtue of my thinking I seemed to myself far removed from their world; indeed, I confess that I regarded

Hasidism not essentially otherwise than Graetz does: I looked down on it from the heights of a rational man. I now saw nothing more of its life, even when I passed quite close to it—because I did not want to see anything.

In spite of this, at that period I heard for the first time, without paying any attention to it, the name that would mean the most precious discovery for me many years later: the name "Besht." This name is composed of the initial letters of the three words *Baal Shem Tov* (Master of the Good Name) and designates the founder of Hasidism, Rabbi Israel ben Eliezer (1700–1760). One of the dairy farms on that estate of my father's was called Tluste Village. In Tluste-City, the market town belonging to it (later well known through the reports from the front of the Russian supreme command, since it was fought over for a long time), the Baal-Shem had lived as a poor teacher of small children. Here, according to the report of the legend, a dream announced to him in the night when he had completed his thirty-third year that the time had come for him to go forth to men.

But it was not Hasidism alone from which I was alienated at that time, but Judaism as a whole.

I had spent my childhood, the time up to my fourteenth year, in the house of my grandfather, the Midrash scholar. The Midrash was the world in which Salomon Buber lived, lived with a wonderful concentration of soul, with a wonderful intensity of work. He edited text after text of the Midrash, those books of Bible interpretation, comparable to no other literature, abounding in legends, sayings, and noble parables. In the Midrash, scattered in a thousand fragments, is concealed a second Bible, the Bible of the exile. Without having ever appropriated the philological methods of the West, he revised the manuscripts with the reliability of the modern scholar and at the same time with the presence of knowledge of the Talmudic master who has directly at hand for each sentence and each word whatever relates to it in the entire literature— not as material of memory alone, but as an organic possession of the whole person. The spiritual passion which manifested itself in his incessant work was combined with the untouchable, inperturbable childlikeness of a pure human nature and an elementary Jewish being. When he spoke Hebrew (as he frequently did when foreign guests visited him from distant lands), it sounded like the speech of a prince returned home from exile. He did not trouble himself about Judaism, but it dwelled in him.

So long as I lived with him, my roots were firm, although many questions and doubts also jogged about in me. Soon after I left his house, the whirl of the age took me in. Until my twentieth year, and in small measure even beyond then, my spirit was in steady and multiple movement, in an alternation of tension and release, determined by manifold influences, taking ever new shape, but without center and without growing substance: it was really the *Olam-ha-Tohu,* the "World of Confusion," the mythical dwelling place of the wandering souls. Here I lived —in versatile fullness of spirit, but without Judaism, without humanity, and without the presence of the divine.

The first impetus toward my liberation came from Zionism. I can here only intimate what it meant for me: the restoration of the connection, the renewed taking root in the community. No one needs the saving connection with a people so much as the youth who is seized by spiritual seeking, carried off into the upper atmosphere by the intellect; but among the youths of this kind and this destiny none so much as the Jewish. The other peoples preserve from dissolution the deep inborn binding to the native soil and popular tradition inherited from millennia. The Jew, even with a newly acquired feeling for nature and a cultivated understanding of, say, German popular art and customs, is directly threatened by such dissolution and abandoned to it so far as he does not find himself at home in his community. And the most sparkling wealth of intellectuality, the most luxuriant seeming productivity (only he who is bound can be genuinely productive) cannot compensate the detached man for the holy insignia of humanity—rootedness, binding, wholeness.

That Zionism seized me and that I was newly vowed to Judaism was, I repeat, only the first step. The acknowledgment of the nation does not by itself transform the Jewish man; he can be just as poor in soul with it as without it, even if, of course, not so rootless as without it. But to him to whom it is not a satiating but a soaring, not an entering into the harbor but a setting out on to the open sea—to him it can indeed lead to transformation. Thus it happened to me.

I professed Judaism before I really knew it. So this became, after some blind groping, my second step: wanting to know it. To know—by this I do not mean a storing up of anthropological, historical, sociological knowledge, as important as these are; I mean the immediate knowing, the eye-to-eye knowing of the people in its creative primal hours.

In this way I came to Hasidism.

In the world of confusion I had neglected my Hebrew, which had been very dear to me as a boy. Now I acquired it anew. I began to comprehend it in its essence, that cannot be adequately translated into any other, at least into any Western language. And I read—read, at first ever again repelled by the brittle, ungainly, unshapely material, gradually overcoming the strangeness, discovering the characteristic, beholding the essential with growing devotion. Until one day I opened a little book entitled the *Savaat ha-ribash*—that is the testament of Rabbi Israel Baal-Shem—and the words flashed toward me, "He takes unto himself the quality of fervor. He arises from sleep with fervor, for he is hallowed and become another man and is worthy to create and is become like the Holy One, blessed be He, when He created His world." It was then that, overpowered in an instant, I experienced the Hasidic soul. The primally Jewish opened to me, flowering to newly conscious expression in the darkness of exile: man's being created in the image of God I grasped as deed, as becoming, as task. And this primally Jewish reality was a primal human reality, the content of human religiousness. Judaism as religiousness, as "piety," as *Hasidut* opened to me there. The image out of my childhood, the memory of the zaddik and his community, rose upward and illuminated me: I recognized the idea of the perfected man. At the same time I became aware of the summons to proclaim it to the world.

But first came the time of study. At twenty-six, I withdrew myself for five years from activity in the Zionist party, from writing articles and giving speeches, and retired into the stillness; I gathered, not without difficulty, the scattered, partly missing, literature, and I immersed myself in it, discovering mysterious land after mysterious land.

My first communication, my "authorship," came about in a remarkable manner. Among all the books, the collections of oral teachings of the zaddikim and the collections of legends from their lives, there was one that was wholly distinctive, wholly separate from the others, and at the same time probably the most popular of all: the *Sippurei maassiyot* (Tales of Adventure), the stories of Rabbi Nahman of Bratslav, a great-grandson of the Baal-Shem. These stories were told by Rabbi Nahman to his disciples, and after his death one of them wrote them down and published them in an obviously distorted form. These were in part pure fairy tales, in imitation, especially, of the Oriental, in other part creations of a special kind—symbolic, at times freely allegorizing tales.

Common to all of them was a not actually didactic but certainly teaching trait; Rabbi Nahman himself had called them the clothes of his teachings, and a comprehensive commentary upon them had arisen from the hands of his disciples. But in them all there also remained the distortion —the distortion of the contents through all kinds of utilitarian and vulgar-rationalistic insertions, of the form through the confusion of lines and the muddying of the pure colors. This one can infer from a few striking parts.

Almost involuntarily I began to translate two of the real fairy tales, hence the unoriginal pieces of the book; if I thought of readers in so doing, then they were none other than children. When I had finished, what lay before me seemed to me paltrier than I had supposed, definitely inferior in quality to the related stories from the Thousand and One Nights. When I saw one of them printed,[2] I was altogether disappointed. It could not work out thus: in the reproduction in a foreign language the distortion was still more visible, the original form still more obscured. I noted that the purity did not allow itself to be preserved in translation, much less enhanced—I had to tell the stories that I had taken into myself from out of myself, as a true painter takes into himself the lines of the models and achieves the genuine images out of the memory formed of them. I began, still shy and awkward, with "The Steer and the Ram." Becoming freer and surer, I turned to "The Simple Man and the Clever Man," then to "The King's Son and the Son of the Maid." "The Rabbi and His Son" was the first which grew unexpectedly into my own work. In the two last, "The Master of Prayer" and "The Seven Beggars,"[3] I experienced, even in the entirely new pieces that I inserted, my unity with the spirit of Rabbi Nachman. I had found the true faithfulness: more adequately than the direct disciples, I received and completed the task, a later messenger in a foreign realm.

I realized my inborn binding with Hasidic truth still more forcefully in the second book, *The Legend of the Baal-Shem*,[4] which sought to construct the inner process in the life of the master out of a selection of traditional legendary motifs which I took from folk books, later also from the mouth of the people themselves. Here too I had begun to translate, a short time after setting down the first tales of Rabbi Nachman. Here too I met with disappointment. The already-existing stories were for the most part recorded in crude and clumsy fashion; they did not become more winged in translation.[5] Thus here too I came to my own narrating in growing independence; but the greater the independence became, so much the more deeply I experienced the faithfulness. And therefore, although by far the largest part of the book is autonomous fiction composed from traditional motifs, I might honestly report of my experience of the legend: "I bore in me the blood and the spirit of those who created it, and out of my blood and spirit it has become new."

Since then, several years after the completion of both books, I discovered another manner of artistic faithfulness to the popular Hasidic narrative. But this no longer belongs to the context of this communication, the subject of which is my way to Hasidism.

But there undoubtedly belongs in this context a humorous and meaningful occurrence which took place in 1910 or 1911, and again, in fact, in Bukovina, not far from Sadegora, in Czernovitz, the capital of the country. After a lecture that I had delivered (it was the third of my *Three Talks on Judaism*), I went with some members of the association, who had arranged the evening, into a coffee house. I like to follow the speech before many, whose form allows no reply, with a conversation with a few in which person acts on person and my view is set forth directly through going into objection and question.

We were just discussing a theme of moral philosophy when a well-built Jew of simple appearance and middle age came up to the table and greeted me. To my no doubt somewhat distant return greeting, he replied with words not lacking a slight reproof: "Doctor! Do you not recognize me?" When I had to answer in the negative, he introduced himself as M., the brother of a former steward of my father's. I invited him to sit with us, inquired about his circumstances of life and then took up again the conversation with the young people. M. listened to the discussion, which had just taken a turn toward somewhat abstract formulations, with eager attentiveness. It was obvious that he did not understand a single word; the devotion with which he received every word resembled that of the believers who do not need to know the content of a litany since the arrangement of sounds and tones alone give them all that they need, and more than any content could.

After a while, nonetheless, I asked him whether he had perhaps something to say to me; I should gladly go to one side with him and talk over his concern. He vigorously declined. The conversation began again and with it M.'s listening. When another half hour had passed, I asked him again whether he did not perhaps have a wish that I might fulfill for him; he could count on me. No, no, he had no wish, he assured me. It had grown late; but, as happens to one in such hours of lively interchange, I did not feel weary; I felt fresher, in fact, than before, and decided to go for a walk with the young people. At this moment M. approached me with an unspeakably timid air. "Doctor," he said, "I should like to ask you a question." I bid the students wait and sat down with him at a table. He was silent. "Just ask, Mr. M.," I encouraged him; "I shall gladly give you information as best I can." "Doctor," he said, "I have a daughter." He paused; then he continued, "And I also have a young man for my daughter." Again a pause. "He is a student of law. He passed the examinations with distinction." He paused again, this time somewhat longer. I looked at him encouragingly; I supposed that he would entreat me to use my influence in some way on behalf of the presumptive son-in-law. "Doctor," he asked, "is he a steady man?" I was surprised, but felt that I might not refuse him an answer. "Now, Mr. M.," I explained, "after what you have said, it can certainly be taken for granted that he is industrious and able." Still he questioned further. "But Doctor," he said, "does he also have a good head?"— "That is even more difficult to answer," I replied; "but at any rate he has not succeeded with industry alone, he must also have something in his head." Once again M. paused; then he asked, clearly as a final question, "Doctor, should he now become a judge or a lawyer?"— "About that I can give you no information," I answered. "I do not know the young man, indeed, and even if I did know him, I should hardly be able to advise in this matter." But then M. regarded me with a glance of almost melancholy renunciation, half-complaining, half-understanding, and spoke in an indescribable tone, composed in equal part of sorrow and humility: "Doctor, you do not *want* to say—now, I thank you for what you have said to me."

This humorous and meaningful occurrence, which apparently has nothing to do with Hasidism, afforded me, nonetheless, a new and significant insight into it. As a child, I had received an image of the zaddik and through the sullied reality had glimpsed the pure idea, the idea of the genuine leader of a genuine community. Between youth and manhood this idea had arisen in me through knowledge of Hasidic teaching as that of the perfected man who realizes God in the world. But now in the light of this droll event, I caught sight in my inner experience of the zaddik's function as a leader. I, who am truly no zaddik, no one assured in God, rather a man endangered before God, a man wrestling ever anew for God's light, ever anew engulfed in God's abysses, nonetheless, when asked a trivial question and replying with a trivial answer, then experienced from within for the first time the true zaddik, questioned about revelations and replying in revelations. I experienced him in the fundamental relation of his soul to the world: in his responsibility.

Each man has an infinite sphere of responsibility, responsibility before the infinite. He moves, he talks, he looks, and each of his movements, each of his words, each of his glances causes waves to surge in the happening of the world: he cannot know how strong and how far-reaching. Each man with all his being and doing determines the fate of the world in a measure unknowable to him and all others; for the causality which we can perceive is indeed only a tiny segment of the inconceivable, manifold, invisible working of all upon all. Thus every human action is a vessel of infinite responsibility.

But there are men who are hourly accosted by infinite responsibility in a special, specially active form. I do not mean the rulers and statesmen who have to determine the external destiny of great communities; their sphere of action is all-embracing but, in order to be effective, they turn away from the individual, enormously threatened lives that glance at them with thousandfold question, to the general that appears to them unseeing. I mean those who withstand the thousandfold-questioning glance of individual lives, who give true answer to the trembling mouth of the needy creature who time after time demands from them decision; I mean the zaddikim, I mean the true zaddik. That is the man who hourly measures the depths of responsibility with the sounding lead of his words. He speaks—and knows that his speech is destiny. He does not decide the fate of countries and peoples, but ever again only the small and great course of an individual life, so finite and yet so boundless. Men come to him, and each desires his opinion, his help. And even though it is corporal and semi-corporal needs that they bring to him, in his world-insight there is nothing corporal that cannot be transfigured, nothing material that cannot be raised to spirit. And it is this that he does for all: *he elevates their need before he satisfies it.*

Thus he is the helper in spirit, the teacher of world-meaning, the conveyor to the divine sparks. The world needs him, the perfected man; it awaits him, it awaits him ever again.

NOTES

1. 1918—ed.
2. In a collection for children, *Heim der Jugend*, with pictures by Hermann Struck; these tales were not included in my book *Die Geschichten des Rabbi Nachman* (1907), reprinted by Fischer Bücherei, 1955.
3. These stories are all included in Martin Buber, *The Tales of Rabbi Nachman*, translated by Maurice Friedman (New York: The Horizon Press, 1956).
4. *Die Legende des Baalschem* (1908), reprinted as a volume of the Manesse Bibliothek der Welt-Literatur (1955), published in America and England as *The Legend of the Baal-Shem*, translated by Maurice Friedman (New York: Harper & Brothers, 1955; London: East and West Library, 1956).
5. One of these translations (although already somewhat free), "Der Zukunftsbrief," appeared in the weekly *Die Welt*, but was not included in the book.

14

Hasidism in Modern Society

Stephen Sharot

Before World War II the main strongholds of Hasidism were societies where the Jews were separated—legally, economically, and socially—from the wider society. The persecution and discrimination of the east European Jews reinforced a separate way of life, but the Hasidim also felt threatened by secularizing and modernizing groups within the Jewish communities. From about 1815 the Hasidim had formed an alliance with their former enemies, the mitnaggedim, against the maskilim. The eastern European Haskalah attracted only a very small minority of the Jewish community, mainly wealthy merchants and professionals. Toward the end of the century, however, a greater threat to the Hasidim was posed by the secular Jewish socialist and Zionist movements, which found support among the Jewish masses. Certain Hasidic dynasties declined in some areas, but Hasidism remained by far the largest Jewish social movement in eastern Europe. The mass emigration of east European Jews to western Europe and the United States began in the 1880s, but Hasidic leaders believed that the comparatively open and secular societies of the West held great danger to their way of life, and they attempted to dissuade their followers from joining the migration.

After World War I the largest concentration of Hasidim was found in the newly independent state of Poland, which had over three and one-half million Jews in 1939. The political representatives of Poland to the Paris Peace Conference had signed minority clauses giving Jews full

Reprinted by permission of the University of North Carolina Press from *Messianism, Mysticism, and Magic: A Sociological Analysis of Jewish Religious Movements,* by Stephen Sharot. © 1982 The University of North Carolina Press.

equality, but these proved worthless, and Polish Jews continued to suffer from legal and economic discrimination, political anti-Semitism, social rejection, and pogroms. There was some development of capitalism and a Christian bourgeoisie in interwar Poland, but the country remained predominantly agrarian, and despite a loss in their share of trade and commerce, the Polish Jews remained a socially distinct urban middleman class. Only a small minority of assimilationists adopted Polish culture with enthusiasm, and these suffered considerable psychological strain from the refusal of the Poles to accept them.

The major division within the Polish Jewish communities was between the religious Jews, largely Hasidic, and the secular Zionist and Jewish socialist movements, which had their own political parties, educational systems, communal organizations, youth movements, and press. The Hasidim responded to the new opportunities for political expression in the Polish state and to the threat of Jewish secular movements by organizing political parties and by participating in the municipal and parliamentary elections. Most of the Hasidic leaders were associated with the Agudat Yisrael (the League of Israel), formed in 1912 and based on the Hasidic dynasties of central Poland. The Agudah announced its loyalty to the state and its support of Poland's parliamentary government, and in 1926 it managed to win some concessions, such as official recognition and support for its schools, by allying itself with a comparatively liberal government. However, the Polish governments defaulted on their agreements, and after 1935 the failure of Jewish political accommodation was made obvious by the passing of anti-Jewish laws and the absence of official protection against the increasingly violent attacks on Jews.[1]

Only a fraction of the Hasidim survived the Holocaust, but the leaders who escaped were determined to continue the Hasidic way of life in new environments, particularly New York and Israel. However, the prospects for the continuation of the Hasidic movement appeared doubtful. Not only were their numbers much reduced, but they were now relocated in comparatively open societies that had no legalized discrimination, were far less anti-Semitic, and offered considerable opportunities for Jews to assimilate into the dominant societies.

Hasidim entering New York after World War II began to settle in three neighborhoods in Brooklyn: Williamsburg, Crown Heights, and Borough Park. Today, the largest Hasidic groups in New York are the Satmar, centered in Williamsburg, which has a total congregation of about thirty thousand, and the Lubavich, centered in Crown Heights, which include about one thousand families.[2] The Lubavich community is less geographically concentrated than the Satmar, and with an estimated two hundred and fifty thousand adherents it is the largest Hasidic sect in the world. New York also has several smaller Hasidic groups, such as the Bratslav, Stolin, Vishnitz, and Bobov, most with less than one hundred families.

Concentrations of Hasidim in Israel are found in the area of Mea Shearim in Jerusalem and B'nai Brak, a suburb of Tel Aviv. The number of Hasidim in Israel is difficult to estimate, but they constitute a large proportion of the approximately fifty-five thousand "ultra-Orthodox" Jews who either support the Agudah party or remain outside the political framework of the society.[3] Perhaps the most important Hasidic sect in Israel is the Gur, whose late zaddik was the dominant figure in ultra-Orthodoxy in Israel for eighteen years: he was the head of the "Committee of the Great Men of the Torah," the most important organization of the Agudat Yisrael, which is the most orthodox of the religious parties in Israel. Outside Israel and New York, there are a few smaller centers of Hasidism, including Stamford Hill, in north London, with over one thousand Hasidic families,[4] and Antwerp, which in 1970 was calculated to have a total of thirteen hundred Hasidim.[5]

In the post-World War II period the Hasidim have had to become more consciously introversionist. The majority now live in large cities in open societies which include considerable social and cultural diversity. According to Bryan Wilson's typology, an introversionist sect is distinguished by an overriding concern with separation from the world: members have a strong sense of the sacredness of the community, and social relationships are confined within the group.

Most of the Christian introversionist sects, such as the Amish and Hutterites, have maintained their religious and cultural distinctiveness in rural environments, where it is easier to preserve the boundaries of the community and isolate it from the larger society. Apart from some limited trade with local merchants, the Amish and Hutterite communities are self-sufficient; the community bears full responsibility for its members, and they do not vote, pay taxes, or accept public services. Members who move away from the rural communities lose their identities, and it is unusual to find a Christian introversionist sect which has maintained its distinctiveness and cohesion in an urban environment.

An exception is the Exclusive Brethren, who have maintained a rigorous separation from the wider society by strict rules that prohibit association with outsiders apart from necessary economic contacts. The Brethren emphasize the spiritual purity of their community, and they seek to maintain that purity by a system of tribunals which admits worthy candidates and expels those accused of false doctrine or conduct.[6]

The Hasidim have no formalized procedures for the acceptance and expulsion of members, but they have achieved great success in maintaining their distinctive way of life. They have almost no defections to the non-Hasidic world, and because they have a high birth rate and, in some cases, recruit from the outside, their number continues to grow. This success may be discussed with reference to three sets of mechanisms: insulation, commitment, and social control.

① INSULATION

Introversionist groups clearly distinguish between their members and outsiders: the Amish refer to "our sort," as opposed to "other sorts of people," and the Hutterites distinguish between themselves and the "worldly people," that is, all those who live outside their communities. Hasidic groups emphasize their separation from the non-Jewish world: gentiles are never befriended or invited into Hasidic homes. Hasidic groups differ, however, in the extent to which they insulate themselves from non-Hasidic Jews.[7] At one extreme are the Satmar, who stress their social and intellectual isolation and are suspicious toward outsiders who visit their synagogues. The Satmar believe that to even talk to an outsider is to risk the dangers of contact with the impure, and they clearly distinguish themselves from most other Jews in their opposition to Zionism and the state of Israel. They believe that a Jewish state must await the messiah, and in Israel they avoid any contact with the institutions of the state: they do not vote, carry the identification cards which are required for all citizens, or make use of the country's courts or legal system. At the other extreme are the Lubavich, who attempt to draw other Jews into Orthodox Judaism. The Lubavich have described themselves as "a mission to Jews by Jews," but they also emphasize their distinct identity as a movement within Jewry.

One important means of insulation is the use of distinctive dress and language to symbolize identity. Like the Amish, the Hasidim wear distinctive clothes, the styles of which undergo little, if any, change from one generation to the next. The Satmar and most other Hasidic men wear the traditional clothing of East European Jews, which was originally derived from the clothing of Polish nobles: long black topcoats and wide-brimmed black hats. From the age of three, boys have their heads shaven periodically except for sideburns, which grow into long dangling curls. Men also grow beards. Most Lubavich men do not wear the traditional clothing, but they tend to dress in the modest and conservative manner typical of many non-Hasidic Orthodox Jews: a narrow-brimmed hat, a dark suit, and a beard. Most Lubavich men do not grow sidelocks, and those that do generally tuck them behind their ears. Female dress in all Hasidic groups is not as distinctive as male dress, and as among non-Hasidic Orthodox Jews, it is governed less by traditional styles than by rules of modesty: arms are covered at least to the elbows, dresses and skirts cover most of the legs (slacks are never worn), and dark stockings are worn even in summer. Women have their heads shaved at marriage, after which they wear a head scarf or wig, but in urban environments, where a considerable number of women wear wigs, this is hardly distinctive. Orthodox Jewish women are more easily recognized in the summer than in the winter, but Hasidic women are not distinguishable from other Orthodox women by their dress.[8]

All Hasidic groups use Hebrew as the language of prayer and Yiddish as the language of everyday discourse. In the West the Lubavich are more likely to be fluent in English than are other Hasidim. In Poland nearly all Jews spoke Yiddish, but in the West and in Israel Yiddish has reinforced Hasidic separation. In Israel, where Hebrew is the everyday language of the majority, Yiddish serves to symbolize the separation between religious and secular life. It is not unusual for immigrant groups to maintain their language, and many non-Hasidic Jews speak Yiddish, but unlike most immigrant groups, the Hasidim have successfully transferred their language as the first language of their children. Insulation by means of language is found also among Christian introversionist sects: the Amish use Pennsylvanian Dutch for everyday discourse and High German for prayer, and the Hutterites use Tyrolese for everyday discourse and High German for prayer.

In the urban environment the intrusion of the outside world is a constant threat, but the Hasidim attempt to limit its influence as much as possible. They have a sense of righteousness in their exclusivity, that they are observing the correct way of life, and that others are living in disobedience to God. They point to crime, drugs, sex, and materialism as signs of the decadence and degeneracy of the outside world, although they are mainly concerned with the consequences of such phenomena on the Jews.[9] Most Hasidic groups do not allow their members to own televisions and radios, attend theaters and cinemas or read non-Hasidic newspapers, fiction, or scientific writings in religiously sensitive areas, such as evolution. In New York some of the Lubavich have television sets, which they watch with moderation; many, especially the women, attend movies; and some of the women occasionally go to concerts and the theater. The stricter attitude of other groups was demonstrated in Mea Shearim, where a woman who bought a television was stoned and required hospitalization. Social contacts with individuals outside the community are discouraged, and endogamy within each Hasidic group is the rule. Since it is presumed that a woman will follow her husband's beliefs, it is sometimes possible for a male to gain approval to marry an Orthodox female from outside his Hasidic group.[10]

The Hasidim have achieved a considerable degree of institutional self-sufficiency, which reduces their dependence on outside agencies and groups. For example, apart from their synagogues, burial society, mikveh, butcher shop, and bakery, the institutional complex of the Satmar in New York includes a school system, an employment agency, a hospital and clinic with female gynecologists, an emergency ambulance and oxygen service, a special nursing service, a large loan society, which gives interest-free loans, a publishing enterprise, which prints a weekly newspaper and books, and a private bus service, which connects the communities in Brooklyn with the Manhattan diamond center on Forty-seventh Street.[11]

The provision of goods for consumption entails a high level of insulation. When purchasing products such as meat, matzah, and bakery and dairy products, the Satmar do not trust anyone except other Satmar and closely related groups. The Hasidim in general put great emphasis on the preparation of kosher foods, and businessmen will sometimes claim that their kosher preparations and provisions are more reliable than those of their competitors. Specialized articles and shops also contribute to economic distinctiveness. For example, leaven-searching sets are produced to prepare for Passover, when the house has to be completely cleaned of leaven. The sets contain a kosher candle, two feathers, a wooden spoon, and a leaflet explaining the laws related to the searching of leaven. In his promotion of the sets, the manufacturer emphasizes that he has exclusive rights within the Hasidic community.[12]

Although the Hasidim produce and prepare their own articles of consumption which have important religious meanings, they are far less self-sufficient and insulationist in their patterns of consumption than the rural Christian introversionist sects. The Amish reject items, such as the automobile, that are part of modern technological society, and their adoption of innovations is slow and likely to involve conflict. The Hutterites select innovations that are consistent with their communal living: they are likely to adopt agricultural innovations, but reject luxury items and labor-saving devices in the house, which are in conflict with their religious standards and work ethic. In contrast to the Amish, the Hasidim do not reject modern technology, and in contrast to the communitarian Hutterites, the Hasidim feel a need to achieve individual economic success. The community makes many demands on the financial resources of the individual, particularly in the area of charity; moreover, the importance of earning a reasonable income has grown with the influence of middle-class patterns of consumption.[13]

Rather than reject modern consumer goods produced outside the community, the Hasidim have transformed some of them from purely secular items to items with religious meaning. Objects that elsewhere have no relationship to religion are adapted for religious purposes and given concrete reference to community values. For example, the Hasidim use an automatic timer on their refrigerators which turns on the motor and prevents the motor from turning on when the refrigerator is opened. This is important on the Sabbath, since starting an electrical current is interpreted as a desecration of the day of rest. Thus, the timer becomes the *shabbos zeiger* (Sabbath clock). The long, black, heavy-gauge stockings ("Hasidic stockings") are another example of the infusion of symbolic meaning into everyday objects; these prevent the exposure of the woman's legs to public view and allow her to be truly modest. An example of the use of technology to reinforce religion is the *shatnes* laboratory, which tests clothes for the forbidden mixture of wool and linen. In its advertisements the laboratory announces that shatnes testing involves skill and that a reliable test can be made only with chemicals and a microscope.[14]

The Hasidim find it harder to maintain their separateness when they enter the urban environment to make a living. The choice of occupations is limited by religiously relevant factors such as the Hasidic clothes, food regulations, and the observance of religious holidays. The limited secular education that most Hasidim receive and the need to reside within the Hasidic community further restrict their occupational choices. A study of the Lubavich in Montreal found that 54 percent of the men were involved in religiously oriented occupations, 20 percent were independent businessmen, and 4 percent were wage earners who mostly worked in companies owned by other Lubavich.[15] Studies of the Satmar in New York found that about one-half worked with outsiders and that a large proportion were engaged in manual labor as operators on piecework rates. As operators, the Hasidim try to make enough money to establish themselves in business within the Hasidic community.[16] An important area of employment in New York and Antwerp is the diamond industry, which provides continuity with the traditional artisan and commercial character of East European Jews.[17]

In addition to their economic involvement in the wider society, and in contrast to the Christian introversionist sects, the Hasidim have taken advantage of social security benefits, external welfare provision, and other governmental programs. The Hasidic community welfare and charity programs are of great importance, and the collection and distribution of money is a regular activity, but even the Satmar in New York have made increasing use of the welfare structure of the dominant society. The Hasidim also participate in the wider political system. At the local level they form a strong voting bloc and have been able to benefit from community-based, city-funded projects. Although in Israel the Satmar reject any involvement with the state, in the United States they make full use of the franchise.[18]

Contact with the wider secular society has required some changes in the organizational structure of the Hasidim in the United States. The Satmar zaddik recognized his limitations in secular matters and appointed an overall community manager to run the affairs of the Satmar court. Since the community manager is a sophisticated man who has contacts and experience with the outside world, he serves as a "culture broker" for the entire community, mediating between the Satmar and the wider society.[19] The Lubavich zaddik, unlike most zaddikim, received a secular education as well as a religious one: he studied mathematics and science at the Sorbonne and was trained as an electrical engineer. With the assistance of a small office staff he directs Lubavich affairs throughout the world from his head office in Brooklyn. The Lubavich are able to point to their zaddik as a man whose familiarity with secular knowledge enables him more fully to appreciate its limitations and dangers.

Solomon Poll has argued that the urban setting has contributed to the growth and development of the Hasidic way of life. Opportunities for the manufacture and sale of the articles and foodstuffs required in their religious style of life are greater in the city because of the accessibility of raw materials and the sizable market. It is doubtful whether the Hasidim could be economically successful in a rural area in modern society, since their economic activities have always been of an urban nature.[20] Problems have arisen, however, in the Hasidic areas in New York City. Williamsburg and Crown Heights, the two major Hasidic areas in Brooklyn, have become areas of major population shifts and centers of the urban crisis in recent years. At the beginning of the 1950s the population of Brooklyn was over 90 percent white, with a large proportion of Jews. During the following two decades the white population declined by 30 percent, and the number of Jewish residents declined considerably. During the 1960s three-quarters of the white residents of Crown Heights moved out and the area became 70 percent black. On one side of the Hasidic neighborhood in Williamsburg is the East River; the other side is the black ghetto of Bedford-Stuyvesant. While most non-Hasidic Jews moved out of these areas, the Hasidim had to consider their need to live in close proximity to each other, their heavy investments in the neighborhood, and the institutions that they had built.

Although some of the smaller Hasidic sects moved out of Brooklyn, the Satmar and the Lubavich decided to remain, and they organized to face the mounting tension in the streets. Friction between blacks and Hasidim began to grow in Crown Heights from the early 1970s. The blacks alleged that the Hasidim received favored treatment in employment and in government loans to small businesses, and their bitterness increased when Crown Heights was divided into two districts after Hasidic leaders expressed a desire for a bigger voice in the affairs of their neighborhood. The blacks organized demonstrations to protest the allegedly cruel treatment of blacks by groups of young Hasidim who patrolled the area; they characterized the Hasidim as "terrorists" and "oppressors," but the violent rhetoric did not develop into mob attacks.

In May 1979 an effort was made to halt the hostility by the formation of a coalition of black and Hasidic leaders, but tension rose again in October when a sixty-eight-year-old Hasid was shot dead and robbed by a black youth. A third area of Hasidic settlement, Borough Park, has retained a larger middle-class population of Jews and Italians, but in December 1978 an elderly man was robbed and stabbed after attending Friday night prayers at a service of the Bobov Hasidim. The Hasidim met to demand increased police protection, and they converged on a police station, where a fight broke out with the police.[21]

The attitude of the Hasidim and the blacks toward each other appears to be one of mutual hatred. The Hasidim see the blacks as the "ultimate goyim,"[22] and the proximity of such a negative reference group may reinforce the social cohesion and feelings of superiority of the Hasidim. However, despite the desire of the Hasidim to be near their zaddikim and the concern of the leaders for their followers to remain in the neighborhood, the physical deterioration and dangers have prompted a number to move out.

Attempts have been made to establish communities outside the city. In 1962 the Satmar bought five hundred acres in Mount Olive Township, New Jersey, thirty-five miles west of Manhattan, but proper zoning for housing was refused. In 1974 they made another attempt in a small town near Middleton, New York; eight apartments and twenty-five single-family houses were built. A successful move from Williamsburg was made by the Squarer (Skvira) Hasidim to a suburban country community in Rockland County, forty miles from Manhattan. The first twenty families moved there in 1957, and after some conflict with the local authority over zoning restrictions and other matters, they achieved incorporation as a village in 1961. The zaddik's house, the synagogue, and the boys' school are found at the center of the village, and one corner of the village is occupied by a shopping center and light industry. Many of the residents continue to work in Manhattan, and they have their own bus to take them there.[23] Finally, though, the large Hasidic sects are likely to remain concentrated in the city, and their suburban offshoots will be heavily dependent on the central communities.

② COMMITMENT

Although the majority of Amish and Hutterites are born within the communities, full membership is dependent on adult baptism, which not only signifies the commitment of the individual but also requires the approval of the community and its recognition that the individual is living in accordance with its rules and ideals. No such formal rite of entrance is found among the Hasidim, but acceptance within the community is dependent on conformity to a strict religious Orthodoxy and a commitment to the particular zaddik. The prerequisites for membership in the Satmar, as stated in its bylaws, include the following: to observe the Sabbath properly; to behave according to the Torah and not willfully violate its prescriptions; to bring up one's children according to the Torah; and, for married women and other women over eighteen, to conform to the prohibition against wearing one's own hair.[24] The strongly introversionist Satmar make few attempts at recruitment, and the line between members and outsiders is clearly drawn. In comparison, the boundaries of the Lubavich are less clear-cut, and it is possible to distinguish Lubavich Hasidism by past family commitment and present commitment. Most of the core group, those who have the closest personal and organizational ties to the zaddik, come from Lubavich families; they are likely to be most resistant to the cultural influences of the outside world. Among those who come from non-Lubavich backgrounds, it is possible to distinguish the members who were raised in Orthodox homes from the *ba'alei teshuvah* ("repentants" or "converts"), who came to Lubavich to learn Jewish law and ritual. Interaction between the three categories is considerable, but members tend to marry within their category. A further category on the outer perimeter includes persons with a wide range of commitments, from those who participate frequently in Lubavich ritual and send their children to a Lubavich school to those whose affiliation is limited to a financial contribution.[25]

Hasidic children are socialized entirely within the community. The agencies of socialization, the family, peer group, and formal educational institutions, emphasize the same values and reinforce each other. The Hasidim have basically two age sets: childhood and adulthood; adolescence is not culturally recognized as a distinct phase of the life cycle, and there is no autonomous youth culture. The Hasidic schools both insulate the young from the non-Hasidic world and help to integrate the community by socializing each generation to the distinctive values, norms, and patterns of behavior.

The Satmar want their schools to serve primarily as agencies to prevent undesirable acculturation. For the boys the schools are a training ground for the study of the Torah, and for the girls the schools are places to learn the knowledge that they will need as adult Hasidic women. Only in a minor way do the Satmar see their schools as places to impart knowledge that will be helpful in any practical sense, such as earning a living. The Satmar are forced by law to provide some secular education, but the boys' school places a heavy emphasis on religious knowledge and gives little respect to secular studies. Since the boys know that lack of attention or interest in secular subjects is unlikely to result in the disapproval of their parents, they tend to be undisciplined in the secular classes, which are taught by outsiders. Young men are encouraged to continue their religious studies, and the yeshivah is a central institution in the community. The Satmar have no tradition of teaching Torah to girls, but the state law requires that girls attend school until they are sixteen years of age, and despite the opposition of the more extreme conservatives, they have a school for girls. The tradition does not provide guidance for an effective Jewish curriculum for girls, and their religious education is kept to a simple level. The secular classes for the girls operate better than those for the boys.[26]

In Brooklyn there are three Lubavich schools for boys, and each family can decide which school it prefers. The most prestigious school has no English studies program; teaching is entirely in Yiddish, and the curriculum is more completely Jewish in orientation. This school is preferred by the core Lubavich members, and it is also preferred by some of the recent converts, who wish to establish their credentials and status within the community. One of the bilingual schools has the advantage of being located in a section of Brooklyn that has better housing and a lower crime rate than Crown Heights. The third school is for college-age boys who have had little or no previous Jewish learning. The one school for girls teaches Jewish studies and an English program that concentrates on reading and mathematics, with little attention to other subjects.[27]

In his study of the Lubavich in Montreal, William Shaffir notes that the Lubavich schools seek to attract students from the larger Jewish community and that only 25 percent of the students are from Lubavich families. Most of the non-Lubavich students come from homes that observe at least the Sabbath and dietary laws, but in contrast to the Satmar, the Lubavich are not selective in their recruitment of Jewish children, since they wish to familiarize children from less religious homes with Orthodox Judaism. The inclusion of non-Lubavich children means that greater consideration is given to a secular curriculum, but although some Lubavich regard the secular studies as an important part of the education, the major emphasis is on Torah education. The school has two streams: in one, instruction is in Hebrew in the morning and English in the afternoon; in the second, instruction is entirely in Hebrew. The community is able to staff the Jewish departments, but it brings in outsiders to teach the secular parts of the curriculum. The risks of Lubavich students continuing their secular studies to the level required for teaching are believed to be greater than any possible deleterious influence from non-Lubavich teachers. The secular staff is expected to remain strictly within the boundaries of their subjects, and directions are given on what they should not teach. The curriculum does not include biology, and any reference to evolution or millions of years is forbidden. A rabbinic college for students between fourteen and twenty-two years of age provides an intensive program of religious studies, and students are strongly discouraged from pursuing a college education outside the community.[28] The Lubavich zaddik grants some children permission to receive a college education if he believes that they are strong enough to resist the secular temptations and that their education will prove useful to the community.[29]

It is important to emphasize what is not included in Hasidic socialization. Children are not taught the skills and knowledge that would enable them to participate successfully in the non-Hasidic world. More important than the lack of a good secular education is the lack of familiarity with the normative patterns of behavior in the larger society, and especially with the more informal and subtle aspects of interpersonal relationships. Young Hasidic adults are ill prepared to handle sociosexual interaction with members of the wider society. The sexes are segregated at an early age, and in some groups there is no period of courting. Most marriages are arranged in part by the parents. Sydelle Levy reports that when the Lubavich parents feel their child is ready for marriage (between eighteen and twenty years for girls, twenty to twenty-four years for boys), they arrange a meeting in the presence of a married couple who know both of them. If the boy wishes to see the girl again, he may call her directly, but while they are dating, they are expected not to touch each other. If they decide to marry, they need only to gain the approval of the zaddik.[30] Israel Rubin notes that the Satmar have little experience in making their own decisions and finds that they are likely to feel threatened if they have to do so. Up to the time of marriage everything is decided by the parents, and upon marriage they transfer this dependence to the zaddik.

The Hasidim are distinguished from other ultra-Orthodox Jews by their commitment to, and relationship with, their zaddikim. The bylaws of the Satmar state that the zaddik is "the sole authority in all spiritual matters. His decision is binding for every member."[31] Shaffir writes that when the Lubavich are asked to comment on what characterizes a Lubavich Hasid, they emphasize the recognition of the zaddik as the central figure in their lives and their willingness to conform to his views and directives. As soon as a child is born into a Lubavich family, the father phones the zaddik. Children are taught to revere the zaddik; there is likely to be a portrait of him in the house as well as collections of his writings. The Lubavich refer to their zaddik in everyday conversation with great frequency; they discuss his teachings and directives and his extraordinary powers of perception and wisdom, and they relate miraculous stories about his activities. They place great emphasis on attending the gatherings at the Lubavich center in Brooklyn on holy days, when the zaddik expounds his teachings. When possible, the zaddik's discourses are transmitted to Lubavich communities around the world, and on the Sabbath and holy days, when broadcasting is forbidden, those present attempt to memorize his words and pass them on to their communities. The process of becoming a member of the Lubavich is characterized by an increasing orientation to the zaddik—an interest in his teachings, a letter to ask for his blessing or specific advice, or a request for a personal audience. A new recruit to the Lubavich community is only considered emotionally and intellectually committed to the movement when he places himself completely under the zaddik's direction and authority.

Hasidim also stress a familiarity with the lives, works, and teachings of the earlier zaddikim. The heritage of the movement is seen principally through the works of those zaddikim, and among the important gatherings of the Lubavich are those that commemorate events in the lives of the movement's zaddikim. The present zaddik, Menachem Mendel Schneerson, was born in 1902 and married in 1926, but is childless. The Lubavich are reluctant to discuss the practical implications of the lack of an heir, and it is often suggested that a possible solution will be the coming of the messiah. When the zaddik himself was asked who was to be the successor, he replied: "The messiah will come, and he will take all these troubles and doubts. He could come while I am here. Why postpone his coming?"[32]

When the Satmar zaddik, Yoel Teitelbaum, died in August 1979, some of the mourners compared the event to the Holocaust. Rebbe Teitelbaum left no heirs and no formal method of succession, and although his followers recognized that there will eventually be a successor, they refused to discuss the matter.[33] When there is no clear immediate successor, some time can pass before a new zaddik is chosen, and during the interregnum the cult of the zaddik often focuses on pilgrimages to the grave of the late zaddik. After the death of Aron Rokeah, the Belz zaddik, in 1957 his followers made regular pilgrimages to his tomb in Jerusalem, principally on the anniversary of his death. The rituals on the day began at the Belz Yeshivah in Jerusalem, the major rallying point, where Hasidim from a number of countries prayed together and renewed acquaintances. A little way before the tomb a small hut was erected where pilgrims could ask for their kvitls to be drawn up in exchange for a pidyan. It was believed that a kvitl drawn up by the petitioner was contrary to custom and lacked efficacy. Both before and after the pilgrims placed their kvitls together with some pebbles on the tomb, they pronounced their personal supplications. The men prayed silently while the women cried, gestured, and implored loudly for intercession. After the visit to the cemetery the women and children went to the house of the widow of the zaddik for a meal while the men assembled in the yeshivah. Several men assembled in the apartment of the widow, where they lit commemorative candles and demonstrated an intense fervor in their belief that the spirit of the zaddik had entered the room. Finally, in a large hall the men participated in a joyous banquet to praise and honor the zaddik.

The Belz Hasidim are widely dispersed, and the pilgrimage helped reassert family and social ties and provided an opportunity for matrimonial agreements. The pilgrimage also had the function of asserting the distinctive identity of the Belz within Hasidism. After 1965, when the young nephew of Aron Rokeah was appointed as the new zaddik, the pilgrimage was celebrated more modestly. The cult of the zaddik returned to its more usual form, focusing on a living personality, and although some of the Belz Hasidim refused to recognize such a young man as their zaddik, by 1969 the new leader had fully assumed the spiritual and thaumaturgic roles of the zaddik.[34]

An additional mechanism of commitment among some groups of Hasidim is participation in proselytization. Although most Hasidic groups are against proselytization because of the dangers involved in contacts with the non-Hasidic world, a few communities have attempted to reach out to other Jews in recent years. The Bratslav, for example, attempt to spread the Torah and the works of Nahman, and they predict that they will become the largest Hasidic group.[35] The "Bostoner Rebbe," Levi Yitzhak Horowitz, leads a community in a suburb of Boston and seeks to attract Jewish students from Harvard, M.I.T., and other campuses on the New England coast.[36]

But by far the largest and most organized proselytizing campaign is that undertaken by the Lubavich. The major stated goal of this proselytizing program is not to add to the ranks of the Lubavich but to draw Jews into Orthodoxy. Thus, they have no prolonged, sustained indoctrination period to process converts into the movement. Their campaign is based on the Lubavich teachings on the need to love all fellow Jews, regardless of their degree, or lack, of religious observance, and the need to prepare as many Jews as possible for the coming of the messiah.

The most widespread and best-known proselytizing activity of the Lubavich is the tefillin campaign, which was started shortly before the outbreak of the Six Day War in 1967, on the initiative of the zaddik. A notice stated that the practice of tefillin was essential as a divine commandment and for its protective quality. Moreover, it would also help "to vanquish the enemy in the course of battle." Since then the practice of laying tefillin has been seen as an effective device to start non-Orthodox Jews on the road to observance. Unlike other precepts (dietary laws, Sabbath observance), it is relatively simple to observe, it requires little time, and it does not involve any initial changes in a person's lifestyle. In the United States, in particular, the tefillin campaign involves many devices, including bumper stickers ("Do your thing. Wear tefillin.") and mobile vans with tefillin booths, which park at airport terminals, on college campuses, and on Manhattan street corners with the message, "Are you Jewish? Have you put on tefillin to-day?" The Lubavich hope that once a man begins to lay tefillin regularly, the observance of additional mitsvot will follow. The Lubavich recommend a gradual adoption of other observances, for they recognize that recruits who try immediately to conform to a completely Orthodox way of life will experience difficulties in their personal relationships. Each recruit is dealt with on an individual basis, depending on his interest and level of Orthodoxy.

All Lubavich are encouraged to become involved in the campaign, but it is mostly the older yeshivah students who are responsible for the major activity of setting up the tefillin booths and persuading Jewish men who pass the location to lay tefillin. Women contribute to the campaign by raising money for the distribution of free tefillin. Shaffir makes the important point that proselytizing is likely to increase the commitment and reinforce the identity of the proselytizers: as they attempt to convince and influence nonobserving Jews, the yeshivah students are influencing and convincing themselves, and the yeshivah students, between fifteen and twenty years old, are at a stage in their lives when their beliefs may require strengthening.[37]

The commitment of the Hasidim to their own group has often been expressed as antagonism toward other Hasidic sects and their zaddikim. In recent years the major tension has been between the Lubavich and the Satmar. The Satmar look with dismay on the willingness of the Lubavich to interact with secular Jews, but the major issue has been over the appropriate Orthodox stance toward the State of Israel. The Satmar abhor the friendly relationship of the Lubavich to the state, which they see as a blasphemy and an abomination. Actions of the Satmar against the Lubavich have included distributing leaflets attacking the Lubavich zaddik, hanging an effigy of the zaddik from a post during Purim, ransacking and later burning the offices of a Yiddish newspaper that was sympathetic to the Lubavich, and burning a candy store in Williamsburg that carried the newspaper. The Satmar were incensed when, in the context of a halachic discourse, the Lubavich zaddik praised the Israeli rescue at Entebbe airport, Uganda, of air passengers captured by terrorists as a miracle from heaven. In a sermon one Satmar likened the Israeli operation to the rescue of Mussolini by the Nazis. In 1977 the Satmar stoned the "Torah tanks" of the Lubavich when they came into Williamsburg, and fights broke out on the last day of Passover 1977 when, despite warnings from the Satmar, the Lubavich arrived en masse in Williamsburg to continue their custom of visiting prayer houses of the area on that day.[38]

SOCIAL CONTROL

Social control is facilitated in the Christian introversionist sects by the small size of their communities. Among the Amish, who have thirty to forty households in each community, failure to participate in religious activities is easily noticed. When a Hutterite community reaches 150 members, it divides, and one section establishes a new community. Sanctions against deviance include public admonition and confession, and for graver offenses the deviant is forbidden to communicate with other members, including his own family. "Shunning" is most formalized in the Old Order Amish communities and somewhat less strictly applied among the Hutterites. There are institutionalized procedures for reinstatement, but if the offender does not show proper repentance or if the offense is too grave, he may be banished.

The Hasidim have a system of rewards and sanctions to ensure conformity within the community, but in contrast to the Christian introversionist sects, community size is not regulated, the urban residential pattern does not allow a strict control over participation, and there is no formalized equivalent to "shunning." The use of the *herem* (excommunication) is a possibility, but it is almost never used. A persistent deviant is, however, likely to experience in less formal ways the rejection of his family and community, and this is a powerful constraint in an inclusive world where the individual is ill prepared for living in the wider society.

Important contexts of social control in the Hasidic community are the synagogue and the mikveh, where deviants are harshly treated through gossip, ridicule, and other treatment. In Satmar synagogues lists of names are occasionally put on the walls to warn worshipers about those currently out of favor. The most damaging gossip is often initiated in the mikveh. Since the individual is part of a dense social network and can only find esteem within the community, gossip can be a very effective means of social control.

Social control is also conducted through material channels. The community assumes responsibility for its poor and sick, and the system of charity applies pressures on both the givers and the recipients. Requests for charity are made individually, and since it is roughly known what each individual earns, members feel compelled to give the stipulated amount. The charity organizations distribute goods and services to needy members, but only to those who conform to Hasidic norms.

Conformity is constantly rewarded by support within the extensive network of social relationships, and, more formally, by ritual honors in the synagogues and at the gatherings of the zaddik. There is a close relationship between social control and social status, since status is dependent on the level and intensity of observance and scholarship.

Nonreligious criteria of status, such as wealth, become relevant only if they are connected to religious behavior. Among the Satmar there is also a relationship between status, social control, and separation from the outside world. A person's status is indicated by the Hasidic clothes he wears, especially on Sabbaths and religious holidays. Those who have the highest status wear "extremely Hasidic clothes," which are most distant from non-Hasidic clothes. The process of gaining recognition in a higher social stratum is a gradual one, dependent on raising one's level of religious behavior, and those who display a higher level of religious observance will be permitted to put on more elaborate Hasidic garments.[39]

It is somewhat ironic that the Hasidim, who in the eighteenth century were accused of deviance and heresy, should have become the major carriers of a traditional form of Judaism. Traditional expressions of Jewish messianism are today also found mainly among the Hasidim, especially in the Lubavich sect. Despite his advanced age the Lubavich zaddik increased his activities in the 1970s in the belief that the Redemption was near and that it was necessary to prepare Jews for the coming of the messiah. The Lubavich made a parallel between Moses as the seventh generation after Abraham and Menachem Mendel as the seventh zaddik of their movement. They argued that the seventh leader received the spiritual strength of the first and that the seventh would bring to materialization the mission of the first. This was taken to indicate that Menachem Mendel would lead the people to redemption.

NOTES

1. H. M. Rabinowicz, *The Legacy of Polish Jewry* (N.Y., 1965), pp. 126–47; E. Mendelsohn, "The Dilemma of Jewish Politics," in *Jews and Non-Jews in Eastern Europe,* ed. B. Vago, G. Mosse (N.Y. 1974), pp. 203–19.
2. S. R. Mintz, "Ethnic Activism," *Judaism* 28 (1979), pp. 449–50.
3. R. J. Simon, *Continuity and Change* (Cambridge, 1978), pp. 1, 29, 31.
4. M. Wallach, "The Chasidim of Stamford Hill," *Jewish Chronicle Magazine* (27 May, 1977), pp. 11–19, 68. According to Wallach, in Stamford Hill there are about 200 Belz families, 200 Lubavich, 200 Gur, 350 Satmar, 100 Bobov, 100 Vishnitz, and some Trisk, Zanz, and others.
5. J. Gutwirth, *Vie juive traditionnelle* (Paris, 1970), p. 51. The Belz are the most numerous Hasidim in Antwerp. The others include Satmar, Vishnitz, and Gur.

6. B. R. Wilson, *Religious Sects* (N.Y., 1970), pp. 118–40; J. A. Hostetler, *Amish Society* (Baltimore, 1963), and *Hutterite Society* (Baltimore, 1974).

7. Much of the following is informed by four community studies of the Hasidim: Gutwirth, *Vie juive traditionnelle;* S. Poll, *The Hassidic Community of Williamsburg* (N.Y. 1962), I. Rubin, *Satmar; An Island in the City* (Chicago, 1972); W. Shaffir, *Life in a Religious Community: The Lubavitcher Chassidim in Montreal,* (Toronto, 1974).

8. S. B. Levy, "Shifting Patterns of Ethnic Identification," in *The New Ethnicity,* ed. J. W. Bennet (St. Paul, 1975), pp. 32–34.

9. Shaffir, *Montreal,* p. 101.

10. Levy, "Shifting Patterns," pp. 36–37.

11. Mintz, "Ethnic Activism," pp. 454–55.

12. Poll, *Williamsburg,* pp. 153–247.

13. Rubin, *Satmar,* chap. 9.

14. Poll, *Williamsburg,* pp. 101–7, 214, 250–51.

15. Shaffir, *Montreal,* pp. 97–98.

16. Rubin, *Satmar,* chap. 9; Poll, *Williamsburg,* pp. 89–90, 93–96, 246–47.

17. Gutwirth, *Vie juive traditionnelle,* pp. 53, 424. A survey of ultra-orthodox in Israel found that 55 percent of the men were employed in a synagogue or religious school, 13 percent had small shops, 11 percent were clerks in government agencies, 15 percent were skilled craftsmen, and 6 percent were laborers (Simon, *Continuity and Change,* p. 80).

18. Rubin, *Satmar,* chaps. 10, 11.

19. Mintz, "Ethnic Activism," pp. 453–63.

20. Poll, *Williamsburg,* pp. 256–57.

21. Mintz, "Ethnic Activism," pp. 455–64; *Ma'ariv,* 11 July 1977; *New York Times,* 26 October, 1 December 1979.

22. Pinsker, "Piety as Community: The Hasidic View," *Social Research* 42 (1975), p. 243.

23. J. Isaacs, "The Hasidim of Brooklyn," in *A Coat of Many Colors,* ed. A. D. Lavender (Westport, 1977) pp. 189–94; H. Steinberg, "New Square: Bridge over the River Time," in *A Coat,* pp. 195–201.

24. Rubin, *Satmar,* p. 66.

25. Levy, "Shifting Patterns," pp. 29–30; Shaffir, *Montreal,* pp. 73–75.

26. Rubin, *Satmar,* chap. 8.

27. Levy, "Shifting Patterns," pp. 39–42.

28. Shaffir, *Montreal,* pp. 110–40.

29. Pinsker, "Piety as Community," pp. 230–46.

30. Levy, "Shifting Patterns," pp. 35–37; Rubin, *Satmar,* chap. 12.

31. Rubin, *Satmar,* chaps. 4, 5.

32. Shaffir, *Montreal,* pp. 52–70.

33. *New York Times,* 27 August 1979.

34. Gutwirth, *Vie juive traditionnelle,* pp. 277–96.

35. *Ma'ariv,* 26 September 1975.

36. *Jerusalem Post,* 19 September 1975.
37. Shaffir, *Montreal,* pp. 180–203.
38. Mintz, "Ethnic Activism," pp. 460–61; *Jewish Chronicle,* 25 February 1977.
39. Rubin, *Satmar,* chap. 12; Poll, *Williamsburg,* pp. 59–82.

Index

About the Editor

Gershon David Hundert is the author of *The Jews in Poland and Russia: Bibliographical Essays* and *Community and the Individual Jew*. Presently Associate Professor of History and Jewish Studies at McGill University, he has been Visiting Scholar/Professor at Yale University, at the Oxford Centre for Postgraduate Hebrew Studies, and at the Hebrew University.